SAM WARD

"King of the Lobby"

Books by Lately Thomas

A Debonair Scoundrel

The Vanishing Evangelist:
The Aimee Semple McPherson Kidnaping Affair

Sam Ward: "King of the Lobby"

SAM WARD

"King of the Lobby"

by Lately Thomas

illustrated with photographs

HOUGHTON MIFFLIN COMPANY BOSTON
THE RIVERSIDE PRESS CAMBRIDGE
1965

First Printing W

Library of Congress Catalog Card Number: 65–10327
Printed in the United States of America

To

ALL DELIGHTFUL PEOPLE

Il faut du courage pour être
romantique; car il faut hasarder.

It takes courage to be romantic;
because it means taking risks.

— Stendhal

CONTENTS

PART I

PART II

PART III

ILLUSTRATIONS

(following page 166)

(following page 390)

PART I

ONE

THERE WAS A TIME . . .

AT THREE o'clock in the afternoon of January 27, 1814, in a small, boxlike house a stone's throw from New York City's Battery Park, there occurred an event which excited no public interest and was of importance only to the few persons intimately involved; these being, principally, three, — a youngish banker, his younger wife, and their first child, a boy, who arrived on that day precisely at the fashionable hour for dinner. Promptness at mealtimes was to be a characteristic of the new arrival through a long and eventful life.

The town, then clustered on the tip of Manhattan Island, had more urgent preoccupations than taking note of a baby. The United States was embroiled in its second war with the motherland, and every morning fearful citizens peered down the Narrows in expectation of sighting an English fleet standing in to ravage their homes. The fear was well founded: rooted in the memories of most inhabitants past middle age were recollections of British regulars marching out of the fire-blackened town at the end of the Revolutionary War, a bare thirty years before. Now a British punitive force was understood to be on the way to America, and New Yorkers were certain that they would be the first to feel Britannia's wrath. This was not because of their city's size — although, with almost eighty thousand population, it ranked second only to Philadelphia on the continent — but because of its superb harbor, which offered shipping facilities surpassed by none.

Until the current calamities, it had enjoyed a thriving commerce; but now, with British warships blockading the coast, trade was at a standstill. Merchants worried, and since bankers are the armorers of business, prospering as trade flourishes, there was cause for care in the little house at number 1 Marketfield Street, on the corner of Broad, when Samuel Ward — fourth of his name in a line distinguished for probity and patriotism — made his entrance into the world. For the infant's father was a banker, partner in the Wall Street firm of Prime & Ward, and since his marriage a little more than a year previously to a lively and charming Boston girl whose vivacity denoted Huguenot heritage, he had been shouldering a difficult task in providing comforts for his little household. Nevertheless, anxiety dissolved into youthful rejoicing over the couple's firstborn.

In August, when baby Samuel was seven months old, a British fleet did appear off the coast, but it sailed into Chesapeake Bay instead of New York harbor, and landed troops who burned Washington. Of this national humiliation the child knew nothing. He did not join in the jubilation over Andrew Jackson's victory at New Orleans, in the following January, or in the celebrations in New York when news of the signing of a peace treaty arrived in February, 1815, and houses were illuminated and neighbors ran from door to door congratulating themselves and each other upon the restoration of prospects for prosperity. Through these events little Samuel slept and fed with normal obliviousness, although many persons who later would bulk large in his affairs were active participants in the historic commotions.

Now there is one part of a biography which, in the words of a man who was to become one of Sam Ward's most loyal friends, as well as prime minister of England, most readers skip over, — namely, that portion in which "the pedigree of the hero is set forth, often in warm fancy, and sometimes at intolerable length." But Sam Ward's ancestry, reaching far back into American history, was a dominant factor in shaping his character and it must be touched upon.

Sam's first impressions of family continuity were gained from his grandfather, Lieutenant Colonel Samuel Ward, a veteran of the Revolutionary War. With this kindly, cultivated gentleman little Samuel lived principally from the time he was five years old. From Grandfather Ward he learned that their line had been founded in America by a captain of Oliver Cromwell's cavalry, Thomas Ward, who emigrated after the accession of Charles II. Settling in Rhode Island, he thrived and fathered sons, who became landowners and merchants. One of his descendants, Richard Ward, married a great-granddaughter of Roger Williams, founder of Rhode Island, and became a royal governor of the colony. One of Richard's sons, the family's first Samuel, also became governor, and during the French and Indian Wars rendered valuable services to the crown. Governor Samuel Ward was wealthy and lived as a farmer at Westerly, but he remained active in public affairs. He signed the charter of Rhode Island College (later Brown University) and was an original trustee.

When the dispute with the London Parliament arose, Governor Ward sided with the colonists, and he was the only colonial governor who refused to enforce the hated Stamp Act. The inevitability of separation from Great Britain he foresaw early and with regret. He was elected a delegate to both the First and the Second Continental Congresses, and in the latter worked closely with the leaders of the independence movement. John Hancock named him to preside over the Congress when it resolved itself into a committee of the whole to debate the issue of separating. He also served as chairman of the secret committee to purchase arms and munitions of war, and was a member of the standing committee on claims. He helped to promote a national navy and backed George Washington for general-in-chief. His fellow delegate from Rhode Island, Stephen Hopkins, being often incapacitated by illness, Samuel Ward took on his work as well, writing reports and carrying on a voluminous correspondence. In the annals of the Congress, few names, outside those of the dominant leaders, appear more frequently than Samuel Ward's. Worn out by his labors, he contracted smallpox in the epidemic of 1776, and died at Philadelphia on March 26, just too soon to sign the Declaration of Independence which he had helped to bring about. His faith in the triumph of the American cause had never wavered, although he had no illusions about the heavy sacrifices that would be required. Shortly before his death he had written to his brother: "That the issue of this contest will be the establishment of our liberties, I as firmly believe as I do my existence; for I never can think that God brought us into this wilderness to perish, or, what is worse, to become slaves, but to make us a great and free people."

Two of Governor Ward's sons served in the American army and one in the navy, one of the soldiers being the second Samuel Ward, little Sam's grandfather. He was graduated from Rhode Island College in 1770, and at the outset of hostilities enlisted in a Rhode Island regiment and was commissioned a captain. He took part in the harrowing midwinter march of Benedict Arnold's force to Quebec, fought in the attack on that citadel, and with some four hundred others was captured when the assault failed. For nearly a year he was held prisoner, transported to British army headquarters in New York, then exchanged. He was at once given a major's commission by George Washington.

During the terrible winter of 1777 at Valley Forge, Major Ward obtained a month's leave, and posting home to Rhode Island wooed and won Phoebe Greene, sister of Governor William Greene of that state and a cousin of General Nathanael Greene, Washington's ablest field commander. When Cornwallis's surrender at Yorktown terminated the fighting in 1781, Samuel Ward retired from the army with the rank of lieutenant colonel.

He found himself an old campaigner at twenty-five, thrown on his own resources for a living, since his father's wealth had been dissipated by the struggle, and there were sisters and brothers to care for. Rhode Island had suffered greatly from enemy depredations, the once extensive commerce of Newport was ruined, and Colonel Ward settled in New York as a merchant. He traveled widely on business, keeping an observant and tolerant eye upon foreign ways and peoples, and in 1788 sailed to Canton as one of the first Americans to visit the Far East. His reports from there helped to alert that insatiable moneybags, John Jacob Astor, to the enormous profit possibilities in the China trade. The paths of the Wards and the Astors were to cross many times in the future.

Colonel Ward was in France during the Terror, and on the day Louis XVI was beheaded he shut himself in his rooms in solemn and compassionate meditation, noting in his journal with disapproval the callousness of some American tourists who took in the bloody spectacle. According to family tradition, upon leaving Paris Colonel

Ward smuggled a French nobleman out of the city disguised as his coachman. This was a stock-in-trade of yarn spinners of that period, but in Ward's case the story may well have been true, for he was no novice at running risks or adopting the ruses of warfare.

A worldly, unspoiled gentleman with urbane manners, Colonel Ward retired from business in 1816 and moved to a farm at Jamaica, Long Island. Of the ten children who were born to him and his wife, seven had attained maturity: two daughters, Katherine and Anne, who never married and kept their father company at the farm, and five sons. These aunts and uncles figured largely in Sam Ward's youth. All the sons stood more than six feet tall, with beam in proportion, like the colonel himself; in the family Sam was to be an anomaly, because he remained comparatively short. His uncles, in order of their ages, were Henry, Richard, John, and William; Samuel, young Sam's banker father, was sandwiched between Henry and Richard.

In his youth, Henry Ward had made the voyage to Madeira and "learned to chew tobacco and abominate the sea." He was socially gay, loved music and dancing, and played the piano and fiddle. A note broker, he was so little pretentious that at his death Sam was surprised to learn he was rich. Uncle Dick, the third son, was a lawyer and a bachelor, haunted by regrets that he had been born too late to fight in the Revolution; by way of compensation he bragged about his father's exploits, to the modest old man's embarrassment. Next in line came Uncle John, easygoing, cheerful, and sentimental; in a crisis, Uncle John was always the one turned to first for sympathy and help. A bachelor, he lived with Richard, and as a Wall Street broker was elected president of the New York Stock Exchange three times, in 1831, 1832, and 1833; his portrait hangs in the Exchange Building today. Youngest of the uncles was Uncle William, a tea importer addicted to lawsuits and somewhat overaddicted to the pleasant "glou-glou" of the bottle. Not that he was often tipsy, but in his case the family partiality for old Madeira sometimes exceeded the bounds of strict decorum.

These five stalwart brothers — little Samuel's father and his four uncles — of a fair Sunday would walk out from New York by the Williamsburg Ferry Road to dine with their father at the farm; and

Sam vividly recalled how, after dinner, a decanter of mellow Madeira (perhaps "Old South Side," plundered by a Rhode Island privateer from a British merchantman in the previous century) would be placed upon the table, and Uncle Henry, as eldest, would lift his glass and propose the toast: "Father, my duty to you. Katie [or Anne, his other sister], my love to you. Boys, better behavior to you." Sam, who had his half-glass, remembered that after the toast "there was not a dry eye or damp glass left at the table."

Two years after Sam's birth a second son arrived in his parents' household; this boy was named Henry. In 1820 a third son was born, and named Francis Marion, in honor of the great ancestor on the maternal side, the "Swamp Fox" of South Carolina in the Revolutionary War. Between Sam and Henry there had been a girl, named Julia after her mother, but she died of whooping cough near her fourth birthday. This gap was filled almost at once by the birth, on May 27, 1819, of another girl, who also was given the name Julia. This second Julia was a tiny thing with reddish hair and bright blue eyes, not a bit angelic, but full of caprices. One day she would be famous as Julia Ward Howe.

The name Francis Marion, which the family would hand down from generation to generation, came through Sam's maternal grandmother, Sarah Mitchell Cutler. She was a niece of the "Swamp Fox," her mother, Hester (or Esther) Marion, being the hero's sister. Hester had been married twice, the first time to John Allston, of Georgetown, a member of the South Carolina planter aristocracy, and after his decease to Thomas Mitchell, another rich Georgetown planter. Sam's grandmother was a child of this second marriage. She had been reared on an Allston plantation, waited upon by slaves, and was imbued with the pride of the leisured Carolinians: to her last day, she never forgot her origin, and she never let anyone else forget it. She, too, had been twice a bride: at fifteen, to a planter named Herne, an officer in Washington's army, and when he died, to Benjamin Clarke Cutler, a Massachusetts widower, sheriff of Norfolk County and a descendant of a Hollander named Messenmaker, or Desmaker, who had settled in the Bay Colony in 1674 and anglicized his name.

Grandmother Cutler was decidedly original. She dipped snuff, and ate with her knife if it pleased her, disdaining forks; what had been acceptable in good society when she was a girl was still acceptable to her, she would shrug. She had been an *élégante* at the receptions of George and Martha Washington, and was fond of recounting the occasion when the First President crossed the ballroom to beg the favor of a dance.

Benjamin Clarke Cutler possessed no wealth, and when he, in turn, made the sprightly Sarah a widow, he left two sons and three dowerless daughters. The second of these girls, Julia Rush Cutler, had been educated in a select boarding school kept by Mrs. Elizabeth Graham in a mansion fronting on Bowling Green, in New York City. There, at the age of sixteen, she caught the eye and fancy of twenty-six-year-old Samuel Ward, banker son of the Revolutionary colonel. Widow Cutler had protested he would rob her nest of its fairest nestling should he marry her, but of course consented: young Ward seemed a solid prospect as a husband. The wedding was in Trinity Church, Boston, on October 8, 1812, and in spite of the outbreak of war with England, was merry. The bride's mother appeared in a theatrically brilliant costume of the previous century, and enjoyed a thoroughly theatrical crisis of tears and joy.

As Sam emerged from babyhood, his anxious mother thought he looked "peaked," that city air disagreed with him, and he was sent to live in the country, on his grandfather's farm. There Sam imbibed health, a sense of family, a taste for good manners, and respect for scholarly attainments. His relations with his grandfather were more like those between chums than between an elder and his prattling scion. Sam soon was enrolled in an academy maintained by Cornelius Eigenbrodt; it was a mile and a half from the farm, and he walked to and from the classes in all weathers.

To launch his namesake properly upon the path of learning, Colonel Ward procured duplicates of Sam's textbooks, pretending that he needed to brush up his own education, and they went over the lessons together daily. The veteran's enthusiasm was kindled when they reached Caesar's *Gallic Wars;* in the fourth book, when they started to construct the bridge across the Rhine — downfall of generations of juvenile scholars — Sam was drilled so minutely that when he was called upon to translate in class, he crossed over smoothly, and sat down amid a buzz of astonishment from his classmates, all of whom had suffered defeat upon that *pons asinorum.* Thanks to his grandfather, Sam came out of the Eigenbrodt academy a sound Latinist for life.

From Grandfather Ward, also, Sam learned the meaning of tact, including the art of paying a compliment gracefully. On one birthday which Sam was spending at home with his parents, the colonel sent his greeting by letter: "This is your birthday. I congratulate you on it and hope you are well and happy. The finest compliment ever paid on a birthday was from Ovid to the elder Germanicus, *Di tibi dent annos a te nam cetera sumes,* which I shall not attempt to translate to you, who, I may now hope, are my superior in the knowledge of Latin. Perhaps in French also. At any rate, I hope you will accustom yourself to speak French, that you may have all the advantages that language can give you . . . Will you excuse me if I express an earnest desire that you may be Mr. Thorough Learned in all your studies as well as Mr. Thorough Good in your life and conversation."

At Jamaica, Sam had boyish adventures, some of which foreshadowed traits observable in his later life. One was a strong streak of credulousness. A mulatto waif named Bilbo, parentage uncertain, lived on the farm, and with him Sam plotted to run away and join a pirate band. They would need money until they reached a suitable pirate's lair, of course; but Bilbo, who understood magic, volunteered to procure this by a simple process: every week Sam was to drop a penny in a hole covered with a flat stone, and by the power of incantations known only to Bilbo, these coppers, at the end of a year, would be transmuted into goldpieces. There was one proviso that Sam found hard, namely — that he should not peep into the hole during the year of waiting, for that would break the spell. But he carried out his part of the bargain, making his weekly offering, bound by a horrible oath of secrecy.

A day came when Bilbo and he decided to make their getaway, and at breakfast that morning Sam developed an appetite so ravenous his Aunt Anne wondered aloud where the boy could be stowing all the bread and butter he was demanding. Sam was stowing it inside his shirt, to serve as provender for the expedition. Off he and Bilbo started on a run, which they kept up for about a mile; then Bilbo — who had assumed command — ordered a halt while he slunk back to see whether they were being pursued. Sitting on a log, Sam felt the pinch of hunger, and started to munch on the commissary supply. Before he knew it, the larder was empty and he was full. When Bilbo learned of this, he vowed to have Sam shot for mutiny, a threat so alarming Sam ran all the way home and confessed everything to his grandfather. The upshot was that Bilbo was bundled off to China as a cabin boy on a warship, and the minute he was sure that Bilbo could not wreak vengeance, Sam investigated their hole-in-the-ground bank. Lifting the stone, he found only a handful of pebbles. From that bitter moment, he contended, dated his comprehension of the Spanish proverb, *Mas vale pajaro en mano que dos en el monte.* Yet, while comprehending perfectly the theory of holding fast to the "bird in hand" and not putting one's trust in promises of gold, he never quite mastered the practice, and to the end of his days the Bilbo trick would be played upon him successfully.

Sam's gastronomical education may be said to date from his experiences on his grandfather's farm, for there he began his lifelong exploration of rare and curious edibles by sampling stewed skunk, prepared by the Indians who worked the land. He found the meat tasty and savored the memory for years.

Another memory never to be effaced was the occasion when his grandfather applied for the arrears of his Revolutionary War pension. This step was taken not on the colonel's initiative, but on that of his sons, who decided that since the national treasury was nearly out of debt, the time had come for their father to file his claim.

> Accordingly, one Sunday [Sam described the scene], my uncles brought down with them [to the farm] Mr. Samuel Glover . . . who enjoyed the advantage of a notary public's seal, to make out the proper petition, with evidence of service, for the authorities at Washington . . . A blush suffused the veteran's cheeks at the idea of being summoned to prove his

share in the Revolution, which might have been rivalled by that of some French émigré upon returning from London after the Restoration, when called upon to produce his patents of nobility to recover his sequestered estates.

There was an old bureau in my grandfather's bedroom, one small drawer of which my boyish eyes had never looked inside of, and to that he forthwith made his way and applied the key. Under the excitement of old memories, he did not notice the noiseless footstep and peering eyes which descried various hitherto unknown objects, — a rosary of tortoise-shell and gold; two pairs of antique gold sleeve buttons; a pair of extra-sized round wooden boxes, such as were made for wafers in those days when envelopes with adhesive gum were unknown, each filled to the brim with glittering silver coins . . . The drawer was evidently pulled beyond its usual limits and the old gentleman, from its innermost recess, drew a sealed packet of papers coated with dust . . . The packet was brought into the parlor and submitted to the inspection of Mr. Glover. In five minutes the expert had become master of the situation and held in triumph the commission signed by George Washington.

Almost equally memorable was another Sunday, when Sam's mother drove out to the farm in her new carriage. In all New York there were probably not a score of private carriages, for distances were short, the city barely extending as far north as Canal Street, and living habits were not ostentatious. The carriage, a ponderous affair slung on C-springs, was banker Ward's gift to his wife to celebrate the birth of a second daughter — a beautiful child, named Louisa for her aunt, Mrs. Ward's younger sister, who had married a lawyer from Savannah named Matthew Hall McAllister. The carriage was a pale lemon color, with bright blue upholstery, and it had cost one thousand dollars. But the Wards could afford an occasional luxury, for on the first of that month the books of Prime & Ward had been balanced, and Samuel Ward was credited with one hundred thousand dollars.

With this rise in fortune and the increase in his family, the banker found the Marketfield Street house too cramped, and in

1821 he purchased one of seven new building lots laid out along the east side of Bowling Green, number 5; Philip Hone, the prosperous commission merchant who soon would become mayor of New York, took up a smaller lot at number 1. A fine brick house soon rose on this fashionable location, and by the end of the year the Wards moved in. For Julia Cutler Ward, the move had special piquancy, because just across the Green was the white-pillared mansion that had housed Mrs. Graham's boarding school. Now it was the home of Nathaniel Prime, senior partner of Prime & Ward (or Prime, Ward & Sands, as the firm had become temporarily), and a lavish entertainer.

But a shadow soon settled upon the new household, when Mrs. Ward developed symptoms of tuberculosis. The disease was so prevalent then that it excited little alarm; among women, the pallor it induced, lighted up by a hectic flush, was esteemed as a mark of beauty. But ill health kept Sam's mother a semi-invalid, and his stay at Jamaica was prolonged. One result was that the years spent with his grandfather always remained warm and vivid in Sam's memory, while his mother, the Bowling Green house, the promenades in nearby Battery Park, where the élite strolled of evenings while little girls twirled skipping ropes and boys played ball on the grass, — these receded with time into an iridescent blur. Even the inmates of the nursery — Henry and Marion and bright-eyed, mischievous Julia — at this period were peripheral images in the camera obscura of Sam's mind. But the farm, the skunk, Bilbo, the gentle, courtly colonel, remained clear-cut, permanently real.

In the course of time Sam outgrew the Eigenbrodt academy, and his father enrolled him in a school that was making a stir educationally, Round Hill School, in Northampton, Massachusetts. Round Hill had been started by Dr. Joseph Cogswell, a former Harvard professor, with the assistance of George Bancroft, the future historian. Sam's mother wept as she kissed him goodbye and put him in charge of his Uncle McAllister for the trip, in the late spring of 1824. Sam set out eagerly.

That summer Mrs. Ward, with the other children, took the country air in a farmhouse far out on the Bloomingdale Road, in upper Manhattan. Returning to town, on November 8, Julia Cutler Ward gave birth to another daughter, and three days later she died. She was only twenty-seven.

Sam could not be summoned back from Northampton in time for the funeral but he received a full account by letter. All his life he would be haunted by a bizarre coincidence: on the way to the burial ground, his mother's cortège encountered a troupe of Italian mountebanks coming from the dock, where they had just landed. The mourners stared in wonderment at the swarthy, gesticulating comedians, who abruptly became silent and gravely lifted their hats as Death passed by.

TWO

ROUND HILL SCHOOL DAYS

THE enrollment at Round Hill when Sam Ward arrived there was about thirty, but during his stay it increased to more than one hundred. Pupils were drawn from north and south, and from as far west as Ohio. They represented the leading families of their communities, and a large number of them would achieve eminence themselves. John Lothrop Motley, the historian and ambassador-to-be, was there from Massachusetts, and other classmates of Sam were Henry W. Bellows, who would organize the Sanitary Commission in the Civil War, and the younger W. Ellery Channing, a poet of note in his day and a friend of Hawthorne. The roster of students might have been taken from a social bluebook. Massachusetts representatives included Amorys, Appletons, Grays, Perkinses, and Peabodys. From Georgia there were Habershams and Bullocks; from Maryland, Tilghmans and Gilmors; from South Carolina a Pinckney-Izard-Middleton-Rutledge-Huger phalanx, to some of whose members Sam was distantly related. The effect upon Sam Ward of immersion in this republic of boyhood was to foster national sympathies and exclude sectionalism, a characteristic that was to mark him always.

Among the New York boys were special friends, like Dominick Lynch, whose father, of the same name, had recommended Round Hill to Sam's father in the first place. Lynch had vouched for the school's social and educational respectability, and on such matters there was no higher authority than the so-called "greatest swell New York ever saw" and recognized leader of the *ton* of the city. A discriminating connoisseur of the arts, Dominick Lynch possessed Continental culture and fascinating manners; he was said to be the first Irishman who *brought* money to this country, and he deserves a nation's gratitude for having introduced Americans to Château Lafite and the Italian opera.

The latter event occurred in 1825. In conjunction with Lorenzo da Ponte — a queer walking relic of the eighteenth century, Mozart's librettist, now diminished into a teacher of Italian at Columbia — Lynch brought from Europe a troupe headed by Manuel García, and coached the singers for their opening in *The Barber of Seville,* at the Park Theater. Eleven-year-old Sam Ward, on holiday from school, attended this performance with his six-year old sister Julia. Never would he forget the shiver of delight (*chair de poule,* literal gooseflesh, he called it) that swept over him when seventeen-year-old Maria Felicita García (afterwards famous as Malibran) rippled ravishingly into "Una voce poco fa." That "divine revelation," as he termed it, made Sam Ward a devotee of music.

Exceptional pleasures like this, however, were few during Sam's first year at Round Hill, and often he complained of loneliness. The abyss of grief into which his father had fallen after his wife's death contributed to the boy's feeling of insecurity: at first the stricken man refused even to look at the baby he blamed for the calamity, but sat in a darkened room, speechless, stupefied by sorrow. At length Colonel Ward intervened: taking up the infant, he carried it to his son's room and laid it upon its father's knees. This action released the banker's tears, and gradually he recovered his equanimity, although his health would remain precarious for the rest of his life.

Morally his character changed, too. Always religious, he became hagridden by anxiety for his children's spiritual welfare. He cherished them more than ever, but insisted on shielding them from possible contamination by worldly vanities, forbidding dancing, parties, and most other social contacts. Otherwise they were stinted nothing, and the banker continued to maintain a domestic establishment of sober luxury. On Samuel, the eldest son, the father fixed his chief hopes, taking it for granted that the lad eventually would assume his place at the head of the Wall Street firm.

Sam's spirits normally rebounded quickly from reverses, but a year after his mother's death he was still shaken. In letters to his father he poured out his craving for assurance of unaltered affection. "It is a long time now since I received a letter from you or anybody else, and on that account I fear that something has happened," he wrote. "I long to know how all the little children are, especially the baby." The baby, who was proving a demure delight, had been named Anne Eliza, after her two aunts; in the family she would be known as Annie.

"Dear father," Sam went on dismally, "I want to see you so much that I would give anything that it is in power to give, in order that we might mutually soothe one another's afflictions. On the 27th will be my birthday [he would be twelve], which will only revive in my mind the sad recollections of my former one spent with so much joy. Your affectionate and unhappy son."

The birthday Sam dreaded brought letters from his grandfather and his father. The older man, understanding a boy's mind, wrote cheerfully from the Jamaica farm:

> My dearest Sam —
>
> This is your birthday and I offer my most affectionate remembrance wishing you many happy returns. "But grandpa, what is this happiness which all my friends wish to possess and which I still more earnestly wish to possess?" Indeed, dear boy, I shall be puzzled to tell how you or any other human being can obtain, or if obtained, can keep it. A poet says, "worthy ends by worthy means to pursue." This places happiness in a steady pursuit of objects in themselves honorable and useful. Your pursuits, I doubt not, are to acquire knowledge and to perfect the morals that your principles may as steady as mortal man's can be. "Ah, grandpa, this is almost too grave for your little boy, and I must put your letter by to go and skate with my school fellows." Well — I bid God bless you, and with my best love I am,
>
> Your most affectionate
> SAMUEL WARD.

More tersely, but no less tenderly, the father wrote, still tormented by thoughts of his lost happiness: "My darling son — Your twelfth birthday fills father's heart with the thought of your angel mother, blest in Heaven. For her, for your poor father, for yourself, and for your friends, strive to be all that is virtuous, good, and wise. Relax not, dearest boy."

As a memento, the father had sent Sam his mother's watch, and in default of a speedy acknowledgement he inquired anxiously: "Is the watch safe? I charge you to tell me if any accident should happen to it. You need not fear that I shall scold you." Sam replied that the watch was unharmed, but he had not been able to get it to run properly. His father counseled patience: "The watch will get into steady motion by and by. It is after all more easily regulated than the human mind."

Like most schoolboys, Sam complained that his spending-money allowance was inadequate, and his father — who was generous but never a Mr. Unthrift — tried to inculcate moderation. "Father lives to gratify all reasonable wishes," he answered, "but is puzzled to know what use his little boy can have for *l'argent.*"

Homesickness dogged the lad, and intermittently he begged his father to take him away from Round Hill. In his second year there (the summer of 1826) he confronted his father with a carefully marshaled argument in favor of his being returned to the Eigenbrodt academy, — a school, he said, in his opinion as good as Round Hill, and possessing the additional merit of being near his grandfather. "I give you my word of honor, dear father," he pledged, "that I will in no wise show myself unworthy of your kindness and that you will never have occasion to reproach yourself for taking me from this scene."

Persevere until the end of the term, his father advised, and Sam was obedient; but in a letter composed half in French, in order to display his proficiency in that language, he renewed his plea: "Le fin du terme s'approache, et vous n'avez pas déterminé encore si je laisserais cette école ou non." Here his pen broke into English: "But if you wish to make me happy, do consider my promises and take me away from here." His father's "no" was put gently: "It is better, my own darling, that you pass one more year at Northampton. You will never regret it." And so it was settled, and gradually Sam became not only reconciled but contented.

Henry Ward had followed him to Round Hill, and the letters from home teemed with exhortations for Sam to set an example of industry, prudence, self-denial, and virtuous conduct for his younger brother. Judiciously Sam reported back: "J'ai le plaisir de vous dire que mon frère Henri est à présent un bien bon garçon." But although Henry "at present" might be "a very good boy," prudence and virtue could not hold back boy nature forever, and there were fights with other students, which, Sam said proudly, Henry won.

Supervision of the younger Ward children had been assumed by Eliza Cutler, the older sister of Sam's mother, — a warmhearted, practical, energetic woman who ran her brother-in-law's household on a sentimental but no-nonsense plan. Her letters to her nephews at school mingled concern over the condition of Sam's clothes ("I cannot understand whether you mean that you cannot find your new nankins, or the old pair you had for fishing") and concern for his morals ("Read the Bible every day. Never forget to say your prayers. Be a comfort to your poor father").

The homilistic vein was even more pronounced in Sam's letters from his mother's brother, the Reverend Benjamin Clarke Cutler, a Congregational divine, of Brooklyn. Uncle Ben could not put off pulpit grandiloquence, even in a letter to a boy he was fond of. A typical lecture ran: "Men may appear to be good, they may profess and practice the virtues of alms-giving and temperance; they may fast and pray and every Sabbath go to church; yet they may be only like sepulchers." This sort of thing, repeated over and over, might have turned a boy less well balanced into a prig or a rebel, but Sam's nature was healthy, and he understood that Uncle Ben loved him in his own way.

Some of the best letters Sam got were Aunt Anne Ward's long, newsy accounts of members of the family. "Marion and Julia took their dancing lesson this morning. Louisa speaks words of one syllable, and the baby is interesting. Julia is very fond of a book," ran one such letter, giving the latest word about Sam's sisters and brother. "Aunt Eliza heard from Savannah yesterday — your little cousins are well and your grandmamma must be delighted to escape the cold weather — as well as to enjoy Aunt Louisa's company. We speak of you every day and thank you for the nuts you gathered for us. Your dear father ate some of them on Sunday."

The Savannah cousins were the children of Aunt Louisa and Uncle Matthew McAllister, who were very close to the Wards. These children were Julian, the oldest, who would attend West Point and serve in the United States and Confederate Armies; Hall, who would become a noted lawyer in early California; and Samuel Ward McAllister — Sam's godson and namesake — who, after dropping his first name, would trip into history as Ward McAllister, the chubby majordomo of *the* Mrs. Astor, and inventor of that cachet meaning the socially elect, "The Four Hundred."

But from his grandfather, still youthful in spirit, Sam received the most welcome letters of all. Become a good linguist, the colonel repeatedly urged his grandson, not neglecting to acquire "the most perfect and accurate or critical knowledge of our language. I have hardly memory in my old age to tell you all that is desirable and even needful to know — from declaiming . . . to the knowledge of mathematics — and I will also add to skate, play ball, run races, hop, skip, and jump, and all needful exercises to make a finished education." Better reading this, than Uncle Ben's fasting and praying and being like sepulchers.

Studies gave Sam no trouble. Less than a year after entering Round Hill, he requested permission to take up an extra subject, Spanish, telling his father that it would be doubly advantageous, inasmuch as (1) the instructor would be his French teacher, who (2) spoke no English, and (3) therefore would be obliged to teach Spanish in French. The reasoning was complicated, but Sam's father got the drift and consented. Only, he cautioned, "Remember, my beloved boy, our conversation together and how much I expect from you. Try hard to have reasonable wants and to make them understood in a manly way."

At the end of Sam's second year at Northampton, Bancroft, the chief instructor, favored banker Ward with an analysis of his son's aptitudes and progress. The summary showed much Yankee shrewdness, but on one point went wide of the mark, stating categorically: "In mathematics he does not excel, nor will he. His mind is not mathematical. He can go through a course with respectability and great advantage to him, but his talents incline him to other pursuits."

Sam's precocity in the field of mathematics had not become manifest when Bancroft wrote; it appeared a few months after that, when he crowed that he was finding geometry "more a matter for amusement than a task which I am obliged to get." And shortly after that: "Geometry I shall soon be master of, and then I intend going into a higher branch of mathematics, viz., the algebra of Lacroix." This, in turn, was succeeded, ten days later, by: "I have just commenced the truly pleasing study of trigonometry, from which I proceed to the higher branches." Sam was fourteen.

In languages also he displayed great facility. French was his best subject, and he told his father he would soon use up "a quire or so of foolscap" in translating Molière's *Les Fourberies de Scapin,* — a choice of subject that was prophetically suggestive. Molière's comedy deals with a lively scamp who thrives by sharp practices, all of which, save one, succeed marvelously, like those of a gambler who cannot lose. A fascinating character to Sam, evidently. He put the rascal's self-portrait into the following speech: "There are few things I find impossible when I choose to take pains. Undoubtedly I received from Heaven a genius adapted to every kind of invention, and to those little genteel tricks, which the ignorant call knavery. And I can say without boasting that you will rarely find a man who is a more skillful contriver of all kinds of intrigues, and who has acquired more glory in the trade than me. But really, true merit is not well enough treated nowadays." The time would come when moralists would elevate eyebrows over some of Sam's "genteel tricks", — not all of which, however, would succeed. Sam was not Scapin.

Round Hill was patterned after a German *Gymnasium,* physical exercise being stressed equally with the stern classical curriculum. In the former department of his schooling, Sam did well likewise, growing "strong as an Apache" and developing a powerful torso and long, muscular arms, but not shooting up to the height of his father and uncles. Boylike, he was always hungry. "Mr. Bancroft IS MARRIED to Miss Dwight," he wrote to his father excitedly on March 11, 1827. "He gave his wedding ball last Friday, to which I and five other boys were invited and had a royal time . . . We had refreshments handed round for the first hour, then went into the supper room, where there was a large table . . . in the middle a wedding cake . . . all around it syllabubs, whips, soft custards, blanc mange, oranges, apples, hams, tongues, sweetmeats, pastries, wine, and champagne."

A quick study in social graces, he added in the same letter: "I had the honor of dancing with Mrs. Bancroft, her sister Miss Dwight, Mrs. Watson, Miss Bates, Miss Upsham, Miss Segur, and Miss Fletcher. We were UP TILL TWELVE O'CLOCK." And by way of postscript he announced his inclusion in a school ballet, "one of the prettiest things you ever saw, a dance of twenty boys."

Every summer the Round Hillers took walking tours, for instruction and recreation, a score of boys setting out afoot, followed by their commissariat in a wagon,—"barrels of biscuit [hardtack], lemons and sugar, and a not too generous supply of plain claret." They covered twenty-five to thirty miles a day with this for refreshment; wayside inns provided overnight shelter. On one excursion Sam went as far as Nahant, on the seashore near Boston, and one of his Cutler uncles took him to nearby Quincy to see John Adams. The venerable Founding Father was seated in a capacious chair surrounded by a crowded library. "He wore a light blue flannel easy jacket and light drab vest and trousers, the former of which seemed to me of excessive length," Sam recalled. "His manner was benign, his eye soft and lustrous." Sam gazed with awe at this living link with his great-grandfather, Governor Samuel Ward.

The final year at Northampton was, for Sam, one of relative contentment. He was permitted to study in Doctor Cogswell's library, which he described as "a small room, filled with the best collections of French, Spanish, Latin, Greek, German, Italian, and English authors, and a splendid collection of minerals [in] 80 large drawers and 65 small ones, and in all of them the minerals are arranged in little paper boxes with the nicest care imaginable." The setting was cozy. In one corner was a little Franklin stove "with doors on an improved style which will heat the room completely in seven minutes, and after that I can open the doors and it is as good as a fireplace. I have a nice little table that I can carry to any place in the room," he went on. "I have my desk in it and am allowed entirely to myself, as no one comes in the room at any time except Henry, who comes in to warm himself sometimes in his play hours . . . I can stay up as long as I please."

He was receiving favored treatment, of course, and was not at all averse to being singled out in this manner. He did not know the reason, besides his aptitude and genuine love of study, that lay behind Cogswell's leniency: because so many parents were remiss in paying their sons' board bills on time, the pedagogue was having a hard time remaining solvent, and banker Ward was assisting quietly with cash advances, gilded to look like loans.

But the next step in Sam's education was at hand, and it was taken for granted that he would enter Columbia College in New York City, of which his father was a trustee. Bancroft estimated that Sam should be able to matriculate with advanced credits, thanks to his more than satisfactory progress at Round Hill. In a confidential letter, the future historian gave Sam's father his considered appraisal of the boy, with recommendations for his guidance from then on. It was a penetrating analysis.

Mental ability, the capacity to learn, was no problem, Bancroft wrote; what Sam lacked was depth and perseverance. His greatest fault was that he was too avid of praise. "When asked a question, he will sometimes hesitate, as if doubtful what bearing his answer will have on the opinion entertained of him. When he fears rebuke, he grows sensitive." Nevertheless, the boy's nature was sound: "Sam always in the main means well; he has no malice and no obstinacy . . . His course this winter has been manly and correct, open, confiding, pleasant, and industrious . . . Yet I am not sure I should say to Samuel himself so much. Praise injures him. He requires just enough to encourage him . . . but too much makes him at first confident, and then careless . . . So far as his mind is concerned, he has so great a facility of acquisition that the pursuit of French and Spanish, for example, however desirable for him in many respects as valuable accomplishments, will carry forward his education as a man very little . . . Pursuit of the easier branches of knowledge is dangerous to him."

Then piercing to the heart of the matter, Bancroft stated his major reservation: "I have said he is often impetuous. He seizes upon a part of an idea in a twinkling, but he is apt to think he has already the whole . . . He is more ready to advance than to secure, to conquer new territories than to confirm himself in the possession of those already entered." In other words, superficiality allied with brilliancy. But Bancroft's last word was favorable: "It is very seldom we are able to say so much good and so little ill of any one as I can safely say of Sam. I have great confidence in him."

Decades hence, Sam Ward's obituary notices would parallel in some respects this remarkably prescient summing up. Sam's character was "jelling" early.

THREE

A YOUNG MAN'S FANCIES

"It is with feelings of great pleasure that I anticipate my career (glorious I trust it will be) at Col. Coll.," wrote Sam ebulliently in the spring of 1829. Glorious or not, his years at Columbia College for the first time made him aware that he possessed a mind of exceptional capacities. The earliest intimation of this came when he romped through the entrance examination, given in the room of Columbia's president, William A. Duer.

"Mr. Cogswell and my father accompanied me," Sam recalled, "and I was immediately put under fire by Professor Charles Anthon, who passed me after I had construed twenty lines of the *Aeneid,* a page of Xenophon, and one of Plato's *Phaedo.* I was then turned over to Professor Henry James Anderson, who, handing me a sheet of paper, a ruler, and a pencil, asked me to solve the forty-seventh proposition of the fifth book of Euclid. This was play for me, and no further questions were asked." After signing the roster of students kept personally in a large folio volume by President Duer, and agreeing to abide by the rules of the college, Sam was registered at the mid-freshman level, although he was only fifteen. The tuition fee of ninety dollars a year was paid cheerfully by his father.

At that time Columbia College drowsed in Park Place, a quiet backwater running from the Park (City Hall Park) towards the Hudson River. Sam described it as "a kind of Sleepy Hollow in the heart of old New York, where, on a lovely lawn, stood the houses of the president and the faculty, flanking on either side the plain central building in their midst, containing the college library and lecture rooms. It was governed," he went on, "by a close corporation of trustees, chiefly of the Episcopal persuasion, and more than half of them members of that New York board of papacy, Trinity Church." In his view, then and later, their outlook was narrow, their minds "as free from receptivity to innovations, or even ameliorations, as the Admiralty of Great Britain or the Naval Construction Board at Washington."

The work of the students was light, Sam discovered. "We got our lessons, or neglected them, at home, where two hours a day were more than sufficient preparation. In fact, we were boys of leisure." That leisure permitted a thorough social and convivial exploration of the attractions of the rapidly growing city. The town had mushroomed in the four years since the Erie Canal had begun funneling the trade of the interior into its harbor, and with the spurt in population fortunes were being made, large landowners, like the Astors, growing astronomically rich. On a reduced scale, banker Ward shared in the prosperity. In hope of escaping the depressing associations of the Bowling Green house (the house he had built for the wife whose death still left him periodically prostrated with grief), he had moved to a new section, so far north on the island that his friends twitted him about moving into the country. Back in 1826 he had purchased several lots on Bond Street, then newly opened. This short street branches off the east side of Broadway just below that thoroughfare's bend at Eighth Street. He paid eleven thousand dollars for the properties, but so swiftly was the city expanding, when he took up additional frontage along Broadway to Great Jones Street (the next above Bond), that parcel alone cost him forty thousand dollars. However, by selling portions to wealthy friends, the banker realized a profit, and the district soon became a hub of fashion. Philip Hone, the former mayor, bought the lot at number 1 Great Jones Street from Samuel Ward and built a fine residence there, and Ward relatives established themselves almost solidly along Bond Street.

While a new home of imposing dimensions was being erected at number 2 Bond Street, on the corner of Broadway, the banker lodged his family at number 16. Old Colonel Ward, finding the winters on the farm trying, moved into number 7 with his sons John and Richard; while another of Sam's uncles, Henry, established himself at number 23. General Winfield Scott lived for a while at number 5 Bond Street. The resplendent hero of Chippewa and Lundy's Lane (two inconclusive battles in the War of 1812) was about as great a celebrity as the nation contained. Sam had been introduced to the mighty Scott at Round Hill — where also he had shaken hands with the friend of Washington, the Marquis de Lafayette, on the latter's triumphal return to America in 1825. Now, in Bond Street, Sam encountered many other famous men, members of the Ward social circle. Bond Street parties attracted figures like Daniel Webster, Henry Clay, and John Quincy Adams, with their wives, daughters, and cousins. At Ward dinner tables appeared the social and literary lions — Dominick Lynch, Lorenzo da Ponte, the rising poet Fitz-Greene Halleck, Washington Irving, and Fenimore Cooper. The mercantile and financial magnates of the city hurried daily along Bond Street's smart, tree-shaded sidewalks. There Knickerbocker aristocrats, like Hamilton Fish, future governor and Secretary of State, hobnobbed with self-made men of importance, like Thurlow Weed, boss of the conservative Whig party, and Weed's upstate protégé, the lawyer-politician, William Henry Seward. On New Year's Day, gouty, dropsical old John Jacob Astor, who seldom ventured out of doors any more, would alight painfully from his carriage in front of number 16 Bond Street to pay his annual call upon the active director of Prime, Ward & King. With many of these men Sam Ward in later life would be closely associated, happily or unhappily; never would wealth, fame, or position awe him, for their possessors he had known familiarly from youth.

There was sound reason why old Astor deemed it fitting to waddle into banker Ward's parlor, after a ride up from lower Broadway where the fur and China trade millionaire had his mansion: Prime, Ward & King had become the foremost bank in New York. A new partner had been admitted, James Gore King, son of Rufus King, who had been United States senator and minister to England. James King had been educated in England (he was a contemporary of Byron at Harrow) and had established a bank in Liverpool with Archibald Gracie, a prominent merchant in New York. King & Gracie were the Liverpool correspondents of Baring's, the great London banking house, and this valuable connection

James King brought with him to Wall Street. From a marble-fronted office at 42 Wall Street, the expanded firm wielded wide influence in the commercial community; a business contemporary recollected that although a rival house, J. & S. Josephs, were the agents of the Rothschilds, they had no such standing in town as Prime, Ward & King.

But with increased business came increased burdens, and banker Ward became more austere, until his family's home life was darkened by his scruples. Worldly frivolities like dancing and party-giving were discountenanced, although the children received dancing lessons privately in order that they might appear properly in adult society. Although Colonel Ward loved his rubber of whist, card-playing was interdicted under the roof of his son, who suffered agonies about the old gentleman's chances of salvation; but the colonel was content to jog towards eternity in his own easygoing way. The Ward uncles were connoisseurs of wine, but Sam's father took up the temperance cause and emptied his cellar of its fine vintages, to the distress of his neighbor, Philip Hone; at Samuel Ward's table, guests were offered tea, coffee, or milk. Another voluntary deprivation was tobacco: the banker gave it up to encourage his sons to abstain. They promised, but lacked his fortitude and often backslid.

Sam's rambles through the city took him especially into eating places, including some that his father would have placed off limits had he known about his son's appearances there. There were oyster cellars, chophouses, taverns, and "ordinaries," many of these hardly respectable. But the most satisfying discovery made by Sam and a few discerning friends was the Continental cafés that had sprung up here and there. In Warren Street was one (nobody was quite sure of its name) where the patrons played dominoes and dallied indefinitely over a newspaper and absinthe, an exotic beverage much esteemed as a stomachic and elixir.

Sam liked best a tiny café on the west side of William Street, between Garden Street and Beaver Lane (later called Exchange Place and Beaver Street), kept by two brothers, John and Peter Delmonico. Half a century later, Sam Ward could still envision the "dim, religious light" and the tranquil atmosphere of that oasis.

He was struck by the prompt and deferential service, "unlike the democratic nonchalance of the service at Holt's Ordinary in Fulton Street, at Clark's and Brown's in Maiden Lane, and at George Brown's in Water Street. I revelled in the coffee, the chocolate, the *bavaroises,* the *orgeats* and *petits gateaux* and *bonbons.* The burgundy disappointed us and did not prove comparable to the Madeira of those days." But in cold weather there was a delectable "hot, rosy whisky punch, sweetened with currant jelly and heightened by a dash of peach brandy. We rose from the table with a sigh . . . We had dined perfectly for half a dollar apiece."

Sam added steadily to his education in good living by the benevolent example of his uncles and their associates. Uncle John was a notable host, his hearty manner at table and beaming countenance attracting gourmets who also liked good talk. He was partial to substantial fare: the beef and turkey he served were roasted to a turn, the oysters impeccably fried, the sherry, champagne, and Madeira of the choicest. Uncle John Ward's recipe for mince pies is used by a New York caterer to this day.

The custom was to serve a glass of Rhine or Moselle with oysters, sherry after soup, champagne with meats, and during and after dessert, Madeira. Among wealthy men there was intense rivalry to buy up the finest lots of the last. The names attached to the shipments, rather than vintages, of Madeira were as picturesque as the wines were seductive. "Rapid," "The Maid," "White Top," "Benefactor," "Black Cork," "The Great Unknown," "The Mob," "The Colt," "All Saints," "The Widow," "Hurricane," "Earthquake," — these were representative. Connoisseurs could mark the subtlest nuances of bouquet, body, and farewell. At a banquet given to honor John Quincy Adams shortly after the sixth President had left the White House, fourteen Madeiras were set on the table, and without referring to the labels, Adams identified eleven of them by sight and taste. Such were Sam's instructors in the arcana of wine.

Home life, thanks to his father's strictness, continued to be excessively staid, but a sparkle that helped somewhat to relieve the gloom was Doctor John Wakefield Francis, the ubiquitous New Yorker whose hand was in a dozen enterprises simultaneously, artistic, civic, and philanthropic. After a long and thorny courtship, Doctor Francis had married Sam's aunt, Eliza Cutler, the year

Sam entered college. The personality of the doctor fascinated three generations of New Yorkers. His practice was large and eclectic, extending impartially to every rank and class. He believed in phlebotomy, and many patients swore he had saved their lives by a timely bloodletting. He enjoyed the company of learned men, and even more that of actors, artists, and writers. One of the last, Edgar Allan Poe, described the doctor's bubbling conversation as "a sort of Roman punch, made up of tragedy, comedy, and the broadest farce . . . His forte was humor, the broadest conceivable." Since Eliza refused, married or not, to relinquish the care of her sister's orphaned children, Doctor Francis moved into the Ward home, where his peculiar vivacity often relieved tension and brought smiles even to the introspective banker.

Time passed swiftly for adolescent Sam amid social, convivial, and academic activities, although the last were too frequently neglected. One subject he let slide was Greek, assuming that he could cram at the last minute; in mathematics he shone almost without effort, or with pleasurable exertion; calculus and astronomy he regarded as fun. But on the eve of the senior tests, he discovered that as a result of ignoring his Greek assignments, Longinus, in which he was to be examined, had become "all Greek" to him, — a blank. "It was a horrible nightmare," he remembered vividly, "to be quite *au fait* in other branches, *facile princeps* in mathematics, and stand a chance of flunking in Longinus!" But he had not translated *Scapin* for nothing. He resorted to a trick — "the first ruse I ever played in my life," he maintained, although he did not pretend it was the last. Feigning illness, he stayed away from the college on examination day. When he showed up the day after, looking properly pallid and languid, the teachers pounced upon him. Luckily, the mathematics test came first, and waltzing to the blackboard Sam "drew a fantastic pigeon-wing." Then, observing the Greek professor making ready, he fainted. The faculty sent him home in a carriage. But he was graduated, two and a half years after his admission.

The engraved invitation to commencement ceremonies on August 2, 1831, bore, as one of the sponsoring committee, the name of his proud father. The banker looked forward to having his son in the countinghouse, now that his education was complete; but

Sam had no intention of buckling down to the drudgery of a bank office if he could prevent it, and he asked his father's permission to study awhile in Boston with Nathaniel Bowditch. The great navigator then was carrying out his translation of the French astronomer Laplace's *Mécanique céleste,* a work Sam wished to sound more thoroughly. Persuaded, perhaps, by the eminence of the teacher, the banker consented, and Sam put in several months at Boston, working hard. He was handicapped, however, by want of systematic guidance, Bowditch being too busy to give more than general supervision. Sam renewed his acquaintance with Benjamin Peirce, a former Round Hill instructor, now at Harvard and accounted the foremost mathematician of his generation in America. As an exercise, Sam published a little magazine called *The Mathematical Diary,* devoted to solving problems stated in previous issues. And he edited a new edition of Young's *Algebra,* for which he was paid. Meanwhile, his morals remained untainted by Boston, he assured his father.

"Do not fear for me," he wrote. "I have copied a great deal of valuable matter out of the Athenaeum books, etc. . . . I have a nice room and am in good health . . . Tell Aunt Eliza that I do not forget anything of my duties in Boston society — also that I keep an exact account of my clothes as they go to the wash." Although he had accepted an occasional invitation to a Park Street party, he pointed out that he had declined many more.

Evidence of his industry appeared in two articles published in the *American Quarterly Review,* a literary-philosophical magazine patterned on *Blackwood's.* One of the articles was a review of a biography of John Locke (concerning which Sam would confess in old age, "It would puzzle me to reproduce, and might embarrass me to understand, today"), and the other, dealing with *The Doctrine of Probabilities,* examined four fairly recondite speculations on the theory of chances as related to problems of insurance. Sam had found Laplace's classic *Théorie analytique des probabilités* more absorbing than a novel, and to the end of his days he would be preoccupied with estimating the probability of the right card turning up for him at the right moment. But his father was calling him home, and to New York Sam returned in the spring of 1832.

The banker was impressed by the compliments he was receiving from studious, respectable men on his son's brilliance, and he was not averse to encouraging it, within limits. An opportunity arose shortly. Sam had run up to West Point, a popular summer resort for New Yorkers then, and was there when the board of examiners appointed annually by the President arrived at the Point to report on the progress made by the Military Academy cadets. These learned and convivial men found in Sam Ward a youth as congenial in serious discussion as he was knowing over a glass, and unanimously they voted to make him an honorary member of their group. As Sam remembered the examination of that year, it was "a kind of frolic" — helped along by the liberal expenses the examiners chalked up at their hotel. Sam admitted that he probably helped not a few of the cadets by "suggestions," — such as the proper line to draw from A to D in order to complete a geometrical figure. In any event, the examination proved to be the most successful held for years, and Sam helped to draw up the report submitted to the Secretary of War. Then he joined the examiners in a celebration at the home of the superintendent, Colonel Sylvanus Thayer. He foresaw what was coming and fortified himself in advance, he said, by swimming the Hudson, across and back; so that after the banquet, Sam Ward was the only man in the party who did not require to be taken back to the hotel in an Army ambulance. That, at least, would be his boast in distant years.

Sam was not surprised, after this escapade, when, a week or so later, his father mentioned at dinner that a couple of gentlemen had called at his office that afternoon with an offer from the Military Academy, — to appoint Sam assistant professor of mathematics, in spite of his being only eighteen years old. (Banker Ward had been told nothing about the sustaining powers of Hudson River water applied externally.) Sam was ready with his answer. There was one branch of the cadets' training about which he knew nothing, he explained, and that was military engineering. However, give him a year of specialized study in Europe, and he might be equipped to take on such a teaching job — at least temporarily — with credit to himself and to his father.

His father was taken aback. A trip to Europe was made by few Americans then, by fewer for purposes of study. Sam ventured that the matter would bear thinking over carefully, and then, the better to think, he retreated to Newport and descended upon his Aunt Louisa McAllister and Grandmother Cutler, who were spending the summer in a cottage Sam's father had rented from farmer George Bailey, "at the third beach."

The woodcock season had opened and Sam did a little shooting, swam in the surf, and loafed, dreaming all the while about Paris. At Round Hill he had surreptitiously read Bulwer's novel *Pelham,* laid in Paris and tantalizingly descriptive of the delights abounding in that witty, wicked metropolis, and Sam was bound to get there. A Rhode Island cousin, George Washington Greene, who had spent some time abroad, fed his imagination with romantic stories about the capital. Sam waited impatiently for his father's decision.

Then fate took a hand in the family affairs. Cholera invaded New York City, and Newport imposed a quarantine on all travel from that area. Sam's father wrote that "we are very comfortable and tranquil in Bond Street," and told him to remain away, for in the city hundreds were perishing, and all who could had fled to uninfected regions. Then, while Sam wondered and worried, another letter came saying: "Your dear grandpa is no more. It has pleased Almighty God to call away his immortal part. His mortal remains will be laid to rest in the same tomb with my and your dear mother this afternoon."

Sitting beside his father's corpse, banker Ward had been racked by reflections upon the fragility of life and the awful nearness of eternity. "Dear Sam," he pleaded, "so be ready when the Bridegroom cometh!" But practical considerations must be faced, and the letter continued: "You will desire a suit of black and some other clothes. I annex a check on the Phenix Bank in your favor for one hundred dollars which be sure you give me a good account of. Get what is *needful,* nothing more . . . Pray be extremely careful in your diet and in exposing yourself."

Sam was shocked by his grandfather's passing, and he wrote to his father at once bewailing the loss of "the instructor of my childhood, friend of my earliest youth, one who, next to you, I esteemed, loved, and reverenced." But there was too much vitality in his nature for him to remain morose long, and some time later, when the cholera abated and banker Ward brought the rest of the family to Newport, Sam's apparent lightheartedness caused a momentary estrangement between father and son. Sam was out hunting when the banker arrived, and he burst in, full of good humor. A scene erupted, his father reproaching him with callousness, and Sam defending his sincerity, for he had been sincere in his sorrow at his grandfather's death. But as with many of Sam's sentiments, melancholy could not last long. At length harmony was restored, and, said Sam, in recounting the episode, "Had we been in California twenty years later, there would have been 'drinks all around.'"

Meanwhile, the hope of going abroad buzzed in his brain, and gradually his father was brought to consider the matter seriously. From that it was only a step to bring him to consent, and in October, 1832, the two returned to New York to procure letters of introduction and make preparations. The first letter was given by a family friend, Albert Gallatin, Thomas Jefferson's Secretary of the Treasury. Gallatin asked young Sam one question: of all the books on analytical geometry then pouring from the French press, which was the best? Without hesitation Sam replied that there was only one perfect book, and that was Biot's. Gallatin clasped the boy's hand in fervent agreement, then wrote a glowing recommendation to his particular friend, François Arago, perpetual secretary of the French Academy of Sciences. Other letters were collected, — a mixed lot, ranging from one to the Duc de Broglie, one of Louis-Philippe's ministers, to a solemn introduction to the president of the Evangelical Missionary Society of Paris. This letter was found unopened among Sam's papers after his death.

Another kind of letter, which Sam accepted as a matter of course but which was to prove his mainstay in Europe, was the unlimited letter of credit his father handed him, authorizing him to draw on the Paris correspondents of Prime, Ward & King, the banking firm Hottinguer & Cie., for funds. For money in hand, Sam was given a pocketful of gold Napoleons.

On October 20, 1832, the packet ship *Havre,* with Sam Ward aboard, dropped down New York Bay, and soon was tossing on the Atlantic, pointed for France.

FOUR

SAM ENCOUNTERS PARIS

SAM WARD's student days in Europe were divided into two parts: a winter of first impressions and conscientious study, and a reprise (or reprieve) of three years devoted to widening his worldly horizon and having a good time.

It was November 28, 1832, when he addressed his first letter home from the "city of sin and science." He was writing from the Hôtel des Princes, one of the most expensive in Paris. The Atlantic crossing had been stormy, but to his surprise Sam had not been seasick; he never would be. He had helped the *Havre*'s skipper, Captain De Peyster, shoot the sun, and had made himself agreeable to the few passengers, some of whom he described as pious and others as gluttonous, but all having good points. With an American merchant named Thomas W. Storrow, who resided in Paris, he struck up a close acquaintance, and the two hurried ashore at Southampton when contrary winds hung up the *Havre* in the Channel. Sam was flattered by the extreme politeness of the waiter who brought his first tankard of English ale, but demerited the skinny cold fowl that the inn served for supper. Dieppe restored his faith in eating places when the *auberge* there produced a prime roast chicken.

Storrow constituted himself Sam's guide for his culinary initiation in Paris. His first breakfast Sam never forgot: in the terms of music, he said, it "resolved the sharp sevenths of my gastronomic experience into the ample major chord of a perfect meal." The place was the Café Véron, in the Passages des Panorames, and half a century later he still recalled the bill of fare. Since this "presupposed a dinner," he said, it was "light and inexhaustive," starting with Ostend oysters, fried smelts, and *omelette aux fines herbes*, accompanied by a Chablis Supérieure, and followed by grilled sausages with truffles, beefsteak *maître d'hôtel* with potatoes, and *pâté de foie gras,* washed down by an excellent Beaune. The finale: coffee and a cigar.

The first weeks spent by "an emancipated youth of eighteen in Paris may be imagined," Sam would recount in the Memoirs he dictated fragmentarily to a distinguished amanuensis in his old age, but failed to finish. "He has to go through various social, artistic, literary, scientific, gastronomic, and bacchic grades, all having the attraction of novelty." With Storrow his mentor, he trod this upward educational path at the Rocher de Cancale, where the kitchens were without peer, and its jealous rival, the Trois Frères Provençaux, where the cellars were unequaled. Endowed with palatal perception and robust digestion, he progressed "through all the degrees of gastronomy according to the text and ritual of Brillat-Savarin," acquiring expertise in "the mysteries and miracles of Parisian elegance, cuisine, and cellars, then the pride of France and the joy of the world."

Sam was blessed in the time of his arrival in Paris, for under the Restoration and Louis-Philippe the city's restaurants reached their greatest vogue and their peak of artistry. Their chefs became legendary in the history of French cuisine: Henneveux, at the Cadran Bleu, reputed to be the costliest eating place in Paris; Hardy, at the Maison Dorée; Buret, at the Café Anglais; the joint hosts at the Trois Frères Provençaux (they were neither brothers nor from Provence), Barthélémy, Maneille, and Simon; and Baleine, the genius of the Rocher de Cancale. And there were many others of almost equal brilliance. Among first-chop establishments, the Rocher was conceded to be favored by the true gastronomes; its three-page menu offered more than one hundred dishes regularly, and special demands were no problem. A waiter there was almost as famous as the restaurant itself, — a *garçon* who would lend a customer the money to pay his bill, and because of his saintly trust in well-fed humanity was known as "St. Vincent de Sole." Sam's initiation into gastronomy, therefore, occurred at a succulent moment. Putting first things first, he applied himself to the savory subject with undistracted zeal.

After a month of delicious cramming, he turned to the business that had brought him abroad. Shortly after his arrival he had left the

Hôtel des Princes, whose charges he knew his father would never approve, for the Hôtel de Hollande, in the Rue de la Paix, where the price was only half as extortionate; now he deserted the Right Bank of the Seine for the Left Bank, taking lodgings in Rue Monsieur le Prince, handy to the Sorbonne. The *pension* was conducted by a Frenchwoman for American medical students, and she turned Sam away at first because of his suspiciously perfect French; but Storrow was able to convince her that his young friend really was American, and merely had a born gift for speaking pure Parisian.

Sam's letters of introduction opened doors to him which few foreigners in Paris entered readily or at all. A rich American youth was a curiosity, and Sam's charm, mental brilliance, and position as heir to a banking fortune, combined to launch him in the ultramoneyed circles that Parisians called the "summits of finance," and in ultraconservative, aristocratic society. His first call, naturally, had been upon Hottinguer & Cie., in the Rue du Sentier, to cash a check. He met Henri Hottinguer, active head of the firm, who at first inclined to be patronizing, but changed his tune when he learned that this surprising young man had studied the profound mathematician Adrien Marie Legendre, and carried an introduction to the formidable François Arago.

Sam's next call was upon Legendre himself, to express his enthusiasm for Legendre's recently published *Théorie des nombres.* Unfortunately, the scientist was ill and could receive no visitors. Sam then presented himself to the secretary of the Academy of Sciences, Arago, who dwelt at the Observatory, in the Luxembourg Gardens. Arago welcomed his youthful caller with simplicity and read Gallatin's letter with great satisfaction. Sam handed him an inscribed copy of the final volume of Bowditch's translation of the *Mécanique céleste,* sent by the translator as a gift to his fellow savant, and Arago chatted familiarly and rather cattily about men of learning whose very names had been objects of veneration to Sam Ward.

In the higher mathematics Sam deployed with ease, but the cash-and-carry of the pocketbook defied his powers of control. Try as he might, and he did try, he was unable to mortise his father's notions of economy into the frame of his spending habits. Before a month had elapsed, the withdrawals at Hottinguer's had assumed a total that Sam knew his father would not approve; so he started in the direction of New York a stream of ingenious explanations to justify his outlay, — explanations which, to his father, a man accustomed to balancing books, explained nothing. "The rate at which I live is an extremely economical one," Sam insisted, at the same time holding out the prospect that he might be able to pay part of his expenses by authorship; John Murray, the London publisher, ought to be willing to pay three hundred pounds for a life of Locke he was considering writing, he said. Meanwhile, his father must bear in mind that he was making extremely valuable connections. He was, for example, received in the literary-musical *salon* of the Duchesse d'Abrantès (Madame Junot), and he attended *soirées* "with several distinguished *savants*" at the home of the physicist Poisson.

Music he was studying diligently. At the Opera he had heard the rage of the season, Meyerbeer's *Robert le Diable,* and in *Le Dieu et la Bayardère* he saw Taglioni dance as a simple member of the *corps de ballet,* keeping in trim while rehearsing her next major role, in *Les Sylphides.* But the harmonic innovations of Meyerbeer and Bellini had not penetrated to New York, and Sam's ears, accustomed to Mozartian melody and the efflorescent jets and cascades of Rossini, were offended by the new style of composition. Feeling he could not afford to fall behind the times in so important a matter, he immediately engaged not one, but two, teachers, — and purchased a piano.

One of the teachers was a violinist and singer named Gear (he subsequently became a celebrated voice coach in London), the son of a double-bass player in the Park Theater in New York whom Sam remembered. Gear began by making his pupil sing, over and over, precisely the music that grated on Sam but that he was determined to admire. Sam worked with Gear on Mondays and Fridays. On Tuesdays, Thursdays, and Saturdays, his teacher was a moody, consumptive German named Lensberg, who expounded Beethoven and Weber with loving insight. Under his tutelage Sam acquired a wide knowledge of music, and sensitive taste; under Gear's drilling he developed an excellent tenor voice.

Sometimes Lensberg would take his pupil to breakfast at the *pension* where he lived with a musical friend, named Franz Liszt. The piano in the sitting room was always open, and Liszt, although never urged, seldom failed to play. "I remember particularly," Sam recounted, "one Sunday morning when the talk ran upon Weber, and during our animated discussion, Liszt stole to the piano and electrified us by the 'Invitation to the Dance.' "

Desirous of showing off his pupil, Gear arranged to have Sam sing at a musicale at the Duchesse d'Abrantès'; she was a noted patroness, and the audiences there were, in Sam's words, "French (which then meant polite) and indulgent." He went through a duet from *Cenerentola* with Gear; then was followed by a Norwegian violinist who also was making his first Paris appearance. This performance was pyrotechnic, and after it Sam observed "the old *habitués,* tapping their snuff-boxes, remarking to each other, '*Il ira loin, ce jeune homme.*' " Which was a true enough prediction: the young man — Ole Bull — did go far, and his path often crossed that of his fellow *débutant,* Sam Ward.

Through Gear, Sam also met the fabulous Nicolò Paganini. Gear had known the great violinist in Italy, and one evening just before Paganini was to appear in a recital at the Tuileries, he took Sam to call. They found the *maestro* seated, with a guitar upon his lap, his "lank body, long skinny fingers, black hair, and burning eyes" making a startling picture. "Your friend is musical?" inquired this apparition. "Fanatico!" replied Gear. "Then he shall hear me practice for tomorrow's concert." And taking up the guitar, he converted the instrument into "an orchestra of sonority." Sam was astounded; he played the guitar and played it well, but certainly not in that fashion. "Now it seemed a battle with the clash of swords, the shouts of the combatants, and the roll of drums. Then wails of pain and grief appeared to emerge from the sounding board, over which his fingers flew like what Western folks would call 'greased lightning.' " This lasted perhaps half an hour, and at its conclusion the perspiration on Paganini's brow, and his disheveled locks, indicated the expenditure of nervous force. "When the *maestro* had received, with a sad smile, our frantic applause," Sam continued his account, "I inquired whether he was going to rehearse on the violin his program for the morrow. He shook his head and said, 'I never rehearse the violin. My practice is the gymnastic of the guitar, to be sure of the suppleness of my fingers and delicacy of touch. My violin never fails me.' "

Such memorable experiences were all very well, but the way money melted in Sam fingers was becoming more and more distressing to his father. Sam was contrite; "I have been very careless in not keeping an exact account of my expenses," he admitted. But he was determined to reform, he insisted, and "I now have a little book in which, at the end of the day, I record my expenditures." Still, he felt he must point out in all fairness that his withdrawals at Hottinguer's had been unavoidable for a dozen reasons, which he listed glibly: "the impositions upon a stranger — the necessity of frequent riding, through ignorance of streets and sometimes detestable weather — my German and music lessons — my *pension* bill . . ."

But backed by that unlimited letter of credit, Sam found the opportunities to spend money only too plentiful. One outlay that raised eyebrows at Hottinguer's was his purchase, all but sight unseen, of the valuable library of Legendre. The scientist had died without Sam's meeting him, and the widow offered the library for sale. Sam bought it intact, for four thousand francs, and wrote his father that "I needed the best books," and that all his learned friends were praising the brilliancy of the bargain, which was "an excellent investment in mathematical stock. I should probably never have such a chance again."

Banker Ward was startled, but Sam's contention was correct — it was a unique opportunity to acquire hundreds of scientific works unobtainable in America. The purchase was confirmed, therefore, and Henri Hottinguer breathed easier; he had feared a blast from the direction of 42 Wall Street. The library, comprising some three thousand volumes, eventually would form the nucleus of the mathematical section of the Astor Library in New York, and later would pass into the possession of the New York Public Library, where the books are still consulted.

Sam's success with the library emboldened him to hint at the possibility of lengthening his stay in Europe beyond the agreed year. "I am each day learning fresh truths in the elementary part of mathematics," he wrote effusively, "and in three years, God blessing my efforts, I shall be capable of effecting an entire reform in American education." To his father such a prospect was thoroughly alarming: why should any son of his aspire to reform the educational system? Sam was needed in the bank. The letters from New York grew severe in tone, and reached a climax in June, 1833, when the banker wrote, not in haste but in exasperation: "The packet of the 16th May brought a letter for Julia, but none for your father, who, however, finds in Messrs. Hottinguer's advices: 'May 10: Pd Mr. S. Ward Jr. frc. 1150.' Now, Sam is it manly, is it honest, is it generous in you to use your influence with Mr. Hottinguer to draw more than you ought to disburse, and to preserve towards your father an entire silence on the subject? . . . You know, my child, that avarice is not my failing . . . The bookseller had but one copy of the book you ask for — price $18, which is double what you named. Pray, my dear, to confine your wish for books to those which are useful. I hope you will not forget the heavy disbursement of Legendre's library." But the letter concluded on a tender note. "If, my dear Sam, there is anything in blood, you have a right to be virtuous. I send you a box with a breast pin containing a precious relic." This was a lock of Sam's mother hair. "Wear it, my dear, on your bosom, and remember it is a talisman — let it not be degraded by any unworthy associations."

Sam had for his father a respect that he termed "almost Confucian," and such reproaches troubled him, — but not for long. Paris was tempting, and the thought of subsiding into the dusty routine of a banking office was repellent. He felt that he must get his father's consent to remain longer abroad. He had done good work, he had been elected to the French Geographical Society, and he wanted to study in Germany, at Heidelberg. But the agreed-upon year was nearing its end. Determined to make a persuasive effort in person, early in July he embarked on the packet ship *Burgundy* for home. In his luggage were presents for everybody in Bond Street, and a special souvenir for his tutor in astronomy, Nathaniel Bowditch, — several glass phials which, just before quitting Paris, he had taken to Père Lachaise cemetery and piously filled with earth from the graves of Laplace, Monge, Legendre, and other famous mathematicians. Bowditch, himself failing towards the grave, would be touched by the gift and the unpremeditated *memento mori.*

Sam found his family vacationing at Newport, and hastening there, opened his campaign. Newport was a rustic resort offering few diversions. One of these was the lively companionship of an old Neapolitan artist, Michael Corné by name, although everybody called him Father Corné. He delighted in serving meals of Italian cooking and dispensing gossip and chatter, wisely and humorously, over spaghetti and polenta. The hearty fare was washed down with rough Catalonian wine, and while soaking up the old man's culinary lore, Sam also imbibed many a maxim about the right use of wine and the abuse thereof. One of these Sam resolved to make his own rule of conduct: "Never to allow John Barleycorn in my house, and to confine Bacchus to the cellar, with the key in my own pocket." It was the only good resolution he ever stuck to, he said. Father Corné, a good Latinist, summed up his easygoing philosophy in the familiar line, *Dum vivimus, vivamus, nam post morten nulla voluptas.* Which Sam translated, *When the fiddles stop, the fun will be over.*

Meanwhile, he pressed his cause with his father adroitly. For previous lapses from financial rectitude he blamed youth and inexperience; this time, things would be different, he promised, meaning every word. The banker was reluctant to part with his son again, but so many men of worth and judgment testified to Sam's exceptional gifts and brilliant promise that at length he gave in, — provided Sam should mend his money courses. The packet *Carroll* was due to sail on October 1, and Sam was already poised to go aboard when the welcome permission came from Newport.

"I am willing, my dear boy," his father wrote affectionately, "that you should engage passage. But in returning to France, Sam, you must carry with you some means of executing your resolutions beyond your previous exertions. I look with pain at your careless and totally uncalled for expenditure — lavishing upon yourself what would have made whole families happy, and this from week to week and month to month, without condescending to offer one word of explanation to your father — absolutely thereby treating him with *contempt* — as if it was your broker's business to furnish money, yours to spend it."

But chastisement administered, father-love took over. "I refer to this, my dear boy, not in a spirit of crimination, but because it is *right* my views should be given you on paper that you may have them visibly to refer to *in case of need* . . . You know of course, my dear, how small sympathy I can have with the French opera or West Point balls. I send you annexed a check for ten dollars."

Resolved to be prudent, thrifty, and a credit to his name, Sam sailed eastward again. But hardly had he reached Paris when the second stage in his Continental education began. This was not prudent, nor thrifty, nor a credit to him, but it was gay.

FIVE

CHAMPAGNE YEARS

THE fiddles would not stop playing, or the fun be over, for the next three years. It would be tedious to follow Sam in all his peregrinations during that time; but there were highlights in the picture, some of which were graphically typical of the turns his character was taking, for better or worse. His studies played a mere rumbling base to shriller pleasures, but his time was not wholly wasted: he acquired (even when not benefiting from) much worldly experience, took on address and polish, and won many friends. He was young, well made, and charming, and he seemed the jolly incarnation of gilded youth, for his pockets were jingling and his hand was extended to give. It was hardly surprising that most of the people he encountered were perfectly willing to be wound around his manicured finger.

His appearance itself was prepossessing. The brilliance of his blue eyes drew attention, and his lips, delicately sensuous, more often than not were parted in a smile. He had grown a wisp of silky, blond beard, and his massive head, showing a noble expanse of brow, was topped becomingly by curls. His wardrobe was that of a dandy, but not extreme; his air and manner more animated than those of a mere boulevard *flaneur*.

This time Sam had armed himself with letters from Doctor Francis's actor and writer friends, less stuffy than elderly scientific celebrities, and without ado he entered Paris's lighthearted upper Bohemia. First and foremost, he struck up a firm friendship with perhaps the most sought after man in the Parisian world of art and gaiety, Jules Janin, short, paunchy, opinionated panjandrum of the Paris stage. Janin wrote, in the *Journal des Débats*, the wittiest, most sparkling newspaper column in Europe. He knew all the popular writers and the prettiest actresses, and he was adept at arranging *petits soupers* of the cleverest and gayest people, where Sam could shine, and usually pick up the check. In time, Janin would put Sam into a book, *The American in Paris.*

Janin introduced Sam to that ageless charmer of the Comédie Française, Mademoiselle Mars, still youthful-appearing despite her nearly sixty years; in Janin's phrase, "an actress in her lightest gesture, her smile, even in the pleats of her dress, in the form and color of her costume, and in the infinite resources of a skill that is never exhausted."

There were girls, of course, for nothing is surer than that virtue too pronounced is a chilling companion at bed or board. Yet Sam's excesses in this line were, so to speak, not excessive. Before leaving home he had exchanged with sister Julia pocket diaries, or "agendas," thin little books bound in red satin; and the names of transitory sweethearts began to appear regularly in his. To "Florentine," on January 2, he noted he had "sent 40 fr. in answer to her request for *un louis.* Went around and paid her a visit." The next day: "Decided not to go to Versailles until I have seen the masked ball. Saw Florentine, etc." The masked ball at the Opéra was a high point in the capital's revels, and Sam attended in "a new coat from Cutler, [and] found it to fit admirably." He arrived in his *coupé* an hour before midnight, and the next morning the diary showed: "Worse for wear. Flor. and Elisa breakfasted with me." On January 28, the day after his twentieth birthday, there was a petulant scribble in a woman's hand: "Je vous aime toujours, et vous ne m'aimez plus." But that had been smoothed over, the line stricken out, and underneath, in Sam's minute script: "Fisher's Ball. Made up with Flo."

Girls and feasting went together, and the diary mentioned "dinner with Storrow, at *Trois Frères.* Drunk 11 bottles." But Sam's carousing was not wholehearted; Father Corné's temperate counsels had taken root in his mind, and among other qualities, inborn or inbred, Sam possessed good taste. It was the spirit, not the vices, of Paris that captivated him, — that spirit of *vive la bagatelle* which a statistician of the time caught when he broke down the average Parisian's method of apportioning his income as follows: "The washerwoman costs more than the schoolmaster; the New Year's gift more than the midwife; the theater twice as much as the nurse; the bookseller half as much as the theater; the bath the same as the bookseller; and the money spent in amusement and luxury considerably more than that expended on fuel, the dearest article of Parisian existence." Opportunities for debauchery abounded, if a rich young man were so inclined, for it was a period of mawkish sentiment and modish profligacy — a time "all champagne and tears," as Henry James described the book that mirrored it, *La Dame aux Camélias*. But Sam Ward was not equipped to be profligate; he oscillated between amourettes and intellectual pleasures. Almost lost among the diary's jottings about "Flo," and "Josephine," and "Paquita" was an entry reading: "Admitted to Société Géologique de France." This acceptance into a second learned society (the first was the Geographical Society) was an incontestable achievement for a youth still too young to vote in his own country.

Keeping up with geology involved keeping in touch with student friends of the winter previous, above all with two Luxembourgers. One, Charles Frederick Mersch, had come to Paris to study mathematics, like Sam; but, unlike Sam, he was a conscientious plodder, incapable of brilliant improvisations. The genius of the youth from New York with his surprising mental reach fascinated Mersch, and wholehearted friendship soon linked them intimately. There was an understanding between them that they should collaborate one day, upon a history of mathematics which Sam longed to write; Mersch to do the research, and Sam to supply the funds and the authorship.

The second Luxembourger to whom Sam was particularly attached was a poor student by the name of Hypolite Mayer. Sam had come upon him shivering in an unheated garret, slaving at his books in order to obtain the degree that would insure him a livelihood. Sam brought the half-starved skeleton into his own rooms, warmed and fed him, and supported him from then on. Mayer was touchingly grateful, and Sam's addiction to primrose pleasures since his return from New York was a grief to this staunch friend.

All this while Sam's father, inhabiting a world remote from students and *grisettes,* was being subjected to progressive shocks. His son's expenditures, instead of diminishing, were greater than before; it was not the total amount of outlay that the banker abhorred, it was Sam's recklessness with money, his inability to govern the urge to spend. But Sam had the bit in his teeth, and light-o'-loves, dinners at the Trois Frères, and so many people less fortunate than he to help out, — all these cost a great deal. So he either evaded acknowledging his father's remonstrances, or replied airily and wide of the mark, advancing specious pretexts for not economizing, and perhaps in the next line mentioning hiring a valet, or begging for a fresh shipment of decent cigars. A factor banker Ward had counted upon to curb Sam was the arrival in Paris of an older relative by marriage, Henry M. Francis, a brother of Doctor Francis. But this worked the other way around: soon Sam was angling with Hottinguer's to get Henry Francis a larger allowance, one that would keep pace with his own overdrafts.

On March 15, 1834, Sam's father wrote with unmistakable displeasure: "The packets have brought me an abundance of letters from you on which I have more comments to make than time to make them. Also one for Julia, which, en passant, had too much Paris frippery and froideur about it. In writing to the children, my dear Sam, put yourself in the place of a parent and write in reference to their moral improvement. Thus, instead of being 'dissolved in tears' when speaking of 'triste B[ond] Street,' you might say youth is the season of study, of [forming] habits."

Then the exasperated sire figuratively took his obstreperous son to the woodshed. "In your letter of the 24th Dec. you speak, as in some previous, of your intentions to make your father your confidant — but in lieu thereof you seem by your drafts upon Hottinguer & Co. — and by them *unaccountably* permitted — to consider your father your *banker.*" This underlining was portentous. "There is a singular incoherence in your letter, a repeated reference to habits of economy and self-denial, opposed by drafts which would shame a spendthrift. You are going to Versailles to write a thesis or a something on heat — but your next letter would lead me to suppose you had hardly left your room for a month. You once refer to getting someone else to take notes at Mr. Poisson's — and you speak of no one thing else that has the least reference to your pursuits." When pressed for news, Sam dealt in mystification, the banker complained. "I ask Mr. Seton about you. He is under the impression that you are bound to Havre. I ask of your health and he speaks of your mustachios. Now, my dear child, what conclusion can I draw? You pass two months at an expensive hotel. You have moved somewhere — but no account where, and I am left in utter ignorance of your residence, pursuits, and associates. You speak of H. M. F[rancis], and after a solemn pledge that you would not do so, you ask his indulgent brother to allow him $400 more per month — as if the fund in our hands must not be responsible for the $600 allowed him. I cannot conceive of a person thus willing, in 'nobility of soul,' to squander the hard got earnings of another."

The banker's sense of honesty was shocked, and he laid down the law: "I desire Messrs. H. to confine their payments to him to the original sum, and yours to 750 francs per month. For if, my dear son, you cannot get along with that, I will make it less . . . As for your servant, I confess I see no use, but the contrary — a ridiculous appanage. As to your presents — I sent you to France to study, not to play the gentleman by becoming a genteel vagabond. As to segars, my dear son, I must see how you come on in matters of more importance."

But nine days later the elder Ward wrote again with tenderness: "No arrivals since my last and therefore without letters from my dear child. Mine latterly, dear Sam, have been written in great distress of mind. Believe me, my own boy — cast away sloth, effeminacy and all that lazy crowd that follow the tracks of a sluggard . . . P.S. I think your presents very dear in proportion to their value."

Yet in spite of this chiding, Sam felt "sure of the domestic rock to fall back upon," and in April he breezily announced that he was leaving Paris for Heidelberg, and was taking Francis and Mersch along.

Off the party set, pausing in Strasbourg long enough to investigate the Rabelasian dishes abounding in that stronghold of *pâté de foie gras,* then rattling on to Heidelberg. There Sam took lodgings for them all, — five rooms on the Kettengasse, midway between the Badischer Hof and the Schloss. With a piano, he settled down to four months of activity that was not, he confessed, "marked by assiduous devotion to any one particular study." He engaged a *privat-dozent* to tutor him in German, and kept at his mathematical reading. Soon his rooms became a focal point for drinking sessions, and in a haze of meerschaum smoke Sam laid in a copious stock of student songs, German, Hungarian, Russian, to supplement the music hall ditties he had picked up in Paris. His hand was always open. Once a month he journeyed to Karlsruhe, where Hottinguer's had their nearest banking connection, and cashed a check to cover expenses for everybody. On July 4 he inaugurated the custom of celebrating Independence Day, firing off champagne corks instead of cannon in a sunrise salute to the Flag, and acting as host to several score students who were invited to partake of unlimited beer, wine, and edibles, without having any notion whatever of what they were celebrating. The next morning Sam's quarters looked like a battleground; but he had maintained equilibrium by recourse to his tried-and-true preventive, — a swim in the river (this time the Neckar) before starting his potations.

Such behavior did not square with his promises to his father, of course, and Sam submitted to the latter's reproaches when he had to. "You may imagine my anxiety to hear from my dear boy at his new quarters," ran a letter that resembled many others. "I trust the next packet will bring what I so much want, a good sound letter. I have suffered a good deal, dear Sam. It is for you by a manly and virtuous course to restore me to myself . . . I want you carefully to review the past few months since again separated from your father and tell me manfully your view of yourself . . . I desire neither needlessly to inflict nor in foolish kindness to spare the rod — nor do I desire to say how much of silent grief I have endured. But if you, dear Sam, have indeed cast off the slough and come out bright and clear, all, all will vanish. I am writing late and will finish in the morning. Good-night, my beloved child." There was a postscript, written the next morning: "I hoped for an arrival today — but no French packet in. I kiss your heart. I send you my blessing."

These appeals — blended love and reprimand — touched Sam, but they could not reform him. Nevertheless, he did make an effort to gratify his father. During a discussion with his pupil about Fourrier's *Analytical Theory of Heat*, the *privat-dozent* mentioned his close connections with the faculty at the University of Tübingen, and suggested that Sam might obtain a degree there, if he would compose a thesis. Setting to work, Sam turned out, in Latin, an extension of one of Fourrier's equations, and forwarded it to the university. In due time he was invited to come to Tübingen and accept a degree as master of liberal arts and doctor of philosophy.

On the way, Sam caught his first glimpse of a Bonaparte — Jérome, who had married the sister of the King of Württemburg — never dreaming as he watched Napoleon's unimpressive brother gallop by that an offshoot of the imperial family one day would marry his youngest sister, Annie.

In October, Mersch went to Luxembourg, Francis set off for Italy, and Sam, who abhorred solitude, accepted the invitation of an eccentric baron, whom he had met at a whimsical fishing party, to move into the latter's semi-monastic villa, in the grand park of Schwetzingen, a former residence of the Grand Dukes of Baden. Baron Emmerich von Wambolt was a caricature of military pomposity. He was tall and portly, and his huge frame soared up to a ludicrously little head thatched with gray hair. On this was usually perched a battered foraging cap, while his costume consisted of remnants of the three uniforms he had worn at different stages of his career, — as an Austrian captain, a Bavarian colonel, and a general of the Germanic Confederation. The jacket was green, the waistcoat red, the trousers sky-blue. He lived alone, except for his cook, Rosine, and Sam became his paying guest.

The baron's habits were peculiar. "We rose in the morning at five and had coffee, cream, and a pipe by candlelight," Sam related, "and talked, read, or wrote as the spirit moved us. Shortly after daylight I took my constitutional in the park, and returned in season to the most serious solemnity of the day, a *déjeuner dinatoire* [dinner-lunch] at half-past ten. This lasted until high noon, for the baron was a trencherman who could have held his own with most of the

Roman emperors. When that meal was dispatched he took a siesta." At half-past two the mail arrived, the baron was resuscitated, and they read newspapers and smoked and talked — about wine or women, old campaigns, politics or religion — until it was time to eat again. As for tobacco, the baron possessed three hundred and sixty-six pipes, one for each day in the year, with an extra one for leap year.

Outside of eating and smoking, the baron's principal occupation was writing a daily three-page letter to his wife, who lived ten miles away at Mannheim; a letter she answered, less voluminously but with strict fidelity. This had been going on for years. Once a year the baron visited her, on All Souls Day; the rest of the year the baroness pursued her own interests, which were poetry, philosophy, and romance. Naturally, Sam wondered why a couple so devoted did not live together.

"My dear boy," boomed the baron in reply, "little do you know the interior spiritual configuration of a childless German woman abandoned to the muses and the philosophers. I live in mortal apprehension lest she should take it into her head some day to renew our honeymoon by a sudden appearance at Schwetzingen. To prevent this catastrophe, you see the length of my daily correspondence, which soothes and pacifies her by its frank confession of sensual materialism. Without this device, which I have ingeniously employed for a score of years, her sentimentalism, which is very tindery, would have long since brought her here to terminate my happy existence."

Baron Emmerich's trencher prowess was matched by his tankard feats, and often Sam would half carry the sodden old toper to bed, where he would snore himself sober. This example of inebriety had a wholesome effect upon Sam, confirming him in his resolve to adhere to Father Corné's precepts. And when summer softened the air, Schwetzingen definitely palled, and in August, 1834, Sam returned to Paris.

With a Latin dissertation and a doctoral diploma in his trunk, a fresh start seemed to be indicated. The red diary was laid aside in favor of a new day-journal, in which Sam noted his doings with the touch of bravado and Byronesque ennui that fashion made *de rigueur.*

Strolling along the boulevard, cigar in hand, whom should he espy, in a pastry cook's shop in the Passage des Panorames, but Florentine! "D'où diable venez-vous?" blurted she, for she had a new lover. Sam bore the blow insouciantly. " 'Twill make no difference in my regard," he confided to his journal, and he went to the Opéra expressly to meet the gallant, who took him backstage. "Much pleased," concluded Sam, as he went solitary to bed.

For some time his father seemed to have fallen silent, a bad sign (actually it was simply that the mails had been delayed), and Sam's conscience bothered him. So, as a propitiatory offering and proof of sober industry, he had made up copies of his doctoral thesis and distributed them among relatives, with three to his father. The diary, meanwhile, was chronicling dissimilar assiduities, concerning "Jeannette" (luscious but no lady), or a visitant with "beautiful madonna face, presence beautiful" (but *chaleureuse,* on the warm side). Nor was Florentine all ice: on one page of the little journal appeared, in shaky spelling, "Florentine bien indulgente, pardonnant les défauts d'autres afin que l'on lui pardonne les siens. Florentine, chez Samuel, à 11½ du matin, le dimanche, 30 août, 1834." What specific shortcomings in others Florentine chose to overlook, on that Sunday in 1834, in the hope that her own peccadilloes might be forgiven, were not listed; the diary simply ended there.

Bills, meanwhile, mounted up — to clothiers and jewel merchants and booksellers, for superb bindings on the books Sam continued to ship home — until Hottinguer's raised stern questions. Sam haughtily reminded them that he was a gentleman and his debts were sacred, — then lit out for Heidelberg, where, in deference to fashion, he was soon complaining of "black boredom" and beseeching his friend Mersch in Luxembourg to rescue him from "*noir ennui.*" Of course he visited Baron von Wambolt and sampled the cook Rosine's repertory of fourteen soups; he even fell in love momentarily with a pretty cousin of the baron, whose appeal was heightened by "an interesting pallor" and a "beatific blush." Planning further travels, he purchased from the baron a ponderous vehicle, a Polish britzka, built long, with a calash top under which passengers could stretch out during extended journeys. In this conveyance he picked up Mersch and a New York friend named Edward Jones — a Columbia graduate two years ahead of Sam — and toured Germany in style.

At Göttingen, he was introduced to one of his idols, Karl Friedrich Gauss, "the Newton of the century," whose *Theory on the Movements of Celestial Bodies* had been published in 1830. The astronomer received his visitors in the observatory. There happened to be a comet visible then, and when Sam alluded to it, Gauss opened the atlas of the stars and showed where he had marked its position the last three nights. "Where will it be tomorrow?" asked Sam. Gauss shook his head and smiled. Deferential but cocksure, Sam replied: "But you have not employed the formula contained in your great book for computing the elements of a comet's orbit. Otherwise, you would be able to mark its next move in the sky. If you have the book, I will show it to you." Aided by a photographic memory — a faculty that would stand Sam in good stead in many a tight corner — he turned to the right page almost at once. The aged scientist, visibly moved, laid his hand upon Sam's shoulder and exclaimed, "This is almost immortality! That a boy from the backwoods of America should call my attention to this equation!"

The britzka's next stop was Dresden, where Sam found time to sit for his portrait to the court painter, Baron Vogel von Vogelstein, who had just returned from England where he had done the portraits of Talleyrand and Princess Victoria, not yet queen. Sam also commissioned Vogelstein to paint the fourth member of his party, his Newfoundland dog, Rover; later the Norwegian landscape artist Dahl inserted this into Sam's portrait. A detour through German Switzerland followed, then Mersch returned to Luxembourg and Sam to Dresden, — only to hurry from there to Berlin, in order to appear *not* to have received a letter from his father, peremptorily calling him home. "It is deucedly tiresome to have to trump one's father's trick, but he is the one who forced this game upon me, so it is his own fault," Sam unburdened himself to Mersch. "No doubt about it, in April I will have to return to the New World, so you can see how much I count on your diligence and application to round out my role of scholar."

Sam himself rounded out his role of *bon viveur* at Berlin, where he attached himself to the American minister, Henry Wheaton, as secretary without salary, thereby acquiring diplomatic status. Outside the legation, he hit the high spots with a contingent of Russian army officers, who had been observing the Prussian maneuvers and were stringing out their leaves as long as possible. One of these, a Colonel Traskine, whose wife was the daughter of the Russian minister of war, Count Czernicheff, tried to prevail upon Sam to come to St. Petersburg, where he promised a splendid career; but Sam understood that for his father, this would be the last straw. He was prepared to make a tour of Russia, however, with a couple of American friends, and he had the britzka partially lined with fur, to form a traveling tent on the long, cold journey. But the plan fell through, and Sam went back to Dresden to enjoy the *gemütlich* amenities of the court there.

An eminently respectable friend of the Wards, George Ticknor, was in Dresden with his wife and two daughters, and he welcomed Sam with the frosty cordiality of the Boston Brahmin he was. Ticknor had resigned as Harvard's first professor of French and German, and was in Europe gathering material for his *History of Spanish Literature*. He proposed that Sam cease his aimless wandering and buckle down to study; but this did not sort with Sam's inclinations at all. Away rolled the britzka, with Sam inside, to Prague and Vienna, where he rattled off a letter for home, mentioning that he ought surely to be in New York by May, — then forgot all about the promise the minute the letter was sealed. Impulsively he returned to Dresden, and there a sheaf of his father's letters did catch up with him.

They were not sedative reading. The banker's patience was fraying. Sam had complained that Hottinguer was making difficulties about honoring drafts, even presuming to lecture him about "lavish spending"; so it was with an effort of self-restraint that his father had written, while Sam was butterflying it in Berlin, that he had at last received a letter, yes, but the only information it gave was that Sam was going to Vienna, "and that my desire for your return home is construed into a free permission to stay until spring! How you arrive at it, my dear Sam, I know not." Regarding the unpleasantness with Hottinguer: "It is you, my son, who have done ill. M. Hottinguer knew the objects for which you went abroad, and he well knew by your wanton extravagance that you had betrayed my trust and disappointed my reasonable expectations. Had you not erred, he would not have censured."

Sam was due for some straight talk, and in a further letter his father delivered it. "I fear, Sam, that you labor under some gross error as to your prospects of independence without labor . . . Perhaps you are not aware that you have not for three months written me one rational letter. Your rhapsodies leave me entirely ignorant of the real position of your mind, and I do not find there an acknowledgment of one line from me — although rarely has a packet been allowed to depart without something from your father. If, my dear, the world had nothing to do but admire your attitudes, it might do very well for a while — but I do most soberly ask you for a little common sense, and pray say if you have received any letters from me during six months past. I love you, my dear son, with all fatherly tenderness — but I do not love your faults."

The reproof was merited, Sam knew well, but he was headstrong, and the opportunity to remain a while in Dresden, hobnobbing with the quavering old king and brushing up on his dancing, was tempting. He had discovered, to his chagrin, that of the mazurka he was utterly ignorant, and even in the waltz, compared with the Germans, he was "nowhere." So he stretched his father's forebearance a little more with only a minor qualm.

Had Sam realized all that lay behind his father's stiffening attitude, he might not have treated the parental expostulations so cavalierly. Some time previously, banker Ward had received a letter from a person unknown to him, the poor student whom Sam had snatched from misery in Paris, Hypolite Mayer. The spectacle of Sam Ward — endowed with such abundant gifts, secure in his social position and basically so good—becoming a profligate and an idler had preyed upon the sensitive Luxembourger until he determined to save Sam from himself. He was aware that interference probably would be resented; still, in halting English, he ventured to address the elder Ward.

"I am a poor German student," he began. "I am bound [to your] son by friendship and by gratitude, for he has done what nobody else would have done . . . Since his return [to Europe] he has been led astray by a set of young men who are no fit companions. It should be a pity that a young man of such moral accomplishments at so early age should be conducted to the wrong way.

"Your son, Mr. Ward," Mayer placed his finger on one source of the trouble, "has a strange mixture of the character of a true and faithful man, and at the same time he is often childish and not able to conduct himself. At the same time he could give you the sagest counsels for managing other people. This is not exactly a fault, but it must be prevented by appointing to him a person who could lead him in your name,—for anything that comes from his father is holy for him. His veneration for his father is one good and eminent virtue he possesses."

Mayer was not proposing himself for the role of preceptor, he made clear, and "Mr. Hottinguer has too much business [to be] able to look after him, and he is too easily deceived by the fair speeches that Samuel makes to him in order to conceal his wrongs. Mr. Henry Francis . . . is too weak and too easily deceived . . . Mr. Ward, you have had the trouble of educating your son well; you have succeeded; and your paternal care has had its reward in producing a son who will do [much] for the sciences and add his name to the most distinguished men of his country. *Let not your work be lost.* The wrong is not yet great; it will be time yet to repair it by holding a stronger leading over Sam."

But this control must be applied circumspectly, Mayer cautioned. "Do not loathe him too rudely or too strongly, it would not do. He will take by kindness what he would not if he were threatened. It has perhaps (as far as I should dare to say it) been a fault committed from his youth,—that you held him too hard. Afterwards, when he found himself alone and owing an account to nobody, he threw off all restraint, and in flying high, he flew, perhaps, a little wrong . . ."

The blame was not all Sam's, Mayer pointed out: his father also had been remiss. "The fault you committed was this," the banker was told: "you gave him too much money . . . The more he has the more he wants. He could live as a man of rank and a student very comfortably with six hundred francs a month. Yet you know he takes at least 1000 francs a month, and with all that he owes his tailor and his jewellers about 2000 . . .

"Sir, I am no ingrate to your son. He permitted me to leave my garret and sit down in his comfortable, warm rooms, in order not to starve by cold, [and] when he saw me study for acquiring a profession that could, in my old days, save me from hunger, he too would not look astray from his books. Many a winter evening has been passed in such labor; but now, as unluck befell me, I caught a violent inflammation of the lungs and the physicians have compelled me to go to my own country in search for health. Here am I now, and my heart bleeding when I think that so promiseful a young man should perish for want of direction. I am Sam's best friend, who pray our Lord the most to keep him in a good way."

This analysis came ruefully close to the truth: Sam *did* venerate his father and shrank from inflicting pain; but he was impulsive and pleasure-loving, and he seemed goaded by an inner need to give pleasure to those immediately around him. His nature, as Mayer had discerned, was a mixture of good intentions and their unfulfillment: what he meant to do, and what he did, often were diametrically opposed. Such was his behavior when he found out about Mayer's "treachery," as eventually he did: he denounced the "traitor" bitterly, then characteristically forgave his "cher Hyp" and continued to send him money.

What Sam's father made of this intrusive communication, whether he answered or ignored it, is not known. But it could hardly have failed to jibe with what his conscience, and his scrupulous love for his son, told him was true. He *had* been indulgent, perhaps too indulgent; yet on the other hand, had he not, at times, been perhaps overstrict? Whatever the father's thoughts, whatever his reticence towards this stranger Mayer, his letters to his errant son became more pointed. Sam's setting of a definite date to be home (Sam had said May) was welcome, the banker wrote, although he had wished him to return the previous fall, "for many reasons." These he did not go into, but one was his uneasiness about the business outlook. New York, and in fact all America, was experiencing a wild boom, and at Prime, Ward & King certain signs seemed faintly visible betokening a coming squall. Under such circumstances, naturally the banker longed to have his son safely at home. Instead, Sam failed even to write, or wrote in such a way as to confuse, rather than enlighten, his father. "I think," wrote the latter from Wall Street, "it is now a year since you acknowledged directly any one letter from me, and I am in entire ignorance of more than one or two having reached you. You will oblige me by putting yourself in so much order as to own the receipt of this. I now, my dear boy, understand that you return in May, and I confirm it. I had hoped you could have seen England, but I cannot extend your time."

But the involvements at Dresden — the balls at court, the belles who were perfecting Sam in the galop and mazurka, and the speculations on celestial mechanics he exchanged with Count Lindenau, the astronomer who functioned as Saxony's chancellor — these all were reasons for not hurrying. Sam lingered on, making himself agreeable to everyone, and finding the life decidedly to his taste.

Should a fellow American show up, he was solicitous to make the newcomer's stay pleasant. There were few of these transatlantic travelers, but one rich young Philadelphian (although by no means as rich as Sam Ward) did come through Dresden with a friend, the actor Edwin Forrest, on their way back from the trip Sam did not make — through Russia by way of Moscow and Odessa, to Constantinople, and across the Balkans to Vienna and Trieste. Five decades later, this traveler would set down in his memoirs the still vividly remembered incident: "We had just finished dinner, when the card of an American gentleman was brought in, who desired to pay us a visit. We welcomed him cordially, and a sprightly conversation followed. He was full of anecdote and piquant remark, displaying acute observation and great independence of character. He was living in Dresden, studying German, and spoke of the gaieties of this fascinating town. This was my first acquaintance with Samuel Ward, son of the New York banker, of the well known house of Prime, Ward & King."

The man who recalled this meeting with such distinctness was Henry Wikoff, who, under the title of Chevalier, would himself become an international celebrity and participate in many of the same historic happenings with Sam Ward, although on a different level and not always as an admired friend.

Still Sam tarried in Dresden, while his exasperated father alternated between reproaches and pleas. "You start for Odessa and land in Vienna," the banker despaired. "I, therefore, when you propose for home, may look for accounts of you from the South Pole! I hope, my dear Sam, soon to receive a clear, distinct annunciation that you have collected your scattered senses and are soberly bound for the land of your fathers!"

Sam sensed that it was indeed time he should start for Bond Street — which for him meant also Wall Street and "servitude" — so, with a gallant goodbye to the Ticknors, he ordered out the britzka. But like a respectful youth who defers to adages, he chose, as the shortest route, the longest way round. It passed through Weimar, where Sam paid duty-homage at the tomb of Goethe and Schiller and kissed Goethe's granddaughter; and Eisenach, where he viewed the Wartburg and meditated in Luther's study; and thence to Heidelberg, where he felt he must bid farewell to his many friends, headed by the voracious Emmerich von Wambolt.

There was an added incentive for rambling the old town by the Neckar once more: Sam's cousin, George Washington Greene, for months had been writing about a friend who chanced to be at Heidelberg, a college instructor from Maine, whom Greene had met in Italy. An extraordinary chap, really, he said, filled with the love of learning and with humor and sentiment, high-minded, generous, a capital traveling companion. Ticknor had spoken eulogistically of the same man, whom in fact he had recommended as his successor at Harvard. The recommendation had been received favorably, and the new appointee to the chair of modern languages at Cambridge was in Europe preparing himself to assume that post. Sam looked forward to meeting this well spoken of scholar, whose name was Henry Wadsworth Longfellow.

SIX

HEIDELBERG AND THE LONG WAY HOME

ALTHOUGH Sam Ward did not realize it, on that day in March, 1836, when his britzka rolled into Heidelberg, he attained the crest of his European passage; from that point on he would descend, with many a slip, a slide, and a slither, towards the fate he dimly descried as *involuntary servitude* in the bank.

At the Badischer Hof he was received royally; then he set out upon his calls. One of the first stops was at his friends', the Zimmern brothers. As he was leaving, Adolph, the elder, pressed him to join a small reception being given that evening for Mrs. William Cullen Bryant, who had spent the winter in Germany with her daughter. At that quiet evening party, Sam Ward met Henry Wadsworth Longfellow. It was "love at first sight," as Sam over and over testified, the commencement of a friendship warm, deep, and lifelong.

The conversation at the reception necessarily was general, but the two young men left together and, moved by the same impulse, adjourned to Sam's hotel. There, over pipes and long-stemmed glasses, they talked until dawn. Rather, Sam did most of the talking, while Longfellow sparkled in listening. Sam told about his encounters in France and Bohemia, described court doings at Dresden and the writers and artists he had hobnobbed with there, and chattered about "Parisian burgundy and French wit, and carousels with poets and philosophers." This was a reviving breath of the great world to Longfellow, who had been stifling for the sights and sounds of social life; Sam's irrepressibility put the moody New Englander in touch again with the world of wealth and activity for which he always had a penchant.

Longfellow was the older of the two, but only seven years senior to twenty-two-year-old Sam Ward. His recent life had been clouded by sorrow. After graduating from Bowdoin College, in Maine, he had spent a happy period traveling in France, Italy, and Spain, mastering the languages and absorbing the enthusiasms of the Romantic movement then sweeping Europe. On returning home, he had taught French and Spanish at Bowdoin, and he had married. But the limitations of a provincial town and faculty became oppressive, and he was casting about for some way of escape when Harvard offered him the chair of modern languages. Gratefully accepting, he stipulated only that he be permitted to spend another year of study in Europe, where he wished especially to perfect himself in Scandinavian.

With his wife, he had sailed the previous autumn. But tragedy overtook them in Holland, where, after a miscarriage, his wife died. The blow aroused the Puritan pessimism that was one element in Longfellow's character; bitterly he blamed himself, and at Heidelberg he had passed the winter in remorseful reclusion, book-cloistered for months. Under Sam Ward's verve and brilliancy, the man's natural cheerfulness rushed back like a New England spring. Their interests were identical — literature, travel, philosophy. Both were intellectual, with scholarly achievements to their credit. Both spoke several languages. Both were classicists. Both loved Horace. Sam's irrepressible vivacity lifted Longfellow out of the doldrums, and they parted only when the sun came up.

The next afternoon Sam burst into Longfellow's study, and again they talked without letup, their conversation growing so animated that Sam took off his coat, the better to let himself go. There was no thought then of future poetic fame: Longfellow had turned out some juvenile verses of complete obscurity, but he had no immediate expectation of writing at all except academically. Sam saw only the gifted, handsome professor, whose lot he declared he envied; if his father would only let him, he was sure he himself would fit best in an academic atmosphere. Longfellow listened with amusement.

For three halcyon days the pair exchanged confidences and outlined their hopes and prospects. Then time (and letters from New York) pressed, and the britzka was put on the road for Luxembourg to pay a visit to that faithful understudy, Charles Mersch. Longfellow came along part of the way, reluctant to say goodbye. At Schwetzingen, Sam introduced his friend to Baron von Wambolt, who regaled them with Pomeranian goose hams and hock, then bade Sam farewell with emotion, feeling they would never meet again. And so it happened: several years later Sam heard of the gourmand's death, — not by apoplexy, as would have seemed fitting, but as a result of losing his appetite and shrinking into his grave.

Rolling down the highway towards Mannheim, Sam and Longfellow made merry over the eccentric baron, Longfellow laughing at the old man's grotesque resemblance to a monstrous greenbottle fly. Longfellow loved a joke, while Sam Ward loved to embroider one.

At Mannheim the friends separated. Returning to Heidelberg, Longfellow wrote to Greene enthusiastically about his new friend. But it was absurd to think of so much exuberance being tethered to the treadmill of teaching, he protested; if anything was certain, it was that after four years of roving France and Germany with carte blanche as to expenses ("and a temperament of at least sixty horsepower") Sam Ward was totally unfitted for the drudgery of a professor's life. What struck Longfellow with peculiar clarity was the marvel of Sam's having retained so much sweetness and purity of character, in spite of having been (as Sam put it) "dunged with flattery."

A series of setbacks awaited Sam, but they would have at least one happy effect, — they would slow still further his snail's-pace progress towards home. The first upset — a literal one — occurred in the town of Trèves. Jumping out of his carriage to greet the innkeeper's daughter smiling in the doorway, he suffered the mortification of catching his heel on that Vogelstein portrait and pitching headlong. A thick fur bonnet (relic of the abortive Russian expedition) saved his skull, but his knee was severely wrenched, and by the time he reached Mersch's domicile in Luxembourg, he had to be carried upstairs to bed. It was three weeks before he recovered. Longfellow sent condolences with the hope that report had exaggerated the injury ("I have not yet made up my mind whether you have lost your leg or not"), and improved the occasion by cautioning his friend against amativeness, recommending that he marry. "Laugh, if you will, at my simplicity," ran the letter, "but by all that is pure and lovely and of good report, think of these things." He forwarded a compliment which, considering its author, seemed almost fulsome: "A letter from Ticknor has just been put into my hands. Hear what he says of you: 'Has young Ward of New York been in Heidelberg, and if so how long did he stay and what did he do there? He . . . left us very anxious to hear good things of him, because he is capable of doing so much.' There is a sugar-plum for you!"

Ticknor's direct commiseration was frostier: "Your letter dated March 26th and postmarked 29th (no need of playing tricks on us) came yesterday . . . If you get from Dresden to New York without more than three weeks of confinement from your own want of *sagesse,* you will at least have exceeded our expectations."

Sam enjoyed the visits of his physician, a Doctor Würth, who had a lively mind. Between them, to kill the time, they conspired to have fun with the credulous Luxembourgers. In Paris just then, a medium named Petit was throwing people into a dither, causing wiseacres to debate furiously the validity of the "phenomena" he apparently was producing. Sam thought it was all a fake, and so did Doctor Würth. To prove themselves right, they worked out a system of signals — taps on Sam's arm, elbow, ear, chin, or nose — by which letters of the alphabet could be telegraphed, while Sam pretended to be in a trance. After rehearsing their act, they invited a select group to a demonstration. With mystic passes the doctor put Sam into a profound sleep, so it seemed to the spectators. His eyes were bandaged, and at the command of the "hypnotist" he identified objects and answered written questions correctly, informed, in each case, by the doctor's fluttering fingers. The séance was so successful it was repeated several times, and Sam's reputation spread.

When his knee was almost healed, the hoaxers decided to give a final performance to which local dignitaries, civil and military, would be invited. Mersch was in on the hoax, but declined to be an active accessory; whenever a séance was scheduled, he went for a walk. On the day of the grand finale, he started out as usual, but a little while later burst into Sam's room with warning of trouble ahead. While passing the *diligence* office, he said, he had seen alight a ribald acquaintance of his and Sam's, a sarcastical, cynical painter named Fresez. The artist had hailed him and announced that he had come from Liége on purpose to show up their friend Ward's pretended powers. Unrolling a sheet of paper he was carrying, he showed Mersch a drawing of himself, done by one of his pupils. Not a soul in Luxembourg had ever seen it, he explained, and he intended to seal the roll, and during the séance hand it to Doctor Würth. "If Würth's mystic passes can force his patient to discover the contents, I shall become a believer," he smirked. Mersch had hurried back to give the alert; the portrait, he said, was really a very good likeness, although the mustache was a trifle overdrawn.

The séance opened before the distinguished audience, and Sam feigned hypnotic slumber. The onlookers were allowed to blindfold him (they almost smothered him, they were so thorough), and in due course he identified watches and handkerchiefs and performed similar tricks. A stir in the room informed him that Fresez had entered. With finger on lips, the painter tiptoed to Würth and with a whisper handed him the rolled-up portrait. Amid tense silence the doctor touched the roll to Sam's head and commanded him to state what it was. Sam protested it was too much to ask, groaned and shuddered and grimaced, while the doctor's fingers wove more potent spells. At last Sam gasped, "It is a roll of paper, on which is a drawing, that looks like a portrait of an artist named Fresez — only the mustache is too heavy."

The effect was sensational, and thirty people left that room firm believers in mesmerism. But the full sequel Sam learned only some three years later. He was in New York then, and he received a letter from Mersch telling of having run into Fresez by accident. "That was a terrible thing you did, you and Würth, with your foolery," the sober Mersch scolded. "You recall what a scoffer and freethinker Fresez was. Well, that trick of yours convinced him that there *are* spiritual forces operating upon our lives, that materialism is not the answer, and he became reconciled with the church and is now a fervent Catholic! He turned Christian!" Mersch said he had tried to undeceive the deluded man by explaining the trick, but Fresez was disdainful. "It is easier to believe in the miracle," he replied, "than in a deception like that!"

Sam left Luxembourg in a blaze of mesmeric glory and careened towards Paris, one stage closer to New York and the "settling down" he dreaded. His father's letters had become exigent. "Messrs. Baring [in London] write that Mr. Ticknor advises them under 23rd January 'that Mr. W.'s son is at Dresden studying hard and quietly,'" the banker wrote. "This, my dear, is the first intimation, save from Messrs. Hottinguer, since 31 December, — when you stated you were in an hour to get into a carriage for Hamburg and England to get a tooth fixed. If I had not learned to trust in Providence . . . anxiety would bear hardly on me."

From the other end of Sam's line of communications, Longfellow pursued him with advice to take a wife soon. "The phantoms of your brain are beautiful but not holy," his Heidelberg friend counseled. "In the silence of the night they visit ladies' chambers . . . Let me speak candidly. Your imagination needs baptism in cool, pure water . . ."

Sam unburdened his hesitations and despondency in letters to Mersch. At Metz, he said, he had been too depressed to "touch the *pâté de foie gras,* for I felt the sentiment rising to overwhelm me the moment the morsel melted in my mouth." Life could not be more dismal. But the mood passed, and soon Sam was bubbling confidently: "There is no doubt about it, we are sitting pretty, my boy, very pretty. We both have great ideas and we know how to carry them out." Mersch must have no doubt about the renown in store for them. "I see two paths my ambition must take: first, I must prepare myself to accomplish great things in my own country; second, prepare to gain an European name . . . I have only one motto, — *Hurrah for success!* At thirty I must be *aut Caesar aut nullus." Caesar or nothing* certainly presented a magnificent scope for action; but in reality Sam's ambitions were more modest. What he longed for, always, was to be popular, to dazzle, and to be adored.

At the moment, two hurdles he must clear before he could embark upon his splendid future were Henri Hottinguer, and his father. From Paris, Sam assured his exacerbated parent that he was not dallying, but on the contrary was making all possible speed. "Why did I come to Paris?" he asked, in order to answer: "Because it seemed the shortest way home . . . You forbade me Paris *unless absolutely necessary* — and so I found it."

But to Mersch, in racy French, Sam unfolded the true nature of the "necessity" that had drawn him to the capital like a magnet. "I am going to the play with Jules Janin, at whose house I dined yesterday, and with whom I am very intimate," he chatted elegantly. "We went to the Palais Royal to see the first performance of *The Cross of Diamonds,* then to the Opéra Comique to see the debut of *The Lutemaker of Vienna,* in which Mlle. Damoreau sang divinely. Then we went to the Palais Royal to eat ices. And here am I, a wreck! . . . Tomorrow I am giving a luncheon for Janin at Tortoni's . . . The next day I dine at his house, and on Thursday next the two of us are going to see the performance of a new drama by Alexandre Dumas, in which Frédéric Lemaître has the lead. It is at the Variétés."

He sent flirtatious remembrances to the girls he left in Luxembourg, to whom he also was forwarding a grand bazaar of gifts, — lace handkerchiefs and perfumed handkerchief cases "costing all outdoors," sheet music, and letter paper for their anticipated replies. His affection for them of course was platonic, for he had formed the virtuous resolve: "I shall wed Science."

That austere alliance must wait, naturally, while Sam trotted off with Janin to the premiere of Dumas's play, *Kean, or the Disorders of Genius.* Lemaître, the epitome of all Romantic acting, bowled over the audience with fiery histrionics, and applause thundered like the surge of the sea. All Paris soon laughed over a sequel to that tumultuous first night. Dumas, who was perpetually broke, had been promised a thousand-franc bonus if the first twenty-five performances should bring in sixty thousand francs at the box office. After steady sell-outs, on the twenty-fifth night the playwright claimed his reward. "Luck is against you," the manager replied; "the total figure is fifty-nine thousand nine hundred and ninety-seven." Whereupon Dumas borrowed a louis, ran to the ticket window, bought a five-franc ticket, and came back crying, "Now it is sixty thousand and two francs!" The bonus was his.

In such an atmosphere — with Janin, the man who held the key to every dressing room in Paris, as sponsor — Sam took his parting fling. Then his leg went bad again, — providentially, however, for now he was able to moan in a long, long letter: "Again on my back, dearest father, and this too for some thirty days to come. My morale laughs at not being able to sally forth in Paris, but what deeply pains me is that I am detained from going home."

How really tranquil this immobilization was Sam reported in a different style to Mersch, giving the events of a single day. "I woke up at seven, read until 9:30, including breakfast, which Henry Francis shared with me, then prepared to write letters. No sooner had I seized my pen than Hottinguer's messenger arrived with the mail. Then in burst Auguste and Pierre, followed almost immediately by Cornille, Captain De Peyster, Potelet, a portfolio salesman, and my old German secretary. My poor bedroom overflowed. I found myself speaking English with the captain, French with Potelet, German with Auguste, and Spanish with Cornille. My servant and the old German were dispatched on continual errands, now paper, now sealing wax, now laces and embroideries, — it was enough to drive one mad!"

At one-thirty this crowd cleared out, but: "A knock: it is Mrs. Brevoort, come to pay me a visit that lasted two hours, her little girl with her. We talked about New York. She brought me news of the marriage of Miss Harriet King, who had waited for my return, tired of waiting, and got herself engaged. I don't feel mournful."

At three-thirty Mrs. Brevoort bade *au revoir,* when: "Another knock: here are MM. Hottinguer & Cie., come to pay me a rather long visit. I converse with these gentlemen on important matters and at five sharp they go."

The subject of this call by Sam's Paris bankers was not spelled out for Mersch, but it was important: it was to present the bill for Sam's vagabondizing. The total came to eighty-one thousand francs, roughly sixteen thousand dollars, or in present-day equivalents around eighty thousand dollars. This for four years of "student life" in Europe.

Sam was stunned. For a moment he panicked. Only his father could save him from a debtor's prison! And to that long-suffering man he wrote, in the accents of the play *Kean* he had just sat through: "Debt! Debt! Debt! The birds of prey fly around me, they shriek, *Debt! Debt! Debt!*" Here a creditor intruded to say a check for three hundred francs had bounced. "Only three hundred francs! Three hundred sins, for every franc is a sin heaped upon my head, not coals of fire, but ashes of lamentation!" How Lemaître could have bellowed these soul-searchings to the gallery! Dumas's rhetoric and Lemaître's ranting had gone to Sam's head, and figuratively he beat his breast, declaiming: "Must my gray-haired sire still labor, in the meridian of his life, while I, who am young and inhale inspiration, genius, with God's air, inhale them but to impoverish him? Gracious Heaven! Is there no recompense? There is a fire within me that can accomplish all that is great. Its fitful flame now gleams with hope, now dies with despair. Here I lie on this sad earth when vainly I would soar! Adieu, dearest father! Thank thy loved sire, my dear grandfather, that until past the age of folly thou atest Spartan bread!"

The afterthought, in a postscript, was like a stab to the heart: "I have received a note from M. Hottinguer in which he requests a list of all my obligations. Folly! Folly! Folly!"

This was not Sam's best vein, and as he lay — not on the sad earth but on fine linen at the Hôtel des Princes — he painted his dilemma pathetically to Mersch: "It is sad to feel indifferent to life and its pleasures at twenty-two." But the pose could not be held, and the next line read: "I imagine Ri-ra-Rosalie could make me feel different if she were here." One of his Luxembourg comforters had been named Rosalie. *"Dieu de Dieu!* Has she beautiful eyes! Oh, well," he sighed, "tomorrow will put me in a better humor."

Sam handed Hottinguer the required notation of his obligations, but accompanied it with a dignified defense of his expenditures. True, he conceded, he had purchased presents for his loved ones at home; but, he asked frankly, "Are these expenses of mine?" He went down the list: "For my eldest sister I have an album of choice drawings and paintings by the best artists of France, which will prove highly expensive . . . The binding of my library is not yet finished or paid for. My tailor's bill will undoubtedly be high, for he has supplied me with articles of attire for my two brothers." As for the expenditures in Germany, he would not attempt to itemize them, merely pointing out that the winter he had spent there had been "a diplomatic, and therefore a costly one." The conclusion was a request for more cash. "Definitely, I cannot leave Europe without having the sum of 10,000 francs placed at my disposal. My debts must be paid before my departure, or I shall not depart. Honor above all things."

So it was up to his father to get Sam home! To that father, the son wrote with contrition. "I slept but little last night, reflecting upon the imprudent phases of my European conduct. I found that affection and indulgence had been repaid by ingratitude and breach of promise, fond hope by sad disappointment, and large advances of money by the contraction of newer debts." Again he repented his errors. "Misconduct is an old story. I am now a man and would blush to take advantage of my position." And he signed himself, "A bankrupt in all save honor."

Yet how would he have explained to his father the companion letter he dashed off to Charles Mersch: "Yesterday a letter of eighteen pages to my father, a sublime epistle . . . I am possessed of the desperation of genius."

This storm, like others before it, blew itself out: Sam's father paid his debts, although in the form of a loan, and on July 22, 1836 (nearly three months after his arrival in Paris for an announced stopover of "three or four days"), Sam went directly from a farewell dinner arranged by Janin to the *diligence* that would carry him to Havre, — the britzka having been sold, at a fearful loss. Did he take ship there for New York? He did not. Still fighting off the inevitable, he crossed to England and made a whirlwind tour of historic scenes there, trying, meanwhile, to gull his father with the pretense that his real purpose was to inspect the heiress daughter of Joshua Bates, a partner in Baring's bank, in order "to convince myself if she may possibly suit me at some future day, or if I may, possibly, win her favor. Ten chances to one," he added, "I shall accomplish, or feel inclined to undertake, *nothing*."

The eruption of calculating amorousness in his gadabout son

might well astonish Ward Senior, but he could not but agree that Sam was wise in bringing to the attention of Mr. Bates "one who aspires to the honor of his future correspondence," through Prime, Ward & King. Sam's next letter stated, with involutions worthy of a diplomat: "If Miss Bates were not so much of an heiress, I might be strongly inclined to become attached to her. But I shall leave England unengaged, save to do honor to my father, my country, and myself. I was entirely wrong in coming here, but once here the best I could do was travel."

Leave England he did, forthwith, and on September 25, 1836, he set foot again on American soil. He rode the omnibus from the Battery to Bond Street, dodged through the traffic of Broadway, and bounded up the steps of the big house on the corner. His heart was pounding as he reached for the silver knob of the bellpull.

SEVEN

MISFIT BANKER

SAM felt that the fiddles had stopped playing and the fun was over all too soon after his homecoming. Put to work in the bank, he was compelled to throttle down his "sixty-horsepower temperament" to Wall Street's jogtrot and struggle with bills and discount rates like any apprentice clerk. Mersch, far away in lovely Luxembourg, was deluged with discourses upon the disadvantages of a banker's life.

At first the letters had been jaunty, like the one in which Sam related the lively manner of his moving into the family home. A housemaid had answered his pull on the doorbell, Sam wrote, and through the open doorway the following colloquy was held:

"Is Mr. Ward at home?"

"No."

"Where is he?"

"At Newport."

"With the family?"

"Yes, with the family. Mr. Ward has bought a magnificent country house there and he will not be back until next week. Doctor Francis is here, as well as Mr. Henry Ward."

"Is there a room vacant?"

"What do you mean, sir! Do you take this house for a tavern?"

"Yes, I do. And I intend sleeping here tonight."

"I think you must be mad!"

"Not at all. I am Mr. Sam Ward, Junior!"

By that time Doctor Francis and brother Henry had popped into the hall to see who might be at the door, and there were "shrieks and vivas, all of us flying about the house, hopping and skipping and laughing and singing and drinking tea and smoking, until three in the morning."

The next day, "I went to show myself in town a bit, and when five o'clock arrived the steamboat carried me to Newport." There he drove up to a big clapboard house on Bellevue Avenue, at Old Beach Road. "The doors open and I am clasped in my father's arms. A crowd of unknown people comes running and surrounds me, and asks me a thousand questions. Three angels embrace me, strangle me, call me 'Brother!' while my soul bathes in so much of unknown delight that I might drown." That Sunday they went to church in a body, and Sam found it "passing strange" that the lesson read was the parable of the Prodigal Son.

During October he remained at Newport, telling his exploits (with suitable deletions) and taking his bearings in the family group again. His sisters he found much improved. Julia, "poor Jule," at seventeen was pert, strong-minded, vivacious, but inclined to be moody; Louisa, smiling "Loulie" or "Weevie," was proud, warmhearted, and flirtatious, although only thirteen; while Annie, ten, was affectionate, sensitive, and demure. The brothers, whom he had left boys, were quite grown into manhood. Henry, who considered himself every bit an adult at eighteen, would soon graduate at Columbia, where Francis Marion, "The General," also was enrolled. Henry was charming and practical, while romantic-looking Marion was all dash and handsomeness, quick-tempered and sporting; in build, Marion was much like Sam, stocky and muscular.

His father Sam found more careworn and reserved. But the banker was cheerful, much occupied with business, and active in philanthropies. He had been serving as librarian of the New-York Historical Society; he was secretary of the recently founded New York University (Albert Gallatin was its president); and he was a diligent supporter of church missionary work, and of the spreading temperance movement. He did not lecture Sam unduly, now that he had the lad safe at home again. But after a month's holiday, he took his son to New York and introduced him into the bank.

Sam was pleased by the family's new home in the city. The great house, number 2 Bond Street, on the corner of Broadway, was sumptuous by New York standards. The ground floor was given over to three spacious rooms, designated the Red, the Blue, and the Yellow from the color of their silk draperies; the Red was the dining room, the Blue was the everyday sitting room, and the Yellow was the drawing room, opened only on grand occasions. The handsome marble mantelpieces had been carved to order by a talented stonecutter employed at Frazee & Launitz's marble works, a young Irishman named Thomas Crawford. Every domestic convenience had been provided, it seemed, from the observatory housing a telescope on the roof, to Doctor Francis's surgery in the basement.

The kitchen appointments pleased Sam particularly. Also commended by him was the picture gallery erected behind the house, along Broadway; it was the first private picture gallery in New York City. Already it held many paintings by European masters and by contemporary American artists as well, for banker Ward generously patronized native art: Thomas Cole, who was bringing into vogue the beautiful landscapes of the Hudson River valley, was under commission for a series of allegorical paintings. But the special feature of the new dwelling was a surprise prepared for Sam. Through a door at the end of the picture gallery he stepped into a library built to hold the books he had sent back from Europe. He had instructed that the boxes should not be opened before he arrived, for he wished to have the pleasure of unpacking them himself; now he found carved mahogany shelves waiting to receive his treasures. In anticipation of the hours of study he would pass in that tranquil setting, he wrote enthusiastically to Mersch: "You shall be the librarian! Only you are lacking, — you and Massa Rover at our feet."

But hours devoted to the bank cut down Sam's time for studious pursuits. He learned that while he had been rollicking in Paris, there had been a rash of business failures at home, and his father had put in strenuous weeks piloting Prime, Ward & King through the financial shoals on which less capably captained firms were foundering. The strain had sapped the banker's vitality and he was now troubled by chronic rheumatism and gout. (Philip Hone, whose new house on Great Jones Street stood back-to-back with Samuel Ward's, concluded that his neighbor must have fallen prey to "poor man's gout," since he drank only water. No such catastrophe threatened Hone: with loving care he had transferred his stock of fine wines — "2180 quarts and 254 half-gallon bottles of madeira and sherry" — from his old residence on Broadway, opposite City Hall Park, to the new cellars, and he was snugly waiting for it to regain the proper repose.)

After these sporadic alarms, the country had lurched into a frenzy of expansion: boom or bust, brag filled the air. New York City's population had spurted above the quarter-million mark and was soaring still; nothing seemed able even to slow it down. In December, 1835, a disastrous fire had wiped out almost the entire business area, but inside a year the property owners had rebuilt more substantially than before. Everybody speculated in something, — stocks, land, currencies, it hardly mattered what.

A new penny newspaper — the *New York Herald* — which a squint-eyed Scotsman named James Gordon Bennett had dared to launch in competition with the thirty-five newspapers already circulating in the city, caught on almost at once because of its voicing the spread-eagle optimism of the moment. "We have eighty-nine banks with a capital of thirty-five millions, a circulation of seventeen millions, specie in vault ten millions, public and private deposits one million, and loaned out at interest eighty-five millions," Bennett crowed, not without sarcasm, when looking over the field of his future operations.

> We have six or seven colleges, all poor and proud, except Columbia, which is rich and lazy, — educating only a hundred students a year, yet complaining of hard work . . . We have in State Prison 1492 rogues, and God knows how many out of prison, preying upon the community in the shape of gamblers, blacklegs, speculators, and politicians. We have 6457 paupers in the poorhouse, and double that number going there as fast as intemperance and indolence can carry them. We have about five hundred dandies who dress well, wear gold chains, spend first their fathers' earnings, then their tailors' and hotelkeepers', and close their careers with a pistol or a glass of laudanum . . . And to close all, we have twenty-three States and three Territories lying to the south, the west, and the east, more or less tributary to New York, getting from us our foreign and do-

> mestic goods, our fashions, our newspapers, our politics, our thoughts, in exchange for their cotton, their rice, their tobacco, their wheat, their corn, their coal, and — though last not least — their electoral votes. Here's an Empire State for ye! And yet one-half of its greatness, magnificence, power, etc., is behind the curtain. Scholars talk and twaddle about the states of Greece — the supremacy of Athens — the moral grandeur of Sparta — the magnificence of republican Rome. Mere shadows to New York as she is and means to be!

This was the prospect — apparently endless growth and limitless prosperity — that greeted Sam Ward on his return from staid, economically stratified Europe. To be sure, there had been those recent flurries and premonitions of setbacks, and a quota of business failures; but Sam's father had weathered the gale and it seemed to the apprentice that no great attention was required to carry on the mechanical trade of banking, — above all at a time when capitalists were multiplying their wealth with facility. An instance that everybody cited was John Jacob Astor, the richest man in America. Now seventy years old, Astor long since had retired from the fur trade, which brought him his first fortune, and from the commerce with China, which had tripled and quadrupled his millions. Now he was buying Manhattan land — farms and empty lots — all over the island. "Buy de acre, sell de lot," the old German would croak in his guttural English; only it was observed that while he bought, he never sold. Sometimes he would even sigh, "If I had only known, I'd have bought de whole island!"

He was not afraid to live up to the standards of lush times, either, as he demonstrated when he erected his monument, — the great Astor House, which occupied an entire block on the west side of Broadway between Barclay and Vesey Streets. The six-story, brick-and-brownstone hotel cost him nobody knew how many hundreds of thousands of dollars, and even jaded English travelers marveled at its luxury: every one of its three hundred rooms furnished with its own key, a water pitcher and wash bowl in every room, seventeen bathrooms, and *free soap!* To make sure the well-paying experiment should not pass out of the family, Astor sold the place, lock, stock, and barrel, to his son, William Backhouse Astor, for "one Spanish milled dollar."

Sam Ward inspected the marvels of the Astor House — richly carpeted, mirrored corridors paneled in black walnut (archly termed "flirtation galleries"), and elegantly upholstered sofas and rocking chairs in the lobby, where superbly gowned women lolled at ease — and he approved. In respect to the civilized amenities, his city was looking up.

It was deprivation of the amenities of Europe that Sam found hardest to bear. Tied to a ledger at 42 Wall Street, when he felt he might be more profitably, as well as more agreeably, employed in construing Plato or consulting Suetonius, he acquiesced in his destiny, but it was out of a sense of obligation to his father, to his family, and even to himself. Prime, Ward & King was flourishing; in January '37 Sam informed Charles Mersch with no little pride that the firm had cleared $216,000 the previous year, and within a year, he had been assured, he would be admitted as a partner. Meanwhile, as a learner, he was drawing no salary, although of course his father did not allow him to be without pocket money. All in all, the prospect was not to be despised, although Sam was repelled by the business of *making* the money he so enjoyed spending. Sam never despised wealth; it was the grasping, mean ways in which money often was accumulated that repelled him. His dilemma was to balance his loyalties and his inclinations, and this necessitated practicing a good deal of reserve towards not only his father, but towards his friends and towards himself: he did not like to face issues squarely. He of course did not see himself whole, and probably his father came closest to comprehending the contradictions at war in his confused and careless son. The medicine of time, backed by the discipline of regular work, might, the banker believed, eventually cure Sam of dilettante ways and turn him into a successful, upright man of affairs.

Lack of salary slightly cramped Sam's style in society, although it could not dampen his enthusiasm for social gaiety. To entertain he deemed a duty thrust upon the rich and well placed members of a community, and he tried earnestly to persuade his father to throw open their home to balls and other festivities. The banker declined.

"Consider, sir, the social tie!" urged Sam.

"The social what?"

"The social tie!"

"I make little account of that."

"I would die in defense of it!"

This so amused the father that for days he went about chuckling, "The social tie — he would die for it!" But there were no balls or receptions or soirées at the Corner House. Now and then the banker presided at a dinner, but these were pleasant, plentiful and sedate.

There was not a fashionable house, however, where young Sam Ward was not welcome. His Parisian accomplishments, his modish dress, cheerfulness, and generally exemplary behavior, all made him popular with hostesses, — and besides, rich and unattached, he was a catch for any marriageable daughter. At parties his high spirits were always on tap, keeping him the center of the liveliest group. He loved to dispense pleasure to all around him; he loved to amuse and fascinate. There was a special quality about him that set him apart from most of the city's gilded youth. This gift, Sam's greatest attraction, was spotted by a West Point graduate, Erasmus Darwin Keyes, the first time he encountered Sam Ward. It was at Dominick Lynch's house, where Keyes, a lieutenant acting as aide to General Winfield Scott, commander of the Army, was a by no means diffident guest. His attention was drawn to Sam when the latter sang a Russian song, "accompanying himself on the piano with a great clatter." Keyes was favorably impressed by the singer's appearance, his "compact form, vivacity of speech, and spontaneous activity." But in addition Keyes noted "an openness and candor" of expression which "denoted that his youth had been blameless." This, the somewhat puritanical lieutenant remarked, could not be said of "ordinary young New Yorkers who were the sons of opulent fathers," and he recalled a saying of Rousseau's, that "young men who preserve their innocence until their twenty-first or twenty-second year are the most attractive and engaging of mankind." Sam Ward, Keyes thought, was such a one.

This air of innate goodness that Sam radiated socially, Longfellow experienced anew when he reached America in October, 1836. From the Astor House (he avoided second-rate lodgings) he sent word instantly to Bond Street, and Sam dashed downtown. Bounding up four flights of stairs (elevators being then nonexistent), Sam found his friend's room empty, and he left a message on the table. He noticed several sheets of paper lying there written over with poetry, but they aroused no curiosity; although, as he was descending the stairs, he did fleetingly hope that Longfellow was not letting verse-making intrude upon serious academic pursuits.

Sam was not aware then that a change had taken place in Longfellow. After the two had separated at Mannheim, Longfellow had undertaken a trip through Switzerland, and there he had met a Boston heiress, Fanny Appleton, who was traveling with her family. It was love at first sight for the future poet, love absolute and irevocable, and thus far without even hope of a happy culmination. Something of the story came out during the few days Longfellow passed in New York, and Sam was sympathetic. But it was necessary for Longfellow to push on to Harvard and take up his teaching. Letters began to flow back and forth between Bond Street and Cambridge, in which the friends unburdened themselves of views on art, philosophy, and love, interspersed with observations upon the dullness exhibited by most bankers, and the irritations that can be caused by campus pedagogues.

This fresh contact with Heidelberg stirred Sam's correspondence with Charles Mersch to new impetuousness. Mersch was waiting patiently at Luxembourg for the signal that would bring him to New York, there to inaugurate his own and Sam's joint career in scholarship. The delay was due to Sam Ward's lack of cash, and by the reverse of enthusiasm he was sure his father would show if approached in the matter. Mersch, of course, would need an income of some sort, for he lived on his salary as a teacher. But Sam thought he could solve this problem. "There are two universities here, and my father is all-powerful in both," he wrote. "I can promise you a professorship at from seven to eight thousand francs to begin with."

But getting Mersch on the spot would be a ticklish affair. "It must be done without arousing suspicion," he advised, and he thought it might be best if Mersch should "arrive at our house as if by accident." He was impatient for that time, he told his friend over and over. "I live upon the hope of the comfort you will be to me and the thought of your constant sympathy . . . Your sojourn among us shall be as long as you like, and wherever I go you shall be my Achates . . . Before all else, I desire that a History of Mathematics shall crown my career and perpetuate the name of my father. There lies my life's work. But I find that wealth is in style everywhere; first I must be rich, and so, for a few years, I must work."

Sometimes despondency overwhelmed him, and then he would write to Mersch that "the future often appears to me dark and inscrutable. Sometimes it seems as if my day had come — and gone . . . Here everything is greed, everything is arid . . . In the office of an American banker, one can but feel that every day is a day lost." And he would caution Mersch to think most soberly about entrusting his career to "a man who up to now has disappointed every expectation of him."

In the midst of these changing moods, a major crisis imperiled Sam's dreamy plan to get rich by a few years of light labor. In May, 1837, the bubble of the economic boom burst; bank after bank went down, business firms toppled, commerce dried up, and the Great Panic spread ruin and misery nationwide. Even Prime, Ward & King was jeopardized when British investors closed their American accounts. On May 10, the banks suspended specie payments, and state after state repudiated its debt. This flagrant dishonesty shocked the banker Samuel Ward, and when New York State tottered on the edge of insolvency, he threw himself into an effort to avert the dishonor of repudiation. James Gore King was dispatched to London to raise tide-over funds, if possible, while Ward exerted all his influence to stave off disaster until help could arrive.

At first King's mission seemed hopeless, but after weeks of parleying, with the endorsement of Baring's bank he succeeded in obtaining from the Bank of England a loan of one million pounds sterling.

The only security offered was the good faith of Prime, Ward & King. In March 1838, when the first shipment of eighty thousand gold sovereigns started towards New York, the governor of the Bank of England wrote King that the advance was being made "on the sole responsibility of Prime, Ward & King, and the guarantee of Baring Brothers & Co. The object of the Bank is not one of profit, the whole transaction is out of the usual course of its operations," the letter explained; hence no date for repayment was fixed. "Having shown your house so much confidence, it would but ill agree with that confidence if I were to prescribe limits."

King sailed with the second shipment. Ward had held the financial and political bellwethers in line. Early in May, 1838, the gold arrived. Young Sam, coming home one evening, called excitedly to sister Julia that he had seen draymen all day carrying into the bank kegs of gold stamped "P W & K." The gold was distributed at nominal cost, and banks resumed payments. New York was saved from repudiation. For banker Ward, the victory was moral and personal; to Sam it revealed the magnitude of his father's power, and his integrity. But the effort cost the senior Ward his health; he was forced to retire to Newport for a long, painful recuperation.

Sam told Mersch that during the touch-and-go weeks, when his own fortunes hung in the balance, he had toiled "fourteen hours a day, doing the work of four men without letup and almost without fatigue" — all "for our future." Now the danger was past, and he daydreamed of Europe again.

"There are moments when, exhausted by heat and drudgery, the cool image of the Moselle rippling through the valley I love so much comes before my eyes, and in my ears is the sound of the Angelus, and I breathe the odor of new-mown hay on the fresh evening breeze. I am so happy." Then "money-bags, accounts, the mire of the office" became more intolerable than ever. "Were it not for that wretched vanity to be better than our other clerks, and the necessity forced upon me not only to shine as an accomplished man of fashion — the perfect Continental — but to prove my ability to become an *American* in every sense of the word, I believe I should fling down my pen and the accounts and become a vineyardist."

But Sam, although born in America, would never be "an *American* in every sense of the word." The time had passed for that: his years abroad, at an impressionable age, had estranged him in some ways from his native habitat and made him a cosmopolite. The irremedial change he had sensed immediately upon returning from France. On the steamboat that took him from New York to Newport, he had regarded the passengers with almost dismay: they had seemed to him alien, although outwardly familiar, — people bent on *getting*, on acquiring, on accumulating, whereas his impulses were to dispense, to spend, to enjoy. How could he establish a genuine sympathy with such a people, he had asked of Mersch. A money-grubber he could never become. American Sam was and always would remain; but not in "every sense of the word." This discrepancy, this jar with the world around him, made Wall Street no more supportable for Sam, once the crisis had passed and the bank settled into the routine of slack times again.

Banker Ward, nursing a gouty knee at Newport, realized his son's restlessness, and he tried to instill patience, preaching the necessity of foresight and the utility of moderation. "The Doctor [Francis] says you are working hard," Sam's father wrote in August of '38. "I solemnly believe, my dear boy, you will never have cause to repent of a year of severe labor, however onerous it must naturally seem to you. Get rid of all romance — but not the sentiment." He asked Sam to say candidly whether he had ever put in a year of hard work in his life; yet years of hard work, he pointed out, were the only means by which to achieve that independence which was the theme of all Sam's reveries.

The banker worried most over Sam's want of orderliness in his personal money habits. "Why do you think avarice a necessary result of following out an honest business?" asked the father. "My dear son, until you become frugal you will *never* be independent. No income can be equivalent to the wants of a person who has not settled principles of expenditure. You had large funds abroad. You came home in debt. This, my dearest boy, you must thoroughly reform. Form no rash plans and try to consider your present trial as a right one. It seems heavy, but patience will see you through it."

But Sam remained impervious to the meaning of system and moderation. His father foresaw inevitable disaster unless the lad changed his thinking, and he bore down hard with counsels of prudence. Apropos of a bookseller's overdue account, he wrote: "I found the enclosed bill of Carroll's laying about. I shall rejoice in the day, dear Sam, when you can on careful deliberation say you are not in debt to anyone, small or large. What fuss, you will say, about a little bill at Carroll's. My dear Sam, 69.75 is not a small bill, and consider how many books you now have. And if it were, the principle is the same. Four packs of cards for $2! . . ."

Yet Sam gave his father cause for pride, too. In October the latter noted: "I received from the executive committee of the Stuyvesant Institute this morning a request that you will deliver the opening discourse." In view of Sam's age — twenty-four — this was a flattering honor and bespoke the consideration he was earning among men of learning and standing in the city. Though he carried his erudition airily, the mind that had impressed the astronomer Gauss was producing an effect upon New York. The Stuyvesant Institute was an association for the diffusion of knowledge modeled upon Boston's celebrated Athenaeum. Towards its establishment Ward Senior had given liberally. He now made a point of coming back to town to attend the ceremonies dedicating the Institute's building, on November 4, 1838.

On that evening, Sam Junior took his place at the lectern, facing an audience of the most distinguished men of New York. He was faultlessly attired (as became an "accomplished man of fashion"), from high white stock to varnished pumps, his gloves immaculate, his bearing modestly dignified. "Gentlemen of the Stuyvesant Institute," he began with the gravity of a divine. "To the deep sense of an unexpected honor are joined in my bosom emotions of pride that there should have been erected in this city, by the voluntary offerings of its prosperous inhabitants, another edifice destined to combine the materials with the opportunity for human enlightenment." In sentences elephantine — and betraying more than a cursory knowledge of the subject — he sketched the barren landscape of Science in America, then bade his listeners look confidently to the future. "Science, whilom companion of the sage and the hidden object of individual devotion, even now seeks among us a permanent abode," he concluded his stately introduction of Minerva to Manhattan. "It has been the object of this brief sketch to show that *we all are bound to welcome her within these walls.*"

The Institute's directors ordered the address to be printed at their expense, and to Mersch Sam exulted: "Behold me launched as a public figure! . . . By and bye I shall be the oracle of scholars!"

This taste of recognition whetted his appetite, and he avowed to his acolyte: "Women no longer appeal to me — the thirst for knowledge alone devours me. Gaiety, pleasures, charming young creatures, daughters of flaming youth, I renounce them all. I shall not marry until I am at least thirty, — except to ambition."

All which was baffling to the prosaic mind of Charles Mersch; for scarcely had this renunciation reached the hands of the stolid Luxembourger when a second missive annulled it entirely. Sam Ward, this communication imparted, was engaged to marry seventeen-year-old Emily Astor, daughter of William Backhouse Astor and granddaughter of old John Jacob. The wedding was to take place on January 25, 1838, — two days before the versatile bridegroom would attain his twenty-fifth birthday.

EIGHT

EMILY

To identify blond, cheerful Emily Astor otherwise than by her family's wealth would hardly have occurred to a New Yorker at the time of her engagement to Sam Ward in 1837. Her grandfather, John Jacob Astor, was the only man in the nation richer than her taciturn, dour-looking father, William B. Astor. Yet Emily had charm and vivacity, she was fun-loving and sweet-tempered, and she captivated her grandfather with her finely trained musical talent; the old gentleman adored hearing her sing German songs.

Sam Ward was like a burst of sunlight enlivening Emily's dull home. The William B. Astor mansion at 376 Broadway (on the unfashionable side of the street) was heavy and forbidding, and was ruled by Margaret Astor, a lady of great weight of dignity. The daughter of John Armstrong, a Revolutionary War officer who had later served as United States senator, minister to France at the time of Napoleon, and Secretary of War in Madison's cabinet during the military disasters of 1812, Margaret Astor in her own estimation was first and always a Livingston. Her mother had been Alida Livingston, and her brothers, Robert R. (Chancellor) and Edward Livingston, were eminent public figures. Thus she had been born into the tight confraternity of Hudson River Valley gentry, and she it was who introduced the *nouveaux riches* Astors into Knickerbocker aristocracy. Old John Jacob was not a bit ashamed of his butcher-shop parents; but after he married his children into the proudest patroon families of New York, his descendants tended to look down on the founder of the fortune and complacently to forget his plebeian origin.

Emily was her parents' eldest child. Younger than she were John Jacob III (the second John Jacob Astor, the founder's eldest son, was feeble-minded and kept out of sight), William B. Junior, Henry, and Alida Astor. They were being expensively reared. Their phlegmatic father, who had been sent to Göttingen for a university education and had imbibed a taste there for scholarly pursuits, upon returning home had submitted meekly to John Jacob's insistence that he assume the responsibility of conserving the millions the old man had amassed. John Jacob Astor used to say of his son, "William will never make a dollar, but he will never lose one he has." This was a fair judgment, and the fact suited the older man, for it permitted him to live on a leisurely, hospitable scale, without oppressive business cares.

Next to getting the better of a competitor in a bargain, John Jacob Astor liked pleasant, witty, clever company: he had persuaded Fitz-Greene Halleck to drop poetry and become his secretary, and Washington Irving often was a year-around guest in the magnate's great house at 585 Broadway (on the fashionable side), where furnishings, food, wines, and service were nonpareil.

The match made exciting talk for New York society. The eligibility of the young man was examined, his pedigree approved, and his wealth deemed no detriment. One of the Livingston girls, writing to a cousin languishing in the country, gossiped:

> I presume you had heard of Emily Astor's engagement to young Ward. I know very little of him having been but once in company with him. He is said to be very clever and well informed — he is certainly very amusing. Tell Aunt that he is a grandson by the mother's side of the Mr. Cutler who married Miss Sheef. Mrs. Ward [Sam's mother] was a daughter of Mr. Cutler by a second wife. Did you ever meet with a beautiful little poem addressed to the North Star, the concluding line of each verse, *Si je te perds je suis perdu?* It was written by Mrs. Ward. I should not omit as a recommendation of the match [this demure gossip went on] that Ward's father is considered one of the wealthiest men in New York, and old Astor's motto is you know *a little more!*

John Jacob Astor liked Emily's choice, as he liked all bright, well-mannered, good-natured young men. And Sam's father, too, blessed the match. "Miss Emily has heart and has something to give in return," the banker had written to his son from Newport, relieved that Sam had not taken up seriously with one of the flirts who had been setting their caps for the heir of Prime, Ward & King. In token of his pleasure he handed Sam an order on Hottinguer's for ten thousand francs, to purchase another fine mathematical library which Sam had coveted. Later, as a wedding present, he would bestow upon Sam a fine house at 32 Bond Street.

Longfellow felicitated his friend upon taking the step he had persistently advised. "May you live very long and very happily with your bride!" came the message from Cambridge, and it was rounded off with a jingle:

> And when with envy Time transported
> Shall think to rob you of your joys,
> She in her girls again be courted,
> And you go wooing in your boys.

An ecstatic Sam responded that "the visions of hope and youth and loveliness have become one glorious, thrilling reality; out of the perfumed incense I have so long burned to my unknown divinity, the goddess herself hath appeared!" Accompanying this dithyramb was an acknowledgment of Longfellow's enclosure of a prospectus for an Anglo-Saxon dictionary: "I shall subscribe to your dictionary and do for it what I can with pleasure."

Mersch, who was in Paris, got instructions to invite three cronies to "a grand dinner at the Rocher de Cancale . . . I enclose three notes of invitation for you to deliver in person. Be all of you very gay! Send me an account of the proceedings, signed by all the friends and edited by Janin!" All at Sam's expense, of course.

The entertainments in honor of the betrothal brought an easing of the social drought in banker Ward's home, to the great contentment of his children. Julia, at nineteen, had her first glimpse of high society at a pre-nuptial dinner given by the bride's parents, and was impressed above all by the firmness of Mrs. Astor's dicta on matters of dress and decorum: glaring colors and vivid contrasts were considered vulgar, and under no circumstances should jewelry be worn during the day.

The Ward girls were much back and forth between the Corner House and Emily's home, or her grandfather's. Bowed with infirmities, racked by gout, dropsical John Jacob Astor enjoyed the young people, and Sam's repertory of old-country songs delighted him; some of them were straight out of his boyhood in Germany. When Emily and Julia Ward paired up for duets, the old man would beat time with his hand, and occasionally would hoist his corpulency out of the chair and join them around the piano, singing words to the tunes in a dialect that only Sam Ward could comprehend.

But with all his liking for this grandson-to-be, John Jacob Astor had no intention of letting the lad lay a finger on his bride's money or any part of the Astor wealth, which had swollen enormously during the panic of '37. In a time of financial distress, properties could be picked up for ridiculous sums, and in a typical deal John Jacob had bought at a foreclosure a block in Harlem that in a few years would be worth a million dollars, paying only two thousand dollars for the land. His holdings in Manhattan included hundreds of lots, large and small. One single property stretched from Forty-second Street to Fifty-first Street, and from Broadway west to the Hudson River, — and in 1838 he inventoried three hundred and fifty-four other separate parcels!

To Emily, when she married or became twenty-one, her grandfather had promised twenty thousand dollars; and this she should have, but tied up in trust for herself and her children. Furthermore, Sam was required to sign an agreement waiving all claim upon the Astor estate, an agreement that was standard practice in that family's marriages. Sam was glad to sign, and this readiness brought a glow of satisfaction to John Jacob Astor's round, jocund face.

The wedding was marred by only one drawback, — the absence of Sam's brother, Henry Ward, who was in Europe on a business tour. Marion, Julia, and Louisa were attendants; Annie was too young to "pair off" successfully. The Reverend (later Bishop) Manton Eastburn read the Episcopal service in the William B. Astor home. Emily, calm and self-possessed, wore white silk and a scarf of old lace in lieu of a veil, and on her forehead blazed a star of diamonds, the gift of her grandfather. Afterwards an elaborate supper was served, the health of the bridal couple was drunk, Doctor Francis regaled the guests with some of his best jokes, and then there was a ball. The dancing floor had been ornamented with floral designs in colored chalks and the music was gay. The festivity was still lively at midnight when father Ward crooked his finger, and Julia and Louisa and Annie were obliged to troop home after him. In a letter to brother Henry, Julia said that although "weddings are in general anything but gay, this was the most cheerful that I ever saw. Sam, Emily, and I are going to sing some grand trios, and when you come home we can have delightful quartets."

Wedding trips were not in vogue, and for three days the honeymooners remained at 376 Broadway; then they moved into the Corner House, taking over rooms that Doctor and Eliza Francis were vacating for a house of their own, directly across Bond Street; the house at 32 Bond Street, which after the wedding Sam turned over to Emily, with love, would not be ready for a while.

The next several months were perhaps the happiest passed by any member of the Ward family for years. As a married woman, Emily could chaperon the girls, and occasional parties ended the long social abstinence. When Emily brought in friends for an evening, Uncle Henry would drop over from 23 Bond Street to play polkas and waltzes, while Uncle John would lounge benignly in the study, pulling on a Manila cheroot and stroking one of the nondescript dogs he usually had at heel. Banker Ward was deeper than ever in business concerns, for he had taken on another responsibility, the presidency of the newly formed New York Bank of Commerce; he had subscribed for thirty-one hundred shares of the bank's initial capital. But on Sundays he joined the whole tribe when they descended upon Uncle and Auntie Henry for tea and music; and when the weary host at last would thump out "The Rogues March" as the signal for going home, the banker would tease his brother with, "No, we won't march yet! Give us half an hour more!"

Sam took his precedence as eldest son seriously. "Our family is growing up," he wrote Mersch, "and my brothers and sisters — two talented boys and three charming girls — need my counsel." But other interests grappled for his attention. For a while he became so engrossed in music that he toyed with the thought of becoming a composer. His father looked askance. "I neither object nor approve," he said. "But I do not want to see you cast among musical men. They are inconvenient and unprofitable, — generally winding up wanting some favor that it is difficult to refuse and that you have no pleasure in granting."

Sam's relations with his father, on the whole, were easier now. To brother Henry, who was still in Europe, Sam wrote: "I have given my dear father my confidence. I have found him liberal, generous, and indulgent beyond belief, and now I know what true happiness is." Meanwhile, he did not forsake literary ambition. He was at work on a novel in French, a frivolous occupation, his father thought, but Sam argued that it helped him to retain fluency in the language. He was also helping to advance the *New York Review,* a magazine of which Cogswell, who had given up Round Hill School, had become editor. Sam solicited Longfellow for articles, but the latter explained that whereas Sam Ward could afford to contribute (as Sam put it) for "no other compensation than the satisfaction of showing that intelligence may be brought to market," a poor pedagogue must write for a paper "where remuneration will be certain, and not so small. This Cambridge is a den of thieves, so I am forced to look for secure returns."

Longfellow envied, he said, Sam's energy. "Are you still a peep-o'-day boy?" he wrote. "Do you work in the morning and go to bed at sunset? I wish I had your temperament. My heart and head are both heavy, and sleep my great consoler. My hours are abominable. Two habits I must break — smoking and late hours. Pray teach me how to do it. Matrimony might cure me." Of which habit, he did not say. But matrimony was denied him, for Fanny Appleton was cool, and for seven interminable years she would keep her lover dangling between hope and gloom.

Sam wrote back that he had so far overcome sloth and self-indulgence that he had given up cigars. As for his hours: "At five I light my candle and am dressed for the day in a quarter of an hour . . . I begin the day with a psalm or a chapter of *Proverbs,* — it is a good composer and nerves the morale. Then I work steadily until eight, breakfast, reach my office between half-past nine and ten, and stay until four." This interruption of congenial activities bore heavily upon him, and he regretted that "sometimes business keeps me until midnight. I reach Bond Street fatigued and unable to study without depriving my dear wife and parlor folk of my society in the evening. I therefore have only my morning hours to do all my study in, and assure you I am half inclined to weep sometimes at the precious hours business consumes. But I begin to perceive my imperfections. The book you heard of [the French novel] is put aside. I am too much amid the dust of the money race to touch it more . . . If there is a man in the world whom I envy, it is yourself. The seclusion, the taste, the instruments, the skill, — all are yours, with ample time to improve and achieve . . . I wish I were a professor."

When summer came, Emily went to "Rokeby," her parents' fashionable country home on the upper Hudson River, while Sam remained "chained to a desk" in the city. Rokeby, a spacious but for the time unpretentious dwelling commanding a noble view of the river and the Catskills in the distance, had been built by Emily's grandfather Armstrong upon his return from Paris, and first occupied in 1815; John Jacob Astor had purchased it for his son William. There Emily felt at peace. Her letters to her husband, perspiring in Wall Street through June and July, were serenely affectionate. Sam was a favorite of Emily's mother, although sometimes rather shocking to that proper lady, and in one letter Emily reported with amusement: "Mother is deep in M. de Balzac's book. When she took it up she observed that it was very audacious of Ward to recommend a book to her that he had forbidden his wife to read." But apparently Mrs. Astor had concluded that "her thirty-nine years would protect her from being harmed by the mischief M. de Balzac scatters so freely." And Sam's ban on Balzac for Emily evidently did not hold, because a few weeks later she told him: "I have been reading *Eugénie Grandet* this morning, and when I shall have finished it I shall write you how I like it."

In town or in country, music was one of Emily's principal resources. Her piano was the best obtainable, a Pleyel, with a range of six and one-half octaves, — almost identical with Chopin's, built to the same model by the same makers at the same time. Julia Ward, whose talent for music had been discouraged by her father, wrote to Emily from the Corner: "I should love to see your beautiful piano and to hear you sing to it. Were it not for the Tenth Commandment I would envy you many things, dear Emmy. Sam certainly is a husband *comme il y en a peu.* He says you have already recovered your color and that your figure is taking on roundness."

This allusion was to the bond that made Emily doubly precious to Sam that summer, and rendered his enforced stay in town doubly exasperating. Emily was expecting their first child, and Sam was so convinced that it would be a girl he already had been billed by a stylish milliner for "one pink hat for baby, $4.00." Emily laughed at this confidence. She, too, deplored their separation, and wrote wistfully after Sam had appeared briefly at Rokeby: "Your visit was so short that it appears to me more like a dream than a reality, were it not for the many tokens you have left of your unceasing affection for me. I fear you were detained a long time at the landing, for I watched for the steamboat until half-past eight, but did not succeed in seeing it . . ."

Sam's replies abounded in endearments, — "My sweet wife," "Dearest love." He ached to be reassured of Emily's health every day: "Since last Tuesday I have received one letter. I feel like one forsaken . . ."

But summer passed, Emily returned to Bond Street, and there, on November 9, the child was born, — a girl, blond and hale like her mother. On January 20, 1840, she was baptized by the same Doctor Eastburn who had presided at the wedding. Named Margaret for her grandmother Astor, the child would be known in the family as "Maddie."

To be young, hopeful, popular, and rich in New York as the decade of the Thirties moved to a tumultuous close was exhilarating. Already the rowdy Presidential contest of 1840 was shaping up, with William Henry Harrison trying to unseat President Martin Van Buren. But for politics Sam had little regard. He had acquired precocious broad-mindedness in that field in 1836, when he cast his first vote, — a ballot for Henry Clay, defender of Whigs and bankers. That effort he saw nullified on the spot when Henry Francis cast *his* vote for Van Buren, who won that round. Bond Street glumly sought consolation in the reflection that, after all, the "Wizard of Kinderhook" was a gentleman, at least, — if only he would cut loose from the Jacksonian riffraff. Sam knew that Henry Francis was "all right," despite being a Democrat, and he could not concur in Bond Street's belief that "Democrat" and "devil" were synonyms. Sam's disenchantment with politics had set in early, and became firmly solidified as time went by.

The interests of his family weighed far more heavily with Sam Ward than public affairs, and gaps had occurred in the circle that brought home to him the debt and responsibility he owed to his line. In 1836 grandmother Cutler had died, sprightly of tongue to the last, and Sam missed her; from her came the French strain that was always so potent in his makeup. Then in July of 1838 Uncle Henry, the eldest and most debonair of Colonel Samuel Ward's five sons, succumbed. While helping to settle his estate, Sam was surprised to discover how rich the piano-playing broker was. The fortune, with the house at 23 Bond Street, went to Aunt Henry, the widow, and their only son, Cousin Henry Hall Ward.

Cousin Henry looked up to Sam Ward, envying his worldly polish. While a student at Columbia College, Henry had brought a classmate — well-to-do George Templeton Strong — to inspect Sam's library, and Strong recorded in the diary he already was keeping, and would continue to maintain until his death, that "in point of show" the collection was "certainly the finest I ever saw . . . Indeed I never saw anything comparable in the way of binding to many of the books there. It is certainly a superb and valuable library . . . a splendid collection, though I fancy more for show than use."

Sam's custom of rising at five o'clock to study before going to Wall Street belied this last guess on the part of Strong; but these two men, moving in the same social world, seldom would find their tastes coinciding. A touchstone was Horace: Sam adored him; Longfellow loved him ("my favorite classic . . . his phrases *stick*"); while Strong detested the Sabine farmer. Sam was no intellectual spectator, and he gave evidence of his scholarly industry in a paper he prepared and read before the New-York Historical Society, on the Battle of Long Island. The affair passed off very well, he assured

Longfellow: "Washington Irving was there, and Samuel Gray Ward of Boston."

This Samuel Gray Ward merits a digression, for he and Samuel Ward of Bond Street have been (and still are) endlessly confused. Samuel Gray Ward was the son of a Boston banker, Thomas Wren Ward, who, like his New York namesake, was a correspondent of Baring's bank in London. As boys, the two Sams were schoolmates at Round Hill. Samuel Gray Ward was a friend of Longfellow and a founder of the famous Saturday Club, where the Boston-Cambridge-Concord literary set foregathered to enjoy good food and better talk. But in respect to temperament, taste, and experience, the Boston and the New York Sam Wards were antitheses, differentiated by their friends as "the good Sam Ward" (Boston) and "the gay Sam Ward" (New York). So close were the two families, although in no way related, at one time Mary Ward, sister of Samuel Gray Ward, was engaged to marry Henry Ward, the New York Sam's brother.

While Sam drudged at his banking tasks, he also followed Longfellow's emergence as a poet with enthusiasm. The month before Maddie was born, a poem entitled "A Psalm of Life" had appeared in the *Knickerbocker Magazine,* and had taken literary New York by storm. Sam heard the verses quoted everywhere, matrons and maidens memorized them, while Fitz-Greene Halleck boldly hailed a new voice. Other poems had appeared serially thereafter, including many that were to become commonplaces of the language, and Sam's admiration overflowed. "Your poetry is beautiful!" he exclaimed. "It will find an echo in every true heart." Mrs. Astor was charmed by the seemingly artless verses, and when Longfellow visited New York in February of '40 Sam introduced him everywhere, heard Emily and the Astors pronounce him delightful, and reveled in his friend's glory. The poet, for his part, expanded under the warmth of praise, and the parties and luxurious living in the Corner House.

During 1839 Longfellow had been occupied with a "romance," that turned out to be *Hyperion,* a book of travel descriptions and fantasy, in which Fanny Appleton, thinly disguised, figured as the unresponsive heroine, and the author, transformed into Paul Flemming, as the ardent hero. Sam read the manuscript of this story of frustrated love in April and triumphantly passed it along to his father. But the banker rejected the work, disapproving of both it and its author. From Newport, where again he was invalided with gout, he sent his opinion: "It is not because L[ongfellow] has curly hair and a little overdresses that I call him a coxcomb. It is because he so introduces himself in his book, with the addition of being taken for Wilhelm Meister (near enough for me). He is constantly presenting himself as a sort of Hero of Romance, parades his thoughts, feelings, affections, love scenes. One such book is enough. As to L., I feel kindly towards him, and should like to see something from his pen which a few years would not lead him [to] desire, as *Hyperion*, to be cancelled and unwritten."

When this failed to dissuade Sam, his father renewed the attack, writing: "Longfellow in *Hyperion* has several touches of great levity, and he evidently desires it to be understood that he could say a great deal more if he had a mind to it in the same style . . . I object not to works of imagination, but to those which soil and vitiate it."

Longfellow's worldly foible was visible even in the Harvard Yard. His students had made up a ditty lampooning his flashy attire:

> Just twig the Professor dressed out in his best,
> Yellow kids and buff gaiters, green breeches, blue vest,
> With a hat on one whisker and an eye that says go it!
> Look here! The great American poet!

And Sam's gullibility in the matter of this goose tricked out as a swan exasperated his father. When a man is nursing a throbbing knee, his temper is apt to fray, and the banker finally blurted: "Sam, do read with the eyes of sense! You and L. flatter each other up to the skies until you are a pair of demi-gods! *You* have some sentiment, though sadly vitiated — L. has *none.* I am surprised at the levity with which you speak of *Faust* . . . For shame, Sam! Are these the results of studies? This your mode of reasoning upon the morals of authors?"

But his father's prejudice did not prevail. Two hours after receiving the first bound copies of the book, Longfellow was on the way to Bond Street, having declined an invitation to spend that August with Washington Irving at Sunnyside and another to be the

Astors' guest at Rokeby, because he preferred to be with Sam Ward when the reviews appeared. Sam dispatched an advance copy to Mersch in Paris, with instructions to secure its publication there. And he tried to obtain for Longfellow a chance to travel and study in Europe for five or six years, on an ample budget, as the tutor of young John Jacob Astor, Sam's brother-in-law. It was the intention to have the youth royally educated, in Germany, France, and England; but at the last minute the head of the family refused to trust "the inheritor of his name and a large portion of his fortune abroad so long." Longfellow's disappointment was keen.

The month that saw *Hyperion* published brought a distinction to Sam, also, when he was elected to honorary membership in the Harvard chapter of Phi Beta Kappa. This was a sweetener for his father, somewhat offsetting Sam's addiction to questionable literature. And with Emily and little Maddie rusticating at Newport, the banker was not discontent. "Emmy and baby have gone to bathe," he chatted to his son. "I have been playing with little Margaret, who seems very happy. She was sitting on the floor, and rolling over struck her head. The quiet, grave manner in which she applied her hand to see what was the matter set me laughing — she looked very sober and quite puzzled . . . No letter from you today. However, I cannot complain. You have been a faithful correspondent, and perhaps not a little sore from father's scribblings, which, however, my dear boy, won't do you any hurt . . ."

But this aura of well-being was deceptive. Although now a full partner in Prime, Ward & King, Sam was no more resigned to his work. "How toilsome is the quest for gold!" he sighed to Longfellow. "I have stopped scribbling . . ." And later: "I am a complete packhorse now, so circumvented by occupations and desires as to fear for all study . . . I am compelled to forgo music." Not only was the bank robbing him of all spare time, Emily and he were moving into the house at 32 Bond Street and fitting it up elaborately, — ordering bronzes and hand-crafted furniture from Paris, and assembling all the paraphernalia of a sumptuous domestic establishment. Everything had to be selected, received, stowed away. Sam had no tranquillity, and from Newport his father watched his fretfulness grow. "I have no quarrel, dear Sam, with your self-dissatisfaction," he wrote. "*Mais courage;* the general disease is an unwillingness to *face it.* You are progressing . . . Aim high. Your father is but a very so-so example and model, unless in love for his chicks."

The deficiencies that were oppressing Sam weighed upon the old man's heart. "Your notions of expense and generosity, permit me to say, are quite inconsistent with common sense," he urged more than once. "Justice and common integrity, my dear Sam, require that you should strive first to build up a capital in order to meet *your share of loss,* when any shall occur, for a long and successful career is no guarantee against loss; it is a contingency you have to count on . . . No true generosity is the offspring of impulse . . . Pray, dear Sam, think and act like a consistent, manly being who has got his part to play in the great drama of the world." Earnest wisdom, but wasted: Sam could not resist impulsive giving or cease to find money-grubbing repugnant. His father perceived one source of the difficulty: Sam's good-natured vanity. "Its dictates will always make you the tool of any who choose to play upon it," the banker warned. "Am I severe? No, my dear Sam — less would not be just . . . Ponder well over this letter, my dear boy, and do not set it aside to say offhand, slappery, dashery, how cruel, how unjust. It is all true, my baby — and if with the Lord's aid you will look manfully into your heart you will find it so."

Yet despite his father's prediction of "small profits this year," Sam's neglect of business duties grew, to the scandal of his partners. An egregious offense at last drew a stern rebuke from his father. "I grieve that you should have given Mr. King just cause to reprove you," the latter wrote. "It was packet day, and *your duty was to have been there.* You are too ready to consider the office secondary, your own convenience and pleasure primary . . . Remember how often you have been late, shamefully late, on a packet morning . . . I freely say that I should not have endured from any young man what has been suffered to be done by you. I shall really have to go back to Wall Street if you are not reliable in the hour of need . . ."

But there was no possibility of the banker's returning to active work. As early as the summer of 1839 he had become, according to Julia and Marion Ward, "very feeble," and Sam, deeply touched, began sending to Newport almost daily remembrances of fruit and flowers. "Pray hold your hand about fruit," his father mustered the strength to object. "A basket of peaches for three successive days and one of melons is an overflow. I like a basket very well now and then, but this is waste. I can buy here." The protests grew milder as the old man's vitality ebbed. On October 7 he wrote: "Your four lines cost 18¾ cents [postage]. Well, well, as they say, it might be worse . . ." And a final gentle reminder: "My letters are all kind if you read them aright."

This closed the father's correspondence with his troubled and troublesome son. His condition grew worse, and he was brought back to New York, where, in his home on Bond Street, on November 27, 1839, the man of integrity died. His neighbor Philip Hone wrote perhaps the neatest eulogy in the words: "He was a rich man, and made a good use of his money." Sam erected his own personal memorial to the father he had revered and loved but could not satisfy. All his father's letters — the chiding letters and the letters filled with yearning, many signed with the exquisitely tender, "I kiss your heart, my child" — these, endorsed in Sam's hand, "From my father," he preserved. They were among his papers when he died.

With his father's passing, Sam moved into the general directorship of Prime, Ward & King. Other burdens also crowded upon him, burdens of family. Once his father had written, "Few families ever loved each other better than ours have, and I trust ever will," and Sam felt the ties of kinship deeply. Brother Henry had taken a leading position in the bank, evincing much ability for business, and Sam had begun to rely heavily upon him for day-to-day decisions. But this help was soon withdrawn: less than a year after their father died, Henry Ward contracted typhoid fever, and with shocking suddenness expired. Sam was stunned, and Julia Ward was affected so profoundly that to the end of her very long life she annually commemorated the date of Henry's death.

Two deaths in rapid succession intensified Sam's sense of being miscast, and almost as shocking was the suicide, under poignant circumstances, of Nathaniel Prime, founder and retired head of the bank. The Primes and Wards had been like one family; a son of Nathaniel was currently a partner in the firm. Old Prime, although a millionaire, had become prey to a delusion that he was fated to die penniless, and in an access of terror he slashed his throat. Sam was as horrified by the deed as if the deranged man had been a relative.

A ray of brightness, set against the gloom of these disasters, was Emily's expectation of another child, due to be born in February of 1841. This time Sam counted on a boy, and to Longfellow he wrote confidently that "in February I shall be a *double papa.*" During the Christmas holidays he stayed at home, to be close to Emily, while working on a course of lectures he had undertaken to deliver for the Mercantile Library Association; his topic was the one that had fascinated him so long, "The Doctrine of Chances."

On February 13 a hasty note dispatched to Cambridge announced the arrival of the baby, a boy as predicted, and said that mother and infant were doing "extremely well." The birth of a son to Sam meant that the family name would be perpetuated, and for two days his happiness was intense. Then, in a letter all but incoherent, he informed Longfellow that infection had set in, and "after but an hour's warning, in the most sudden and awful manner," Emily Ward had died. Sobbed Sam, "I am heart-broken!"

Three days passed, and on February 21 he wrote again, somewhat less desperately: "The deplorable incidents of the past week have not a little unnerved me. Tonight my beloved mother-in-law left me for the first time since death robbed my home of its gentle mistress. I am alone, and how lonely I need not say to you. I thank God my little babe is doing well . . . I have been shattered root and branch."

A postscript, penned the next morning, read disturbingly: "I fear we shall not be permitted to raise the little boy."

The day thereafter the catastrophe became complete. A note to Longfellow said: "A little after three o'clock this morning our little sufferer left us to join his mother."

Within fifteen months, Sam Ward had been deprived of four sources of affectionate attachment, four steadying influences: his father, his brother, his wife, his son. To Longfellow, whose mind and heart could comprehend grief and loneliness, he uttered a cry of despair: "I feel crushed and worthless. God knows what will become of me!"

NINE

POETRY AND BUSINESS

THE Astors were kind to Sam in his grief, in which they participated. Mrs. Astor's sustaining sympathy moved him to gratitude; she helped him by her display of fortitude. On the day the baby died, he had conveyed the dreadful news to a cousin of Emily, at Charleston, in a note penned on heavily black-bordered paper: "This new blow comes hard, but Mrs. Astor endures it with becoming resignation not having left me scarcely since my bereavement." And as the shock grew less, he continued to be much in the homes of both William B. and John Jacob Astor. Little Margaret, for her part, was taken to her grandmother's heart and treated like a child of her own.

But it was to Longfellow — "Longo," as he had been affectionately dubbed — that Sam turned instinctively for understanding. "What a dreadful week! What an eternity of misery! What a troubled ocean of life seems before me!" he unburdened his grief during the first days of his bereavement, and letters expressing utter hopelessness followed. "I feel as one shipwrecked . . . Sometimes I am cheerful with the family at the Corner, and then come home sick at having smiled or mingled in mirth . . . I find myself towards night excitable and a little unhinged. My little girl is my main comfort, and my business my only distraction. Thank God the little girl is well . . . Her education shall be my special and prayerful task."

Longfellow's gentle, grave verses had been collected in a slender volume titled *Voices of the Night,* and in this Sam found solace. With Mrs. Astor he read over and over "The Reaper," "Flowers," or "Footsteps of Angels," and told the author, "For all this we feel deeply indebted to you, my dear friend."

Business preoccupations helped to keep him from brooding. Besides the affairs of the bank, which were onerous enough, there was the formidable undertaking of settling his father's unwieldly estate. A strange rumor had spread, just after the banker's death, that he had died "not worth a groat." George Templeton Strong heard the story and scratched in his diary: "Startling news . . . that Sam Ward's estate is going to turn out absolutely *minus*, and that proceedings have been instituted against the property settled on Sam Junior by prior creditors — absolutely incredible and astonishing, though stated on good authority." How the canard gained currency, who can say? Perhaps the free-and-easy habits of Sam himself had provoked suspicion.

Just how large the estate was cannot be determined accurately now, but it was valued in the millions of dollars. Years afterward, Sam Ward reminded his sister Julia that "maladministration" by a subordinate had cost the family "six million dollars." At least, so he said. In any event, Sam, his brother Marion, and the three girls had come into formidable wealth. Mainly the fortune was invested in real estate, and neither Sam nor his Uncle John Ward, who had been named joint executors, professed to know anything about that business. Acting in what they believed to be the most prudent way, they proceeded to sell off such property as they could, and reinvested the capital in stocks and bonds, about which they knew a great deal. The Newport house was the first to go. Its disposal Marion Ward protested, pointing out that Newport was steadily growing in popularity as a fashionable resort, and that property values were bound to rise; but Marion Ward was in New Orleans, where he had entered business independently after taking a master's degree at Harvard, and his advice was overruled. The Newport house was sold for ten thousand dollars.

Uncle John gave up his home at number 7 Bond Street and moved into the Corner House, in order to keep an eye upon his orphaned nieces. Sam took his meals there, returning at night to number 32, ownership of which had reverted to him upon Emily's death. But before long the great mansion on the corner was found to be too commodious for the diminished clan, and it too was sold, fetching sixty thousand dollars. Uncle John and his bachelor brother Richard then took over number 8 Bond Street, while Julia, Louisa, and Annie moved in with Sam and Maddie at number 32.

Leaves taken from two of the numerous diaries that Sam Ward began and abandoned sporadically provide an insight into the changes that had been wrought in him during the brief span of his marriage and its termination in multiple bereavements. The first entry, dated April, 1839, was written when Sam had been the husband of Emily Astor for more than a year, and their daughter, Maddie, was several months old. The previous summer had been one of frustration and elation as Sam toiled in the torrid city, separated from his bride, who was at Rokeby, awaiting the birth of their baby. The 1839 diary recounts a weekend trip up the Hudson River to Rokeby, where again Emily was installed, but now under circumstances of benignity and no apprehension. Charles Mersch was taken on this outing; for soon after he had been accepted into the bank as a partner, Sam at last had brought his studious friend (familiarly called the "Professor") to the United States. Sam wished to introduce Mersch to old General Armstrong, who was still the nominal laird of Rokeby although the estate was owned by the William B. Astors. The entry started cheerily:

> We embarked on board the *De Witt Clinton* at 5 o'clock. It was a fine afternoon. The river craft, hardly thawed out of their winter quarters, peeped forth here and there, and there was quite a show of steamboats. The boat was crammed, and I had an opportunity I had often wished for, to show Mersch an American steamboat, steaming with aborigines upon an American river. The spring had hardly opened its green eyes and the sky was not like an October one. The air was keen and clear. After supper we came on deck. The moon shone brightly and the sky twinkled with stars.
>
> I rapidly ran over last summer — the excursions to my dear wife's country home, the romance and agitation, the anxiety and hope, the strangeness of that early destiny, hardly married before I was severed from my blessed one, to pass in the fever heat of New York a summer half madness and half joy. "No longer," I thought, "shall I find Emmy in white, childish and playful, awaiting me in that pleasant circle. Little Margaret, too, will now assert her claims, and that undivided devotion is impossible."

As we sailed through the Highlands, passing West Point, Mersch was undoubtedly struck by the beauty and grandeur of the river — far finer, said he, than the Rhine. Newburgh, which by day is ugly and unpicturesque with its white-painted and white-washed houses, looked at night like an ancient Roman city, with its amphitheatrical outline and villas nestled among the trees.

We came to Barrytown [the landing for Rokeby] at 1½ A.M., landing in the small boat of which the bottom was frozen. We went to bed at the inn, and I awoke at 7 A.M. Sunday morning with the sun staring me in the eye. We soon arose, dressed, and learning that Mr. and Mrs. Astor had arrived and gone to Rokeby, we hastened up there to demand breakfast. I was glad to find that I knew the old paths of last summer and safely guided the Professor to the château . . . We came in sight of the white mansion, and I then made Mersch aware of the character and fortunes of the interesting being [General Armstrong] we were visiting. And what on earth can be more interesting than a man born in 1758 — a distinguished actor in the American Revolution — who knew Washington and had been in battle beside him . . . We found the old soldier in his basement room, writing. He looked up from his manuscript, welcomed me cordially, and gave M[ersch] a civil reception. We sat down and conversed for 3 hours. The room was warm but the old man's stories were still warmer.

Move on, now, to the diary undertaken in the spring of 1842, three years later. Now there are severe changes. Sam's father is dead, Emily Ward is dead, Sam's infant son is dead, Henry Ward is dead, and Sam has been placed under an unexpected burden of responsibility as executor of his father's estate and guardian of his sisters. Following weeks of anguish, Sam has recovered his poise, but his tone is graver, his manner more terse and sedate, his hopes humbly expressed. Yet in the medley of his interests there is an incongruity (science and singing lessons) peculiar in a banker or a thoroughly domesticated family man. The page, torn out of the original book, is headed in Sam's best script, "The Winter of 1841–42," and the entry reads from that heading:

has passed quietly by. A climate of unexampled mildness, indeed unlike any winter I have known. Some gaiety in our fashionable circles. Constantly increasing gloom in our foreign manufactures. Our currency in confusion worse confounded. *Lord Morpeth* and *Dickens* our visitors, the former a gentleman of education, the latter an impulsive genius. Recently Mr. Lyell [Sir Charles Lyell, the geologist], a more instructive person than either, has given interesting geological lectures — 2 last week, which I attended promising myself the pleasure of attending the remaining 6.

March 17 — The Girls left the old homestead [the Corner House] to sleep for the first time beneath my roof. I trust they will not leave it but for a better one. Uncle John joins us in a few days. They appear quite pleased with the house and I am invigorated by their presence. I have made a very comfortable bedroom of the small chamber adjoining my library. Maddie has learned to spell and grows apace. She bids fair to make a fine woman if spared to me and from spoiling.

March 21 — Lost $200, by an order to buy stocks from old Mr. Astor. Dined at 3 with Mr. Wm. A[stor] and Uncle Koosy [James Kosciusko Armstrong, General Armstrong's bachelor son] at the Astor House. They came to my library and sat smoking until near 7. Took my singing lesson. Mrs. Astor moved today to Lafayette Place [the new William B. Astor mansion]. Tomorrow they breakfast with me.

I have read this winter the following German books —

Goethe — Wilhelm Meister
Götz von Berlichingen
Faust
Iphigenia
Torquato Tasso

Wieland — Aristipp — 1st vol.
Jon: von Müller — Alg: Geschichte

Schiller — Robbers
Kabale & Liebe
Don Carlos
Brant von Messina
Wallenstein
Maria Stuart
Fiesco
Wilhelm Tell
Briefe Über Don Carlos
" von Julius & Raphael
Dreisigjahrig Krieg
Revolt of the Netherlands

Sam's interior and exterior condition at the age of twenty-eight is summarized in this self-revealing leaf from a diary he soon cast aside. Through it we see him through and through — his tastes, his prejudices, his sympathies, his scholarly ideals, his restlessness, his fine intentions, his friendliness, his ineptitude with money, his incapability of holding a grudge, his universality, his innate craving for affection from those around him. We see his attractiveness and appeal. We detect his appreciative eye for the social gaieties, in which, this season, he had taken little part. He worries about the business outlook, not profoundly. He displays a more than dilettante interest in scientific topics and in literature. He reads to purpose and systematically. He radiates family concern. The simplicity of his personal needs is exemplified in that unpretentious bedroom fitted up next to his library, which was the heart of his home. He is delighted with little Maddie, and determines that she shall not be spoiled. Without repining, merely as a matter of record, he jots down a loss of $200 to his cheerfully greedy grandfather-in-law, who never allowed personal considerations to stand in the way of adding a dollar to his pile. Sam finds congenial the sober talk and meditative company of his staid, fact-obsessed father-in-law and enjoys a pipe with Emily's genial "Uncle Koosy," after a dinner at the best hotel in town. All this a jumble of inclinations and tendencies, none dominant yet, but any one of them potentially apt to assume an ascendancy crippling to the rest.

For Sam, every cranny of the house at 32 Bond Street was redolent of Emily. Mementos lay everywhere. There was, for instance, the death mask he had taken of her features, put by with long strands of her golden hair. (Two decades hence that waxen image would be shown to Sam suddenly by a niece, who did not understand its significance, and the wound would be reopened.) For a while, Sam clung to these bittersweet souvenirs, but gradually the exuberance of his sisters, and his intellectual distractions, enlivened him and drew him away from introverted brooding upon his sorrows. The drawing was not hard.

The Mercantile Library Association lectures he delivered, and they were well received; Sam shared the association's platform that season with such luminaries as Longfellow, Ralph Waldo Emerson, Charles Francis Adams, and Horace Mann. Next he sketched out a series of analytical lectures upon the history and theory of music in its several forms — ecclesiastical, choral, operatic, symphonic, and folk — the talks to be interspersed with musical illustrations. Much research was done for this project — it would mark his final appearance as a lecturer, Sam stressed — and again the temptation to turn composer beckoned enticingly. "How brilliant and delightful to be the first American composer!" he mused to Longfellow, but admitted that it probably was "a little late to think of the *gai science*." His ardor for everything that pertained to music was vivid, and on a visit to Rokeby, during the first summer of his widowerhood, he did write — working in the handsome octagonal library there — a monograph on Beethoven for his friend Cogswell and the *New York Review*.

In this and other scholarly work he now had the assistance of Charles Mersch. The friend of Sam's Heidelberg-Paris days was older and calmer now, but still unfailingly loyal. He lived at 32 Bond Street as a companion-secretary, engaged on numerous projects begun by Sam. One of these was assembling data on Tycho Brahe, the Danish astronomer, whose biography Sam was in hope of writing. (By coincidence, Longfellow, towards the close of his career, seriously considered a long poem on the same subject.) Plodding and conscientious, grown rather pious and even ascetically inclined, Mersch was a sane influence upon Sam, acting as a brake on the latter's vagarious impulses. It was Sam's hope to place Mersch on the faculty at either Columbia or Harvard, a position for which the scholar was completely qualified. Longfellow joined in pulling wires, and at one point it seemed probable that Mersch would be named to Harvard, after Sam had offered to donate his library to the university, and to add a liberal endowment for a chair; he knew that if the offer were accepted, New York's learned institutions would cry "treason," but for his friend's sake, he was willing to face this wrath. Yet in spite of every effort, Mersch could not be fitted into a professorship.

During these negotiations, when Sam was casting about to raise a considerable sum in cash, should Harvard prove amenable, the situation at the bank became strained. Sam was irritated by the deliberation of certain of his associates, notably James Gore King, who Sam felt was overcautious and lacking in progressiveness. King was a banker after the pattern of Sam's father, conservative and scrupulous, and Sam's readiness to act on snap decisions often shocked the older man. Flighty notions about what constituted a reasonable, safe investment always alarmed King, and he kept a sharp eye on Sam's apparent eagerness to play fast and loose with the bank's funds. The fact was, of course, that Sam wanted to make money quickly, ignoring the inevitable multiplication of risks that high-yielding speculations involve, while King was geared to make money slowly and surely. Marion Ward, in New Orleans, received many a letter of complaint from Sam, reporting the dissension and throwing out hints that it would be better for all concerned to dissolve the partnership and set up independently in business. This seemed to Marion the extreme of folly, and he lectured Sam severely. "It is your ambition that makes you think your position is undesirable," read one sharply worded note. "You caution me often against a disposition to change my circumstances and occupation. Do not suffer uneasy ambition or restlessness to affect your better judgment."

Marion's acumen was greater than Sam's, and his younger brother's opinion Sam valued highly; a reprimand from Marion he would submit to meekly, when he would not accept reproof from his uncles or business friends. After a scolding from New Orleans, therefore, Sam would subside for the time being; but the reform was not permanent. The truth was that Sam was fed up with banking and longed for leisure to study, contemplate, travel, and enjoy life, pleasures that were denied to him by his responsibilities to family and his social position. Again and again his mental gaze turned hungrily towards "Longo" and the poet's supposedly ideal existence in Cambridge's supposedly placid groves.

But Longfellow's life was not as uniformly pleasant as Sam imagined it. The poet suffered from the normal campus irritations, and more keenly from the coyness of Miss Appleton. Essentially he was a domestic man, at his best only in a sympathetic home circle, and marriage was needful to him. But marriage was denied. He was lodged in a superb house — the Craigie House, that had served as Washington's headquarters during the siege of Boston in 1776 — and between there and Bond Street flowed a stream of correspondence, — frank, chatty letters, telling each other's troubles and frustrations, and otherwise canvassing every subject of interest to the two gifted men. The compatibility of the friends was almost without flaw. They used pet names for each other, Sam calling Longfellow "Longo" and "Longobardus," while the poet saluted the banker as "Dearest Sam," or "Most amiable and beloved Sam," and "Best of Sams!" Ward was amused by the popular notion that Longfellow, being a poet, must be lank and lorn, and he regaled the Craigie House dandy with an account of how he rebutted this fallacy when a young lady asked whether the author of *Voices of the Night* was not "a tall, thin man, quite emaciated, with great, melancholy eyes?" Replied Sam, "He is as round as a barrel and as rosy-cheeked as yourself, and his eyes, 'Oh, they resemble blue water-lilies' . . ."

"But isn't he often very unhappy? Doesn't he sit abstractedly, with his eyes fixed, musing mournfully to the tune of the 'Psalm of Life?' "

"Not that I ever saw, ma'am. He is generally merry and cheerful — likes a smiling chat and a good glass of wine with a friend, or half a dozen."

"Dear me!"

And Longfellow retorted that he would tell the next woman who asked about Sam Ward that "you are only five feet three, with a white swelling on your knee, and the erysipelas in your face." Surrounded by earnest, high-minded, and dogmatic disputants in Boston, Longfellow gave thanks that in Sam Ward he possessed one friend who never talked "as if he were the Pope."

Sam formed the habit of running up to Boston over weekends,— a long, tedious trip by steamboat in those days. But he would burst in, brimming with vim, singing a student song and flourishing a bottle of Rhine wine. The friends would greet each other in hearty Heidelberg style, with a kiss on each cheek and one on the mouth, and then would hold forth for hours of talk and tobacco, over the long-stemmed green glasses that Longo had brought back from Germany. These intervals snatched from prosaic activities they both treasured — "the wine of life, the Gold Seal Johannisberger 1834 — *cabinet-wein*," Longfellow labeled them. His letters teemed with injunctions to "come soon." "When can I make up your bed at Headquarters?" "It is a long time (three days) since I heard from you." "I hope you will drop suddenly upon me next Saturday, it would delight my weary heart exceedingly." "Pray come soon." There could not be too many visits.

Sometimes the poet summoned Sam to pass judgment upon some new poem, especially if it were one of which his Cambridge friends thought little. In this way Sam first heard "The Skeleton in Armor," an experiment in ballad form which the poet had been advised was below his usual standard. In response to the call, Sam reached Craigie House before breakfast, and after eggs and coffee Longfellow brought out the manuscript. Sam listened while the author read, until excitement drove him to spring up, snatch the manuscript, and (as he recounted the incident) to "read it with more dramatic force than his modesty had permitted him to display. When I came to the crescendo —

As with his wings aslant,
Sails the fierce cormorant,
Seeking some rocky haunt,
  With his prey laden, —

So toward the open main,
Beating to sea again,
Through the wild hurricane,
  Bore I the maiden —

he sprang to his feet and embraced me. The doubting Thomases were at a discount that morning!"

Sam insisted that he be permitted to place the poem with a New York magazine, promising to get fifty dollars for it. This was unheard of munificence, for in spite of his popularity with readers and editors, Longfellow had never received more than twenty-five dollars for a poem. But Sam Ward was a salesman.

The most influential judge of poetry in New York was Fitz-Greene Halleck, and to Halleck Sam went directly. He found the ex-poet studying a ledger in the dingy Astor countinghouse in Prince Street. Sam read the poem aloud, and Halleck's enthusiasm flared up. At Sam's bidding, he wrote at the foot of the manuscript: "I unhesitatingly pronounce the above to be, in my opinion, Professor Longfellow's finest effort." Equipped with this testimonial, Sam attacked Lewis Gaylord Clarke, editor of the *Knickerbocker Magazine,* and before the latter could quite grasp what was happening, Sam had sold the poem to him for fifty dollars. Sam remitted a bank draft to Cambridge that evening, proud of the achievement. Clarke was aghast at his own liberality, but Longfellow thenceforth accepted with gratitude the services of one of New York's more prominent bankers as literary agent, to market poems, dun editors, and advise on publication generally. Sam was delighted to do it all.

He went further: out of his multilingual reading he culled themes for poems that Longfellow worked up effectively. "The Luck of Edenhall," and "The Phantom Ship" were subjects suggested by Sam. When he received from the Swedish minister at Washington a copy of the poems of Esaias Tegnér, he sent them to Longfellow, urging that he put Tegner's "Nattvardsbarnen" into English. The result was "The Children of the Lord's Supper," which Longo forwarded with a letter "penned with the very ink that wrote the last words of it . . . The poem is indeed very beautiful . . . I am blinded with tears."

In pure affection, Longfellow rendered into English verse Pfizer's "Junggesell." Sam had asked it as a favor, shortly after Emily and the baby died, but for a while the poet was unable to find the right words. Then one day came a note from Cambridge with the version complete, explaining: "Sitting sad and sorrowful the other morning, I felt the mood come over me. You now have the piece entire." It was titled "The Two Locks of Hair," and it brought comfort to Sam.

Sam's sanguine temperament speeded his rebound from moments of depression, and he laughed heartily with Longo over a gay evening spent with a ventriloquist, who had "devils coming down the stairs and chimney, changing his face, playing the drunken man, etc." Sam was impatient to take the fellow over to call on John Jacob Astor and make the old man "think he has a cat in his belly." And from such foolery he would turn to serious matters and impart the wisest counsel to others. When Longfellow groaned about hardships and the bitterness of having to pass half his waking hours in the company of callow, unfurnished minds, and vowed he intended to throw up teaching and come to New York and earn a living by writing, Sam called him to order with sound sense. The city was overrun with starveling scriveners, he pointed out, and even the talented found it impossible to earn a livelihood by their pens. Consider the case of Fitz-Greene Halleck: once acclaimed the hope of American letters, Halleck, for the sake of security, had descended to "toiling at Mr. Astor's books, carying forward million after million to page after page, *and this another man's wealth.* Think of him, receiving such a pittance as two thousand a year, chained to the oar, until he drops from the galley bench into the sea of death!"

Sam got good counsel from Longfellow, too, when he wrote that he had half a mind to throw up banking and retire to a farm, there to devote, "ere it is too late, three or four years to study, reading, and meditations." Marion Ward had looked over the ground in western New York State, Sam said, and reported that ten thousand dollars would buy a fine farm there, with a stone house, where a man could fancy himself a prince. (Marion's interest in the region arose from his being in love with a Genesee County belle, Elizabeth

Wadsworth.) It sounded all very fine, Longfellow replied astringently, but he was willing to wager that Sam would become thoroughly sick of his "Genesee farmer-prince" fantasy within a year.

Each man took the other's advice: Longfellow did not desert teaching, and Sam did not retire to farming and meditation.

Both went much into society, and they exchanged candid comments upon the characters they encountered there. Sometimes their preferences did not jibe. When Charles Dickens visited America in 1842, Longfellow found him "a glorious fellow," and wrote from Boston: "You will be delighted with him, Sam. I have promised him a letter to you, and want you to see him first in New York — before any one has laid hands upon him . . ."

But Sam was less than overwhelmed by the famous, and it seemed to him somewhat fatuous, celebrity. Dickens accepted, and then was forced by sheer pressure of the lionizing he received in Manhattan to back out of, an invitation to dine with Sam and a few choice spirits in Bond Street. Sam bore the slight with equanimity, for it was commonly known that Dickens was not a well-bred man. He wrote to Longo that sister Julia had breakfasted with the great author at James Gore King's, but "I would say that I am not altogether *delighted* with Dickens . . . He did not call upon me, and if he were the Emperor of Russia instead of Grub Street, I should insist upon being civilly treated."

Sam's and Longfellow's reactions to another notorious visitor from overseas — Fanny Elssler, the ballerina, on a triumphant tour of the United States — differed also. Longfellow had read to Sam, some time previously, the first draft of his dramatic poem, "The Spanish Student," and Sam affected to believe that the chastely hoydenish gypsy dancer of the play, Preciosa, was modeled upon the sultry Elssler. "You, who can believe Elssler virtuous!" he scoffed. "She has been bought and sold as often as absolution from and by priests!" And he proceeded to recount her reputed love affair with the young Duke of Reichstag in Vienna, and her other amours, one of which had resulted in an embarrassing souvenir which she prudently parked with a nurse in England before embarking for Puritanical America. Sam had seen Elssler at Dresden and knew all the scandal about her, and when Longfellow reprobated the taking of liberties with a lady's name and reputation, he hooted irreverently, "Enfin, amigo, you used to like a merry tale or an amorous one as well as another!" And twitting Longefellow's naïveté, he sent the poet a plaster statuette of the dancer, of the sort that was being sold by the hundreds, with instructions that it be placed above "Longo's" bed, where it could be warranted to give the poet troubled dreams.

But seldom did the two friends have even so mild a disagreement. The only time Sam Ward's high spirits really provoked Longfellow was one occasion when, during a convivial party, Sam read a poem of his own and attributed it to "Longo." Never, never do that again, came a stern rebuke from Craigie House, and repentant Sam never did.

Out of the correspondence over "The Spanish Student," which Sam praised, urging that it be published, grew the friends' custom of signing their letters with the names of the student comrades in that drama, — Sam calling himself "Hyplito," and Longfellow, "Victorian." The letters themselves became more and more occupied with the activities, in New York or Cambridge, of a circle of Longfellow's friends, who had been introduced to exuberant Sam and immediately embraced him as one of their own. Two special intimates were Cornelius C. Felton, professor of Greek at Harvard, and the rising Boston attorney and public-spirited intellectual, Charles Sumner.

Felton had been an instructor at Round Hill in Sam's time, but now they met on an equal footing. The professor was gregarious, and he became an immediate favorite in Bond Street, where he reveled in the cosmopolitan society and expanded wittily at the well-furnished table. The Ward sisters quite bowled him over. The "Three Graces of Bond Street," he called them, or the "Water-witches," and Julia he termed "quite the most remarkable person I ever knew; I am astounded that all the unmarried men are not piled up at her feet!" With each visit he marveled more at "the wit, accomplishments, lively sense, and domestic enjoyments [of] your little circle," he assured Sam. "The hours I have passed in your home seem a pleasant dream, so unlike are they to the commonplace of society." And he told Longfellow he must be "the most insensible block in existence" if he did not fall in love with one of the "Immortal Three."

On one of his trips to New York the poet, resolved to languish no longer for his Fanny, did reputedly propose to Annie, aged fifteen. "Oh, Mr. Longefellow! Think of the difference in our ages!" that miss was said to have murmured before fleeing upstairs. From Cambridge Longo did subsequently send back by Sam "a Swiss basket for my sweet Annie," but nothing came of the romance, if there was one: Longfellow was committed beyond redemption to his coy, cautious, contrary Fanny Appleton.

Sumner and Sam hit it off capitally, although at base their temperaments were poles apart. The Bostonian gave promise of being a physical giant, but was still slender and boyish-looking, with handsome features, possessing an imposing manner and a mind astonishingly stocked with information about almost every subject known to man. Morally earnest, he was already an abolitionist, and tending towards that Olympian haughtiness that later would mark him in the United States Senate. A vestige — barely discernible, and startling when detected — of frisky humor he still retained; this would evaporate completely when fame should crown him with moral martyrdom. Sumner's loyalty and sincerity never were questioned, and when a principle was not under challenge there was a surprising sweetness in the man. "A noble heart and an equally noble intellect," Sam wrote enthusiastically to Longfellow. "His only defect is an organic indifference to the fine arts, especially music." Although Sam did not mention mathematics, their mutual friend, Benjamin Peirce, who had instructed Sumner at Harvard, had been driven once to despair that "no matter how fine I whittle a mathematical idea, I cannot force it into your brain!" Sumner and Sam disputed often, but never permanently quarreled; and at the summit of his reputation for unbending dogmatism, Sumner would concede that although he disagreed with Sam Ward on almost every known topic, "when I have talked with him for five minutes, I forget everything save that he is the most delightful companion in the world."

The liveliness, social ease, good nature, and exhilarating conversation he found in Bond Street captivated this magisterial Bostonian. More than that, it humanized him. "Such an ecstatic visit to New York as our last!" read one Augustan epistle of appreciation dispatched to Sam. "We returned plethoric with happiness. Cornelius enjoyed himself more than tongue can tell, and heaped happiness upon happiness by a dinner at his house where we drank the punch and Prince Metternich Johannisberger. Your health and that of your fair sisters floated in our glasses." Still dazed, he added: "My last game of blind man's buff, before the one in Bond Street, was in 1836. When shall I have another?"

To inveigle Charles Sumner into joining a game of blind man's buff was a feat no one after Sam Ward could claim.

In one respect, the future senator's convictions coincided perfectly with Sam's, for Sumner also was unmercenary. He approved — on the highest moral grounds, of course — Sam's urge to relinquish banking for literature and science. "What you say about yourself and your feelings for business has my highest respect," Sumner wrote. "I think you, dear Ward, fitted for better things than Wall Street."

Sam followed the doings of these Cambridge friends when they were at home with as much avidity as when they were camping with him. Longfellow was continually prodded for news. "It is a rainy Sunday," responded the poet in a typical verbal vignette. "I am writing on a small round table near the window. Behind me sits Charles Sumner, reading the *Sketch Book,* and exclaiming, 'I wish I knew Irving! How shall I get acquainted with him?' I reply, 'By means of Sam Ward.' Then he asks, 'When is Ward coming here?' I ask the same question. Let the answer come soon — and you with it, *old gentleman.* What would I not give to hear the tramp of your boots on the stairs, and your inspiring voice singing '*Was kommt dort von der Höhe?*' The truth is, you must come here for a few days."

But these pleasures of friendship were becoming difficult for the poet, because of his uncertain health. Sleeplessness, intermittent melancholy, nervous debility — these symptoms the doctors could read, but they could not diagnose the cause. Sam blamed Fanny Appleton's caprices. But all treatment having failed, Longfellow decided to try a water cure in Europe, and in 1843 obtained a leave of absence. Sam made the travel arrangements, securing a berth on a desirable packet and providing introductions, especially one to George Sand, whose praise ("superior to Balzac") he had been singing; Jules Janin would be charmed to present Longfellow "to *him*," said Sam, "and I candidly think *her* worth seeking." His own health, he reported, was fine; but he was not dangling after any woman. True, he had been indisposed recently and reduced to a "meek, mouse-like, wine-and-coffee-less state," but he had recovered his vigor to the point where, as soon as he had posted that letter, "four of us are to walk to Harlem for dinner and return on foot in the evening, fifteen miles before nine tonight."

Longfellow stayed several days at Sam's in New York on his way to take ship, and he described the life there in a gay letter to Sumner: "Sam as multifarious as ever; in the morning he reads Livy an hour before breakfast with Mersch, then hurries down to his business; rides on horseback before dinner and sings Italian duets after. It is nearly one o'clock and at this very moment two voices are singing under the window: 'Thou, thou reignest in this bosom.' A serenade to which one of the three sisters? If to Julia they will not gain by the transaction — they sing too horribly out of tune."

In Paris Longfellow presented Sam's letter to Janin, who welcomed his friend's friend. "He asked many questions about you," was the report Sam received. "He has quarreled with George Sand, Victor Hugo, in fine, with all the literary characters, says he does not like them and does not wish to visit any of them. I asked him if he knew Alexandre Dumas, who is at the Hôtel de Paris, where I lodge. He had known him, but they had quarreled." Longfellow called at Sam's old *pension* and found "your memory there as fresh and green as the peas we had for dinner . . . Madame Michu was particular in her enquiries after you. You have left the odor of sanctity behind you in that habitation."

Restless himself, Sam tried an excursion into the deep South, to visit relatives in Georgia. Marion went with him, on the way back to New Orleans after a vacation at home and a courtship visit to the Genesee country, and they passed a delightful week, "riding, laughing, joking, shooting snipe and quails, and, to conclude, killing a noble buck in the forest to the music of the hounds' voices and returning in triumph to the castle with honors and pack and the stag across the crupper of the huntsman's horse, to find the windows thronged with ladies waving handkerchiefs and sparkling congratulations. And oh, the delight of that climate, of the *dolce far niente* that it wraps around you, placing one, as it were, in a cradle!" He visited his Aunt McAllister and the cousins, young Hall, younger Ward, and the rest, and returned north "strong and hearty."

He also brought back convictions about the great issue that was agitating the nation, — slavery. "It is a sad object," he held. "But though I sympathize with those human beings so degraded, I feel infinitely more for their masters than I agree with the abolitionists. I entertain unmitigated detestation for their doctrines — not in the abstract, for I would not own a slave — but for their fanatic and bigoted interference with the rights and property of other men. If they but knew half the annoyance and vexation these semi-humans occasion their owners, and how fluctuating and uncertain a thing the largest income is, at the South, they would not be brutally libelling the motives and feelings of those who have inherited this curse, but would, rather, sympathize with their 'forlorn, disheartened brothers.'"

Sam had relatives and a wide acquaintance in the South — in Georgia, South Carolina, Alabama, and Louisiana — and his attachment to both segments of the Southern population, masters and chattels, was steadfast and warm. When Longfellow, upon returning from his water cure, issued his *Poems on Slavery* — his single propagandist writing, which abolitionists like John Greenleaf Whittier considered good but not half forceful enough — Sam sent copies to his Southern friends and talked the book up in New York. But, like most people in both the North and the South, for abolitionists and their doctrine he had abhorrence; he could not believe that wise policy lay in the confiscation of property, legally acquired, without compensation. To him, always, extremists in anything (except the spending of money) were anathema.

But public issues could arouse Sam Ward to fervency only spasmodically: he was essentially a private man. As time healed over the wounds left by the loss of his wife and kin, he subsided into what he imagined would be his permanent groove, — business, poetry, and mathematics. "Do you know what I have been doing lately?" he queried Longo. "Reading geometry. Paganini used to play upon the guitar before he took hold of the violin."

In a way, Sam felt that he was plucking the guitar in preparation for some virtuoso performance upon the stage of life; that had been his dream, which still lurked nebulously in his thoughts. In what form his virtuosity ultimately would display itself he guessed at differently from day to day, and never hit upon the truth. He was still practicing; the crystallization of his unique talents would come about as a result of wider, richer experiences that rapidly crowded upon him.

TEN

MEDORA

That Sam Ward, debonair widower, not yet thirty, in possession of health, wealth, good looks, a position in society, and charm, should remain romantically unattached indefinitely was not to be expected. He was not fitted to be an anchorite, and mental stimulants alone could not nourish his whole being. He had a heart and sense (as well as senses), and he craved affection. It was no wonder, therefore, that two years after his shattering bereavement, Sam's friends should be talking about his involvement in what some of them deemed a dubious adventure.

In July, 1843, Charles Sumner, writing to Sam in regard to the proper entertainment of a mutual friend (Professor Francis Lieber, the historian and political writer), admonished with preceptorial waggishness: "More than the frolic wine, he loves the sweet countenance of woman. Does he not join you, fair Corsair, in admiring the fair mistress of the Island?"

The allusion might seem inept (Sumner's elephantine raillery often was inept), for there was nothing piratical about Sam Ward: jolly he might be, but he was incapable of enlisting under the Jolly Roger. Yet the allusion was clear. In the afterglow of the Byronic age, "The Corsair" was a poem still avidly read, and the name of the heroine of its turbulent heroics was Medora. The attraction that euphonious trisyllable held for that generation is attested by a Medora, Kansas; Medora, Illinois; Medora, Indiana; Medora, North Dakota; and Medora, Manitoba, — souvenirs of the nineteenth century frontier's groping towards an ideal of beauty. Sam, it was rumored, was attracted to a Medora, too. And Sumner's "Island," both men understood, meant "Staten."

Behind this newest vagary of Sam's lay a fascinating and quite improbable story. During the early years of the century, there had lived and prospered in Orange County, Virginia, a planter named John Randolph Grymes. A Tory during the Revolution, he had fled to England and forfeited his Virginia estates; but possessing adaptability, upon the resumption of peace he returned and acquired another plantation. His younger son, also named John Randolph Grymes, was a lad of no promise, spending his time hunting, fishing, and loafing, indifferent to the call of ambition.

At twenty-two this idler traveled with his brother Philip to the Louisiana Territory, which the United States had just bought from France. In New Orleans, the brothers were admitted to the bar, and Philip, the industrious one, shortly died. John Randolph survived, and sloughing off his aimless indolence, discovered a talent for activity and legal success that, by the time he was twenty-six, made him district attorney for New Orleans Parish (county). In that capacity he won for the city a famous suit to take title to the "batture lands," — new ground built up by the Mississippi along the waterfront.

The Territorial governor, William C. C. Claiborne, was being harassed by an equivocal character named Jean Lafitte, whom people styled variously "merchant," or "smuggler," or plain "pirate," according to their interests and points of view. At Claiborne's urging, Grymes procured Lafitte's indictment for a variety of offenses, principally the studied avoidance of collectors of customs duties. Jean had not risen to his thriving state by being dull-witted, and he approached the prosecutor with the offer of a fancy fee to defend him against the allegations which Grymes himself had framed. John Randolph Grymes resigned his official position and took the case. His associate counsel was Louisiana's most eminent attorney, Edward Livingston, a member of the aristocratic New York family, and incidentally the great-uncle of Emily Astor Ward. Edward Livingston had come south in the backwash of a financial scandal that had erupted while he was mayor of New York City; the guilt was a subordinate's, but the political odium fell upon Livingston.

Before Lafitte's case could be tried, the Battle of New Orleans intervened. Grymes and Livingston served as volunteer aides to General Andrew Jackson, and Grymes won the general's lasting admiration by his handiness in dashing off martial proclamations. Grymes it was, according to hearsay, who talked the reluctant Jackson into accepting Lafitte's offer of himself and his ragamuffin crew to help fight the British. For this display of patriotic belligerency, the smuggler-merchant-pirate was granted remission of all statutory sins and his slate was wiped clean.

Although his attorneys had not brought about this pleasing consumation strictly by due process of the courts, Lafitte insisted that they accept their fee in full, and he invited them courteously to collect it at his piratical hideaway in Barataria Bay, in the Gulf of Mexico. Livingston mistrusted his client, but Grymes was game for any gambol; he sailed down the Mississippi to collect for them both. Lafitte entertained him royally for several days, then started him back to the city in a boat manned by a hand-picked crew. Stowed in kegs and jewel cases was the fee of twenty thousand dollars (in moidores, doubloons, and pieces of eight, let us trust), which Grymes and Livingston were to divide equally. But during the slow voyage up the river to New Orleans, Grymes gambled away every picayune, — his own and Livingston's, too.

For feats like this, John Randolph Grymes had become celebrated as the "second greatest gambler in Louisiana," his only superior being the spendthrift creole, Bernard de Marigny, who inherited seven million dollars at seventeen and died a pauper, stripped of everything except princely airs.

To the dissipations of New Orleans — the racetrack, the cockpit, the dice table, the dueling ground — Grymes was ardently addicted. He also was an assiduous devotee of the opera and balls. His legal adroitness was prodigious, and his fees no less, reported to range up to one hundred thousand dollars for a single brief. But no matter how large his income, he was always in debt. And about debt he was nonchalant.

In his person he developed eccentricities that set him apart even in that community of randy personalities. He never wore the same suit two days running, and commonly dressed all in a single color, from hat to shoes, — one day green, the next brown, the next white, and the day after that, perhaps, in a chromatic medley — green coat, buff pants, red neckerchief, white hat, and lemon yellow shoes.

But no matter how showy or absurd his costume, his manner was always dignified and grave; sidesplitting ribaldries he would relate with a perfectly expressionless countenance. He lived lavishly and entertained in a style above all individualistic. The city long talked about the peripatetic dinner he tendered to a visiting German duke. The table was set in one end of a room divided in the center by folding doors. When the meal began, the doors were closed, but at the end of the first course they were thrown open, revealing a second table, set with the next course. The guests shifted over to fresh chairs and ate their way through the second relay of delicacies. Then the doors were opened again, and the guests moved back to the first table for the next round; thus jogging back and forth through anything but a jogtrot repast, right down to dessert, coffee, liqueurs, and cigars. The duke was enchanted. Afterwards Grymes took his guest to a Quadroon Ball and enchanted him even more.

Grymes's duels were notorious. An attorney who taunted him with taking Lafitte's "bloodstained lucre" he challenged and deliberately shot in the hip, so as to cripple him for life. While a member of the Louisiana Legislature, Grymes shot the Speaker in the buttock over a point of order; arraigned before the bar of the house for violation of the rules, he claimed privilege, argued his case, and was sustained.

He could also carouse. At a club (the Elkin) which he organized with John Slidell, the future senator and Confederate emissary, Grymes won a much vaunted drinking bout. Several members undertook to consume twelve bottles of wine apiece, and top off with a quart of anisette, the last man on his feet to take a purse. At the end, Grymes and Slidell were the only contestants still in sight, and Grymes was the only one on his feet.

Not until the 1830's did John Grymes marry; then he took to wife the widow of Governor Claiborne, a creole beauty of a family more Spanish than French, née Suzette Bosque. As the governor's third and terminal lady, Suzette Bosque Claiborne gave rise to a legend of loveliness which still lingers in New Orleans. In later years she ceased to be dazzling. She liked to describe herself loftily as the daughter of the last Spanish and the wife of the first American governor of Louisiana, an assertion that was exactly one-half untrue. However, her daughter by Claiborne, Sophronia, was married to Mandeville de Marigny, son of the state's prime spender, Bernard de Marigny; thus by her marriage to John Randolph Grymes, Suzette could rightfully claim a direct link with Louisiana's two first gambling families.

Suzette and Grymes had three children, a son, Alfred, and two daughters, the elder of whom was baptized Marie Angéline, and the younger, Athénaïs. Marie Angéline was her father's darling; and possibly considering the dainty syllables of her Christian names too feebly French, he transmogrified her into the Byronian "Medora." And Medora she remained all her life, except when signing property settlements.

The girl's extraordinary beauty as she matured excited admiration even in a city overrun with pulchritude. Her face was oval, her skin glowed with a creamy pallor, and her dark olive eyes dreamed under long lashes, or suddenly darted piercing shafts of bewitching flame. Dark, luxuriant hair framed her languorous creole features; her mouth, rather too small but voluptuous in outline, pouted provocatively; and her figure and carriage were the perfection of seductive grace. Women might term her insipid, but men were ensorceled by her, and when she burst upon New York during the 1842–43 social season, artists could only describe her as "the modern incarnation of Aphrodite," while old stagers and men of the world vowed that she had never had more than one rival in the city for sheer beauty, — the daughter of the keeper of Brown's restaurant in Water Street (where Sam Ward had dined in student days), over whom young August Belmont and madcap Ned Hayward of Charleston had fought their duel; Belmont being shot in the thigh, but suffering no injury otherwise except to his *amour propre.* But the Brown beauty strictly was no longer in the running, having declined into bourgeois mediocrity as Mrs. Oscar Coles; whereas Medora Grymes — charming, witty, radiant, exchanting Medora — was the toast of every gallant, the envy of every debutante, and the despair of every mama with a marriageable daughter.

To be sure, there was one drawback about Medora, and that was her mother. After twenty years of second marriage, Suzette

Grymes was no longer the belle of tradition: time and her temperament had defaced her image ruthlessly, and the Spanish traits of her nature had almost wholly superceded whatever French *gentillesse* she had once possessed. She had grown strident, brusque, and apt to lapse into a vocabulary more masculine than elegant. But on state occasions she could still assume a *grandezza* that was imposing, and at such times her beauty, weathered though it was, seemed temporarily recreated; but ordinarily she went about unkempt and slatternly, and disconcertingly rude. This alone might have been endured, although not condoned. But New York society heard that Suzette Bosque Claiborne Grymes was (let the word be whispered!) *divorced.* At that time, among respectable people, divorce was a condition too dreadful to contemplate; the word was never mentioned in polite drawing rooms, and certainly was not fit to be uttered in mixed company. Manhattan's dowager-ruled society therefore drew the line sternly at Mrs. Grymes, even in those daughterless homes where Medora was graciously received.

Rumor maligned Suzette Grymes: there was no divorce in her background. She and her high-rolling husband had merely agreed that their union would be the more firmly cemented if they should remain a thousand miles or so apart during most of the year. So Suzette had brought her daughters to the rich marriage market of New York, and Grymes had purchased for her a plot of ground among the fashionable villas on Staten Island; where Suzette herself supervised the building of an ample residence, stamping about in men's boots, gruffly keeping the masons and carpenters to their tasks.

John Randolph Grymes might lose thirty thousand dollars at a game of bagatelle and *call* it a bagatelle, but his wife was dollar-rapacious. She had experienced up-and-down opulence, and she wanted none of that for her daughters: she intended that Medora and Athénaïs should marry men who had wealth and knew how to keep it. This was no caprice: the girls had always lived extravagantly, spoiled by a doting father, and to them money was a necessity. Medora's inherited and inbred defects, stemming from indolence and undisciplined self-indulgence, were to become apparent later, under stress; but for the present, her gentleness, vivacity, and beauty attracted the roving eye of Sam Ward, who was lonely, bored by business, and irritated, just then, by some stuffy objections made by his Astor connections over a mild flirtation he had been carrying on with one of the Livingston girls.

Sam knew about the Grymes family. Marion Ward belonged to John Grymes's clubs, and William V. Lanfear, head of the New Orleans firm with which Marion was associated, had long been a friend of the Wards. Medora found Sam sensitively compatible; his sparkling French and musical aptitude matched her own (she, too, played the guitar and sang), and his social polish put her at ease. Sam was such an amusing talker! And he seemed to know everybody worthwhile. Soon ripples of gossip were spreading as far as demure Cambridge regarding Sam Ward's eagerness to bask in Medora's sultry smiles. Longfellow shook his head dubiously, and was relieved when Sumner passed along a later rumor that the fascinator had become engaged to marry "an old Frenchman in New York," named Delauny.

Now Sam's letters grew sluggish. Although he said nothing about the cause, Longo divined that his friend was smarting under a setback in love. "From my heart of hearts I sympathize with you, dear Sam," the poet wrote, "yet . . . I am not sure that this is not one of those disappointments that are 'better than events' . . . Make short work of it. Nothing is really so bad as it seems."

Sam's injured vanity, or sting of rebuffed ardor, was rendered more painful by the swirl of romance that had been agitating the Bond Street household for some time. Julia was in love. "Dudie," or the "Diva," had become engaged, after a stormy courtship, to a real-life adventure hero, Doctor Samuel Gridley Howe of Boston. Two years before, while visiting her Boston friend, Mary Ward, Julia had met the tall, dark, handsome doctor when she had been taken by Sumner and Longfellow to the Perkins Institution and Asylum for the Blind, in South Boston, where Howe was director. He was forty and Julia twenty-two when she first glimpsed him, astride a superb black horse, and her fate was settled then and there. Howe came to Bond Street with Sumner, and Sam pronounced him "a grand fellow."

In his youth, Howe had fought for six years with Greek guerrilla bands in Greece's War of Independence against Turkey. He had brought back from Missolonghi Byron's very helmet of steel and gold, with its blue plume, and had been accorded a Greek decoration that carried the title Chevalier. This his friends shortened affectionately to "Chev." During the 1830's he had served as a secret agent for the insurrectionary Poles, and in Prussia had been imprisoned while carrying revolutionary dispatches. Upon his return to New England, he had directed his rather overpowering energy and idealism into humanitarian causes; and as director of the Perkins Institution had won worldwide fame for his success in bringing human understanding to children who had been born blind and deaf, and consequently had grown up as apparently imbecilic mutes. These waifs of fortune had been treated as idiots, incapable of establishing rational touch with life; but by ingenuity and the exercise of almost superhuman patience and perseverance, Doctor Howe had succeeded in communicating with them through a touch alphabet. The success he achieved with a girl named Laura Bridgman was as widely acclaimed as the later miracle accomplished with Helen Keller; Howe was the groundbreaker in this field, and Annie Sullivan, Helen Keller's teacher, learned Howe's methods at the Perkins Institution.

The imperious Chevalier was high-minded in purpose and authoritarian in manner, and like some other reformers, vainly proud of being above the vulgar scramble for riches. Before asking Julia the all-important question, he had written to Sam and Uncle John Ward, her guardians, honorably laying bare his circumstances and prospects, the former consisting of his salary at the Institution (three thousand dollars a year), and the latter boiling down to unremunerative labor on behalf of assorted reform projects. The letter provoked whistles at Bond Street. "A mere pittance," Sam termed the salary, while Uncle John smelled a fortune hunter.

But Julia was of age and knew her mind; in fact, she had put her uncle and brother in their places when they had presumed to instruct her in how to observe the proprieties while visiting Boston. "What on earth has possessed you with the idea that at twenty-two I am not able to take care of myself?" she had retorted. "I really want to laugh at you for a couple of old ninnies. Cannot I be trusted away from the shadow of your wing?"

The engagement was announced early in 1843, with Howe pressing for an immediate wedding. Sam sympathized with this impatience, although he told his sister: "We are all somewhat taken aback with surprise. But I approve most cordially." With everything turning out rosily, Julia then opened her heart to "Bro. Sam": "The Chevalier says truly — I am the captive of his bow and spear . . . Dearest brother, let me tell you that although I have chosen for myself an older and more experienced guide than yourself, I do not expect to find anywhere a kinder friend than you have been to me."

The wedding took place on April 26, 1843, in Uncle John's parlors at number 8 Bond Street, although at the last moment it looked as though it might not come off. This was because Howe refused to sign an agreement placing Julia's considerable wealth in trust, with Sam and Uncle John the trustees. Julia owned building lots on Fifty-eighth and Sixtieth Streets uptown; on Maiden Lane, Exchange Place, Beaver and Pearl Streets downtown; on Second Avenue and Eighth Avenue; as well as a tract running from Thirty-fourth to Thirty-fifth Streets west of Eighth Avenue; plus more real estate shared jointly with her brothers and sisters. In addition, she possessed stocks, bonds, mortgages, and miscellaneous securities. The management of this fortune called for skill and familiarity with local conditions, neither of which Howe could provide. But stung in his pride, of which he had an overdose, the doctor protested that he had never dreamed Julia was rich and in fact would have preferred her penniless. Here Uncle John looked skeptical, and the debate grew acrimonious, with Howe insisting that the custom of the period prevail and his wife's property be vested in him, to do with whatever he might choose. Sumner, speaking as best man and also as Howe's legal adviser, argued that for the bridegroom to sign away his conjugal property rights would be demeaning.

But at length, with Sam the peacemaker, a compromise was reached: Julia's property would remain in trust, and three thousand dollars of the annual income would be paid to her, to match Howe's salary; any surplus income would be invested. In addition, ten thousand dollars would be paid to Howe on demand to furnish a home. Inwardly fuming, Chev gave in and signed. Sam, who was to have the responsibility of making the payments, began to gather what Marion Ward had meant when he had spoken of Howe as "that confounded bit of New England granite." Once the agreement was signed, Uncle John made the best of the situation and extended hearty blessings.

The day ended happily for everybody. Julia wore her mother's diamonds, and Longfellow was relieved that her sometimes elvish humor did not mar the solemnity of the service. Already Howe had felt compelled to lecture Julia against her habit of teasing, a treatment he could not tolerate, and she had promised to amend; but during the supper she could not resist slipping two silver spoons into Sumner's pocket when his head was turned, and giving the company a laugh when he discovered them. Sam kissed the bride goodbye (Julia tiny beside her six-foot husband) and wished them joy on their honeymoon in Europe. They were taking Annie Ward with them, and on the Cunarder going across would have for traveling companions the Horace Manns, themselves newly married. From London they would proceed to Rome to spend the winter.

Soon after Julia's wedding, Sam's sister Louisa took little Maddie to Rokeby for the summer, and he was left alone. He had not forgotten Medora, and he began to be seen in her company again, regardless of her announced bethrothal to the Frenchman Delauny. Longfellow heard slurring rumors, but Sam assured him, "I am prudent and discreet." At the same time, he heightened Longo's alarm by hinting: "If a certain heart should prove to be wholly and devotedly Hypolito's, would you have him refuse the beautiful casket in which the gem is enshrined?"

Really, this sort of behavior was unworthy of Sam, Sumner and Longfellow decided, and they took it upon themselves to sift the situation. Was Medora leading Sam Ward on, to jilt him at the last? Was Sam Ward acting honorably towards a woman promised to somebody else? There was a *tante Espagnole,* a Madame Caldeor, who sometimes chaperoned Medora at parties, and from her Sumner tried to ascertain the true state of affairs. Madame Caldeor told Sumner "something about the engagement to Delauny," Longfellow wrote guardedly to Sam. "There were *fainting fits* on the night of the acceptance of the old Frenchman's suit . . ." And Madame Caldeor was "grieved and disappointed . . . for she hoped Medora would marry . . . Sam Ward."

This fitted in with certain rumors to the effect that Medora had been dragooned by her mother into accepting Delauny. Suzette Grymes had brought her daughters north to marry rich men and she was not disposed to be thwarted. Longfellow's anxiety mounted. "Have you been flirting?" he tried to pin Sam down. "Have you not reason to feel remorse? Write me long and loud on the subject, not in Sphinx's riddles. Don't keep me in the dark."

Longo himself finally caught a glimpse of Medora when she visited mutual friends in Boston. "She is lovely, truly so," the poet conceded to Sam, "but I have had no chance to say more than two words." Miserable in New York, Sam waited for more explicit news, and to drown his misery, got drunk. "A deep carouse upon Johannisberger last night for the first time in six years has given me a headache which at Heidelberg I should have cursed as Katzenjammer," he confessed to Longfellow. "I hear nothing, I ask nothing, but await patiently."

Back came Longo's report, this time more ample and favorable to Medora, although salted with cautions. He had met Medora again, he wrote, and had sat on an ottoman beside her, and thus had been subjected to the full effulgence of her charms. "She was dressed in white, with a little Greek cap on the side of her beautiful head. We first spoke Spanish, but she soon unsheathed her flashing and trenchant French. She is a wonderful girl!" The poet had ascertained, he told Sam, that Père Grymes, in a "beautiful and touching letter," had withheld his consent to the Delauny marriage, "at least until he comes on in June." But Sam was importuned to go slowly. "Your duty to Medora, your duty to yourself, your duty to Delauny require you to pause, to remain perfectly quiet. Do not interfere in any way, neither by word, nor letter, nor the language of books, nor the language of flowers." (Considering Sam's penchant for sending sumptuous bouquets to pretty women, with or without a convincing pretext, this admonition was timely.) "From your own lips I read you a homily: *Les choses sérieuses de la vie, pour la vie, ne devraient pas se décider dans un moment.* Let this imbroglio unravel itself. Patience and the passage of time! . . . Come to me soon. My heart is too full to write. I must see you, to talk of all your affairs and my affairs . . . In hottest haste, yours, Victorian."

The poet's reference to his own affairs, of which his heart was "too full to write," was blithe indeed, for at long last Fanny Appleton had said "yes." With all his soul Sam rejoiced in his friend's happiness, and in June he traveled to Cambridge for the wedding. In a letter to sister Louisa he described the festivities gaily: "I was master of ceremonies and helped demolish the wedding cake. We drank champagne to their felicity until midnight. They called upon me for a toast, and I gave 'The Ashburn Treaty.' "

Sam was in fine form: the Webster-Ashburton Treaty, recently concluded between the United States and Great Britain in settlement of the northeastern boundary with Canada, was said to have been "floated into port on a sea of champagne," so libatiously had Lord Ashburton been dined and wined during the negotiations.

From that scene of nuptial joy Sam returned to New York, where he found Medora more alluring than ever. In the meantime, her mother had been evolving schemes. Although Monsieur Delauny undeniably was rich, Sam Ward was richer, a millionaire, and at the top of the social heap, and so . . . Suzette Grymes could distinguish between a good bargain and a better one. Soon, therefore, Sam — spurred by bravado as well as by a passion now deep-rooted — appeared to his relatives to be rushing towards a misalliance that portended grief and even disaster.

Of all the family, Marion Ward was the most sympathetic; yet, viewing the situation rationally, he could not approve. Marion had gone to Europe on business and could only communicate his fears by letters; to his sister Louisa he wrote candidly: "Sam is entirely beyond our control, and indeed beyond self-control. Something *must* sober him a little, for he is perfectly among the clouds. It may be marriage, it may be disappointment. Whichever it is, I hope it will come soon . . ."

Marion was sure that Medora was not the woman to make Sam happy. "M[edora] is intelligent, witty, and passionate, and perhaps ardently attached to him, but neither in herself nor in her letters could I see anything noble or exalted," read another letter. "True, to please him, to secure his hand, she makes every promise he can require. But what will not a woman do, to attain the object on which she has set her heart? I do not wish to accuse her of hypocrisy," he added in fairness. "I only say that he has required, and she has promised, more than she can perform."

It was inevitable, at the rate things were going, that society should assume that Medora Grymes would *not* wed her betrothed lover, Delauny, but would instead become the bride of dashing Sam Ward. John Randolph Grymes came north to look into the matter. For him, his daughter's mere caprice had always been decisive; and when her preference was made clear, Delauny, somehow, became eliminated without fireworks. Medora's betrothal to Sam Ward then was announced.

Society generally was disapproving, although highly diverted by the tableau. Sam's relatives did not favor the match, although they could see that he was desperately in love. From Europe the disheartened Marion made a final attempt to alert Sam to the danger of the step he was about to take, conveying his apprehensions once more through Louisa: "Sam has not demanded too much to secure their mutual happiness, indeed he has hardly demanded enough; but they are too differently situated for their union to be a happy one. She has not the necessary ingredients in her character to carry her through the trials she must undergo . . . I should be glad if Sam would read the foregoing lines, for I have not the heart to strike a direct blow at the root of any attachment to which he may have surrendered himself, — though I long to set him right." But Marion quailed at the thought of antagonizing Medora, and he doubly and triply underlined the warning: "Do not, however, trust this letter out of your sight, for should M—— know that I have endeavored to thwart her wishes, it would sow the seeds of a deadly discord between us which could not but make Sam unhappy. He is careless with papers, therefore do not forget to follow my instructions strictly."

Despite all head-shakings, preparations for the wedding went forward. The date was September 20, 1843, and the place, Capo di Monte, as Suzette Grymes had named her home, although locally it was known as Grymes Hill. The guest list was small: there was no representative of New York's upper crust, and no member of the Astor family. From Cambridge came the loyal Sumner and Longfellow, although Mrs. Longfellow did not accompany her husband. Uncles John and Richard Ward were on hand, and Doctor Francis, with Cogswell and Professor Lieber. Sam's sisters Julia and Annie of course were in Rome, and Louisa was at Rokeby with Sam's daughter, Maddie. But cousin Hall McAllister was there, with Medora's sixteen-year-old brother Alfred Grymes ("decidedly a hard character," in the opinion of seventeen-year-old Hall McAllister). The bride's mother was haughty in high heels and mantilla, and her father stood needle-slim in his nattiest attire. The Episcopal service was read by the Reverend (later Bishop) Jonathan Mayhew Wainwright, of fashionable St. Paul's Chapel, New York, an urbane and convivial parson who had long been under obligations to both Sam and his father.

Hall McAllister described the affair in a letter to his brother Julian, a cadet at West Point. The guests rode the ferryboat to Staten Island (their fares thoughtfully paid in advance, Hall noted approvingly), and Uncle Richard was "quite sober." During the ceremony "Sam looked remarkably well and was perfectly self-possessed. Medora trembled a little but was quite composed." When she trembled, the parure of diamonds, sapphires, and emeralds that were Sam's gift flashed exceedingly. Sam got the first kiss after the responses had been made, the parson took the second, Mrs. Grymes the third, Uncle Richard the fourth, Uncle John the fifth, and so on, not even Sumner declining the privilege. Hall McAllister was bashful and hung back, but during the dinner he pondered ways and means of claiming his portion, and "succeeded in the following manner. Mrs. Grymes and the bride were standing near the door bidding adieu to the company. I was standing near Mrs. Grymes. Uncle John was just giving a smack to the bride when I observed to Mrs. Grymes that I felt quite affectionately disposed towards the bride. 'Oh, then,' said the old lady, 'go ahead and take a kiss, you are a cousin.' Upon the strength of this I marched up to the bride and respectfully took her hand and raised it to my lips. She, seeing no doubt that modesty was my failing, said: 'I'll allow you to go further.' You may be sure the words had scarcely left her mouth when I was inflicting sundry delicious smacks on her beautiful phiz."

The party did not break up until seven, and a chartered ferry carried the guests back to New York, "the regular lines [explained the impressed Hall] not running later than half-past five. Carriages were provided for our use and everything was *comme il faut.*"

The next morning, Mr. and Mrs. Grymes left the house to the newlyweds. Grymes Hill was to be the scene of much happiness, and much bitterness, to Sam Ward.

ELEVEN

DEBACLE

ALTHOUGH Sam Ward did not realize it, his three-day honeymoon with Medora on sylvan Staten Island marked the beginning of a greater alteration in his life than mere matrimony might have produced.

John Jacob Astor, old and palsied, had been dying by degrees for years. Philip Hone observed the senility at table ("his head down upon his breast, the saliva dropping from his mouth, and a servant behind him to guide the victuals which he was eating, and to watch him as an infant is watched") and reflected that some people would think Mr. Moneybags had lived long enough. But Hone also noted that Astor's mind remained clear, "his observation acute, and he seems to know everything that is going on."

He certainly knew about Medora. Sam Ward's folly in marrying that "fast woman" from New Orleans he might have dismissed as inconsequential, so long as money was not involved. But disinterest ceased when Sam bestowed upon his new bride, as a wedding gift, the house and lot at 32 Bond Street. This galvanized the patriarch into action, for he considered the property — since it had once belonged to Emily Astor Ward — to be Astor property irrevocably and not disposable by Sam. A rumor somehow circulated that the house had been given to Sam by the Astors originally, although the records showed that it had been presented by banker Ward to his son. But half society believed the rumor.

The squabble rejuvenated Astor. Washington Irving, then in Europe, was a friend of everybody concerned, and he got the details from his and Sam's letter-writing friend, Henry Brevoort. "Old Mr. Astor still holds out and is better, body and mind, than he was before you left us," Brevoort reported chattily. "An ontoward event has just happened in his family, which has stirred his ire, a thing which always does him good. Master Sam Ward has married Miss Medora Grymes and settled upon her *his* house in Bond Street, which house had been purchased and previously given, or settled, upon his first wife, but by our laws became his after her decease. This affair sticks deep in the old gentleman's gizzard. He views it as a sort of impeachment of his accustomed sagacity; a sort of outwitting and overreaching in the art of bargaining. Previous to the marriage he sent for bold Samuel — not to remonstrate with him upon the step he was about to take, but to warn that unless his great-granddaughter [Maddie Ward] was not . . . placed in the hands of her grandmother Mrs. W. [B. Astor], means would be adopted to deprive him of the property he had accidentally acquired." In other words, a lawsuit was threatened, with the possible corollary that Maddie's Astor inheritance would be jeopardized. "To this Master S. bowed submission. William's family have taken this new alliance in great dudgeon, and have resolved never to hold intercourse or to speak to their much overrated son-in-law . . . Sam, albeit not one of the wisest of men, has probably made a silly marriage — but the resentment of the Astors is, I think, carried beyond all just bounds, unless there are causes for it unrevealed in this pigmy world of ours."

The extent of the William B. Astors' dudgeon was shown when word of the marriage reached Rokeby. Louisa Ward was there with Maddie. William B. Astor stepped into the hall, rang for the butler, and ordered the carriage to be brought around at once — "Miss Ward is leaving." Thus was sentence of banishment passed upon Sam and his kindred. Louisa never saw Rokeby again.

But victory did not perch upon the Astor banner always. Brevoort favored Irving with another chapter in the great to-do, recounting an encounter by the contending parties at a garden party given by James Gore King. The affair was at King's country place, "Highwood," on the heights of Weehawken, and some five hundred guests were invited, among them Mr. and Mrs. Astor and Mr. and Mrs. Samuel Ward. Medora was making her debut as a married woman. While promenading in the garden, the couples inadvertently came face to face, and the enthralled spectators craned to watch the outcome. As Brevoort described the ensuing scene to Washington Irving: "There was no recognition, and the A.'s left the field very prematurely to the victorious Sam, who, with his wife, were the lions of the day."

But the Astor confrontation was not the only dramatic moment of that afternoon. The letter continued: "Mr. Delauny, who had been jilted by Sam's Medora, approached her with the true French nonchalance, took both her hands and congratulated her very warmly upon the happy event (not of his having been jilted), and clapping his hand on Sam's shoulder, exclaimed, *Eh, bien, mon ami, comment ça va?*" And as a *bonne bouche,* Brevoort passed along this tidbit: "The trousseau which he had ordered from Paris arrived very opportunely before the marriage, and the jilted man wrote a polite note to his rival, offering to sell him the said trousseau, which was *accepted,* and the bride was made doubly happy!"

At home or in society, Medora perfectly satisfied Sam. He wrote to Howe in Rome that "I admire her more as a young wife than as a *fille à marier,* and that is saying a great deal. Tell Dudie [Julia] and Annie that I am as happy and serene as it is possible for a man to be, and that I see in store for me a continuation of more felicity than I deserve. I know you will rejoice heartily that I should be at length at peace."

The family, however, remained divided about the marriage, and on returning from Europe, Marion Ward frankly confessed, "I tremble for its consequences." Yet such was Medora's charm, he soon found himself acknowledging thankfulness to her for imparting a little sparkle and gaiety to the stodgy decorum of Bond Street. Louisa's flirtations had been giving Uncle John sleepless nights, and she had been packed off to Rome to join the Howes and Annie, and to her Marion wrote consolingly: "Medora is all gentleness and love and longs to have you back again. She has got Uncle John pretty much under her control, and says that you shall dance as much as you please and not fear putting him into fits any more . . . I hear from impartial people that the Astors are making themselves ridiculous, and that public sympathy seems to be entirely with Sam." But the outlook in regard to Maddie, who was now claimed absolutely by the Astors, troubled Marion. Sam must "rescue her," he said, — "if not at the moment, at least in the course of the next two or three years, before her charming little disposition can have taken the stamp of the Astors. I try not to despise them, but it is very hard."

Sam's Boston friends generally accepted the marriage. Medora was capable of captivating any man, and Sumner was willingly charmed. True, he did privately admit to Howe that he had reservations: Sam's choice, he felt, was "beautiful and clever — with a large brain and a highly nervous organization, animated by strong health . . . I wish she loved her husband as much as he, evidently, loves her." When Sam brought his bride to Boston, Sumner dined with them twice at the Tremont House and observed with a trace of malicious gusto Medora's failure to win over dour, strait-laced Mrs. George Ticknor, who had been so *simpatica* with Sam in Dresden, years before. During a tea at the Ticknors', Sumner told Howe, Medora had grown "excessively displeased with Mrs. Ticknor's manner towards her, and vowed never to cross her threshold again. She said Mrs. Ticknor's countenance seemed filled with ill-nature, 'If you stuck a pin in it, vinegar and verjuice would have spirted forth.' "

Longfellow, ideally happy with his Fanny at Craigie House (old Mr. Appleton had presented the place to them), was warmed by Sam's contentment. There was less letter writing back and forth between the friends, but considerable visiting — Longo to ride Sam's fine saddle horses on Staten Island, and Sam and Medora as guests in Boston. Sam was continually sending presents to Cambridge. "Medora herself selected your *pâtés de foi gras,*" ran a note to "Victorian." "They have not been made more than three months and are from the best oven of the most noted Strasbourg baker. They cost $20. They should be opened six hours before use and the grease scraped off the top."

When acknowledgment of this remembrance lagged, he wrote to Fanny Longfellow ("Dear Ladye"), not to complain, he made clear, "of the want of the pleasant epistles which used to make even Wall Street paradise . . . but, I pray you, send me copies of what my poet has written." Yet though the carefree ardor of comradeship had begun to subside, both men remained steadfast in friendship. "Hardly a week passes without my heart's sending you affectionate greetings, though I do not write you with my pen," Sam assured Longo. "Thank you for 'Rain in Summer.' I have read and studied this new gem, placing it in every possible light, as a man does a ruby . . . I met Halleck in Broadway and the first thing we spoke of was you and 'Rain.' He knows it by heart. He says 'the fenceless fields of air' is one of the finest lines in the English language." Sam still gladly hunted out editors and pushed Longo's reputation on every occasion. But "hang it, one cannot write as fast as one can talk," he exclaimed. "When I get into your armchair, with one of those Salem cigars in my mouth, I feel like a full-bred pointer dog for whom no field is too long or too broad."

The arrival of children in both homes also tended to keep the friends apart. Sam's happiness was crowned by the birth of a son, hearty and strong, whom he named Samuel, the fifth of the name in direct line; among the family, the boy would be called "Wardie." A year later a second boy was born, one who took after Medora, and he was named John Randolph, for his grandfather in New Orleans.

Marion Ward, still living in New Orleans, often saw the old dandy there. "Grymes is looking remarkably well and plays his rubber at the club as regularly as if his mother knew he was out and didn't expect him back," reported Marion. "He listens with avidity to anything I can recall of home . . ." But on a trip home, Marion found Grymes's daughter a little less beguiling than she had seemed at first. "Were she all Grymes I could understand her, but it is the mixture of her mother's race and disposition that makes her inexplicable to me," he confessed to Louisa. The fits of temper she was coming to display he attributed to her being "a different person in town from what she is on Staten Island," where she was under her mother's influence and nagging. However, Marion concluded, "she makes Sam very happy, and if she is inclined to be extravagant, it is more his fault than hers."

Louisa — dear "Loulie" — was another to present a family problem, when she capped her stay with the Howes in Rome by falling in love with Thomas Crawford. He was the journeyman stonecutter who had carved the mantlepieces in the Corner House, but now he was a sculptor. He was Irish, and there was some mystery — perhaps deliberately fostered — about his parentage: rumor had it that he might be the son of an Irish nobleman and a cook or laundress. While he had a mother and sister living in New York, the latter averred that all family records had been destroyed in a fire, and there was no evidence either to confirm or to confute the legend.

Crawford was possessed of intense drive and ambition. He had gone to Italy, financed only by his meager savings as a stonecutter, and had been accepted as a pupil by the Danish sculptor Thorvaldsen. His talent was undoubted. Charles Sumner had encountered him in Rome, and was magnetized by his personality and power. He did a portrait bust of Sumner, and through the latter's enthusiasm had been enabled to procure several commissions from wealthy Bostonians. His "Orpheus" was creating an artistic sensation in that city when suddenly he showed up at 32 Bond Street, quite uninvited, to demand Louisa's hand, making no apology for his antecedents or lack of fortune. Uncle John smelled another fortune hunter; but Crawford was aggressively independent and scorned to benefit from Ward wealth; he eagerly assented to the same trustee arrangement for Louisa's property that Howe had boggled at.

Sam liked the bold Irishman. Uncle John hung back but finally consented, and a year after Sam's marriage, Louisa became a bride in a ceremony at 8 Bond Street. For their honeymoon, Sam procured the use of Hamilton Grange, the former country home of Alexander Hamilton on upper Manhattan Island, which had been acquired by Sam's Uncle William Ward after Hamilton's death at the hands of Aaron Burr. The grounds covered several city blocks overlooking the Hudson River north of 141st Street. Then, with pockets crammed with more than fifty thousand dollars worth of commissions, Crawford embarked with his wife for their permanent home in Rome.

A third wedding took place in Uncle John's parlors when Annie, youngest and shyest of Sam's sisters, became the wife of Adolph

Mailliard, a dapper Frenchman, whom Sam had known since his days in Europe. Mailliard's grandfather was Joseph Bonaparte, brother of Napoleon and onetime King of Spain. Joseph had a son by a woman whom, for dynastic reasons, Napoleon forbade him to marry; the boy's parentage was no secret and was considered no blemish. Louis Mailliard, as he was named, grew up in his father's household and became his man of affairs. After Waterloo, Joseph settled temporarily at Bordentown, New Jersey, and when he died in 1846 Adolph Mailliard, Louis Mailliard's son, came to New York to consult with Prime, Ward, & King about the hundred and sixty-two thousand dollars of Bonaparte funds invested with the bank.

Adolph had been born in New York, although reared in Europe, and his good looks and social graces conquered Annie. Sam was enthusiastic for the match, and in June, 1846, the wedding took place. Julia attended (she and Chev had returned from Rome with their first child, a girl whom they named Julia Romana), and in a full report to Louisa, Dudie wrote that their little sister had looked very beautiful in a dress of white tulle trimmed with lace "that cost two hundred dollars or more." The company was gay, and there were "oceans of fruits and ices." Uncle John cried when he handed Annie into the traveling carriage, and Annie cried, too, but tears of happiness, as the bridal pair rolled away in style to their home at Bordentown.

The Howes went back to Boston, and Sam and Medora were left with their boys at 32 Bond Street. The correspondence between Sam and Julia became lively as their compatibility took on depth and richness: now she was the "Old Bird" in his letters ("venerable but still lovely and always beloved"), while for "Bro. Sam" Julia employed her own tender diminutive, "Bunny." Big brother signed himself "Sambo," and snatched moments from his moiling in Wall Street to post her bulletins: "Medora is well . . . Our boy walks and sings . . . I began this at ten, and now it is half-past three! . . ."

With Samuel Gridley Howe, on the other hand, Sam Ward's stock had plummeted to a ruinous low. The doctor was overbearing and egotistical by nature, and like some other humanitarians delightful when he could dominate, but umbrageous when he felt that he was being slighted. That trust agreement debarring him from the control of his wife's property which other husbands exercised had rankled, and his resentment broke into the open shortly after he and Julia returned from Rome. The immediate cause was trivial. During the stay abroad, Howe had overdrawn his letter of credit upon Baring's bank in London by some three hundred dollars, and upon reaching home he had dropped a note to Sam Ward instructing that this sum should be advanced out of Julia's next-year income. Without thinking about the matter particularly, and sensing no urgency in Howe's request, Sam had replied with businesslike brevity that there was nothing due on Julia's account at that moment. He had not meant to be curt, but had merely answered a business communication in a business way. But Howe's pride, always sensitive, was stung: he chose to regard Sam's answer as cavalier and insulting.

Thereupon all the latent dislike he had accumulated against this top-lofty, airy-minded, too-rich brother-in-law boiled up, and Howe consulted Sumner about breaking the prenuptial agreement. Sumner told him honestly that it could not be broken, certainly not with honor; whereupon Howe consulted a second lawyer about the right of the Wards (Sam and Uncle John), as trustees, to keep Julia's money in their bank. This attorney said their action was perfectly proper. Howe then made up his mind not to touch Julia's income, — and not to let her touch it, either!

Julia had been receiving the agreed three thousand dollars a year from her estate, and the need of this supplement to Howe's salary had been emphasized by the birth of their second child, — a daughter, whom they baptized Florence, in compliment to an English friend, Florence Nightingale (not yet celebrated as the Lady of the Lamp). Howe demanded of Julia that she sign a power of attorney turning over to him every cent she was due to receive thenceforth. As generous as was her brother Sam, Julia complied. Then Howe wrote to those high-handed New York Wards that he would decline to receive Julia's income. When, notwithstanding, a payment was forwarded, he sent it back with a letter excoriating Sam.

Now Sam was incensed: how, he asked, were the Howes to live decently if they cut their income in half at the very time their family had increased? Already he had been pained by the way Julia had been constrained to live for a while, — in one wing of the drafty Asylum, smelling of disinfectant, in rooms presided over autocratically by Howe's spinster sister, who had no use for the society bride her brother had brought back from New York. And now Julia was not even to be told that her husband was spurning her income rather than have anything to do with Sam Ward! Julia was informed, Sam saw to that. Back came a furious letter from the offended Chev, addressed to Uncle John, railing about his "self-denial" being made a subject of conversation and "talked about in the family. I never told Julia about it, nor my best friend." Now that she knew, she would "suffer vexation," but, he protested, "*this is not my fault.* Though it makes me sad to have anything displease her, it cannot make me change what has become to me like a principle. Mr. Samuel Ward's views differ so much from mine as to what is delicacy and self-respect that we had better never have any business relations . . . If Julia's income were the equal of John Jacob Astor's, and I could have it by submitting to be advised and tutored by Mr. Samuel Ward, I would reject it." He hoped, he added, that Julia would "love me enough to prefer to live with me in poverty than to ask me to submit to what I must deem humiliation."

Julia did love him, to extremities, and she could laugh in spite of tears. "Bro. Sam" did his best to mollify the enraged Chev, but the breach remained. Ever after, Samuel Gridley Howe would be for Sam Ward a hair shirt. And no wonder Chev was chronically tortured by agonizing headaches that resisted medical skill.

Coincident with this family tension, differences were developing between Sam and his partners at Prime, Ward & King. The chief dispute was between Sam and James Gore King. The older banker clung to the conservative practices of Sam's father; Sam wanted to make millions quickly and retire from business. King had become more and more alarmed by Sam's attempts to persuade the partners to risk the firm's capital in shaky speculations and in December,

1846, he decided to expose himself to financial legerdemain no longer. There was a showdown, and King withdrew from the bank. A terse statement was given out that "a diversity of views as to the proper scope of the business" had made the separation necessary. King, with his son, A. Gracie King, and his son-in-law, Deming Duer, set up a new bank,—James G. King & Sons. Edward Prime, son of the founder, Nathaniel, joined Sam and Uncle John Ward, William Greene Ward, and Robert Ray, a distant relative socially and financially prominent, to carry on the business of Prime, Ward & King under a new name,—Prime, Ward & Company.

The upheaval spread dismay throughout Sam's personal circle. His friends could not comprehend the reasons for it, for James Gore King enjoyed immense respect. Sam sensed the tacit censure of those closest to him, and he was hurt. "Have you forgotten those who love you and live in Bond Street?" he wrote to Julia reproachfully when the new firm was already a month old. "Is their welfare so indifferent to you that you have not the curiosity to inquire whether there is anything left of them after the *King's* displeasure? . . . A few years ago, any event, joyful or sad, found an echo in the bosom of my friends, and letters came dancing back from Longo and Felton and Sumner and Chev,—yet, within a month, an event of considerable importance to me has passed by without eliciting a single inquiry from Boston or Cambridge." Well, he was not to be daunted. "Hereafter we mean to dispense with a *King*." Illness had aggravated the worry and harrassment of the crisis, he said. "Medora has been in bed since New Year's with a severe cold. Wardie too is not very well. I was very sick last week: my head gave out after thirty nights of but three hours sleep each."

The outlook for the newly aligned bank appeared hopeful. Times were brisk for trade, the war with Mexico was in full swing, and army contractors were getting rich. Food was in demand, and the new firm speculated in wheat and other commodities. All seemed well,—until September, 1847, when Wall Street was stunned by the news that Prime, Ward & Company had crashed.

George Templeton Strong—he was a Wall Street lawyer now and saw Sam Ward regularly—had heard that the firm was in trouble, but refused to credit the rumor. "In the case of any other house I should say the diagnosis was very unfavorable, but those people are strong enough to weather a good deal" he had noted. Conviction came on September 11, when the authoritative newspaper, *Niles' National Register,* published a bulletin that was worded almost apologetically: "The old and respectable house of Prime, Ward & King [sic], a firm that has stood *firm* amid all preceding storms, we most sincerely regret to announce, has found it necessary to stop payment, in consequence of the return of protested bills from England. They have published a card [notification] to that effect, dated September 9th." The slip in regard to the name of the firm was a testimonial to the prestige the famous bank had carried: the new name, Prime, Ward & Company, had hardly registered on the minds of Wall Streeters yet.

Strong next heard that Baring's bank had taken up "a whole ream of bills" to help out their New York associates, largely as the result of personal intercession by James Gore King — "very creditable to him, especially considering the circumstances under which he went out of the concern and that he's now the leader of a rival banking house. Common report says the Barings accepted all the bills that were out. But I know of one batch ($15,000) that came back."

For several days the news fluctuated: Prime, Ward & Company would pay, would pay in part, would pay nothing. On the 25th *Niles' National Register* heard that friends were rallying to the assistance of the partners and that all bills outstanding (more than half a million dollars) had been paid. This reported bailing out of "one of the oldest, and certainly one of the firmest and most deservedly credited banking houses in this country," was commended. But by the middle of October, *Niles'* published the grim truth: "The failure of Prime, Ward & Company proves disastrous in the extreme. It is the impression that the general creditors will get nothing, that the preferred class will swamp all assets."

Mused diarist Strong: "John Ward retires from his house, a bankrupt, the other partners carrying on as best they may. Wonder who'll go next."

Then, for Sam, disaster was heaped upon disaster. A few days after making the above entry in his diary, Strong noted briefly: "Marion Ward, I hear, is dead of yellow fever at New Orleans."

Francis Marion Ward had fallen victim to the great epidemic

that scourged New Orleans that summer; according to report, he "left his office as well as usual at eleven, and was dead at six"— only six days before the final collapse of Prime, Ward & Company. At the moment of his greatest need, Sam thus was deprived of the support of his level-headed and loyal brother.

In the Ward family circle, the crash caused consternation, and some of Sam's kinfolk were quick to load him with reproaches; for not only had he, they felt, sullied his father's honored name, he had tumbled their own wealth into ruins. Uncle John Ward, although himself vexed with his nephew's business maladroitness, was too downcast to do much expostulating. Julia hastened to New York to learn the full extent of the catastrophe at first hand. Uncle John she found "in great agony and distress of mind. Poverty is little to him, but bankruptcy looks hideous and frightful. He has given up everything to his creditors. Prime & Ward is utterly broken up . . . ruined by a very extravagant speculation in flour and by holding a large amount of paper of houses which have failed in England. People blame Sam excessively for these speculations," she protested. "Sam was but one of three, and Uncle and [Edward] Prime, who knew him so well, should have looked after him sharply and restrained him." Sam himself she quoted as pleading in extenuation: "I have committed a grievous error, but it was the business of these gentlemen to hold me back. I have done nothing to which they have not assented."

Howe felt no compunction about tossing aside such excuses. Finding himself in a position to rowel his despised brother-in-law, he made the most of the opportunity. He had always suspected that if he put his mind to it, he would make a better judge of investments than Samuel Ward. In the formal notification of the collapse, Uncle John Ward had made clear that neither Julia's nor Louisa's property was intermingled with the bank's obligations, hence these trusts were safe; however, both he and Sam resigned as trustees of their sister's estates at once. Howe went to New York to take over Julia's portion, and from there reported that "poor Uncle John" was "deeply distressed" at being forced to face creditors — small tradesmen — who had been his friends for years, whom he now saw ruined; but that "poor Sam" was merely "fidgety and trying to be cast down!" Howe took over as administrator of his wife's fortune, and chose a Boston banker, James K. Mills, for his associate. Convinced that New York City would never build up as far north as Sixtieth Street, they sold the Manhattan real estate and sank much of the proceeds in South Boston property, which eventually proved a heavy loss. And in time Mills went bankrupt.

Her son-in-law's debacle outraged Suzette Grymes. After she had married her daughter to one of New York's richest men, he had had the temerity to pauperize himself and his wife! Suzette was pitiless. Medora's house at 32 Bond Street, it was true, had been kept out of the hands of Sam's creditors, but with no money to keep it up, it was hardly an asset. Sam managed to rent it for twelve hundred dollars a year, but this was a trifle compared with the income Medora had grown accustomed to.

Having no other home, the Sam Wards moved with their children to Grymes Hill; Medora was made welcome, but Sam got a sour reception. Daily he smarted under rasping taunts by his mother-in-law, until to Julia he confessed himself as bewildered as he was depressed. Two months after the breakup, on a day "stolen from the torments of business, the importunities of duns and creditors," he wrote to "dearest Dudie": "Times have changed, dearest, but not our hearts, and while these remain true to their warmer and native impulses, the former roll on with or without fortune." Easy to say, but the practice he found excruciating.

Longfellow's tact evoked gratitude. "You did well to send me, in the midst of the misfortunes that surround me, but shall never overwhelm me, a line of poetry instead of condolence," Sam wrote to his best friend. The "line of poetry" was "Evangeline," and in reading it Sam for the first time suffered doubts of the poet's inspiration. "The metre fills me with apprehension. Any production of yours which should not find its way to the hearts still throbbing with the 'Psalm of Life,' and become as popular, would break my heart." But his fears soon were dissipated. "Medora thinks 'Evangeline' your best effort, she has read it twice," he reported happily. "[August] Belmont compares it to 'Hermann and Dorothea.' My little daughter Maddie read it with delight."

Though "constantly engaged in annoying occupations," he had taken up poetry himself,—seriously, he assured Longfellow, sending samples for his friend's inspection. "I feel somewhat awkward in the dress of the Muses," he admitted, "much as a man must at a masquerade rigged out in petticoats." But he hoped, with Longo's encouragement, to "get above mediocrity, which Horace recommends in everything save poetry."

While smarting under daily castigation which he thought hardly merited, Sam kept casting about for some means, if not to retrieve his fortune, at least to maintain himself. He thought he might lecture, but dropped that notion when Medora protested that the appearance of her husband as a speaker *for pay* would ruin her socially. Yet, being "a poor man with two bairns to support," he was obliged to earn money, he told Longfellow, and he wondered about writing for magazines. "What does the *North American* pay? Would they like an article on Gastronomy? I have materials for a sublime dissertation upon that sublime topic, the sixth Fine Art . . . I want to turn a penny."

Howe's contemptuousness provoked an expostulation to Julia ("with a pardonable stock of indignation") over not having received so much as an acknowledgment from Chev of Sam's final accounting as trustee of Julia's property. "But," he concluded, "as Mr. Toots says, 'It is of no consequence.'" Yet he was deeply hurt when Chev found a new way to express his disdain: not until a month after the event—and then only through Julia—did Sam learn that his sister had given birth to a son, whom she had christened with the names of the brothers she and Sam loved—Henry Marion Howe. The Chevalier had not bothered to inform the baby's feckless uncle.

And all the while the Astors regarded Sam's predicament with detachment. The William B. Astors had forsaken noisy Broadway for sequestered Lafayette Place, and from their Florentine mansion they extended cold sympathy, but nothing else. Mrs. Astor kept up an appearance of liberality in regard to Maddie, now and then allowing the child to cross to Staten Island with Nancy Richards, a trusted retainer who had been Emily's nurse; but Maddie was forbidden to spend a night under the same roof with Medora Ward.

To Sam's wife the Astor door was resolutely closed. Yet, characteristically, old John Jacob Astor, who was nearing his end, was able and willing to differentiate between the reprehensible businessman and the responsible scholar in his son-in-law, and he retained Sam's name on the roster of distinguished citizens named as trustees of the great Astor Library he would found and endow in his will.

In the fall of 1848, Suzette Grymes packed Medora and the boys off to New Orleans to stay with Medora's father, and ordered Sam to grub for himself. He went to live with Annie and Adolph Mailliard at Bordentown, where he was heartily welcomed. Annie's property had not been placed in trust at the time of her marriage, and she had suffered severely in the crash; but she would not judge her brother harshly. Mailliard had an ample income, and by the timely sale of some of his wife's holdings he had salvaged twenty-seven thousand dollars from the wreck. Mailliard's passion was horses: he was building up a stud of thoroughbreds, and Sam shared his appreciation of fine horseflesh.

Too resilient to remain downhearted indefinitely, Sam evolved a plan of action. The great national excitement was the discovery of gold in California. Where better could a man hope to strike it rich than in a land teeming with gold? Sam asked himself this alluring question, which thousands of other Americans, and indeed adventurers all over the world, were asking then. Even though it might not be true, as some newspapers were asserting, that nuggets were to be picked up in the streets of San Francisco, there was gold in California, and plenty of it. Hall McAllister, at twenty-three a lawyer without a practice, had caught the fever and was hot to try his luck, although his father, Judge McAllister of Savannah, and his younger brother, Ward, warned that he would starve in the savage West. Even Charles Mersch, a creature of phlegmatic impulses, was caught up by the excitement. And so was Sam. These three decided to head for the goldfields as allies. It would be first come, first served, so in order to get ahead of the stampede, it was agreed that Mersch should hurry on by the fastest route, across the isthmus of Panama, while Sam and McAllister shipped around Cape Horn; they could get berths on the new steamship

Panama, about to make her maiden voyage, and beat the sailing vessels already laboriously en route, by weeks and months.

Sam had to get clear of creditors and raise a stake; but he found that obtaining capital for a flyer in El Dorado was ridiculously easy: everybody wanted to share in the golden shower. Early in 1849, preparations were completed and Sam wrote jauntily to Julia: "The weather is fine, my spirits are indomitable as ever, my wife an angel, boys cherubs, purse empty, but head and heart pretty full; health tip-top, prospects so-so; Annie sweet, Uncle John cross, Louis-Philippe dethroned, Aunt Henry charitable, Uncle William rheumatic, and old Mr. Astor dead."

But the final goodbyes were not so light-hearted. Sam made the trip to Boston to take leave of Dudie, and Julia described the parting in a letter to Annie. Sam seemed "much subdued in spirit," she wrote, "and yet in a more natural state of mind than at any time in latter years. The visit was altogether a sad and solemn one, — it seemed like an eternal farewell. He was busy yesterday morning, and I saw him but little, but he came back to dine at five o'clock. Longo came to meet him. We were all very friendly, but very sad. In the evening he left me for a little while, but came back and stayed until half-past twelve. We sat at the piano and sang two or three of the old songs. We began with that farewell *Bemooste Bursche nun zeich' ich aus,* but poor Bunny cried as if his heart would break and we could not finish it. He then went upstairs, kissed all my children, we exchanged our final kisses and benedictions and parted, perhaps for the last time.

"Dear Annie, we have all been too hard upon poor Sam," she urged. "His faults are infirmities, not wickednesses, and can be entirely accounted for by the irresolution of his character . . . Let us think tenderly of him. He is our only brother and has in his time shown us great kindness . . ."

To his friend of friends, Longo, Sam sent a last word on the eve of sailing: "Adieu, dear Longo. Write to me when you have time and inclination. Would that both came oftener. What felicity I have enjoyed under your roof! . . . I have quit the Muses. I ought to have cultivated versification ten years ago. . . . If I write, it must be in phosphorescent characters upon the wall of the banqueting room. Adieu . . ."

And on a blustery day, the 18th of February, 1849, the *Panama* cast off, carrying Sam Ward away from all he knew and cherished in this world. He was fortuneless, for the time being wifeless and childless, estranged from his family, outcast from his social sphere, dishonored, and contemned. At thirty-five, with half his life spent, Samuel Ward was a flat failure. Yet released at last from the constrictions of conventional thought and customs, he was headed (although he did not know it) in the direction where he would find fame and fortune. Fame ultimately, fortune twice.

PART II

ONE

A LONG WAY FROM BOND STREET

NOT every American was elated by the discovery of gold in California. Word of the strike had been published in the Eastern press late in 1848 without creating any special enthusiasm, but upon President Polk's guarded confirmation in a message to Congress on December 5, 1848, and his placing on exhibit three thousand dollars worth of gold washed from the placers of the Sierra Nevada, hysteria exploded; thousands of hitherto sane, collected citizens made hasty preparations to depart for the fabled land. Five days after the President's announcement, diarist Strong noted that "the gold mania is rising fast" — and three days later, "California gold fever raging furiously." Within a month he had become seriously concerned about so much inflationary wealth undermining the whole national economy, — if not the economy of the world: "This California business worries me sadly, though I hope and believe that the stories afloat are nothing but the wildest exaggerations." At the close of January, 1849, his gloom was intensified by the arrival of the steamship *Crescent City,* bringing a consignment of several hundred thousand dollars in new gold. "The frenzy continues to increase every day," he noted. "It seems as if the Atlantic coast were to be depopulated, such swarms of people are leaving for the new El Dorado."

Soon thereafter, the side-wheeler *Panama,* with Sam Ward and Hall McAllister aboard, was bucking a late February gale on its way south towards Rio and Cape Horn. The first few days of the voyage were extremely rough; everyone was seasick except the captain (David Dixon Porter, late of the United States Navy) and, of course, Sam, who was immune. Hall McAllister lay in the cramped, airless stateroom he and Sam shared and agonized until the ship entered warmer latitudes and the weather bettered; then, with the other passengers, he emerged on deck and took stock of their fellow travelers.

There were fifty-seven of these, but some were booked only as far as Rio de Janeiro. Most of the California-bound emigrants leaving eastern ports had headed for the short route, across the isthmus of Panama, in preference to the tedious, fifteen-thousand-mile haul from New York to San Francisco by way of Cape Horn. To make this dreary passage, sailing ships required from six to nine months. The fast steamer *Panama* could cut that time in half or less, so Sam and his cousin still were traveling with comparative speed and in fair luxury. Their ship was new and seaworthy, their officers were congenial, and Captain Porter personally vouched for the food and wines as "Astor House fare." He promised all aboard "a jolly time." Most of the passengers were men of substance, for the very cost of a ticket ($600) eliminated the impecunious.

Twenty-six days out, on March 16, the *Panama* churned into Rio harbor, and the sea-saturated travelers stretched their legs on land. There was much in the exotic, tropical city to inspect; Sam piloted parties to Faroux's, a restaurant opposite the landing wharf, where he could chat with the proprietor in Portuguese, a working knowledge of which he had picked up during the voyage, and add to his gastronomic lore. The ten-day layover at Rio was enjoyable.

The next leg of the journey — down the coast to the Strait of Magellan — proved to be tempestuous; but on April 6, after twelve days of tossing, the *Panama* entered the Strait. From this extreme southerly point, Sam wrote to his sister, Annie Mailliard, a letter filled with misgivings and with yearning for all he had left behind.

"We made Cape Virgenes, the N.E. entrance of the Straits, at nine this a.m., and entered on our path to the Pacific at twelve o'clock," he wrote. "Tomorrow at daybreak we enter the first narrows — nine miles long and half a mile wide — and we hope to be able to continue our course without anchoring tomorrow night. This will bring us to Cape Pillar on Sunday morning, and turning that corner we shall be upon the broad bosom of the Pacific. I have enjoyed good health, never been seasick, and suppose this voyage and the sea air will land me in good physical order for hardship in California. As far as the mind goes, I have done little else than read, and that with the voracity of a man who dreads to think."

Momentarily the future looked as forbidding as the Patagonian landscape visible through the porthole. "So bitterly have I been schooled in misfortune," he wrote, "that I cannot see any bright prospect ahead. What all this California business will amount to I no longer pretend to divine. When I think of the mass of emigration, it seems to me an insanity, and yet the Professor [Mersch] and others have reached there before now and our chance is as good as any. I am too old to hope and not old enough to be indifferent. Dearest sister, accept these lines as proof that when farthest from you, dear sister, you were present in my thoughts. I hope that while I am away you will not hesitate to send for Maddie whenever you come to town. Heaven bless you, dearest. Keep a little corner of your heart warm for your affectionate Bro. Sam."

Too old to hope and not old enough to be indifferent . . . The gap of years that divided him from his shipboard companions depressed him. He was thirty-five, and these rivals in the race for gold averaged about twenty-six years of age. He had lived a full life in cultured, monied, influential society; their lives lay before them. They, unlike himself, had no defeat to live down.

At the western end of the Strait a sudden Antarctic gale almost swept the *Panama* upon the rocks of Cape Pillar. Captain Porter stood by in the engine room for twelve hours, often with a crowbar in hand to help pry the great piston crank past dead center when it threatened to stall. After the crisis was weathered, the captain admitted that several times he had given up hope. A hurricane then carried the ship most of the way to Valparaiso, where a halt was made to take on coal and supplies. An American couple, a Mr. and Mrs. Hobson, came aboard there; and with a lady in their midst the passengers suddenly became mindful of the compact they had virtuously signed at the commencement of the voyage, — to abstain from swearing, a habit "alike contrary to the precepts of morality and good breeding."

The pause at Valparaiso was brief. Sped on by friendly salutes from the French and British frigates lying in the harbor, the *Panama* steamed north to Callao. Here McAllister, aching for the feel of firm ground under his feet, spent a night in a tent on the beach, and damnationed the fleas that kept him scratching. On May 15 the steamer anchored off the city of Panama.

For two months, California-bound Argonauts had been trekking across the isthmus, only to find themselves blocked at Panama City. There were no ships going north to San Francisco, and hundreds had been stranded in the fever-ridden town. In January, the Pacific Mail steamship *California,* on its way up from the Horn, had picked up nearly four hundred at Panama, and a month later the *Oregon,* its sister ship, took aboard another complement; but throngs remained. Although the *California* and the *Oregon* had been scheduled to return immediately, weeks passed and neither ship reappeared. Nobody knew the reason. What had happened was that when the *California* dropped anchor in San Francisco Bay on February 28, the crew deserted as one man, to hurry to the gold mines. Also, supply ships bringing coal had not arrived, and the *California,* crewless and without fuel, was marooned. When the *Oregon* entered the bay, her captain, foreseeing trouble, boldly steered alongside the United States warship *Ohio,* and, reporting his crew in mutiny, requested that they be held prisoners until he was ready to sail. But the failure of the coal ships to arrive immobilized him, also, although more than two thousand emigrants were clamoring for passage at Panama City.

When the liner *Panama* appeared, therefore, the rush to get aboard was like a stampede. Tickets exchanged hands for as much as a thousand dollars, and any accommodation, even a spot on the bare deck, was accepted. When the steamer cleared on May 18 (under the command of Captain Bailey now, Captain Porter having gone back across the isthmus to take over a steamer on the Atlantic run), two hundred and ninety passengers were crowded in space designed for half that number. As many as possible were squeezed into cabins already filled. Others slept in hammocks slung between davits, or huddled on the deck and in the passageways. The newcomers were of all sorts, the obscure and the eminent, and in the doubling-up Sam Ward and McAllister drew the most distinguished passenger of all, — Thomas Butler King, millionaire planter of St. Simon's Island, Georgia, who was traveling as President Zachary Taylor's personal emissary to investigate conditions in California and make recommendations for the territory's government. The King and McAllister families were Georgia friends, and Hall McAllister jotted in his dairy: "T. B. King has the lower berth, Sam Ward the upper, and I the bunk."

Almost as prestigious as King was Doctor William McKendree Gwin, a tall, handsome Southern politician and land speculator, who was hail-fellow with all the giants in Washington, — Calhoun, Webster, Clay, Douglas, Benton. During a game of cards on deck, Gwin predicted that California would be admitted to the Union as a State within six months, and said he would be its first United States senator. Endowed with great wealth, and a master of political tactics, Gwin, an impressive man, with a leonine air, looked capable of succeeding in whatever he might undertake. He and Sam Ward became friends, and as a fellow clubman of John Randolph Grymes he was able to give Sam some scraps of news about Medora and the boys: Sam's wife, he said, was staying with her father on an upriver plantation, and from all accounts was as fascinating as ever.

Another passenger who was glad to get aboard at any price was Major Joseph Hooker (the "Fighting Joe" of future fame), on his way to a military assignment at San Francisco. And there was the very official boundary commission of military men, sent to survey the line between Mexico and the United States as set up in the recent peace treaty. Most warmly welcomed by the Cape Horn passengers, however, was frail and ailing Jessie Benton Frémont, on the way to join her famous husband, John Charles Frémont; their six-year-old daughter, Lily, was with her. To give her air and privacy, Captain Bailey rigged a tent on the afterdeck by stretching a large American flag over the spanker boom. Four other women, Army officers' wives, also had found places aboard, and they all were gallantly attended by the male passengers. Sam wiled away the time for Jessie Frémont by talk about mutual acquaintances and did his best to make the trip supportable; she was touched by his thoughtfulness. The sea fogs soon brought on a lung hemorrhage that left her listless and weak.

On June 1 the ship made San Diego Bay, where the boundary

commission was put ashore. Sam and McAllister had time to make a literary pilgrimage to the Bryant & Sturgis hide-house on the beach, where Richard Henry Dana had put in the winter he described in *Two Years Before the Mast.* Sitting in the room where Dana had slept, surrounded by some thirty thousand hides stacked up, awaiting shipment, Sam and his cousin were refreshed by a tumbler of "the most delicious water I ever tasted, clear as crystal and cold as ice." The passengers had worried lest the gold strike might have played out before they could reach the scene, but at San Diego they were told that, far from abating, the excitement was mounting daily. Everybody was flocking to the northern mines; labor could not be hired, even for twenty dollars a day. Heaps of cargo strewed the San Diego beach because there were no hands to carry it into the warehouses. The whaleboat that took Sam ashore had barely touched the beach when a sailor leaped out and scuttled off, heading for the gold country; pursuit was useless. Before the boundary commissioners were fairly landed, half their military escort had deserted.

During the last day of the run up the coast the *Panama*'s coal supply gave out; to keep up a head of steam, all loose lumber about the ship — crates, boxes, barrels, extra spars — was fed to the furnaces. With the last of this motive power, at daybreak on June 4, 1849, the *Panama* moved slowly through the Golden Gate. A cold, foggy wind was blowing from directly astern, and the shivering passengers hugged the rail, looking for habitations and seeing none. Fear arose that the mines had indeed played out and the long journey had become useless. Ahead, Guano Island (later paradisaically renamed Angel Island) seemed to block the entrance to the bay; but as the sun burned through the mists, barren hills took shape on either side. Then, to starboard, appeared the adobe structures of the Presidio, but still no settlement. Those on the liner felt their hearts sink. Another headland was rounded (Telegraph Hill) and suddenly a forest of masts was revealed. This was the ghost fleet of abandoned ships, left to rot when their crews bolted for the mines.

Dotting the treeless hillsides were rude huts and tents and, down in the cove, a cluster of miserable shacks knocked together out of timbers stripped from the ships; many were festooned with tattered blankets. Boats shot out from the shore, and in a few minutes welcomers began piling aboard. One was a midshipman from the sloop of war *Warren;* he was mobbed by questioners until he gave assurance that the mines were still productive; those hovels ashore, he explained, were patchwork shelters erected by the hundreds of men who were awaiting conveyance to the placers. As the sun topped Mount Diablo, one young passenger pointed towards it and asked a grizzled fellow: "Is that the way to the mines?" "Yes, that's the way," came the response, — "Are you going to the mines?" The lad — he was eighteen — nodded. "Then," said the old-timer, looking his questioner up and down, "my advice to you is not to go, for I don't think you are a man calculated to succeed in the mines." The boy saw that the man was crippled, and his determination wavered, — but just then the sun burst through the fog, burnished like a gold plate, and confidence was rekindled.

The first necessity was to get ashore, and after breakfast Sam and his cousin were deposited on the beach. The summer wind blew piercingly, whipping up clouds of blinding dust, and fog streaked across the surface of the bay. It seemed a long way from Bond Street or the boulevards of Paris.

At once the newcomers learned that one commodity which was cheap in San Francisco was money. McAllister hailed a man hurrying past and offered to pay him for carrying their dunnage to a hotel, only to be rebuffed with: "No, siree! This is my play day! No ounce for me!" So the two men shouldered their portmanteaux and, avoiding collision with mules laden with mining tools, dodged through the choking dust to the store of Dewitt & Harrison, on Montgomery Street, where they had been recommended. During that day they climbed Telegraph Hill to take in the sweep of the bay, and dined in a tent, on an upturned barrel, — bill of fare: pork and beans; cost: half an ounce, or eight dollars. The Mexican gold ounce, equivalent to about sixteen dollars, was the accepted monetary unit, and no coin smaller than a two-bit piece (twenty-five cents) was recognized.

Charles Mersch, Sam found living in a tent, into which McAllister and he were fitted, and immediate preparations were started to launch a commercial venture. Mersch had put in his time usefully, studying the needs of the place. It had been understood that Sam Ward was not going west to broil under a tropic sun, stand in icy water, or sluice particles of gold from grit and sand; back at Bordentown it had been reasoned that a new country would require almost every commodity and article of manufacture in use by civilized man. Therefore the capital that had been rustled up by Sam had been invested in an assortment of merchandise, which was being shipped around the Horn. Soon the tri-weekly *Alta California* published an advertisement: "WARD & MERSCH, commission house," offering for sale "upon the arrival of the ships *Albany*, *Brooklyn*, and others, a wide variety of stores — much hardware and tools, pumps, lead pipes, blacksmith's tools, a circular saw with frame ready to use, two Jersey wagons with harness, a small stock of bar iron, etc." Sam was embarked as an importer and commission merchant, with the "Professor" his partner.

From July through October, Ward & Mersch continued to advertise utilitarian and in the main disposable merchandise, and trade was good. They made their share of blunders; Sam groaned when he paid the freight on a cargo of obsolete stoves that could not be given away. Once a month, on "steamer day," balances had to be struck, remittances made up, often with cash borrowed at usurious rates, and orders written to replenish stock. It was a hustling life and Sam entered into it zestfully, with Mersch his balance wheel. But by commerce alone, the fortune Sam had come in search of would accumulate with insufferable slowness; so he arranged to tap other and more lucrative sources of profit.

Not all the passengers brought by the *Panama* scattered to the gold regions; some had other purposes in mind, and of these William McKendree Gwin was one. Establishing himself in a shack — palatial accommodations for the time and place — he plunged into political maneuvering. T. Butler King also showed himself politically aggressive, and as the White House representative he rated privilege. And Sam Ward still retained imposing connections back east that might be useful to a Washington politician. Political advantage and moneymaking went hand in hand, and soon, through

King, Gwin, and other friends situated like them, Sam was taking part in get-rich-quick speculations in city lands.

The town of Yerba Buena, as the hamlet was known in Mexican days, had been laid out in lots of fifty and one hundred varas each. A fifty-vara lot measured 137½ feet by 137½ feet, and these lots originally had sold for sixteen dollars (one ounce), the cost of filing a deed. But with the gold stampede, and a city springing up, ownership of a building location on which some sort of flimsy structure could be run up and rented for a fantastic sum was a shortcut to wealth. Any room or tent forty by sixty feet would bring a thousand dollars a month. A lawyer needing office space considered himself lucky to get the use of a cellar at a rental of two hundred and fifty dollars a month, although the place was only a hole dug in the sand underneath a gambling saloon.

There was, of course, finagling in the land trading, as in every other activity in the roaring settlement. By law, no one could own more than one fifty-vara "in-lot" and a single hundred-vara "out-lot"; but the use of dummy purchasers was winked at, and large-scale operators were gobbling up the choicest properties. Small investors rode the boom as well as they could, and one of these was an old friend of Sam's from New York, Captain Erasmus D. Keyes, the former aide to General Scott. Keyes had put in the war years as a cavalry instructor at West Point, where he had taught and come to esteem Julian McAllister. Army and Navy officers at San Francisco were at their wits' end to subsist on salaries that had become ridiculous in the face of the astronomical cost of living, and they were hiring out as engineers and taking flyers in the land boom simply to eat. There was a consumptive-looking lieutenant of artillery who refused to join the good-times parade, and who took as an insult to his intelligence his friends' urging that he buy city lots; before the gold rush, he pointed out, lots had gone begging at sixteen dollars, and he predicted that the day the mines petered out, and the emigrants sailed for home, the land would be worth about that much again, or perhaps less. Even Sam Ward could not persuade this stubborn doubter, whose name was William Tecumseh Sherman.

One paying job that Keyes talked himself into was the construction of San Francisco's first wharf. He introduced Sam Ward to the principal backer of the project, a New Jersey man named Rodman McCauley Price, who was the Navy's fiscal agent on the West Coast and a member of the municipal council. In the latter capacity, Price was an "insider" when it came to land deals, and it was believed that he had succeeded in acquiring more real estate than any other man in town. Price had heard about Sam Ward: as a Navy ship's purser, he had been stationed at New York for a year, although Bond Street had been above his social level then. But in San Francisco's ferment and turmoil, social distinctions were sheared away, and Sam and Price became friends. Soon Sam's real estate operations, disclosed or subterranean, assumed pleasing proportions; and his knowledge of banking and his intimacy with Eastern and European bankers proving another asset, in the summer of 1849 a partnership was formed — Ward & Price, mercantile and auction house.

The helter-skelter agglomeration that was San Francisco — an inchoate congeries of men, calling itself a city but exhibiting none of the marks of stability or permanency — brought out in Sam Ward, as in other inhabitants, qualities which he had not known he possessed. The minute-by-minute improvisations essential to survival stimulated his energy and at the same time widened his mental horizon. His sense of humanity was innately spacious, but it had been cramped within the limits of a pleasant, genial, but formalized society; now he found himself among men of the most disparate origins — sternly puritanical and starkly criminal — under conditions demanding the utmost flexibility and sympathy. His own marked personality was not submerged or adulterated by the experience; rather it was enriched and matured by the new demands laid upon it. Every demand was an opportunity: Sam found himself as much at ease sharing a drink and a gossip with a deckhand, a miner, or a monte dealer as in discussing the calculus with scholarly Charles Mersch.

One liberating benefit conferred by immersion in this mixed, virile environment was freedom from reminders that in the business world he had proved a failure. In the new West there were no failures: wealth, honors, power were up for grabs, and every man had a chance. There were no established reputations to be venerated, and no vested interests to be coddled or kowtowed to. What a man had been was of slight concern in a community where every one was passionately preoccupied with what he, his neighbor, or his associates, might become tomorrow. There were no precedents, there was merely the chance to create them. The present was transitory and nonessential, only the future counted, and in the sparse luggage brought ashore by each ship-arriving emigrant, or laboriously carted across the plains and mountains, there was no room for that superfluity, a past.

Sam, naturally curious, convivial, and avid of new ideas, entered into the fascinations of the camplike settlement with gusto. Gambling and drinking were the inhabitants' chief diversions, almost the sole ones; and for a while Sam lived in a ramshackle hotel called the Parker House, next door to the half-tent, half-barn that housed the gaudiest gambling establishment, El Dorado. There the dice never stopped clicking, and the cards slid slickly out of the faro boxes night and day. Sam liked to gamble (the laws of probabilities absorbed him), but he was not a winning player. Fortunately, his inbred sense of good taste and style, and his adhesion to the Horatian ideal of the golden mean, saved him from succumbing conspicuously to the lure of cards or gross vice.

Although the population was rowdy and brawling, between individuals courtesy prevailed, because every man carried a pistol to command it. Sam wore a revolver, too, and became a crack marksman, although he was never forced to draw the weapon in earnest. Somehow men cottoned to him, as he to them, his charm, versatility, and willingness to please, making him popular. In the numerous French colony, especially, he met a warm welcome; but Sam could pass for a Frenchman easily at any time in his life. With these exiles, many of them tragically frustrated by their failure to find fortune in the mines, he established enduring friendships. One of these was with a ruined nobleman, Count Gaston Raousset-Boulbon, who knew of Sam's brother-in-law, the sculptor Crawford, in Rome. The count was given to rhodomontade, but Sam divined a genuine elevation of spirit in him, too.

In a community made up predominantly of young men (the average age of the San Franciscan of 1849 was calculated at twenty-six),

Sam Ward's relative maturity projected him into public activities he would hardly have imagined himself capable of a few months previously. Seven days after he landed from the *Panama,* he joined other "prominent citizens" in a call for a mass meeting in the Plaza to consider "the necessity of electing delegates to a convention to form a government for Upper California." Gwin had engineered this move, with his own political advancement in view. In July Sam joined in the appeal issued to all peaceful citizens to organize a "law and order society" to deal with a gang of desperadoes calling themselves "The Hounds," whose assaults and robberies had passed the limits of toleration. This movement — a forerunner of the later Vigilance Committees — set up a people's court, with Gwin one of three presiding judges, and tried the ringleaders and drove them out of town. Pushed forward by Sam, Hall McAllister appeared as a prosecuting attorney in these impromptu trials, and in consequence became favorably noticed and began to receive legal business.

A civic function with which Sam surprisingly was identified, for it was out of character, was participation in the First California Guard, the region's earliest home-grown military organization. The martial role was foreign to Sam's nature; but in Eastern cities it was the custom for young bloods to join some militia company, preferably one with a brilliant uniform, and discharge their civic obligations by marching splendidly in parades. The same duty seemed incumbent upon the "best citizens" in the West, and presumably Sam gave the impulse his support by enrolling himself among the sixty privates and thirteen officers of the California Guard who were pledged to drill once a month and to parade as required. (The relative importance attached to the company's two main functions was clearly indicated by the scale of fines for breach of duty established in the by-laws: the penalties ranged from two bits for a private's absence from drill, to twenty dollars for the commanding officer's nonappearance in a parade.) Lackadaisical diligence in discharging military obligations was an old story with Sam Ward, however: back in 1840, the Tenth Brigade of New York State Infantry had gravely receipted "Mr. Samuel Ward" for "fourteen dollars and 35 cents, being the amount of fines imposed on him by the brigade court-martial of this brigade."

Probably the First California Guard succeeded no better in getting Sam to heel and toe across dune and hill in a vainglory of perspiration.

He was too busy getting rich to waste his time in such antics. And rich he was growing as the incredible city assumed shape. The amount of wealth he acquired cannot be gauged accurately, for money values expanded and contracted from day to day and bore no relation whatever to standards of wealth elsewhere; but within several months Sam credited himself with a quarter of a million dollars — the equivalent, perhaps, of a million dollars today. The studious Mersch shared in this general prosperity; and with a competence in hand he permitted himself the luxury of undertaking a systematic examination of the Chinese language.

Sam, for his part, kept his social wits from rusting, and one of his feats was talked about, probably, for nearly a week, — a small eternity in that time and atmosphere of daily fresh excitements. This came about when the merchants of the city proposed to tender a banquet to the officers of the warships in the harbor. They rented the only building large enough to hold the gathering, a long, low, narrow, gloomy warehouse of rough planks. Oil lamps proved inadequate to light the interior, but Sam offered to "enlighten" the feast satisfactorily, if the arrangements committee would resign the difficulty to him and ask no questions. When the guests arrived, they were startled to behold two rows of classically draped, marble-white statues ranged along the walls, each figure holding a flaming pine knot; and they were heartily amused when they realized that the statues were stevedores, whom Sam had stripped to the waist and whitewashed. The flambeaux-lighted party proved a rousing success. Barrels of liquor were consumed, some guests got spifflicated and some got drunk, and Sam was the toast of the carouse.

Subtler satisfactions befell him, also. In August the mail steamer brought a letter from Medora, and with it a copy of Longfellow's new book, *Kavanagh*. The poet's prose romance awoke memories of *Hyperion* and Bond Street and Sam's father, and with his reply to Medora went a letter to Craigie House that bridged the gap in that correspondence.

"I have read 'Kavanagh' through with much pleasure," he wrote to the author, under date of August 31, 1849, "and I have sent it to Mrs. Frémont, who has what we call in the geometry of curves 'a point of contact' *à votre sujet.* Nevertheless you were wrong not to send me a letter. The copy I have is from Medora, who contrived, from the interior of Louisiana, to get it and send it to me, through New Orleans. We have also had the pleasure of 'Resignation' and 'Sands of the Desert in an Hour-Glass,' the former in your best vein."

These poems Sam had come upon in magazines, and his reaction to the poignant "Resignation" was personal. The poem had been written after the death of Longfellow's little daughter Fanny, but for Sam it stirred overtones of his own losses:

> There is no flock, however watched and tended,
> But one dead lamb is there!
> There is no fireside, howsoe'er defended,
> But has one vacant chair!

Sam felt his friend's sorrow, but also, it had been just about this time of the year when Marion Ward died . . . He was moved to assure Longo that the "multitude of wifeless, woman-forsaken men" among whom he moved had become repellent.

But the letter closed in the old, bantering style: "And now, Hyperion, my best beloved, fare thee well. Let thy heart sometimes beat in the direction of the Sierra Nevada. Were it not for business and partners, I would winter there, and tame two grizzly bears for my companions on my return home. Imagine what a sensation a chap with such an escort would make on Broadway! Perhaps there are some they might take hold of in welcome—perhaps not!" He signed himself, as he had not for a long while, "Hypolito." The thought of parading grizzlies down Broadway made him chuckle; but an edge came into the chuckle when he imagined a possible encounter with William B. Astor.

Fits of depression could not withstand the brilliancy of that autumn's weather, and business prospects seemed as bright as the cloudless, cobalt sky. Hall McAllister was looking forward to en-

Lieutenant-Colonel Samuel Ward, Sam's courtly, kindly grandfather, who taught him patriotism, Latin, and good manners. *Artist unknown. Reproduced from an illustration in* Uncle Sam Ward and His Circle *by Maud Howe Elliott. The Macmillan Company, Publisher.*

Sam's banker father, Samuel Ward, a founder of Prime, Ward & King, the first great banking house in New York City. *Artist unknown. Reproduced from an illustration in* Uncle Sam Ward and His Circle *by Maud Howe Elliott. The Macmillan Company, Publisher.*

Julia Rush Cutler Ward, Sam's mother, who died when he was ten. *Artist unknown. Reproduced from an illustration in* Uncle Sam Ward and His Circle *by Maud Howe Elliott. The Macmillan Company, Publisher.*

Above: Henry Ward, with cup and ball; Samuel, with guitar; and Julia Ward, with pet dove, in a miniature painted by Annie Hall, a relative by marriage.
Courtesy of John Richards

A miniature of Henry and Samuel Ward, painted on ivory at about the time of the miniature by Annie Hall.
Rokeby Collection.

Sam Ward, young prince of science and society, at Dresden in 1836, the year he met Longfellow. Portrait by C. Vogel von Vogelstein, the court painter, who had just completed portraits of Talleyrand and Princess (later Queen) Victoria. *Courtesy William S. Mailliard. Photograph by Frick Art Reference Library.*

Bridal portrait of Sam and Emily Astor Ward, a miniature painted by Annie Hall. Sam regretted that Emily did not wear orange blossoms at the wedding, but a diamond parure given by her grandfather, John Jacob Astor. Sam insisted on being painted holding the blossoms over Emily's head. *Rokeby Collection. Photograph by Frick Art Reference Library.*

"The Corner," at Bond Street and Broadway, where Sam lived until his marriage to Emily Astor in 1838. This watercolor of the house was painted by Hosier ca. 1835. The pillared extension on the Broadway side was the first art gallery in New York. *J. Clarence Davies Collection, Museum of the City of New York.*

Mrs. William B. Astor, née Margaret Livingston Armstrong of the Knickerbocker aristocracy of New York, mother of Emily, Sam Ward's first wife. Photograph by Brady, New York, about 1865. *Rokeby Collection.*

Sam Ward's father-in-law, William B. Astor, son of John Jacob Astor. The richest man in America, he left an estate of upwards of one hundred million dollars. Photograph by Brady, New York, about 1865. *Rokeby Collection.*

Rokeby, the country estate of William B. Astor on the upper Hudson River. This painting of Rokeby was done at about the time of Sam's marriage to Emily Astor. *Rokeby Collection.*

A miniature of Margaret Astor Ward, "Maddie," the only child of Emily and Sam Ward. *Rokeby Collection.*

A painting of Maddie done by a member of the nineteenth-century American school. *Rokeby Collection. Photograph by Frick Art Reference Library.*

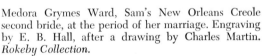

Medora Grymes Ward, Sam's New Orleans Creole second bride, at the period of her marriage. Engraving by E. B. Hall, after a drawing by Charles Martin. *Rokeby Collection.*

Silhouette of Sam Ward—banker, society man, aspiring intellectual—made by a French artist, Auguste Edouart, in New York on October 30, 1840, about one year after the deaths of Sam's father, his brother Henry, and his wife Emily. *Reproduced from an illustration in* Uncle Sam Ward and His Circle *by Maud Howe Elliott. The Macmillan Company, Publisher.*

“Wardie,” Sam’s elder son, when about thirteen. The boy was the fifth in direct line to bear the name Samuel. *Rokeby Collection. Courtesy the late Mrs. Richard Aldrich.*

The sons (below) of Medora and Sam Ward about 1855. Randolph, on the left, who resembled his mother, and Samuel, called in the family “Wardie,” who resembled his father. *Courtesy Mrs. Thomas Clark Howard.*

Sam's daughter "Maddie," Mrs. John Winthrop Chanler, holding her son, John Armstrong Chanler, Sam Ward's first grandchild. Photograph by Brady, Washington, about 1864. *Rokeby Collection. Courtesy the late Mrs. Richard Aldrich.*

Sam Ward's son-in-law, John Winthrop Chanler, photographed by Matthew Brady, at Washington, about 1864, when Chanler was a member of the House of Representatives from New York City. *Rokeby Collection. Courtesy the late Mrs. Richard Aldrich.*

The only known likeness of Sam Ward at the time of his greatest flourishing as a lobbyist in Washington, during the Andrew Johnson Administration. The only print of this photograph found bears an inscription on the back, in Sam's handwriting, to his young grandson, Marion Ward Chanler, dated "Washington, 27th April, 1869." *Rokeby Collection. Courtesy the late Mrs. Richard Aldrich.*

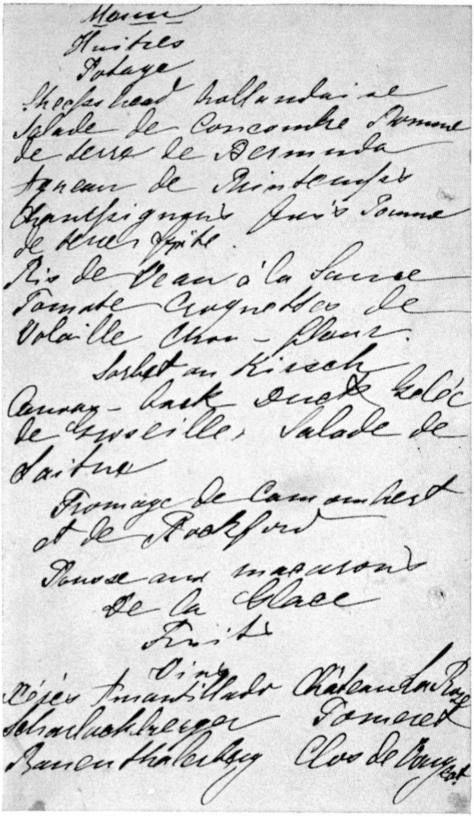

Menu
Huitres
Potage
Sheepshead hollandaise
Salade de Concombre Pomme de terre de Bermuda
Agneau de Printemps
Champignons farcis Pomme de terre frite
Ris de Veau à la Sauce Tomate Croquettes de Volaille Chou-fleur.
Sorbet au Kirsch
Canvas-back duck Gelée de Groseille. Salade de Laitue
Fromage de Camembert et de Rockford
Pousse aux macarons de la Glace
Fruits
Vins
Xérès Amontillado Château La Rose
Schwarzhofberger Pommard
Rauenthaler Berg Clos de Vougeot

A "king card" at Washington during Sam Ward's reign there. On the face, a pen-and-ink drawing of "The King," and on the reverse, the menu for one of Sam's carefully composed lobbying dinners, written in his own hand. (This menu is reproduced on pages 414–415.)

joying an income of one hundred thousand dollars a year; Mersch was contented with his philological pursuits; and Price was talking about giving up his Navy job and going home to enter politics. Since Sam, too, was in the chips, why not return to New York and open an office of Ward & Price there? The notion seemed feasible, and Sam wanted little persuading. The crudities of frontier life were beginning to be wearisome.

A few interludes recalling the pleasant intercourse of sophisticated life were provided by the Frémonts during those clear autumn weeks of 1849. The great Mariposa grant which Frémont had bought for three thousand dollars before the gold discoveries bade fair to become the richest strike of all; men were speaking with awe about millions in gold that lay in the earth there, and experts were rating the Mariposa as probably the most valuable single tract owned by one man in the entire world. Frémont had brought his wife from Monterey to San Francisco, and there had acquired a knocked-down house imported from China. It was a bandbox affair, quaintly fitted together without nails, the walls and floor dovetailing and the windows and doors sliding in grooves, and it had been set up at a distance from the noisy Plaza (on ground where the Palace Hotel later would stand).

To this toylike home, friends of the couple would resort of an evening, — hardy men and picturesque adventurers, who had roamed China, India, South America, and could spin true tales of palace intrigues and stealthy dealings; educated men who could discuss books and art and famous personages they had known with fluency and insight. The future Army general, "Joe" Hooker, was nearly always a guest, and Sam Ward, also. The men would ride in from several directions and gather around a campfire, beside which the dinner would be served. A pile of shingles substituted for a table, and the choicest delicacies would be laid out there, with first-rate Burgundies and champagnes. The conversation would glow like the sun setting in a blaze of apricot and mauve and pomegranate-red, and Jessie Frémont, who pined for urbane, witty, civilized company, would expand as Sam and others tossed the ball of allusion and reminiscence back and forth. At length the horses would be brought around, and one by one the guests would ride away across the dunes into the cool, clear night. Jessie Frémont treasured those magic evenings in memory all her life.

But November came, and with it, rains, — torrents and deluges, that dissolved the dusty streets into knee-deep mud. Mules that fell were sometimes drowned in the sludge, and riders risked the same fate if their mounts should slip; young Lieutenant Sherman was frankly scared every time he had to ride through the town. Nothing would pave the slough, it seemed, although surplus merchandise — bales of tobacco, bolts of cloth — was tossed into it in vain attempts to provide solid footing. Here and there packing cases formed precarious stepping-stones from side to side of a street.

Sam and Price made up their minds to leave. Mersch opted to continue his Chinese researches, and McAllister said he had settled down to stay. But Sam was ready to go: after six months of strenuous activity, he had piled up a snug fortune, and his self-respect and self-confidence were restored. In December Price began to wind up his accounts, and that month Sam made a final purchase of a lot on Mission Street, paying twelve thousand dollars for it; then he arranged with the bankers Godeffroy & Sillem, the Rothschilds' agents, to manage his affairs during his absence, and booked passage to Panama on the steamship *Oregon*. This time he would be taking the isthmus route, because time — his time — now was worth money.

The *Oregon*'s passengers included California's first Congressional delegation, bound for Washington. Gwin had proved a true prophet. In September a constitutional convention had assembled and adopted a form of state government, and Gwin and Frémont had been elected senators. The self-proclaimed state had yet to be admitted to the Union, but the delegation was hastening to Washington to spur Congress into action.

On New Year's Day, 1850, the *Oregon* nosed seaward through the Golden Gate with Sam Ward aboard. In the ship's hold was the largest consignment of gold yet sent out, — somewhat overestimated by Bayard Taylor, the *New York Herald*'s reporter, sailing for home, at two million dollars. On January 2 the *Oregon* paused in Monterey Bay, and there, in slashing rain, the Frémonts were handed over the side. Frail Jessie Frémont, desperately ill, was carried aboard in her husband's arms. Another passenger coming aboard at this point was Lieutenant Sherman, on his way to Washington with dispatches for General Winfield Scott.

From San Diego to the isthmus the run was made in fine weather. At Panama the Frémonts decided to rest, and wait for the next month's steamer; but Sam and the others made the muleback ride to Cruces, on the Gorgona River, whence *pungo* boats ferried them down to Chagres. A mile offshore, the steamer *Crescent City* rolled in the swell. The travelers were paddled out in canoes and clambered up a Jacob's ladder swinging over the stern. The few women passengers were given a lift, — hoisted up in a tub slung from an overhanging boom; the crew laughed heartlessly at the struggles of one fat, flustered female to wrench herself out of the tub after it thumped down on deck.

It was the end of January when the *Crescent City* docked at New York. Sam Ward was home, — accompanied by no grizzly bears, it was true, but his self-assurance needed no such protectors. Just short of eight months previously he had landed in California, a castoff and a failure. He had touched bottom, and had shot to the surface again with both hands clutching gold. His pockets jingled with souvenir nuggets, and soon some of Sam's old acquaintance would revive the saying that Sam Ward could strut even when sitting down.

TWO

MIRAGE OF PROSPERITY

IT WAS dark when Sam stepped on the dock at New York. The eaves of Manhattan's houses were blotted out, but his interest did not lie there. Taking along a shipboard companion, a prospector who had cleaned up at the mines, he headed for Staten Island. Apprised of his imminent arrival, Medora had come back from Louisiana to Grymes Hill. Obtaining transportation across night-shrouded New York Bay consumed time, and when Sam and his friend trotted up the driveway of Capo di Monte the house was dark; all were asleep. But Sam knew Medora's bedroom, and standing beneath the window he flipped gold nuggets against the pane. After some time the sash was raised, and the hard-bitten miner, straight from the placers of the Sierra Nevada, never forgot the vision of loveliness that appeared: Medora, in filmy peignoir and charming disarray, leaning out to see what was disturbing her slumber. It was Danaë responding to the golden shower. The door opened and Jovian Sam entered the tower.

Suzette Grymes was reserved in her welcome the next morning; she was suspicious of this night-flitting son-in-law and his mysteriously sudden wealth; she had had experience with slippery riches in New Orleans. But nothing could dampen Sam's joy in coming back a conqueror.

His sons he found prodigiously grown. Wardie, at five, was a heavyset, sturdy child, already showing Ward family characteristics, while Randolph, at three, was a high-mettled creole, with dark, lustrous eyes, petulance, charm, vivacity, and a flash-point temper. Sam brought them souvenirs of California, — gold nuggets to play with.

A grand surprise was his reunion with Louisa. She and her two little daughters, Annie and Jennie, were visiting Uncles John and

Richard Ward at number 8 Bond Street, while Crawford was in Virginia arranging the contract for an equestrian statue of George Washington to be erected at Richmond. The commission would mean fifty-two thousand dollars, and would bring the sculptor fame and orders for decorative statuary for the Capitol building slowly taking shape in Washington: a frieze for the north pediment, bronze doors leading to the Senate wing, — and, most importantly, the figure of Armed Liberty that would surmount the dome. Louisa Sam found brimming with contentment now that fortune was flowing towards her husband. Crawford himself was delighted to hear about Sam's return. "The old house will be ringing again with merriment," he wrote from Richmond. "A hearty shake of the hand for Sam!"

Louisa and her children actually were spending more time with Annie and "Uncle Do" Mailliard than in Bond Street, and at Bordentown Sam was received royally. Mailliard, a princely dispenser of hospitality, had tastes comparable with those of Sam, and Annie was no longer shy, but self-possessed, — "even in front of her servants," Sam twitted her. In hours of good talk the family's Argonaut told tales of the mines with such vividness that ever afterward his kinswomen believed he personally had washed out the nuggets he had brought back. These trophies he had had mounted handsomely in jewelry, something for everybody, but a specially sumptuous bracelet for Julia, and for Medora a high comb studded with raw gold.

Julia was expecting another child in Boston. While Sam was in the West, she had suffered from an attack of scarlet fever, which had left her depressed and nervous; but her surroundings had brightened, for she had been delivered from the Asylum and its lurking smell of water closets. Howe had bought an old house in South Boston, planted amid fruit trees and flowers, which Julia gratefully christened "Green Peace." Chev, however, was still tortured by nervous headaches and was meditating whether a water cure in Germany might give relief. Ignoring former unpleasantness, Sam forwarded to the prickly doctor his cheerful greeting; but Howe viewed the reappearance of his thriftless brother-in-law with no enthusiasm.

On behalf of Ward & Price, "bankers and California agents," Sam opened a business office at 40 Wall Street, next door to the old address of Prime, Ward & King; and when the chill at Grymes Hill did not thaw sensibly, he engaged rooms at number 30 West Seventeenth Street, a genteel neighborhood, and brought Medora and the boys there. The old house at 32 Bond Street was still let; and Sam, who might have to go back to California, was uncertain about the length of his New York stay. Price was on his way eastward, would arrive in March, and they could decide their business course then.

There was one aspect of his rehabilitation about which Sam was apprehensive: what would be his reception by the Astors?

William B. Astor was not at all perturbed over the inflation bogey conjured up by California's gold. His wealth, of which since his father's death he was sole master, was invested in land, and as money depreciated, the dollar value of his properties rose. And so did the rents he could exact. Collecting rents had become his life: if he had profound feeling for anything except property, he did not show it publicly. How rich he was nobody could more than guess; but John Jacob Astor had left upwards of twenty million dollars, the bulk of which went to the already enormously wealthy William, and since that time the fortune had grown formidably. In the 1850's, while men who lived on fees, wages, salary, or other fixed incomes steadily grew poorer as the buying power of their dollars shrank, Astor grew richer, both in the appraisal or market value of his land holdings, and in the dollar income he drew from them. He scrutinized every detail of his business himself. There was a common saying that at any moment Astor could tell you how many panes of glass there were in the windows of buildings he owned, and how many of them were broken. The town guffawed when one bold enterpriser tried to extort fifty thousand dollars from the city's "Midas." Even G. T. Strong smiled that "none but a genius in rascality, a Michelangelo of swindlers, could have conceived so sublime an idea!"

Sam's daughter Maddie was firmly adopted in the Astor home on Lafayette Place, but he hesitated to call there; instead, he dropped around to the Astor countinghouse at 87 Prince Street, where he was certain to find his father-in-law any day. William B. Astor looked up from a ledger, stared at his far-roaming son-in-law, and his dour features creased into an unaccustomed smile. Sam was touched: affection he could never resist, and his father-in-law's pleasure in seeing him went to his heart. Astor assured him that the door at Lafayette Place was always open for him to see Maddie, and father and child were quickly reunited.

Margaret had grown into a cool-mannered, diffident girl of eleven, primly correct and dutifully acquiescent; but from her nervousness it was easy to deduce that little good had been told her in that house about her flashy, ne'er-do-well father. Nor was the dilemma exclusively the child's. Sam had returned to the setting in which he had been reared, impulsively hoping that with his new prosperity, and the demonstration that he could make good financially, he might be accepted once more into the mores and cults of his social peers. William B. Astor's readiness (now that his son-in-law was again respectable, i.e., solvent) seemed to justify that expectation. But the route, he found, was blocked by the obstinacy of Mrs. Astor, who had not weakened a jot in her refusal to admit the existence, socially, of Sam's Medora. And Sam could not go back to ways of thinking he had outgrown as a result of broadening experiences in the West; his meetings with Maddie, under the circumstances, became so constrained and difficult that finally, for the child's sake as well as for Medora's, he almost ceased to call.

On the first of March, Julia Howe gave birth to a third daughter, who was named Laura, after Laura Bridgman, Doctor Howe's famous pupil. The Chevalier was becoming less and less flexible in his personal relationships, and Crawford, tied down at Richmond by the negotiations over the Washington statue, was moved to protest Howe's peremptorily bidding Louisa to come to Boston for a visit. "It is quite impossible for you to rush on to Boston in chase of the Doctor's whims," the sculptor fumed. "I am sure you would have been ill after it, and much as I wish you to see Julia, I think your health is of greater importance." At Chev's talk of taking Julia to Europe so soon after the new baby, Crawford exploded. "I am almost inclined to believe the Doctor is really insane! Why

Julia should be dragged about the world in this manner is more than common sense people can determine!" With Sam and Medora, however, Crawford was entirely compatible, and he came to New York whenever he could. After one such visit, returning to Richmond without his cravats, he explained the oversight by the reasonable excuse: "Medora being at the house the day I left interfered with my memory somewhat."

Then Julia descended on the Mailliards at Bordentown with her four children, baby Laura scarcely three weeks old, and there was a joyous reunion of the three sisters. Brother Sam flitted in and out, bubbling with good-nature, scattering gifts among toddlers and grownups alike, and they all sang Sam's student songs, while "Uncle Do" beamed.

But Sam's bubble was about to burst.

The affairs of Ward & Price were not prospering as had been expected. And during March, Price reached New York, bringing dismal news. The steamboat on which he had been coming up the Alabama River had caught fire and sunk, taking with it all his valuables — records, vouchers as Navy purchasing agent — everything, in fact, but his life. This directly affected Sam's affairs, for upon leaving San Francisco, Price had advanced to his successor in the Navy post seventy-five thousand dollars to carry on with until a fresh requisition should arrive from Washington, and this money had been borrowed from the funds of Ward & Price. Now, in default of the vouchers or other records, the Treasury Department was refusing to reimburse Price for the loan.

In addition to this, Ward & Price were uncertain how to conduct business while the question of California's admission to the Union hung fire. All that summer the debate raged between the slavery and "free soil" factions. The occasion marked the last appearance together in the Senate of the three giants, Calhoun, Webster, and Clay; Calhoun died before the session ended, and Clay and Webster would soon follow him. Gwin, impatient to take his seat in the Senate, kept Sam informed of the changing trend from week to week, but business more or less marked time until the issue should be decided. To meet accumulating bills, Sam raised loans, including one of forty-five thousand dollars on notes endorsed by

Francis Griffin, a partner in G. T. Strong's law firm; relatives and speculators also provided some cash.

On September 9, 1850, California at last was admitted, as a free state, and Gwin and Frémont were sworn in as senators. The end of the political stalemate was bound to bring about changes in the situation on the Pacific Coast, and Sam and his worried partner agreed that one of them should return to San Francisco. Price was needed in Washington to press the claim for seventy-five thousand dollars, so Sam was elected to go. Parting from the family would be less of a wrench for him, because the members were dispersing: Louisa and the Howes, with their children, were sailing for Rome, and Annie and Mailliard would go later. Already Crawford had preceded them to prepare his studios for the work he had under contract. Sam felt lonely and restless.

The alteration in his attitudes that had been wrought by his Western experiences was permanent and deep-seated; somehow the stratified society of New York no longer seemed all-important. By both business necessity and personal choice he had been brought into association with men and women who could never be accepted in the stiff Knickerbocker world, but whose abilities he admired and whose company he enjoyed. His mental and emotional scope had been enlarged, and he was finding New York a trifle fusty. Snubs he could detect with sensitivity and resent properly; the Astors' ostracism of Medora was one. But for the most part, social distinctions disturbed him very little any more.

Preparing to sail, he paid a farewell visit to Craigie House, and was struck by Longo's growing resemblance to the poet's seafarer ancestors: with his ruddy complexion, blue eyes, and muttonchop whiskers, Longfellow looked more like a whaler captain than a famous literary personage. Sam, too, looked different: he had discarded the under-the-chin ruff of whiskers he had worn during the Forties in favor of the standard Western adornment, — a Southern planter's flowing mustache above a goatee or imperial. It was a style popular among the new aristocracy of the Golden Shore.

Sam saw San Francisco again on January 4, 1851. During his year's absence, the town had changed radically. Now it numbered nearly forty thousand in population, and there was evident a harshness and disorderliness (not the mere clutter and confusion of the early days) that had not been prevalent in '49. Rough, lawless elements swaggered through the streets, the word "hoodlum" would soon be invented for the toughs who infested public places, and a crime of violence a day had become commonplace. Several fires had destroyed property, and these fires were believed to have been started by arsonists from an encampment of criminals, prostitutes, and escaped Australian convicts at the foot of Telegraph Hill, who called themselves the "Sydney Ducks." The motive of the arsonists was supposed to be hope of pillage.

Sam found business hesitant. He quarreled with Godeffroy & Sillem over what he believed had been mismanagement of his affairs; however, he had given the bank authority to act in his stead, and there was no redress. "Steamer day" produced a crisis, and in order to discharge pressing obligations Sam accepted a loan from Charles Mersch. The Luxembourger, who so long had lived on Sam's bounty, was happy to help, and was able to conveniently, for he was comparatively rich. A booklet published late in 1851, entitled *A Pile, or a Glance at the Monied Men of San Francisco and Sacramento City*, would list Mersch in the select ranks of the wealthy and credit him with fifty thousand dollars. Hall McAllister also would be put down as being worth thirty thousand dollars. But Samuel Ward's name would not appear in the booklet, for by the time it was issued, he was again without a dollar.

Impoverishment came as abruptly as had his wealth. On May 4, the town was swept by a fire that left almost everything in ashes. Sam's fortune went up in the smoke. Others suffered just as severely. Captain Keyes, for example, estimated that on May 4 he had possessed a rental income of one thousand dollars a month, and on May 5 his income was thirty-seven dollars. Keyes recouped; but before Sam could fight clear of the debts overhanging him, word arrived from the East that Price had closed their New York office. He had made no progress towards collecting the seventy-five thousand dollars from the government (he never would collect it), and the news of the disaster in San Francisco had frozen possible investment assistance in the East.

Sam was snowed under by claims, harassed by men as desperate for funds as himself, and litigation piled up. Ward & Price was bankrupt. But a letter from Price opened a way for Sam himself to get clear of the wreck; his partner offered to assume the firm's debts, if Sam would sign over to him and to Francis Griffin, a major creditor (himself hovering on the verge of bankruptcy), all that Sam possessed in the way of property in the West. Sam's confidence was gone; he saw no way to rebuild without capital. That unlucky seventy-five thousand dollars might have pulled them through, but as matters stood, creditors were clamoring for payment and there were no funds to pay them. Making the best of a sorry bargain, Sam chose peace of mind, and closed the deal with Price's agents.

Sam was down to rock bottom again, overwhelmed by misfortunes which, he felt, had sprung up around him "as suddenly as a crop of mushrooms." Yet the bitterest blow had come from New York and it did not concern Ward & Price. In New York City a suit was filed, petitioning the court for permission to sell Sam's last vestige of property, real and personal, there. The assets involved were his library, and a small life interest in a fragment of the property his father had bequeathed. The petition alleged the necessity of raising money to pay delinquent taxes, and the petitioner was Margaret Astor Ward, Sam's daughter, acting through her wealthy guardian-grandfather, William B. Astor.

This action by his Midas father-in-law stirred the gall in Sam, and he would never forgive it. San Francisco might rise from the rubble, but he was washed up, deserted by all. Medora? Why, Medora was in Paris, with her mother and her sister Athénaïs and Sam's sons, reported to be living gaily.

Sam's vein of luck had run plumb out.

THREE

AN ARTIST AMONG THE PRIMITIVES

Nate-mi	*to know*
Nate-ma	*I know*
Nate-se	*thou knowest*
Nate-ko	*he knows*
Nate-ti	*we know*
Natey-noma	*ye know*
Nat-hen-po	*they know*

THIS was Potoyensee Indian talk, and Sam was writing it on a crude table in a cabin on the Merced River in the interior of California, two hundred miles from San Francisco, for his sister Julia Ward Howe to show to Greek scholar Felton with the observation that the form of conjugation strangely resembled the Greek. And in faraway Harvard Yard the learned Felton would adjust eyeglasses, study the linguistic novelty, and exclaim to Charley Sumner (a *Senator* now), "Bless my soul, it's true! Quite so!"

How the devil did Sam Ward come to be among the Potoyensee Indians, and why was he bothering to write down their gibberish? There were several stories afloat about this and none of them hit on the truth; although, as Sam himself was wont to observe, "The goddess who is said to reside at the bottom of a well, if not always stranger than fiction, is at times quite as interesting."

Sam had ridden out of San Francisco to try placer mining, and had found nothing to encourage him; he picked up a trifle of "dust" and drifted back to the city, where Captain Keyes, returning from a military expedition to the pueblo of Los Angeles, came upon him morosely muttering that he had a mind to "light out for Alaska" and take a chance with the polar bears. Keyes judged this to be melancholy engendered by obsession with a sonorous line of poetry — "The wolf's long howl on Analaska's shore." But howling wolves were not to sample Sam.

The gold excitement had shifted from the streams of the north to the quartz deposits at the southern end of the "mother lode" that underlay the Sierra foothills. In placer mining, particles of loose gold that have been eroded by the friction of running water and carried downstream are separated from the gravel in which they lie by a process of shaking and sieving, simple and inexpensive. Quartz gold is embedded in the rock and must be dug or blasted out, the ore then crushed to a powder, amalgamated with mercury, and passed through a retort to extract the pure metal. This requires machinery and heavy costs for labor and materials.

There is a Spanish proverb, "It takes a mine to run a mine," and when Sam hit San Francisco again he learned that Frémont was proving the truth of the saying in his attempts to mine the Mariposa grant. Besides machinery, Frémont needed capital to fight off rival claimants to the land, who were alleging flaws in the title. To obtain capital, he had resorted to leasing tracts to investors as distant as London, and at San Francisco there was active speculation in the shares of the mining companies thus promoted. Some of Sam's acquaintance were interested in the Washington Vein, near the settlement of Mariposa; but before putting up their money, they wanted a trustworthy report on the ground. Sam, at a loose end, undertook with two companions to make the survey.

In August the three started out, and for ten dollars traveled a hundred miles inland to Stockton, on the San Joaquin River, aboard a teakettle steamboat, the *Sophie*. From Stockton they rode another hundred miles across the parched interior valley, where the temperature hovered around ninety degrees and there was no water; had they not been provisioned, by Sam's forethought, with "a small cask of very tolerable claret," they would have suffered painfully from thirst. They were headed for the hills beyond the Merced River, and at a point on that stream known as Belt's Crossing (the present site of Merced Falls) they came upon a village of Indian hogans, or brush shelters, strewn untidily around the ferry and a trading store. These Indians had been herded there after a series of attacks upon settlers, and their main occupation was panning the river for gold in small quantities. Sam's party paused to watch the tribe at work, — naked children scooping up sand, squaws twirling gravel-filled baskets with patient dexterity, and men standing waist-deep in the frigid water, prying up rocks beneath which the eddies might have swept a bit of "pay dirt." Sam thought they eased the boulders out of their sockets "as tenderly as his first-born removes the outer seal from the will of a millionaire," although their takings were never more than a few dollars a day. This was immediately traded for meat, brown sugar, and raisins, the most prized variants from their natural diet of acorns, grasshoppers, and grass.

Sam and his companions then passed along to Quartzburg, a mining camp, where they inspected the outcroppings of the Washington Vein. They returned to San Francisco with a favorable report, and the capitalists thereupon bought the claim. Sam was let in for a few shares, and was offered employment as operator of the ferry and store at Belt's Crossing.

Hard up, dispirited, and longing for solitude, he accepted this chance to get away from reminders of his failure. His duties would be minimal: maintaining the ferry, which was a scow looped to a cable and hauled by hand back and forth across the deep, narrow, boisterous stream; managing the store; purchasing cattle; chaffering with the Indians for their "dust"; and acting as a subrepresentative of the United States agent who was supposed to look after the wants of these disinherited victims of progress. A friend donated a brass bed, others undertook to provide cigars and tobacco, he was "found" in coffee and white sugar, and although dressed lumber cost four hundred dollars per thousand feet, he succeeded in procuring a rough table. His diet would be meat — often horsemeat — bread and beans, with execrable whisky and an infrequent — very infrequent — bottle of almost as execrable wine. On September 10, 1851, the state of California being one year old, he moved into the frame cabin that contained the store and cut himself off from the annoyances of civilization.

His worldly possessions he inventoried: a mule, a saddle, a bridle; a revolver, which never left him in that country, and a double-barreled gun; two trunks one-quarter filled with nearly worn-out clothing; his father's watch, that had once belonged to brother Marion; two finger rings; a locket sent to him in Europe containing his sisters' and brothers' hair; an Indian bow and arrow; three or four ounces of gold of his own washing; and a few books. He had the use of a *cavallada* for saddle horses, and if he cared to ride five miles over rough trails to Quartzburg, or twenty miles to the Frémont ranch at Mariposa, he might enjoy the company of an educated white man.

At first the tranquillity was "refreshing to one who had just quitted the carnival excitement of San Francisco existence," Sam decided. "There were no unsaleable goods to be 'worked off.' There were no 'steamer days' calling for heavy remittances from an exhausted treasury; no fever from the infection of 'good things.'" Life was reduced to food, sleep, and exercise.

The day started with a plunge into the snow-fed Merced, whose waters were usually about forty degrees Fahrenheit. Sometimes he spent an entire day in the saddle, roaming the hills and practicing his pistol marksmanship. In this he became so skillful that he won bets in shooting matches with passing Mexican *vaqueros*. The five or six hundred simple-minded Indians he considered his wards, and he made a friend of their chief, named Bautista, who had been brought up (more or less forcibly) by the mission padres and spoke bastard Mexican; respect for the Madrid Academy forbade Sam to call it Spanish. He observed that white men who had lived among them for years often were unable to speak their language, and one day jokingly wagered with a teamster that he could learn Potoyensee in a month.

His method was simple and direct: he invited the mission-bred chief into the cabin and plied him with "claret sangaree" to keep him talking. After that, he maintained, all that was required was "a good memory and flexibility of tongue." He won the bet.

This put Sam in the tribe's confidence, and his generosity in bartering for their gold won their gratitude; so much so that he was permitted, on one occasion, to witness the cremation of a deceased brave, a ceremony normally taboo to whites. On the night before the rites, he was kept awake by the keening of the squaws,—a harrowing chant he described as commencing with "a shrill wail, that fell in minor triplets until it reached a 'sensible note,' which was repeated with an intervening appoggiatura. The voice then rebounded, as if from the ground, to the initial wail, and renewed its descent, until, like a ball at the end of its tether, it was once more caught on cup or point, and again released." This outcry was accompanied by a dance, "a series of violent revolving jumps, with closed feet, executed with an energy nearly approaching fury . . . The dance and chant grew in violence, until the wail became a shriek and the phases of the cadenza as sharply accentuated as the tap of a drum." When one squaw dropped exhausted, another took up the wail.

After being subjected to hours of this ear-torture, Sam entered a grove where the cremation was to be performed. On opposite sides of a clearing were ranged the men and women of the tribe. In the center, upon three logs laid crosswise over two others, lay the corpse. An Indian who was a stranger to Sam stolidly heaped brushwood about the pyre. Then at a signal the men one by one placed some trifling token upon the body, and the women followed. The attendant applied the torch; and as the flames crackled, the wailing of the squaws rose again, while the men moaned. Sam thought of the pyre of Patroclus, and of Shelley and the Gulf of Spezia, and looking around at the mourners, he found the scene moving beyond expression, "their grief, I am not ashamed to say, infectious. The only external emblems of sorrow were the women's blackened faces, and it was heart-melting to realize the indigence of a race too poor to indicate their bereavement by the slightest change of dress. A pocket handkerchief would hold the worldly chattels of any woman of the tribe." In an hour the mourners crept away, leaving the attendant to gather the bones in a basket and carry them by night to the burial grounds, the site of which was concealed not only from whites but from the young people of the tribe.

The progress made in mining the Washington Vein Sam followed with the hopefulness of a stockholder. For a while it appeared that he might be drafted to operate the business, despite his unfamiliarity with machinery; but a Yankee Jack-of-all-trades turned up with recommendations from the San Francisco shareholders, and he was hired. This spare New Englander had two prime qualifications for a position of trust: he drank nothing more inebriating than milk, and he never gambled. There was something about the man, though, that grated on Sam; he was reminded of his brother-in-law, Samuel Gridley Howe.

In his own bailiwick he lived serenely. He took the Indians' gold in exchange for the dainties they coveted (they gluttonized on raw beef tallow), collected ferry fares, shot rattlesnakes, drank with the few travelers, and planted a melon patch. He also constructed a log canoe and taught the Indians to paddle it; they had never seen a canoe before. His health was magnificent and his appetite for horsemeat, gristly beef, and hardtack unfailing. In magazines which the freight wagons occasionally brought he read *Bleak House* in installments, and he had Virgil's *Eclogues* to teach him rusticity, and the songs of Horace to teach him philosophy.

Talleyrand, Sam was fond of saying, divided mankind into two classes: the friends and the enemies of baked apples. Sam might have divided mankind into the lovers and the haters of Horace. With the first he would always be *simpatico;* with the latter, always at loggerheads. Longfellow, of course, loved the Alban singer; Jules Janin published paraphrases of the odes; and Sam, in his high-roller days at Washington and London, would sign telegrams to cronies to buy or sell, "Flaccus," and be understood; a Secretary of State and a President of the United States would receive such wires, and reply in kind and in Latin. For Sam among the Potoyensees, Horace was like a handclasp with a world of wit and manners.

The day came for the Washington Vein's first "clean-up," which would tell whether the mine was productive. Sam hastened to Quartzburg to witness the critical test. When approaching the camp, he noted that the hundred-and-twenty-five-pound "stampers" that pulverized the ore were silent, and he found the Yankee superintendent already scooping a muddy mixture of ground rock and mercury into an iron pan. In a side room waited half a dozen stockholders. Sam joined them, and they watched tensely while the superintendent poured the contents of the pan into a buckskin held by the corners, which were then brought together to form a bag, and the hide was squeezed. Under the pressure the mercury passed through, the gold amalgam remaining inside.

"Miners," Sam recounted this moment of suspense, "are generally satisfied when the residuum which refuses to pass through the 'chamois' is no bigger than a hickory nut. An English walnut produces palpitations of the heart, and any larger mass brings on delirium. Our first ball was the size of a pippin! The next five showed no diminution, — and even the mercury from the six lower tubs [second drainings] gave us as many filberts! What a dessert!"

The party watched the further operation of sublimation in a retort, and finally saw the pure metal patted into little loaves or balls ("like butter — the little jokers"), which were weighed and came to three hundred and sixteen ounces, equal to more than five thousand dollars! Such a bonanza called for drinks all round, from which the superintendent begged to be excused, no milk being at hand. But during the backslapping, Sam overheard the Yankee inquiring "what time the Stockton stage goes through tomorrow," and in a flash he guessed that the superintendent was planning a little coup, — intending to send word to friends in San Francisco to buy up the mine's shares before word leaked through of its richness.

Saddling his horse, Sam took leave, saying he was going to Mariposa to call on a friend. Mariposa lay to the south, in the opposite direction from Stockton and the steamboat to San Francisco, and he saw the superintendent smile as he loped away. Once out of sight, he made a wide detour and reached his cabin, where he picked up a remount and rode hell-for-leather to Stockton. He arrived there at ten o'clock the next morning, and ascertained that the stage had not yet come through. The steamboat *Sophie* was due to cast off in about two hours, and Sam spent the time hunting up holders of Washington Vein stock and taking it off their hands at the going price. In this way he picked up a hundred and fifty shares.

The next day at dawn he reached San Francisco, where he planned to stay hidden. He went to the home of an Army friend, Captain Charles Pomeroy Stone, told him the story, and sent him out to corral shares. The captain managed to pick up fifty more for Sam. Twenty-four hours later the stage mail arrived, and suddenly there was a demand for Washington Vein stock. The superintendent's message had come through, — too late. In the brisk market Sam unloaded his shares at a fine profit, and had the satisfaction of having outsmarted a milk-drinker and a Yankee. The buyers of Washington Vein stock at this time were to be disappointed, for the vein was not a continuous ledge of ore, but a scattering of isolated "pockets" of gold-bearing quartz, buried in masses of worthless slate. By chance one of the richest of these "pockets" had been struck at the start. When this was stripped clean, the search for new leads ate up profits and required further investment, until the disgruntled shareholders sold out. Had the first proprietors been patient, they would have been rewarded — Sam among them — because other "pockets" of gold were located from time to time, and eventually the Washington Vein yielded some two million dollars.

November's rains flooded the Merced at Belt's Crossing, swept away the ferry, and drove the Indians to high ground. There was much misery among them, for hunger always stalked these primitive people, who knew nothing of agriculture and subsisted on nuts and herbs. Every winter brought the specter of famine, and the tribe looked forward every spring to the run of salmon coming upstream to spawn. Then the tribe grew fat with feasting. This spring, however, the salmon failed to appear, and scouts reported that a dam thrown across the river several miles downstream was holding the fish back. The tribal fathers appealed to Sam, and he reconnoitered the obstacle himself. It had been built by half a dozen Germans "under a chaotic impression that there might be gold in that bend of the river, and an equally idiotic determination to turn the river from its channel," he told the story. The riverbed failing to show gold, the builders had decided to use the dam to turn a wheel, although there was neither wood to saw nor grain to grind in the entire countryside. Then they thought of using the dam as a salmon trap, and for that purpose it was working only too well.

Sam pondered the dilemma. He reasoned that "Dutchmen are no very formidable adversaries in the absence of lager beer, and these poor devils had not even sauerkraut." He also doubted that "a party who had committed two such egregious blunders as to attempt to turn a stream which contained no gold, and to erect a mill where there was nothing to grind," would hardly be likely to think as fast as he could talk. So he approached the dam's proprietors with a constructive suggestion.

"If you open the dam and let the salmon swim upstream," he counseled, with the knowing air of an old fishing hand, "once they are all up, you can close the dam again and you will have them at your mercy. But if you prevent them from going up, they will soon turn tail and swim away to another spawning ground."

The "Dutchmen" rose to the bait, opened the dam, the fish swam past, the Indians waxed fat, and Sam, according to his account, was hailed as the tribe's great white father. The outwitted victims scratched their heads a long time before they perceived the hole in Sam's line of reasoning.

But all was not always friendliness between Sam and the Indians, and one brush he had with them nearly cost his life. On a trip to San Francisco he took along a relative of the chief, a youth named Sacate, to show him the wonders of the white man's world. The creaking, groaning, shivering steamboat *Sophie* terrified the savage, although with racial stoicism he concealed his demoralization. In the city Sacate astonished beholders by his ability to stow away food. Then he disappeared, and although the sheriff was notified, no trace of him could be found.

Sam headed back towards the River of Grace with misgivings. A ferryman warned him to be prepared for trouble if he returned without his companion; but resolving "for once to indulge the luxury of a stainless conscience," he continued his way. Chief Bautista heard Sam's story and said he understood perfectly. But that night Sam was kept awake by the keening of squaws; and when he went to the window to look at the moon, an Indian rose up from the ground, as though he had been posted there; and in the morning, when he opened the door, an Indian was lying athwart it. Several days went by and Sacate still did not reappear, nor was there any word of him. Tension mounted, for it was plain that the tribe suspected the unfortunate youth had been either murdered or sold into slavery, — a fate that had befallen other Indians who had vanished with unaccountable suddenness.

Then an uncle of Sacate, who lived at a distance, showed up drunk and brandishing a pistol. He took a shot at Sam, — "a very fair line shot," Sam described it, the bullet plugging the wall three feet above his head. Sam had the Indian covered with his own six-shooter and was ready to fire — any other white man would have done so in the circumstances — when the thought of the vengeance that would be taken on the whole tribe, should the attack become known, restrained him, and he ordered the drunk trussed up. The terrified Indians pounced upon the offender with vim. And that night Sacate reappeared, gaunt and famished, but driving a remuda of horses he had rustled from ranches on his slow march back from the city. He had been so long, he explained, because he was afraid to travel in the daylight; and besides, he had tarried to do a little horse-trading with Mexicans heading south. He had run away, he said, because the wheezing and snorting *Sophie* put him in fear of his life; he was afraid that Sam would take him aboard that devil-craft again. Amid the tribe's rejoicing, Sam ordered the uncle to be untied and driven out of the village, deeming that and the poor fellow's hangover to be punishment enough.

In February of 1852 Sam was agreeably surprised to receive a letter from his sister Julia. She was back in Boston, after having spent the previous winter in Rome. Without delay Sam sat down at his table of unplaned boards and wrote a reply.

"Dearest Dudie," he began. "Your sweet letter came to me this a.m. It was the first word I had received from home, dear old home, since my arrival back in California." A period of disappointments, he termed the interval, and then described his surroundings. "This savage life does not contrast so unfavorably with civilization as one might think. Strip the men and women of the society surrounding *you* of tinsel and conventionalities, and what remains but a crowd who eat, drink, and are clothed, lodged, and amused better than my Potoyensees? . . . My health is good and I take much exercise. Physical fatigue deadens reflection, and at night I retire early. I have a copy of Horace and of Virgil which I am reading in order to be able some day to teach Wardie and Randolph. I do not know what *avenir* Fate has in store for me, but I am growing strong and bracing my nerves to every kind of physical danger. I may now say from my experience and actual test that I fear neither man nor beast. When I first came I suffered greatly in the ascent and descent of steep mountain passes, when a misstep of my mule would have made poor Medora a widow. Now I gallop up and down like any other Indian."

He had taken stock of himself, and reported his findings as truthfully as he could. "This cultivation of physical courage and the development of endurance are the only symptoms of improvement of a positive kind. Negatively, a profound contempt for the world and its opinion, a savage indifference to all save those who are kindly disposed to me, complete the picture. I have sown to the wind and am reaping the whirlwind. I have scattered flowers in summer bowers and am reaping the withered leaves."

But there were still a few accomplishments in which he could take satisfaction. "I now speak Spanish as fluently as French. I can make a good Indian speech, and I would stake my pile that in one month I could learn to speak enough of any language for all the common purposes of life . . . Sometimes when a motley throng of travellers assembles at the store I am talking, at the same time, English, French, Spanish, German, and Indian. I have mistaken my vocation. I should have been a linguist."

His success with the Indians was a source of genuine pride. "The chief tells me that if I could lay aside my anti-polygamic ideas and marry into the tribe they would make me an *Oyani*. But I flatter myself that I have retained as much of the dignity of a gentleman as can be maintained by a pauper. You know that in my palmy days I had none of the repulsive vanity of riches . . .

"Whatever may have been my sins towards heaven and my ingratitude," he summed up, "my resignation to my present expiatory sacrifice of comfort, affections, and happiness is proof to me that I bow down to its decrees as just. I have never sinned towards mankind as far as I can remember. I have always been liberal, hospitable, sympathizing with the unfortunate, and, perhaps, generous. I have rarely found gratitude and have ceased to expect it . . . I eat only what is needed to support life, and gourmandise is out of the question . . . This is the longest letter I have written for two years . . .

"Adieu, dear Julia. Kiss the bairns, and particularly dear little Harry for me. Remember me kindly to all inquiring friends. Tell Longo . . ." Abruptly he broke off. "Remember me kindly to Chev, and believe me, dearest Dudie, ever your affectionate *Bunny.*"

Soon after receiving this word from home, he began to yearn for city life. Since he needed a stake, he decided to wash out some gold for himself, and going into the river with the Indians — pretending it was a joke — he labored in the frigid water one day. Then he contracted with several Indian children to pan the gravel he dredged up, and after a fortnight found he had acquired a little less than fifteen dollars. That ended that splurge of activity.

He won a shooting match with a happy-go-lucky Mexican drifting through, — and a couple of days later helped direct a posse to where they ran down the same *vaquero* for killing a teamster not far from Sam's store. The culprit got the usual short shrift at the end of a rope; he went out jauntily.

Sam met mountain men and Indian traders, figures famous in frontier lore, and participated in at least one Homeric feast with some of these legendary heroes. A heifer was lassoed, butchered, and slabs of the dripping flesh tossed on a campfire with a rapidity that amazed him. The half-raw, half-charred meat was snatched off the coals and devoured ravenously, in enormous quantities, seasoned only with coarse salt. The greatest guzzler of all was one of Frémont's guides, White Elliott; by Sam's guess, Elliott consumed twenty pounds of gory beef, and wound up spattered with blood, and, although a tireless chatterer and windbag, bloated into a stupor of silence.

With health robust and optimism sprouting again, Sam yearned for civilization and San Francisco. The store was doing well, but he was surfeited with solitude. So, in the fall of 1852, he rode back to the city, no richer in purse but greatly enriched in experience and the widening of his sympathies. Less than ever — far, far less — did he resemble the Sam Ward of Bond and Wall Streets who had stepped into this Western world of mirage and magical fulfillment back in 1849.

FOUR

MEXICO — PARIS — NEW YORK

When Sam Ward returned to white men's haunts in 1852 after vegetating among the Potoyensees, he found San Francisco in still a new phase. The First Vigilance Committee of 1851 had cleared the town of its more odious hoodlums, but now a different lawless element was infiltrating under the direction of an alumnus of Tammany Hall, David C. Broderick. This ambitious politician had introduced Tammany-style organization, and was fastening a vise of corruption on the city that would be smashed only by the Second Vigilance Committee in 1856. Broderick operated behind a screen of thugs, who rigged elections, terrorized opponents, slugged, crippled, and practiced playful mayhem in the stews of the Barbary Coast. One of the bully-boys had brought his own ballot box with false bottom across the plains; another was the ferocious midget, Billy Mulligan, a bantamweight who tipped the beam at less than a hundred pounds, but when on a bender was feared more than any two badmen in town. Sam Ward once saw Billy Mulligan chase Johnny Morrissey, two-hundred-pound heavyweight champion of the ring, out of a saloon and down a flight of stairs, armed only with a billiard cue.

Sam transacted a little business towards the close of 1852, selling some lots on Telegraph Hill, but without great benefit to himself. Hopefully he retained a tenuous connection with the East through a New York business address, listing himself in the Manhattan directory as a "merchant," with offices at 35 South William Street. His address in San Francisco for a while was the Franklin Hotel, on Sansome Street at Pacific; but as his resources grew slimmer, he moved into a shack owned by Rodman Price. From the East his former partner was inquiring through friends: "What is Sam Ward doing? Is he making anything, or has he made any?" Sam had not, and his despondency was not alleviated by the reports that Price had ridden adversity into Congress, and was pulling clear of business embarrassments.

News of friends back east made his eclipse more difficult to bear. Charles Sumner was a United States senator now, having succeeded to Daniel Webster's seat, and Sam heard that his friend was making himself unpopular even in Massachusetts by his denunciations of the "lords of the lash," Southern slaveholders. Sam was gratified by Sumner's rise to eminence, but he deplored the swing towards fanaticism: *Surtout pas de zèle,* he agreed with Talleyrand.

There were members of Sam's family circle in San Francisco who took much the same detached view of the national crisis. Hall McAllister had persuaded his father and brother, Ward, to share his lucrative fees, although both suspected they were foolish to leave assured positions in Savannah. Their qualms were vanquished when Ward brought back the retainer in their first case, — four thousand dollars in gold. As he counted out the ounces, tied up in leather pouches, on his father's desk, the old judge danced a jig for joy: verily this was the land of Cockaigne, where gold could be scooped up in the streets!

Another link with dear ones was Adolph Mailliard, who had been induced to come west by Sam's glowing accounts of the richness of the Mariposa vein. By the time Mailliard arrived, that prospect had, in the mining phrase, gone into *borrasca,* or an unprofitable streak; but there were other investment opportunities. The country was filling up, and land values were rising steadily. With a view to possibly settling in California later on, Mailliard bought some acreage in Marin County, north of San Francisco, Sam procuring it at bargain prices for his brother-in-law; some of the properties had come into the possession of Ward & Price in settlement of debts.

In a short while, Judge Matthew and Ward McAllister decided they had made their "pile," and departed for the East. Ward would not return; but his father, after a ruinous speculation, would obtain from President Franklin Pierce appointment as the first United States judge in California, and finish out his life there. Sam was sorry to see the McAllisters leave, and to keep Hall McAllister company he moved into the latter's house on Pike Street, — a lane, long since built over, in what is today the heart of Chinatown. By his own account, Sam spent most of the winter of 1853–54 in Hall McAllister's library. But he was no recluse; a call to social duty would bring him bustling into activity. Captain Erasmus Keyes recalled that during the first half of 1854 he saw Sam Ward almost daily, and spent much time with him in "feasting and vain discourses"; and that while Sam was deficient in the most ordinary rules of prudence, the variety of his accomplishments was astonishing.

An instance was a dinner that Hall McAllister gave for a dozen worthies. He told Sam to arrange everything, and on coming back from his office that afternoon (Hall had become San Francisco's district attorney), he was startled to find that the kitchen range had been ripped out and workmen were installing a new one, under Sam's supervision. The dinner was cooked on the new range, by a new cook, who resisted Sam's authority, but without avail; he was flattered, cajoled, beguiled, or fooled into doing what Sam wished, while the odors emanating from the battleground tantalized the waiting guests. When the *pièce de résistance* was brought to the table, all tried to identify it, and failed; Keyes could describe it only as "a dish superladen with ornaments." Sam was appealed to for information. He examined the concoction gravely, then announced, "Gentlemen, the name of this dish, the basis of which is beef, is not found in any of the catalogues, but it is composed in the fashion of Béchamel." Name or no name, it melted in the diners' mouths.

Sam could cook up journalism as deftly as ragouts. In "forty-five minutes by the watch," he composed a review for the *Alta California* of the first operatic performance in San Francisco, — a performance of *Norma,* at the Metropolitan Theater, on Montgomery Street, on the evening of Sunday, April 30, 1854. The singing he criticized lightly and expertly, but he paid tribute to the audience, which he found far more sophisticated musically than New York audiences had remained for a long while after the initial appearance of the García-Malibran troupe. In the house, "packed from pit to paradise," he doubted that there were a hundred persons who had not heard the opera in New Orleans, New York, or Paris. This sketch of what he designated a "historic solemnity" marked the first time in ten years he had put pen to paper on the subject of music.

But the effort put nothing in his purse, and a birthday note to Julia in mid-May betrayed his depression and aimlessness. "In ten days, amidst the flowers of Green Peace, the summer breeze will greet thee on thy thirty-fifth birthday," he wrote. "I urge my fervent prayer that many happy anniversaries may crown thy gentle and classic head . . . I am thinking of some lectures upon California, but Medora will not relish it . . . The truth is that I have never had any heart since poor Marion's death, nor any head since I parted with my books."

The reference to Medora was mild bravado: Sam was too proud and too loyal to acknowledge the gossip he had been hearing. For a long while Medora had been uncommunicative, but Sam knew that she was still in Paris. The rumors reaching New York from the French capital were noted tersely by G. T. Strong in his diary: "Mrs. Sam Ward, who's living in Paris while her husband's in California, said to be the mistress of a Russian prince." The "prince" was Paul Demidoff, enormously rich but a prince only by self-styling, and a rake as handsome as he was depraved. Strong's diary was no compendium of tittle-tattle, and his mentioning the rumor at all was proof of its wide prevalency in New York. Of course the gossip seeped back to Sam, and he suffered cruelly; even though there was more than a likelihood that it might be false, he mistrusted Medora's compliant nature, for he knew how necessary wealth and luxury were to her. Still he maintained, as well as he might, the appearance of ignoring what was being said around him covertly.

The principal social centers of San Francisco were its multitude of bars, and over the cocktails there was much talk about the filibusters who were making sporadic raids on Latin American territory, hoping to carve out principalities for themselves in the pattern of the *conquistadores*. Not all these daredevils were Americans; they came from many nations, and in San Francisco the adventures of two daring Frenchmen were attracting much attention. Both had fitted out expeditions in California, with designs upon the Sonora territory in northern Mexico. One of these bravos was the picturesquely ruffianly Marquis Charles de Pindray, and the other was Sam's friend, Count Raousset-Boulbon.

Since the termination of Spanish rule in 1821, Mexico had been torn by revolutions, one dictator succeeding another. The province of Sonora had long been virtually taken over by fierce Indian tribes — Yaquis, Apaches, and others — and Mexican authority had almost disappeared from the area. In colonial times the gold and silver mines of Sonora had been among the richest in the world, but since the country had fallen into savage hands, the mines had been abandoned. The existence of this immense treasure in the forbidding mountains of the Sierra Madre was the bait that lured first de Pindray and then Raousset.

The former, a nobleman who had run through a fortune in France with the Demidoff crowd, then had turned Rocky Mountain hunter and Indian fighter, recruited a band, mainly of Frenchmen who had failed at the placers, and sailed from San Francisco under an agreement with the current Mexican dictator to "pacify" Sonora, in return for permission to work the abandoned mines. The group landed at Guaymas on Christmas Day, 1851, and were welcomed with feasts and fandangos. Marching inland, they got as far as Arispe, where they ran into Apaches and suffered casualties. One morning de Pindray was found dead with a bullet in his skull, and the expedition fell apart.

The disheartened survivors straggled back to the coast, on their way meeting a company led by Raousset, who had come from San Francisco to share in the gold they were confident of finding in Sonora. But the political situation in Mexico City had changed, and Raousset encountered only harassment by the Mexicans. Rashly proclaiming the independent Republic of Sonora, he stormed and captured the provincial capital, Hermosillo, — an astounding feat by his handful of ragged men, armed only with rifles and knives, charging against artillery and twelve hundred trained troops. But this expedition, too, then fell apart because of bickering and indecision, and Raousset returned to San Francisco to gather a new force and try again.

He was hailed with salvos of applause. "Manifest destiny" was written on the hearts of most Californians in the 1850's; an American named William Walker already was organizing his own raid on Mexico, which would fail, a year hence, but would spur him to his later, spectacularly successful attack on Nicaragua. Sam Ward listened to his friend Raousset describe the opportunities awaiting bold men in Sonora; he admired the count, believing him motivated by an elevated, if anachronistic, code of honor, and more avid of glory than of gold. Raousset urged Sam to come with him, and Sam was tempted, for his luck had run out in California; but his instincts were pacific, and in 1854 Raousset sailed without him, after circumventing all obstacles raised by the United States authorities. The outcome was disastrous. At Guaymas, Raousset was overwhelmed by the Mexican garrison, and he and a number of his followers were captured. Among the prisoners were several American citizens, and it was said that all would face a firing squad.

News of the catastrophe shocked San Francisco, where Raousset-Boulbon was widely known and liked. The dictator controlling Mexico at the moment was vain, treacherous Antonio López Santa Anna, and he vowed he would exterminate the invaders, once and for all. The count's friends thereupon laid plans to ransom him, if possible, and Sam Ward was invited to carry the ransom offer. Santa Anna was arrogant and he hated gringos; but Sam spoke Spanish fluently, and he looked like a Frenchman. Sam accepted the mission, willing to do what he could on behalf of his valorous but deluded friend.

A letter was drawn up stating Sam's purpose, which was to proceed to Mexico City and procure a delay in the proposed execution of the count until a ransom could be raised. "We have no doubt that if the sum be in any way moderate or in reason, we can raise it here among Raousset's friends," the letter promised; and since it was written on the stationery of Adams & Company, San Francisco's leading bankers, the promise should carry weight. In deference to the United States neutrality laws, the letter was not signed. It was Sam's only credential. He set out at once.

Sam's objective, put bluntly, was to bribe the self-styled "Perpetual Dictator" of Mexico, and that wily tyrant could be touchy about appearances. Sam realized that he would have to move swiftly, delicately, and amid risks.

The news he received on reaching Mexico City was grim: on August 12th, Count Raousset-Boulbon had been led from his cell at Guaymas and shot. But Sam set to work to save the count's followers, for whom Santa Anna had decreed a special humiliation: they were to be paraded in chains before the vainglorious conqueror in a Mexican approximation of a Roman triumph. Already the men were being marched ignominiously towards the capital.

In diplomacy, intrepidity may be a winning gambit, like dash upon the battlefield, and when combined with tact and adroitness it may succeed brilliantly. A diplomat, on the other hand, may approach his objective circuitously, by cultivating a general aura of sympathy; and for carrying on such a program Sam Ward was ideally equipped. To start with, his polish and vivacity bespoke Paris, that lodestar of cosmopolitan Latins; even his idiomatic Spanish had the twang of the boulevards, for Sam spoke Spanish with an accent distinctly French. Exactly what *démarches* were set in train by Sam Ward during the weeks he spent in Mexico City never transpired; but, then, cards dealt under the table are supposed to remain hidden from view.

Sub rosa, he collaborated with the French consular authorities, who were desirous of sparing their compatriots a public degradation, even though the offenders technically had forfeited French protection. Consular aides had access to the Palace, where words might be dropped into receptive ears, while Sam Ward held aloof. His care was to devote himself genially to brightening the social atmosphere of the remote and insipid capital; for leading politicos and diplomats he gave dinners artfully composed and prepared, while to delight their ladies he organized a dancing class and instructed them in the Redowa, the latest rage in Paris. Bouquets and bonbons were rained upon the female population, while men of consequence in and out of the government stroked deliciously stuffed rotundities and expanded in a haze of cigar smoke and sparkling conversation about chefs, savants, and grizzly bears.

There were moments when Sam despaired. On the day when Santa Anna was expected to give a definite "yes" or "no," Sam sat tensely in the diplomatic club for an hour waiting for his agent to return with word from the Palace. At length the messenger appeared; but Sam, who always dreaded to hear bad news, kept on reading a newspaper, unable to ask the crucial question. At last his vis-à-vis suggested they take a stroll, and as they stepped into the street Sam ventured: "Well? I suppose that proposition went through?"

"Not by a great deal," came the answer. "We are put off until the Greek Calends" — until never-never time.

Yet from this setback Sam, with his inborn optimism, rebounded, and on the next day regrouped his forces and won his objective. How he did this he never divulged, but Santa Anna called off his Roman triumph and the prisoners eventually were released. Sam's chief memento of this hazardous service was a chronic case of "Mexican ague," or malaria, that would plague him for years.

At the end of November, Sam Ward left the capital, taking with him a few relics of the unfortunate Raousset, which he promised to deliver to the count's brother René Boulbon, in France. He kept the promise. He had a business mission to carry out, too. The international commercial interests operating in Mexico maintained a sort of diplomatic corps of their own, and Sam had been engaged to act as negotiator between investors in Europe and agents in America. At Vera Cruz he boarded a ship for New Orleans, where he could catch a steamer direct for France.

At New Orleans, however, he was met by news that sharply affected him: his father-in-law, John Randolph Grymes, had just died, and the newspapers were filled with accounts of the old dandy and his career. Sam was reading the tributes with mixed emotions when a sentence in the *Picayune* caused his heart to leap: Medora was in the city! "Mrs. Samuel Ward of New York had arrived in time to watch by the sick man's bed," the paper said, and Sam riffled through the other journals for amplification. The *Weekly Delta* provided details: Grymes's last moments, it said, had been

> cheered by the sight of her — his own "Medora" — for whom through his long and eventful life he had cherished a romantic affection, — the more striking for its contrast with his general

> stoicism . . . Never was man's heart so utterly bound up in the life of another as this father's in his favorite child. To the griefs and joys of others he remained comparatively indifferent; but the mere mention of her name would send the blood quicker through his veins and arouse him to tenderness and gentleness at once. There was something chivalric in this steady, tender, delicate, undivided affection. It was surely a happy circumstance that the last face he looked upon in life was the beautiful inspiration of this passionate, paternal love.

In much agitation, Sam attended the funeral the next day in the Grymes house on Conde Street, and there he saw Medora. She had not known of his arrival; they met in public, and their greeting was reserved. But that evening, while Sam was weighing his course of action, tortured by remembrance of the Paris gossip and resenting his wife's silence and their long separation, the door opened and there stood Medora, suppliant in her mourning. Silently she glided into his arms, and past anguish was passionately obliterated.

His sons Sam found wondrously grown; Wardie was ten, and Randolph eight. But he could not remain with them long; after spreading word among his sisters of the happy reconciliation, he had to take off for Europe, in obedience to business demands. From now on, he would never remain long in one place.

A warmhearted letter from sister Louisa overtook him en route. "We scarcely dreamed how soon your sorrow and exile would be turned to joy and home," she wrote. "After the long separation, in which Medora has seen so much of the world, and suffered so deeply, you will both be infinitely happier together than you have ever been. She can now appreciate you as man, husband, and friend . . ." By way of personal news she added: "Perhaps some one has written you of the birth of my little boy, and how he is called Marion, the beloved name. Even if you should never see him, the name will endear the little fellow to you."

The newcomer was six months old when his mother wrote this letter; his full name was Francis Marion Crawford, and his Uncle Sam would not only see him, but in the course of time would launch him on a career as a famous novelist, — F. Marion Crawford.

"Frankino," as the baby was called, was Louisa's second additional child since Sam had gone west again; another daughter had arrived three years before, and although christened Mary, she seldom would be called by any than her "made-up" name, "Mimoli."

By mid-May, 1855, Sam, back from Europe, was staying at the Mailliards' home at Bordentown with Medora and the boys. To Longfellow he described his first glimpse of the Continent since student days: the one biggest change, he wrote, was finding Longo's poems "printed, reprinted, embellished, and set to music" everywhere. He recorded the pride he had taken in "glorifying my intimacy with you, — I, who would never boast of being received at this or that court, or by such and such a potentate." "Dear old Germany" he pronounced doubly picturesque with railroads, "which I had feared would rob her landscape of many a charm. The tracks are enclosed with pretty railings and the embankments are decorated with flowers. The stations are graceful chapels in red stone, green with ivy, and in harmony with the ruins that crown the crags."

Mersch had made a pilgrimage to Heidelberg with him, for the "Professor" was now in Luxembourg, living on his California winnings. "I pointed out your abode and narrated our meeting and those long, bubbling, effervescent conferences we held," Sam chattered to Longo with the old freshness. But, alas, two decades and "the mighty waste of my chequered life" had divided him from that carefree time of youth. And Paris under the new Empire of Napoleon III had tired him, — "the rage of the people after amusement . . . they resembled a parcel of maniacs in straitjackets, allowed the diversion of dancing by some superintendent of a first-class *maison de santé*." But Jules Janin was still the same, the critical sultan of the stage. "I breakfasted with him every morning. In his rooms I saw Béranger, Lamartine, Ristori, Rachel, in a word, all the clever people of the day." Hugo, Eugène Sue, and others too tenaciously opposing the Napoleonic dictatorship were in exile.

"How I long to clasp your hand and look into those blue eyes!" Sam concluded. "I could afford to entertain you in the style you used to like. I came back attired like a jockey in variegated colors. But already the dust conceals the bright velvet of my cap and the perspiration has stained the jacket . . . The future is still an enigma," he confessed, but not ungaily. "I am like the mariner who has misplaced his sealed orders . . . or the Flying Dutchman, eternally trying to double the Cape of Good Hope, and yet so used to uncertainty its pangs are now become a necessity. Adieu, dear Longo. I place on Fanny's lap a garland of sweet flowers for the happiness she has wreathed around your life. Annie and Medora send love."

Sam's reunion with his daughter Margaret again proved unsatisfactory. At sixteen, Maddie was a poised, cultivated girl with reddish-gold hair, who received her raffish father with an assumed air of interest and some condescension. Sam was pained but understanding. "Not in the way of reproof or censorious comment, but to check a tendency which my own sad experience has shown me to be injurious in the long run to both character and self-respect," he sent her the next day "a few words of comment on your remarks . . . Do not think, dearest child, that I snap at an unguarded expression or feel vexed with you at having allowed it to escape your lips. You have so much that is womanly and charming in your nature . . . There is no need of diplomacy, no need to flatter or to blame people . . . I know that within the past year you have gradually emancipated yourself from conventional thralldom and taken the habit of saying what you think about many matters . . ."

(The tone was that of Sam's father, writing to his wayward son in 1836, so far had the wheel of time and circumstance revolved.)

The impasse between Mrs. Astor and Medora troubled him. Late in May, he visited Rokeby (it would be the last time he would see the estate) and discussed this with his daughter. But Maddie supported her grandmother, saying that having once taken a stand, Mrs. Astor should not be asked to reverse it. Sam dropped the subject. He would soon be off to Europe again anyway.

The sources of Sam's sudden exhibitions of temporary affluence were a mystification to his friends and family, and probably were misty to himself. Who or what provided the means for this new European jaunt is not known. The trip in some way was connected with business on behalf of, or perhaps merely with, Baring's bank in London, where Sam was still well acquainted. Or perhaps he had negotiated a loan from one of the solvent Wards, as now and then he did, — with consequences which would crop up disconcertingly years afterwards.

In any event, Sam obviously was in the chips, for he supplemented his official travel with another swing around the Continent, which assumed the aspect of a holiday outing. Charles Mersch met him at Antwerp, and the friends "did" the picture galleries there together. Then they proceeded to Cologne, where they "inspected old churches and cathedrals," according to Sam. The next stop was at Düsseldorf, where they heard Jenny Lind sing in a great music festival. Along the route they encountered numerous acquaintances from New York, about whom Sam wrote to Julia, — this one grown pompous and stupid, that one trying to get rid of sciatica, a third struggling with German verbs. The Rhine Sam found more bewitching than ever ("Mersch almost fell in love with a fräulein on the boat — a sweet blonde"); and so to Heidelberg, the irresistible goal, where the ruins looked the same but "the town and landscape younger and fresher, while I have grown old and stale."

At Heidelberg Sam fell ill — "had to lie a week or more on my back, won the unsuspecting heart of Rabbi Bronson, who came to read Hebrew with me every a.m. and his sons to entertain me every eve," a letter to Julia reported. "Mersch and I had a good old-fashioned time, all enthusiasm for science and study, did me much good. Two weeks at Heidelberg, an hour in Baden-Baden, time enough to spend twenty francs in the d—— restaurant, and then to Strasbourg, travel all night, reach Paris. Old quarters, Hôtel des Princes. Jules Janin hugs me. See the operas, the 'Vêpres Siciliennes,' 'Étoile du Nord,' 'Prophête,' all the theaters and the divine Ristori, the queen of tragediennes. Breakfast with her at Janin's. Fell sick in Paris with a relapse of Mexican ague, very miserable."

But not too miserable to enjoy ("when I have no shake") the society of a congenial new ally, William Makepeace Thackeray. While finishing *The Newcomes,* the novelist was in Paris with his mother and daughters, and Sam sensed a kindred spirit even before Thackeray related a funny anecdote. In December of 1852, while Sam was hibernating among the Indians, Thackeray had paid his first visit to the United States, to lecture on *The English Humorists,* and in New York one day he had asked George Bancroft in all innocence, "Who is a Mr. Astor who has left a card for me?" Thackeray could not place "William B. Astor," and he was totally unaware that the bearer of that name had an income of a million dollars a year. Sam laughed heartily, picturing his old Round Hill tutor's shocked embarrassment; he felt vindicated.

Ward's gourmet tastes were Thackeray's own. They joined forces in "researching" Paris restaurants, where they presented a striking contrast: Thackeray tall and loose-limbed, Sam short, stocky, and brisk, but both jovial, quick-witted, and exuding good cheer. *The Ballad of Bouillabaisse* Thackeray offered to give to Sam, and they collaborated upon a "roll of honor" of superlative cooks they had known; they could not recall the name of one whose genius reached sublimity in salads, so Thackeray put him down as "Sultan Saladin." At the close of a banquet at the Café Foy, the novelist confessed to Sam his real ambition: "Before Charon ferries me across the Stygian stream, I should like to write a story that will live for several centuries."

"Why," cried Sam, "you did that when you presented us with *Henry Esmond!* It will live as long as *Don Quixote, Tom Jones,* or *Ivanhoe!* Can you ask for more?"

All Sam asked for at the moment was the check, which he paid.

"Too much burgundy, too much bordeaux," lamented Thackeray the headachy morning after; but he roused himself to send a note to Sam at the Hôtel des Princes: "My dear Ward — One or two friends dine with me at Voisin's at 7 o'clock today. Will you be des nôtres?" On another day Sam took Thackeray to Janin's, where they were entertained merrily.

During a performance of *Phèdre* at the Comédie, Janin took Sam backstage to Rachel's dressing room, and when the great actress entered bade him feel her costume: it was soaking wet. Yet Sam had seen her declaiming, almost without a gesture, without physical movement; his memory flashed back to Paganini's outpouring of nervous energy during that guitar rehearsal, until the sweat spangled his brow.

A friend of both Thackeray and Sam was Henry James, the

Swedenborgian philosopher (father of the novelist), who had brought his sons, William and Henry, to imbibe European culture. The elder James was a dear associate of the Howes in Boston (Julia always regarded the father as superior to either of his famous sons), and Sam and Thackeray saw much of him. The James lads, twelve and thirteen, were about the age of Sam's boys. They had visited in Bond Street, and young Henry always remembered Ward households as exuding an "atmosphere of apples and nuts and cheeses, of pies and jack-knives and 'squrruls,' of domestic Bible-reading and attendance at 'evening lectures,' of the fear of parental discipline and the cultivated art of dodging it, combined with great personal toughness and hardihood." The description would have fit Sam himself.

One evening in June, Sam escorted Thackeray's mother and daughters to the theater to see Ristori in *Mary Queen of Scots,* in order to let William write the last chapter of *The Newcomes* without distractions. Thackeray completed the story "with a very sad heart," said a prayer of humility, and went to a music hall, where he slept soundly. "I thought it would be much pleasanter to see a clown jump through the window than to see a queen have her wicked head chopped off," he told a friend.

But Sam was "still in harness," he informed Dudie, and must hurry along to London. He promised to squeeze in a visit to Lord Morpeth, the literary-minded peer whom Sam once entertained in Bond Street and who now was Lord Lieutenant of Ireland. "He has written to invite me to Dublin," Sam said. "I am all philology and Christianity. Béranger and Paris did not repaganize me. Was Puritanically decent. Assisted at the conclusion of *The Newcomes,* thought the old fellow at one time would require forceps, *dreadful accouchement.* Best regards to Chev. Kisses to the babies. Your loving Bro. Sammy."

Late in July he sailed for home on the Cunarder *Asia,* looking forward to spending some time with Julia and Medora and all the children at Lawton's Valley, the Howes' summer home on Aquidneck (Newport) Island. Just how he would continue to make a living he was not sure, although for the moment he was solvent.

California no longer seemed the thing: business had gone into depression there since the gold mines had passed their productive peak in 1853. New York offered better prospects, and life with his family, in his own home, loomed attractively. He had written to Longfellow that "Consuelo [Medora], henceforth the companion of my wanderings, clings to me as the ivy round the oak." But trouble developed with that perennial antipathy, — Medora's mother.

While Sam was in Europe, Suzette Grymes had tried to turn Medora against him, dinning that Sam Ward, who had lost two fortunes, would never get another. The nagging was incessant, and Medora was easily swayed. But her father had left some property, and that, combined with Sam's windfalls, served to provide her temporarily with the luxury she required; no break threatened immediately. But Grymes Hill, where Medora and the boys once more were installed, was no haven for Sam. His mother-in-law frankly did not want to have him around. She was in process of marrying her daughter Athénaïs to a wealthy German, Baron von Hoffmann, and under the circumstances she frequently suggested that Sam spend more of his time in Manhattan. He would move over to the nobby New York Club, of which his cousin, Henry Ward, was president; but the vacuity of club life repelled him, and back he would drift to Grymes Hill, to meet a stormy reception.

In self-defense, he developed protective techniques which a friend was allowed to see in action one day. The friend had been invited by Sam to come along with him to Staten Island; and he was amazed to hear Sam shout, the minute he stepped inside the door at Capo di Monte: "Who has been drinking my Chianti? Who has been using up my olive oil?" Knowing that he would be assailed on sight for some offense or other, he employed this stratagem to spike Suzette's guns before she could open fire. Sometimes the ruse worked; but Sam was coming to detest this mother-in-law.

The gap between Maddie and her father was another point that rankled. In a letter to his daughter written in French (Sam relapsed into that language readily), he protested that no consideration of mere consistency should prevent Mrs. William B. Astor from receiving Medora and treating her at least civilly. "You judge and condemn without a hearing one who is worthy of every consideration. What a way of thinking for a Christian woman!" he exclaimed reproachfully. "You humiliate her with your disdain. Ten years go by, — and your pride, your piety, or your vanity prevents you from holding out your hand?" He felt that he could no longer accept social favors at a house from which his wife was excluded, particularly since, "I swear, my dear child, she is worth a thousand times more than I am!" To continue to spin pretexts as to why Medora did not call with him at Lafayette Place would be insulting to her and demeaning to himself, he concluded; therefore he would stay away. But he promised to see Maddie whenever he could, and to send word to her of times and places where they might meet.

Painful to write, this was a letter painful for a daughter to read.

Then, in August, came a brief holiday, when Sam, Medora, and the boys passed delightful days at Lawton's Valley. That spot was Julia's domain. Restlessly taken up with his crusades (he was getting deep into militant abolitionism), Howe seldom was on hand, and at Lawton's Valley Julia and the children romped without constraint. She had five little ones now, the youngest, Maud, having been born during a temporary return to the Asylum the previous November. "I don't know how I keep alive," she wrote gaily to sister Annie. "The children seem always waiting, morally, to pick my bones, and are always quarreling over their savage feast . . . Were it not for beer, I were little better than a dead woman, but, blessed be the infusion of hops, I can still wink my left eye and look knowing with my right, which is more, God be praised, than could have been expected after eight months of Institution. I have seen opera of 'Trovatore'," she breezed along. "In bonnet trimmed with grapes, I went, bonnet baptized in 'oh d-Cologne' . . . Chev feeling very ill just at opera time, but making himself strangely comfortable after my departure with easy-chair, footstool, and unlimited pile of papers. Well, dear, you know they would be better if they could, but somehow they can't — it isn't in them . . ."

This was the spirit of Lawton's Valley, and it suited Sam. The plain farmhouse had been furnished in part with the two hundred dollars Julia earned by her book of poems, *Passion Flowers.* A little stream wended through the dell in which the house stood, and there was a dam that had formerly turned a wheel, and the mill itself had been fitted up with iron bedstead and a battered dresser. Sometimes Sam slept there, alternately lulled by the rustle of water in the race, and irritated by the thump of the ram that pumped water to the house. Medora charmed everyone — "very beautiful," Julia assured Louisa, "and Sam winning himself golden opinions from many people, prejudiced as the world has been of late against him."

The Howe children were delighted — and often equally shocked — by Sam's lack of reverence for serious subjects. Emerging from church one Sunday, after sitting through a tedious sermon, Sam murmured fervently to Dudie, "*Ce pauvre Dieu!*" to the giggling scandal of the small fry. Another time, after a man named Potts had crucified them with an opinionated lecture, Sam let loose a diatribe against the fellow until, running out of breath, he caught himself up with, "Where are we?" "In Potsdam, I think," Julia had replied gravely, and Sam's mellow laugh had led all the others. Life moved merrily when "Uncle Sam" was around, the Howes found, and Wardie and Randolph got along swimmingly with their cousins, envied for the splendid gift of their father's, — a pony and pony cart, with a silver-mounted harness.

In September Medora and Sam came back to Staten Island for Athénaïs's wedding, and Suzette Grymes heated up the old complaints. Now the effect on Medora was more pronounced, for Sam's money was giving out, and Medora froze at the very thought of poverty. Sam found Medora was eluding him, and often there were flare-ups on both sides. Sam was dabbling in Wall Street, with only so-so success, and also was in touch with William Walker, the "gray-eyed man of destiny," who in the most spectacular filibustering expedition had seized Nicaragua, proclaimed himself President, and was angling for recognition by the United States. In October Thackeray plopped down in New York for more lectures and provided a genial interlude. "Waiting for Sam Ward, who is to breakfast with me," the author wrote from the Hotel Clarendon directly after landing; and a month later: "A very pleasant evening with Sam Ward and a party at Delmonico's."

But Sam was much alone. One November evening Strong observed him at a concert, "looking deteriorated and debased from the Sam Ward of fifteen years ago." But even a Mozart quintet could not compensate for the domestic disharmony at Grymes Hill. There never had been much compatibility of temperament between Medora and himself; now there was almost none. Incapable of accepting privation, or even considering it, she taunted him with his lack of means. Sam was furious when he found out that she was airing their money disputes among her friends.

The spring of '56 found the Crawfords once more visiting Annie and Adolph Mailliard at Bordentown, while Thomas Crawford supervised the erection of his Washington statue at Richmond. Family indignation ran high in May over the assault made upon Charles Sumner in the Senate, when a Southern hothead caned him savagely in retaliation for Sumner's denunciations of slaveholders. The Wards trembled lest Sumner's injuries prove fatal; as it was, he was years recovering. For public affairs generally Sam had no heart. He refused to be drawn into the tug-of-war between the South and the North; Southern fire-eaters and Northern extremists he found equally obnoxious. Back in the Merced Indian days he had stated his creed: "To me a Bostonian is a Bostonian, and a Virginian a Virginian; together they are Americans."

As his purse grew emptier, Medora's respect for him vanished. It required so little, as she saw it, to make her happy — affection and money — and she could not see why her husband should not provide both. The house at 32 Bond Street had reverted to her, and for a while they lived there; it was cheaper than renting rooms. Sam, with his excitable imagination, felt like a revenant in the ghost-peopled place, but Medora luxuriated in the setting, which seemed to shut out the specter of poverty. In such surroundings, in lulls between the storms, she was charming. Mimoli Crawford, "going on six," was taken to visit her Aunt Medora there, and never forgot the experience. Because Wardie and Randolph Ward, with whom she played, were such great hulking boys, the child had expected to see a withered old woman; but she was greeted by a lovely lady, who brought her right into her boudoir and talked simply and sweetly, in a low, rich voice, while arranging her hair, standing before a Louis Quinze dressing table and regarding herself in the mirror. The little girl noted that her eyes were large and dark, and her coloring was like a rose. A plate of strawberries was on the dressing table and the air was filled with unfamiliar perfumes. Medora was wearing an embroidered white muslin peignoir with an under-robe of pink silk, just the color of her cheeks.

"The sun came into the big luxurious bedroom through green Venetian blinds, and one long shaft lay on the moss-green carpet," Mimoli remembered that scene. "She smiled at me and held out the plate of strawberries, saying, 'Sit down on the floor, my dear, and eat them while I finish doing my hair.' It was such a delightful way of receiving a child. No putting one on one's best behavior and making one answer a lot of stupid questions,—just the fragrant fruit and the soft carpet and the stealing sunshine, and her beautiful hair to look at in happy silence. When she had finished her toilet and I the strawberries, she got out her guitar and sang to me the songs that had sung her into my uncle's heart,—'Oh, bring to me my Arab steed,' 'The minstrel boy to the wars is gone,' 'My earrings, my earrings, I've dropped them in the well,' and I don't know how many more. . . . I felt with a certainty that, though she was so beautiful and looked so grown up, she was in reality not much older than myself, so completely had she understood my childish inclinations and sympathies."

But between Sam and Medora there was no such rapport, only bickering, that stemmed from the only too plain circumstance that his money was gone, and he was in debt. By the close of 1856, the dissonance had become so strident that Julia wrote from Boston in distress: "My poor Sam, why not make the best retreat you can and pitch your tent elsewhere? You surely need repose and comfort. These you can have under my roof." But with Samuel Gridley Howe master under that rooftree? Sam knew such an arrangement was infeasible. Julia pleaded. "You have been unfortunate, I suppose—always too sanguine, elated by a little success, running terrible risks, perhaps misled by the figures which do not always rightly show the chances. My poor brother, you have still many years of life and vigor to expect; you have many good gifts, you still have friends who really love you, — health, uncommon talents, acquirements, and accomplishments. Save these things from the wreck. Most of us are shipwrecked more than once. Begin a right and simple life with the capital you have, — yourself. Take anything you can get, a Western professorship, some lectures, accounts of your Indian and Californian experiences. Brush away the ruins and rubbish of these disastrous years, and let the fountain of your true nature have room to rise."

She administered reproof, too, but with love. "You have gathered strange views in these years, so I hear at least. Your worst tendency is vanity, — and even this has its good as well as its bad side. But you must come out of the atmosphere of torments in which you now are, dear Sam. Come back to the old Puritan morals . . . Shake yourself loose from this nightmare. Wake up, and find yourself all that you ever were, — the honest son of an honest man. Go back to your grandfather's poverty, and dignity, and sweetness. . . . For God's sake, my dear brother, listen to these true words from a heart true to you. Come here and share my simple life!"

But for Sam to return to a simplicity he had never possessed was impossible. His own troubles and perplexity he did push aside for the moment, to turn his attention to helping and encouraging Dudie. Julia had written a play, *The World's Own,* which had been produced in New York and mercilessly attacked; both because it was written by a woman (a most unladylike impropriety) and because its heroine, named Leonora, was a "woman betrayed," who wound up not in repentance and the gutter, but rich and respectable. This flouting of an ethical cliché infuriated the critical martinets, but Sam wrote sturdily in March, 1857: "Leonora still draws the best houses. Hardly standing room Friday night . . . As for the attacks, smile serenely. If you talk about the affair, say you stood up for woman's rights and had in view to show how abominable our sex can be and how abused yours is . . . As to not reading criticism, — it is too much like my lying perdu and opening no letters. But *I* have no hope of recovering money or position, and therefore am indifferent and callous. You have a *future.* Grub Street — filthy, venal, tobacco-chewing, gin-drinking Grub Street

— merits reproof for crying out 'indecency,' 'lady author,' etc. . . . Be of good cheer. Leonora beats all Bulwer and Sheridan Knowles. I add the forbidding face of E. B. Browning." This rousing encouragement he signed, "Your old Sambo." But the play folded.

Sam's personal fortunes were at rock bottom. The very letter containing the above gave Julia news of the definite wash-up of his marriage. Annie Mailliard had been trying to bring about a reconciliation, but Sam wrote to Julia: "I saw Medora this a.m., cold and argumentative. I tried to behave well, but was not in the vein. I was cold, quiet, and natural. Avoided anything theatrical and neither strove to be tender nor pathetic. Annie was present. Medora goes to Europe with her mother. I fancy my goose is cooked . . ."

The calamity was general. Sam's finances were at the last gasp. Longfellow was startled to receive a cry of desperation, seeking a quick loan of cash. The poet (who so long had been Sam's protégé) received the letter at Nahant on a Saturday, and replied speedily: "I am ashamed to ask you to wait, even a single day, for so small a sum; but I have it not with me, nor have I any deposit in the bank to draw upon. Can you wait until next week? I shall then go back to Cambridge and will send you two hundred and fifty if you can make that do. I would send the whole sum, had I not been straining a point to oblige a neighbor and lending him all my available funds (and more, too) to redeem his house and garden. Ah, dear Hypolito, it makes my heart ache to think of your calamities and perplexities. Can you wait the little while I ask and will you forgive my sending the smaller sum of the two?"

If Sam's weakness was vanity, it was being mortified. Did he recall the many times when he had opened his purse to Longo? Probably not; that was not Sam's way. But Longfellow remembered — how Sam had surreptitiously slipped a thousand-franc note into his wallet when the poet set out for Germany in '42 — how often Sam had urged his poorly paid friend to "draw on me" for the cost of a trip to New York — the gifts, rare and beautiful — that glorious set of Molière in the "cream-and-molasses" binding which had arrived in the midst of writing *Hyperion* . . . Longfellow remembered these and innumerable other instances of Sam's open-handedness, and he suffered for "Sambo." Tactfully he assured the hard-pressed petitioner: "Your secret shall be safely kept. I will not mention to any how much your letter touches me." He signed himself, as with a handclasp, "*Siempre tu amigo, Victorian.*"

Five days later, "scribbling in haste standing at my study window," Longfellow forwarded from Craigie House the promised sum: "I wish I could double it, but cannot." By way of news from a mutual friend he added: "I had a note yesterday from Sumner, dated 'Hôtel de la Paix, Rue de la Paix.' What a murmuring sound of rest there is in those words!"

In the midst of these trials, Death again moved close to Sam Ward. Thomas Crawford, complaining of headaches, had gone back to Europe, after completing the Richmond work, and in Rome a surgeon had diagnosed cancer in the left eye. Louisa was with her husband when he died in London in October, 1857. The catastrophe cast gloom over all the Wards.

But Sam possessed the gambler's — and the romantic's — elasticity in rebounding from defeat, and just at this dismal moment, the tide turned. On October 17, 1858, Sam sailed from New York, aboard the United States frigate *Sabine,* a member of a diplomatic-naval mission to Paraguay. Overnight he had acquired a salary, official status, respectability, and the key that would open the door to greater opportunity. Once more confident, he could wink at Fate.

FIVE

A SECRET AGENT'S SECRET

When a man's luck is out and creditors rise up against him, the acquisition of a stated salary, even if it be small, may enable him to stave off catastrophe and give him time to catch his second wind. This was the case with Sam Ward in October, 1858: his berth with the Paraguay expedition was a godsend, for it carried a salary of fifteen hundred dollars a year (a trifle by his former standards), and would transport him temporarily far from the daily scrimmage to make ends meet. His appointment was not twenty-four hours old before he had mastered the intricate background of the international crisis into which he was being levered, and perhaps even in that time — with his promoter's instinct — he glimpsed a chance radically to improve his personal affairs.

The Paraguay crisis had been building up for years. When James Buchanan, Pennsylvania gentleman farmer and "Old Public Functionary," was Secretary of State in the cabinet of President Polk, he had had a diplomatically hair-raising experience with an American apostle of direct action named Edward Augustus Hopkins. The son of the Episcopal bishop of Vermont, Hopkins at seventeen threw up a humdrum job as church organist and enlisted in the Navy as a midshipman. He was assigned to the South American squadron, and during the next five years managed to be court-martialed three times for insubordination. He proved refractory to all discipline. His commanding officer finally recommended that Hopkins be dismissed from the service, but such were the tempestuous twenty-two-year-old's persuasive powers, he was permitted to resign without prejudice. And the very next day President Polk appointed this rebellious middy a special United States agent to investigate the readiness of Paraguay for recognition as an independent nation. It was a mission calling for tact, restraint, and cool judgment,

— all qualities in which Edward Hopkins was notably deficient. Buchanan had recommended him for the job.

In his letter of instructions, the Secretary of State had cautioned the headstrong emissary to watch his temper, act prudently, and commit the United States to nothing. No sooner said than undone.

The fact was that Hopkins had fallen desperately, incurably, and even practically in love with the vast emptiness of South America, particularly with the idea of that hermit nation, Paraguay, which he had never seen. Lying a thousand miles inland, cut off from communication for years, Paraguay presented a challenge to an explorer and exploiter. Hopkins was both.

In the chaos succeeding the disintegration of Spanish hegemony in South America and the subsequent interminable warring between rival despots, Paraguay had declared itself independent, and because of its inaccessibility its bellicose neighbors had let it alone. The country had been ruled by a dictator named José Gaspar Rodríguez Francia, a dry pedant, who styled himself El Supremo. He had quarantined his people against the infection of unsettling ideas by prohibiting all intercourse — commercial, diplomatic, or personal — with the rest of mankind. Once a year a single ship was allowed to ascend the Paraguay River to Asunción, the capital, bringing the few articles of foreign provenance deemed indispensable; all other needs of the population were supplied by crude native manufactures. Foreigners were not permitted to cross the frontier without permission from El Supremo; and once inside the country they were sometimes detained for years.

When Francia died in 1840, he was succeeded by a bluffer, heartier despot named Carlos Antonio López, who contented himself with the less ornate title of President. López had glimmerings of the benefits that might accrue to the country, and more specially to himself, by limited commerce with other nations; and the United States was prepared to enter into friendly relations if the conditions warranted. But in Washington nobody knew the real situation in Paraguay, neither Francia nor López yet having deigned to send diplomatic representatives abroad. Hence Edward Hopkins's fact-finding mission in 1845.

In June of that year he set out from Rio Grande, Brazil, and pushed on foot and horseback more than a thousand miles through jungles and over trackless mountains to Asunción. He arrived there in November, and three days later obtained an audience with López, whom he startled by flatly announcing that "the next Congress of the United States will recognize Paraguay's independence." The Paraguayans had thrown off Spanish rule in 1811, but in the confusion of Southern American fighting its independence had never received recognition, nor had Francia sought it.

López was corpulent but wide-awake; he was willing to barter. Unfortunately, he was handicapped at the moment by a war of sorts with the bloody-minded tyrant of Buenos Aires, Juan Manuel de Rosas, who had blockaded the mouth of the Paraguay River, thus preventing the passage of any commercial vessels. On behalf of the United States government, Hopkins offered to mediate this quarrel; and when Rosas brushed aside this unaccredited offer by a brash stripling from nowhere, that dictator was read a lecture by Hopkins in a letter which for impudence could scarcely be improved. Which would he prefer, the *gaucho caudillo* was asked point-blank — to go down to posterity as the benefactor of his people, or to perish knowing that "I have desolated my own country, impoverished it, ruined it, and gloated in the blood of my enemies?" Such was Edward Hopkins's cut-and-thrust diplomacy.

Two months later, back in Rio de Janeiro, he proudly reported his action to the agitated Secretary of State, assuring Buchanan that "next to our own country, Paraguay is the most united, the richest, and the strongest in the New World." Repudiation of Hopkins followed swiftly; but Buchanan had had his attention called to Paraguay in a lasting way.

Rebuffs did not daunt the young adventurer. For five years he campaigned, in South America and at home, on behalf of a "good neighbor" policy of mutual trade and assistance between the two continents, and in 1851 a commercial treaty with Paraguay was negotiated, largely as a result of Hopkins's prodding, by the United States minister to Brazil, — a Hoosier politician named Robert Cumming Schenck, who was well known to Sam Ward. Hopkins, who had badgered successive Presidents and Secretaries of State relentlessly — with the help and blessing of his father and influential New England friends — was appointed American consul under this treaty, and in Asunción he obtained in short order authorization from President López to organize an American company to start industrializing Paraguay; the company would operate river steamers, build factories and sawmills, and engage in trade on a wide scale. Hopkins had been in touch with another South American devotee, Samuel G. Arnold, lieutenant governor of Rhode Island; Arnold had visited the La Plata region and was enthusiastic about its potentialities. In 1853, the Rhode Island Legislature chartered the United States and Paraguay Navigation Company, with an initial capital of one hundred thousand dollars and the right to increase this to one million. Most of this capital was provided by Rhode Island investors. Edward Hopkins was named the company's general agent.

A river steamer was bought, renamed *El Paraguay,* and loaded with an assortment of merchandise and tools, — road scrapers, knocked-down boats, steam engines, a sugar mill, seventeen kinds of Yankee clocks, chessboards, candles, and church organs. With an equally burdened schooner, *El Paraguay* started southward in March, 1853, encountered frightful gales off the Brazilian coast, was half wrecked, run ashore, and abandoned. The schooner alone reached Asunción, and López sympathetically helped make up the company's loss by a loan of ten thousand dollars and the granting of further concessions. Soon a brickyard, cigar factory, and sawmill were in operation, and success seemed certain.

But Hopkins's irascibility and arrogance were defects that doomed the enterprise. When a soldier, in a fit of anger, struck Hopkins's brother, Clement E. Hopkins, with the flat of his saber, Edward galloped to the President's house, and still wearing muddy boots and flourishing a riding crop, burst upon the dictator and demanded instant punishment of the soldier and a public apology in the government newspaper. The outraged López revoked Hopkins's exequatur as consul and ordered him out of the country. The departure was made in a manner as offensive as possible to the President, and López thereupon canceled the company's privileges and the enterprise collapsed. Crying "Foul!" the Rhode Island investors petitioned the State Department to exact redress for their losses, real and putative. These they pegged at nine hundred thousand dollars, but later revised the figures upward to a million and a quarter.

A year later the State Department had taken no action. Then, in 1855, a fresh provocation stirred up official Washington. The United States ship *Water Witch,* a rakish paddlewheel steamer, while exploring the Upper Paraná River, which divides Argentina and Paraguay, came opposite the Paraguayan Fort Itapirú and was commanded to turn back, in default of written permission from President López. The skipper of the *Water Witch* rejected the Paraguayan commander's note for the odd reason that it was in Spanish, and ordered full steam ahead. Whether this defiance constituted the height of insolence or the depth of ignorance the Paraguayan officer did not pause to puzzle out: he opened fire, smashed one of the *Water Witch*'s paddles, and killed the helmsman. The crippled vessel drifted downstream and the incident moved into the realm of international diplomacy.

Further to roil the situation, Washington was irritated just then over President López's refusal to ratify the commercial treaty he had approved and signed four years before.

Since the contretemps of 1845, James Buchanan had served as minister to Great Britain (narrowly missing drawing Ward McAllister as legation secretary), and in 1857 he was the occupant of the White House. The time had come, he judged, to settle all differences with Paraguay, and in December of that year he asked Congress for authorization to exact satisfaction from López "in a firm but conciliatory spirit," but with power to "use other means in the event of a refusal." Congress obliged, and the mightiest naval force the United States had ever assembled was got ready. This task group mustered two frigates, the *Sabine* and *St. Lawrence;* two sloops of war, the *Falmouth* and *Preble;* three brigs, the *Dolphin, Bainbridge,* and *Perry;* nine armed steamers, including the *Fulton* and *Water Witch;* the revenue cutter *Harriet Lane* (gallantly named for the bachelor President's niece and White House hostess); and two armed storeships. The armada mounted two hundred guns and carried twenty-five hundred sailors and marines, under the command of a tough sea dog, Commodore W. B. Shubrick. Also aboard was a commissioner to conduct the negotiations — a reliable stump orator, James B. Bowlin, of Missouri — and, as secretary and interpreter, the bustling Samuel Ward, of New York.

Sam had got the job through personal and political influence. Some of the complaining Rhode Island investors were his distant relatives, and the company endorsed his appointment. In many respects his qualifications were incontestable. His fluency in Spanish and persuasive personality were in his favor, and he even knew something about Paraguay, more, in fact, than anybody else in the expedition knew; Robertson's *Paraguay*, one of the few books describing that country, had been in his Bond Street library. Secretary of State Lewis Cass therefore was satisfied when Commissioner Bowlin notified him on October 11, 1858, that he had engaged Mr. Samuel Ward as secretary and translator.

Aboard the flagship *Sabine*, Bowlin and Sam left New York on October 17. The frigate in itself showed how thoroughly the Navy had pressed into service every available warship to give the expedition impressiveness, for the fifty-gun vessel was old, and this was its maiden cruise. Built in 1822, it had lain at the Brooklyn Navy Yard, its size rendering it unsuitable for use in the Mexican War. The *Sabine* looked old-fashioned and lubberly among the trim modern steamers, a leviathan among minnows.

Before Sandy Hook had been passed, Sam was on good terms with the officers and crew. Both were of the type of Yankee sailors then known in every port in the world, for this was the high noon of the United States' maritime glory. Commodore Shubrick and Sam talked about California; the former had served in the Pacific area during the war with Mexico and knew many of the military and civilian personnel Sam had consorted with there. Of course Sam kept a journal (he jumped in and out of diaries with the agility of a cat) and right off his mathematical mind calculated the ages of the crew: "Average age of cabins and wardroom — 21 people — 40 years, 5 months, 6 days. Ditto of crew — 25 years. A pretty old set!" And he verified that he was the only man in the expedition who spoke Spanish well.

Seven days out, the *Sabine* ran into a hurricane, and for three days was so battered she was forced to put into Bermuda for repairs. Thus when the flagship reached Montevideo in December, most of the fleet was already assembled there. The brig *Dolphin,* Captain Charles Steedman in command, had gone a hundred miles farther up the Plata estuary to Buenos Aires, and Shubrick sent Sam to recall her to Montevideo.

Commissioner Bowlin had been given secret instructions defining what he was to demand and accept, and these had been read, presumably, only by himself and his secretary-interpreter. Bowlin was to demand that López apologize for the attack on the *Water Witch;* indemnify the family of the helmsman killed; negotiate a new treaty of commerce and friendship in lieu of the one López had flouted; and secure some settlement of the claims of the United States and Paraguay Navigation Company. On this last point Bowlin was given leeway: he was authorized to demand one million dollars, but should this be refused he could scale the amount down to half a million. Should it prove impossible to agree on the sum to be paid, then, if López would admit liability in principle, Bowlin might consent to have the amount of the damages arbitrated by an impartial commission.

At Montevideo it was reported that López was showing fight, and target practice became a part of the fleet's daily drill. The appearance of this concentration of naval power had thrown the whole Plata region into dismay, for the objective of the armada could only be guessed; all the petty *caudillos* were in a panic. In Argentina, Rosas had been supplanted by the more enlightened Justo José de Urquiza, and his trepidation was especially keen because as President of the Argentine Confederation he was about to engage in a showdown with the now mutinous state of Buenos Aires.

Sam found Captain Steedman enjoying the amenities of Buenos Aires, such as they were. They dined together, and well, at the Hôtel de Rome and took in a passable performance of *Nabuco* at the opera house. The next day they were guests of the American consul, whom Sam sized up unfavorably. Steedman entered in his journal that they had had "some pretty drinkable claret," and after two days' acquaintance he was "favorably impressed by Mr. Ward."

Then the wheels of intrigue began to turn. By some means, a copy of Bowlin's secret instructions, revealing the real objectives of the expedition and the terms on which the United States would settle with López, was smuggled to General Urquiza at Paraná, then the Argentine capital. The copy was in Spanish. Whether this occurred at Bowlin's instigation no one knows; all that is certain is that Urquiza received the copy in Spanish, and that Sam Ward was the only capable writer of Spanish attached to the fleet. Sam Ward had read Bowlin's instructions. And the copy reached Urquiza while Sam Ward was at Buenos Aires, which was in Argentine territory.

Suavely, General Urquiza came forward with an offer to "arrange" matters with his fellow President, López. Bowlin declined this offer courteously. But Urquiza set out for Asunción on his own responsibility, fortified, of course, by his knowledge of what the commissioner was going to require.

On December 30 Commodore Shubrick transferred his flag to the steamer *Fulton,* which was capable of navigating shallow waters, and taking along Bowlin and Sam Ward — Sam and the *Dolphin* had returned a day or two before — left Montevideo and headed up the Paraná River towards Asunción. Accompanying the *Fulton* were the *Water Witch,* another light-draft vessel; the revenue cutter *Harriet Lane;* and the brigs *Bainbridge* and *Dolphin.* At the mouth of the Paraná, the *Fulton* took the two brigs (sailing ships) in tow.

The panorama that unfolded on either bank of the river amazed the American crews. Aboard the *Dolphin,* Steedman recorded his impressions: "On our left, farm lands of the province of Buenos Aires, and upon the plains as far as the eye could reach the land was covered with herds of cattle and horses. On the right, it was still low and covered with creepers, weeping willows, and beautiful flowers. During the whole day I never left the deck, I was so enchanted with the scenery, it was so new, so little like anything I had ever seen. Time after time I caught myself saying, 'By heavens! What a country and how little anybody knows of it!" Every evening Steedman found his pleasure of the day continued when Sam Ward would row over from the *Fulton* for a glass and a chat.

On January 4 the ships anchored off the town of Rosario, and Steedman was told that the *Harriet Lane* would take over the towing, while the *Fulton,* with the commissioner aboard, pushed on ahead. This was an irritation for the *Dolphin*'s sociable skipper, for it meant parting company with the delightful Sam Ward,— "a charming, agreeable, and intelligent companion, one who seems never satisfied unless he is contributing to the pleasures and comforts of others. I shall miss him very much," the captain registered his regret in his day journal.

Before separating, the two comrades took in the sights of Rosario, dined "tolerably" in a hotel, and after siesta sauntered through the dusty, sunny streets. "We met several pretty women and the extent of their crinolines rivaled that of a New York belle's," Steedman's sailor eye noted. "I observed that most of the women were treating themselves to a cup of maté." This tealike beverage, brewed in a pipkin or gourd and drunk through a tube called a *bombilla,* Sam tried and found pleasantly invigorating. "This is the last night I had Ward with me," Steedman's account of that day concluded. The next morning the *Fulton* steamed up the river, and suddenly Steedman found the mosquitoes and continual grounding of the *Dolphin* on snags and sandbars an infernal nuisance.

In this way the flotilla reached Corrientes, in Argentine territory, at the confluence of the Paraná and Paraguay Rivers. From Corrientes, on January 21, Commodore Shubrick, Commissioner Bowlin, and Secretary Ward departed aboard the *Fulton* on the final leg of their journey up the Paraguay River into the heart of the continent; the *Dolphin, Bainbridge, Harriet Lane,* and *Water Witch* were ordered to remain at Corrientes in readiness for action, and to carry out war drills by marines and target shooting by the crews regularly. Rumors from Asunción said Carlos López was becoming more belligerent, and the Americans wished to make clear that they were prepared to fight, if necessary. Patriotic fever ran high. A song composed at Corrientes and sung throughout the fleet expressed the spread-eagle spirit:

> At Corrientes lies a fleet from o'er the distant sea,
> Their bunting sure proclaims them the nation of the free;

How proudly waves the Stars and Stripes — 'twould seem a gala day!
This is the Yankee fleet, my lads, that's bound for Paraguay!

Then tremble, General López, for freedom's sons are near,
Who'll change your high-toned vaunting to cowardice and fear!
Judge Bowlin's up the river, and at an early day,
There must be peace or war, my lads, twixt us and Paraguay!

This cheerful bellicosity did not frighten the Argentines of Corrientes, and Captain Steedman, in command of the ships there, found his evenings brightened by a succession of balls, tendered first by the townsfolk to the officers of the fleet; then by the officers in grateful acknowledgment; then by the townsfolk in reciprocal courtesy. "I danced two quadrilles with the prettiest and most stylish woman in the ballroom," Steedman set down in his private log. "Made her a belle, for it is not usual for married women to dance."

On January 29 came a letter from Commander Drayton of the *Fulton,* reporting their unobstructed passage up the river, "everybody excessively polite, no impertinent questions asked . . . Got to Asunción at 10 o'clock on the 25th. The audience [with López] has not yet taken place, and there are all kinds of reports about town . . . Urquiza is here with his very pretty wife and says he will stay until things are settled one way or another . . ."

In a supporting show of force, Steedman sounded general quarters every day thereafter and kept the crews hard at target practice.

Then on the 2nd of February a steamer was descried coming down the Paraguay, flying General Urquiza's flag. The American ships manned their yards and fired a twenty-one-gun salute as the Argentine President landed; he brought word that peace had been concluded with López and all difficulties had been settled amicably. Confirmation of Urquiza's news came to Steedman in a laconic note from Sam Ward, dashed off the day previous at Asunción and endorsed "*Private*":

"My darling old Mess-mate: — After a sharp engagement of some three or four days fighting, peace was concluded today at noon. Particulars in a few days. Your affect. S.W."

And on St. Valentine's Day, February 14, the *Fulton* and *Water*

Witch — the latter having been dispatched to escort the flagship down the Paraguay — returned with official confirmation of the "spirited, successful engagement" and its happy outcome. This called for a celebration, and the people of Corrientes gave still another ball, at which Sam Ward whirled pretty girls through polkas and waltzes with a light step and twinkling eyes. Steedman thought everything was in the very best taste, and concluded that "it will be many a day before *los oficiales Americanos* will be forgotten by these really kind and hospitable people."

Then the flotilla headed back towards Montevideo, while the *Fulton* took Commissioner Bowlin, his indispensable secretary, and Commodore Shubrick on a state visit to President Urquiza. The latter was so relieved to see the Yankee host depart he presented Bowlin with a diamond-studded gold snuffbox valued at five thousand dollars, and addressed a letter of highest commendation to the "distinguado Señor Don Samuel Ward, Secretario de la Legación de los Estados Unidos en Paraguay." Steedman later observed that Sam was wearing a ring set with a brilliant sapphire that the captain had not noticed before.

Among acknowledged trophies, Sam brought away an assortment of utensils for making maté, a supply of the leaves of the yerba plant which are the basis of this brew, several sprigs of jessamine, a silver flagon, won, he said, in a shooting match, and of course romantic memories.

He also brought away something that may have contributed to his buoyant mood on the homeward voyage — something neither Steedman nor any other member of the expedition ever learned — a secret agreement with President López to lobby on Paraguay's behalf at Washington.

The four-day skirmish in Asunción might have terminated less speedily had anyone save Sam Ward been calling the plays. A winning hand had been dealt to López before the negotiations opened, through his exact knowledge of Bowlin's instructions. López was convinced that the Yankees meant business, and he did not relish the thought of those warships at Corrientes starting up the river towards his capital with guns blazing. He knew he could not hedge on the apology for the *Water Witch* affair, the indemnification of the family of the slain helmsman, and the new treaty. He also believed that he would be compelled to pay the evicted Rhode Island company something. The question was how much.

Sam Ward was the only member of the American negotiating team with whom López could talk colloquially and confidentially, with no third person present. Sam Ward, therefore, was the one person who might ease the dictator's dilemma; and without Commissioner Bowlin, Commodore Shubrick, or anyone else in the American party becoming aware of what was happening, a private arrangement was reached between the trepidacious President and nimble-witted, needy Sam Ward. This taken care of, López was in a position to put up a token resistance to Bowlin's demands, and then capitulate graciously. He apologized for the *Water Witch* attack and agreed to pay the heirs of the unlucky helmsman ten thousand dollars; he signed a new treaty of friendship and commerce; but Bowlin's demand for a million dollars for the Rhode Island investors he rejected vigorously. Bowlin cut the figure in half; whereupon López grumbled that Paraguay owed Edward Hopkins's associates nothing, — but to get rid of a nuisance he would give them a quarter of a million dollars; if that was not acceptable, let the amount of the indemnity be determined by arbitration. A convention then was drawn up providing for an impartial commission to study and rule on the amount of the indemnity; this commission to be composed of two members, one appointed by the President of the United States and the other by the President of Paraguay. The commissioners would meet in Washington, examine the facts, and fix the sum Paraguay should pay the clamoring stockholders. If the two arbiters disagreed, they were to select an umpire, who would cast the decisive vote.

Bowlin himself had begun to have doubts about the justice of the company's claim, and he was delighted to have the issue taken out of his hands. He felt that in Washington he would receive credit for a diplomatic victory, and the onus of deciding against his countrymen would not rest on his shoulders.

What Sam Ward got out of his private arrangement with President López was this: a cash payment of one thousand pounds sterling, for which he undertook to smooth the way for speedy ratification of the commercial treaty and the arbitration convention by the United States Senate; and thereafter he would use his best efforts to hold to a minimum the award the arbitration commissioners might make in favor of the Rhode Islanders. For this contingent service he would be paid a commission of two per cent of whatever sum he might succeed in slicing off the starting figure of five hundred thousand dollars. In true conspiratorial style, he was to correspond with President López directly, under a pseudonym, and the President also would conceal his identity under a pen name, in making his replies. Two of the most common names in Spanish-speaking countries were chosen, López camouflaging himself as Nicolás Pérez, while Sam Ward was transmogrified into plain Pedro Fernández.

The first extended halt on the long voyage home was at Buenos Aires, and from there, on March 4, Pedro Fernández warned Nicolás Pérez that Edward Hopkins (no *nom de plume*) was in the Argentine city stirring up trouble, denouncing the settlement, the terms of which he only guessed at, and attacking Bowlin for gullibility. Pedro Fernández advised his correspondent, Señor Pérez, that the details of the arbitration agreement should be kept secret for the time being, "first, because it is better to hold your aces until the game has begun; and second, in order not to draw suspicion upon Pedro Fernández," who was doing his utmost to counteract Hopkins's propaganda. The writer intimated that there was a plot afoot in Buenos Aires to assassinate the President of Paraguay, and suggested that the United States consul there might be employed in an effort to scotch the danger; the consul, the letter explained only too candidly, probably would welcome a chance to pick up some cash. "He is a spendthrift, owes a lot of money, and at any time may go broke. His tastes are those of a *grand seigneur*. He is crazy about women, and is a man with plenty of vices, but all of them the vices of a gentleman."

While on the subject of money, Pedro Fernández confided that his own necessities were pressing, and therefore would Nicolás

Pérez kindly instruct P. & A. Blyth, in London, to pay Fernández one hundred pounds monthly until the convening of the arbitral commission. The Blyth banking firm served as the Paraguayan government's fiscal agent in London; they were instructed as Pedro Fernández requested.

At Montevideo, on March 8, a further report was prepared by Sam, in his Pedro Fernández capacity, saying that Hopkins was still furious with Bowlin. Among the officers of the American fleet, however, the letter went on, it was generally felt that the Rhode Islanders had overreached themselves in stating their claims; in fact, during discussions in the officers' mess, Nicolás Pérez was assured, both Bowlin and Commodore Shubrick had indicated that they were beginning to suspect López had been "taken." Sam-Fernández told López-Pérez: "All today are against the company, which they regard as having used the most unscrupulous lies. The same idea has permeated the whole crew. The officers are going to give a dinner in honor of the commissioner and commodore to celebrate the peace with Paraguay . . . and next Thursday, the date of the dinner, they will pledge themselves to defend the Paraguayan government against the company. Will you permit me to engage the lawyer recommended by the commodore? His name is J. Mandeville Carlisle. At present he is legal adviser of the British legation in Washington." This last query indicated that Commodore Shubrick had come around to the point where he was anxious to do whatever he properly could to assist the Paraguayan cause; possibly the amusing hours Shubrick passed with Sam Ward were having an effect.

After giving López-Pérez this bracer, Pedro, alias Sam, offered some comments concerning money. The sum he was to receive, he said, would be in part payment for his "moderating influence in the past" (which could only mean services rendered during the Asunción negotiations), and in part compensation for future "maneuverings." He had in mind, should the arbitration commission deadlock, having himself chosen as the deciding umpire. But in order to carry out his mission, he would need immediate cash, since he must clear up debts he owed to "important friends" and spruce up his wardrobe so as to appear *rectus in curia* at Washington ("beyond any suspicion") before the Paraguayan commissioner should reach the scene. With the deftness developed by practice he explained that he would not settle all his debts at once, but would pay each creditor separately; in this way giving the impression that he was paying out of his official salary, while each creditor would think he was receiving preferred treatment. Sam had mastered most of the shifts to which necessity can impel a generous man.

In his pseudonymous reply, López wrote that inasmuch as Señor Fernández had not made clear how much cash he stood in need of, the Paraguayan member of the arbitration commission, Don José Berges, would be authorized to handle the matter.

All this correspondence passing back and forth between Montevideo and Asunción was entirely without the knowledge of other members of the American party. The officers of the fleet found Sam Ward a charming and stimulating companion, and Captain Steedman had competition in preempting the secretary's time and versatility. Sam enjoyed the stay in port. When the day of departure neared, he was delivered back aboard the *Sabine* by Steedman in his own gig — an open whaleboat — after a lively scamper across the roadstead. "Cracking breeze," noted Sam. "Close-reefed big sail. She flew over the water like a shell ricocheting. Though nervous about upsetting in small boats since the cyclone at Bermuda, all apprehension soon disappeared in the fascination of the motion." They luffed too soon and fell short of the frigate's companionway, and the sailors had to pull hard to bring the boat alongside. On the *Sabine* Captain Adams welcomed Sam back in the heartiest fashion. There was a final dinner with Shubrick, Steedman, and Captain Jenkins of the *Preble,* and then the *Sabine* heaved anchor for home.

Sam's thoughts raced towards the future. And not towards the future only: Medora still troubled him. "Dreamed last night I was again in love with Medora," he jotted in his shipboard journal. "Had a wretched time of it. Reflected on waking that her indiscretion in communicating to others my affairs had been ruinous. Instead of sending for advisers, why did she not come to me? This she never did, save to ask questions and to scold, and to raise the devil. All vanity, some pride, more haughty than self-respecting, and not a bit of heart! Always posing for others and *jouant la comédie* with me. A complete sell, from A to Z! The loss of fortune which I have several times experienced never gave me one-tenth the sorrow I have felt at losing a woman's affection." But all that was finished now.

While homeward bound, a shipmate "lost the number of his mess," and Sam participated in a burial at sea. He saw much target practice, and calculated the cost of firing one hundred and thirty-three rounds at a floating target to be four hundred and thirty-four dollars and eighteen cents. He took part in a call to general quarters in the middle of the night — "prepare to repel boarders" — a fire alarm; and on April 23, during serene weather, recorded: "Saw last night the Great Bear facing the Southern Cross. Odin, Jesus Christ — the Vikings, the Popes — Scandinavians and Rome — the emblems of the great struggle of European civilizations. Strange that I should never before have seen these two constellations in the same firmament."

There was sentiment, as well as wonder. The jessamine plants he had brought aboard withered in the salt air, all save three, one of which put out blossoms, "like some stout heart that has kept warm through the storms of adversity." Four days before reaching New York the lookout cried "Breakers ahead!" and the wardroom emptied in a trice. But it proved to be a mirage of fog, so Sam and a lieutenant "crushed a bottle of sherry" between them, and by the time a second had been opened Captain Adams came down from the deck to explain the hallucination.

On May 9, 1859, the *Sabine*'s hook splashed into New York Bay, and James B. Bowlin, diplomatist, and Sam Ward, secret agent, were rowed ashore.

SIX

MAN ABOUT WASHINGTON

In New York City, on June 26, 1859, Sam Ward sat writing a message to a particular friend, scrawling on faintly blue-lined stationery bearing the letterhead, "United States Assay Office":

Dear Barlow,

The delay is not mine but the silversmith's — with this little instrument of exhaustion your maté establishment is as complete as any in South America.

Directions

1. Introduce the Bombilla.
2. Drop in 3 lumps — not too large — of loaf sugar.
3. A tablespoon of yerba.
4. *Boiling* water.

Drink hot. Make it stronger if you please.

Semper idem
Sam Ward

He was introducing a novelty brought back from Paraguay to a friend who was interested not only in Sam's travels, but in Sam's talents and tastes, as well, for these coincided pretty much with his own. The note, sent with an exquisitely chased silver maté pipkin, was the first in a correspondence that would be ended only by the writer's death. Samuel Latham Mitchell Barlow was the recipient.

S. L. M. Barlow had been named for his grandfather, who in turn had been named for Doctor Samuel Latham Mitchill, a versatile genius who speculated upon such diverse subjects as "the phosphorescence of the waters of the ocean, on the fecundity of fish, on the decortication of fruit trees, and the anatomy and physiology of the shark." He was professor of chemistry, natural history, and agriculture at New York College, and a United States senator. In 1795 he published *The Life and Exploits of Tammany, the Famous Indian Chief; Being the Anniversary Oration Pronounced Before the Tammany Society or Columbian Order,* the earliest connected account of the supposed character and career of the patron saint of New York's Democracy. He also produced a book of poems, *Epistles to His Lady Love.*

Although the Barlows were a Massachusetts family, with this background in his baptismal names young S. L. M. Barlow naturally drifted to New York, where at sixteen he took a job sweeping out a law office and running errands for one dollar a week. During his seven-year struggle to gain admission to the New York bar, he suffered many hardships; but once he was launched as an attorney, the upswing of his prosperity was marked clearly by his successive listings in the New York City directory. In 1848, when Sam Ward was preparing to migrate to the goldfields, Barlow was living on the Bowery; in 1850, when Sam returned from San Francisco the first time, Barlow had offices on lower Fourth Avenue, a high-rent district, and was living at Delmonico's Hotel. By 1858 he had his own law firm and was wealthy, and from then until the end of his life he denied himself no luxury that money could procure. In matters of aliment, he thought as one with his fellow Sam; and New York newspapers would state with awe, in obituary notices that would appear in the late Eighties, that "in his tastes as an epicure," S. L. M. Barlow "almost rivalled Sam Ward." No praise would have been more keenly relished by either man.

Barlow's great gift lay in his ability to reconcile apparently irreconcilable claims, and thus avoid, rather than promote, litigation. He was a lawyer who almost never appeared in court. He had a knack of piercing to the heart of a complex dispute and coming up with a solution acceptable to all concerned. At one time William H. Aspinwall and Commodore Vanderbilt, bitter shipping competitors, became involved in a quarrel so furious they ceased to speak to each other. Barlow invited them to dinner, fed them, and proposed a truce on terms that both liked so well they shook hands then and there, and handed their host their checks for five thousand dollars each on the spot.

In the era of railroad building, Barlow's business lay principally in that field, but he was active in shipping lines and international financing, too. His earnings were commensurately large; a single trip to Europe on behalf of the Illinois Central was said to have netted him fifty thousand dollars. But his hand was in innumerable enterprises, and in many men's pockets, to their and his own benefit. Jokes were cracked in Wall Street about this, a favorite being a story of two men sauntering along Broadway, when one exclaimed, "Do my eyes deceive me? Do you see what I see?" "What?" asked his companion. "There, ahead of us — Sam Barlow — with his hands in his own pockets!"

Having a taste for politics, Barlow by 1859 had become a leader of the Democrats in New York. He had backed James Buchanan for the Presidency; in fact, at the 1856 convention that nominated the self-styled "Old Public Functionary," Buchanan's floor managers mapped their winning strategy under Barlow's roof. Consequently, his influence at the White House and among Washington's dominant political group was decisive; it had been largely through wire-pulling by Barlow and Senator Gwin of California, Sam's fellow Forty-niner, that Sam had been attached to the Paraguay expedition.

Sam Ward now was a welcome, admired guest at Barlow's fine home on lower Fifth Avenue, where another intimate in regular attendance was the equivocal genius, William Henry Hurlbert. Thirteen years Sam Ward's junior, Hurlbert was a slender, silky, dark journalist and master of amazing erudition. He was the son of a Unitarian preacher-schoolmaster, who spelled the family name "Hurlbut"; while a student at Harvard, William Henry had been struck by a printer's error on his calling cards, and had retained the form "Hurlbert." Although he had been born and reared in Charleston, Hurlbert's family were New Englanders, and he was sent to Harvard, where he had studied divinity and law. The fascination he exercised over some of his fellow students amounted almost to idolatry; one of them, puritanical Thomas Wentworth

Higginson, recorded that Hurlbert "seemed to know everything in advance, without study"; and by way of illustrating his uncanny power to charm, said that he "could not stop to buy an apple of an old woman on the sidewalk without leaving her with the impression that she alone had really touched his heart." That organ, incidentally, many people who knew Hurlbert did not believe he possessed, even vestigially.

For a while he had preached as a Unitarian minister, although not ordained, and had written hymns that were long popular. But the fleshpot allurements of life discontented him with moral austerity in Boston, and he had come to New York and entered the office of the Manhattan district attorney, the flashy A. Oakey Hall. "The elegant Oakey" combined poetry with politics, and in time would become mayor of New York and Boss Tweed's "front man." Hurlbert wrote for magazines; visited Cuba and wrote a book descriptive of the island which evoked the praise of as strict a critic as John Greenleaf Whittier: "The man who wrote that can write anything he pleases." Hurlbert also tried his hand at dramatic criticism, traveled in Europe (on money advanced by the family of a young lady of Salem, whom he was engaged to marry), met the Brownings and saw Tennyson, and returned home (deciding not to marry the Salem miss after all), and wrote a successful comedy, *An American in Paris, or a Game of Dominoes.* In 1858 he became the chief editorial writer for the *New York Times.*

Convivial and ingratiating, he was a brilliant table talker, noted because he seldom raised his beautifully modulated voice. He was to appear in widely different guises in three novels during his lifetime; serving as model for both the hero and the villain of the plot in one, and in the other two as a puzzling, egotistical, Satanically gifted "villain." In New York he was popular, although by some persons considered pushing; and in consequence of certain episodes in his career not openly advertised, a few persons loathed him. One of these was G. T. Strong, whose execration (for reasons stated in his diary) reached the pitch of physical revulsion. "The glass from which water was given to this dog I have smashed," Strong wrote after one distasteful interview.

William Henry was not the only odd fish of his family. He had a half-brother, Stephen Augustus Hurlbut, who retained the family spelling of the name. Stephen became a political associate of Abraham Lincoln, a Civil War general, first commander of the Grand Army of the Republic, and minister to Peru. His reputation, like William Henry's, was brilliant and spotty. A story told of the brothers in later years cast light on this point. It had to do with William Henry's sending a reporter to Chicago on journalistic business. There the reporter happened to encounter Stephen Augustus, and they adjourned to a bar.

"And how is William?" asked the ex-general over the cocktails.

"Mr. Hurlbert was very well when I left New York," was the reply.

"A remarkable man, that brother of mine," said Hurlbut, after a moment's silence. "A man of extraordinary gifts. He could have been anything he aspired to, if he were not such an infernal thief."

When the reporter got back to New York he mentioned that he had seen Hurlbut.

"I'm glad you found Stephen well," said Hurlbert. And, after a moment's silence: "A remarkable man, that brother of mine—a man of extraordinary gifts. He could have been anything he aspired to, if he were not such an infernal liar."

But all this lay in the future, which was to be by no means dull.

In Hurlbert Sam Ward found a personality vastly different, but not greatly inferior to his own, and a mind upon which he could sharpen his wits. With Barlow a congenial triumvirate was formed.

When Sam landed from the *Sabine*, he found the Rhode Island stockholders of the United States and Paraguay Navigation Company impatient for a report, and he gave the company's New York agent a rundown on the arbitration agreement. In his next letter to President López, he said he had been sounded out on his willingness to serve as either arbiter or umpire! He even guessed the directors might send him to Paraguay to work out a compromise before the arbitration commission could meet.

One service he did accomplish at once, through his friendship with Hurlbert, and that was to stop the campaign of vilification of López that Hopkins had been carrying on by means of letters to the *New York Times.* Then, on journeying to Washington, Sam found the Buchanan Administration jubilant over Bowlin's achievement, in spite of opposition howls that the expedition had cost the taxpayers three million dollars and had produced no more tangible results than a gold snuff box in the pocket of the commissioner. Sam advised López-Pérez to provide his representative with "a full purse," because heavy outlays might be required.

Bustling between Washington and New York, Sam buttonholed anyone who might help, without revealing his own stake in the settlement. He was still drawing salary as Bowlin's secretary, and receiving a hundred pounds a month secretly from López's London bankers, so his circumstances were easier and his creditors were placated. This renewed prosperity was manifested in a flow of presents to friends and family, presents he could ill afford but could not resist the pleasure of giving.

His activities also drew him into closer association with S. L. M. Barlow, whose political influence was considerable and whose business interests were far-ranging. The attorney was always on the lookout for profitable investment openings abroad, and Sam had made himself an authority on the La Plata region of South America. Sam's relations with Barlow were fortified by the fact of their being fellow members of New York's Holland Lodge of Freemasons, — the lodge to which John Jacob Astor also had belonged, through whose sponsorship Sam himself possibly had been admitted. A note written by Sam to Barlow at this time echoed a notorious incident of the anti-slavery agitation just before the Civil War, — the affair of the yacht *Wanderer.* This sleek, fast vessel had been used to run a cargo of African slaves into Alabama in contempt of the United States law prohibiting the trade. The *Wanderer* had been registered as the property of a member of the New York Yacht Club, although in reality it was owned by Southern hotheads, who hoped by their rash action to discredit the honesty of Northern opponents of slavery by demonstrating that these men were ready to profit from it. Sam's note concerned two applicants for admittance to Holland Lodge, who were being opposed because of a suspicion that they had been connected with the *Wanderer* scandal.

"My dear Namesake," the message read: "It occurred to me after we separated that I had forgotten something which I ought to have told you." Then he explained that the real purpose of the candidates was "to get up a lodge at Islip, where they have property . . . We should rarely see them at Holland." And it had been represented to him, Sam said, that "no complicity in the *Wanderer's* cargo has ever been *proven,* and so grave and solemn a rebuke as a refusal to admit a man of fair standing to the house of Masonry should not be administered upon hearsay."

But such concerns were by the way. The Paraguayan member of the arbitration commission, Don José Berges, was slowly approaching Washington by way of London, and in 1859 Sam Ward went abroad to meet him. He also paid another visit to Heidelberg, where his elder son, Wardie, was studying under the care of Charles Mersch, and narrowly missed encountering Medora, who arrived at the university one day after he had left. "Suzette [Grymes] thinks she wanted to see me and would have come back to me!" Sam wrote incredulously to Julia. "That nasty little Athénaïs appears to have made much mischief. The ungrateful little wretch!" He had been "wise, not clever," in avoiding temptation, he said, admitting frankly: "I now sometimes think I should like to have her, or some one of her sex, to cheer my loneliness."

In London he had a foregathering with Thackeray, and Anne Thackeray noted in her diary for January 1860: "Sam Ward said he hoped to get a divorce shortly and I should hear from him." She was twenty-two, he was turning forty-six, but Sam never shrank from proposing to a pretty girl, youth no bar.

Thackeray showed his ubiquitous friend literary London, and a legend began to crystallize about this beaming apostle of good cheer who seemed to have traveled everywhere and known everybody — who conversed like an angel, was a man of distinguished deportment in any society — who discussed business with bankers, theology with divines, equations with mathematicians, literature with authors, music with virtuosi, all with equal fluency and authority — who sparkled with backstage anecdotes when among actors and swapped wilderness adventures when among explorers — who saluted ladies with bouquets and verses, recited Horace and Homer, told a gay story with an irresistible twinkle, and when among *bons vivants* dilated upon vintages and chefs in masterly fashion. Sam had become a legend-creating man, and Thackeray for the nonce was his acolyte.

At ten o'clock one Sunday evening the novelist trotted Sam across Onslow Square to the home of William Howard Russell, who had become the world's first war correspondent by his reporting of the Crimean conflict for *The Times,* of London. Russell heard the doorbell ring, and as he did not wish to be disturbed, signaled to the servant that he was not at home; but already the door was open, and (as Russell wrote) "a voice I loved dearly cried: 'Only five minutes, William! I have brought an American friend who desires above all things to see and know you!' It was Thackeray, who was always welcome. Taking my hand in his and putting it in the palm of his companion's, he said: 'This is Mr. Sam Ward, of New York, nominally a citizen of the world; the rest you will find out for yourself.' It was nearly two o'clock in the morning ere the visitors left."

Russell understood vaguely that Thackeray had met Sam Ward "somewhere abroad, driving a coach and four on a pleasure tour." This was a detail in the growing legend, inaccurate but sufficiently likely to be accepted as true; actually, Sam, as he perfectly well recalled and more than once mentioned in letters, had first met Thackeray at a dinner at the Garrick Club in London. But the yarns circulated about Sam during these years were many and varied; one — perhaps apocryphal, placed sometimes in Europe, sometimes in South America — pictured him traveling in a coach with a female companion disguised as a man, — the disguise apparent only to Sam. True or not, these yarns were relished. On occasion Sam himself would supply others just as piquant, some of which were absolutely true.

The meeting with José Berges enabled Sam to hold up his end socially while in London. This was because he touched López's emissary for five hundred pounds, which was handed over without question, although the autocrat in Asunción, in privately instructing Berges "to liquidate the bills presented to him by Mr. Samuel Ward, asking for a report about his activities," had thought it useful to insert a caution that "you should not be tricked." Sam received assurances that as soon as the commercial treaty and the arbitration convention should be ratified, he would receive another five hundred pounds; meanwhile, there would be smaller, interim payments to cover expenses.

In a farewell call upon Thackeray, Sam found the novelist in the midst of writing tributes to Thomas Babington Macaulay and Washington Irving, both recently deceased. Sam was chatting with Anne when her father entered the room, exclaiming: "There! I have just built a monument to Macaulay, and I am now going to finish a bust of Washington Irving. The idea and comfort," he added, "of having to write the obituaries of two authors whom no hat was handed around to bury or to provide for their families!" Like Sam, Thackeray had been separated from a patrimony and had known the humiliations of poverty.

In mid-January, Berges and Ward sailed for New York, where they landed January 30, 1860. Sam was at once waylaid by an attorney for the Rhode Island company, who subjected him to a long interrogation, the gist of which, set down in dialogue form, Sam forwarded to Nicolás Pérez, alias the President of Paraguay, in Asunción. The lawyer's name was Charles Bradley, and if the dialogue was reported correctly, he got anything but satisfaction. In courtroom parlance, Sam was a "good witness," volunteering nothing, answering readily, but disclosing not a scrap of information he did not wish to disclose.

"Do you think Commissioner Berges has enough authority to conclude a friendly settlement for the company?" asked Bradley. Sam's reply: "To a certain extent, yes."

"We are here to discuss the pros and cons of the situation," the lawyer went on. "Are you free to work for us?"

Sam: "I am free to do my best in the search for a just and honorable settlement."

Bradley: "You haven't answered my question. I want to employ you with us, and pay you a good commission."

Sam: "Thank you, but you come a little late. What would you expect from me?"

Bradley: "I'll tell you frankly: we are informed López is ready to pay seven hundred fifty thousand dollars indemnity."

Sam scoffed. "That figure is not only an impossibility but an outrage!"

Bradley pointed out that the higher the figure, the larger the commission would be, but the "good witness" brushed that aside.

"It is not a matter of some illusory and ridiculous commission, but of something practical," he said; in other words, not hypothetical percentages, but definite cash.

The company had witnesses and a wealth of evidence to support its claims, Bradley warned, but Sam laughed. "If I were the Paraguayan government, I should laugh at your witnesses and evidence!"

"We are sure we will secure the appointment of a friendly commissioner and an umpire favorable to us," Bradley went on, "so we can count on two votes to one."

"If I believed in such an infamous possibility," retorted Sam, "I should tell the whole world that my country has sacrificed justice and honor to the baseness and greed of a few persons unworthy of the name of American!"

Bradley: "So you reject our proposition?"

Sam: "That kind of proposition I do reject."

It made wonderful reading for President López. And for Sam the comedy of the company's offering to pay him to run the amount of the indemnity up and up, while López was paying him to cut it down and down, must have brought amusement.

Ratification of the treaty with Paraguay and the arbitration convention posed no problem: at the beginning of March the Senate approved both perfunctorily, and on March 6 Don José Berges was received officially at the White House. Sam collected the balance of his fee for this accomplishment, which, to tell the truth, had required little effort on his part, — five hundred pounds. About this time President López, becoming exasperated with the Pérez-Fernández rigmarole, began to call Sam "Sam," right out, protesting that all the double-naming "makes my ears ache." But an air of mystery appealed to Sam, and in his communications to the President he continued to sign himself Pedro.

Berges retained as counsel the attorney recommended by Commodore Shubrick through Sam, J. Mandeville Carlisle, and he proved to be the best possible choice. In May Congress authorized the appointment of an American arbiter to serve with Berges, and Buchanan selected a friend in whose integrity he placed full reliance, Judge Cave Johnson of Kentucky; Johnson had been Postmaster General in President Polk's cabinet when Buchanan was Secretary of State. Named secretary and translator for the arbitration commission was Samuel Ward of New York: had he not, months before, from Montevideo, promised President López that he would do some "maneuvering" in Washington?

On June 22 the commissioners met in the Treasury Building and took an oath to "fairly and impartially investigate, adjust, and determine" the amount of claims due the Rhode Island company, and Samuel Ward swore "faithfully to discharge the duties of secretary and interpreter." Arguments were presented by both sides. Bradley, for the company, asked an award of more than one million dollars, while Carlisle, disdaining to quibble over the size of the settlement, denied that a single penny was due, and contended that the Paraguayan authorities had acted within the letter of the laws of their country. With a wealth of evidence he demonstrated that the confiscated lands, which Hopkins had valued at tens of thousands of dollars, had cost the company seventy to eighty dollars all told; that the factories were insignificant; that the estimated profits could never have been realized; and that the claim for damages was "inflated, fictitious, and worthless."

On August 10 Cave Johnson entered his decision: it virtually annihilated the company's position and closed with the words: "For the reasons above given, I am clearly of opinion that the award should be in favor of the Republic of Paraguay, and against the claimants, who have not established any right to damages." Three days later Don José Berges was charmed to concur.

The "Old Public Functionary" in the White House was furious,—betrayed by a friend, he almost wept. The justice of the Americans' claims had not been submitted to the arbitrators, he protested; that question had been settled at Asunción, and the commissioners had willfully exceeded their powers, and, well, the whole thing was a disgrace and simply went to show to what a deplorable level honor among politicians had sunk since Andrew Jackson's day. Sam dined with the President and sympathized with his host's lamentations. He could afford to commiserate, for he was collecting — how much? There is no positive proof, but correspondence between Berges and Carlos Antonio López "closing out Ward's account" indicates that the agreed commission was paid — two per cent of whatever amount should be shaved off the starting figure of five hundred thousand dollars. Since the amount had been cut to zero, the difference was five hundred thousand dollars, two per cent of which is ten thousand dollars.

Thus, presumably, Sam Ward, who less than two years previously had been on his uppers, in the space of a few months had pocketed (aboveboard or presumptively) at least eighteen thousand dollars, plus perquisites and extras. He was in business again, and apparently by sheer luck, for there is no evidence that his exertions affected the outcome of the arbitration, one way or the other. Paraguay won the case on its merits, and Cave Johnson's integrity never was questioned. James B. Bowlin — who had no inkling then or ever of Sam Ward's understanding with President López — wrote to the latter, after the decision was announced: "I pledged myself to your Excellency that you would have nothing to fear in submitting these particulars to the impartial justice of my countrymen, and I feel now that that pledge is redeemed fully in the result."

International jockeying suited Sam Ward, and the plums were worth picking. The inner contentment generated by his restoration to affluence assumed outward and visible forms, especially in the splendor of his dress. Sam dressed to the nines, — brilliant cravats, immaculate linen, diamond studs, rings on both hands with the great sapphire eclipsing lesser stones, invariably a rose in his lapel. It was a time when men wore jewelry, and later his nephew, F. Marion Crawford, would repeatedly observe that to the end of his days Sam Ward was the only man who could wear jewelry without appearing vulgar. His ties, which would have outblazed any lesser personality, on him looked jauntily right. For daytime his suits were British tweeds, London-tailored; his evening wear was conformable to the muted dignity of a legation dinner. The slight bandiness in his legs had been stitched out by English pantaloon makers. With the years he had taken on weight, but he moved with firm stride, erect and vigorous. His face was round and jolly, his blue-gray eyes of extraordinary brightness. The sweeping mustache and elegant goatee were turning gray, and his massive head was bald except for a fringe; but the crown of his dome gleamed with the reflections of good living. Sam had acquired an air, a posture, and a patina, built up layer by layer through his many experiences. That air, that presence, that tact, that social deftness, that superlative gift for friendship, he now put to work. In the house he had rented in Washington, he spread himself, that year before secession.

SEVEN

"BOHEMIA IS RISING IN THE WORLD"

TO BE in Washington in 1860, in the thick of the political turmoil that was boiling up to an explosion, was exhilarating. Sam Ward responded with gusto. He was busy with the Paraguayan arbitration, carrying on a huge correspondence, and hobnobbing with senators and others whose names would soon become historically famous. The center of his activity was the house at 258 F Street that he sublet furnished from his friend Barlow; it was owned by a widow named Mrs. Euridice P. Simms, a character straight out of a Dickens novel.

Sam plumed himself a little to Julia over his comeback, writing to the "dear Old Bird":

> I have my own crockery and a set of silver marked S.W., which I earned by the sweat of my brow and the oil of my tongue . . . Here I sit at my old trade, but solemn and more quiet than I ever expected to be, no *entrain* and no *afflatus*. This is partly because I am old, partly because I am more respectable, and a good deal because, for the past three months, I have been in company with Paraguayans who speak neither English nor French. I have slept, washed, eaten, and drunken Spanish until the formal dignity of that language has shaped and demurred me. But what progress I have made! I speak it as fluently as French and write it faultlessly. Pretty good for forty-six years. The other day at the State Department they asked me to put a protocol into Spanish. I did it offhand, without grammar or dictionary, and my work remained without a single correction. I dined with old Buchanan Friday.

Society, politics, and business all commanded his attention. Behind the scenes of the intensifying crisis he moved agilely, at peace with himself and benevolent towards everyone, — except his mothers-in-law. "Why recapitulate the sufferings of the last five years which have left me houseless, childless, friendless, and penniless — at war with Lafayette Place and not at peace with Staten Island?" he observed to his closest adviser, Barlow. Even a long-standing quarrel with August Belmont, the New York banker-politician who was the Rothschilds' American agent, Sam was happy to end, after deft intervention by Barlow and Hurlbert; he was heartily relieved to put aside "all this damnation." Belmont was a leader of the Democrats in New York and shortly would become the party's national chairman; his financial and social prominence rivaled that of William B. Astor, and his dinners were far more entertaining.

The dinners Sam presided over at 258 F Street were becoming known in the capital, not only for the peerless fare, prepared under Sam's watchful scrutiny, but for the eclectic guest lists. Although an active Democrat, Sam permitted no party divisions at his table. Men of all factions gathered there in harmony, — the two California senators, Gwin and Milton S. Latham, both Democrats, sitting alongside the Republican-abolitionist senator from New York, William Henry Seward. The Northern Democratic maverick, Senator Stephen A. Douglas of Illinois, sat down amicably at Sam's board with such Southerners as Senators Robert M. T. Hunter and James M. Mason, of Virginia, and Senator Jefferson Davis, of Mississippi, and the urbane, aristocratic Senator James H. Hammond, of South Carolina. Moderates or hotheads, all shelved their differences at 258 F Street and enjoyed Sam's hospitality.

This was particularly welcome because socially the capital had become dull. Until that year, Northern and Southern representatives had maintained relative peace outside Congress, and Washington society had flourished. The city's social life had always been Southern in tone, hostesses from the slave states setting the pattern. For sheer magnificence, nothing had equaled — nothing would equal for the rest of that century — the masquerade ball Senator Gwin's wife had given in her great house at 19th and I Streets, from dusk till dawn on April 9, 1858, with President Buchanan receiving at the hostess's side. Gwin, owner of a slave plantation in Mississippi although representing free-state California, was said to have spent at the rate of seventy-five thousand dollars a year during the high noon of Buchanan's term, and other cotton magnates poured out their money almost as recklessly. But those times had passed; as the clashes between Northerners and Southerners in Congress grew more violent, social mingling all but ceased.

Senator Latham, who at thirty-three was personable, wide-awake, and eager to be in the swim, had come to the capital fresh from a five-day tenure as Governor of California. He lost no time in obtaining an invitation to dine with Sam Ward, who kept his California connections bright, and he promptly noted in his diary that Mr. Ward seemed to be "a most remarkable man." On Sunday, March 25, Latham was a guest at F Street with Baron Salomon de Rothschild, a younger son of the Paris branch of the banking dynasty, with Gwin, Representative "Sunset" Cox of Ohio, and William M. Browne, editor of the *Constitution*, the official Buchanan newspaper. It was a select company, — assembled, Latham surmised, for a purpose, which he put down as "desirous of hiving."

The baron's visit in advance of a Presidential election caused much speculation; some newspapers were denouncing his supposed sinister designs. (In New York, G. T. Strong had snubbed the French visitor for a different reason, namely, because he was "immoderately given to lewd talk and nude photographs," Strong confided to his diary.) In Washington, Sam, prompted by Belmont and Barlow, introduced the young Parisian to the leading men, such as rakish John Slidell, a senator from Louisiana, who was Mrs. August Belmont's uncle; and Judah P. Benjamin, his colleague, "silken and Satanic" in his pro-slavery reasoning; and Vice-President John C. Breckenridge, of Kentucky, whom the baron found "charming, full of fire and intelligence, and — a rare thing — a perfect gentleman." Slidell gave a dinner for the visitor and the Russian minister, Baron Stoeckl, at which Sam was not required to serve as interpreter, for everybody chattered in French.

Rothschild had left Washington by the time Sam organized a cruise down the Potomac for Miss Harriet Lane, the White House hostess, eliminating the possible mischance, remote enough, of any indelicate overtones; the party included Latham again, the

Gwins, and one of Sam's McAllister nieces from Savannah. It was such a success Sam was moved to memorialize the occasion with a poem, "Impromptu After a Pic-nic — Potomac River."

In the midst of this socializing, there occurred the Democratic national convention at Charleston, which gave a premonition of the imminent breakup of the Union. The delegates assembled in April, 1860, with secession sentiment in South Carolina rampant. Washington waited tensely to learn the party's selection of a candidate for President. Douglas of Illinois was the front runner, but the South was furious with him because of his espousal of "squatter sovereignty," the doctrine that the people settling in a new territory should themselves decide whether the area should be free or slave. Pro-slavery Democrats contended that they had no right to do this, and that issue, added to others in the long, complex controversy, had split the party wide open. For Presidential candidate the South was demanding the nomination of a vigorous supporter of their interests; Vice-President Breckenridge was supposed to be their choice.

On April 30 the Douglas forces won the first round by jamming through adoption of their platform. Thereupon the delegations from six States of the deep South marched out of the convention hall, followed by stragglers from other States.

On May 1 balloting for the nominee began, and although Douglas took a commanding lead, he fell short of the required two-thirds majority. James Guthrie, of Kentucky, who had served as Secretary of the Treasury in President Franklin Pierce's cabinet, surged up as a compromise candidate; but ballot after ballot proved inconclusive, and adjournment was taken until the next day. Then voting was resumed, and Washington was filled with conflicting rumors.

Sam Ward trotted here and there, gathering news where he could. Gwin was vitally interested, because his term in the Senate was nearing an end and his hope of political survival depended upon Douglas being eliminated. But Guthrie was not acceptable either; years before, Gwin and Guthrie had been on the verge of a duel, so intense had been their dislike of each other.

On the evening of May 2, the Gwins dined with Senator Hammond of South Carolina. Other guests were Senator Albert G. Brown of Mississippi, a rabid secessionist; Secretary of the Treasury Howell Cobb of Georgia; W. W. Boyce, a fire-eater Congressman from South Carolina; and Vice-President Breckenridge and his wife. Also on hand were Senator Latham, a Mrs. Eve of Augusta, Georgia, and her daughter, Miss Eva Eve, — "a beautiful flower," sighed Latham as he took her in to dinner. Except possibly for Latham (he had no further political ambitions and planned to utilize the senatorship as a springboard for entering large-scale business), there was not a friend of Douglas in the company.

In the midst of the meal Sam Ward appeared. He had a bulletin from Charleston for Gwin: "Douglas has withdrawn, and Guthrie has 196 votes, six short of the number needed." Sam hustled off immediately to gather details, and Gwin, masking his disgust at Guthrie's strength, relayed the news to the entire table. There was a moment of shocked silence, during which Latham felt he could hear Mrs. Breckenridge's heart thumping, while her husband grew paler and paler; the Vice President had felt sure that if Douglas could be sidetracked, the convention would turn to him, and to have the prize go to another man from his own state was a bitter pill. Hammond, Brown, and Boyce looked grim, for Guthrie was no secessionist, and the rest of the meal passed in smothered gloom.

Latham and Gwin left together and hurried to Sam's house to learn what further he might have heard. Nothing, Sam told them. What had been the source of the message about Douglas's withdrawing? they asked. The White House, he answered; and so, despite the late hour, the two senators posted there, while Sam went in search of Jefferson Davis, who might possibly have received some word directly. The President, who hated Stephen A. Douglas, told his callers that he had received no such dispatch as Sam had relayed. Then Ward and Davis came in while he was speaking, and questioned him. Perhaps some other source at the White House? . . . Buchanan shook his tilted head and looked vague.

Giving up on him, the senators and Sam repaired to the home of Howell Cobb, to see whether he had received any amplification of the news. Cobb was not there, but his wife said no message had come through. The four men next tried the Virginia senators,

Hunter and Mason; Hunter was out, but Mason said he had received the same information as Sam's, and he didn't relish the prospect of having James Guthrie as President. Then Hunter and Cobb came up together, with a direct dispatch: "Douglas 150½ and Guthrie 68, adjourned until tomorrow." So Douglas had not withdrawn, and Guthrie was still trailing far behind. "Damn the luck!" swore Gwin. "I've made a pretty fist of it today, sure!"

The truth was that the deadlocked convention had adjourned, not overnight but for six weeks, during which period the Douglas managers would strive to nail down the few votes their candidate still lacked.

Through these momentous happenings, Sam Ward moved easily, meeting everybody and being everywhere welcome in the tension-ridden capital. On the floor of Congress, Bowie knives might flash and enraged antagonists hurl spittoons, but at 258 F Street all was harmony and peaceable digestion. On May 6, with the dust at Charleston still unsettled, Sam was host to an old Bond Street diner-out, General Winfield Scott, commander of the army. This marked a real triumph, for Scott, who fancied himself to be the foremost gourmet in the land, had, with years and dropsy, grown so fat he seldom summoned the energy to leave his own quarters, in the house of a noted French chef; any dinner that could entice him abroad must offer more than ordinary promise.

Another venerable figure at the board was Senator John J. Crittenden, of Kentucky, whose career of public service included several cabinet appointments. John Van Buren, the vain, hard-drinking, ladies-man son of former President Martin Van Buren (called "Prince John" because of his imperious manner) also was a guest accompanied by "Constitution" Browne, Buchanan's editorial mouthpiece. As by right, the two California senators completed the company, and Latham voted the group "one of the most interesting dinner parties ever assembled." The dinner he greatly admired; it "was gotten up in the most exquisite style, and the wines were pronounced by General Scott and Crittenden as very rare and exquisite in taste." One novelty that astonished the Westerner was "milk punch, *a year old,* in color very much like rich Hock wine." There also was a bottle of "Rhenish wine which Mr. Ward had brought in his trunk from Germany, which for aroma and delicacy of taste seemed to me to be incompariable [sic]." In compliment to the guest of honor, the dessert was "a pyramid of candies representing the different battles in which General Scott had been engaged, surmounted by the Goddess of Liberty with the American flag in her right hand and in her left the scales of justice." This put the old warrior in a storytelling mood, and Latham listened agog to Scott and Gwin exchanging off-the-record recollections about Andy Jackson and his terrible temper. Scott reminisced about the war in Mexico, telling how General Harney hanged several Irish deserters, and dropped the last three "just as they saw the American flag supplant that of Mexico over Chapultepec Castle." Sam was a self-effacing host, pouring *"milk punch a year old"* and saying little. But he wrote about the dinner to Julia, telling who was there, — all people who mattered. "Bohemia," he preened, "is rising in the world."

He had been writing quite a bit of poetry, he also told Dudie, and he sent her a sample, "a gypsy song which came while I was humming a waltz the other day. I like it better than the others. Does it show progress? A lady was quite astonished to hear from her husband that the *stout Mr. Ward,* who gives dinners, writes poems. If Longo should come your way, would it seem vain in me to have you show him one or two of my jingles? If you knew what a home lover I am becoming, how much I read and think, and all the mischief I keep out of, your moral sense would be gratified."

Sam's poetry *was* showing progress, within its limits. His style best suited the light tone of gallant addresses to ladies known or unknown, a form of verse that requires deftness and brevity, and which was popular in that day. Verses signed "Rosario" were appearing in New York and Washington newspapers, and Sam preserved these anonymous outpourings of his in a clipping book. The waltz-inspired effusion which he forwarded to Julia — and which Longo eventually read — was a fair specimen of Sam's touch, — half a dozen couplets, graceful, unpretentious, and playfully tender. It was titled "Lines Written to a Young Incognita."

I cannot doubt that thou art fair
As roses and as lilies are,

Nor that the lustre of thine eyes
With the bright gaze of Venus vies,
Nor that a form of lissome grace
Sustains the radiance of thy face.
But be thy hair of gold or jet,
Hazel thine eyes or violet,
Queenly thy stature, or, it seem,
A sylph's, ethereal as a dream, —
Thy youthful charms an old man sings
With blessings on thy wanderings.

What mischief could such a poetizer get into? Was doing a favor — for pleasure or profit, but more by far of the former — was lending a hand, brushing aside an obstacle, uttering a mild cajolement, — were these mischief? For Sam Ward they were acts of living. Take Thomas Crawford's unfinished commission for the bronze doors to the Senate wing of the Capitol; the modeling had been interrupted by his death, and opposition had developed to accepting them. Even Charles Sumner, Crawford's hearty admirer, disliked the sketches. But in the same letter in which Sam told Julia about his verse-making and dinner-giving, he added the promise, "I shall get Crawford's doors taken." First, for the honor of his brother-in-law, and second, because Louisa Crawford would need the money. And the doors *were* taken and paid for and installed, thanks in part to Sam's maneuvering. And proud he was when he saw that in one panel the sculptor had placed portraits of several members of Sam's family, from Colonel Samuel Ward of Revolutionary times to the baby features of Francis Marion Crawford.

On business deals involving the government, Sam worked closely and successfully with his New York friend, S. L. M. Barlow. In June of 1860 he wrote to Barlow: "I am always happy to be useful, and particularly to my friends, and to few so much as to you who have laid me under obligations of gratitude for past sympathy and kindness. I cannot get away this p.m. because I have an interview with the President tonight." And apropos of the purchase, apparently by the government, of a building for which the owners were asking one hundred and fifty thousand dollars, came a scribbled message marked "*Private*": "I've got our affair so near you had better draw up papers so there can be no mistake . . . I think we can allow them $110,000 — and of the balance $15,000 apiece for us and $10,000 for other purposes and parties." What and who the "other purposes and parties" were he did not put on paper.

Again: "My dear Barlow — It has taken me a week to corral my Congressional elephants and I am at length able to write you favorably touching both your projects. I can get the furniture bill passed any day. Touching the other, *my man* tells me . . ." and he listed figures on the cost of repairing a delapidated building. "Keep these figures to yourself and call at the New York Hotel on Monday at 10 a.m., when you will find me at breakfast, and I will unfold to you my *plan de campagne*. In haste, yours fraternally, S.W."

Envious tongues may have clacked, for in one instance Sam wrote aggrievedly to his opposite Sam: "With every disposition and desire to serve you, I fear that the program of *usefulness* which you developed when I saw you last has been made impracticable by the manipulation of a bitter and unjust hostility towards me on the part of those with whom you propose cooperating. A calumnious accusation, repelled indignantly — which I have the means of disproving by evidence, but I have done nothing more than deny it — evinces an animus which neither inspires me to be useful, nor with the faintest hope that my usefulness would be appreciated. At the same time, so far as *you* are concerned, command my services as you have a right to do on the □, and are entitled to do by the many obligations under which you have placed me.

"On the □" was the Masonic sign that put a communication under seal of strictest secrecy. Sam wrote "On the □" at the top of numerous letters to Barlow relating to ultra confidential matter.

Throughout the fall of 1860 Sam vibrated between Washington and New York. The Presidential campaign unrolled, with no less than three Democratic candidates in the field, — Douglas, repudiated and reviled in the South; Breckenridge, the champion of the Southern extremists; and John Bell, Tennessee moderate, acceptable to neither faction, thinly disguised as the choice of the hastily formed Constitution Union Party. On the Republican side was Abraham Lincoln, rawboned Westerner disliked and distrusted by the East.

Seward had believed he had the nomination in his pocket when the Republican convention opened in Chicago, and his chagrin at missing the prize had been keen. But Seward was above all a politician and a party regular, toughened and disciplined by frequent manhandling at the polls; recovering his aplomb, he loyally supported his successful rival, counting upon playing a dominant — if not in fact the commanding — role in the new Administration, should Lincoln be elected. Sam Ward was in and out of all camps, and in October wrote realistically to Julia:

"We shall have trouble with the South if Lincoln carries New York. Nor do I blame them, for with all their violence and vaporings they have vested rights, and if they submit to the irrepressible conflict, after all their declarations, they will stultify their records and become ridiculous. I anticipate a commercial panic that will shake Wall Street to its foundations. The North is playing with fire and a powder magazine." The crisis, he maintained, as he had so many times before, was "due to demagogues," ranting abolitionists and fire-eating slaveholders alike. He had no affinity for either, and he observed gloomily that "it is a melancholy retributive consolation that they who sow the wind reap the whirlwind."

This viewpoint was hardly acceptable to a woman whose husband was a militant abolitionist, whose convictions she had come to share. Doctor Howe had gone to Canada precipitately, on advice of counsel, when he was accused (apparently on good grounds) of complicity in organizing John Brown's fanatical raid on Harper's Ferry; he would remain across the border until that tragic episode was swallowed up in the greater tragedy of the war. Sam Ward and his sister Julia had drifted far apart on the issue of slavery, and for a while a coolness developed between them. It was not a rupture, but their letters became less frequent, and that summer Sam stayed away from Lawton's Valley.

Seward and Sam had become very friendly. Sam kept the senator informed about railroad stock quotations; and when Lincoln was elected and it appeared that Seward would become Secretary of State, Sam's ubiquity enabled him to be of service in various ways.

The national crisis was rapidly moving to a climax. In December,

1860, South Carolina made good its threat and seceded from the United States, setting itself up as an independent republic. The vital question was whether other States would follow; and in January, Mississippi, Florida, and Alabama did go out, with Georgia, Louisiana, and Texas shortly joining them. The northern tier of slave states — Arkansas, Tennessee, North Carolina, and Virginia — hung in the balance. In February, while Lincoln was journeying towards Washington, where rebellion was rife, the seceding States set up their own government at Montgomery, Alabama, and elected Jefferson Davis (the Mississippi senator with whom Sam Ward had trotted through the night seeking confirmation of Douglas's rebuff at Charleston) President of the Confederate States of America. Disunion now was a fact.

Sam prepared to dig in at Washington. "How much rent do you pay for this house? And what do you value the furniture at?" he inquired of Barlow on February 15, three weeks before Lincoln's inauguration. "In case I get a lease for another month, would you mind staving off your sale?" The capital was seething with political guesses, and Sam intended to stay on the spot. In letters to Barlow he relayed his own surmises. "Lincoln indicates that events will shape his policy. That's good. In my mind the future depends upon England and France. If they, especially England, should be driven by fear of bankruptcy to recognize the new Confederacy, we have lost the Gulf States forever . . . Kindest regards to Mrs. Barlow, whose charming face gleams from the paper as I write her name."

Seward, who was to be Secretary of State, it now had become definite, was in a quandary. As he saw the situation, he faced two necessities: one was to guide the inexperienced Lincoln in shaping the policies of the Administration; and the other was to convince his former associates in the Senate, who now headed the insurrectionary Confederacy at Montgomery, that Washington would initiate no hostilities against them, but would follow a policy of conciliation and friendship. Seward wanted Jefferson Davis, Judah P. Benjamin, and the others to understand clearly that he would be the chief architect of Administration policy; and further, that they could rely on his assurance that this policy would be one of peace, not provocation. In this, of course, he spoke only for himself, but he was confident that he would be able to shape Lincoln's view of the situation; Lincoln, he reasoned, was unversed in statecraft, and would be grateful for expert leading by a thoroughly practiced Secretary of State. Seward's sincere conviction was that the problem of secession, like all other human disagreements, could be resolved by reasonable discussion among reasonable men. Hotheads in both North and South were temporarily in control; but if these could be held in check until passions cooled, then men of good will and statesmanlike dedication on both sides could work out a practical settlement.

One wing of the Republican party was howling for the forcible suppression of "treason" in the South; this wing was led by Salmon P. Chase of Ohio, and to them Seward's conciliatory views were themselves barely removed from treason, — if removed at all. Therefore Seward was in a most delicate and even dangerous position. For him to communicate directly with the men in Montgomery might be construed as "communicating with the enemy." If he were to communicate with them at all, he would have to work through an intermediary whom both he and the Southern leaders could trust. In his dilemma he appealed to his Senate associate and personal friend, Senator Gwin, to act as go-between. Gwin, whose term as senator was due to expire on March 4, hesitated to assume the responsibility and risk; for he realized that his intimacy with Seward was appreciated at Montgomery, and that the leaders there probably would accept at face value anything he might relay as coming from the prospective Secretary of State, and might base their own policy of belligerency or reconciliation upon it. Also, personally he still wavered about deciding on which side of the national quarrel his own best interests lay. He yielded to Seward's persuasion, however, and wrote to Davis, conveying Seward's assurances that Washington's intentions were peaceful. The mails had not yet been interrupted, and Gwin's letter went through undetected by Seward's opponents and detractors, in or out of the party.

But Gwin's value as an intermediary was limited. He and Seward could not afford to be seen conspicuously together, for Gwin's close ties with Southern extremists were well known, and newspaper reporters swarmed in Washington. To circumvent this obstacle, Gwin suggested that they reach each other through a mutual friend, Sam Ward. Any man might drop in at Sam's house on F Street without incurring suspicion that he was looking for anything but a good dinner.

The arrangement was agreed upon, and Sam became the go-between for the go-between in a high-level political maneuver. Soon notes were passing from 258 F Street to Seward's house nearby, cryptically noncommittal but enlightening to the parties concerned. "Dr. G[win] desires to see you and begs you will be kind enough to send me word as early as you please at what hour it will be convenient for you to meet him at 258," read one message. And in mid-February: "Dr. Gwin dines alone with me today at five and thought that, if not elsewhere engaged, you might find it a relief from cares and questions to join us, which I should esteem a great pleasure as well as a high honor. There will be no other guest."

The messages were not always political. With a case of wine, Sam wrote: "The accompanying box contains tears not crushed from the wine press, but 'by the bruiséd grape in mercy dropt to man.' Unlike the New England rum, which is reported to have taken the Malakoff [fort at Sebastopol in the Crimean War], the inspirations of this wine are pacific, though it came not from the vineyards of Los Angeles. Its soothing effect upon our friend Dr. Gwin in some of his most irascible moods sustains this theory. Yet while tempering the passions it promotes virtue, and I wish I had a shipload of it to send to Montgomery. It is better for being *well cooled.* Drink, but don't take the trouble to acknowledge."

Whatever information he gleaned from his own widespread correspondence he also forwarded to the secretary-to-be, on the theory that "to the navigator, the faintest scud may sometimes prove the direction of the upper currents, and a cloud no larger than a soup plate a meteorological indication."

When Lincoln slunk into Washington in a distressingly pusillanimous manner (or so it seemed), supposedly to foil an assassination plot, Sam was disgusted. Commanding the District of Columbia Volunteers, whose duty it was to preserve the peace in the city, was Colonel Charles P. Stone, the friend with whom Sam had lain doggo in San Francisco in 1852 while carrying out that coup in Washington Vein stock. Stone's loyalty came under fire, and Sam defended his fellow Forty-niner vigorously. Associates from '49 were turning up in Sam's path continually, many of them now men of substance and influence. The Forty-niners always considered themselves rather special, and a strong sense of camaraderie linked them in a Freemasonry of their own.

Lincoln's inauguration passed off tensely: Pennsylvania Avenue and the Capitol bristled with sharpshooters posted by General Scott, as if in the midst of an enemy. But in effect Washington was such, — an enemy camp. Seward became Secretary of State, but balanced against him in the cabinet was Chase, leader of the war radicals, as Secretary of the Treasury. On inauguration day Sam sent Seward a lengthy resumé of his gleanings of March 4.

"I visited Dr. G[win] this p.m. and found Senator Hunter [of Virginia] in his study. Neither had read the inaugural, and my account of it confirmed the impression they had received from Mr. Bright [Democratic senator from Indiana] and another senator whose name has escaped me. Whilst we were discussing the probable action of Virginia, which Dr. G. maintained *would not go out*, Constitution Browne came in from the p.m. train, fresh from Montgomery." "Constitution" Browne, an Englishman who had lived in Ireland before migrating to the United States, had "gone Secesh" with a vengeance. "I propose," Sam then ventured, "intruding upon you with the rough sketch of the salient facts and speculations of the dialogue that ensued.

"1. Mr. Davis had shown Browne a letter received from Dr. G. some days since, foreshadowing peaceful policy on the part of the incoming administration. This announcement has given Dr. G. great satisfaction. He, too, was in favor of moderate measures and eliminating angry words, threats, and bluster from 'the situation.'

"2. There is perfect unanimity in the Southern Congress — no jar. All is harmony. Tom Cobb, a cleverer man than his brother [Howell Cobb], is the leader of debate." Thomas R. R. Cobb had been making stump speeches in Georgia four and five hours long calling for secession, and crowds had listened to him raptly.

"3. Toombs is the master spirit of the new government." This was the impression blustering Robert Toombs of Georgia liked to foster. Toombs's extravagances had long been the butt of Washington wits. Once at the dinner table of Hamilton Fish, then a senator from New York, the "coarse, loud, and triumphant" Toombs spouted that the South would "relume the torch of liberty upon the altar of slavery," and had been deflated by Mrs. Fish's winning exclamation: "Oh, I am so glad to hear you say that again, senator, for I told my husband you had made use of exactly the same expression to me yesterday, and he said you wouldn't have talked such nonsense to anybody but a woman."

Sam appended a list of political appointments made at Montgomery, with details about the Confederate Constitution, and wound up with Browne's report on the widespread "submissionist," i.e., anti-secessionist, feeling in two border States: "In Tennessee Browne did not see a man, woman, or child who was not a submissionist. (Here he groaned in spirit.) In Virginia he found people shockingly submissionist save at the University (Charlottesville, I believe) and in Richmond."

Seward was juggling a hot potato tossed to him by three commissioners whom the Confederacy had sent to Washington to treat for the peaceful surrender of United States forts in Southern territory, principally Fort Sumter at Charleston, and Fort Pickens near Pensacola, Florida. The commissioners — Martin J. Crawford, John Forsyth, and the French-speaking Louisianan, André B. Roman — were well known to Sam, and he tipped off Seward that "Mr. Crawford . . . has full powers without his two colleagues. He will instantly apply for a reception. If he goes back unacknowledged as commissioner, President Davis cannot hold back the people from attacking the forts. Dr. Gwin and Hunter think the question had best be referred to the Senate. They say it is a risk you must take. You can count on twenty-two Democratic votes."

Sam also touched on the surprising election of a political nonentity to Seward's seat in the Senate, — an obscure judge named Ira Harris, about whom no one seemed to know anything. Harris had defeated New York's most eminent barrister and public orator, William M. Evarts, a man of tremendous ability, prestige, learning, and dry humor, — and a warm friend of Sam Ward. The election had been rigged, of course, by Thurlow Weed, the former Whig boss of New York State who had put on Republican harness; in fact, the story convulsing Washington was that when a reporter had asked Weed in all innocence whether he knew this man Harris, the boss had replied: "Do I know him? I should rather think I do know him. I invented him." Sam's comment to Seward read: "Hunter thinks it was to be regretted that you could not leave your mantle upon the shoulders of a man of nerve to sustain your measures in the Senate." The understanding was that Weed preferred to have a voting senator, rather than a man of brilliance, as Seward's successor.

The secretary kept stalling the Southern commissioners with excuses — pressure of patronage demands, the delays attendant upon settling into departmental routine, and such pretexts. He could not receive the commissioners without recognizing the government behind them; yet he did not wish to send them back to Montgomery in anger. He still believed he could shape Washington policy, and that peace would prevail.

Gwin and Sam Ward continued to be two principal intermediaries through whom Seward's evasions and the heckling demands of the commissioners were transmitted. But the inclusion of Chase in the cabinet alarmed Gwin. Lincoln had said nothing yet, beyond his restrained inaugural speech, and Seward was insisting that conciliation would be the policy adopted; yet in view of Chase's militant views, Gwin became increasingly uneasy. The Confederates were pressing hard for the surrender of all Federal property in their states, especially Forts Sumter and Pickens. Whether these would be given up peacefully — whether their garrisons would be strengthened and supplied — whether they would resist, if attacked — these were questions to which no one in Washington had authoritative answers.

Gwin was now an ex-senator, and he determined to withdraw from the affair. But to protect himself against any imputation of having misled his Southern friends, he drafted a telegram to Jefferson Davis, saying that now, in view of Chase's position in the government, the prospects looked like war. Gwin sent Sam with this draft to Seward, to check its accuracy. But Seward by erasures changed the wording so that it read: "Notwithstanding Mr. Chase's appointment, the policy of the Administration will be for peace and the amicable settlement of all questions between the sections."

Sam brought the altered telegram back to Gwin, who accepted it as a true reflection of the feeling inside the government, and authorized Sam to send the message as Seward had changed it. A few days later, however, Seward developed a suspiciously sudden illness that prevented him from keeping an appointment with Gwin in reference to the commissioners; and the ex-senator, scenting a sharp veering of the political wind, abruptly left Washington to make a swing through the South for the purpose of appraising the South's prospects himself.

The sequel of that final telegram to Jefferson Davis — at least the sequel that Gwin surmised — may have had a bearing on the subsequent relationship between William Henry Seward and Samuel Ward. Seventeen years later, in 1878, Doctor Gwin dictated his memoirs; and speaking in the third person, he then revealed his innermost thoughts: "Dr. Gwin has been of the opinion for a long time that this dispatch, which was taken to the telegraph office by his mutual friend [Sam Ward], was copied by that mutual friend and Dr. Gwin's name signed to the copy thus sent to Mr. Davis. The original dispatch of Dr. Gwin, as altered, he has always believed was retained in the possession of this gentleman, who, although a pronounced Democrat, was a man of great power with Mr. Seward during the whole term of his occupying the position of Secretary of State."

The man dictating these words made no direct accusation of any improper use having been made of the altered telegram; but he did record that "whether his [Sam Ward's] power originated from the confidence with which he [Seward] had entrusted this gentleman, although a Democrat, previous to this date, or through the medium of this dispatch, which placed Mr. Seward in a perilous position after the Civil War broke out, is mere conjecture." The suspicion that there was some connection between that dispatch, addressed to the President of the Confederacy and bearing Seward's handwriting, pledging that Washington would follow a policy which proved to be directly contrary to the one that was followed — a dispatch entirely outside the bounds of propriety and even of the constitutional right of a cabinet member to send at all — the suspicion that this dangerous document exerted some influence upon the Seward-Ward relationship was never eradicated from Gwin's mind.

And it is true that the dispatch was the only *written* evidence that Seward is known to have allowed to escape him, showing that he was in direct, personal communication with the head of the insurrectionary movement, without the knowledge of President Lincoln. The construction that could have been placed on such clandestine communication, had it become known, would have been fatal to Seward's position in the government, and might have incited a charge of treasonable conduct. With other private intermediaries acting on behalf of the Southern commissioners — notably Supreme Court Justice John A. Campbell of Alabama — the secretary had dealt both verbally and in writing; but none of these possessed a scrap of writing addressed by the secretary to Davis himself. Hence the draft telegram that Seward handed so nonchalantly to Sam Ward — bearing alterations in the telltale handwriting — may have been an imprudence, if not an egregious blunder, that the secretary regretted almost as quickly as it was committed. On the other hand, his apparent carelessness may have been another evidence of the extraordinary confidence Seward reposed in Sam Ward's discretion. Either way, it is a fact that all through 1861 and 1862 the relationship subsisting between Sam Ward and Seward was intimate, ambiguous, and strange.

EIGHT

PEACE AND WAR

In mid-March, Sam confided to Seward the contents of a letter that revealed his own direct link with sources of information inside the Confederate capital. "The following extract from a letter I have this moment received from New York may interest you," he wrote, and then gave the extract, as follows: " 'I wish I could think that there would be no fighting at Pickens, but I am skeptical about the possibility of preventing it. Benjamin [now attorney general in Jefferson Davis's cabinet] writes Barlow (received yesterday a.m.) in the most emphatic manner as to the dissatisfaction of the government at Montgomery with things at Washington, and their intention not to await events.' "

Whether to surrender the Southern forts, or to reinforce and defend them, and thereby risk war, was still undecided. At Charleston the dapper creole General Pierre Gustave Toutant Beauregard had ringed Fort Sumter with artillery, ready to open fire on Major Robert Anderson and his handful of Federal troops the moment the order should come.

Just then an overseas development projected Sam Ward deeper into the complexities of the great drama unfolding. In London, in February, 1861, the editor of *The Times,* John T. Delane, requested William Howard Russell to go to America and report what really was happening in that incomprehensible country. The regular *Times* correspondent in New York was writing like an abolitionist, Delane grumbled, for it seemed hardly credible that the slave states seriously contemplated pulling out of the Union permanently, or if they did, that they had less than a preponderance of right and justice on their side. Russell, who in reporting the Crimean War had virtually invented the profession of war correspondent, was highly respected and his dispatches would be read as authoritative. But Russell was averse to accepting such an assignment. He knew nothing whatever about American politics, and about slavery only what he had gathered from *Uncle Tom's Cabin.* Thackeray decided him. Over a dinner at the Garrick Club the novelist insisted: "You must go. As to waiting until you understand the political questions, you will never do it here. You must go out and see them at work on the spot. Don't delay. I will give you letters." One of the letters was to Samuel Ward.

When Russell landed at New York on March 16, knocking promptly on his door at the Clarendon Hotel was Sam. "That wonderful Sam Ward!" Russell jotted in his ever-present notebook. "I was trying to recall a line from Dante, when in walked Sam, and gave me the line straight out of his memory, and half a dozen others, too." Sam took Russell in charge, introducing him to important people and opening doors to firsthand information. They began by an evening at the Lambs Club, — "very pleasant and very late." Thereafter Russell's days and nights were filled with invitations, callers, and what to him were utterly mystifying "clarifications" of the much roiled controversy.

With S. L. M. Barlow, former Governor Horatio Seymour, George Bancroft, Samuel J. Tilden, and Hamilton Fish, Russell dined at the home of William Butler Duncan, a banker and good friend of Sam's, and was surprised when nobody seemed to be unduly concerned over the Southern secession. The dinner was "such as bankers generally give all over the world," the household charming, kindly, well informed, and the guests all men of prominence; yet the table talk, when gradually it drifted to politics, was mere special pleading for the South, spiced with disparagements of the new President and his government. Russell did not at first grasp that, except for Hamilton Fish, all the guests at that dinner, like the host, were pronounced Democrats. Later he realized that while they admitted the South had meditated "treason against the Union for years," they could not bring themselves to "allow their opponents, the Republicans, now in power [to use force] against their brother Democrats in the Southern states." Russell listened to legalistic hairsplitting until he wondered whether he had strayed into a polite lunatic asylum, where everybody spoke fluent gibberish devoid of common sense.

After ten days of this, he moved to Washington, where Sam again procured him instant access to the leading government figures. At the Willard Hotel the swarm of office-seekers bowled the Britisher over, but he pluckily fought his way clear, and made the rounds of the capital, from the White House down, — advised, prompted, and seconded by the ubiquitous Sam. "Russell makes 258 his living place and dined with us yesterday and the day previous," Ward informed Barlow. "He says there is no truth whatever in the report of English and French feeling against this country."

With Secretary of State Seward, Russell dined several times, on terms of striking intimacy, and he was astounded by the secretary's genial brushing aside of the whole secession turmoil. "Why, I, and all my brothers and sisters, seceded early in life," Seward scoffed with an airy wave of his cigar. "But we all came back. So will the Southern states." As Russell was leaving, on the occasion of the first interview, Seward remarked casually: "You are invited to dine with the President tomorrow. It is his first dinner with his cabinet ministers, and you will meet them all, — nobody but ourselves."

The British minister, Lord Lyons, raised eyebrows when Russell informed him of this invitation. "It is a great honor they do you," he said, thereby increasing the correspondent's trepidation, for he feared that among so many practiced politicians his ignorance of American political questions would be embarrassing. Sam Ward reassured him. "You will find them ordinary people, — good honest folk, most of them," he said. "Chase is a remarkable man and worth talking to. He won't praise all his colleagues. Cameron is as cute as any Yankee dead or alive. Smith and company are just respectable people." Simon Cameron, the Secretary of War, was Pennsylvania's political boss and had a reputation for trickiness; Caleb Smith, Secretary of the Interior, fairly fitted Sam's description as "respectable," nothing more. Russell came away from the dinner with a liking for Mrs. Lincoln, whom he considered maligned by supercilious Southern hostesses, and with respect for the President, in whom he sensed a loftiness of character and a political flair that were apparent to few observers at the time.

Sam was in high fettle as he piloted his friend around the city, and he kept Barlow minutely informed. "Russell dined with Lord Lyons on Sunday and met Sumner, with whom he went home and took black pills for an hour or so, and then came in to me to work off the effects with whisky in place of Congress water. Yesterday I took him to see Mr. [Stephen A.] Douglas, who talked for an hour and a half with wonderful nicety and clearness, giving him an historical sketch of the present row and analyzing its occult springs with impartiality and honesty . . . He had an interview with the Southern commissioners, of whom he liked Roman best." This meeting took place at Gautier's, a French restaurant on Pennsylvania Avenue where the fare was vouched for by Sam.

Douglas fascinated Russell — "a small man with a large head and flashing eyes, full of energy, subtle and overflowing in speech." But Sumner failed to impress him. He conceded that the senator had "a fine presence and imposing manner;" but when Sumner felt it incumbent upon him, as chairman of the Senate Committee for Foreign Relations, to give the visitor a rundown on his view of British public opinion, Russell's esteem evaporated. When the latter alluded to the possibility of armed conflict with the South, the senator broke in with almost febrile emphasis: "Never! They are too crafty! Bullies! Bullies! Braggarts! They would be assassins of some sort if they dared, — but fair fight, never!" Russell recalled that Sumner had had personal experience of the system of assault favored by the more violent Southrons.

On the last day of March, Sam took pleasure in writing to Barlow, in formal chirography: "I had yesterday a visit from our joint landlady Mrs. Euridice Simms, in quest of her monthly rent. After I had paid her, she remembered with becoming diffidence that there was a balance due from you, touching which she begged me to write, as the 'seven daughters' she has to feed and clothe make heavy demands upon her slender resources." The situation in which "Mrs. Euridice P. Simms" (the name rolled under Sam's pen like a *bonne bouche* over the tongue) had placed him tickled his sense of the ludicrous, and he proceeded with the urbanity of a diplomat: "Had you not intimated when I last saw you a consciousness of this obligation, and a laudable desire to fulfill it, not even a trace of her motherly garden should have tempted me to the ungracious office of a *dun*. I enclose her 'wee bit supplication,' and if you will send me a check to the order of Mrs. Euridice P. Simms I will promise to mail you the receipt for the enclosed bill."

So much for fun and personal matters. Political chatter followed. "'Abe' is getting heartily sick of the situation.' It is hard for the captain of a new steamer to work his own passage. On Friday he confessed to a friend of mine that he was 'in the dumps,' and yesterday Mrs. Lincoln told Russell that her husband had 'keeled over with sick headache' for the first time in years, — all on account of the gloom and worry of politics. This I interpret favorably for peace."

Although Mrs. Euridice Simms's demure requisition was presented the day before April Fool's Day, her bill was honored, and two days later an uncompleted note came to Barlow from Sam. "Russell is not up yet and I reply to your letter before breakfast in case he should persist in visiting Mount Vernon today," the letter began; then was taken up by a housemate of Sam's, who endorsed it: "As Ward anticipated, Russell came and without giving him time to finish his breakfast they rushed pall-mall to Mount Vernon. He desired me to enclose the receipt for the rent, which I have accordingly done."

The question still unresolved at the White House was whether to reinforce and if necessary defend Forts Sumter and Pickens, either or both, or to abandon them. Sam, however, again assured Barlow that Lincoln's policy was *peace,* there would be no hostilities. In candid discussions with Seward and other government men, Russell himself gleaned the impression that no fighting was intended; and while he divulged no information imparted to him in confidence, nevertheless over a whisky at 258 F Street conclusions could be conveyed tacitly, and they all strengthened Sam's belief.

The New York stock market was jumpy, for war would vitally affect the city's commerce. Much of New York's prosperity rested on its trade with the South, and stoppage of the supply of cotton from that region would mean bankruptcy for many enterprises. Or at least such was the expectation. Equipped with knowledge of Seward's conciliatory pronouncements to Gwin and others, Sam counseled Barlow to buy stocks.

Then there was a stir of activity at Brooklyn Navy Yard, and simultaneously a clampdown on news. Without Sam's knowing it, Seward had swung around, after discovering that Lincoln intended to make his own decisions, and was now involving the President in sending an expedition to reinforce Fort Pickens, — not with aggressive designs, Seward maintained, but simply as a defensive precaution. At the same time, Secretary of the Navy Gideon Welles, also having procured Lincoln's assent, was fitting out separate transports and men-of-war to relieve Fort Sumter. The confusion in Washington was staggering, with Seward and Welles issuing contradictory orders, neither aware of what the other was doing. Meanwhile, the loading of transports went ahead in tight secrecy, partially under the direction of Sam Ward's California companion, Captain Erasmus D. Keyes.

On April 4, the frigate *Powhatan*, under Captain Samuel Mercer, steamed out of New York under sealed orders. When the ship came abreast of Staten Island, a comedy of command took place on her deck. Emerging from a stateroom where he had been concealed, Lieutenant David Dixon Porter handed Mercer an order prepared by Seward, but signed by President Lincoln, instructing Porter to take over the ship from Captain Mercer and head for Fort Pickens, — instead of Fort Sumter, which Mercer had gathered would be his destination. Mercer, deciding that the President outranked the Secretary of the Navy, under whose orders he had been proceeding, yielded the command, and was rowed ashore.

At that moment Porter was handed an urgent telegram reading: "Give the *Powhatan* up to Captain Mercer — Seward." Porter observed that this order was signed by the Secretary of State, whose authority over Navy officers seemed dubious, to say the least; deciding that the instructions from the President remained in force, Porter steamed away for Pickens.

What had happened was that Seward had been caught meddling with Navy affairs, there had been a row with Welles, with Lincoln ruefully admitting he had signed conflicting orders without understanding them, — and the President had told Seward to countermand the order instructing Porter to take the *Powhatan* to Fort Pickens. Whether Seward deliberately signed the countermanding order with his own name, instead of the President's (as he should have done to make it valid), is a matter for speculation. All that is certain is that Sam Ward's seagoing friend, Porter, who had skippered the *Panama* around the Horn in '49, possessed a world of nerve and was not afraid to act. He had come back into the Navy when it looked as if he might get action and he was not going to be euchred out of it.

Meanwhile, the separate expedition to relieve Fort Sumter got under way, the *Harriet Lane* (how well Sam remembered that saucy cutter from Paraguay days) sailing on April 8, followed by transports loaded with troops and stores. What was their destination? The newspapers could not find out, but Sam advised Barlow that "Sumter will not be voluntarily evacuated." The news blackout, he added, was impenetrable: "The reporters are looked upon as spies and excluded from the departments." At State, "no clerk is allowed to admit a stranger to his room without Seward's permission, under pain of expulsion. All are now on their p's and q's for fear of dismissal." Every reporter he met had told him "the cabinet was as impenetrable as the Council of Ten at Venice. The oldest rats and foxes can glean nothing. To gain time is evidently one great object of the government."

With political intuition sharpened by the tension, he saw the Administration's dilemma; and he pointed out that "Lincoln, before the people of the world, can justify his course by his oath of office and the Constitution and the want of any authority to deal with revolution. His executive impotence should be taken into consideration by reasonable men, and if disregarded by violence *will react in his favor.*" Quoting Seward, he told Barlow: "Let the doctrine of secession spread, and you will have your nursery seceding from Mrs. Barlow under a sense of oppression!" Quoting two mutual friends, he postscripted: "Russell proclaims the whisky execrable and John Doyle anathematized it as flavored with neutral spirit! Alias fusil oil!"

With matters thus at touch and go, Sam had an inspiration: he would go south on a peacemaking expedition of his own, talk over "the situation" unofficially with men of sound judgment there — men whose intimacy he had long enjoyed, friends and family connections — and perhaps might come up with some last-minute solution. He mentioned the project to Russell, and the correspondent was ready to go with him, in order to view the crisis from the opposite end of the political spectrum.

On April 9, Sam wrote to Seward: "I have resolved — perhaps under the inspiration of vanity — to set forth for Montgomery on a peace errand in the morning. I have made out and signed my own roving commission and should esteem it a great favor if you could afford me the honor of a five-minutes interview this p.m. at any moment convenient for you." This request he signed formally, "With great respect, your friend and servant, Samuel Ward. 258 F Street."

Presumably he saw Seward, for later that day he scrawled to Barlow: "I am off for Richmond in an hour and only write to you to explain a telegram which I took the liberty of sending you. It is that I am *convinced* Mr. Seward is sincere in his assertion that 'no hostilities will be provoked by any of the war movements which have been in progress for the last five days.' How I know this, no matter — I do know it and recommend you to keep cool and buy stocks, and if they drop to go on buying."

But he did not get away immediately. "The storm flooding the railroads held us back yesterday," he wrote the next morning. "I shall leave today or tomorrow at 6. Keep cool and don't despair of the Republic."

Barlow was anxious, for the stock market remained jittery, and it seemed ominous that two of Seward's close associates — Thurlow Weed and Sam Blatchford, a lawyer who had been Seward's secretary when Seward was governor of New York, and who now had one foot in politics and the other in Wall Street — that these two presumptive "insiders" should be selling. Barlow wired Sam, who referred the query to Russell. The correspondent had had still another dinner session with Seward, and back came his response: "Benjamin is a Hittite and Barlow is a dweller upon Jordan . . . I never left that —— Sec. till 12:30 this morning. I went to your house and pulled the bell — leastways I induced the handle to make music — but not a soul came, and so I went off into the darkness cursing and howling like an evil spirit. Will you help me pack my clothes this morning? Will you help me to get my clothes mended? Will you help me to get needles, thread, and buttons? I will say a word when I see you — even now will I utter it — there are no hostilities meant."

This positive information Sam relayed in profound secrecy, marking his letter to Barlow both "*Private*" and "On the □:"

> I am grieved that your friend should be menaced with a loss and that my sanguine advices are the cause of it. My belief in the pacific policy of the administration was derived from Seward's intimations to Gwin in the first place, and in the second by the whole tenor of his discourse to Russell, with whom he has had four long interviews. Russell was too honorable and I too discreet, he to reveal or I to inquire, but after each he has come away satisfied with this, — that there will be nothing done by the government to provoke or even to assist a collision.
>
> He was with Seward night before last until 12:30. In the a.m. I wrote him a note referring to your answer. I enclose his answer, the conclusion of which refers to the pith of his previous night's powwow with the Secretary. Keep the letter as an autograph . . . If I am wrong, I have been *fooled,* and Mr. Seward is keeping the truth for the benefit of his friends, [like] Blatchford, who sold out last week and went short, as I hear from Hurlbert. But I can hardly believe that the Secretary would send for a man like Gwin and pour volunteer lies into his ear, or that he would solicit the presence of Russell to deceive him with purely fictitious revelations!

He gave Barlow positive assurance on one point which political wiseacres would not grasp for some time to come, — namely, that in spite of initial friction, there now was perfect harmony between President Lincoln and the Secretary of State. "Rest assured," Sam wrote, "that on no point of policy has there hitherto been nor is there likely to be any difference — not even the slightest — between Seward and Lincoln."

This superconfidential note was dated April 10, 1861. The expeditions to reinforce Forts Sumter and Pickens already were on the way. On April 11, George Templeton Strong noted in his diary, at New York: "Nothing from the seat of war (wherever that is)," and then turned to the dinner he had just attended at William B. Astor's, a dinner given in honor of the judges of the court of appeals. The guests had included legal luminaries like Hamilton Fish, William M. Evarts, the eloquent Charles O'Conor, and Common Pleas Judge Charles Patrick Daly. "Mrs. Astor and Miss Maggy Ward gave us the light of their countenances," the diarist recorded; little suspecting that even as he wrote, General Beauregard at Charleston was demanding the surrender of Fort Sumter, or that at three-thirty on the morning of April 12, Major Robert Anderson, commanding at Sumter, would be notified that shore batteries would open fire on the fort in exactly one hour.

While Margaret Ward was "lending the light of her countenance" to her grandfather's judicial guests, her father, unjudicial Sam, was in a train clattering across the trestles spanning the Peedee River swamps, coasting jerkily through the piney barrens of South Carolina, hurtling on towards the marshes environing Charleston.

NINE

BEHIND THE LINES IN SECESSIA

At 4:30 A.M. on Friday, April 12, 1861, the first Confederate shell arced high and exploded like a signal rocket above Fort Sumter.

In New York, that day, George Templeton Strong wrote with mingled relief and incredulity: "*War* has begun, unless my *Herald* lies, and its Charleston dispatch is bogus . . ." The day following, the news was confirmed beyond a doubt, and Strong penned the most momentous entry in the chronicle of his life.

"April 13. Here begins a new chapter of my journal, entitled WAR — EXSURGAT DEUS *et dissipentere inimici ejus, et fugerunt qui oderunt eum a facie ejus. Amen!*" [RISE UP, LORD, and let thine enemies be scattered, and let them that hate thee flee before thee. Amen!]

The "Amen!" would have found a fervent echo in the heart of Samuel Ward as he checked into the Mills House in Charleston. Fort Sumter was ablaze, pounded by Confederate guns, and Major Anderson was on the point of capitulation.

Sam witnessed the final phases of that dreadful drama. He saw women huddled in the corridors of the hotel, proud and prayerful. He mingled with curious crowds observing the awesome spectacle from rooftops. And the sight of the Stars and Stripes being shot down aroused in him the ardor of his Revolutionary ancestors. When Russell, who had been detained in Washington by a last-minute invitation to dine with General Scott, overtook Sam at the Mills House, the latter gave a description of the bombardment and capitulation of the fort that was not sparing of the aggressors, in spite of Sam's strong sympathy for all the people of the South. While the cannonade was still shaking the hotel, he had given vent to his sorrow and indignation in a poem. "The Old House Servant," expressing the bewilderment of a loyal slave, who was prepared to follow his master to death if necessary, but wondered why he should be called upon to fight the men who wished to make him free.

Russell had been astounded by the virulent hatred of Yankees he had encountered everywhere south of the Potomac. In Charleston, Sam Ward's connections were of the highest, comprising not only kinfolk but friends since Round Hill school days, and he was able to put Russell quickly in touch with the leading actors in the drama — Beauregard, the military commander; Francis W. Pickens, the State's blowhard governor; William Porcher Miles, beau ideal of Southern hauteur and elegance; and others in the top tier of South Carolina. Sam's discretion and entrée to such circles permitted him to move freely around the city at a time when strangers in any way suspected of Northern leanings were in danger of being lynched.

Russell had brought letters of introduction, particularly one from William Henry Hurlbert to James Louis Petigru, a close friend of the Hurlbut family and an old and admired acquaintance of Sam's. Petigru, the state's foremost lawyer, revered alike for his character and his attainments, had opposed secession with obstinacy and wit. When the state had declared itself an independent republic, he had remarked, "It won't work: South Carolina is too small for a republic and too large for a lunatic asylum." But his had been one voice raised against a hurricane; the hotheads tolerated him as amusing and harmless.

Petigru gave a dinner for Russell attended by all the notables; the *Times* man gathered that except for his host, not a Carolinian present felt anything but abhorrence for the United States. Old Petigru's intellectual clarity and vigor greatly impressed Russell, who expressed surprise that a man of such endowments should have remained relatively obscure, in a provincial city. Replied Petigru, with a laugh: "When the same remark was made to my friend Plutarch, he said, 'I live in a small town, and choose to live there lest it should become still smaller.' "

All that he saw and heard, Sam was relaying secretively to Seward at Washington. The Secretary's blind spot in respect to the true feeling in the South Sam had long tried to overcome. Seward was stubbornly persuaded that there existed a strong undercover Union sentiment throughout the seceded states, which needed to be encouraged; Sam and others better informed understood that attachment to the Union in the South had shrunk to nil.

In communicating with Lincoln's cabinet leader, Sam was in a ticklish situation: should his messages become known, his liberty, if not his very life, would be jeopardized; certainly his freedom to observe without hindrance would be forfeited. This he undoubtedly foresaw before leaving Washington; and by evident prearrangement with Seward, he addressed his report on Southern activities not to the secretary directly, but to Seward's trusted friend and subordinate, George Ellis Baker. As a further precaution, the letters were signed with a pseudonym.

Some of the reasons for this concealment were obvious; there may have been others, tenuous, but quite as compelling. Seward himself was in a ticklish situation; and it may be that he still felt uneasy about that altered telegram to Jefferson Davis, with revisions of the wording appearing in his own handwriting. By nature and long practice, Seward was a wily, wary political strategist; he knew only too familiarly the seamy side of politics. Perhaps the thought crossed his mind that one incriminating document linking him in a dubious relationship with Sam Ward was error enough, the blunder should not be repeated. Not that he would ever suspect Sam Ward of being less than a thorough gentleman, but . . . The reasons behind more than one devious action on Seward's part never have been satisfactorily clarified, and it may be that he welcomed Sam's indirect method of dealing with him from secession territory, through an intermediary and under a feigned name: it reduced risks all around.

What is not speculative is that Sam's reports from the Confederacy, in the weeks just after Sumter, were sent to George Ellis Baker; that they were signed "Charles Lopez"; and that they were smuggled out of the Confederacy under cover of Russell's dispatches to *The Times.*

George Ellis Baker was an able admirer of Seward, with whom he had been associated politically and personally for years. In 1853 Baker edited the three-volume *Works of William Henry Sew-*

ard, and in the eighties, after Seward's death, he was to issue a *Life and Works of William Henry Seward,* utilizing the Seward papers. In 1861 Seward appointed Baker the State Department's disbursing agent, a position of great trust because it carried control of the department's "secret fund," for which no accounting was required. Baker had an office close to Seward's, and in Washington he was accepted as a sort of administrative officer to the secretary.

That the letters Sam Ward sent to George E. Baker, beginning with the salutation "Dear George," were nevertheless written for the secretary's eye, and that they were read by him, is placed beyond doubt by internal phrasing that could apply only to Seward, and by the penciled endorsements and comments in Seward's handwriting that appear on some of them. It is also significant that they were preserved among Seward's papers (not Baker's), and were retained there by the secretary's literary executors, Baker and Frederick Seward, the secretary's son. That Sam Ward wrote the letters is beyond question, for the handwriting is unmistakably his, and there are many identifying allusions in the text. The pseudonym "Charles Lopez" was an obvious mental throwback to Sam's Paraguayan game of hide-and-seek; he loved a mystification. And the protective enclosure within Russell's dispatches of the highly indiscreet rundowns on Confederate plans and doings was a precaution taken against Southern vigilantes, who were ransacking the mails in their hunt for spies.

Sam began his reports on April 16, writing to "Dear George" a description of the bombardment of Fort Sumter and the reasons for its surrender, all of them, according to Sam, attributable to the ignorance, incompetence, neglect, indecision, or procrastination of the Washington authorities. He told of discussions with leading secessionists, including the tigerish former senator from Texas, Louis T. Wigfall, whom Sam and Russell encountered, tipsy and stumbling over his long saber, while inspecting the ruins of Sumter. The Texan had bragged to Sam that in his company of volunteers, there was not a man but was "ready to fight a rattlesnake and give him the first bite." As for Beauregard, the general seemed delighted to meet Mr. Ward, with whose three sisters he remembered dancing at Newport when he was a West Point cadet. Sam described the general as "young, active, strong; he reminded me more of commanders I have read about than of any I have seen." (Russell rated Beauregard "very intelligent but not very determined," and remarked the nosegays lying upon the military maps, tributes from Charleston belles.)

Sam warned Seward-Baker: "While you are planning, these people are acting. They have been anticipating every contingency for months, perhaps years, and have concerted measures for every emergency . . . The *New York Herald* this a.m. says, 'Recruiting [in New York] has been unusually brisk at Chatham Street station — thirteen men enlisted for Governors Island.' What a mockery!" Russell he reported "fighting secession sword in hand. He attacks these gentlemen with great vigor, — stigmatizes the whole movement as impolitic and suicidal and invariably has the better of the argument."

During these verbal jousts Sam observed a discreet neutrality outwardly. But he told Seward plainly: "I feel convinced that the people *here* will *never* come back. They are as ready for the stake as the Smithfield martyrs. Had slavery been let alone, the Negroes would have bought themselves free in three generations more. But there is no use crying over spilt milk. I am opposed to abolitionism."

He did not hestitate to forward all information about military preparations he could gather. "I hear they are building gunboats in New Orleans . . . Major Whiting has gone to Montgomery to organize the engineering bureau of the C.S.A., which is in confusion . . . The army of the C.S.A. has had no pay yet. I know one officer of four months service who has not received a dollar . . . I commend to you the ship *Archer* in Baltimore as likely to be the first [Confederate] privateer. She is the only vessel I saw at the wharves that seemed to be fit for the business." And Confederate army men were making speeches saying "Washington must be taken."

Sam wanted Russell to see the gracious aspects of Southern living, also, and on April 22 they left Charleston in a coastal steamer for the Pringle plantation, above Georgetown, on the Peedee River.

This was the home country of Sam's grandmother, Sarah Mitchell Cutler; there was a Charleston attorney named Mitchell in the party, and many of Sam's remote cousins remained in that region. At the Pringle estate, Russell's luggage was carried by an old Negro in livery into "a low room hung with colored mezzotints, windows covered with creepers, and an old-fashioned bedstead and quaint chairs." The dinner was excellent, cooked and served by slaves, and it was accompanied by claret mellowed by the Carolina sun and Madeira brought downstairs lovingly, "as in the days of Horace and Maecenas, from the cellar between the attic and the thatched roof." Their host was anxious to get away to Europe, where he had already sent his wife and children, but was afraid of being mobbed in New York if he took the steamship there. "Some of the guests talked of duels, and of famous hands with the pistol in those parts," Russell recounted; the conversation "had very much the tone which would probably have characterized the talk of a group of Tory Irish gentlemen over their wine some sixty years ago, and very pleasant it was. Not a man — no not one — will ever join the Union again! 'Thank God!' they say, 'we are freed from that tyranny at last!'" The slaves seemed to Russell to be apathetic, "neither seeking nor shunning us." He was struck that their master knew nothing about his chattels personally except the household servants.

Expectation that Charleston harbor might be blockaded momentarily hastened the return, and during the run down the coast eyes strained seaward to catch sight of an intercepting man-of-war, but none hove into view.

On April 25 Sam wrote again from Charleston to "My dear George" — "The blockade and the word *insurrection* in the President's [Lincoln's] proclamation have produced a commotion here. Some of the more rational people . . . confess that with power and ingenuity the North may render the South very uncomfortable. . . . The uprising [of patriotic fervor] at the North, the large sums of money offered to the government, and the heavy fall of State stocks afford food for reflection. . . . The same men fear now a protracted war because of the North's unfitness for the field, — the cohorts unwieldy, inexperienced, and unofficered must get the worst of it in the beginning, and hostilities will only terminate when they have learned their strength by discipline and experience."

This was a farsighted view, although rejected by politicians and populace in the North, where it was believed the rebellion would be crushed in three months. Sam clinched his warning: "No one pretends to say that the North will stay whipped. They know she is slow to anger, and, once roused, hard to cool, but they maintain that all this will not bring back the seceding States . . . I hear that two Louisiana regiments have gone up to Memphis . . . I was told yesterday by a graduate of West Point that the resignations of officers have 'drawn the back teeth' of the U.S. command. Lee and [Albert Sidney] Johnston are great names and great talents . . . I may be wrong, but I look with dismay upon these defections. These men know all your secrets — all your power and all your weakness — and they have every deviltry of war at their command . . . I shall go south tomorrow and address you the news I get at every opportunity."

This dispatch, forwarded under cover of Russell's news letters, was itself one "deviltry of war" in operation: as an intelligence agent, Sam was supplying the United States government information of a sort that would have justified the Confederates, had they discovered the letters, in employing the short word "spy." Nevertheless, on the next halt, Savannah, where Sam was well acquainted, he continued his surreptitious communications to the Department of State.

Their host in Savannah, Charles Green, was a British-born merchant, whose red sandstone mansion afforded one luxury rare in Southern homes, — bathrooms and plenty of cold fresh water. Georgia military men showed Russell and Sam the city's defensive works, and they were regaled with horrendous stories of the consternation and anarchy supposed to be sweeping the North, — Lincoln and Seward taking to drink, and a renegade Massachusetts Democrat named Ben Butler leading a horde of ruffians to lay waste the South. Sam lost no time in giving "George Baker" the number of volunteers drilling nearby, and he described the activity at Fort Pulaski, which commanded the Savannah River, stating the quantity, caliber, and placement of its armament. "I think Pulaski impregnable and that none but iron-plated steamers could risk going up the river," was his opinion. "The tactics of the C.S.A. since the New York demonstrations [monster patriotic rallies] have changed from *invasion* to *defense*. So far so good." As for political developments: "A law will be passed by the present [Confederate] Congress making it death to export a single bale of cotton by sea or rail to the North. . . . I saw an important and reliable letter today from one of the most prominent men of England, who says: 'Here we are all disposed to recognize the C.S.A. *as soon as we can do so with decency*. Of course we prefer the North's and South's cutting each other's throats to ours . . .' Remember that blockade, but be actual — a gun a mile."

From Savannah Russell and his "secretary," as *The Times* man introduced Sam, pushed on to Montgomery, and at that point Sam relayed a budget of military and political news gleaned on Jeff Davis's doorstep. The travelers talked with Davis, Benjamin, Toombs, Beauregard and Wigfall again, and heard their candid estimates of the Confederacy's chances of success. Soon George Ellis Baker would be reading in an office just down the hall from Seward's, in a letter dated May 9: "Fort Monroe will be attacked within ten days. There is a scarcity of powder in the Confederacy. They have all the ingredients save sulphur, which they hope to get from Mexico. The C.S.A. can get all the volunteers they want for this war . . . They say that by spring they will have an army of 100,000 soldiers and will then cross the frontier and show you the difference between soldiers and railroad passengers. Northern soldiers will not compare with the tough and sinewy men I see here."

Towards the close of this letter was a paragraph that Seward would recognize as intended for him personally: "Judge Campbell has possessed the President [Davis] with all the details of his interviews with the State Department, most of which was submitted to Congress yesterday and will soon be published." This was an oblique reference to Campbell's angry version of his pre-Sumter talks with Seward, in which the secretary had given positive assurances, the judge said, that the fort would be evacuated peacefully. Sam was placing Seward on his guard against the storm that would follow Campbell's disclosures, that did, in fact, raise a hue and cry against Seward throughout the South, and that furnished ammunition for his opponents at home.

Russell desired to inspect Fort Pickens, over which such a pother had been made; that fort was still in Federal hands, and Union warships were blockading Pensacola. General Braxton Bragg had thrown up batteries menacing the fort, but no attack had been launched. Sam and Russell went to Mobile, to carry out the Pickens inspection, registered at the Battle House, and came under the scrutiny of a surly vigilance committee. But Sam's "well known Southern proclivities," backed by the good offices of secessionist friends in the city, saved them from active molestation. John Forsyth, one of the rebuffed Southern commissioners to Washington, for whom Sam had acted as a transmitter of messages to Seward, was publisher of the *Mobile Register;* he escorted them himself through Fort Gaines and Fort Morgan, which defended Mobile Bay. They witnessed great activity in progress, to strengthen these formidable works. Judge Campbell, who had resigned from the Supreme Court to follow his state into rebellion, entertained them with a denunciation of Seward, after which they chartered a schooner and set out to run the blockade of Pensacola and visit Fort Pickens.

An overnight sail brought them in sight of the Federal warships, and they were taken aboard the *Powhatan,* where Captain Porter (as he had been promoted) received them like old friends. Porter's ship was taut and ready to engage at a minute's notice. Porter signaled the flagship — none other than the frigate *Sabine,* in which Sam had sailed to Paraguay — and the visitors were transferred there. Captain Adams was still in command; he welcomed them heartily and gave them the best his ship contained. But he was no more the jolly sea dog of former days.

His distressful situation was common enough those days. He was a Pennsylvanian, had married a Louisiana woman, and had lived and reared a family in her state. Now one son had joined the Louisiana troops, and two others had enlisted under Lee in Virginia. And a letter Sam brought from Mobile added to the father's grief, for it was from his daughter, announcing her election as *viviandière* of a New Orleans regiment, with which she said she was about to march to Washington and "get a lock of old Abe's hair." The letter concluded with the fervent hope that her father might starve to death, if he persisted in his "wicked" blockade. Adams was resolved to do his duty. "But God knows," he exclaimed, "when I open my broadside, but that I may be killing my own children!"

Adams consented to their proceeding ashore, if they could make it; but he warned them to fly a flag of truce, because Bragg had threatened to shoot at any craft approaching from the fleet. Off Sam and Russell started in the schooner, hoisting a white tablecloth as a sign of peaceful intentions. They were permitted to land on a sandspit where a battery was being erected, to bear on Fort Pickens, a few hundred yards away across an inlet. General Bragg greeted them and rode with them over the entire Confederate works, explaining their strategic value and purpose. Then the two observers sailed across the inlet to the fort, where, after a challenge, they were received and taken through the installation, top to bottom. This inspection completed, they returned to Bragg's camp for the night, and the next morning received a copious briefing on the Confederates' plans from several officers who helped to put away a bountiful breakfast of fried ham, onions, biscuits, coffee, claret, and ice water, served from the schooner's well-stocked food locker, which Sam had personally seen filled. General Bragg gave Russell letters to the authorities in New Orleans, and the sail back to Mobile proved uneventful. From there the two men traveled aboard a steamboat to New Orleans.

In that city, or in visits to country estates nearby, they tarried until June 11, being everywhere entertained with the warmest hospitality. Sam was the guest of a railroad tycoon, a Major Ranney, where he enjoyed delicious dinners at the price of listening to muddleheaded reasoning on the question of the hour. The people of Louisiana were as bellicose as South Carolinians. The home of John Slidell, former senator, resounded with good French and bad fighting talk, while the ladies spent their time scraping lint. But creole cookery was a noncontroversial blessing that Sam Ward was proud to place before his London friend, and Russell voted the terrapin soup excellent (although he was advised by Sam that it could not touch the best turtle), the soft shell crabs beyond praise, and pompano the finest dish of all, while the wines, in his opinion, upheld the gustatory reputation of the town. Military activity was so intensive that Russell was unable to find a seamstress who would mend his shirts, — they were all busy stitching Confederate flags!

The passage up the Mississippi was made by stages, with frequent pauses at seigneurial plantations . . . the André Roman estate, whose cultured, wholly Gallic proprietor Sam and Russell had last seen in Gauthier's restaurant at Washington . . . the Manning and Burnside plantations, enormous tracts planted with cotton and sugar cane, worked by gangs of slaves . . . and so to Baton Rouge and Natchez. Everywhere they noted the Southerners' eagerness to fight, and their ignorance of the real power of the North. At Vicksburg the travelers took the train to Jackson, Mississippi, and found everything in turmoil there, but everybody confident. Thence they continued by train to Memphis, where they checked in at the Gayoso Hotel. Memphis was the headquarters of General Gideon J. Pillow, a lawyer, who had been wounded in the Mexican War, — a fact he never failed to mention before a stranger.

Sam had been forwarding reports to Baker-Seward assiduously, but he suspected that some of the letters were not getting through. At Memphis, therefore, he composed an omnibus letter, recapitulating his previous dispatches for the benefit of "My dear George." The information he gave in this digest was almost wholly military. "*Fort Pulaski* can only be taken by an approach by land by forces landed at Thunderbolt Bay, where a channel leads into the Savannah . . . *Beaufort, Port Royal,* and *Broad River* [on the South Carolina seaboard] have only slight defenses. Unless blockaded, arms and provisions might easily be smuggled in that region . . . *Fort Morgan,* Mobile, can be approached from the north by land and taken (when I saw it) by 2000 rifles . . . *Fort Pickens* was safe when I was there on the 17th ulto., and General Bragg claimed 8000 rank and file, having really, as I made it, less than 6000. His forces have since been reduced by two regiments, one of Mississippians, fine soldiers, and the other of Louisiana Zouaves, fire-eaters, who have been dispatched to Richmond . . . With 1000 more soldiers and the aid of the *Sabine, Brooklyn,* and *Powhatan,* Colonel Brown [commanding Fort Pickens] might take the [Pensacola] navy yard when he pleases . . . The spirit of our men upon the ships was highly gallant, ardent, and patriotic." Washington could depend on the Navy, what there was of it.

Sam went on in this fashion, methodically compiling military intelligence. "*New Orleans.* The Washington Artillery, 240 men, 8 howitzers, *and no horses,* left for Richmond while I was there. They are the only *soldiers* I have seen in the South . . . At *Camp Moore,* eighty miles above New Orleans, there are 3100 volunteers, most of them the scum of the levee, relieved here and there by a few country companies who keep aloof from the rabble . . . The New Orleans papers claimed 5000 troops there, and you can always estimate half, or three-fifths at most, of what the Southern journals claim to be true . . . Excepting a small company of cavalry near Donaldsville, I saw no military movement along the Mississippi from New Orleans to Memphis."

The personal nature of some of his sources of information was indicated by reference to "a regiment of Greeks, Sicilians, and other foreigners in process of formation at New Orleans, under the auspices of Emile Lesine and Mandeville Marigny." Mandeville de Marigny was the husband of the daughter of Suzette Grymes by her first husband, Governor Claiborne. Sam said that de Marigny "told me with delight that 'his men were sure to fight well, for two of them had already cut each other to pieces with knives this a.m.' "

"At Memphis," he continued, "I saw General Pillow, who ought to be called 'Bolster,' for he is as great a braggart as ever, and if you listen long enough will tell you that he led every charge and commanded every movement in Mexico." Pillow's forces were enumerated, including "a variety of artillery to prevent passage of gunboats and flotillas down the Mississippi. From the artilleristic capacity evinced by his command yesterday, when it took them five minutes to get a gun off, I would rather be without than within the fort."

Still no pay in the Confederate army, Baker-Seward was told, but "plenty of tall, sinewy fighting men . . . I think the camp at Union City [Tennessee] has as fine military material as there is to be found in the world. There was a company of 120 in the 13th Regiment each of whom had either killed his man or been shot in a personal encounter," and the officers complained that their recruits "were amenable to order in the inverse ratio to their fighting accomplishments."

Sam was earnest in pointing out the initial edge the Southerners would have in the clash of armies. Of the soldiers he had seen, he said, "a majority [are] far superior in familiarity with danger, self-reliance, disregard of peril, and indifference to the sight or production of bloodshed, to any Northern forces brought against them. In a hand-to-hand encounter, or in the open field, these men would better than double their number of inexperienced recruits . . . Rifled cannon with shrapnel are the only weapons to demoralize them . . .

"While these fellows are spoiling for a fight, and talk with a ferocity which, although heightened by whisky, I am sure they feel, no such reckless spirit of daring pervades the councils of Davis, Lee, and Beauregard. The military chiefs of the C.S.A. play at war as they would at cards, and do not intend to run the smallest unnecessary risk. Their cause cannot afford to suffer defeat. They have no army, but plenty of armed humans ready to fight. Your only safety is in masses and discipline and artillery . . . They lack arms and have more shells than powder to fill them. Fifty tons of brimstone were sold in New Orleans last week for $250 a ton. There is no more in private hands. They hope to get sulphur from Mexico via Texas. Coffee is likewise scarce." Sam quoted Russell's expert judgment of the possibilities at Memphis: "R. says that a French general with two gunboats and 5000 troops could take Memphis in a week!"

The signature on Sam's dispatches to the State Department had remained "Charles Lopez"; he may have hoped that "Lopez" would start a train of thought in Seward's mind which would lead to Sam's being given a diplomatic appointment, perhaps as the United States' first minister to Paraguay, under the treaty he had helped to negotiate. There is no doubt that Sam would have welcomed the assignment; and in view of his background, and his acceptability to President Lopez, there is no doubt that he was qualified. The appointment lay in Seward's province, but Sam would not importune, and the secretary gave the post to Charles A. Washburn, a Republican from Maine. Sam hid his disappointment, merely commenting in a subsequent letter to Washington that "I am sorry you have given away the Paraguay mission, which is useless to the incumbent." Sam had known Charles Washburn in California when the latter was editor of the *San Francisco Times,* and he had a poor opinion of the man's ability and discretion. Sam proved right in this instance: by clumsy intriguing, arrogance, and ineptitude, Washburn gave United States diplomacy a bad name throughout Latin America.

Sam's next letter was posted from Cairo, Illinois, in Union territory. Russell had become uneasy about being trapped behind the Confederate lines, unable to communicate with his paper, and the tour had been abbreviated. Whether to signal his emergence from rebel country — or whether for any reason at all except whim — at this point Sam altered his pseudonymous signature from "Charles Lopez" to the more correctly Spanish "Carlos Lopez." But he continued to address the reports intended for Seward's eye to George Ellis Baker. From Cairo he forwarded a warning of a Confederate scheme to lure the U.S. warship *Brooklyn* aground and attack her with light-draft gunboats and a masked battery; and again he attested to the ferocity of Southerners as fighters. "I cannot better explain my view of the difference between the aggressive tiger man of the South and your soldiers fighting for an abstract question than by reminding you that I have seen Billy Mulligan on two occasions clear out a bar room. These men, with their yells and Bowie knives and bloodthirsty manners, will take by surprise the bravest men who are unused to such riot . . . Your men here [at Cairo] are full of zeal, [but] should a meeting take place tomorrow, it would be the odds of horned cattle against beasts of prey. Nothing but the mob of Paris in the Reign of Terror can equal the savage ferocity and sanguinary bitterness of the Southern troops. Your men will get their blood up by and by and prove the more unrelenting of the two, but it will take lots of blood to bring them to such a diapason."

One chord Sam struck again and again was exactly what William Tecumseh Sherman would be pilloried as "insane" for saying a short while later: "For your purpose, you will need 500,000 men and a million in all before the end of the year. This, with half a million reserves, will give you a butcher's axe to draw upon when you fight an engagement. It must be a bloody riot that lands you in Richmond." Yet all over the North the cry was "On to Richmond!" and within a few weeks political pressure would force General Irwin McDowell and his raw troops into the bumbling mistake of Bull Run.

Lincoln's commissioning of political generals aroused Sam's alarm, and in some cases his disgust. As a New Yorker, he bridled especially at the bestowal of a brigadier general's commission on Daniel Sickles, the Tammany lawyer and good-looking philanderer who had achieved the ultimate in disreputability by shooting his wife's lover within sight of the White House. Exploded Sam: "Dan Sickles at the head of a brigade of 500 men! Good God! Fancy him caught in a tight place by Davis, Beauregard, Lee, or Whiting! Do you believe in miracles and that the Lord of Hosts will select Sickles's head and heart as His tabernacle for the nonce?" But he groaned that "it is useless to publish such truths, and I only impart them to you as a caution that you cannot exert too much power in behalf of discipline, nor be too cautious in selecting the most skillful *military* men to be on the staffs of your citizen generals, to whose appointment to posts of high responsibility I am bitterly opposed."

Sam and Russell next went to Chicago, where the former relayed to the State Department confirmation of the rebel plot to attack the U.S.S. *Brooklyn* — "which certain descendants of Lafitte have offered to capture for $200,000 — no cruiser — no pay." From Chicago the pair journeyed eastward, took in Niagara Falls, and reached New York on July 2, 1861.

The change in public sentiment there they could hardly credit. Whereas in March Russell had been treated to philosophical disquisitions on the right and even the inevitability of disunion, now the same persons were demanding that the rebellion be put down by any means. That this end would be achieved in the swift and easy manner envisaged by press, pulpit, and politicians, Russell did not for one minute believe. "Assuredly, they will not have it over the South without a tremendous and long sustained contest, in which they must put forth every exertion, and use all the resources and superior means they so abundantly possess," was his prediction to his newspaper. Sam Ward was on record with the same unpopular belief.

TEN

SAM AND SEWARD

THE file of Sam Ward's outpourings of information and advice to Secretary of State Seward is remarkable in one respect, namely, that not only are there no replies, but there is no direct reference anywhere to an acknowledgment from the secretary himself; allusions to responses do occur, but only to responses relayed through an intermediary, not to any letter from Seward himself. The relationship between the two men during 1860, 1861, and part of 1862 was one of admiration, confidence, and cordiality on Sam's part, and on Seward's, cordiality, at least. Whether Sam's letters were solicited is not known; certainly the tenor of his communications from Secessia can hardly have been welcome, for Washington had embraced the fallacy that one quick knockout blow would terminate the rebellion. Sam preached the contrary, and Cassandras are never popular, — above all, when they prove to be right.

There are several possible explanations why the surviving Ward-Seward correspondence is entirely one-sided. Seward's replies may have been destroyed (if there were any replies), for Sam did destroy, and instructed his heirs to destroy, documents the publication of which might embarrass others. Then again, assuming that Sam's letters were answered, the answers may not yet have come to light, for Sam's papers were widely scattered and left in great confusion. A third possibility is that Seward purposely and scrupulously refrained from making any direct acknowledgment of Sam Ward's communications, because he was chary of again committing himself in writing with this man; he had done that once, it may be inadvertently, and once bitten, twice shy. Whatever the explanation — and it is all guesswork now — letters continued to flow from Sam to Washington, and continued to be read and sometimes annotated by the Secretary of State.

Upon his return from the swing through the Confederacy, Sam visited Washington and was depressed. War had torn the face of the city, and where twelve months previously he had mingled with wits, sophisticates, and statesmen, now brilliance was gone and the town was uncouth with military encampments, the government in the hands of men unschooled in manners, often deficient in education, though forceful and committed to their cause.

Sam talked with Seward and returned immediately to New York, leaving a note urging that every courtesy be extended to Russell, "as good a Northern man as you are." Sam was past fighting age and had no qualifications as an officer; but he had other talents, and these he proceeded to put at the service of the Union. In New York he installed himself at a hotel (the New York Hotel) much frequented by Southerners and Southern sympathizers; and from there, on July 15, 1861, he wrote the first in a succession of letters that would pour into the State Department for months, crammed with rumors, doubts, opinions, and sometimes valuable intelligence picked up in that nest of copperheads.

That he had reached an understanding to do this seems unquestionable: he had just conferred with the secretary and would hardly have omitted imparting his plan and soliciting Seward's consent. Certainly he would not have proceeded with his program, in the cordial tone of his letters, had Seward objected. The channel of transmittal through George E. Baker was retained, Sam writing at the outset, "Any communications had best be addressed by G.E.B. to me in my own name at the New York Hotel. It is a good gleaning ground." He continued to sign his letters "Carlos Lopez." Rarely would he vouch for the accuracy of any report he forwarded, observing sensibly that "I have no time to sift the truth of such matters as command my attention, when it is so easy for you to verify them." Seward had many informants, and Sam simply added his "pacotille" for what it might be worth.

One member of Sam's circle about whose whereabouts Seward was curious for more than personal reasons was William Henry Hurlbert.

The brilliant but erratic editor had made himself more or less famous in New York by an editorial *gaffe* that had appeared in the *New York Times* on July 16, 1859, during the war between France and Austria. On the basis of a laconic cabled announcement of the Austrians' defeat in the battle of Magenta, Hurlbert had dashed off an analysis of the military situation under the heading, "The Defensive Square in Austrian Italy."

Newspaper associates had long marveled at Hurlbert's ability to compose simultaneously several articles, on unrelated topics, writing a sentence of each in succession and sending the sheets directly to the composing room, supplying several printers with copy. It was a time-saver when a deadline was near, and Hurlbert had never got his topics mixed. But in this instance his versatility betrayed him.

On the day of inditing "The Defensive Square," he attended a going-away party for a friend sailing to Europe. There was much champagne, and when the editor arrived at his office to do his last-minute stint, he was so confused he wrote several editorials, instead of one, and ran them together. *Times* readers were startled to come upon non sequiturs such as: "If we follow the windings of the Mincio [River], we shall find countless elbows formed in the elbows of the regular army"—an observation that was repeated later on, altered to, "we shall find innumerable elbows formed by the sympathy of youth." The caution was offered that "notwithstanding the toil spent by Austria on the spot, we should have learned that we are protected by a foreign fleet coming up on our question of citizenship," followed by the reassurance that "a canal cuts Mantua in two; but we may rely upon the most cordial cabinet minister of the new power in England."

Now, early in 1861, Hurlbert, with his flair for the inexplicable, suddenly had left New York. He was in Secessia, and Seward was somewhat concerned, because as a propagandist Hurlbert could be formidable.

On July 15 Sam informed the secretary, through the medium of Baker, that Hurlbert had told a friend he was going south "to obtain the privilege of representing, overtly or covertly, the Richmond clique in Mexico." Hurlbert felt sanguine of the cordial acceptance of his services, volunteered to undermine the efforts of Thomas Corwin, Washington's minister to Mexico, this friend said; but now,

Sam went on, "the British consul at Charleston writes me that H. has been paying a visit to Mrs. King — the only secessionist of the Petigru family at that place — and was on his way to New Orleans when he backtracked to Richmond."

Five days later Sam heard "from pretty good authority that Hurlbert has made his peace with Davis and taken a charming cottage near Richmond, where he is giving dinners which have been more than once partaken of by Davis, who is said to be 'quite fascinated with the fellow.' You know he took with him $7000 made on the fall of stocks after that of Sumter, and taken out of the pockets of Blatchford, Weed, and others. He is also sustained in Richmond by the Jewish bear clique of Wall Street. It is even intimated that his pen may be traced in the message Davis delivers today in Richmond."

Sam's "pretty good authority" in this instance went astray. Hurlbert was not ghost-writing the Confederate President's messages. He had been received with hostility in Charleston, where the sincerity of his change of colors was doubted. In Savannah, on June 24, he had narrowly escaped being lynched as a suspected Northern spy; only his arrest by the authorities saved him. Taken to Richmond, he was held prisoner there, and friends high in Confederate councils were afraid to intercede. One who did act was old Petigru, at Charleston; not, he told his daughter, from reluctance to see "the deserter deserted," but from love of justice and affection for Hurlbert's deceased father. But Petigru's petitions to Richmond went into a pigeonhole. In New York, S. L. M. Barlow went to work on the turncoat's behalf; he was in touch with Judah P. Benjamin, Davis's attorney general; and in these maneuvers Sam Ward assisted discreetly, but no *démarche* brought immediate success.

Whatever had been Hurlbert's intention when he went south, it was canceled by the reception he got, and a letter which the unhappy man smuggled to Barlow was vituperative against secessionists. "As you have never been in prison, you can't 'appreciate the feelings' of a gentleman who is," this letter started; "so I will not describe them to you . . . I have no words for the conduct of your 'friends' here." They were, in Hurlbert's opinion, all "blockheads" and "bullies." "Benjamin has behaved better than anybody, but he is not strong in the cabinet. As for [Constitution] Browne — but why should I find fault with a poor fellow so placed that if he loses his actual clerkship to Toombs [Secretary of State], he will never have so much as the hope of a carpet for his wife to scatter her h's upon? And a conjugal rain of aspirates upon a bare floor—what man can be expected to love such a prospect as that?" Hurlbert's pen could sting; he could brush and leave a scar; his feather-touch was often tipped with acid. "In truth this whole country is under a reign of terror," he went on. "I have it, thank Heaven! in black and white over Toombs's own signature, that I have been imprisoned here 'through fear of the rabble,' that 'the authorities have not and never had any charge against me,' and that to 'release me would be for the government to incur the charge of complicity with a spy!' Bah!"

"Where are you all now?" he sighed sybaritically. "In some lovely place by the shore? Well a day, all these things must be, and there's an end of it. Yet I assure Mrs. Barlow that I fully anticipate the pleasure of putting myself in front of the fire, *en cravate blanche*, at her first Sunday dinner next fall. I think I prefer the still champagne, but I insist on the Chancellor madeira . . . Don't be surprised at anything you may hear of your friend."

The substance of this direct salutation from the dubious but diverting journalist Sam relayed to Seward, with the further information that Hurlbert had been told that should he attempt to escape to the North he would be hanged, "because possessed of so many plans and secrets of the C.S.A. This precaution is needless," Sam scoffed, "as H. is too near-sighted to be able to see his way home."

In the same letter Sam said he had just spoken with a friend "arrived from Mobile by way of New Orleans . . . who expressed surprise that the North had not given out yet." This friend was willing to bet that the Union blockade of Southern ports would be lifted before the coming January 15, because "Charles Heidseck, the champagne broker, and other French agents were in the South selling their wares with the guarantee that they would be delivered by December 15th next, which French commerce has fixed upon for the opening of the blockade."

As the weeks went by, Sam was beset by an old personal problem: his money was running low. He was dabbling in stocks (with him this was always a sign of shrinking fortunes), dealing through a broker cousin, Charles Ward, who had an office at 54 Wall Street. (Charles Ward was one of three sons of Sam's Uncle William; the other two — William Greene Ward, who became a brigadier general, and John Ward, a colonel — were in the Union army.) Sam lived handsomely, and he needed to live on such a scale; for much of his value as a gatherer of intelligence depended upon his ability to mingle socially with men of wealth and large affairs, and in cultivating a wide acquaintance. Undoubtedly his eye was cast towards the diplomatic service: with his command of languages, his experience, and his firsthand knowledge of Europe and Latin America, he was eminently fitted for a diplomatic post, and the dignity and honor attaching to a diplomatist had appeal.

Hints regarding his availability for remunerative official employment popped up periodically in his letters to the State Department, and from hints he progressed to open bidding for a job. "Will not Dr. Mackie's temporary absence create a vacuum in your department which I might help to lessen?" he queried. "I only suggest this in case I might be of service." This represented a comedown from Sam's recent aspiration to the Paraguayan ministerial appointment, for Dr. James S. Mackie was one of three State Department clerks staffing the diplomatic division, drawing a salary of a mere eighteen hundred dollars a year. However, it would be a foot in the door, and Sam was in need of some stated income. To all such nudges, however, Seward remained obtuse; there was no response.

Whenever information turned up that Sam deemed too "tindery" to entrust to the mails, he would take it to Washington himself, and at such times he had access to Seward, who seemed cordially glad to see him. Seward loved good talk, and Sam Ward was one of the brightest conversationalists in America. Usually they met at the secretary's home, on a social footing. "I shall be in Washington tomorrow and unless unexpectedly detained I shall return in the P.M.," Sam would write, typically, in arranging these get-togethers. "Something is transpiring in New York which I should like to compare notes with you about. I will call at your residence and should feel obliged by your leaving word at what hour I can have the pleasure of seeing you."

Although this and other, similar letters ostensibly were sent to Baker, there is no doubt that Sam proposed to call, in a manner as unobtrusive as possible, on Seward, and that the private information he was conveying was for Seward's ear. There was no compelling reason why Samuel Ward, whose acquaintance in Washington was exceptionally wide, should not call at the State Department office of George Ellis Baker, a subordinate functionary, and excite no special comment; but a formal visit to the Secretary of State, at the latter's official address, might easily start the tongues of gossips wagging. A call at Seward's home, however, would seem a mere civility, for Seward entertained much.

On these trips to the capital, there is no evidence that Seward ever flatly turned down Sam's bid for some accredited employment; on the contrary, it is apparent that the secretary, who was noted for talking at large and at random, while promising nothing definitely, led Sam to believe that the door to preferment was always open. But quite apart from personal considerations, Seward was hedged by political obstacles. Sam Ward was a Democrat, and in New York he associated flagrantly with Southern sympathizers. He also was an intimate of such Northern Democrats as S. L. M. Barlow, August Belmont, and Manton M. Marble, the editor-publisher of the *New York World,* which often vituperated the Administration. Some Republicans would howl at Sam Ward's being taken into government service.

And even had these objections been surmountable — which was most unlikely — there remained subtle personal factors. In view of that unfortunate misstep of the altered telegram to Jefferson Davis, it may have been that Sam Ward had become an embarrassment to William Henry Seward, — one which the secretary would be glad to be rid of, if that could be accomplished without open affront. The secretary could not know whether Sam in fact had held back the original copy of the incriminating document (and Sam might have done so magnanimously, intending to *shield* both Gwin and Seward by covering their part in framing the telegram); but even the possibility was painful to think about, and to admit a suspicion would be insulting to Sam. The secretary, realizing that he could not afford to ask the question, may have resorted to the device of letting matters coast along, trusting to time to eliminate Sam Ward in some way or other, without the necessity of direct action. Whatever the secretary's motives, the net result was that Sam was kept in suspension, hopeful ever.

During the visits to Washington, Sam developed his friendship with the secretary's son and Assistant Secretary of State, Frederick W. Seward. Father and son worked closely together; they shared the same office, and passed papers back and forth without the need of intermediaries. This opened up to Sam a more immediate link with Seward than that provided by Baker, and gradually the communications from the New York Hotel became addressed to Frederick Seward; Sam could expect the letters to find their way into the secretary's hands almost upon receipt.

In view of his own financial stringency (he was becoming fretful over the rapid depletion of his stock of choice wines), Sam must have relayed with a touch of ruefulness the gossip concerning his Croesus father-in-law. Edward Schermerhorn, a New York millionaire, had told him that "Mr. William B. Astor's remittances to England amounted to $3 millions of money he was putting out of the way of war and taxes. I have no doubt that there is some foundation for the story," Frederick Seward was informed. "Vanderbilt has stowed away a million, and most people of means have laid by a golden nest egg of greater or less magnitude."

Added to Sam's other anxieties was constant fear of exposure. "Returning last P.M. from Long Island, I received your kind message," he wrote with relief to young Seward, "which sets matters right, as I was nervous lest my notes had fallen into wrong hands, which would have impaired the usefulness you are pleased to approve, by depriving me of a certain class of confidences from which it has derived . . . I do not mention names because much of my information is Masonic, and that involves the sacred condition of safety to the communicant." This was just after he had talked with "another Southron just arrived from Lee's command"; and the explanation instances an element of incurable naïveté in Sam, — for the Secretary of State had started his career in politics as a candidate of the short-lived anti-Masonic party, — professional Mason-haters.

"Sorry to have missed your father and sorry to say that your silence is discouraging," ran another message, "for with any decent stimulus I could be *useful*."

On every side he was witness to open or covert undermining of Union morale. In the wake of the first major battle of the war — Bull Run — the spirit of defeatism had proliferated through the shocked North, and one casualty of that confused encounter had been Russell. The *Times* man had written a brilliant, accurate account of the Federal rout as he personally saw it, and when copies of the newspaper reached the United States from London a few weeks later, Russell became an object of execration. He was excluded from society, threatened with assassination, and cold-shouldered by official Washington from Lincoln down. Some military men, among them William Tecumseh Sherman, corroborated the report in detail, but "Bull Run" Russell was hated by every "decent patriot" in the North. Sam protested, but the hysteria ran wild.

A few weeks after Bull Run, Sam tipped off Seward that Southern sympathizers were anticipating an attack on Washington; he outlined the strategy he said would be employed. He did not vouch for the truth of this alarm, but merely passed the rumor along for Seward to sift, explaining that his method in "gleaning" was "to evince no curiosity when told the most incredible things," and to ask few questions. This attitude of the noncommittal, sympathetic listener became so habitual with Sam, it characterized him the rest of his life.

The psychological warfare being waged against Northern morale worried him. "I was just putting my foot into a carriage for the depot when a secessionist passed by and accosted me with an intimation that in the next fight some of our troops would rather join the enemy than have another battle," he alerted Washington on August 24. "Are secessionist emissaries at work secretly to demoralize our lines?"

Then a "friend of Commodore Vanderbilt, who was bitterly pugnacious and uncompromising when I met him in New York on my return from the South, told me in the Street this 2 P.M. that he 'began to think those fellows could whip us.' I reasoned with him upon the time requisite to form soldiers. 'But,' he said, 'they all seem soldiers down south.' "

And on October 25 he wrote in deepest gloom to Frederick Seward: "As I was on the point of leaving town Saturday, I received a note from Barlow pressing me to dine with him yesterday. I left his house last evening in greater tribulation than I have felt since I saw the flag shot down at Sumter." Foreign diplomats in Washington, "without exception," were saying that the blockade would be broken by January; the British minister at Washington, Lord Lyons, had informed his government that Seward was "assuredly bent on provoking a war with England"; Lincoln was said to be only waiting for one military victory to offer the South a settlement, — there were five closely written pages of such disheartening table talk, some of which was lent weight by Sam's explanation that "the presence of Stoeckl in New York and his intimacy with Barlow would seem to warrant the surmise that the diplomatic *on dits* were derived from him." Edward de Stoeckl, the Russian minister, was supposed to be well informed and well disposed towards the North; otherwise, the Italian minister alone excepted, the entire diplomatic corps was partial to the Southern cause, holding the national rupture to be irremedial and the North vindictively persisting in a senseless fight.

Stoeckl was the hero of an anecdote Sam Ward liked to tell. A regiment of a thousand Frenchmen had been raised in New York, and the proud colonel invited Stoeckl to dine in camp. This would have been a breach of diplomatic propriety, and Stoeckl suavely declined with, "Ah, colonel, how could I, with my bald head, appear before your brave contingent, which numbers five hundred hairdressers?" "Then let me dine with you," proposed the colonel. "Impossible, my dear fellow! How could I presume to offer a dinner to you, who have five hundred cooks at your command?"

Sam had constructive suggestions to offer the Administration officials who were struggling with problems for which there was no precedent, nor, for all anybody then knew, any solution. When Secretary of the Treasury Chase cast about for some means to pay the astronomical costs of the war, Sam forwarded to Seward, for transmittal to Chase ("should you think it worth consideration"), a broad plan for issuing Treasury notes exchangeable for bonds bearing interest payable in gold. "My past career has made me unprofitably familiar with financial questions," he explained with a certain wry humor. Whether the program was ever sent to Chase is not known; Sam quite overlooked the fact that any proposal emanating from the Secretary of State's office would probably receive short shrift at the Treasury, in view of the strained relations between Chase and Seward. Nevertheless, the Legal Tender Act, voted about a month after Sam's communication, did embody some of the key features of Sam's plan.

In October, 1861, he came up with a brilliant idea, and wrote to Frederick Seward: "My old uncle, John Ward, says this struggle will never be settled until the South shall be convinced that the world can be supplied with cotton elsewhere. The belief that they have a monopoly of a product essential to the American and European governments underlies the whole conspiracy. Destroy that faith and they are powerless." Had the secretary, he then asked, observed that "400,000 bales of cotton were produced by free white labor in Texas last year?" Well, "the Pacific Mail steamer *Constitution* sails on the 15th of next month for San Francisco, via Rio de Janeiro, Straits of Magellan, Chile, Peru, and Panama. I have a great desire to make that voyage with a view to ascertain the cotton capacity of South America. I should get information in Brazil, and landing at Valparaiso travel along the base of the Andes into Bolivia through the native regions of the *cotton tree* and ascertain how far it can be transplanted with success.

"It strikes me that this object is one of great political importance, and that familiar as I am with the people and languages of South America I might accomplish it, and that you might dispatch me on this secret service, allowing me the customary *per diem* of such traveling agents. I should feel gratified to add this feather to your political cap and proud of the confidence it would betoken. I should bring back seeds and plants so that the Patent Office might teem with the means of trying the experiment upon a grand scale next spring. Will you lay this matter before the proper authorities?

My record of active and energetic service in Paraguay and my familiarity with travel and hardship are pretty well known. I need not say that I should feel truly grateful."

This suggestion was given official scrutiny, and Sam's hopes were high as he acknowledged a response from Frederick Seward: "Accept my grateful thanks for having entertained the proposition as to the *Argonautic* voyage (for cotton seems to be the *Golden Fleece* of the day), and should anything come of it I shall feel quite proud at being indebted to you for a piece of rare good fortune." Inasmuch as Confederate raiders were known to be lurking in the Pacific, he suggested that it might be wise to put aboard the *Constitution* "fifty well drilled marines and forty sailors and four cannon, which that number of 'salts,' under the charge of a passed midshipman or a second lieutenant of ordnance, would be able to handle. The crew would also be drilled man-of-war fashion, and my experience in gun-work aboard the *Sabine* might even render me of service."

Unfortunately the government was coping with far too many crises during those months of defeat for this scheme to get off the boards, and Sam was doubly disappointed; for not only would it have provided a means for his active participation in the war effort, it would also have solved his pressing personal problem, — want of an income, as his funds sank lower every day.

He did not allow disappointment to blunt his assiduity in forwarding to Washington news and views upon public developments, and his extensive acquaintance with many of the men coming to the fore in the wartime upheaval gave his opinions some value. Frequently his comments on the political shuffling were pungent. The replacement of Simon Cameron as Secretary of War by Edwin McMasters Stanton particularly struck Sam. Stanton, a prickly character, had been a staunch Buchanan Democrat and attorney general during the closing weeks of that Administration. Previously he had incurred widespread unpopularity by his high-handed method of disposing of land-title frauds in California; undoubtedly innocent claimants had suffered with the guilty. Some of the victims of Stanton's ruthlessness were Sam Ward's friends, and in 1860 Ward had been credited with authorship of an anonymous pamphlet (*The Exploits of the Attorney General in California — by an Early Californian*) which had charged Stanton with rapaciousness, jealousy, and revenge, pointing out, among other odd circumstances, that Congress had appropriated fifty thousand dollars for the undertaking, of which Stanton had pocketed one-half. In one case — the New Almaden quicksilver mine controversy — the pamphlet charged that Stanton had previously appeared as attorney for the parties who were trying to seize the property.

"Mr. S. is said by his friends to possess pluck and energy and to lack cupidity," Sam advised Seward upon the cabinet appointment. "To me he is personally distasteful from the bitterness and injustice with which he persecuted some of my California friends." Recalling a dinner conversation of years before, when Senator Gwin had said that "Stanton was a dangerous foe, — a sleuthhound sort of man who never lost his scent or slackened in his purpose," Sam cautioned the Secretary of State to keep on good terms with his new colleague. And when William Howard Russell, bitterly disappointed by Stanton's denying him permission to accompany McClellan's advance into Virginia, sailed back to England in disgust, Sam told Seward that "the prophetic words of Dr. Gwin, 'He will tomahawk them all,' came back to my mind. However, what with his [Stanton's] vanity and his obstinacy, I am in hopes that with all the rope he now has he will soon hang himself. If so I will give $1000 to witness his suicide."

The world was topsy-turvy, and full as his hands were with his own affairs, Sam still found time to help some of the sufferers from the topsy-turveydom. Sometimes this necessitated a direct approach to the Secretary of State with a formal petition, and such letters, carrying no allusion whatever to Sam's undercover activities, were signed plainly, "Samuel Ward."

In one of these he asked Seward for a pass to permit Miss Fanny Butler, daughter of Fanny Kemble, the actress, to visit her father, Pierce Butler, imprisoned in Fort Lafayette, — the fortress in New York Bay that was used for political prisoners. "I should be happy and proud to serve the young lady, who is young, pretty, and intelligent," Sam wrote. The pass was forthcoming and Butler soon was released.

On another occasion a Southern-born midshipman in the Navy was thrown into Fort Lafayette when he resigned his commission with the announced intention of joining the secessionists of his state. Sam interceded, writing to Seward that the lad had merely followed the example set by older officers who had been permitted to quit without recrimination; he recollected one instance himself, when a North Carolina lieutenant resigned from the *Sabine* the day before Sam had visited the frigate off Pensacola.

In October, 1861, Sam again wrote to Secretary Seward directly: "I am not partial to Mrs. Gwin, but to her husband I owe a debt of gratitude for past affection and kindness, — the only class of debts save death I am able to pay. She meant to pass the winter in New York, but finds herself lonely and uncomfortable, and would return to her Mississippi plantation if she felt confident of reaching it. She has inquired whether, in case of need, I would be willing to accompany her, and I, of course, had but one answer, 'Certainly.' I mention the subject thus early so that His Excellency may have his reply ready should I apply for a pass. In the act itself I should doubtless acquire much *useful* and *valuable* information, as it would lead me through Kentucky. I should of course return in time for the 'voyage after the Golden Fleece.'"

In a separate letter to Frederick Seward, Sam suggested that Mrs. Gwin's despair over the success of the Confederate cause would make her an excellent propagandist for the North. "Mrs. Gwin proposes going to Washington towards the end of the week to dispose of her furniture," he added. "She has already sold her wines. Does Mrs. Seward want her piano at $300? It cost $1000."

Doctor Gwin had last been heard of in San Francisco, and Sam had no idea where the ex-senator might be now. In mid-November he found out in a startling way. A long, tense letter went to Frederick Seward on November 15: "On my way to breakfast two hours ago I was surprised by a summons to Mrs. Gwin's parlor to see my old friend the Doctor [Gwin], who briefly stated that he was under arrest, and requested me to meet Messrs. Brent and Benham [arrested with Gwin] at 11 o'clock and hear and see all the details of the case."

While aboard ship traveling from San Francisco to Panama, Gwin and his companions had been arrested by a military officer, General Edwin V. Sumner, on suspicion of harboring designs inimical to the United States. Sam gave Seward a full account of the arrest, which had been made in a highly irregular manner, General Sumner's order stating as grounds that the three suspects were "prominent members of the Democratic party in California."

"Dr. Gwin's first impulse was to write to the secretary, upon whose friendship he could rely for fair play," Sam went on. But this course had been rejected as premature, and "Dr. Gwin expressed earnest hope that his old friend the secretary would do nothing in haste." This communication was signed openly, "Samuel Ward."

Gwin's arrest carried more than ordinary significance, for on November 8 a United States warship had halted the British mail steamship *Trent* north of Cuba and had taken off former United States Senators Slidell and Mason, who were on their way to represent the Confederate government in France and England. An international storm burst over this high-handed action, with England demanding the return of the two men and apologies by Washington, and jingoists on both sides talking hotly of war. Mason and Slidell were incarcerated in a fortress at Boston when Gwin, a close associate of the Confederate envoys, appeared under arrest at New York. Sam's intervention, therefore, touched upon an international crisis that had public and official opinion inflamed. The next day he wrote Frederick Seward in great distress that the United States marshal had "spirited away Dr. G. and his friends, and left me the melancholy consolation of having done all in my power for my old friend. I shall charge your department for an unexpected drain upon my slender stock of wines and cigars."

The sudden emergence of Gwin and Ward in a situation fraught with overtones may have caused Secretary of State Seward some anxious moments. At all events, after a brief detention Gwin and his companions were taken to Washington, accorded a hearing, and released. The ex-senator immediately went south to Mississippi, and Sam Ward wrote to Frederick Seward: "I am overjoyed at Dr. Gwin's release, and only sorry that I had no 'finger in the pie' that might have testified my desire to serve him. . . . Present my compliments to the secretary, and beg him not to forget that I am at all times anxious to serve him." From this time forth, all Sam's letters to the State Department would be signed "Samuel Ward."

At about the same time, the *Trent* crisis was settled by the United States yielding to British demands: Mason and Slidell were released and sent on their way to Europe, and war with England was narrowly averted. Sam Ward was forced to weather a minor scandal when he was accused of profiting in Wall Street by advance information about the settlement, information relayed by "Bull Run" Russell. Sam's bank balance, a thing of shreds and patches, was evidence to him that he had benefited by no such clandestine maneuver, but the story was widely circulated, and it rendered him increasingly dissatisfied with his anomalous position. "Since my fiasco in the attempt to serve my old friend Gwin I have rarely left my study, and occupied myself with the more congenial pursuit of letters," he wrote circumspectly to the younger Seward. "Present my compliments to the secretary and beg him not to forget that I am at all times anxious to serve him." At Christmas time he sent Frederick Seward "a saddle of venison for Mrs. Seward. Had there been war, I should have sent a quarter of bear — in the absence of tiger meat, which the Chinese eat to sustain their courage. P.S. I send you a *jeu d'esprit* which may amuse you. I have a volume of songs in press. Idleness has driven me to this folly."

In the midst of the Gwin-*Trent* furors, Hurlbert, the unpredictable, turned up in Washington looking surprisingly sleek and healthy. Barlow received an exuberant letter from him: "'Who would be free themselves must strike the blow.' So, having weighed all things I left my trunks in Richmond on Friday last, hired a buggy, and have turned the Confederate pickets — crossed the Potomac — walked from lower Maryland to this city — and I hope ere long to have the pleasure of seeing your excellency. I can a tale unfold, as you may guess, and shall. How anxious I am to see the delightful groves of Gotham once more [and] you in a white choker dispensing still champagne!" As for "our friends down South — a more abject set of poltroons and pirates never existed."

The story Hurlbert told in Washington was that he had at last wangled a parole, rented a buggy, and taken French leave, — although his passage through both armies undetected, and his blooming health, caused cynics to hint that he might have been "leaked out" of the Confederacy, as it were; that is, "escaped" by connivance of the rebels, possibly to double as a spy for the South. G. T. Strong contemptuously wondered whether the "ambrosial Hurlbut" — he whom James Gordon Bennett in the *New York Herald* called "The Reverend Mephistopheles" — had indeed "ratted again."

Before long Sam Ward would be writing to Barlow in terms that indicated that they had played a decisive part in delivering their peculiar but inseparable friend: "What does he not owe to you and me for steering his helmless bark through that black and stormy night and the strange currents and eddies of the succeeding days! Will he be grateful? No! Never! And yet you and I would do the same thing over again, though foreseeing the inevitable result in such a compound as he is."

But whatever he might have been able to do for Hurlbert, Sam still could not do what he wished for himself. Reminders to Seward of his availability for profitable employment grew more pressing. "If you set one-tenth the store by my tact and persuasive skill that they who know me do," he wrote Frederick Seward as 1862 rolled in, "you would turn me to good account in London or Paris, where as a savant and man of letters I may say without vanity that I hold a desirable position." In February he tried once more: "I am thinking of taking a run over to Europe. In Paris I might be useful. Why not suggest this to the official mind?" But a fortnight later he canceled the suggestion, writing: "To my inexpressible joy and delight, the lady whom I felt bound to escort to France released me from my engagement yesterday A.M. I anticipated the voyage with great discomfort at this critical moment." The lady in question was Mrs. Gwin, who with her daughter left at that time for permanent residence in Paris. And the moment was indeed critical, for General Grant had captured Fort Henry on the Tennessee River and was investing Fort Donelson. The omens for Union success were not favorable, and Sam had written his letter during the morning of February 16, just a few hours before General Simon B. Buckner surrendered Donelson to Grant with fifteen thousand Confederate troops. It was the first solid Union victory after a long succession of defeats and paper victories. Sam's spirits, with those of the entire North, revived.

In default of public employment, Sam sought to fatten his checkbook by private means, and from Washington scribbled to Barlow a note marked "*Private*": "See Commodore Vanderbilt or send Dick Schele to see what price he will pay cash for the defeat or withdrawal or death by inaction of Senator Sumner's bill to repeal all laws trammeling the carriage of mails and freight to San Francisco via Panama by foreign steamers. With you I will divide the spoil, to Schele I will give one-quarter of the plunder. I can do it." Vanderbilt of course was vitally concerned with maintaining his grip on the shipping trade to Panama. But mindful of the Commodore's slipperiness, Sam added this caution to Barlow: "Make his contract binding. Better you than Schele as he would be less apt to *throw* you, and Schele might deceive us. Lose no time. Say 1 to 5000 $ or more — no cure no pay."

But this hope also proved delusive, and a few days later he told Barlow: "Vanderbilt had an interview with Stanton — I dare say about ironclad boats — he kept very dark here — I did not see him. No matter about Vanderbilt." The behind-the-scenes views of the progress of the war he relayed to his New York associate. While dining with the Spanish minister, Topara, and the French minister, Henri Mercier, he had heard nothing but confident predictions of catastrophe for the Northern cause. In strict confidence ("Can you keep a secret?") he divulged to Barlow that Mercier had returned from a visit to Richmond "warmed into admiration by the indomitability of the rebels and entirely of the opinion" that they would never be subdued. "Wigfall told him peace would not be made south of Philadelphia." This letter closed with an observation that for either of these Epicurean Sams must have seemed a perfect Q.E.D.: "Mercier did not taste tea, coffee, wine, or brandy while in Dixie. All Richmond could not furnish him a cup of coffee or a bottle of claret. The courage, confidence, and serenity evinced by *bons vivants* under such *trying* circumstances had a great moral effect upon him."

Considering all the indications, Sam told Frederick Seward that he had "a dumb apprehension — atmospheric perhaps — that we are on the eve of some disaster. I hope my superstition is foolish." But he passed along information that proved of value, too. As early as November 6, 1861, he had alerted Seward regarding the design of the French Emperor Napoleon III to install a puppet emperor in Mexico. "Since my residence in the city of Mexico, I have kept up my relations and correspondence with some of the enlightened and influential friends whom it was my good fortune to make in that capital," this letter had read. "Although it has hitherto been only my province to advise you of such matters as pertained to the Rebellion, I think it my duty to say that I have received information that it has been settled at Paris and Madrid, and not discountenanced in London, that the 'Mexicans shall have a throne—republics having proved all folly and failure.'

"I will vouch with my life for the accuracy of my informant. I have mentioned and shall mention this to no one, and should have withheld it even from you had it not seemed a crime of less-allegiance to suppress a fact of such interest to the secretary to whose fortunes I have expressed a willingness to attach my own."

Four months later he reminded Frederick Seward, not without satisfaction, that "the papers of this A.M. confirm what I wrote you long ago about the Franco-Spanish project of forcing a crowned head upon Mexico." A joint French-Spanish-British expedition had seized the customs house at Vera Cruz to compel payment of Mexico's foreign debts, and Sam had a proposal to make. "A large party of my Mexican friends . . . sail for Cuba in the *Columbia* en route for Vera Cruz, where they have intimate and friendly relations with the chiefs of all the Allied expeditions. My opportunities for observation would be unequalled, and as I perceive by the papers that the Honbl. Secretary is now busied with the contemplation of Mexican affairs, I write to suggest that it may be agreeable and useful for his department that I accompany this party."

Attempting to promote this mission to Mexico, Sam passed several weeks in Washington. The consternation caused by the Confederate ironclad *Merrimac* and its forays upon the Federal warships at Hampton Roads was the big news, and he told Seward that the betting in New York was four to one that the *Merrimac* would yet sink the *Monitor*. The panic of Stanton and other dignitaries in the capital during the first alarm over the *Merrimac* Sam described richly to Barlow, adding that "Mr. Seward alone is serene in his optimism. He considers the price of Confederate bonds the criterion of our success and their defeat. He says that at 55 the C.S.A. can go on . . . but that when their scrip falls to 25 their cause will have become hopeless."

Barlow utilized Sam's presence in the capital to forward political advice on how the Republicans could hold the support of the Northern "War Democrats," who were in favor of prosecuting the war, but not in favor of abolition or reprisals against the South. To one such communication Sam responded: "I was so pleased with your letter that I took it at once to the State Department and showed it to Mr. Seward. Though busy with his foreign dispatches, he took it with avidity and read it through with earnest and deliberate attention. He thanked me for the perusal and observed that 'it was an extremely beautiful and classical letter and that the Paganini simile of the *one string* was novel and striking.'" In the ensuing discussion, Sam said, Seward had repeated his often expressed belief that had the South been permitted to withdraw peacefully, it would have drifted back into the Union within two years and "saved us all this trouble, blood, and expense. I differed from him, and said that I had found at Montgomery, among the leaders, a malignant bitterness and contemptuous hatred of the North which rendered this lesson necessary. Within two years they would have formed entangling free trade and free navigation treaties with Europe, and have become a military power hostile to us." Sam's insight had been clearer than that of the Secretary of State.

"After the war" was a problem already bothering official Washington — assuming that the North emerged the victor — and Sam told Barlow that Seward considered "the future of our conquest as difficult to predict as it would have been a year ago to prophesy when it would begin — that the question was not what we should do with the subdued South, but what they would do with themselves when subdued."

This uncertainty worried Senator Sumner, too, and in a long conversation with this old but much altered friend, and with Samuel Gridley Howe, who was in Washington on business of the Sanitary

Commission, Sam had the issue out frankly. "Your letter," he reported to Barlow, "made the two abolitionists wince. He [Sumner] spoke with great despondency of the low ebb of Union feeling in the border States. Howe spoke bitterly of the aversion of women and children to our troops and officers. 'Why then,' asked I, 'did you provoke the issue? Six months ago you were all for war. You have raised the demons Mars and Bellona, and now find that you should have invoked Mercury and Minerva.'

"Sumner confessed the same doubt as to the future he had before expressed. 'Granted,' said he, 'that we shall conquer them by arms, — what is then to be done? We shall only have a bitter, sullen, rebellious, and probably conspiring faction, — breeding discontent and breathing a hatred the malignity of which will have been intensified by defeat.' "

Sam had responded that there must be a "magnanimous and merciful" way; that the rebels should be treated as "wayward children, until by moral suasion or Divine guidance we can give their 'new hearts' the religion of the Union." But Sumner was bitter against "traitors" who had "violated their oaths"; these, he contended, must be forever excluded from the government. "The Republican party will be very cruel upon the South — cowards are always vindictive," Sam predicted.

The squabbling over command and the conduct of the war Sam found almost as repellent as the political fumbling. The partisan meddling by Congress with military operations aroused his wrath. "Oh! for a Napoleon and a Brumaire to scatter the pack of Congressional asses to their districts!" he cried out, favoring Seward with his estimate of the two generals whose lobbies were at loggerheads, — McClellan and Frémont. The latter Sam had known since California days, and his opinion was stated bluntly: "There is nothing of Frémont save a capacity to endure privation and fatigue . . . He is so great a humbug that anything like ordinary contact with the people would betray his vapidness and wear out the prestige which he only sustains by the mystery of silence and invisibility . . . People in the East think the struggle for the next Presidency will be between Frémont and McClellan. Mark my words — by that time they will both be shelved."

McClellan's elevation to command of the Union forces Sam had welcomed at the time. Bursting in upon Russell shortly after Bull Run, he had shouted, "McClellan's the man!" but that was infection from the popular enthusiasm which was magnifying two minor victories in western Virginia into major triumphs. Months of observation had moderated Sam's approbation of "Little Mac." "McClellan is not a giant, although plenty big enough to do anything if he can get his army in hand," he was telling Seward late in 1861. "But Frémont is a pigmy, and if you will only give him plenty of rope, he will execute lynch law upon himself." Early in 1862, before the start of the disastrous Peninsula campaign, Sam was willing to agree that "McClellan knows his business, but I wish he had more dash."

With not a few of the military figures who were forging into the spotlight Sam had personal acquaintance, and his opinion of these he expressed candidly. It was not always flattering. When General Henry W. Halleck was summoned from the West to command all the Union armies, Sam predicted to Seward that "Halleck will disappoint you far worse than McClellan. As a soldier he is inferior to Buell, as a captain to Rosencrantz [sic] and others. I will offer a reward of $100 to anyone that shall prove that man, woman, child, or dog ever loved him. He is cold, heartless, cruel, and avaricious . . . Pope is another mistake. He is of small caliber and given to vainglorious mendaciousness."

But of all the military leaders, Ben Butler was becoming Sam Ward's "loathing stock." Butler's abuses as military commander in New Orleans, and the quite shameless rapacity of his brother, A.J. Butler, aroused Sam's deepest disgust. "A.J. Butler, buying blackmail in New Orleans under cover of brother Ben's guns!" he fumed. "He says he is not working from mercenary motives, 'but he needs all the money he can get to help make brother Ben President!' . . . That horse-whipped gambler has control of the commerce of the town, and I saw a French gentleman from there this A.M., who told me, in the presence of the [French] consul, Montholon, such a series of stories of their joint rapacity and venality as spoiled my appetite for breakfast." Thus to Frederick Seward, croaking, "I shall have to sign myself your *Raven.*"

This outburst the Secretary of State — who by now was quite aloof from poor Sam, although he gave no sign of telling him so — endorsed in pencil in the upper left-hand corner of the first page: "This letter would be alarming if Mr. W—— had ever been able to write a cheerful one even under the brightest skies."

The meaning of Seward's impenetrable indifference Sam could not longer ignore. Still friendly, frank, and seemingly sympathetic in personal conversation, the secretary remained blandly oblivious of Sam's necessities. These had become desperate. Barlow was treated to a wild appeal for help in a letter marked "On the □" and signed "fraternally:" "I have lost nearly all my *ready* in that d——d specie speculation. See if Travers [a Wall Street broker] will admit me to a short interest in Government or C.S.A. securities upon the strength of this letter and some details of a melancholy foreshadowing which I will send on Sunday if he agrees to such a proposition. I have means of information unsurpassed by anyone save Blatchford . . . My first venture not less than $10,000."

Plainly put, the proposition was to swap tips on secret developments in Washington and Richmond, either or both, for a margin account, opened on credit. His sources of prospective information were impressive — Seward in Washington and Mercier and perhaps Benjamin for Richmond — and he was willing to play bull or bear, deal in the securities of either government. It was the sort of speculation that was being carried on by more than a few Americans, operating through foreign agents; Confederate bonds were available and were being traded in Europe. "I lost in November and December some $2500 and never made a winning, which may dispose Travers to help me get even, when he can do it at a profit to himself," Sam concluded this appeal.

By return mail Barlow counselled caution. He may have offered to tide Sam over. In any event, Sam repented and canceled the rash overture. "No matter about the speculation," he replied. "It is undignified to make propositions which may be declined; and is, besides, a *confessio paupertatis* which it is best to avoid. To you, my steadfast friend, I shall take pleasure in unfolding news and views out of which poverty, and not avarice, was prompting me to try to make some money. Let the golden dream pass."

Two days before that frantic appeal to Barlow, Sam had sent a letter to Frederick Seward that revealed his need almost as explicitly. "I saw a letter from Dr. Gwin this A.M.," this communication began. "It was without date or place, but I imagine it to have been penned in Richmond last week." Had it been carried through the lines by Mercier? The timing would seem to point to that possibility. "It was devoted to the expression of his gratification at being once more free and among friends and of his regard for the friends he had left at the North. The concluding phrase was, 'Farewell. We shall meet again. This war cannot last forever, for this people cannot be conquered, nor will they ever consent to a union with their former associates.' I mention this for you and the secretary alone. Pray don't have it mentioned in the cabinet, for *Carnot* [Stanton] is quite capable of abusing my confidence, — if he be not already abusing that of the country and the Administration."

Then Sam proceeded to make the most energetic bid he had yet ventured for some gainful employment. "Six weeks ago I put in a suggestion that I might be of service in Mexico, and I recently saw that you had sent Mr. Plumb on an errand I should have been glad to have performed." E. L. Plumb had been named secretary of legation at Mexico City. "I am aware that a republic is the last place in which 'a diffident dog can hope to grow fat.' And yet I am loath to think that my experience and tact, coupled with some acknowledged ability, will continue to suffer neglect because I have neither bored nor importuned my friend. Is there no merit in the patriotism and self-respect which have refrained from having a finger in contracts? I am a man of letters, and my zeal would make me grateful for employment. Excepting Russian, Turkish, Chinese, and Manchu, I speak and write all the languages of the governments at which you have missions. How many of your envoys know any other tongue than our own? Try and keep this in view when anything offers in my line."

How much Seward tried can be judged only by the results — a complete blank. "Diffident dogs" were at a discount while profiteers grew fat on war contracts, and Sam had too much heart for the sufferings of the troops to stoop to that game. Perhaps Sam's appeals troubled Seward's equanimity. Perhaps not.

In July, Sam wrote to Seward: "I am going to Newport. Though not likely to be wanted, I continue to advise you of my desire to be useful." Barlow he told wistfully, "I might have joined you at Saratoga but for the *res angusta domi* [money stringency]." His nerves were jangled, and Seward's immovability was humiliating in view of some of the men who apparently were riding the crest of favoritism in official circles. There was Henry Wikoff — the same Henry Wikoff to whom Sam had offered his services in Dresden thirty years before, and who since had become internationally notorious because of various scandals, including the abduction of an heiress and a subsequent term in prison. Now Henry Wikoff, self-appointed social adviser to Mrs. Lincoln, was intimating that he would soon be sent abroad on a mission for the White House! This filled Sam's cup of bitterness to overflowing. "Wikoff to be sent abroad on a secret mission!" he retched verbally. "I hope not! He is perhaps as insinuating as a snake, but also quite as slimy. I never trust a pimp or a pander."

To the cool cordiality of Seward he opposed a sense of "mortification, tempered by humility, that the writer, who volunteered nothing that he would not have tripled in his performance, was not deemed worthy to serve his country in his capacity of linguist, diplomatist, poet, and philosopher." Then, with the urbanity of a diplomat, if not with the trappings, he closed his account as a State Department informant (unsalaried) in a dignified farewell to Seward's son. "In any new combination for the future, I trust to enjoy more of the private than I have of the public confidence of the secretary, who, if my correspondence has been of service, will owe me a certificate that it has been disinterested; although I have felt at times no little mortification at his having ignored — not my claims — but my zeal and ability. Pray do not leave my letters at the State Department."

This request, like the others, dropped unacknowledged into the bulging file. Everything was preserved.

ELEVEN

EXIT MEDORA

SO ONCE again Sam Ward was rejected, dejected, and next door to broke. But in compensation, time and suffering had brought him closer to Longfellow, the comrade of his youth.

In July of 1861, Fanny Longfellow had died a shocking death, burned fatally when her dress caught fire from a candle. The poet himself had been severely burned in attempting to beat out the flames. His recovery was slow, and the tragedy altered his appearance permanently: because of facial scars that made shaving painful, he grew the patriarchal beard with which he would be identified thereafter.

Sam had suffered with Longo throughout the terrible ordeal. "Since the genial evening I spent with you an awful shadow has fallen over you and yours," he wrote. "I, who used to associate your name with perfect bliss, never think of it now without speechless sorrow. I have had my fair share of sorrow, but nothing compared to yours. God bless and strengthen my dear old Viking."

To help keep Longfellow from brooding he sent letter after letter, chatting about himself, about the war, about his own poetical stumblings; and Longfellow drew comfort from Sam's vitality and worldly good sense. When the poet's son wanted to enlist in the army, the father turned to Sam for counsel, and the latter advised that the boy be allowed to fight, if he wished; "campaigning will make the lad more reasonable." He promised to watch over the recruit, and did.

The subject of the war inevitably filled pages of the friends' letter-talk. "We are impoverishing ourselves to enrich contractors and speculators, and were I a capitalist I should feel very uncomfortable," Sam commented. "But enjoying neither rents nor the privilege of taxes, I sit in the stage box like old Goethe [watching Napoleon], with this difference, — that excepting Presbyterian, psalm-singing Stonewall Jackson, all this chaos has not turned out a soldier or a statesman worthy of the tumult. . . . Tom Appleton [Longfellow's witty brother-in-law] is here, rosy and happy," he went on. "I am neither, having had the misfortune to fall in love the other day. I now discover that I am not as old as I ought to be. Of course, there are no bars to my carrying the caprice to the altar, — save poverty, my fifty years, my hair (or no hair) and teeth; and, easiest to overlook, the participation in my fancy by its object. But I am weary and lonely. Ever and ever thine, Sam."

The times were grief-saturated. From Fitz-Greene Halleck, living in retirement, watching his world go up in smoke, Sam heard the lament: "Almost every letter I receive comes to me with crape upon its left arm. Tell me the whereabouts of your accomplished acquaintance, W. Hurlbert," the poet begged. "Since I read, in some anti-Southern paper, that, like a certain gentleman of old, he had 'gone down from Jerusalem and fell among thieves,' I have heard nothing of him."

Hurlbert, Sam could reply, had gone to Memphis, Tennessee, after the battle of Shiloh, on a cotton-buying excursion financed by Barlow, in the wake of the Union army's advance into Mississippi. And he had succeeded — slipped in and out of repossessed rebel territory and collared bales that sold to Northern mills at tremendous profit. Hurlbert had joined the staff of the *New York World,* and had taken time out for this quest of the Southern Fleece because (as he put it boldly to Barlow): "Money I must and will make, and if not here I will go to Mexico or Mozambique in search of it. I never cared for it before in all my life. Now — but I love you too well to make myself a bore deliberately."

But Sam's luck was out. All during 1863 he avoided his customary haunts, — his habit when he was unable to pay his way socially. He found some little comfort in occasionally seeing his daughter Maddie, who was married now to John Winthrop Chanler, a handsome young lawyer, of a socially well connected New York and Charleston family. Released from the domination of her grandmother, Mrs. Astor, Maddie had made an effort to comprehend her father, with only partial success. Molded by conventions which

Sam transgressed, apparently with the utmost aplomb, she was baffled and repelled by his bohemianism. His manner on all occasions was perfect, but his associates, or some of them, at least, were rather to be deplored. Chanler was if anything more conventional than his wife, and there never could be any real sympathy on his part with his shady father-in-law. When Tammany elected Chanler to Congress, he and Maddie moved their home to Washington; but even so, Sam saw them hardly at all.

But his relationship with Julia was back on its firm basis of mutual understanding and unbounded affection. Julia Ward Howe was more than the "Old Bird" now: she had become famous with her "Battle Hymn of the Republic," which was sung everywhere, and Sam was proud of her celebrity. Julia had schooled herself to judge her extraordinary brother not by his actions, nor by his utterances, but by the inner light of the essential character that shone through his divagations. By that light she judged him true and sweet, and infinitely kind. On vacation visits to Newport, Sam found escape from the miseries of the times with Julia and her children, and with the other relatives gathered there. "Nineteen members of my family" on hand, he gaily told Longo — Greenes and Rays and Ward McAllister (Julian McAllister was in the Confederate army now), and the family of Samuel Ward Francis, one of whose daughters was named Medora. Old Doctor Francis had died on the eve of Sumter, almost his last words being the despairing question, "Have I still a country?" Chiefest of the numerous clan, for Sam, however, were the Howes at Lawton's Valley.

Julia's brood was growing up, and the older children now could appreciate their Uncle Sam, who came and went so suddenly and unaccountably and brought so much brightness. They never knew when he would appear. On a summer morning they might be wakened by a voice singing under the window:

> Noble châtelaine, voyez notre peine,
> Et dans votre domaine
> Rends charité.
> Voyez le disgrace qui nous menace
> Et donnez par grâce
> L' hospitalité.

On the doorstep would be Uncle, a basket of peaches beside him, while his voice trilled like the lark's. "Uncle Sam!" Squeals of joy and a patter of feet to the door as they ran to let him in. At breakfast he would talk tirelessly, and pull presents out of pockets for everybody. The squirming children would gaze in awe at the powerful, thick-set physique, long arms, hands that gesticulated with Latin grace, and sparkling hazel eyes and kindling smile. He was a sight to spread cheer, their Uncle Sam! And his attire! Striped cravat, elegantly tailored tweed, rings on his fingers, a great sapphire flashing on one hand, a diamond stud, and a rose in his buttonhole! When Julia would command, "They want you to sing, Sam," he would be pulled to the piano, and striking the keys with his jewelled hands would troll out song after song, especially one in Russian that the children loved best. To them it sounded like:

Roda bim bamboola,
Roda bim bagataga,
Roda bim bamboola,
Batherusea schengo!

And it closed with a triple giant sneeze, "Schengo! Schengo! Schengo!", and a wink. Half a century later, Maud, the youngest of those children, would recall that wink: "Just as Sam could wear gorgeous clothes, neckties, and jewels without being flashy, he could *wink* and remain a courtly aristocrat. Such a humorous, kindly wink, never to be forgotten, — like his great resounding laugh, or the gesture of rubbing his hands as if washing from them every trace of soil." When he departed, suddenly, at any hour, seldom giving notice that he was leaving, heading away on mysterious errands, the children felt a regiment had decamped.

But Sam was adrift, heading nowhere, — caught up in a revulsion of disillusionment. Then S. L. M. Barlow, practical and watchful, came forward with a proposal that appealed to Sam's need of a change.

For several years the transit route across Nicaragua between the east coast and west coast had been closed, in retaliation for the killing of a Nicaraguan by a Yankee ship captain. A new shipping combination wanted to negotiate a renewal of the permit. It was a task for a diplomat who spoke Spanish and who could rough it, if necessary. Barlow nominated Sam Ward, pointing out that while in Nicaragua, Sam also could inspect gold mines in which Barlow's clients were interested, to determine whether the ore could be brought to a seaport for shipment. Sam was offered a retainer and stock in the new shipping line: Barlow thought it might make Sam rich in a few years. Disenchanted and purposeless, Sam accepted the offer. He placed his sapphire (described by some Central Americans once as "big as the Pope's") for safekeeping in Mrs. Barlow's hands, paid a last visit to Craigie House, and sailed for Panama. From there, on December 15, 1863, he wrote to "Longo" in no very lively mood:

"It is now more than fourteen years since I first trod the ramparts of this old town, and it is less changed than I am. I have had my surfeit of the whole belt of this continent between the Isthmus and the River Plate. In these three lusters my life has vibrated between the zenith of wealth and the nadir of poverty." And yet, it seemed to him, he was "happier than when my note was worth 50,000 pounds. I have as many friends, more true ones, and what I have accomplished has been the result of my own efforts." The letter closed with thoughts about his family: "My oldest boy is nineteen and the youngest sixteen, and I am the grandfather of two little boys, the beginning of my daughter's family. God be with you!"

The next report came from Managua; it was to Barlow, dated January 27, 1864: "Still waiting for a Congress. Hope to get through next week and then start for Choluteca. I hear of few developments there, but of mines no end, and do not doubt that, were I twenty years younger, I could bag a million in five years. But I am fifty years old today, — entering upon the Sahara of age and infirmity, and probably unfit for the privations and toils of discovery . . . Not a line from a soul since I left New York fifty-five days ago. Write me care of Panama. I kiss Mrs. Barlow's hands."

This letter, scrawled on vile paper with a viler pen, bore a postscript: "I am told of an Indian who offers for 100 head of cattle (no cure no pay) to show *una laguna d'oro* [a lake of gold]. But the journey is almost as rough as any fabled voyage through the opal mountains. This is for your private ear. If I go a little beyond my depth and can see a prospect of a *seguro,* I shall draw upon you for my contingent remainder . . . Interim, I prefer the Yacht Club chowder (as supplied by S.L.M.B. last summer to W.H.H. and S.W.) to any mixture of pork and bananas this country affords."

The 13th of February produced a second letter, this one penned compactly on small notepaper to conserve space; it recounted a fresh instance of the versatility that had been the wonder of Sam Ward's friends so many years. All his buoyancy seemed to have been restored.

Dear Barlow,

Thanks for your letter of the 12th ult. which was handed to me by a courier near the top of a mountain which commands an enchanting prospect of Lake Managua. I rode on the 29th of January — fifty years and two days old — from here to Granada — seventy-two miles in eleven hours upon the same horse — and came back on the 1st quite fresh. I went to look up some senators who were hanging fire, as we thought, under the pretense that their families were sick. I found no humbug, but a serious eruptive malady with often dark — instead of red — blotches and tending to degenerate into typhus.

The very night of my arrival I consented to a consultation with the doctor of Señor Ballaverez' family over the panting and death-stricken frame of a sweet little girl of ten years, comatose since morning. The practitioner was young, had taken his degree in Guatemala and had never been outside of Central America. So I felt quite safe. I found the little sufferer towards sunset in a dark room, her bed curtains and the windows closed. On either side of the room were half a dozen or more ladies in blue and yellow, friends and relatives of the family, musked to kill all the moths in a July muff.

I instantly threw open the windows, made rags of the curtains, and ordered the room to be cleared of the scented señoritas. But alas! it was too late. I called for stimulants and there were none, — not a drop of elixir, cordial, or ether in a Spanish city of 35,000 souls with a cathedral and fifty churches. I called for wine, — there was none, although the father is rich to the extent of 10,000 cattle. I went all over the town, which had but one hotel, and inquired at stores and houses for wine, and all I could find was some German-manufactured "port" tasting of whisky, logwood, and molasses. So I made, with the remnant of some New York Hotel brandy in my traveling flask, and some Angostura bitters, a palatable cocktail to see to what extent consciousness could be restored. But the little girl could no longer swallow. Stimulus a day or even half a day earlier might have saved her. But she was beyond human aid. I told the father and mother recovery would be a resurrection, and left them all in gloom.

The next day I repeated my visit to see whether they had been able to arouse her to swallow her elixir in the night. When I came into the patio, I was thrilled into hope by the sound of joyous voices. A group of girls, boys, and one or two young ladies was busy around a table on which I saw a silver crucifix, with flowers, long tapers of wax, ribbons, and all the appliances of a fête. It was, alas! the fête of the little girl's funeral they were preparing!

I went to her room. There was no one in it but an old nurse. Her eyes were sunken and her breathing more feeble. "How long will she live, Señor Doctor?" "Until the hour of sunset." I mounted my horse to return hither, and passing by the house, learned that she had expired at two o'clock. The father has seven children left. These people think nothing of a child's death. The priests assure them that she has gone straight to Heaven and they accordingly deck the body with flowers, stretch it upon a bier, a procession bears it through the streets, headed by priests who stop to chaunt at every corner. The mother sheds a tear at home and the father suppresses a sob; but to the family and friends it is the pleasantest thing next to a wedding or a baptism.

I imitated our friend Elliott [a physician] so admirably that I was overwhelmed by visits and consultations. But what could I do without remedies, and the only apothecary in town a widow who sold her husband's drugs by the phial and guesswork? So I concluded to run away from those I had no means of helping. But before I could get out of town I could not help seeing a number of cases which I reserve for . . . the next time we meet with a bottle of the evanescent Grinnell madeira between us. I say "evanescent," because those aldermanic decanters of yours are so unfair to absent friends that I meant to entreat you to suppress them until my return.

Prospects for the mining business looked doubtful, he added. "An old California friend who made fair wages up there" said canoes might transport ore from the mines three or four months of the year, but rapids in the Coco River would necessitate portages, and it seemed unlikely that "such heavy cargo as ours would pay for the risk."

The transit permit business detained Sam several weeks longer, —"a sharp running fight against intrigues and opposition," he reported, although he had "lassoed and corraled" one rival for the franchise by tactics "unheard of in Elmir-y, and as much vigilance as around the polls in a close election." Politically he paid his disrespects to "Don Strabismo" (Ben Butler) and predicted that "one thing is certain: if the Democrats do not elect Grant, the Republicans will re-elect Lincoln."

For Barlow's eye only, he put down "one suggestion that comes to me out of my Central American successes, which have not been inferior to the Paraguayan captures—namely, that I will undertake to prevent the repeal of the Panama Railroad charter in 1869, *if they will pay me for it* . . . If you will sound out the matter, we will share. My knowledge of Spanish and of the people who count on this continent, and a variety of other qualities which I am not vain enough to mention," led him to believe that "I can capture Bogota and defeat John Bull and the [British] South Pacific Steam Ship Company. Have this little job cut out against my return and I will show you 'a watch as shall do you credit.' I shall come jumping in some Sunday P.M. with a load of coffee and chocolate to remind you that I have been in the land of the citrons and myrtle."

And so he did, early in June, 1864. He retrieved his sapphire from the kindly custody of Mrs. Barlow, and while levying toll upon those "aldermanic decanters" of his attorney-businessman friend, unfolded tales of his latest adventures.*

But almost immediately after returning to New York, he reeled under a fresh shock, — this one combining cruelty with bereavement.

Death had pierced Sam Ward many times, — in the loss of his mother, his father, his brothers, his wife Emily, and their son. And the separation that deprived him of Medora and his two boys he had felt almost as keenly as death. After each bereavement, Sam, who lavished affection and required it from those around him, had believed he could not suffer more shatteringly. He was to learn he could.

On Wednesday, June 9, 1864, while glancing through the *New York World* — a newspaper he was in the habit of sending to his sons, who were studying in Luxembourg with Charles Mersch — his eye was attracted by a familiar name heading the obituary notices: *Delmonico.* Aline Clemence, three-year-old daughter of Constant and Louise Delmonico, had succumbed to diphtheria, and friends were invited to attend the funeral mass at the Church of St. Vincent de Paul, on Twenty-third Street, the following day. Sam's eye strayed over the other names — there were only five in the list — *Onderdonck,* a fine old New York family . . . *Smith* . . . *Sprague* . . . *Ward* . . . Incredulous, he read: "WARD — On

* Sam Ward's sapphire ring, so widely known and so frequently mentioned in his day, was examined by an authority on precious stones just a century after Sam reclaimed it from Mrs. Barlow's safekeeping, and the following exact description of the jewel was procured. The plain gold ring is set with a "beautiful five-carat 'Burma' sapphire," of brilliant deep blue, oval in shape, and surrounded by forty-two minecut diamonds in two rows with an additional tapering cluster extending down five rows on either side. The sapphire itself measures seven-sixteenths of an inch long by five-sixteenths of an inch wide. The overall measurement of the setting, including the two bands of surrounding diamonds, is five-eighths of an inch, the long axis of the sapphire. This is hardly a gem "as big as the Pope's;" but the stone's exceptional brilliance, heightened by its cincture of diamonds, causes it to appear larger. It is also likely that Sam, who had a flair for jewelry, wore the ring with an air that increased its impressiveness. The ring is a treasured heirloom, now owned by Mr. Lawrence Terry, Samuel Ward's great-nephew, and most of the time it reposes in a bank vault.

the 26th of May, at Luxembourg (Grand Duchy of Luxembourg), John Randolph Ward, son of Medora Ward and grandson of the late John Randolph Grymes of Louisiana."

That was all.

Two weeks previously, his son — his Randolph — bright, vivacious, petulant, romantic-looking Randolph — had died, and Sam had not even been told! The wording of the notice — "son of Medora Ward and grandson of the late John Randolph Grymes" — no mention of the boy's father — seemed so cruel he thought it must be a hoax, and he hastened to the *World* office, where a clerk produced a letter that had arrived by the steamship *Asia* two days before; it read exactly like the printed wording, and Sam saw (as he poured out his shock to Longfellow) that it had been written "in a steel pen, in Mrs. Ward's sharpest hand. What think you of the bitterness that could brandish a hatchet at the father over his boy's corpse? My poor Randolph! With his brother Wardie he had been for a year residing at Luxembourg, attending college there. He was precocious and charming, but ambitious, and, I fear, overworked himself."

Later he was able to write the details, as conveyed to him sympathetically by Mersch: Medora "had come on to take Wardie to the School of Mines at Freiberg, Saxony, on the 20th of May. On the 24th Randolph felt unwell and remained in bed. He breathed his last in thirty-six hours, very much as poor Marion died in New Orleans in 1847."

Dudie and Sam's daughter grieved with him. Maddie wore mourning for her half-brother, and to Julia Sam gratefully wrote: "Thanks for your sweet note, which is rivaled by two Maddie has written me in spontaneous sympathy and human *épanchement.* Her consolations are all from the Sermon on the Mount, yours from a doctrine of wider horizon; yet both reach my heart, just as I presume Christians and Buddhists alike reach Paradise. I begin to think her a little trump of a daughter." Mersch, he said, involuntarily had widened the wound by writing: "I have a considerable sum left out of your remittances, which were given but sparingly to your boys. After defraying the modest expenses of poor Randolph's sepulture, I am directed by Mrs. Ward, whose wishes I must respect however much I regret them, to hold the balance at *your* disposal." Medora had found another way to hurt the father of her child, and in the midst of his grief, Sam learned that Medora's relatives were accusing *him* of dictating the notice published in the *World!*

This spelled the end of Sam's association with Medora. He never saw her again, although in time he was able to think of her with detachment and a faint glow (how could he help it?) of his youthful affection. But towards Medora's mother, Suzette Grymes, he was unforgiving. "I'll outlive her!" he would exclaim, and he did.

He heard about Medora, though, after '64, — too much, in fact. She was living at Nice in a cosmopolitan set, "a society composed of the froth of all grades, and no one cared what became of the froth after the bubbles burst," as her best friend, Helene von Racowitza, described it. Helene herself was the *femme fatale* who caused the duel in which Ferdinand Lasalle, the German Socialist leader and her impassioned lover, was killed; then she married his killer, a tubercular, dreamy youth who himself was dying rapidly. Helene, who has been summed up as "a raving beauty, a colossal fool, and something of a well known international slut," retained vivid memories of the parties (*orgies,* others termed them) given in sumptuous villas along the Riviera, and of how, afterwards, a few kindred souls would adjourn to Medora Ward's for after-the-party frolics, carried on under the cynical eye of Suzette Grymes. Now nearly seventy, this "chaperone" was rated by one observer as "little but an old pander," but Helene found her fascinating, — "still more beautiful than her two daughters, who were noted beauties. When, on grand occasions, she put on full dress, one could hardly imagine anything more distinguished or more elegant." But around the house she was slatternly, in faded cotton dresses and down-at-heel shoes. Helene conceded the old woman was hot-tempered, but she was clever and full of fascinating anecdotes.

Medora's nest on the Riviera was frequented by political and religious spies, titled wastrels and profligates, to whom she told a pathetic story of her sufferings, — how she had been married very young to "one of New York's richest and fastest men," and had been forced to endure "everything possible in a short time," while her husband squandered his money on cards, women, and drink. In spite of this dolorous past, Medora seemed able to lead a carefree life: she was witty, seductive, and amiable, and when set off by, perhaps, a Mexican costume of yellow and gold, with a gold-studded comb and lace mantilla, she was the attraction at any ball. How she and her mother paid the bills was a matter for gossip. Although Athénaïs von Hoffmann lived with her husband on the Riviera, von Hoffmann was reputed to be parsimonious; in any case, the couple had their own daughters to provide for; one of these was named after her aunt Medora Ward.

But the life of champagne and gaiety did not last long. Two years after Randolph's death, Wardie died in Europe. He had been completely estranged from his father. By Sam's direction and at his expense, both his sons were interred in Père Lachaise Cemetery at Paris. Medora did not long survive. Her burial place is not known.

Sam was old when he received a telegram informing him that he *had* outlived Suzette Grymes, and he scandalized a niece by capering like a boy, shouting, "I have outlived her!" But as for Marie Angéline, otherwise called Medora, there had been too much tenderness during their loving years for Sam to harbor bitterness after she was gone.

TWELVE

SAM MARRIES THE MUSE

AT THE peak of his grief over Randolph's passing, Sam was prepared to leave the United States for good. His friend Gwin was in Mexico to promote a vast scheme of colonization in Sonora, under the benevolent sponsorship of Napoleon III; if successful, the project would mean millions to the organizers. In July of '64 Gwin wrote to his son in Paris that he had "received a long letter from Sam Ward, who says he will join me in September." But Gwin's plans foundered on the inability of Maximilian to come to any decision. Meanwhile, Sam had suffered another financial débâcle.

The cash he had earned by the Nicaraguan mission he had invested in shares of the Gould & Curry mine, on the Comstock Lode in Nevada. The Comstock was booming, and for a few months Sam collected regular dividends; then the vein petered out, and Sam wrote Barlow glumly: "I heard yesterday that Gould & Curry sold at $1600 last week, and Baum sold me out at $2200. Some of my shares cost me $3900 and others $5000. I had only just got a letter speaking in glorious terms of the duration of the mine and its paying dividends for years to come. Damn the world — it is all turning topsy-turvey! I thought I should have no more work after January, and by this I lose $1500 a year in gold!"

Before that disastrous month ended, he was reduced to thinking about pawning or selling his sapphire in order to raise a thousand dollars. But by then he could describe his predicament humorously. "Some people seem only destined to be *gotten* with fortune, and to collapse at the end of the parturition period. It seems I am one of them. I had a charming *grossesse* of about twelve months — the elephant's term — and now behold me in the straw!" Well, at least he had derived a poem from the fiasco, "The Dead Sea Apples of Gould & Curry Lake." He hoped Barlow liked it.

Being a man of many moods and many impulses, of course he had other irons in the fire. He tried "making a market" for the shares of the Central American Transit Company, the Nicaragua shipping line in which he held an interest. As usual, he was bursting with enthusiasm. "Sam Ward is in town and thinks Transit sure to go to 75, which is as much as to say he is in excellent health," Manton Marble, of the *World*, chuckled to Barlow. Sam's friends were peppered with promises of fortunes: "Do not fear for Transit; it will pay . . ."

Yet little more than a month later — after dining with George Augustus Sala, the London journalist (who told ribald stories about Alexandre Dumas), and with Hurlbert (who dashed off an editorial for the *World* between courses), and after running around to his daughter's of an afternoon when one of the babies fell ill — a month later Sam was moaning: "I have never been more worried than by the present market . . . No sale for anything save gold, and that at 260. I am nailed to the cross here . . . I am still short $1800 — with my money locked up in Transit at 41! Where are we all coming to?"

Letters to Longo now went "from the corner of a broker's desk," or "from a counting house." "I have been working for bread since I last wrote you . . . The d——d mine in which I had invested my totality caved in and left me once more as poor as a poet. *Mais toujours gai!* When I feel gloomy I take up my pen and write a song."

At the holiday season, that disastrous year of 1864, he sent the Barlows "Sam's Christmas Poem." It was engrossed in his finest penmanship, on large, blue-tinted paper; its theme, as he explained in a covering letter brimming with affection — "I, who had felt as rich as a Jew, become once more pauper." It began:

To toil and hope is not to win,
We end not all that we begin,
  Nor gather all we've earned. . . .

and continued to the heartfelt close:

Men hold it ill at fate to rail,
  When all is ruled by Heaven;

And yet when — at our best — we fail
And, trim we as we will our sail,
On rocks and shoals we're driven —

Though we may feel 'tis Heaven's high plan,
And bend beneath our lot,
Yet — if we be no more than man —
Resigned we may be, if we can —
Contented we are not.

To excel as a poet was an ambition never entirely stilled in Sam Ward's heart. Apart from the satisfying sense of achievement it would bring, a firm literary accomplishment might vindicate the errors that had marked and often marred his life. He had dabbled in verse ever since his youth; when he was courting Medora he composed a long poem entitled "An Excursion to Staten Island"; and in California nosegays and "impromptus" had been offered to more than one pretty woman.

In 1860, however, Sam had succumbed to what he termed a serious "relapse of the Muse fever," and for a while he wrote poetry (or at least rhymes) copiously. Some of his verses appeared in *Porter's Spirit of the Times*, a New York sporting journal, to which he also contributed, just before he set out for Charleston and the swing through the Confederacy, a series of lively sketches of his life among the Indians on the Merced River. "Incidents on the River of Grace," the series was called, and he signed it with the nom de plume "Midas, Jr." — a gentle sarcasm directed at the nickname bestowed on his multimillionaire father-in-law, William B. Astor, whom the city knew as "Midas."

In view of his nearly fifty years, his stoutness, his thinning gray hair, and the battering he had taken from life at many stages, Sam was self-conscious about his belated poeticizing. "I am still pursued by Euterpe," he gaily told Longfellow, "and have done nothing of profit since we parted save boiling my old bones down to the glue of rhythm. I find peace in the pursuit, though I follow it as awkwardly as he who should resolve to learn the mazurka at fifty . . . If my life is spared I hope to do better."

He explained his vagary in a rhyme:

You ask me why, to rhyming given,
I perpetrate at forty-seven
The follies of eighteen? . . .

And answered himself that it was in part want of an incentive, in part lassitude:

But when of losing one is weary,
Confess — it were too sad and dreary
To try and fail again . . .

Driven in upon himself by want of employment in the active world, and aware of the decline of his physical robustiousness, he took refuge, he said, in the citadel of his mind:

My body is a castle, hoary
With wasted years, if not with glory,
My brain its citadel . . .

The poetry was indifferent, but the sentiment was plain. Sam was growing old, and he felt that he had accomplished nothing; so he took to expressing his disillusionment in rhymes. These he distributed impartially among friends and acquaintances. Secretary of State Seward had received occasional verses; Barlow received many, and Barlow encouraged Sam's avocation. "I send you the *verses,*" had run a typical scribble to Barlow, mailed from Washington early in the attack of Muse-fever. "If you think them worth keeping, pray have them copied for yourself and send the transcript to my daughter, Miss Ward, 32 Lafayette Place, New York."

In '61, William Howard Russell had been struck by one of Sam's effusions, entitled "Time the Auctioneer," and had recited it at stag dinners with telling effect:

Stands a clock within the hall,
Like a monk against the wall,
Like a hooded monk, with eyes
Owl-like, spectral, solemn, wise,
In whose sockets moon and sun
Mimic phase and season run;
While beneath the face austere,

"Going! Gone! Going! Gone!"
Time, the ruthless Auctioneer,
Sells the minutes, one by one . . .

Time his hammer raps again:
"Going! Gone! Going! Gone!" . . .

Russell twitted "most egregious Sam" about the versifying, maintaining that "the puerperal symptoms after poetical partuition are very dangerous, and the condition of the patient requires constant watching, great stimulation, and a severe course of criticism . . . I am grieved that I am not enrolled among the number of those who will be made famous as the genius who discovered S.W."

Longo, of course, was favored with many specimens of Sam's struggles with "the eels and anacondas of rhyme"; and America's premier poet usually contrived to find some phrase, or line, or conceit, that he could honestly praise. To this criticism Sam submitted meekly: he was not verse-proud. And he persevered. "I am on a new poem which keeps me happy and unconscious of the ills the purse is heir to," he could inform Longo genially. "It is a healthful occupation and keeps one away from mischief, whether to one's self, in the way of grosser pleasures, or to one's neighbor, in the artful dodge of money-making. And if with me it should never rise above the dignity of a harmless hobby, it has served and still serves to procure — forgetfulness . . . I am bound to make a spoon or spoil a horn. If my attempt succeeds it will do me credit; if it fails, no disgrace. Will you let me come to you in October, bringing my little *pacotille* for friendly and critical adjudication?"

Longfellow's smooth mastery of his craft caused Sam to despair at times. "What is your secret?" he marveled. "Is it lyrical ventriloquism?" Then, when a hiatus would occur in Longfellow's stream of productivity, Sam would inform him bravely, "If you will no longer pipe for me to dance, I must pipe whether anyone dance or not." And soon he was reporting, "I have now nearly ten thousand lines, enough to burn half and leave perhaps enough for a small volume."

There it was — Sam's intention to present himself publicly in the role of poet. On his way to Nicaragua, he had written to Longfellow about this perhaps rash plan, taking refuge in the novel defense: "I intend to put forth my little volume as a protest against the enemies who slandered me as having fallen off from culture and into the worship of Epicurus."

The closing days of 1864 found Sam reading the proofs of his book, which Appleton in New York, and Roberts Brothers in Boston, were to bring out under their joint imprint. S. L. M. Barlow was underwriting the cost. Longo received an exuberant letter from "Sambo" announcing: "When we meet again I shall have been delivered; whether boy, or girl, or stillborn, I intend to have my caudle and you shall partake of it. My title page motto is:

> Je vous donne avecque ma foy
> Ce qu'il y a de mieulx en moy —

from an old French love song I remember seeing in the library of my green-bottle fly, the Baron of Schwetzingen."

The book, got up in handsome style, appeared in January, 1865. Its publication was an event of great emotional importance to Sam Ward. Let it be said at once that he did not disgrace himself; Julia Ward Howe, who already had two books of verse to her credit, had hardly done as well. But Sam was cagey about exposing his inspirations to critical testing, and played safe by a number of sly devices. The title of the collection, *Lyrical Recreations,* itself seemed intended to disarm the censorious by implying that the contents were not to be judged as serious productions. Then Sam prefixed to many of the lyrics personal dedications, to friends and relatives, which would preclude harsh judgments at least by those so signalized. Poems were inscribed to members of Sam's family, first of all: to Julia and her daughters, Julia Romana and Florence; to "My Daughter, Mrs. Margaret Astor Chanler"; to cousins William G., Charles H., and Richard Ray Ward; and to Uncle John Ward, "The Honored Patriarch of the New York Stock Exchange." Old friends were honored, including Joseph Cogswell (but not George Bancroft), William Henry Hurlbert, and Fitz-Greene Halleck. The book as a whole was dedicated to Sam's Bond Street cousin, Henry Hall Ward — "Treasurer of the New York Society of the Cincinnati, President of the New York Club, Familiae Capiti, True Gentleman,

Kinsman, and Friend." And the opening poem, "The King of the Troubadours," paid homage to Sam's oldest and dearest friend, Henry W. Longfellow.

The preface was addressed to S. L. M. Barlow, in the form of an open letter. It began "When a bachelor, over-ripe, takes to himself a wife in the bud, he is apt to imagine he owes his friends some explanations. It is the privilege of youth to woo Euterpe, and my hair is gray." He had contracted the lyrical fever, he said, "in the natural way," that is, without forcible inoculation, in the spring of 1860. "In mining parlance, the discovery of this unexpected 'pocket' of verse afforded me equal pleasure and surprise. It is true that the bonanza barely held out two years, and then 'split up into horses.' But all veins, alas! too often 'peter out,' and if mine be, perchance, another Mariposa, there are no other stockholders to be caught by the collapse . . . I have, here and there, inscribed a lyric to some one of those whose friendly lamps have lighted me through the dark, when, like the foolish virgins, I have suffered my oil to burn to waste . . .

"Inviting a party of friends to assist at the launch of a sloop, and then carrying them to sea against their will, is, perhaps, sharp practice; but should the frail craft founder, they must remember, with good Sir Humphrey Gilbert, that 'Heaven is as near by sea as by land'; while if the cruise terminate in the Fortunate Isles, they will, perhaps, thank me for a pleasant episode in the Voyage of Life, and I shall be overpaid."

In this preface, Sam confessed failure in an experiment he had tried (like many other poets of all degrees of skillfulness) to naturalize the meters of Horace. As evidence, he included a specimen or two; they were very bad. One, "The Tree and the Shadow," ran, in part:

> The oak still haunts the grove
>   From which poor Joe,
>   Ten years ago,
> Took the leap of death, for love.
>
> The woodsmen's loud alarm
>   Drew young and old,

Where stiff and cold
Joe hung on that oak's right arm.

The moon was in Orion
When from his breast
The love supprest
Leaped like an ambushed lion . . .

It may have been this attempt that caused Julia to remark, after she had been favored with the first bound copy of the book, that Sam's output exhibited "more human than literary quality." It had "surprised" Chev. Retorted Sam, "I should be glad to have it do the same to Ticknor, who has been snubbing me horribly since my fortune fell."

But not all readers were severe, and Sam was happy that "my daughter, who, two years ago, had been taught to eye me askance as a disreputable old Bohemian, has written me a letter full of praise and pride in my book. This alone is no small recompense." William Cullen Bryant had complimented "the grace and brilliance of my treatment of my themes," he further crowed. And Oliver Wendell Holmes had called it "a lovely volume. He got it Saturday, read it Sunday, and wrote me the same evening." Fitz-Greene Halleck had pronounced it better than anything by Tennyson (whom he detested), and the Laureate himself, "in a long and kind letter," had asked Sam to translate into French "the *Jubel-Gesang* in 'Maud.'" This suggestion Mrs. Tennyson tactfully squelched by observing that her husband's "stately oaks cannot be transplanted into Sèvres pots with success, unless by the Chinese process of dwarfing." Sam was flattered just the same.

Unfavorable reviews of his book he magnanimously ignored, although he did remark that James Russell Lowell had "not behaved well in refusing to mention its existence in the *Atlantic* or the *North American*."

Not all the commendation was prompted by mere friendliness. Sam had a gift of expression, hurriedly and sparsely as he had cultivated it in the midst of his multitudinous interests. Poems he scratched out swiftly. Constantly on the move, he wrote poems on the backs of Western Union telegraph blanks, on hotel stationery, steamboat letterheads, the stationery of the Census Bureau and the Internal Revenue, on menus and calling cards. Man being a rational animal governed largely by irrational impulses, and Sam Ward being a compendium of some of man's most engaging foibles, he substituted *will* for *work;* the result might be felicitous or a dead failure, but it exhibited spontaneity. "Impromptu" was Sam's favorite title-word.

When he stuck to light, graceful themes, Sam's verses often turned out very well. A major poet he never would be, but a skillful writer of society verse, in the manner of a Sir John Suckling or Richard Lovelace, he might have become. Some of his bilingual trifles — rhymed in English, then duplicated in French — were charming and effective.

AT LAST!

What care I whence the cold wind blows,
Or if yon skies be drear,
Now that my longing arms enclose
Her whom I hold most dear!

What care I for the wealth and power
That light an emperor's throne,
Since that kiss made — 'tis scarce an hour —
Those tender lips my own!

ENFIN!

Qu'importe d'où souffle la bise
Qui teint en gris les cieux,
Puisqu'enfin, dans mes bras, Élise
Repond a tous mes voeux!

Qu'importent la puissance et l'or
Qui luisent près d'un Roi,
Puisque, cèdés leurs doux trésors,
Ses lèvres sont à moi!

Nor in respect to some other themes was Sam's Euterpe uniformly disdainful or coy. Now and then she favored his fumbling ardency, as in "The Hebrew Alphabet" —

Come, my little Hebrew lad,
On thy task look not so sad.
Only learn it, and thou'lt feel
Writing is in prayer to kneel;
Writing, in His sacred tongue,
Words His holy prophets sung.
Writing out the Law, bequeathed
Unto Moses, when He breathed,
Near the burning bush, the Word,
Then, as now, "I am the Lord."
First we'll learn to spell the name
Sinai saw in clouds and flame.
Write the *Aleph* — every sign
Let thy pen with love design.
Aleph is bright Eden's token,
Ere our race by sin was broken.
Daleth follows in the spell,
Loved in Heaven, feared in Hell.
Aleph, Daleth, then again
Aleph taketh up the train.
Aleph, Daleth, Aleph: now
On our bended knees we bow,
Ere unto the Holy Rune
We append the closing *Nun.*
Adon, Adon, clap your hands
Hills! while joy elates the lands!
Aleph add, and, with a *Yod,*
Tremble at the name of God!
God with whom none others vie,
God of Israel! ADONAI.

Contrasting with this gentleness was the bite of wit in a footnote referring to William Henry Hurlbert: "At that time imprisoned at Richmond, expiating his defense of human liberty by the loss of his own." And the tailpiece of the volume, "Sub Tegmine Fagi," addressed to Uncle John Ward, the ancient of the family, betrayed Sam's deepening inner melancholy:

You marvel I should bid farewell
To cities and to men —

At fifty — and contented dwell
  Within the lonely glen.

Long be it ere afflictions give
  Your undimmed faith the lie,
And teach you it is hard to live
  Where those you cherish die!

While here I drew, with every breath,
  Of life a balmy share,
Your city seems a haunt of death
  When to it I repair.

So many of its palaces
  Are sepulchres for me,
Of those who shared a happiness
  That never more will be;

That when my footsteps pause beside
  Some old friend's dwelling-place,
A gravestone seems the door, once wide
  With welcoming embrace.

And e'en the living few, of all
  My comrades I yet meet,
Seem tottering to a funeral
  Along the callous street.

It was not at all times *toujours gai.* And yet, as he trotted to Washington, to Boston, to Newport, to New York, he could feel that his little testament to eternity was not futile, although his fortunes were flat. From New York he wrote to "Dearest Dudie" at Newport: "On returning [from Washington] I do not find my trunk, which I begged you to have expressed to me at 720 Broadway. I had to go to bed to have my shirt washed. Please send the trunk!" So destitute was he, he added: "I have to go back to Washington Monday to get some money. But for you and Louisa, I should have been stuck fast in Philadelphia. All my bank accounts are overdrawn."

Lying in bed, waiting for that shirt to be laundered, and ruminating on the debits and credits of his career, he reflected — and jotted down the thought — that "eighteen hundred years had failed to produce a second Horace, and as many more might elapse before the appearance of another Béranger." Perhaps he had not done so badly.

And there was consolation in the feeling that somewhere his poems were being read and admired, preferably by a pretty woman. Preserved among his papers was a copy of a presentation poem, written out elegantly in violet ink —

To Miss G——
with a copy of my book

To her who shows with artless grace
The freshness of life's June,
I send these bits of rhythmic lace,
With ties and points of tune.

No spells their meshes lie within
To loose the magic chords
That soared last night in Lohengrin,
Above the clash of swords.

But, as within the psalter old,
Round which bald friars pant,
When from their pallets rudely tolled
By bell of matin chant,

In pensive hours her eye may light
Upon some gentle strain
In tune with fancies, sad or bright,
But human in their vein.

S.W.

The good and the horrendous of Sam the poet lay embalmed and capsuled there.

PART III

ONE

PROMETHEUS IN THE KITCHEN

"I HAVE shed as many tears for Mr. Lincoln as for any sorrow since my brother Marion's death," exclaimed Sam Ward on April 21, 1865, one week after the President had been fatally shot by John Wilkes Booth. Sam had not been partial to Lincoln and had criticized him unfairly. So had most Democrats. So had many Republicans. But in the 1864 election campaign, Sam had taken no active part, either against Lincoln or on behalf of the Democrats' candidate, General McClellan. His close friends had been most active: August Belmont and S. L. M. Barlow had been instrumental in winning the nomination for McClellan, and in the *World* Hurlbert had scathingly attacked the "coarse, vulgar" team of Lincoln and Andrew Johnson. Sam heard McClellan speak, and commented upon the general's "cultivated and scholarly periods, conveying gentlemanly, patriotic, and Christian sentiments." But more than that seemed to be required in a candidate, and Lincoln and Johnson had won hands down.

There is no indication that Sam Ward viewed McClellan's defeat as a national calamity. On the contrary, Johnson's moderate policies while wartime governor of Tennessee Sam several times had recommended to Barlow's consideration as offering the basis for a wise reconstruction policy after the conflict should terminate. Now that Lincoln was dead, Sam grieved for both the North and the South; for coupled with his detestation of the assassination itself was his feeling that Booth's bullet had rung up the curtain on a period of intense turbulency, and even anarchy.

Sam, however, was not one to repine; continuous emergency and continuous change had become his way of life. Therefore, when the new era offered him an opportunity to join the ranks of those who were marching onward if not upward, he stepped into the opening with aplomb and alacrity.

The talisman that procured Sam Ward's introduction into the inner circles of the Johnson Administration was the friendship of Hugh McCulloch, Secretary of the Treasury. McCulloch was an anomaly in Washington, — a man without a political past, and with no ambitions for a political future. He was in politics at all only by a fluke. In 1862, while president of the Bank of Indiana, he had come to Washington to oppose Secretary Chase's pending national banking bill. The bill passed, but Chase had persuaded McCulloch, who was a skillful, widely respected banker, to inaugurate the new system as Comptroller of the Currency. In 1865, after Chase's elevation to the Chief Justiceship, Lincoln named McCulloch Secretary of the Treasury, and President Johnson continued the appointment.

The youngish-looking secretary (at fifty-seven he was six years older than Sam Ward) faced the Herculean task of bringing order out of the hodge-podge of wartime financing. His first concern was to retire, in a systematic manner, $450,000,000 in greenbacks (stopgap paper money) that had been put into circulation. Congress was notoriously skittish on questions of financial policy, and in order to ease his program through House and Senate, the secretary called in as liaison man the best inducer of goodwill available, Sam Ward. Nowadays there are Presidential assistants and other officials who act as links between the legislative and executive branches of the government; in 1865 there were none.

Sam's task was to bring balky, and sometimes doltish, legislators to a realization that contraction of the currency was salutary and imperative to the nation's credit and well-being. To accomplish this laudable end he resorted to the least disingenuous of tactics: he gave dinners. The technicalities of finance he had at tongue's tip himself, but to introduce such abstractions into the skulls of rustic Catos would seem to require trepanning, at least, he was convinced. Therefore, being a humane man, he ruled out surgery, dismissed all thought of appealing to repellent reason, and proceeded upon the comfortable axiom that the shortest distance between a pending bill and a Congressman's "aye" lies through his stomach. On this thesis Sam Ward constructed a career unparalleled in the history of Washington, D.C.

Since the inception of the Republic, the comestibles situation in the nation's capital city had been deplorable. Barrooms there were, in superfluity, but dining rooms were few and for the most part rough-and-ready. The Solons of the new nation may have been bursting with high resolves, but they did not burst with good cheer. They subsisted precariously in boardinghouses and communal "messes" which were egalitarian, to be sure, but primitive, rude, and unseductive: decade after decade, Dyspepsia had crouched fearsomely upon the steps of the Capitol.

Here and there occurred oases in the desert, but they did not reflect the tone of the town. One exception to the general rule of gastronomic simplicity was the table set by the banker, W. W. Corcoran: his entertainments were notoriously lavish and his Johannisberger was nonpareil, but the guests did not unbend at a Corcoran banquet. The cuisine at the White House under Buchanan was French and the Madeiras nutty and mellow, but these advantages were nullified by stiffness and formality. In the homes of more opulent members of Congress, particularly among the Southern contingent, fine regional cookery prevailed, and a fashionable caterer for those inclined to sample the exotic was Gautier, prized above all for his elaborate setpieces, — pyramids and pageants in meringue and spun sugar. Some of the more adventurous hostesses entrusted their dinner parties entirely to Gautier, although their robuster husbands hardly encouraged the practice. Not only were these hosts nonplussed by the names of strange dishes proffered by Gautier waiters, on Gautier china and Gautier napery, they sometimes were even at a loss how to get a fork into an unrecognizable creation.

Few residents emulated Daniel Webster's wholesome custom of touring the markets in the early morning to select in person the provender which his African-born cook, Monica, would transform into succulent, if superabundant, repasts of patriotic American fare, — Maine salmon, New Jersey oysters, Florida shad, Kentucky beef, Delaware canvasbacks, Virginia terrapin, South Carolina rice-birds, and the prime of fruit and vegetables in season.

The obligatory official dinners prescribed during the sessions of Congress were dismal affairs, all of a pattern. One survivor of the grim ritual — Ben: Perley Poore, the politician-journalist — recalled that guests dining in rotation at different houses saw the same rented table ornaments, were served by the same waiters, and ate, or affected to eat, food prepared, or desecrated, by the same cooks. "A watery compound called vegetable soup was invariably served, followed by boiled fish, overdone roast beef or mutton, roast fowl or game in season, and a great variety of puddings, pies, cakes, and ice creams . . . Champagne, without ice, was sparingly supplied in long, slender glasses, but there was no lack of sound claret, and with the dessert several bottles of old Madeira were generally produced by the host, who succinctly gave the name and history of each." The older men would linger to "discuss the wines *ad libitum,* if not *ad nauseam,*" while the young bloods, having escorted the ladies home, would gather at an oyster house and stoke up for a lark, shouting popular songs, breaking windows, wrenching knockers off doors, sending doctors on fools' errands, and jumbling signboards.

This was the prandial side of Washington high life, as recounted by a participant, at a period only shortly before Sam Ward appeared to lighten the darkness, — a Prometheus of the kitchen, who brought the fire of divine cookery, superlative conversation, and temperately Elysian, not merely overstuffed, dining into the diatetic wasteland. Taking for his theater of operations a shabby little house on E Street, number 1406, he there gave dinners of a sort and to such purpose that he rapidly acquired the reputation of a latter-day Lucullus. But he was better than merely Lucullan: he was Sam Wardian, and in that benevolent capacity he was unique.

The occupation of host — with the United States Treasury defraying the cost of his entertainments — provided scope, at last, for Sam to deploy and bring into brilliant play his diversified tastes and long perfected talents. Sam Ward's dinners were more than ambrosial food and the subtlest of wines, offered with artistry; they combined with such provender Sam's personality, his superb tact, and some of the finest table talk to be heard in the United States.

The rule at 1406 E Street was *absolute discretion,* and this promoted expansiveness, both physical and mental. Nothing ever said there in confidence leaked out. There were no women on hand to overhear and perhaps tattle; waistbands might unbutton communally. Sam permitted neither gambling nor any excess, simply such food as Washington had seldom known, a cellar stocked with the choicest vintages of Europe, and a host who laid himself out to be sympathetic, genial, and entertaining.

For filling such a role, no man alive was better equipped than Sam Ward, nor more consummately trained. He had been (or seemed to have been) everywhere, had known everybody, and had experienced everything. He entered eagerly into social enjoyment with others; his bright eyes would sparkle with unconcealed relish as he chatted about diplomats and actresses, scholars and steamboatmen, or alluded familiarly to Astors, Vanderbilts, and Bonapartes he had known. He would dilate with equal gusto upon cooks, comets, clocks, or cockfights — upon Juvenal or penny-dreadfuls, Homer or "cookers" of dice — upon musicians, pugilists, astronomers, sea captains, and society swells. He knew the occult history of salt and forgotten usages of champagne. He could cite proof or refutation, as need be, of the existence of ghosts or the efficacy of prayer. He could mingle admiration of his own heroic family tree with appreciation of men whose pedigrees began and ended with themselves. Snobs or soul-savers, languages or loves, saints or charlatans, whatever the topic might be, Sam could discourse upon it mathematically, philosophically, and wittily, and never be a bore. His tone was that of good company, never emphatic, never intrusive; he trod on no corns, seldom argued except jocosely, confined his raillery to the mildest sarcasm, and listened with flattering attention when others assumed the floor. In a hard-drinking age, his repasts were temperate; his guests might take on a beatific glow, but they never reeled away from his door. The rule inculcated by old Father Corné at Newport in Sam's youth — never to permit John Barleycorn in the house and to keep Bacchus locked in the cellar — was piously honored; while to overfeed a guest would have been, in Sam's eyes, an offense as blatant as diluting oatmeal with Château d'Yquem.

The most cynical Washington observers never intimated that Sam

Ward took or offered bribes: no consciences were racked, no impertinent challenges were thrust at a man at 1406 E Street. The only inconvenience (and few found it that) which a Congressional dallier at Sam's table might look forward to would be the receipt, on the morning of the day when a measure in which Sam Ward was interested came up for a vote, of a gay little note, on delicately tinted blue paper, reading: "This is my little lamb. Be good. Sam Ward."

During the first session of Congress under President Andrew Johnson, Sam's reputation as a gourmet who loved to share sapidity and sapiency with his fellow man became firmly established. By adjournment time invitations to the house on E Street were more eagerly sought after than a summons to the White House, and at one time or another all the best and brainiest, as well as the most powerful, men in Washington were to be found at Sam's board. Secretary McCulloch watched, approved, and paid the "dinner expenses." These, it was rumored, totaled twelve thousand dollars for the session. Sam was silent on the point; he never liked to minimize any rumor that magnified his prestige.

Beyond contesting, Sam Ward had become the capital's "man to see" if one had or hoped to have any remunerative dealings with the government. His influence, reputed to be immense, in some instances was so. And his industry was amazing. From breakfast to dinner time, his compact figure and massive bald head might be seen anywhere within a mile radius of the Capitol, hurrying on errands not divulged, yet always ready to pause for a chat and a whispered confidence, for a sounding out of views, for a sparkle of repartee. His carriage and high-stepping trotters (a gentleman was judged by his equipage) were at the service of anyone needing assistance. Let some stranger accost him in a Capitol corridor, and he would listen alertly, then perhaps scribble a line on his card and instruct the suppliant where to take it to attain his end. "Happy to oblige," he would wave aside the astonished thanks of a person accommodated in this offhand, magical way, and the special thing about Sam Ward was that he meant it.

Sometimes he worked for goodwill; sometimes he worked for

fees, — and good round fees they were, for he could command them. To Sam there was no impropriety in accepting recompense for professional services rendered. He helped, for a consideration, in maneuvering certain bills through Congress, sidetracked others, pushed claims before government bureaus, and by way of personal business speculated on the New York Stock Exchange, chiefly in the fluctuating price of gold. His facilities for ascertaining the day-by-day intentions of the Treasury to buy or to sell gold were an invaluable asset. He had the run of government offices, and wrote personal letters on whatever stationery was at hand. "House of Representatives . . ." "Committee of Ways and Means . . ." Office of Internal Revenue . . ." read letterheads on which he outlined lobbying proposals. The penmanship of these letters was equally varied, depending upon the pen he picked up: some nibs sputtered, others were judicially smooth-flowing.

"Weed [Thurlow Weed] has just received 10,000 Russian cigarettes of the old brand. They have been out of the market for a year and a half. If you want any send word. They are very fine." This was dashed off on taxpayers' notepaper to his crony Barlow. Regarding a bill Barlow hoped to have approved: "To accomplish such a result will cost some money and dinners — not more than I am giving of the latter, but more of the former than I have to spend." Appended to a communication marked "*Confidential*" and written on "House of Representatives" notepaper: "Have that bottle of Montrachet brought up from your cellar and laid upon its side in your pantry against my next call for it. *Les petits cadeaux entretiennent l'amitié.*" Then, in an outburst rare because it was one of the few instances where Sam Ward violated the convention requiring words of profanity to be indicated by dashes: "I wish you would order a dozen copies of my book sent to me by your 50% friends Appletons god damn them." But this concerned Sam's poems, and a poet must be allowed his temperament.

In a few days there followed a note in lighter vein, written on "Treasury Department" stationery: "Don't forget that Montrachet, and whenever you feel prompted to send me wines, liquors, or cigars, remember that Adams Express knows my address." Next, a word regarding some pending legislation: "I can stave it off in the House. This is easy to smooth. As for the fee, I don't know what to charge, as I am doing no end of similar things daily without recompense." On the letterhead of the "Office of Internal Revenue": "I am sorry I took that bottle of Montrachet — fruition dispelled my bright imaginings of its charms. Perhaps I had a bad bottle. Perhaps it is a summer wine. But it certainly was not the nectar of which Mercier spoke in such raptures . . . Give my love to the children, and assure Mrs. Barlow my chivalrous reverence, ardent admiration, and tender affection."

Business, gourmandry, and chivalry, — they were all, not jumbled, but harmoniously blended in Sam.

Sam's operations on behalf of McCulloch's measures bore fruit when the greenback retirement bill cleared the House. But it was killed in the Senate. At the next session, however, despite obstinate opposition, the secretary did obtain authorization to retire a limited amount of the paper currency over a term of years. Sam's performance pleased McCulloch, whose endorsement brought other major lobbying assignments. One of these was for John Morrissey, the prizefighter known as "Old Smoke." Morrissey, a Tammany stalwart, was the kingpin of the lotteries and gambling houses, and he conceived the patriotic notion, he said, that inasmuch as every business ought to bear its fair share of the burden of the war, lotteries should be taxed, also. His real reason for promoting a tax on his source of revenue was that he saw a way to put his competitors out of business; the size of his operations would enable him to pay a reasonable tax, but his less affluent rivals would be driven to the wall. The tax was voted, and thereafter the word circulated in New York's political and financial circles was that Sam Ward could "get results" at Washington.

At various times Sam also represented foreign interests, mainly British, in such matters as tariffs, shipping rights, and claims against the government. In those days Congress was in session only three or four months of the year, and as soon as the session ended, Sam would hasten to Europe to drum up commissions and investigate the latest inspirations of Parisian chefs. In his word, he "vibrated" from side to side of the Atlantic, materializing when and where least expected, but always bringing cheer, good humor, and stimulation. Royalty and soubrettes knew him, young people loved him for his overflowing sympathy, and older folks for his bonhomie, astuteness, and witty charm.

His travels took him far afield in this country, too. He performed some service for Brigham Young — its nature is mysteriously vague — and a pair of bronze eagles outside the entrance to a public building in Salt Lake City remained as a token, — the gift of Sam Ward. Sometimes the fees he collected for his services ran well into five figures, for Sam never depreciated his own worth. But richly as he took, he spent even more lavishly. His style of living was regal. Starting out in the morning with a thousand dollars in his pocket, by evening he might have lent or given away everything, including the use of his carriage, and be without even money to pay cab fare home. But every hackman knew him and Sam never walked if he chose to ride.

Pensioners, parasites, and panhandlers found him an easy mark, and there was always a cluster of hangers-on to be seen at 1406 E Street. Out of his liberality, Sam succored and supported them all. Anyone in distress, it seemed, might turn for help to Sam Ward, and seldom was anyone refused. One day Medora's half-sister, the wife of Mandeville de Marigny, showed up with her ailing child, begging the means to get back south; her husband was penniless as a result of the war and his father's squandermania. Sam had no cash at that moment and scribbled a hasty appeal to Barlow to remit a small sum, in recognition of a service that had cost Sam time and trouble. "You might as well say $25," he wrote, "which I will give to my wife's wretched half-sister, to get her South with her dying little daughter. Strange that with von Hoffmann opulent, and Alfred Grymes comfortably off, I should be the only Samaritan she can find." This appeal he signed, only half in fun: "S. de Bazan, Bohemiae Patriarchus." Five days later, he sent an acknowledgment on "Jay Cooke & Co." stationery: "Thanks for your letters and contents. I gave your check and $100 more to Madame de Marigny. I wrote entreating letters for aid to Alfred Grymes and von Hoffman and here are their replies!!!" They were a frigid "no." This note Sam signed more gaily: "Love back at the ranch, S.W."

He had a staff to assist him in his gadabout activity. Besides the chef — the keystone of his semi-domestic arch — this comprised

Jerry, the valet, a pale, sandy-haired Irishman, and James E. A. Valentine, a well-known horse handicapper and sporting-sheet writer, who functioned as Sam's secretary. Jerry kept a valise packed at all times, so that Sam might dash off to any quarter of the globe on the instant. Valentine, who was splendidly humorous, served as Sam's ear-to-the-ground in the capital's plethora of barrooms, where politics was always being discussed, and not always soberly.

A virtual extension of Sam's E Street headquarters was Welcher's restaurant, a landmark in Washington from the close of the war until the middle of Grant's second term as President. During that time, it was said, there was no great question of policy but had been discussed — and often decided upon — at Welcher's, in either the public or one of the private dining rooms. And never did anything uttered in these high-level confabulations leak out.

For Welcher's was largely the creation of Sam Ward. Stories differed as to how John Welcher got started in the business. At times he was described as a wine importer in New York, who, finding trade slack, came to Washington and opened an eating house as an outlet for his wines. Another version pictured Welcher as a German cook, who was operating a modest restaurant that Sam chanced to pass. Sniffing the aroma of good German cooking, Sam entered and found a diamond in the rough, — a born culinary genius, needing only polishing and instruction in the highest reaches of the art. Taking this peerless prospect in hand, Sam taught him the *haute cuisine,* and personally spread his protégé's fame. Whatever its genesis, Welcher's became the fashion, and differed from other eating establishments in the capital in that food was its only allure; there was no carousing or gambling. Its menus compared favorably with those of Delmonico's. So perfectly at home seemed Sam Ward at Welcher's, the impression arose that he was the proprietor, or at least a partner. But Sam had no pecuniary interest in the business; he merely patronized the place, and he used it for his purposes with consummate skill.

A Congressman, for example, might drop in and from a side table Sam Ward would be seen to rise and go to greet the new arrival with a beaming welcome; he would find a table for the Congressman, and stand chatting for a few minutes, perhaps to recommend the best on the bill of fare that day. Then he would bow pleasantly and retire to his own unobtrusive seat. But by some mysterious concatenation, the Congresman might find seated opposite him, after a while, a man with whom he particularly wished to talk in some neutral and irreproachable setting. One thing would lead to another, and the conversation might drift into serious discussion of a mutual problem, legislative or personal. Sam Ward, meanwhile, would appear to be oblivious of the happy encounter, absorbed in his coffee and meditations; yet perhaps he had been paid precisely to bring those two men together in an apparently accidental manner, and then fade out of the picture. Such arrangements were a specialty of Sam's, and they were carried out so pleasantly and naturally that to suspect an ulterior motive seemed ungracious.

Sam was a shrewd promoter of publicity when it could further his projects, and he was fortunate in being able to command the cooperation of the *New York World,* thanks to his friends Hurlbert, Barlow (a part owner of the *World*), and the newspaper's editor-in-chief, Manton Marble. Hurlbert's articles in the *World,* although never signed, were easily recognizable for the airy persiflage with which he treated the most solemn political and moral questions. Hurlbert it was who recommended that a certain politician, who persisted in opening his mouth and saying the wrong thing, ought to be "gagged with his own foot."

Barlow had moved into a brownstone mansion at number 1 Madison Avenue, where he housed his superb library of Americana and his art collection; and there, because of Barlow's dislike for dining out, Sam and Hurlbert became constant visitors. The once slim attorney had grown exceedingly corpulent, although he had tried every expedient to constrain the all-conquering fat. At one time, for instance, he had taken up horseback riding, on his doctor's advice, but abandoned that when he found he had gained five pounds and his horse had lost fifty. Thereafter, letting nature take its course, he dispensed hospitality at home, or at "Elsinore" his country estate at Glen Cove, Long Island. For years Sam Ward passed every birthday with the Barlows; theirs was the only domestic hearth with which he had regular touch.

TWO

THE LOBBYIST AND THE PRESIDENT

While Sam was enjoying a position of acknowledged power in Washington, the political horizon had darkened, and early in 1868 the storm broke. President Johnson and the so-called Radicals of the Republican majority in Congress were locked in a pitiless struggle. Essentially the issue lay between a runaway Congressional clique on one side, and the executive authority on the other; and the Radicals, infuriated by Johnson's attitude of moderation towards the defeated South, had become determined to strip the Executive branch of independence and reduce it to a rubber stamp for Congress. This was nothing less than a conspiracy to scrap the Constitution — a palace revolution by *coup d'état* — to be followed by a dictatorship wielded by a committee. This, Sam Ward — with other men of honest vision — saw and resisted.

Sam already was a partisan of the President for numerous reasons. Johnson was a Democrat from Tennessee, who had been elected with Lincoln on a "unity" ticket. He had remained loyal to the Union throughout the war, the only slave-state senator to do so. Moreover, Sam was in full accord with McCulloch on most issues, and the Treasury Secretary stood firmly by his chief despite what he believed to be Johnson's blundering handling of the crisis. Finally, in the camp of the Radicals were men whose venality and unscrupulousness Sam knew thoroughly, and whose subversive intentions he fully comprehended.

The role he played in the culminating drama Sam was proud of, — prouder, he said, than of any of his "ground and lofty tumbling." That role took shape in February, 1868, when the antagonism between the President and the Congress came to a head. Sam remembered it was on February 22, Washington's birthday — a Saturday — that the Radical leaders in the House of Representatives decided to press to a vote their motion to impeach Johnson. He got the word at Welcher's, where a number of leading Democrats had met to canvass the prospects for their next national convention. In the House, debate (it was less a debate than the haranguing of a hate-maddened mob) even then was in progress, and Sam heard that the schedule set by the Radicals was to "impeach the President in three days and try him in four weeks." Actually, the impeachment motion was voted by the House on the following Monday. (Vengeful Thaddeus Stevens, leader of the Radicals, ordered the House clock stopped so that officially the thirteenth President of the United States might be impeached on the birthday of the first.)

"It was I who carried the first tidings to Secretary McCulloch," ran Sam's account of that fateful Saturday. "I took a card from him to the President, whom I did not know. He was entertaining the diplomatic corps at dinner, and I had an hour to spare which I consumed in seeing Chief Justice Chase, to whom the news was a surprise. It was also news to the President, when I found him at ten o'clock, and told him to secure the ablest counsel, half Democrats and half Republicans."

This policy, whether or not on Sam's advice, was adopted by Johnson, and one of the Republican defense attorneys selected was Sam's good friend, William M. Evarts.

The President's trial opened before the Senate, sitting as a court of justice, on March 5. The House managers (prosecutors) were headed nominally by Stevens, who was old and feeble, but pushing to the fore as the loudest and most vituperative of the deputy managers was Sam's bugaboo, Ben Butler.

Butler had exacerbated Sam Ward — and a host of other Americans — ever since his notorious exploits at New Orleans. In the later fighting of the war he had covered himself with anything but glory, and had suffered a humiliating repulse in the attempt to capture Fort Fisher, where it was charged he showed cowardice in the face of the Confederate resistance. The fort later was taken by General Alfred H. Terry, commanding a force no greater than that Butler had failed with. In 1866, when Butler took advantage of a freak provision in the Massachusetts election laws to jockey himself back to Congress as a Radical Republican (he had been a leading Democrat before the war), Sam boiled with indignation, and had begged Barlow: "Have Marble or Hurlbert give the [election] district anathema for making their representative helmet out of a *pot-de-chambre!*" His epithet for Butler was "The Great Unscrupulous" —

> Whom friends and foes alike despise,
> Whose soul squints through his demon's eyes,
> In which and in his face you see
> The Devil's likeliest effigy.

The trial of President Johnson was a farce-tragedy. The impeachment was strictly political in nature and its disguise as a judicial proceeding paper-thin. The articles of impeachment were vague and unsubstantial, representing little more than the Radicals' anger at the President's exercise of his constitutional powers. The only substantive charge was that Johnson had violated the Tenure of Office Act, which was a trap that had been set deliberately to goad Johnson into an overt act of defiance. This law forbade the President to dismiss any appointive official, including the members of his cabinet, without the consent of the Senate. Edwin Stanton, the holdover War Secretary, was not only personally obnoxious to Johnson, but he was acting as a barely concealed spy for the Radicals, betraying to them everything that passed in cabinet sessions. Finally Johnson fired Stanton; but the latter refused to accept dismissal, and the Radicals blocked an appeal to the courts that almost certainly would have thrown out the law as unconstitutional.

In the House the Radicals commanded an overwhelming majority, but their strength in the Senate, while predominant, was less topheavy. A vote of two-thirds of all the senators would be required to convict, and the impeachers felt sure of almost that number. Consequently, during the weeks while the trial was unfolding before the Senate, a tug-of-war went on elsewhere to beg, bribe, or coerce wavering senators into line. Both sides were active in this canvassing, and no holds were barred. Men were subjected to every possible pressure, they were hounded, smeared, and threatened with ruin and assassination. Even the sanction of religion was enlisted by the Radicals, with Johnson-hating Bishop Matthew Simpson of the Methodist Episcopal Church, North (this church had split over slavery into Northern and Southern wings), pushing through the church's General Conference a resolution calling for prayer "to save our senators from error." The resolution was aimed at deeply religious Methodist Senator Edmund G. Ross of Kansas, who had intimated that he believed Johnson was innocent. It was adopted without a dissenting voice.

Balloting on the verdict was scheduled to start on Tuesday, May 16, and up to roll-call time the betting odds shifted continually. Handsome, foul-mouthed Ben Wade of Ohio, president *pro tempore* of the Senate, would automatically become President should Johnson be convicted. Wade was swaggering sure of victory.

At the outset of the fight, Sam Ward had not been hopeful; he had expected a speedy conviction of Johnson. On February 25, the day after the impeachment motion was voted by the House, he had written to Barlow: "Make your calculations upon having Ben Wade President by the 30th March, probably the 15th. The cabinet will be changed . . . with that d——d reptile Stanton as figurehead or manager . . . There is more volcanic danger today than when South Carolina seceded, — more than in the first French Constitutional Assembly." This warning had been written on stationery headed: "House of Representatives, 40th Congress of the United States."

Two days later, on a letterhead imprinted, "Treasury Department, Office of Internal Revenue," Sam toned down his forecast of disaster. "The chances since yesterday are rather favoring the President. If the conservative Republicans limit the bill of indictment to the Stanton removal count, that count will not command a two-thirds vote . . . How can Ben Wade vote upon a question which is to raise his salary from $8000 to $25,000 a year?"

Sam suggested that the *World* help with "a nice cartoon of Andy on his back, trampled and beaten and bleeding, and Wade and Sumner and Thad and Ben rushing up to finish him. Let him press on his breast a roll marked 'Constitution.'" Wade and Sumner, Sam's old friend, were the impeachment leaders in the Senate.

On the 4th of May, while counsel were summing up interminably, Sam again became doubtful of the outcome. "I don't believe in the President's conviction," he protested to Barlow, "but if it should occur, I think that on the day of the crime all Democratic papers should appear in black — the deepest mourning. The flags at Tammany, the Manhattan [Club] and City Hall should be at half mast to call public attention to the murder of the Republic." The Manhattan Club was the socially elect Democratic counterpart in New York City of the Republicans' Union League.

On Tuesday, May 16, in an atmosphere of intolerable suspense, the senators voted, taking up first the article of impeachment drafted by Thad Stevens; a catch-all indictment, it was the one on which the managers believed they had the best chance to get a "guilty" verdict. The roll was read alphabetically, and Chief Justice Chase, sitting as presiding judge, put the question solemnly to each senator as his name was called. Telegraph wires had been installed at the Capitol, and over these Sam Ward kept his cousin, Charles H. Ward, the Wall Street broker, apprised of the voting almost minute by minute. Wall Street, of course, was tense and sensitive to each shift in the news.

Sam had wired "Cousin Charley" several times during the last few days his opinion that Johnson would be acquitted. At 11 A.M. — half an hour before the Senate convened — he telegraphed, using the pseudonym "Prescott": "Vote will be taken. Will be close. Not more than two one way or another. My opinion unchanged." At eleven-thirty he wired: "Potter feels more confident this morning." "Potter" was code for McCulloch; there had been a rumor that the secretary was despairing, and every rumor was being reflected on the stock exchange. A few minutes after this message, another telegram to Charles Ward advised: "The last vote on the list has the cast. He was safe last night." This referred apparently to Sam's own list of possible waverers; but long before the roll-call was completed, the Radicals conceded defeat. When Senator Ross voted "not guilty," President Johnson stood acquitted by one vote.

Just before the final tally was announced, Sam wired his cousin:

"Butler just passed, looking like Fort Fisher not taken." Sam gloried in Ben Butler's scowl.

His contribution to the foiling of the cynical attack upon constitutional government was a source of immense satisfaction to him; he had been intensely active behind the scenes, exerting influence, helping to raise money, bringing sympathetic factions together adroitly, and never openly exposing his hand. It was lobbying of a high order, and for a cause to which he subscribed with all his heart. In the chaotic aftermath of the war, with venality and political degeneracy corroding almost every aspect of public life, it was a truism that every sore could be salved with an embrocation of pelf. Sam recoiled from accepting this; and by his activities in the impeachment crisis he helped to preserve the liberties his ancestors had helped to gain. Years afterward, he would record: "I am prouder to have countermined that vile intrigue . . . than of any other event of my life. I contributed my money and efforts and we won, and I saved the country from being Mexicanized." His father, his grandfather, and his great-grandfather, who presided over the Continental Congress, would have approved him.

They called Sam Ward the "King of the Lobby," and he was. Henry Adams, surveying the Washington scene, found "few figures on the Paris stage more interesting and dramatic than old Sam Ward, who knew more of life than all the departments of government put together, including the Senate and the Smithsonian." All during the seventies, "The King" was as much a sight for tourists as the Patent Office. He enjoyed prerogatives accorded to few government leaders; and when, at the close of an arduous session, he tendered a dinner to the Speaker of the House of Representatives, James G. Blaine, and presented him with a silver loving cup engraved as the gift of "Rex Vestiari," few moralists were scandalized. When Sam asked a favor now, as he often did, he need not supplicate: his tone was that of one dignitary addressing another. In 1867 he sent to Frederick Seward, who was still Assistant Secretary of State under his aging father, the name of a friend whom he recommended for diplomatic preferment, and the spirit of the letter was far removed from the humility of those appeals of 1862. "I *do* hope," he concluded, "that for the honor of the guild of honest brains, to which we both belong, you will be able to make an exception of merit versus the hackneyed title of political consideration."

In both Washington and New York, "The King" entertained on a scale befitting his eminence as a potentate of the table. He favored most Wormley's Hotel, in the capital, or Chamberlain's (the select gambling house that doubled as a social club for top-drawer politicians), or the Metropolitan Club. And at Welcher's he was on display daily, while for dinners of special importance he used his house at 1406 E Street. In New York he was a pillar of Delmonico's, but he also frequented the Brevoort House, where the cuisine was scarcely inferior, and his downtown headquarters was Sutherland's, on Liberty Street. John Sutherland, a witty Scotsman, became Sam's devoted friend, and when "The King" dined at Sutherland's, John himself would hover solicitously around the table, insisting upon serving his most distinguished and appreciative patron personally. Sutherland's cuisine was récherchée: one specialty was Braised Beaver Tails *Béchamel.*

Although political corruption in Washington and all over the nation was attaining a pitch of brazenness without modern parallel, Sam Ward contrived to remain unspotted. He was frank about his occupation, so frank and free-spoken, in fact, that he disarmed critics. Everywhere he was called "Uncle Sam," a title bestowed with as much affection as jocularity.

Of course, all was not smooth sailing, for Sam had enemies. The part he had played in discomfiting the Radicals during the impeachment attempt drew down on him the wrath of that camp. Ben Butler was furious at being deprived of the cabinet post he had counted upon enjoying — Secretary of State in Wade's administration — and he tried to make capital of his opponents' "irregular" activities. On his motion, the House authorized an inquiry into "the raising of money to be used in the impeachment," and Butler headed the investigation. The Senate also created a select committee to look into "whether improper or corrupt means have been used to influence the votes of members of the Senate in the trial of impeachment" — quite an undertaking, since both sides had been equally unscrupulous in their methods. The Senate inquiry languished and no report was filed, but Butler pressed his campaign, calling numerous witnesses. Among these was "Uncle Sam" Ward.

Butler confronted the imperturbable Sam with telegrams the latter had sent during the crisis; Sam said they were business communications, — he had been speculating in gold at the time. Butler was amused, and he pointed out how blandly Sam had combined his two purposes in Washington — "to aid the President in his trial, and to furnish information by which the gold market in New York was manipulated."

Ben put into the record a telegram reading: "May 18 — Charles H. Ward, 54 Wall Street, New York: Potter will be quiet all this week. Advocate my cause. Measure low enough. Prescott." Why, that, Sam testified, was a business code message, which signified: "McCulloch will not sell gold all this week. Buy me $50,000. Gold is low enough. Sam Ward."

Other telegrams were produced by Butler, signed "Prescott," or "O," or "S," and Sam conceded that he had sent them all. One of these, signed "Prescott," had gone to "Cousin Charley" Ward, saying: "Potter says not a particle of truth in the rumor you mention, and recommends demurring dondea Bengal." Decoded, said Sam, this would read: "McCulloch says not a particle of truth in the rumor you mention, and recommends selling gold on the prospects of the acquittal of the President." Sam was quite at ease in the witness chair, even when Butler showed him two telegrams that had been exchanged on May 12 between someone signing himself "Evri," at the New York Hotel, and Sam Ward, in Washington; the date was four days before the impeachment vote. At 11:22 A.M. "Evri" had wired: "Telegraph to the hotel quick if rans oder rein." And at 11:30 A.M. the answer had been dispatched: "Gans und volkommen rein." All which, Butler said, meant: "Telegraph to the hotel quick if guilty or clear," and "Entirely and completely clear." Ben added, with real or pretended incredulity: "Ward swears that he did not and does not know who 'Evri' was nor what his telegram meant — yet he answered it in eight minutes!"

One incident on which "Don Strabismo" hammered was a dinner Sam had attended — and possibly had arranged — at Welcher's, on the evening before the senators voted. The guests had comprised a regular grab-bag assortment — officeholders, axe-grinders, agents of the Whisky Ring, betting men, and Evarts (Johnson's counsel) and Sam Ward. Sam had occupied the host's place, although ostensibly the dinner had not been given by him. Some of the men present at that dinner, Butler maintained, were betting two to one on Johnson's acquittal; and "that the dinner was to bring together those principally engaged in procuring it is apparent from the card of invitation issued to Mr. Evarts by Sam Ward, under the feigned name of 'Horace.' "

With a smile the inquisitor handed Sam the very invitation Evarts had received. "Uncle Sam" glanced at it and said that he did not know to whom it was written, or "anything about it." "Is that your signature?" Butler pressed. "I think it is." "Is there any doubt about it?" "No, I do not think there is." "Did you ever sign your name 'Horace?' " "Not that I am aware of." "Did you ever use that *nom de plume?*" "I do not know that I have. I use a great many, but I do not remember having used that."

Sam's famous memory seemed to have passed into eclipse; he remained impenetrable, and Butler was unable to educe any proof whatever of bribery.

Nonchalant as he appeared on the stand, Sam nevertheless had experienced some harrowing moments. He confided to S. L. M. Barlow, in reporting the ordeal: "I was two hours before Butler yesterday, and trembled about that d——d telegram of 'Monkshood' [a code signature] . . . But it escaped notice." Butler's shamelessness in making friendly gestures towards the winning side — in this instance represented by Sam and his Democratic coterie — Sam set down marvelingly. "He treated me with a cordial urbanity which took the starch out of my stomacher. Today I revised my testimony and found he had cooked it up as though he had been my counsel . . . Butler is a strange compound, and if he could jump Jim Crow into Tammany he would do it."

At Welcher's, Sam shrugged that he had appeared before "that strabismal inquisition" and had given some testimony, but that it was "not worth the mileage." The mileage allowance — ten cents a mile each way between Willard's and the Capitol — totaled twenty cents. Sam said that since his fare by omnibus was only twelve cents, round trip, he had remitted eight cents to the Treasury as conscience money.

THREE

"TOUJOURS GAI"

WHEN Grant took office as President, some of Sam's political power was shorn, for the Radicals then were in the saddle. However, there was a respectable Democratic minority in Congress with whom Sam cooperated effectively; and his social popularity never flagged. Always he seemed to be on the go. To Longfellow he grumbled: "I spend nine nights out of ten in the cars, one foot in New York and the other — where? I was Count Almaviva once. Now I am Figaro, old, grizzled, *factotum della citta,* whose *bodega* is half infirmary and half almshouse. The word fun has disappeared from my vocabulary."

But this was not strictly true, for after promising Longo that "the mystery of my Washington work shall entertain you, some evening, with a bottle of burgundy and two glasses between us," he rattled on with a chuckling account of one exploit too good to hold back. It concerned "a client, eager to prevent the arrival at the committee of a certain member before it should adjourn at noon, who offered me $5000 to accomplish his purpose, which I did by having his boots mislaid, while I smoked a cigar and condoled with him until they could be found at 11:45! I had the satisfaction of a good laugh, a good fee in my pocket, and of having prevented a conspiracy!"

"Sambo" and "Samilasso" were the jaunty signatures appended to these notes that streamed into Craigie House, bringing Longo a breath of a world remote from backwater, narrow-horizoned Cambridge. With their mutual friend, Sumner, Sam's relations had become less cordial, since the senator's activity in the impeachment trial; yet he and Sam remained friends, albeit opposed on nearly every political issue.

* * *

Sam's restless toiling had brought him money, — money whose principal virtue, in his eyes, was the power it conferred to scatter presents. The scope which these attained exceeded all previous bounds. Wines, and California olive oil, which he purchased by the case; rosewood furniture for Barlow's home, although Barlow was several times a millionaire; an ingenious "traveling lamp" for S.L.M.B., made by Tiffany and requiring wax candles that Sam imported from Italy; a bolt of seersucker cloth for summer suits, together with instructions on how to remove the sizing without causing shrinkage; books, flowers, fruit, candy, and of course cash, — this would be a mere fragmentary list. A dozen bottles of Tabasco sauce were sent to a dinner acquaintance whose remarks about food Sam had appreciated. He imported green coffee by the sack and distributed it among his sometimes baffled relatives; the Howes wrestled with this awkward commodity for years. Jewelry, tea by the chest, a cane, a watch, a diamond, a puppy, a span of horses, a house, a ranch, annuities, — it was so delightful to spread happiness, and Sam deprived himself of not one particle of pleasure that could be procured by this means, whether he could afford the expense or not.

With a basket of refreshments to a friend starting a long train journey, Sam sent a twinkling note: "I am very fascinating on the cars as a caterer, if not as a companion." Gail Hamilton, a Washington writer, interviewed Sam Ward at the Capitol, and was startled upon leaving to have a ripe banana pressed into her hand; the next morning a messenger brought her a large box of candied fruits. Once a stranger accosted Sam in a railroad car, thanking him effusively for the watch Sam had given him years before; Sam shook his head in mystification, and afterwards told the niece who was traveling with him: "I must know that man, for he says I gave him a watch, but I can't remember ever seeing him before."

When friends remonstrated against his haste to get rid of money, he pleaded that "piety, like Scotch whisky, may mellow with years — not so champagne, which loses, like me, its sparkle with time."

Shortly after Grant's inauguration, Sam made his will, being then in the happy position of having something to bequeath; Julia he named his beneficiary. Sister Annie Mailliard already was provided for, and sister Louisa had an income from her own property; but Julia was poor and hard-pressed.

"Dear Old Bird," he wrote from the Manhattan Club in New York. "Having recently resumed my carrier-pigeon trips to and from this place and Washington, and feeling that age as well as the possibility of accident make it prudent for me to put my affairs in order, I executed yesterday at Washington a will in your favor, which I will send to you under Granny Sumner's frank to whatever address you may indicate. It is now in the safe of John Welcher."

But no income, least of all one as irregular and capricious as Sam's, could withstand the drain of his lordly generosity, and within a twelvemonth he was obliged to inform Dudie that her prospective inheritance, like another will-o'-the-wisp, had glimmered away. Duns were hounding him, he wrote, and with impeccable logic he explained: "My poverty compels me to live at the Brevoort, where no creditor would think of looking for me, as it is the dearest hotel in New York."

His rooms at the Brevoort he maintained permanently, — a basement suite, soberly furnished, distinctive only because of the books that littered tables, chairs, and shelves. These included many editions of Sam's passion, Horace, from Elzeviers to elephant folios, sumptuously bound.

At the Brevoort Sam snatched such privacy as he could. His niece, Maud Howe, who had become a devotee of her Uncle Sam, arrived there from Boston one morning unexpectedly, bouncing in at seven o'clock; he was already at work, wearing a monk's habit and sandals. That was the only time Maud ever saw her uncle in anything but the most correct attire; his code demanded that he appear fastidiously dressed for every occasion.

Maud had begun to sense how special Uncle Sam was when she was about eleven years old. Sam was not being hounded by creditors just then, and he was not cramped in his style. And what a style it could be! Julia's life had become clouded by the death of her youngest child, Samuel, at the age of three. In hope of rousing her out of despair, Sam treated her and Maud to a holiday in New York. It was the first time Maud had seen Uncle Sam in his own setting, and the thrills began the day after their arrival, when he drove up to their hotel in a smart turnout, punctual to the minute, and handed Dudie a large bouquet, and Maud a smaller one. Then he whirled them out to fashionable Islip, on Long Island, where squads and companies of obsequious, smiling servants seemed eager to do Sam's bidding. With a wave of his jeweled hand he conjured up mouth-melting foods and sparkling wine, all with an air of careless expenditure that took Maud's breath away, it ran so completely counter to every precept of thrift she had been taught. His costumes, varied from day to day, left her speechless with admiration — "checked trousers, superb waistcoats, handsome rings and scarf pins, an overcoat of pale gray box cloth with large white pearl buttons, unmistakably from London." On any other man his cravats would have appeared garish, but everything he wore suited him perfectly. A delightful hubbub of excitement surrounded him, through which he smiled and nodded and told stories and passed out compliments that brought the color into Julia's cheeks and rekindled the twinkle in her eyes.

A visit to Washington followed, and Maud was wafted to the seventh heaven of bliss by Uncle Sam's buying her unlimited fried oysters (oysters were never *fried* in Boston) from white-coated vendors who passed through the railroad cars. It was dark when they arrived, and Uncle Sam's first words were, "Look up!" There was the illuminated Capitol dome, topped by Thomas Crawford's Armed Liberty. Maud felt a surge of pride, felt herself to be a part of the place, — which revolved around Uncle Sam, it seemed to her. They stayed at Wormley's, where Sam was more at ease than the proprietor himself, and he took them to see his house on E Street. There an incident occurred that Maud remembered later as having lifted the veil Sam usually drew over his griefs and frustrations. Julia had brought along a girl with a sweet voice to sing for them, and Uncle Sam applauded warmly until a French song (*"Si tu savais comme je t'aime"*) brought him bounding out of his chair with the exclamation, "That song again! I have heard it too often!" The song, Maud guessed, must have been one that Medora sang. The visit broke up prematurely.

* * *

These glimpses of an inner life of hurts not healed were reserved, normally, for the very few to whom Sam could expose his heart. Longo was chief of these, and to a lesser extent, Barlow. Business was taking Sam to Europe frequently, and he told Longfellow frankly that he found little pleasure any more on the Continent. Too many old friends, like Béranger, were missing, and Jules Janin was crotchety and dyspeptic, although rejoicing in the downfall of Napoleon III. The capture of Paris by the Prussians depressed Sam. On January 29, 1871, he told "Mi Querido Dueño" (Longfellow): "I completed last Friday my fifty-seventh birthday, ever memorable to me as the future anniversary of the capitulation of Paris . . . This fearful war symphony has saddened the last six months of my life."

His melancholy deepened as that year advanced, and from the Brevoort he wrote to always understanding, indomitable Julia: "I long to see you and am harder at work scratching than ever. Sometimes, like Sisyphus, back rolls my stone . . . Imagine an old seagull, with nothing but the sea to rest upon, following eternal steamers, and you have my case."

But for most people Sam remained buoyant and irrepressible. He now had his own stationery to supplement that provided by the taxpayers or some steamship line; it was engraved with the device of a compass, the needle of which pointed to SW; and on this he wrote with bravura to Barlow from Washington: "I have directed a demijohn of old Stauffer Rye, nine years old per pedigree, to be sent to you at Glen Cove. While the last Congress was a ragged campaign, it is proper to add that such small hits as *were* made owed their reaching the bull's-eye to this particular brew. Reserve it therefore as a persuasive element in delicate negotiations."

The Barlows being about to sail to Europe, Sam forecast a royal progress for them, and to Elsie, their young daughter, he sent a special going-away wish culled from his favorite poet—

Sis licet felix ubicumque mavis
Et memor nostri, Galatea, vivas
Tecque nec laevas actet in picus
  Nec vaga cornox.

"I'll give her a metrical paraphrase of these loveliest of Latin verses on her return," he promised, — and then, with characteristic precipitancy and verve, put down, "The Muse is too strong for me," and improvised this translation —

> May you be happy wherever you go,
> Now and then mindful of me your old Beau,
> And may the ill-luck of magpie or crow
> Never thwart your journey.

Mid-winter of 1871 found Sam making another whirlwind tour of Europe. This time his business took him to Italy, where he hoped to talk with the Emperor of Brazil on behalf of certain British railway investors. Dom Pedro II was at Florence, but with Sam family claims took priority, so he went first to Rome, to pay a long deferred visit to Loulie and her brood. Louisa had remarried after Crawford's death, and her husband now was Luther Terry, an American painter resident in Rome. They had a son and a daughter — Arthur Noel and Margaret ("Daisy") Terry — whom Sam had never seen.

Twenty-year-old Mimoli Crawford was nervous about meeting her uncle again — she had not seen him for years — and it was with some misgivings that she ran to the door of the family's apartment in the Odescalchi Palace when the bell rang. But immediately she heard a well-remembered voice call out, "Mimoli!" and she was crushed in a bear hug against a shepherd's plaid bosom. "I should have known you anywhere!" was Sam's hearty exclamation when he released her, out of breath. Then, reaching into his waistcoat pocket, he dropped into her palm a pearl. It was so large and lustrous, she gasped.

"Have it set as a ring," he ordered briskly. "It's a stud now."

Next Louisa laughed and cried a little as she hugged "Bro. Sam," and the servants scurried to prepare a room, while the cook whipped up "a dream of a breakfast" for the so much talked of uncle.

Sam had grown older, his relatives noticed first: he was stouter, and the light brown hair, except for a graying fringe, was gone, and the sweeping mustache and imperial were silvery white. But his eyes still sparkled. He wore a dark red tie and a rose in his lapel, and the famous sapphire gleamed on his right hand.

The day unrolled like a dream in motion. Rome was new to Sam, and he wanted to see everything. Although the Vatican was closed, they took him through St. Peter's and the Forum excavations, where he delighted the curators by his apt Latin quotations. All day he was amusing and effervescent, although Mimoli liked best his grave mood in the evening, when "in the fading twilight he took his Horace from his pocket, and, without opening the worn volume, began to repeat the description of the Sabine farm . . . He told us all that Horace had been to him through life . . . 'No one can ever be sad or lonely who *possesses* Horace,' he said. 'All my life I have carried him about with me and he is the most faithful and sustaining of companions. Some day I may show you my Horaces, as the greatest treasure in my library. I have all the first editions known to exist, but this little brown volume is the dearest of all. It never leaves me."

Sam's business brooked no delay, so "after his *café noir* and cigarette," Louisa wrote to sister Annie, "our fascinating guest was driven to the station in the family landau, taking an affectionate leave with the assurance that he would be back in the spring and 'bring his knitting.' Never was brother more brilliant, more intelligent, more loving. Truly, a golden-lettered day . . . One Sunday only, scarcely twelve hours, yet looking back on it that visit seems to have comprised a month of happiness. Many springs may, I fear, come before he will return, but one must not expect a comet yearly."

The "comet" flashed next over Florence, to cheer another niece, Julia's daughter Laura, who was spending her honeymoon year there with her student-architect husband, Henry Richards. The couple were poor and happy and in love, shivering through a bitter winter in "a little stone room in a stone house with a little stone fireplace" that gave out tepid heat. Then, as Laura remembered it — "Suddenly it was summer, for my Uncle Sam came in."

He could spend only twenty-four hours in Florence, he told them, and hustled off at once to see the emperor. Dom Pedro was traveling *incognito*, and sent word that he could not receive Mr. Ward. But against such a contretemps Sam was prepared. The emperor, he knew, was an ardent bookman, and Sam had brought an autographed presentation copy of Longfellow's latest volume. He sent this to the emperor with a graceful note: doors flew open, and Dom Pedro and Sam chatted for an hour. The emperor expressed admiration of the poet and said he hoped some day to meet him. Nothing simpler, responded Sam, and from talk of poetry they progressed to matters more immediately connected with Sam's call, and parted friends for life.

Back to Laura and her husband came the uncle, laden with good things to eat, and regaled them (sworn to secrecy, of course) with a racy recital of how he had won over the Emperor of Brazil. The next morning Laura received a bouquet "a yard around," with a paper frill, and a check almost as sizable. The newlyweds guessed that the money was intended to procure them a warmer lodging; but with Sam's own recklessness they bought a statuette instead, and continued merrily to freeze.

Sam's route taking him to London, he telegraphed ahead to his seventeen-year-old nephew, F. Marion Crawford, then studying in England, to meet him at the hotel; and from there Sam praised Marion to his mother, regretting that "the people with whom I had business were so jealously greedy of my time that I could not make the dear boy as happy as I wanted. He *is* a splendid fellow, and his likeness to dear Manny struck me in the bull's-eye of the heart."

On the ship coming home, he found a New York acquaintance "with his lovely daughter Virginia, whom I forthwith christened Ariel when the first wave drenched us as she was taking a stroll, on my arm, on the upper deck." Ariel, he informed his sisters, had drawn "fresh sparks of poesy out of my dilapidated heart. I don't think I have ever been so deeply smitten since 1843"—the year he courted Medora Grymes. But susceptible Sam was in for disillusionment: Ariel "never told me that she was engaged to be married to a gentleman she had met at Canton." Reproachfully he sent her the following impromptu:

Pourquoi me cacher ce secret,
  Pour mon coeur une épine?
Que mon Ariel avait laissé
  Son petit coeur en Chine?

"So you see," he wound up the episode in a letter to Julia, "the *folle du logis* has not deserted my poor old brain. If I had time I might yet do something nice."

"Do you know that I am nine times a grandpa?"

Longo received this query soon after Sam's return from Europe. "Six boys and three girls, all fine children and admirably reared," Sambo particularized. "They senilize me with the title 'Grandpa.' "

A superficial harmony had developed between Sam and his daughter, and Dudie received periodic bulletins, such as: "I have dined with Maddie twice since my return." Or, "Her children certainly are splendid, and she is quite affectionate." Yet Maddie's conventionality could not bridge the gap: her father's manner of living she never would condemn, but to her it was incomprehensible and frightening. Neither could John Winthrop Chanler be at ease with his wife's brilliant but really too bohemian parent. Chanler disapproved of lobbying, especially by his father-in-law; it was a disreputable trade, he believed, and certainly degrading to a gentleman. Sam took no umbrage; he seldom encountered Chanler socially, except at the latter's own home.

Once when an opportunity arose to do his son-in-law a political service, Sam embraced it eagerly. It occurred just before an election: Chanler's "corporal's guard" of Democrats holding jobs at the New York Customs House were to be turned out of their places in favor of Republicans. Sam appealed to Barlow to intercede. "It is the only favor I have ever had the chance of doing Mr. Chanler, who has always treated me with remarkable courtesy," he wrote, "especially when the hostility of Lafayette Place is taken into account."

The matter was satisfactorily adjusted, and Chanler was appreciative; but still no real intimacy or mutual trust was possible between the men, and in September, 1874, Sam blurted the truth to Longfellow: "I am a moral nomad, homeless and comparatively childless, for my daughter is in the enemy's camp and I rarely see her now." This sense of failure oppressed him. "My life is an eternal Sisyphism," he wrote to Julia, reverting to a familiar metaphor; "always rolling stones up mountains until they grow to avalanches, and are dashed to pieces in the valley. Still, I sing as I roll, never say die. I enclose a real impromptu written by me New Year's night to a lady. It is pretty straight French and some song. But I have no rest, although pure as the highest snowflake."

A few months later, nothing had improved: "Maddie has asked me to be her guest at Newport, but I am ever scratching for worms to catch my fish with." And to Longfellow he sighed: "Here I am, in the *Salle des Pas Perdus,* on the banks of the Styx, waiting to be ferried over to Fortune. I am like one of those couriers whose horses always stood saddled in the courtyard of the first Napoleon, ready to mount at a moment's notice for Moscow or Vienna."

Rhyming was his pastime, and on Dudie's fifty-fourth birthday he sent her a lilting tribute, which contrasted, however, her life of achievement with his own —

Six times nine are fifty-four!
May you live years many more!
Dearest, dearest sister mine,
I have loved you six times nine! . . .

Wise ones say I've lived in vain
Through life's calm and hurricane,
All my voyage wayward sport,
With no cargo brought to port,
Save upon the barren deck
Someone rescued from a wreck.

Yet who may the story tell
Must avow my craft sailed well.

And on his own fifty-ninth birthday he philosophized to Longo: "I hear Mr. Astor is worth $160 millions. And that one item of his fortune is thirty-three thousand houses in the city of New York. I might have been absorbed in the Nirvana of that golden essence. I prefer my own individuality." This declaration of independence sounded hardly enthusiastic. He put a poser to his poet friend, whose optimism was unquenchable: "You have always maintained that whatever *is* is right. How, then, can that which *was* be wrong?"

More and more, in introspective moods, he harked back to places and people he could not forget. So many associates of his youth were dead. His memory of Medora had softened, and her name appeared now and then in his letters, without rancor. When he was past sixty, he could express to Longo the hold her name still retained on him, writing: "This is the anniversary of my marriage to Medora, thirty-one years ago, and I am invited to dine in the very house, this P.M., by its present owner. What an episode!"

Yet outwardly he was debonair; and though the nation was laboring in a great depression and well-paying lobbying assignments grew scarce, socially Sam Ward's popularity did not wane. He had no opportunity to mope or grow stale. His friend Hurlbert was in Mexico untangling an investment snarl for Barlow and buying porcelains and paintings on his own account ("a real Holbein," he gloated), while sermonizing Sam on the vanity of riches. "All good things are dreams, although all dreams are not good things," he counseled. Sam reported back that he himself was dull, although still subject to "occasional fits of rhyme."

Longfellow's steady flow he followed avidly. He resumed the role of literary broker for his friend and sold publication rights to Longo's latest poem, "The Hanging of the Crane," to Robert Bonner, eccentric publisher of the *New York Ledger*, for the unheard of sum of four thousand dollars — $3.16 a word, or $20.20 a line — the highest price ever paid to a writing man, "Samilasso" glowed. One thousand dollars of the price was Bonner's commission to Sam, who accepted it as honestly earned. Longfellow was awed: "It is a great sum," he noted in his journal. "It was not my asking, but his offer." When Sam came to Craigie House to extend congratulations in person, the poet remarked that he looked "like a prime minister or a European diplomat." On his side, in the midst of a dozen barely sustaining tasks, Sam growled to Longo: "I am so jarred by circumstances that thought has no more chance to crystallize than the taker of tickets at Barnum's Hippodrome has to remember the 119th Psalm."

Sumner died in 1874, and although their friendship had cooled, Sam felt the snapping of this link with his confident youth. He communicated the details to Longfellow, who was prostrated. Sam had been in the bath, he said, when a friend brought word that Sumner was alarmingly ill. Upon reaching the senator's home, Sam found him *in extremis,* and the end came shortly thereafter. "A vast crowd of freed men with the gloomiest faces darkened the street before his door. The last audible words he uttered, with the old ring in his voice, were, 'Don't let the bill die!' Shortly after, again in a loud voice, 'I mean the civil rights bill!' "

The grief Sam felt was deep and sincere; but as time went by, the poignancy subsided into "a lonely feeling of privation, which has a melancholy charm when I pass twice a day before his dwelling, and recall his sweet and gracious ways," he told Longo. Now Sam Ward was Longfellow's most ancient, most closely clasped friend.

FOUR

A PARABLE OF PIGS' EARS

THE city of Washington, where corruption throve, was a poor habitat for sentiment; as 1875 dawned, investigations into some of the more noxious scandals already were under way. In one of these Sam Ward came under fire. Friends were startled when he was summoned to testify before the House Ways and Means committee regarding his lobbying affairs; this would never have happened during the Johnson Administration. Sam was not perturbed.

The outrage under scrutiny was the asserted use of large sums of money to obtain for the Pacific Mail Steamship Company a subsidy to carry the mails to China and the Orient, in ships to be constructed for that service. The circumstances were complex, so intricate, in fact, that the report ultimately submitted by the committee would fill six hundred and thirty-two pages of fine print.

The inquiry had dragged along for weeks, prodded by several newspapers and particularly by the *New York Tribune,* which openly charged that a million dollars had changed hands corruptly. Although "the evidence has led to the very doors of Congress, there it has been stopped," the *Tribune* complained.

The bagman in the supposed sordid transactions, according to testimony, was a Colonel Richard B. Irwin, a man whom, in the *Tribune*'s words, nobody had ever taken for a fool, since he was "a gentleman who knows Washington as well as his own pocket, who has been on the inside of three or four Administrations, and who is hardly the sort of person to throw a whole prize beef to a cur who would be made happy with a shin bone." This allusion was to a couple of House doorkeepers, who had been thrown, by this same Irwin, $4500 and $11,000, respectively, apparently for doing nothing. They testified they thought the money was a tip!

Day after day, witnesses wandered afield, challenged the committee's power to pry, and misquoted themselves and each other. At length a second-string payoff agent produced a list of persons who had shared in the distribution of one sum of $120,000; they were newspaper editors, Washington correspondents, ex-postmasters, a former marshal of the Supreme Court, a former mayor of Washington named James G. Barrett, and Sam Ward. Barrett and Ward were said to have split seven thousand dollars between them.

The *Tribune* made merry hay over this disclosure, facetiously conceding that the handout to Barrett probably had been justified, "for he is one of the handsomest men now living, and his beauty is of incontestable value to any cause he espouses." Sam Ward unhesitatingly told reporters that, yes, he had received four thousand dollars, and no doubt had spent it at Welcher's long ago, but he would go cheerfully before the committee at any time.

Barrett was called and proved himself a windbag and a braggart, and the committee elicited nothing to the purpose from him. Then Sam was summoned, and what transpired the *Tribune* reported, the next day, under the headline, *"A Noted Lobbyist's Testimony"*:

> Samuel Ward, famous for his grand entertainments and convivial qualities, was the most amusing and frank-spoken witness that has yet helped to enliven the proceedings of the committee. Mr. Ward gave his testimony — or rather, delivered his humorous lecture — standing at the end of the table, with his eyes twinkling, his face beaming with good humor, and his whole person presenting evidence of his being, not only in belief but in practice, a disciple of the science of gastronomy. He kept the members of the committee and a numerous audience in constant laughter.

The chairman opened by saying he supposed the witness knew why he was appearing.

"I received a subpoena about an hour ago," replied Sam, "particulars not specified."

How much money had he received in connection with the Pacific Mail subsidy?

"I think it was after the first failure of the measure in the House that Mr. Barrett called at my rooms one afternoon, and said that he had been requested to see if I would accept a retainer to help this subsidy along. I asked him how much." Sam spoke rapidly and without reserve. "He said $500, and $5000 contingent on success. I said, 'All right.' He sent me, that afternoon or next morning, a check for $500, signed by a gentleman I had never seen, Mr. R. B. Irwin; and some days after Congress adjourned I was agreeably waited upon by Mr. Barrett, who said to me: 'They have cut us down $3000, and there is only $7000 to be paid; shall we insist on more?' I said, 'No, let us take what we can get. It is all right.' He handed me $3500 in bills, and I went to New York that night."

"Now," said the chairman, "I suppose it is unnecessary to ask you if you retained all of that sum and applied it to your own uses?"

"I did," replied Sam. "I must say that it was a very liberal compensation for the moderate amount of work which that subsidy seemed to require."

"State the nature of the services rendered by you."

"Simply stating on all occasions when it was proper to do so," Sam waved a hand, "that I was in favor of the measure, that I thought it a good measure."

He had a special right to express an opinion on this particular subject, he elaborated, "because, as an old Californian, having sailed often on those steamers, I had a sort of friendship for them. I thought well of the line; I thought that it was a great national undertaking; that our shipbuilding was going to the dogs; and that if those ships were to be built in this country, it would give an impetus to iron shipbuilding. I thought that a subsidy to the Pacific Mail Steamship Company was a proper thing, particularly as the Cunard Steamship Company had a subsidy from the English government and had attained a colossal success. I wanted to see the American flag flying again on the seas, and I would have helped the Pacific Mail Steamship Company subsidy without one cent of compensation."

Nevertheless, the chairman asked, Sam did use his influence to secure passage of the subsidy?

"Certainly," rejoined the witness. "There was not much time to act, only a fortnight, I think. I was rather agreeably surprised at being retained, because that clinched my determination to do what I could for what I regarded as a great national enterprise."

"Do you know of any other sums of money being paid to any parties for their services in procuring the subsidy?"

"I never heard of any, and, until I was surprised the other day by that list, which I saw in the *Star,* I never knew who was in the combination. I did not know there was any combination, except that I found people generally very favorably inclined towards the bill. I never saw Mr. Irwin till the day the vote was taken, when I saw a pale man standing around this corner, and was told it was Mr. Irwin."

The chairman brought the witness back to the question, whether he knew of "any sum of money being paid, directly or indirectly, in connection with the subsidy?"

"Not a penny." Sam was positive. "I might have been at liberty to suppose that the whole thing was confined to Mr. Barrett and myself."

"Do you know of any money being paid to any member, officer, or employee of either house of Congress in connection with the subsidy?"

"No, sir," said Sam; whereupon a member of the committee broke in with a diversionary question. "I have heard it suggested," he said, "that you have remarked that there was a great deal of difficulty in a gentleman living in Washington on the oxygen of the atmosphere, and that a gentleman was obligated to do something."

Sam's glance lighted upon this questioner. "This business of lobbying, so called," he said disarmingly, "is as precarious as fishing in the Hebrides. You get all ready, your boats go out — suddenly there comes a storm, and away you are driven." He was off, speaking vividly, gesticulating, giving a rundown on his method of earning a livelihood. "Everybody who knows anything about Washington, knows that ten times, aye, fifty times, more measures are lost than are carried; but once in a while a pleasant little windfall of this kind recompenses us, who are always toiling here, for the disappointments. I am not ashamed — I do not say I am proud, but I am not ashamed — of the occupation. It is a very useful one. In England it is a separate branch of the legal profession; there they have parliamentary lawyers who do no other business. There the committees sit all day to hear these lawyers, and they sit in Parliament at night, whereas here committees are only allowed to sit for an hour and a half; so that it is very hard to get through four thousand bills in a session. The disappointments are much more numerous than the successes. I have had many a very pleasant 'contingent' knocked away—" Here the committee members broke into audible laughter "—when everything appeared prosperous and certain, and I would not insure any bill, if I were paid fifty per cent, to secure its passage. That is the general rule. In this matter I think that the gentleman [Irwin] paid more money than he need have paid."

"And he distributed it rather badly?"

"I am satisfied with what I got."

The admission, made with good-humored candor, was refreshing to the committee, after weeks of witnesses who had slithered, dodged, and prevaricated.

"You got much less than the others got," the chairman prodded.

"I don't know," answered Sam. "I was retained, I suppose, because 'the king's name is a tower of strength,' [Laughter] and I am known as the 'King of the Lobby.' But I am not the Treasurer of the Lobby, that is certain. If you were here for entertainment, I could entertain you with histories of well concerted plans which all disappeared just at the crack of one member's whip; perhaps a matter of caprice, perhaps a matter of accident; you can't tell which.

"We who are of the 'regular army' know when we are whipped," he conceded, to the chuckling accompaniment of his listeners. "But gentlemen of little experience come down here, and peg on and peg on until the end of the session, and never understand when they had better go home." Sam recapitulated the woes of the harried lobbyist. "To introduce a bill properly, to have it referred to the proper committee, to see that some member in that committee understands its merits, to attend to it, to watch it, to have a counsel to go and advocate it before the committee, to see that members of the committee do not oversleep on the mornings of important meetings, to watch for the coming in of the bill to Congress day after day, week after week, to have your men on hand a dozen times, and to have them as often disappointed; to have one of those storms which spring up in the Adriatic of Congress, until your men are worried, and worn, and tired, and until they say to themselves that they will not go up to the Capitol today, — and then to have the bird suddenly flushed, and all your preparations brought to naught, — these," he exhaled, "these are some of the experiences of the lobby."

The stenographer was obliged to interpolate the note "Laughter" again at this point; it was the fifth repetition, and there would be as many more before the close.

"Another point," Sam went on briskly, "the question of entertainments is spoken of. There is nothing in the world so excellent as entertainments of a refined order. [Laughter.] Talleyrand says that diplomacy is assisted by good dinners, but at good dinners people do not 'talk shop.' But they give people who have a taste in that way the right, perhaps, to ask a gentleman a civil question, and to get a civil answer; to get information which his clients want, and that can be properly given. Sometimes a railroad man wants information. Sometimes a patentee wants his patent renewed, — that is a pretty hard fight. [Laughter.] Then a broker wants to know what the Treasury is going to do about a certain measure. Sometimes the banker is anxious about the financial movements in Congress, or a merchant about the tariff. All these things we do constantly, and we do not make any charge for them. We keep up a certain circle of friends, and once in a while an opportunity comes of getting something that is of real service, and for which compensation is due and proper. But the entertainments are proportioned to the business of the session. When the business is good, so are the entertainments, and when the business is not good, the entertainments are meager."

His listeners, most of them, had stretched their legs under "Uncle Sam's" table, and had not found the fare meager. It is possible that they looked skeptically amused. At any event, Sam launched into an anecdote, a puzzler, like some of the conundrums he threw out at his dinners to give his guests a thought to mull over on the way home: let them extract the meaning from it if they could.

"Washington Irving tells a story about the king of Spain, who was lost in the woods with his hunting party. He ordered one of his attendants to climb a tree and see whether there was any building in sight. The man saw a château on the top of an adjacent hill, and the king said, 'Let us go there.' They went and were received at the door of the château by the grandee, with his head uncovered. The king announced who he was, and said the party wanted dinner. The family had dined an hour before, and the servants had consumed everything that was left. The cook was sent for, and said his majesty would be served in an hour's time. They had a very pleasant dinner, and the king was rather surprised by the taste displayed in some of the dishes. After dinner, commending the excellence of the repast, he asked what it was composed of. The grandee sent for the cook, who came in and said, 'Your majesty, no animal has contributed its life to your dinner,' and he went to the window and showed the king fifty-two pigs with their ears all cut off. Said the king, 'A man who can make such a repast as that from the ears of fifty-two pigs should be made a governor of a province!'"

Sam looked around with a twinkle as a burst of laughter greeted this. A sour member broke in with a question: "Is there not a great deal of money wasted on good dinners?"

Sam's riposte was rapier-swift: "I do not think money is ever wasted on a good dinner. If a man dines badly, he forgets to say his prayers when going to bed, but if he dines well he feels like a saint."

The chairman then plumbed the good humor and geniality of the witness with one final question: "Were you aware that Mr. Barrett, in point of fact, had received $10,000, instead of $7000?" In other words, that the man of portentous beauty had cheated in his split with Sam?

"No," came the cheerful response. "I did not know anything about it until I saw it mentioned in the papers. It is quite all right; he probably did more work than I did. I was quite satisfied with what I got."

Instructed to step down, Sam left the room with triumphant tread, and the air, it was said, of a French marshal.

FIVE

HARD TIMES AND FAME

THIS unconventional hearing took place in January, 1875, and Sam Ward's parable of the pigs' ears set the country laughing and trying to ferret out its significance. Who were the fifty-two pigs who lost their ears? Who was the cook capable of concocting a succulent and tasteful dish out of such unlikely provender? Was Sam vaunting his own skill? Was he conveying to the well-fed, negligent Congressmen that a purveyor of dinners as remarkable as his was worthy of official employment? It was all a riddle and a guessing game in which the newspapers joined, and the *New York Daily Graphic* cartooned "Uncle Sam" in a chef's cap stewing pigs' ears marked with dollar signs presumably for Congressional palates. Sam smiled and said nothing.

His extraordinary performance on Capitol Hill boosted his renown all over the nation. "Everybody knows Uncle Sam Ward," was the way gossip columnists referred to him, and in New York the *Graphic* followed up its cartoon with a handsome portrait and a full-length word sketch. "He is a good-natured, Pickwickian old fellow, apparently about fifty-five but in fact close upon seventy," the *Graphic* said. "A perfect specimen of vitality, fat and solid — just such a 'right jolly little elf' as is described in 'The Night Before Christmas.' He has jocund little eyes that laugh over smooth delicately red cheeks and rounded jaws. Wit, scholar, and poet, gourmand and political intriguer, he has seen about as much of the world as any man living. Sam inherited a large fortune, but this was naturally enough melted away by his youthful gaieties, and he has been engaged in a multitude of more or less lucrative pursuits. Usually dressed in flashy style, and making lavish display of funds, he steps from the Brevoort House in this city, or Welcher's in Washington, looking as if he were at peace with the world.

"Samuel is decidedly eccentric," this pleasant if superficial delineation continued. "One of the most genial and hospitable of men, ever ready to do a graceful or kindly act at just the right moment, he has yet a restless, roving disposition. As a lobbyist he holds that the first step towards inducing a senator or representative to vote in any desired way is to clear his judgment and vanish his prejudices by a comfortable dinner. His now famous story of the king of Spain and his fifty-two pigs has been studied as though it were a riddle of the Memphian Sphinx."

The perfume of such acclaim Sam savored appreciatively, and to Longo he wrote proudly that "a business which people imagined must have been unpleasant has turned out profitably." That "saucy testimony" of his, he said, had "a certain humor, which I can no more suppress than a stammerer can suppress his stuttering, and it has made me famous. And what is more, highly honored. My box is full of letters of congratulations and my fingers sore with hand grips. I told you I wanted a chance for assertion and vindication . . . I have had offers for a book from several publishers and have felt half inclined to ramble on with my pen . . . but I am a prey to beggars and bores and cannot leave the market until March 4th. You said to me once, 'Write your memoirs, beginning now and going back.' Do you still recommend this?"

"Beginning now and going back . . ." It was a beguiling temptation.

To a Wall Street acquaintance — Edmund Clarence Stedman, who combined stock brokerage with versifying — Sam now made the only public defense he ever offered of his lobbying activities.

"I feel tenderly touched by your kind note," Stedman was told. "When I appeared at the short summons of the committee and gave my testimony I had no idea it would spread throughout the land. This ignorance was the probable cause of my untutored simplicity, to which is due the popular success of my narrative.

"I quite agree that the profession of lobbying is not commendable. But I have endeavored to make it respectable by avoiding all measures without merit. In the struggle for existence, to which I was not born, my various chances and mishaps have landed me upon that shore, — like the émigré who escapes the guillotine to make a good living by compounding salads.

"I began life with prospects of a brilliant and happy career. But I was divested of my library and my studio by the ill-advised pertinacity of Mr. Astor, who insisted on my going into business. Unluckily, I resolved to keep up my culture and for five or six years rose at 5 A.M. and got in three hours of study before breakfast. In fact, knowledge was my only ambition. This absorption of my mind and feeling was unfair to my business, which was generally a purely mechanical pursuit, until the death of my father and my wife compelled me to take up the pursuit more actively. But, just as I was becoming something of a banker. . . ." And he summarized his successive disasters. "I tried my hand at various things, but never got to the north of independence, then came to Washington, first on one errand, then on another, until finally I made this place my headquarters and Congress the theater of my employment. I hope soon to retire, for the life is distasteful to me."

But the widening of Sam's reputation contributed nothing to that ability to make "a lavish display of funds" which the *Graphic* had advertised. At sixty-one, Sam was still scratching for a living. The depression that followed the panic of 1873 — one of the most severe and protracted in the nation's history — had tightened purses, and Sam's correspondence throughout 1875 constituted a Jeremiad of hard times. The party in power was not his party, he groaned; he had been "driven from the [Treasury] Department by rings and the ill-will of secretaries." He beseeched Barlow to find him gainful work. "If you know of any cotton or other cases now in the court of claims on which it is desirable to dismiss appeal, I can do miracles for a consideration — no cure no pay." When Ben Butler introduced a "blackmail" bill to punish a person who had refused to hire him to lobby a shaky fifty thousand dollar claim, a spirited attack against such iniquity was led by the "King of the Lobby."

"I can defeat it in the Senate," Sam wired the intended victim, "but time is as valuable as a hairdresser's on the day of a court ball." Forty-eight hours later he was able triumphantly to announce that he had "saved the bacon," adding that "the battle was won by Garfield and Blaine. The Speaker supped with me at 2 A.M. and I injected him with the right ideas." But this victory, when all accounts had been settled, not only brought Sam no tangible profit, — it left him two hundred and fifty dollars out of pocket.

One close friend who had helped in this tight scrimmage was James A. Garfield, a fellow Latinist and enthusiast of Horace; Garfield and James G. Blaine were the undisputed Republican leaders in the House. Notes passed between Sam and Garfield in a stream. "Come up to the Library and drink a glass of champagne and smoke a cigar," Sam would write, and Garfield would reply in Latin. Many such letters and telegrams were exchanged, some in code and dealing presumably with legislative questions, although no cryptographer has deciphered them yet.

Garfield figured in one of Sam's most striking feats as a "gastronomic pacificator," which was Sam's own description of his function. Garfield and another wartime political general and fellow Congressman — Robert Cumming Schenck of Ohio — had quarrelled to the point where they refused even to speak to each other. Both were influential Republicans, and the party deplored the breach. Sam invited the two men to dinner at E Street, telling neither that the other would be present. The enemies met in Sam's vestibule, glared, — then Sam made a well-timed entrance, beaming hospitably, took each by the arm and led them to the dining room. There a truce was imposed by good manners, and by the time the dessert arrived, differences had vanished in the foam of the wine, and the antagonists departed arm-in-arm. On occasions of importance, such as this, Sam made a practice of dining in advance on a simple mutton chop, a baked potato, and a glass of Burgundy, so that he would be free to devote himself to the comfort of his guests.

Later, when Schenck was appointed minister to Great Britain during the agitation over the *Alabama* claims, Sam brought together the new minister and William M. Evarts — who was to be the United States counsel in the arbitration hearings — for a briefing on the issues and personalities involved. Sam excelled as a "gastronomical explicator" as well.

Under all his sympathies and preoccupations, money embarrassments continued to harass Sam Ward that year of 1875. His letters to Barlow, a man of resources with whom he worked closely, were a mixture of affection and scouting for money, and of course they were replete with mentions of presents. In these letters S.L.M.B. had come to be saluted as "Sambo," "Sampayo," or "Sambolio," while the sender signed himself "Sambo," "Sambonio," or, oftenest of all, "Uncle Sam." Thus "Sampayo" might be alerted: "I took the liberty of sending you from Baltimore last night a pair of superb canvasbacks shot yesterday morning"; after which business affairs would be discussed with serio-comic cries for relief; and the letter would conclude: "Pray say to dear, dainty, sweet, and good Lady Alice [Mrs. Barlow] that the telescope was my New Year's offering to her. I am not making a dollar here and only hold on for patriotic motives, as a volunteer *cantinier* — the *père,* not the *fille du regiment.*"

Evarts thanked "Uncle Sam" for "the boys' knives — so fine Mrs. Evarts had been unwilling to expose them to a public school, and they are in chamois bags!" Again, "in regard to Max [a grandson], you know he runs to animals. If you want to send him a coop of live ducks it will please him."

Senator Thomas Francis Bayard, a high-principled, sweet-tempered man, third of his line to sit in the Senate for Delaware, acknowledged receiving "the shaded candlestick for my poor old eyes." And apropos of Sam's excruciating account of the demands made upon him for time, money, and energy: "I never thought you a 'financial pool of Bethesda,' nor do I suppose the fellows who troubled you were angels, but I laughed over your description of it." When saddened by the carnival of corruption in Washington, Bayard turned to Sam: "There are few to whom my society is not oppressive; but you — my many-sided friend — allow me to feel that I do not trouble you when I unpack my heart of words."

Friend or stranger, any applicant for help got what Sam could provide. He laid himself out to push a Peruvian guano claim in which "I have no earthly interest except to guide these bewildered people into the safe haven of your office," he told Barlow. He helped to engineer the selection of a reasonably honest receiver for a bankrupt railroad "to keep it out of the jaws of the sharks here, who would have made mincemeat thereof." He rescued "a blasted Britisher's $900,000 without his paying for it." And while shepherding around New York a visiting social lion and jovial admirer, Lord Houghton (the poet, Monckton Milnes), he reassured "Sampayo" that "I think you can nail Houghton for Monday evening. Hurlbert has taken the sulks at his accepting for Tuesday P.M. a reception at the Union League and has broken up the contemplated ovation for Monday at Delmonico's." Coincidentally he sighed: "Events advise me to refrain from jogging the sugar men for money at present. Love to all at Glen Cove. Your old Cove, Sambo."

So intermingled were his moods, in the midst of a complaint to Longo about hard times Sam could interject: "I sent you some of the Khedive's finest tobacco. If its caress inspires the true Nirvana I will steal some more for you . . . The session just closed was a failure as a harvest, and I have been obliged to grow root crops to keep the wolf from the door of the retainers. It is hard for a fashionable bootmaker to be compelled to take to cobbling, but I have the health and spirits of your old blacksmith . . . With Charley Sumner gone, the grace of public life has left this den of cut (the public) throats." He visited Cambridge, and on coming away wrote with tender feeling: "I hope you are mellowing gently. The bottle of Avignon was too troubled to be uncorked. It does not do to go to the confessional while your adversary's blow, or your mistress's kiss, is still moist upon hand or lip, and I thought it unjust to the papal grape to submit it to the critical test of my palate, without giving it time to recover its serenity." After three months of repose, the wine being serene again, a note came to Longo: "We drank your health in the Avignon wine. God bless you, my dear boy! Samilasso."

A further break in Sam's family circle occurred that summer, when Cousin Henry Hall Ward died. The pain of Henry's death was sharpened by a money disappointment and a severe humiliation to Sam's pride.

Cousin Henry's story had been decidedly odd. For thirty years he had paid court to the woman of his choice, Miss Élise Partridge, a cousin, who lived in Carroll Place, not far from Henry's home at 23 Bond Street. But his mother, Sam's Aunt Henry, had forbidden the marriage, and Henry had meekly submitted to his mother's domination. For thirty years he called every afternoon on Miss Partridge, remained an hour or so, then repaired to the New York Club, of which he was the president, and sought gentlemanly solace in the bottle. At seventy-six, Aunt Henry at last consented to expire, and the family believed that Henry and Élise would marry at once. But then Henry was stricken ill, and in August Sam told Longfellow: "Poor Cousin Henry is at Saratoga Springs adying. Life to me, without him, will be most lonely. I held him in my arms on the day of his birth, and counted on his reciprocating this act of cousinly affection by burying me."

Élise Partridge hurried from New York to nurse the dying man, and Sam told Dudie that he "became quite attached to her, and was so deeply touched by her devotion that I sent her a lovely tortoise-shell necklace, cross, and earrings." But Henry died.

When his will was opened, the family was startled to learn that he had left everything to his unofficial fiancée of three decades. "Everything" included not only Henry's house at 23 Bond Street, which was stocked with Ward family heirlooms, but also Sam's old home at number 32. As Sam explained to Julia: "You are aware that when Medora died, the house at 32 Bond Street reverted to me." To settle "some old Ward accounts — quite as much through their *ineptic* speculation as my own" — he had transferred title to that house to Cousin Henry. "I learn — *entre nous*, with some surprise — that Henry [in his will] does not mention me, his oldest and most unselfish friend. In his previous will he bequeathed me an annuity of $500, which was the interest of the $5000 left him, at my suggestion, by poor Marion. His leaving me out in the cold is a strange practical joke." What hurt most was the realization that still another member of his family had failed to show him devotion equal to his own.

Unexpected humiliation followed. Miss Partridge sent for him — at 23 Bond Street — and informed him that on his deathbed Henry had told her: "I leave Sam in your charge; whenever he needs money, supply his wants." She said she would write a check for whatever he might need immediately, and give him an order to draw so much a month thereafter. The thought of becoming a pensioner upon the charity of a woman who was not allied to him by either kinship or intimacy galled Sam, and he replied that "while I had brains and health I could take care of myself, and needing no money I could not accept any." But he was upset that Julia should suffer from this whimsy of Cousin Henry's, for now Sam's own will was valueless; he had no property and no prospect of acquiring any to bequeath to anybody. "You and I are approaching the Patriarchate," he told Dudie dolefully. "I have just seen mention in the papers of the death of our old minister, Bishop Eastburn." Doctor Eastburn had married Sam Ward and Emily Astor in 1838.

One by one the leaves were falling; but Sam clung still to the hope of eventual happiness with his daughter. Her affection he craved, yet despite his best endeavors, the frostiness in the Chanlers' household had never been entirely dissipated. Maddie was dutiful and considerate, but her large family (there were eleven children all told) absorbed her attention. The youngest baby she had christened Emily, and when that child died, Sam wrote wistfully to Julia: "Maddie has given me no token of her existence since little Emily's funeral. I hear confidentially that Chanler is ill. Poor Maddie. I might give her the few remaining years of my life, but for the hostility of her kin. This nervousness of her husband explains her strange behavior."

Chanler's "nervousness" was his apprehension that any partiality shown to his improvident father-in-law might antagonize the Astors, and with ten living children to provide for, and no fortune of his own, he felt he could risk nothing.

The letters Maddie wrote to her father from 1871 to 1875 Sam preserved jealously. They were not many, and most of them were acknowledgments of presents received, mere snippets of notes, reserved and kindly but not outgiving. With almost little-girl primness, she signed herself "Your loving Child," or "Your affectionate Child," and Sam was always "Dear Papa." The Chanler town house was at 192 Madison Avenue, and they had a villa at Newport, Cliff Lawn; she wrote from both places. "Dear Papa: I am doing well but not yet move about [sic]. Margaret is well. Her silver is marked and is lovely. Thanks for your handkerchiefs and the pretty card. Your loving Child." ("Margaret" was Margaret Livingston Chanler, a baby then; she would marry Richard Aldrich, for many years music critic of the *New York Times.*)

Penciled on the back of a calling card was a scribble from Chanler: "For Mr. Ward. Please let Maddie see you as soon as you can after your arrival. She has been very anxious about you. Hold yourself free to dine with us. You name the day."

In another note Maddie begged "dear Papa's" forgiveness for not having received him when he had called, "but just as you came, a lady came by *my appointment,* and I could not break off our interview." So Sam was turned away from the door. "Tomorrow I hope to open the *tempting* box you have sent," Maddie's apology continued, "for which I thank you heartily. Write and console your affectionate Child."

Thanks for gifts — this was the theme of most of the letters Sam received from his "Child." "Thank you, dearest Papa, most gratefully for your lovely birthday note. It is put away among my *personal* treasures . . ." "The poem is *lovely* — how pleasant to have inspired so affectionate and graceful an effusion! . . ." "The pears have not yet come . . ." "The cheeses are delicious! they arrived this morning in perfect order . . ." "I forgot to thank you for the lovely book you gave me — which is a perfect work of art! . . ." "I will be very happy to see you tomorrow at *half past five* o'clock — for we have our engagement at 8 o'c. . . ." And at Christmas time, a gift from Maddie: "What pleasant letters you sent me! I send you a little seal for your watch charm and have adapted your happy conceit of a *compass.* I hope you will find it useful, and I sincerely hope that *all* winds will blow good for you . . ."

The immaturity of some of these brief communications pained and baffled Sam, and when he was invited to Cliff Lawn occasionally in the summer he would turn his attention to the children; he would line them up in order of their ages and silently study them, seeking family traits, then suddenly would smile, rub his hands, and begin to amuse them. It was from Newport, on the eve of her father's projected departure for Europe, that Maddie wrote one of her warmest letters: "Now in regard to a dress for me — please don't bring me so costly a thing, for I really don't need one — and do pray *don't,* dearest Papa. My gloves must be 6 and 3 qrs. But oh I trust you won't go at all. Mr. Chanler and the children send their love to you and say Bon Voyage most heartily. May God bless and keep you, dearest Papa. Don't wear yourself out, but live more slowly for the sake of your loving Child."

Thus matters stood when, on the day before Thanksgiving Day, 1875, a major change occurred in Maddie Chanler's life. On that day the New York newspapers announced the death of "a noted citizen," William B. Astor, aged eighty-two. For years, "Midas" had trailed a care-worn figure, stooped under a burden of gloom, from home to office, where he balanced ledgers mechanically, — ledgers that always balanced. Mrs. Astor had died several years previously, and Sam Ward had not seen the old man for a long while. The press did its valiant best to discover some interest other than dollars in William B. Astor's life, and reported his stately funeral with unction. Near the head of the long file of carriages that followed the hearse to Trinity Cemetery, far uptown, in a bluster of sleet and rain, rode Mr. and Mrs. John Winthrop Chanler. (In the eleventh carriage were the deceased's three doctors; and in the fifteenth and last, placed behind the household servants, rode the staff of the Astor Library.)

The newspapers stated that "it is supposed that Mr. Astor leaves an undivided estate of one hundred million dollars." The will was opened on December 7 amid much public curiosity. The bulk of the Manhattan real estate had been left to the dead man's three sons, John Jacob III (as eldest, he received the largest portion), William B., and Henry Astor. Next after these, the relative remembered most liberally was Margaret Astor Chanler, "only surviving child of my deceased daughter, Emily Ward." Even in death Astor avoided naming excommunicated Samuel Ward.

In sum, Maddie was left an estimated five million dollars — the house at 192 Madison Avenue; Rokeby and its furnishings, with three hundred acres of land; improved property to the value of $175,000; the income of $375,000 held in trust; three houses and lots on Fifth Avenue at the corner of Thirty-fourth Street; improved real estate to the value of $40,000 to be selected; $30,000 in money; one-third of another sum of $50,000 — the tabulation went on and on.

It had been understood that Maddie proposed to "do something" for her father when she should gain control of her estate; as long as her grandfather lived, this had been forbidden. Now she was mistress of great wealth and she was independent; friends waited to see what she would do.

Maddie had come home from her grandfather's burial chilled and feverish, and Sam, after condoling with her briefly, had returned to Washington. The story goes that Maddie lost no time in putting her plan to help her necessitous father into effect, and with this in view sent for her attorney.

Two weeks passed. On December 13, Sam came back to his E Street house after a round of morning calls and found three telegrams. "Three black crows!" he mentally murmured, with a presentiment of evil. They were from New York, and informed him that his daughter was gravely ill . . . was feared dying . . . was dead. She had expired at six o'clock that morning, from pneumonia brought on by exposure at the Astor funeral.

Sam caught the first train and reached New York that evening. Even then business crowded upon his grief, and he posted to Barlow a report on the status of several claims on which he had been working: "Having before me three days of sorrow, I hasten, before the sad events in prospect shall unnerve me, to give you an account of my stewardship." The day after, from the Brevoort, came a further message: "Dear Sambo — Sorry I was not here to shake your hand yesterday, when I was stouter than I am today. Sorrow does not improve upon acquaintance."

Maddie's funeral was held two days later. After the services, in St. Mark's Church, Sam made the long, cold ride to the cemetery.

When Maddie's will was opened, it was found she had left her father an annuity of one thousand dollars — by Astor standards, about the bequest that might have been bestowed upon a faithful upstairs maid.

A tradition was handed down among Margaret Chanler's descendants that during the lifetime of her grandfather, who controlled her property absolutely, she had been prevented from making any will; and that when, in her last illness, the family lawyer arrived to consult about whatever arrangements she had in mind for Sam Ward, she was already so near death a document was hastily drawn up leaving everything to her children (the eldest of whom was only thirteen) and her husband.

The record does not bear out this version of the event. Margaret Astor Chanler's will had been executed on April 20, 1872, more than three years before her decease, and of course during the lifetime of her grandfather, who may have dictated some of its terms. The will had not been altered or amended in any way; there were no codicils. It did provide for her father, but in language that could hardly have been more wounding. The second clause directed that there should be paid "an annuity of One Thousand Dollars to my father, Samuel Ward, Esquire, the same to be paid to him in quarterly payments, commencing the first payment in six months after my decease, and to be paid so long as he shall be able to enjoy and receive the same without the interference of any creditor, receiver, assignee, or other person than himself, the same being intended solely for his own personal use and enjoyment during his life."

Except for a few token bequests, everything else was left to the husband and children.

This public pointing up of dun-ridden Sam Ward's waywardness with money furnished grist for spiteful talk, in print and out. The phrasing of the bequest, quite as much as its mediocrity, stung Sam, and he blamed the Astors, not his daughter, for the gratuitous slap. Harried as he was, he would have welcomed a substantial bequest from his daughter, both for itself and as evidence that he had conquered her love and confidence. Being cut off with a pittance, in what seemed to him a contemptuous manner, was a blow: generous to a fault himself, he had difficulty in condoning the want of generosity in others, and in the first flush of his resentment he spoke plainly. Some of his remarks were published. In consequence, Sam received a notification that henceforth the Chanler door would be closed to him.

This denial of access to his grandchildren he could scarcely credit. From the Brevoort he wrote to his son-in-law: "I have awaited your pleasure until now and have no doubt fretted very foolishly at not hearing from you. I have been yearning to see the children and resisting this longing out of apprehension lest my unexpected presence might interfere with something or somebody. All this, while you have probably been too much absorbed by sorrow to care to 'put yourself in the place' of one interdicted your house for reasons which now will probably remain forever unexplained. The *res angusta domi* compels me to return to Washington tonight," he concluded. "I can defy fate, as I have nothing left to lose. But I should be glad to take my leave of you and your dear motherless ones, even should inclination or policy decree that this shall be my last visit."

There was no meeting. From the moment of his wife's death, John Winthrop Chanler was haunted by dread lest his Protean father-in-law, by some unpredictable transformation — of which Chanler believed Sam Ward fully capable — should gain some control over Maddie's legacy, and then, *vogue la galere!* — goodbye to solid investments and slow but certain accruals. The possibility of this never entered Sam Ward's head, and it was never out of John Winthrop Chanler's.

To Longfellow Sam unpacked somber thoughts: "I am alone in the world. My old heart has been seared until it has lost nearly all its susceptibilities, but its isolation renders it more alive to the sorrows of the few remaining for me to love . . ." The years behind him and before looked bleak — "a lunar landscape, nothing remaining of the volcanoes but craters and fissures . . . Had I not been pulled hither and thither by the Furies and the Fates, I might have done something. But it is too late. Orestes, become gray and abandoned by his tormentors, is too restless for repose." Yet clinging still to affection, he closed, "I shall see you as usual Christmas morning," and signed, "Samilasso."

To Barlow went word: "I go to Washington tomorrow P.M. to renew my burrowing . . . I expect henceforth to paddle my own canoe harder than ever."

One year after Maddie's death, Sam tried to reopen communication with his estranged son-in-law, scratching out the draft of a letter that exposed his heartsickness.

"On this agonizing anniversary," he commenced, recasting every second phrase . . . "I have suppressed my craving to see your children . . . feared to be intrusive or I felt, when I last saw you, on the 18th December last year, that my presence might perhaps be a multiplication of your grief . . . I knew at the same time that you could not doubt my readiness to devote what remains of my life to yourself and your children . . . that, under this conviction, you would not hesitate to summon me . . ." All this was interlined and written over almost beyond legibility. He went on to assure Chanler that he had been "happy to hear from our new mayor-elect that he saw you in good health and brave spirits at Tammany Hall," and spoke of "the slough of despond" of politics. Regarding his own prospects, he said: "I am weary of ceaseless and unrequited labors for others. I don't complain, for I am not covetous, and ambition for wealth has long been eliminated from the equation of my life . . . while cramped as my means have been for two years past, I have had the comfort of relieving a good deal of distress. But age is stealing over me, and I foresee that I cannot live in this country and continue my charities. So I shall probably seek some quiet and economical residence abroad, where I can wind up my old age decently and philosophically on my meager allowance, satisfied to await the —"

The draft broke off here, as though discouragement had halted his pen. The useless letter was never sent.

SIX

"THE MENDACIOUS CLUB"

SAM WARD did not write Emerson's essay on "Compensation," he lived it. But the swings and counterswings of his career were not always consecutive or of equal duration: sometimes the arcs overlapped and blurred in a crosshatching of contrasting experiences. Out of the barren years of the war had come Sam's poems; and during the vicissitudes of the seventies — the public acclaim and the private sorrow — a kindly twist of fate brought one compensation that applied balm to his battered heart.

In 1875 a British peer, young, handsome, rich, and unattached, visited America, — the Earl of Rosebery. Although only twenty-six, and thus thirty-three years Sam's junior, Archibald Philip Primrose found complete compatibility in Sam Ward. His background, personality, and temperament were quite as extraordinary as Sam's own. At Eton, the future peer had distinguished himself by braininess and aversion to study, and a tutor there had tagged him with the phrase that would stick all his life, — describing the lad as one who, in the race of life, "would like the palm without the dust." However, the same tutor had credited him with "wonderful delicacy of mind, penetration, flexibility, capacity for friendship, — all but the tenacious resolution of one that is to be great . . . a born Latinist . . . original all day long . . . the wisest boy that ever lived, and full of fun, too . . . He will be, if not a poet, such a man as poets delight in."

At Oxford, Rosebery had applied himself to serious study even less, and after two years he had withdrawn rather than obey the order of the university authorities to divest himself of his small string of racehorses. The turf would be a lifelong enthusiasm of Rosebery's. Shortly after succeeding to his title (at the age of twenty-three) he had startled the House of Lords by a witty speech in defense of horse racing; to attempt to put down gambling by abolishing racetracks, he said airily, would be as ridiculous as to attempt to abolish rain by eliminating gutters. This cheeky performance by a peer who looked like a stripling and spoke with the assurance of a man gave a foretaste of that rather gay disregard for inherited opinions that would characterize Rosebery always.

This young man, remarkable in almost every way, accorded Sam Ward an admiration steadfast and unbounded, for in the old man the younger saw much that he would like to be. He immediately elected himself the foremost of "Uncle Sam's" many adoptive nephews. Of course the fascinating, high-spirited visitor was lionized in New York, where he found doors opening magically at a wave of the Wardian hand. And the convivialist who most perfectly matched Rosebery's penchant for persiflage was Sam Ward's particular and peculiar friend, William Henry Hurlbert, now editor-in-chief of the *World* and a New Yorker of consequence.

A British writer had described Hurlbert as "the most distinguished and visionary journalist in the United States, a man of immense but erratic information, a charming talker, — a little mad." The description was not amiss, and Rosebery encountered nowhere any subtler or more stimulating table companion than this egregious individualist. The three men — Sam Ward, Hurlbert, and Rosebery — were soon so firmly knit in compatibility they formed what they called the most exclusive club in the world, since its membership was limited to themselves. They named it the "Mendacious Club," and devised a rigmarole that made Sam the "President," Hurlbert the "Member," and Rosebery the "Sycophant." S. L. M. Barlow was honored with the title "Perpetual Candidate," although never admitted as a member, and occasionally some congenial spirit, like Lord Houghton, might be invited to attend the club's sessions (which always coincided with dinners), but only in the capacity of observer. It was reportedly at a session of the "Mendacious Club" that Rosebery made his famous boast, — that he would marry the richest heiress in England, win the Derby, and become prime minister. He made good on all counts, and won the Derby three times.

After a lively stay in the United States and Canada, during

which, with Sam Ward's help, he met celebrities from Longfellow to Ben Butler, Rosebery sailed for home, leaving a doggerel salute to "Uncle Sam" that found its way into the newspapers. The lines, widely quoted, went, in part:

Alas! my Samuel, when I think
I stand upon the ocean's brink,
The time is near, full is my cup,
The bouyant *Russia's* steam is up,
And I return, an unlicked cub,
Leaving the great "Mendacious Club";
Thy tales no more my mind shall fill,
And Hurlbert's brilliant voice be still! . . .

No more shalt thou approach my bed,
A bandit's hat upon thy head,
Beneath whose brim there beams an eye
That puts to shame the brilliant tie.
Beneath one arm a trout, alack!
The other holds a canvasback.
The pockets bulge with products rare, —
French novels, prints, and caviare,
Two manuscripts of odes and bets,
Old bills of fare and cigarettes,
Two thousand-dollar notes — ye gods!
Welcher's accounts, green pepper pods,
And pressing calls to various duties,
From railways, senators, and beauties.

And then, perhaps, thy bursting brain
Reveals its treasure-room again,
And recollections, lightly wove
With tales of horror or of love,
Carry the listener swiftly through
From Cochin-China to Peru;
And further yet, as in a trance,
From memory sprightly to romance,
He hears thee clothe the arid fact
And scorn the fools who are exact!

"King of the Lobby"—the Sam Ward of legend. Impeccable tailoring, jaunty tie, diamond stud, rose in buttonhole, massive, gleaming cranium, proudly lifted head, brilliantly twinkling eyes—the hallmarks of the "universal uncle." Photograph by Sarony of Boston in 1874. *Reproduced from an illustration in* Uncle Sam Ward and His Circle *by Maud Howe Elliott. The Macmillan Company, Publisher.*

Sam Ward's heiress daughter, Mrs. John Winthrop Chanler, in a portrait posed for fashion's photographer, Sarony, at New York, about 1874, one year before her death. *Rokeby Collection. Courtesy the late Mrs. Richard Aldrich.*

Rare snapshot of "Uncle Sam" in convivial company. On left, William Henry Hurlbert, editor of the *New York World* and a founder with Sam and Lord Rosebery of their three-man "Mendacious Club." On right, Lord Houghton (Monckton Milnes). The seated young man receiving Sam's mock blessing is not identified. The picture was taken during Houghton's visit to the United States in 1875. *Courtesy Mrs. Thomas Clark Howard.*

Sam Ward, the chef-lobbyist, cooks $1000-pigs' ears for Congressmen in this cartoon appearing in the New York *Daily Graphic* on December 20, 1876. Sam had just lectured the House Ways and Means Committee on the hazards of lobbying and the peculiar meal served to a king of Spain. *Reproduced from an illustration in* Oscar Wilde Discovers America *by Lloyd Lewis and Henry Justin Smith, Harcourt, Brace, and Company, Publisher.*

Sam Ward at sixty-eight, mentor of Oscar Wilde and "host of New York." Restored to wealth, he moved, it was said, with the dignity of a diplomat and the tread of a French marshal. Photograph by "Marc & Schlum, 14 & 16 West 14th St., N.Y.," about 1882. *Rokeby Collection. Courtesy the late Mrs. Richard Aldrich.*

Sam Ward, "uncle of the human race," depicted by the famous London caricaturist "Spy" in *Vanity Fair*, January 10, 1880. The rotund, bustling figure was as familiar in London social circles as in New York.

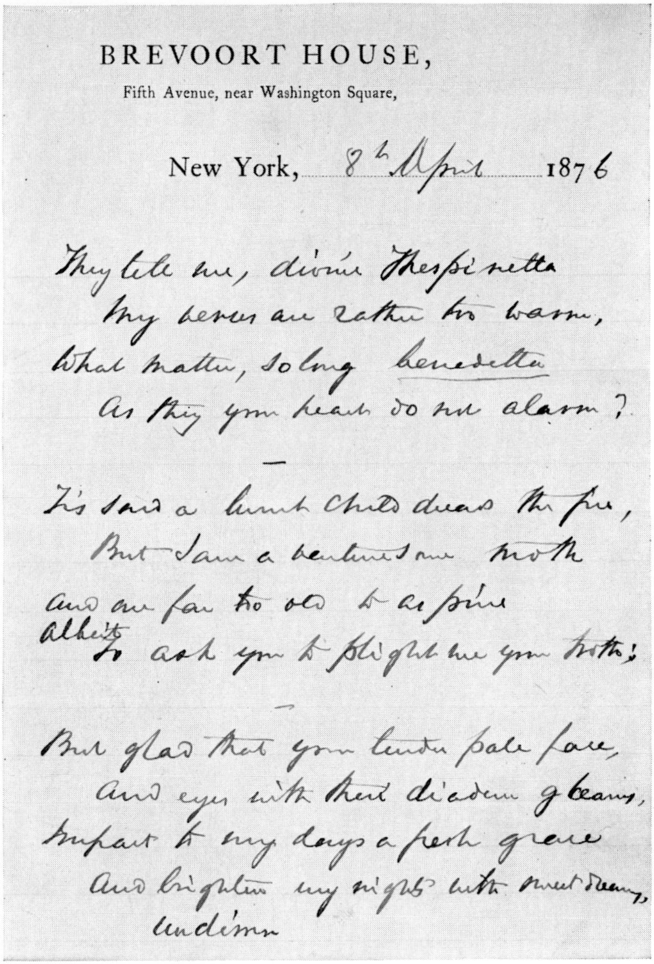

BREVOORT HOUSE,

Fifth Avenue, near Washington Square,

New York, 8th April 1876

They tell me, divine Thespinetta
My verses are rather too warm,
What matter, so long benedetta
As they your heart do not alarm?

—

'Tis said a burnt child dreads the fire,
But I am a venturesome moth
And am far too old to aspire
Albeit
To ask you to plight me your troth;

—

But glad that your tender pale face,
And eyes with their diadem gleams,
Impart to my days a fresh grace
And brighten my nights with sweet dreams,
undimm

("THESPINETTA" AUTOGRAPH POEM)

A specimen of "Uncle Sam's" impromptus, which he sent to pretty women with bouquets of appropriate size—to a young and pretty woman, a large bouquet; to one not so pretty, a larger; and to one who had suffered the double misfortune of losing both youth and loveliness, the largest bouquet of all. Interesting because it is written on a Brevoort House letterhead—doubtless the paper handiest—and because of the indecision about two lines, which is probably why this copy was never sent. Transcribed, it reads:

They tell me, divine Thespinetta,
My verses are rather too warm,
What matter so long, *benedetta,*
As they your heart do not alarm?

'Tis said a burnt child dreads the fire,
But I am a venturesome moth,
And am far too old to aspire
To ask you to plight me your troth;

But glad that your tender pale face,
And eyes with their diadem gleams,
Impart to my days a fresh grace,
And brighten my nights with sweet dreams.

José Villegas's painting (almost identical to one painted by his pupil, John Elliott), for which Sam Ward posed as model in Rome during the last winter of his life, 1884. The figure shows Sam idealized as a meditative, secretly amused sage. He wears the famous sapphire on his right hand. *Courtesy Lawrence Terry.*

Strikingly resemblant portrait bust of Sam Ward made in Rome in 1884, at the same time as the Villegas painting. The sculptor was the Spaniard, Mariano Benlliure y Gil. The bust shows Sam still hearty and debonair, his noble dome of baldness, flowing imperial, and eyes observant and friendly, set off by "laughter wrinkles." *Courtesy Mrs. Thomas Clark Howard. Photograph by John Hopf, Newport, Rhode Island.*

Samuel Ward's grave at Pegli, near Genoa, Italy, with the plain stone cross erected by his friends, Lord Rosebery and William Henry Hurlbert, and his nephew, F. Marion Crawford. Photographed seventy-eight years after Sam's death by one of his many great-great grandsons. *Courtesy Rear Admiral Hubert W. Chanler.*

He's borne aloft from Piccadilly
To California, willy-nilly;
He sees thee change, without a creak,
To banker, sportsman, or cazique.
He sees thee read with deep emotion
The burial service in mid-ocean,
Or play, with one hand on thy knife,
A ruined miner, for thy life.

By Tennyson or Longo sought,
Probing a jockey's inward thought,
Counselling statesmen on finesse,
Counselling ladies on their dress, —
A wit, a scholar, and a poet,
A rake we fear, a friend we know it;
It is the lion and the lamb,
And there's your portrait, Uncle Sam!

Some foolish fancy dims my eye,
As, for a time, I say "Good-bye!"

Counterbalancing the heart-lift given by this youthful ebullience there came another bereavement for Sam, when Julia's husband, Samuel Gridley Howe, died in January, 1876. Between Howe and Ward there had never been a strong community of affection, but this brother-in-law, once gone, Sam could think of only with kindliness. The fact was that both men had mellowed, — and Sam mellowed very easily. But their characters had remained basically antithetical. To Longfellow, so many years Howe's dear friend, Sam wrote in consoling sympathy, "We differed so widely upon public matters that I never knew how truly I loved him until told by my own tears." And to Maud Howe he spoke glowingly of her "preux Chevalier" father — "brave as a lion and tender as a woman, a noble heart applying a mighty will and a high intellect to mitigate the sufferings and relieve the infirmities of humanity."

The tie with Dudie was drawn closer with the passing of the only man she had loved more than her brother. "Memory transported me this morning to those old days in Bond Street, musical with youthful joys and warm with thoughtful aspirations, when Sumner and Chev were inseparable," he wrote her gently. "Now you and Longo and I are the only ones that remain, save for Annie and Louisa, of that happy period."

The political scene, meanwhile, had become almost insupportable to him. The Tilden-Hayes Presidential scandal filled him with alternate sadness and disgust; yet when it was settled, Sam drew comfort from President Hayes's selection of William M. Evarts as Secretary of State. This vindication of his friend rejoiced Sam, for Evarts had steadily opposed the Radical faction in his party. Barlow was told that Evarts "is happy and his family and [law] partners are wretched. He has at length the recognition so long craved in vain, and is even with Grant and Butler, who have ignored and humbled him."

With Evarts installed at the State Department, a new period of regular correspondence with a cabinet member opened for Sam Ward. But unlike those letters that had been sent for Seward's eye, Sam's communications now dealt with personal and business matters, such as the purveyance of wines and superintending stock transactions as Evarts's proxy. The secretary also utilized Sam's skill and eagerness diplomatically, dispatching him on confidential errands. One of these was to ascertain adroitly what Ferdinand de Lesseps was up to in his proposals for a canal across Panama. "I know no one who can make this inquiry more completely and with less ostentation than yourself," the secretary wrote. "Any expense you are put to, send me a memorandum of."

Evarts called on Sam liberally in regard to table fare, and many letters came to the Brevoort on "Department of State" stationery, conveying acknowledgments and requests like the following: "The sherry (two cases) arrived last evening, for which I am much obliged . . ." "The last cigars you sent me are better than the others, although all are fine . . ." "The cranberries came yesterday . . ." "I got your Latin telegram and was able to understand it . . ." "I have received two cases of wine from New York, but no advice whether from you or not . . ." "Please have the box of Beychevelle sent here by express . . ." And Evarts could turn a compliment in Sam's own vein, on occasion: "I received a basket of very nice peaches and pears from New York a few days ago without notice from whom. I suppose, as the peasants do, that all good gifts are from the King, that they come from you . . . Your good deeds always outrun your friends' desires."

In view of this mutuality of tastes and frankness, Sam's hopes revived for obtaining a regular diplomatic appointment. But, alas, he still was a Democrat, and politics supervened. No offer was made, and Sam neither would nor could demand.

Meanwhile, the *res angusta domi* was becoming acute, — rendered more so after the death, in 1877, of John Winthrop Chanler. Sam was saddened, despite Chanler's estrangement, and he told Barlow: "Pray say to dear Mrs. Barlow that I have been since Chanler's death and my demoralizing puzzle about those grandchildren as much out of spirits as the cellar of a teetotaller." A board of trustees was appointed to supervise the upbringing of the Chanler children, and these guardians voted to protect their charges from possible contamination by their wastrel grandsire: Sam was still shut out.

The Astors' obduracy Sam felt again when Chanler's will failed to mention him, and the executors construed that as authorization to discontinue Sam's annuity. Slight as the sum had been, this privation hurt, for again all Sam's money schemes were going awry. "I have been more busy than usual with dead horses this session," he moaned to Barlow. "Nothing has passed to serve my purpose, and everything has gone wrong politically."

To Maud Howe he described himself as "working against wind and tide in my old scow, to which the barnacles cling, and have hardly time for individual thought and feeling. I sometimes think of running away to recultivate my own acquaintance, and cancelling my charitable impulses to keep the crowd of suppliants, who absorb my time, sympathy, and 85% of all that I earn." But he could bravely thank Maud for her present, on his sixty-second birthday, of "a lovely flask . . . I shall not fill it with anything younger than myself." Appended to this acknowledgment was a remonstrance: a young lady, a friend of Maud's, had sent him "some exquisite flowers," and had cruelly "added a year to the number I mourn over. Hand her the enclosed lyrical reproaches." As he took on age, his gallantry was becoming more pronounced; his nieces were resigned to his proposing marriage to every young girl they introduced him to, even those who were plain.

Few who observed "Uncle Sam" flitting from London to Washington, to New York, to Paris, on errands unexplained and some of them perhaps inexplicable, could believe that he might be suffering from a chronic constriction of the purse. He moved with the air of a millionaire, if not with the substance, and he exercised the open-handedness of a Maecenas to the extent of his resources and beyond them. He seemed always provided with cash or credit sufficient to do the honors in splendid style for the stream of notables who knocked at his door. Many of these were sent by his irreverently affectionate disciple, Rosebery. "As pants the hart for cooling streams, so pants my heart for thee, O Samuel!" closed a spirited communication from "Thy fellow liar (but not on this occasion) — A. Rosebery."

Even the earl shared in Sam's largesse, and in bidding "Uncle" hurry back to England pledged that "I shall not touch one drop of the liquid gold you have so kindly sent me. It will be like producing a quart of my heart's blood when I bring out a bottle of *that* madeira. I boasted of it last week, when the Prince of Wales vaunted his. There was a look in his eye as if he expected me to pass it on to him. Let that look remain! No drop shall flow down a royal throat!" But Rosebery did part with two or three bottles to Gladstone, at a moment when both the "Grand Old Man" of the Liberals and Disraeli, the Conservative prime minister, were cultivating the young peer as a likely political recruit. Rosebery recommended the vintage to Gladstone as "specimens of possibly the only aristocracy that the United States deigns to recognize"; and wound up his report to Sam with, "My dear Uncle and eternal President, do let me have a photograph of you, and a good, long letter. My homage to the King! *Citizen R.*"

So conspicuous was the procession of titled Englishmen whom Sam piloted through the social mazes of Washington and New York, a suspicion arose in some quarters that the old man was maundering in the last throes of a violent attack of Anglophilia. More cynical observers deduced that "Uncle Sam" was using his noble visitors' prestige to push his own dubious enterprises. Neither supposition met the facts of the case. Sam Ward was a staunch American, although never a bigoted one. He was widely known and esteemed in London socially, and in addition Rosebery was diligently preaching the gospel of "Uncle Sam" in the highest circles there. At the time, there was much interest among the British aristocracy regarding America and things transatlantic, and it was inevitable that any of Rosebery's friends who might be contemplating a visit to the United States should be sent by the earl directly to his own mentor. Typical of many letters that were handed to Sam was the following gay salutation from his "Sycophant":

"When I am asked by the rising youth of this country to give them an introduction to the principal poetical, theological, and political celebrities of America, I invariably surprise them by giving them one simple note with your image and superscription upon it. When I am asked the reason of my giving only one letter, I reply that under your sombrero may be found an epitome of all the poetry, theology, and politics of America . . . Besides that, there are some sparks of geology, philosophy, facetiae, gastronomy, and philoprogenitiveness. You have studied in its native wilds that savage and ferocious animal, the mother-in-law. You have, moreover, moulded the millionaire, cauterized the courtesan, and probed the prig. Hail! Representative of the highest Culture! Allow me to present at your feet Captain George Algernon Percy of the Grenadier Guards, — nephew of the Duke of Northumberland. If you can instruct him in the way he should go, you will have gratified his contemporary at Eton and your affectionate disciple, A.R., Sycophant, M.C."

Needless to say, George Algernon Percy made the rounds from Sutherland's to Delmonico's, and was introduced to available heiresses.

A more artistic introduction was brought by Lord Ronald Gower, sculptor son of the Duke of Sutherland, who had been assured by Rosebery that to meet "Uncle Sam" was a liberal education. Gower found that it was. Dined and entertained to satiety, he was grateful, towards the end of his stay, for a day of relative inactivity passed with Sam at the Jerome Park racetrack. As the last race was going off, Sam remarked that Gower could not think of leaving the country without meeting Longfellow. Gower regretted that insufficient time remained, for his ship was to sail in two days and he had to pack. "Nothing simpler," said Sam. "We will leave New York tonight by the ten o'clock train, breakfast at my club in Boston tomorrow morning, drive over to Longfellow at Cambridge, catch the midnight train, be back in New York the next morning; and that will leave you time to pack up and start for England later that day."

That schedule was carried out, to the Englishman's astonishment. They dined at Delmonico's, slept in a Pullman on the way to Boston, breakfasted sumptuously at the Somerset Club on Beacon Street (Gower never forgot the quality and quantity of that breakfast), then drove across the river to Cambridge where they came upon Longfellow out walking with a daughter. The two old men embraced, and in Longfellow's study at Craigie House, surrounded by literary and historic relics, the visitor was treated to "as pleasant a conversation as I ever heard . . . Ward's flow of recollections and reminiscences was amazing, and Longfellow, although no great talker, proved himself to be a capital listener." The return trip was completed in plenty of time for Gower to board his steamer leisurely.

The Earl of Dunraven — a sporting Irishman whose *Valkyrie* challengers for the America's Cup were the yachting sensations of their day — found "dear old Sam Ward genial, quick, very sagacious — a *bon viveur* and a very staunch friend." Dunraven, an outdoors man, was headed for big game hunting in the Rockies, and Sam gave him a letter to that universal genius — geologist, mountaineer, author, wit, art connoisseur, hail fellow — Clarence King.

And on the other side of the Atlantic, Sam's hearty welcome among the exalted of the earth was not confined to England. In 1877 ex-President Grant started on a tour of the world, and in Rome he paid his respects to King Humbert. What was Grant's amazement when the king's first question was regarding his "dear friend, Sam Ward of New York. He is a man whose friendship is an honor," Humbert remarked, adding with evident eagerness that he hoped to entertain Sam that summer at one of his castles in Piedmont.

In London, so thoroughly "Pallmallmerized" had Sam become, *Vanity Fair* published his familiar bustling figure in a caricature by "Spy." The accompanying text boldly proclaimed Sam Ward the "protector of the English and uncle of the human race." Nothing could have been more pleasing to its subject than this editorial accolade. "According to the almanac, Mr. Ward may possibly be somewhere near sixty-five, but in health, energy, and spirits he is not more than three or four and twenty . . . If he has a fault, it is that there is no knowing at any moment precisely where to find him. A few days ago he was the honored guest, with Mr. Gladstone, at Dalmeny Park [Rosebery's Scottish residence]; now he is in Washington, having flown off at a moment's notice to extricate some friends from an old standing difficulty.

"There is no man alive who has performed such generous acts, or thought so lightly of them afterwards," the tribute went on. "The prince of good livers, a delightful companion, a ruffler in his day, a sound scholar, a thoughtful reader, a man of much experience, observation, and wisdom, he is yet seen at his best in some act of gentle kindness to the poor and afflicted. That it gives the means of doing such good work is one of the greatest merits of money in the eyes of Sam Ward. His very presence in a room is enough to put everybody in a good humor; his wit is ready, and his good nature so great that most Englishmen who have seen New York bring back from it, as one of the most pleasant of their reminiscences, the memory of Uncle Sam."

How Sam contrived to maintain his gadabout resplendency on resources as meager and chancy as his own, neither friends nor family could fathom; they were not privy to the stratagems to which he often was reduced. But friends feared for the collapse that seemed inevitable. Then, as had happened before in Sam's checkered existence, the right card turned up, his luck changed, and he was in the chips again. Not on a small scale, either: the bank balance he was able to maintain at J. P. Morgan and Company stood — in cash — around three-quarters of a million dollars.

Sam's acquaintances early heard of his good fortune. Evarts wrote heartily from Washington, where he was nearing the end of his term as Secretary of State: "I ought to have inferred that you had gone to Europe, or the North Pole, from your long and silent absence, but I have been pleased to hear that you are present, prosperous, and plethoric in purse, if not in power." From Rome, where she was spending a season with the Terrys, Julia wrote that "latest advices confirm that a wealthy Californian, in recognition of your great kindness and devotion, has settled upon you a certain modest but comfortable income. We all hailed this information with great joy."

What had happened made a story that went far back in Sam's past. During the fifties, in California, he had come upon a young man who was desperately ill, alone, and friendless. This man was James Robert Keene, a Liverpool Irishman who had emigrated to California at fifteen and had been knocking about, trying to earn a living at half a dozen occupations, without much success. Sam nursed the stranger back to health. It was the sort of Good Samaritan act he performed on a number of occasions, and for which he took little credit. After Sam had left the West, Keene struck his *métier,* — the most successful stock plunger ever seen in San Francisco. He became president of the San Francisco Stock Exchange and amassed a fortune of four million dollars.

In 1877 Keene wound up his affairs temporarily and with his wife headed for a long vacation in Europe. Thoroughbred racing was his hobby, and he looked forward to picking up a stable in Ireland and perhaps running the best of the lot in the United States.* At New York, he stopped over long enough to greet old friends, among them Sam Ward.

Keene was anxious to meet some of the noted plungers of Wall Street, especially Jay Gould, and Sam, who knew everybody in the financial and social worlds, introduced the pair. Immediately the itch to take a hand in the Wall Street game developed in Keene, and instead of going to Europe he undertook to master the intricate

* In time, Keene realized this ambition and assembled perhaps the most remarkable single racing stable in the history of the American turf. Colin, Sysonby ("the best horse that ever was or ever will be"), Foxhall, Domino, Cap and Bells, Hornpipe, Ballot, Voter, Spendthrift were a few of the thoroughbreds that carried Keene's "white, blue dots," to innumerable victories. Near Lexington, Kentucky, Keene established a noted stud farm; Keeneland racetrack stands on a portion of that land today.

complexities of the New York stock market. In twelve months he ran his four millions of capital up to thirteen millions. Wall Street had never seen anything to match this spectacular success, and it was observed that as Keene's daring combinations paid off, the prosperity of Sam Ward, his friend, mentor, and guide, seemed to grow proportionately.

Not all the comments passed upon this phenomenon were charitable. Henry Clews, a clever and rather spiteful little Englishman, who himself had achieved a considerable fortune as a stockjobber and was as gossipy as a cricket, drew conclusions not at all complimentary to Sam. In Clews's opinion, Sam Ward was a portly parasite on Keene's bounty. Ward, he sneered, had originally been "forced into prominence by his marriage to Miss Astor," and since then had been able to maintain his social reputation only in Europe, where presumably his antecedents were not known. Mr. Clews, however, thought he had penetrated the mystery of Sam's technique. "This celebrated society man," he sniffed, "recognized Keene's worth, and wherever Keene appeared it was safe to bet that Ward's shadow would soon be seen . . . Whether it was uptown or downtown, at Newport or in London, at the Derby or the Grand Prix, it was all the same, — where Keene was, there Ward soon appeared."

The truth of what had befallen Sam was fantastic but not at all mysterious. With James Robert Keene, it had long been observed, gratitude was not a word; yet Wall Street was agape at his liberality in every direction. Keene felt that he owed his life to Sam Ward. When Sam's Astor annuity was stopped, the stock plunger filled the vacancy (according, at least, to Henry Clews's well-founded belief) by creating a trust fund of gilt-edged securities, the income of which was to be paid to Sam for life. Clews heard reliably that the fund was fifty thousand dollars, and the income Sam received was three thousand dollars a year.

Keene went even further. Notoriously secretive in business transactions, he quietly earmarked for Sam Ward a block of railroad stock which he was manipulating, held it for the rise, sold at the right moment, and handed Sam the profit, — nearly a million dollars.

Once Rosebery had asked "Uncle Sam" jocularly: "What would you do, if Providence were to bestow upon you a third fortune, say of a million sterling, tomorrow?"

And Sam had replied without a moment's hesitation: "Why, appoint three trustees at once and have myself declared a lunatic; otherwise it would all be got out of me in a week."

SEVEN

THE FAIRY GRANDFATHER

WITH this dramatic alteration in his circumstances, Washington saw little of Sam Ward any more. The city had lost its last charm for him when John Welcher died, and while the widow continued the restaurant, the genius of its kitchen was gone. New York became Sam's headquarters, and from there he continued his ceaseless bustling, to the concern of his friends. Sam in the money was cause for deepening anxiety, in view of his scatteration habits. One of his best counselors, the banker, William Butler Duncan, suggested confidentially, on the strength of their twenty-year friendship: "Your generous soul is about as fit to be trusted with money as a child's. If you can't spend it yourself, you will give it away . . . Won't you let me act the part of a true friend, and salt some of it quietly away for a rainy day? No one need ever know of this but you and me." But Sam felt that he had been strengthened by long struggle, and he told Longfellow: "One good effect of my prosperity is that it has chastened me more than adversity ever did, and I feel the grave responsibility of one of the stewards of the Most High."

His outpouring of physical energy alarmed his circle quite as much, and when he suffered an accident and was bedridden for several weeks (a rare experience for him), Senator Bayard took him to task. "You dear old fellow! What an ugly, ripping fall you had! Don't you know that only *young* boys can fall, and that old boys must not?" At least, Bayard hoped, the tumble would compel Sam to think about "a certain person of three score years, with a fine big brain and a broad and tender heart, living a most feverish life, with no time for rest and recuperation — a bundle of odds and ends of hours, and *not one he could call his own* . . . You have now a substantial pecuniary independence. Pray tell me you are well."

Rosebery kept badgering "Uncle Sam" to hurry back to England, scoffing at proffered excuses: "I expected you July 20. I told Dunraven to expect you. We all expect you, and you put us off with Mendacious Club drivel!"

Sam was sincere in avowing to Longo his feeling that benevolent fate — Providence — some occult power — had caused the revolution in his affairs. For some time he had been studying Oriental mysticism, led to it by two intellectual discoveries made at about the same time — the *Rubáiyát* of Omar Khayyám, and Theosophy. The *Rubáiyát,* as transmuted in mellifluous quatrains by Edward FitzGerald, Sam had read in the first flush of its dawning upon literary England. The work had been pointed out to him by Lord Houghton, one of the coterie comprising Rossetti, Morris, and Swinburne, who pioneered the fame of FitzGerald's marvelous adaptation of the ancient Persian poet. Sam was captivated by the artistry of the poem, and even more by the uncanny way the lovely lines expressed his own hedonistic, fatalistic, tolerant beliefs.

A suspicion was germinated in his mind that, by some miracle of transmigration, he might in fact be a reincarnation of Khayyám. This was not a passing fancy: the similarities seemed too pat to be coincidental. Had not Omar been a mathematician? Had he not written an algebra, like Sam? Had he not experienced prosperity and penury, by turns? Had not his poems suffered disesteem in his own time? The longer Sam pondered these parallels, the more persuaded he became that he was more than merely akin to the philosophic tentmaker, — he was Omar Redividus. And the *Rubáiyát,* with its preachments to enjoy the blessings of life here and now, its sweetness streaked with melancholy, took its place with Sam's Horace as a pocket breviary, into which he dipped at spare moments for moral refreshment.

The new cult of Theosophy had drawn Sam's attention at about the same period. The Theosophical Society was launched by Helena Petrovna Blavatsky in New York in 1875, and for a while it had a vogue among the city's intellectual swells. Sam had been attracted to it by curiosity, but he read the society's publications and gradually became a convert to its essential teachings, — to the annoyance of his relatives. He was too old to become an "adept," he conceded, but he continued to give the creed his entire sympathy.

* * *

As a sign that he had indeed reformed and entered upon a settled mode of living, Sam gave up his basement quarters in the Brevoort House and took a permanent apartment at 85 Clinton Place, — a fashionable street (today West Eighth Street) just north of Washington Square. From there he wrote to Longo that he was "comfortably lodged for the first time in many years. I hardly know the faces of my books, after so many years of separation. I, who for forty-five years have been fighting not only the wild beasts of Ephesus, but fathers-in-law and mothers- and brothers-in-law, have been weaned from my vocation. After nearly half a century of the life of a galley slave, I have suddenly become quite independent."

Of these Clinton Place rooms of "Uncle Sam's," his nephew, Marion Crawford, left a graphic picture. One noticed first their odor of Russian cigarettes, which Sam smoked incessantly. The walls were covered with pictures wherever they were not covered with books, "and there was not an available nook or corner unfilled with scraps of bric-a-brac, photographs, odds and ends of reminiscences, and all manner of things characteristic of the occupant." The furniture was comfortable, but there was no display: between the windows a worn sofa, and in the center of the sitting room Sam's armchair and writing table. Everything in the rooms "was good, much of it was unique, and the whole harmonious. Rare editions were bound by famous binders."

Sam's deportment was energetic and animated. He chatted with visitors while tramping around the room, "leaving a trail of white smoke in his wake, like a locomotive . . . He wrote endless letters, and his correspondence was typical of himself, — the scholar, the wanderer, the diplomatist, and the priest of Buddha by turns, and sometimes all at once." Seated at the cluttered table he would dash off a poem, an invitation to dine, a book review for the *World,* or, if a letter of introduction were in question, a line addressed to almost anybody from the Czar of Russia to an ex-miner in California, — all equally friendly, respectfully familiar, and often amusing. "There, I think that will draw sparks," he would say. "Put that in your pocket and keep your powder dry."

But Sam was no stay-at-home. Periodically Europe still saw him — saw him more than ever, in fact — and in 1879 and '80 he romped through the famous Midlothian campaign in which Gladstone, who had retired once, staged a tumultuous and successful bid for re-election to Parliament, with Rosebery acting as his manager. Dalmeny Park, Rosebery's home near Edinburgh, was turned into Gladstone's headquarters, and Sam entered enthusiastically into the excitement.

The spacious house was presided over now by Rosebery's gracious wife, Hannah, whom he had married the previous year. The only child of Baron Mayer Amschel Rothschild, of the English branch of the banking dynasty, upon her parents' death she had inherited one of the largest fortunes in the kingdom. The marriage had been opposed by both Rosebery's relatives and the Jewish community, but it had been carried out with éclat, Disraeli, now Lord Beaconsfield, giving the bride away, and the Prince of Wales signing the register. "Uncle Sam" was delighted with the couple's evident happiness, and Lady Hannah declared herself an adopted niece on sight.

Just after Midlothian, Lord Ronald Gower, at Windsor, received a flying visit from "Uncle Sam," and found the old man "as perfect as ever, as full of pleasantry and stories as formerly, and, as he always is, overflowing with human kindness." Sam spoke enthusiastically of Gladstone's verve in the campaign, and delighted another visitor at Gower's cottage just then, young Oscar Wilde, who had brought along an Oxford friend, James Rennell Rodd; the latter aspired to be a poet, but was destined for a diplomatic career. Rodd became another of "Uncle Sam's" devotees on the spot.

Then in London, Sam turned his energies to pampering Mimoli Crawford. Mimoli now was the wife of Hugh Fraser, a British diplomat, and for four years they had been stationed in Peking. Returning home in 1879, Mimoli had come to London in search of advice by medical specialists, and found that her Uncle Sam had arranged everything. The Harley Street expert made his report, and then for two weeks Mimoli was royally entertained by Sam and "Uncle Do," Adolph Mailliard, who also happened to be in London, shopping for thoroughbred stock for James R. Keene. To Mimoli it seemed that Uncle Sam was the most sought after man in London, but he was never too busy to spoil her. Her uncles formed a contrast — Uncle Do tall, slim, white-bearded but handsome as ever, and quiet in manner; Uncle Sam short, thick-set, vivacious, "bubbling over with sociability," and frankly enchanted by the good time he was having. One day he was late for a luncheon appointment — a rare breach of social responsibility on his part — and came in five minutes behind time beaming. From under his coat he whisked a Camembert cheese. "Only one place in London where you can get the real thing," he crowed. "I've carried it all the way down Piccadilly." And to his niece: "I wonder if *you* would have the courage to do that?"

A pathetic reunion with one of Sam's granddaughters took place during this London visit. Young Elizabeth Chanler, Maddie's eldest daughter, was attending a school on the Isle of Wight. The child suffered from a "hip disease" (possibly a tubercular infection of the bone) which her guardians had been assured would prove fatal, and through Julia's intercession, permission was granted for Elizabeth to meet her grandfather in London, when she was taken there for a medical consultation. Both Sam and the guardians believed that she was dying.

In point of fact, Elizabeth would live for many years, and long afterward she set down the vivid impression her grandfather made upon her in 1879. He had arranged accommodations for her at ultra-respectable, gloomy Brown's Hotel, and after the Harley Street physician had paid his call, she was sitting listlessly in the sitting room of the suite, only mildly interested in meeting the grandfather whom she vaguely recalled having seen when she was quite tiny.

Then — "There was a knock at the door. Mr. Ward and Mr. Mailliard ('Uncle Do') were announced, and in they came. They looked to me incredibly old, one with a long white beard, the other — my grandfather — with a white mustache and imperial, above which glistened and gleamed the most brilliant eyes I have ever seen. They both remained standing, looking at me intently, asked a few polite questions, and presently said good-bye." The brevity of the visit did not surprise the child, for it seemed to fit into the general desolation of the hotel.

Half an hour later came another knock, and a messenger handed in a small parcel. Pills from the doctor, Elizabeth thought, and opened the package with little curiosity. "Beneath the paper lay a small purple velvet box, and inside the box was a ruby ring of such astounding beauty I could not believe it was for me. There must be some mistake; I was thirteen years old, and this was a woman's ring. But I was left in doubt only a minute, for another knock admitted the two old gentlemen again, come to see my pleasure. I hope I conveyed it properly, and I think I must have done so, for grandpa's eyes sparkled more brilliantly than ever, and though he and his companion hardly spoke a word and quickly withdrew, they left me with a sense of fairies in the air, and an earth capable of yielding magic happenings.

"I had hardly learned the beauties of the ring, flashing it back and forth to catch the gleam of its diamonds and gazing into the depths of its central ruby, when another knock at the door announced another parcel, this time a large one. I was beside myself with anticipation as I opened it. This grandfather knew how to give presents! And there it was — a grown-up traveling bag of beautiful shiny leather, lined with maroon watered silk, and fitted with all proper cut-glass bottles, capped with gilt.

"I think my excitement was even greater this time, for this second manifestation of his powers proved — definitely proved — my grandfather to be more than mortal. He and Uncle Adolph returned shortly to again inspect my pleasure, said hardly a word, twinkled, and disappeared. Two more presents came within half an hour, a wonderful camel's hair traveling rug rolled in its strap, and a great basket piled high with hothouse grapes and nectarines. My grandfather and uncle returned, after each gift had arrived, to see my joy, and departed as swiftly as they had come . . . That London visit was what I felt it to be, — a thing whose delicate roots shot back into fairyland, and whose very gifts drew their glory from the imaginative regions in which their giver lived."

Elizabeth was to see her grandfather once more, the next autumn, when she was lying ill at the Brevoort House in New York. He came for a few minutes, by special dispensation of the guardians, and his visit was followed by "a great basket of rare fruits, and plovers' eggs, and other dainties that he knew best of all living men how to provide. I never saw him after that." Elizabeth Chanler, granted these glimpses of her grandfather only because she was believed to be dying, recovered and became Mrs. John Jay Chapman. "The magic impression he made on me never faded," was her tribute to Sam Ward.

On Sam's return from England, he told Longfellow that he was still "quite dazed by the overwhelming kindness" he had encountered. "There is nothing more certain than that I have been the object of some supernatural intervention, — yet I sometimes think it is a mockery to be made rich just as I am going off the stage."

Now, at last, he could distribute presents on a scale commensurate with his imagination. In California, sister Annie had fallen in love with her home on the ten-thousand-acre San Geronimo ranch in Marin County, north of San Francisco, but Adolph Mailliard — who possessed not a scrap of business capacity — had mortgaged the place, and in disgust was talking about selling it and moving to Hawaii. Annie was despondent, until Sam, by a stroke of his pen, paid off the encumbrances and placed the property firmly in her name. Now she could live out her days among the California hills, as she desired.

Julia Howe's situation had grown more and more precarious. Chev had left nothing to her, all his property (there was little enough) having been willed to his daughters. She lived by her pen, and was hard put to make ends meet and provide for an increasing brood of nieces, nephews, and grandchildren, whose education she considered her special care. Lawton's Valley had been sold; her summer home now was a simple farm near Newport, called Oak Glen. While she was there, "Bro. Sam" surprised her with the present of a fine house on Beacon Street in Boston — number 241 — and all summer he shipped lamps, curtains, rugs, and other furnishings from New York, so that in the fall she could step into a completely furnished, commodious home of her own. There the "Old Bird" would spend the coming thirty years, through the loving generosity of "Samilasso."

Nor was Louisa neglected. Sam underwrote summers in Switzerland for her family, sent checks, and poured out advice and encouragement. The Terrys were feeling the pinch of hard times, for most of Louisa's property had vanished in the panic of '73 — thanks to rash speculations by Cousin Charley Ward, not Sam, this time. They had been compelled to give up their splendid apartment in the Palazzo Odescalchi and move into modest quarters in the Altemps Palace. (Marion Crawford was in India, editing a newspaper in Allahabad and studying Sanskrit; he was a born linguist like his uncle.) Daisy Terry, struggling with the uncertainties of youth, was studying the piano in Rome. Her teacher took her to see Liszt on his sixty-sixth birthday; they heard the aged abbé play, and afterwards Liszt walked Sam Ward's niece home.

In 1881 Louisa and Daisy were brought to America by Sam for a visit with relatives, east and west, and while they were in Boston Sam arranged a surprise. Secretly calling Annie Mailliard from California, he whisked her to Boston for Dudie's sixty-second birthday. Louisa almost fainted when Annie walked in, and Sam beamed while the three sisters chattered as if they were girls in Bond Street again. "The first time in twenty-five years we four have all been united," he glowed in a note to Barlow upon returning to New York. "I return thither in a day or two, and have great pleasure in sending you two fresh jars of Russian caviar."

Months after receiving his third fortune, Sam still had not certified himself a lunatic, and the well of prosperity seemed to run plentiful and clear. To cap his good fortune, on March 4, 1881, his "dear Garcampus," James A. Garfield, was inaugurated as the twentieth President of the United States. Of all Sam's political cronies, Garfield was the only one who really intended to utilize, by a major appointment, what was probably the best diplomatic talent at large.

EIGHT

THE GREATEST GASTRONOMER*

JUST as Sam Ward had been accorded the title "King of the Lobby," so, in the seventies and eighties, was he recognized as America's premier authority on all matters pertaining to food and wine. His principal renown, then and since, rests upon his eminence as a connoisseur of the *haute cuisine,* its preparation and service.

During more than a decade, when he was most active as a gastronomical panjandrum, his authority was absolute, never successfully disputed; although, as occurs in all instances, a few rivals felt that Sam's reputation was overblown. But jealousy among experts is an old story. And Sam Ward's beneficent influence upon the eating habits of the nation can hardly be exaggerated. Largely because of the impetus he provided, the American understanding of what is proper to put into a human stomach was revolutionized: from the horrified Frenchman's "country of fifty-two religions and one soup," the United States became a land where a civilized man could dine.

When Sam began to give dinners in Washington, the staple diet of the nation ranged from grits and sourbelly in the South to New England turkey and Indian pudding, while whole sections of the hinterland eked out life dyspeptically with a frying pan. Even that postwar phenomenon, the new millionaire and his socially pushing wife, had no clear notion of artistic dining. A New York hostess ordered her dinners sent in from a caterer or bakeshop, and menus plodded along in the unfussy, substantial ruts worn by generations of feeders. Then came a curious combination of three personalities

* This chapter, dealing exclusively with Sam Ward in his aspect as a host and gastronomer, is an interpolation in the story of his life. While it may interest those who have a leaning towards this specialized field — since it contains much material taken from unpublished sources — readers not so inclined may safely turn to Chapter Nine, where the narrative is resumed.

— Sam Ward, his cousin Ward McAllister, and *the* Mrs. Astor, Sam's stiff-necked sister-in-law by marriage, who never gave him a nod of recognition — and society's dinner tables were transformed into sophisticated triumphs of gourmandizing. The vogue starting among the upper crust percolated down through successively lower echelons of the social scale, and in time respect for the highest culinary art was won.

A glance at Mrs. Astor is germane. Although she never vaunted herself upon possessing a delicate palate, she was, in her heyday, society's most powerful arbiter of taste; her fiat determined the fashion in entertaining. Born Caroline Schermerhorn and married to William B. Astor II, she had embarked, after the Civil War, upon a planned career of ruthless social domination that ultimately enshrined her in American mythology. Although she was the wife of only the second of William B. Astor's sons, and hence outranked by the wife of John Jacob Astor III, Caroline Schermerhorn Astor beat down all opposition, decreed her own rules of precedence, and emerged as *the* Mrs. Astor, without qualifier or adulteration.

During most of her august reign, her obsequious majordomo was Ward McAllister, a snob of snobs, bemused by the pomps and rituals of society. In her behalf Ward McAllister coined the phrase "The Four Hundred" to designate the fortunate few whom Mrs. Astor condescended to receive at her balls and soirées. Ward McAllister was fastidious about food, and under his leadership elegant feasting became an essential element of social prestige. In 1890 he could look back to a scant twenty years before when not one fashionable household in New York had maintained its own chef; whereas by 1890 a *cordon bleu* had become a *sine qua non* if one hoped to survive in society. Yet Ward McAllister was proud to boast that everything he knew about the arts of the table and the cellar he had learned from his "distinguished cousin," Sam Ward; he could offer no higher credentials.

Sam cared nothing for the social values of his quite undistinguished cousin. One day the two men were driving up Fifth Avenue and passed Mrs. Astor's brownstone palace at Thirty-fourth Street. "Why do you like to frequent that house?" inquired Sam. "Because," drawled the Autocrat of the Drawing Room, "I meet the best people there." Sam was merely amused; he felt no deprivation by his exclusion, and was wholly untroubled by "Aunt Lina's" frown.

Dining, to Sam Ward, was more than a palatal exhilaration or mere exploration of suave flavors and tantalizing aromas. One of his more discerning admirers evolved the axiom: "There are two ways of dining — dining with Uncle Sam and dining without him." And its corollary: "For those who have dined with him, all other arrangements are an empty sham." For Sam Ward was more than a gourmet: he was that higher and rarer manifestation, a gastronomer.

The gastronomer excels the gourmet as the gourmet excels the cook. Antonin Carême, most illustrious of French cooks, was learned in the chemistry of foods, yet he survives principally as a text for specialists and antiquarians. But Jean Anthelme Brillat-Savarin, inferior by far to Carême in the technical mastery of cooking, continues to expound to generation after generation the whole gospel of gastronomy, — its philosophy, its utility, its mysticism, and its most subtle delights. A roving, well furnished mind, social assurance, much wisdom, fine manners, tact, innate cheerfulness and sparkling table talk — these go to make up a gastronomer, along with an educated and exquisite discrimination in taste. And in all these qualities Sam Ward abounded. He gave his guests and fellow diners articulate, intellectual nourishment with the varied and superbly served creations that emanated under his direction from the kitchen.

In the composition of dishes, he preached and observed moderation, order, harmony, his taste, like his mentality, being broad in scope, but rational, balanced, and sane in expression. Although he had sampled skunk and other repellent curiosities, he reprehended overrefinement and degeneracy of taste, such as the preference for ultra high, that is, semi-putrid, meats. Such indulgences can be cultivated and intensified, but they are essentially morbid, indicative of the breaking down of healthy standards, the abandonment of median pleasures, and the rejection of gustatory limits. Great gastronomers have always been open-minded but inherently conservative.

* * *

According to Sam, the preparation of a dinner must begin with the marketing; the ingredients must be of the choicest quality, and a host should attend to this matter himself. Siro Delmonico, of the famous family, did his own marketing every day, and Sam wrote poems to Siro Delmonico. The next step was to *compose* the menu, and this should be done in consultation with the cook. Ward McAllister reported Sam's practice. First, the chef should be brought to "fever heat by working on his ambition and vanity. Impress upon him that this particular dinner will give him fame and lead to fortune." At this point — according to McAllister — Sam would "bury his head in his hands and (seemingly to the chef) rack his brain, seeking inspiration, fearing lest the fatal mistake should occur of letting two white or two brown sauces follow each other in succession, or truffles appear twice in the dinner. The distress his countenance wore as he repeatedly looked up at the chef, as if for advice and assistance, would have its intended effect on the culinary artist, and *his* brain would at once act in sympathy."

Nor, once the dinner was achieved, should the chef be stinted of praise and criticism. "Above all things, you must know how to criticize," McAllister enjoined. "No French cook will take any interest in his work unless he receives praise and criticism. If he finds you are able to appreciate his work when good, and condemn it when bad, he improves, and gives you something of value."

In his own writings Sam Ward laid down the broad rules that should govern the organization and presentation of a dinner of merit. In the first place, "the host must feel that for the nonce he is Aladdin served by the genii of the lamp, in his own palace." Next: "The menu is the plan of campaign, dependent upon the numbers of the enemy who will be reduced to capitulation by the projected banquet. The host will inspect it and suggest changes, often an abridgment, but if wise, rarely an enlargement. People who have come into an unexpected fortune, or have stolen a railroad, may take needless pride in exuberant, costly, and ostentatious plenteousness. But the elect require an early inspection of the plan, and ponder thoughtfully the affinities of its details, the harmony of the ensemble, and the selection and distribution of the wines, which may be likened to the application of algebra to geometry. The whole should be suitable to the prevailing season, and last, not least, to the temperaments of the guests."

Sam took pride in his menus. Many of these he filed away, with a methodicity unusual in him, in a folder labeled: "*Menus of a few of the dinners wherein the Honbl. Samuel Ward took part — or partook of, as you like it.*" The menu cards were elaborate. The card for a banquet at the Union Club on St. Patrick's day, 1877, for example, was decorated with a water color from Tiffany's studios. Another, for a dinner given on June 14, 1879, at Pinard's restaurant, by the eminent New York attorney, Charles O'Conor, in honor of Chief Justice Morrison R. Waite, was printed on gilt-edged parchment embellished with a songbird in feathers. Sam planned this affair and sat at the speakers' table with such worthies as Joseph Choate, S. L. M. Barlow, August Belmont, Samuel J. Tilden, James R. Keene, and William Waldorf Astor (Sam's nephew by marriage). Secretary of State Evarts, regretting that he had been detained in Washington, the next day congratulated Sam upon a "magnum opus," as reported in the *New York World*. This menu, which Sam contemplated with pride, merited the secretary's encomium by reason of its happy adaptation of the classical rules to American tastes and materials, in part. It read, and the meal was marched through, course by course and vintage by vintage, as follows:

Little Neck clams
Montrachet

Potage tortue vert à l'anglaise
Potage crême d'artichauts
Amontillado

White-bait Filets de bass, sauce crevettes
Rauenthaler
Concombres

Timbales à la milanaise

Filet de boeuf au madère

Pommery sec
Selle d'agneau de Central Park, sauce menthe
Moët et Chandon Grand Crémant Imperial, Magnums
Petits pois   Tomates   Pommes croquettes

Côtelettes de ris de veau à la parisienne
Cèpes à la bordelaise

Asperge froide en mayonnaise

Sorbet au marasquin

Pluvier rôti au cresson
Château Margaux
Salade de laitue

Fromage varié
Old Madeiras, Charleston and Savannah
Bombe de glace   Fraises   Pêches   Gâteaux
Raisins de serre
Café
Cognac et liqueurs

Menu cards for less formal dinners Sam sometimes wrote in his own hand. Here is one for a dinner, undated, in Sam's minute penmanship, written on the back of a card bearing a pen-and-ink drawing of a brace of casks labeled "The King":

Menu

Huîtres
Potage
Sheepshead Hollandaise
Salade de concombres
Pommes de terre de Bermuda
Agneau de printemps
Champignons
Riz de veau à la sauce tomate

Croquette de volaille
Choux-fleurs
Sorbet au kirsch
Canvasback duck, gelée de groseille
Salade de laitue
Fromage de Camembert et de Rockfort [sic]
Pousse aux macarrons [sic]
De la glace
Fruits

Vins

Xeres Amontillado	Château La Rose
Scharluckberger	Pomeret [sic]
Bauenschalerberg	Clos de Vougeot

Another menu, written by Sam on a card gay with a tinted picture of eighteenth century children inspecting sweetmeats on a table:

Menu

Soups — Clear Green Turtle
Consommé à la royale
Fish — Chicken halibut à la Parisienne
Cusk à la crème
Petits pâtés à la Beacham
Ravioli
Braised stuffed capon
Roast saddle of mutton
Quenelles of grouse en belle vue
Sweetbreads in baskets
Artichaux farcies
Roman punch
Canvasback ducks
Walnut pudding
Soufflé de chocolat
Ice cream
Fruits
Coffee

The accompanying wines: Château d'Yquem 1868, Johannisberger, two sherries, Château Mouton 1858 and Château Lafite 1858, Veuve Cliquot for champagne, and three Madeiras, Gordon Duff 1818, Phelps Raye 1828, and June Packer 1823.

Professional chefs were respectful of Sam Ward's inventions. At the Souper of the Société Culinaire Philanthropique, held in the Academy of Music on February 5, 1878, Sam was given star billing. This charitable affair — not a dinner but an elaborate buffet — brought out creations by member chefs, each attempting to outdo his colleagues in novelty and richness of fancy. Under the heading, *Service Froid, Grosses, Pièces,* was Sam's principal entry — "Gourmandises à la Sam Ward sur Temple de la Liberté." There were twenty-five entries competing in this category, some of the others being "Hercule Portant la Terre," "Cirque d'Apollon," and "Bacchus et le Vin." Among the nineteen *Entrées* submitted were "Langue de Buffalo à l'Indienne" and "Quartier d'Ours à l'Oncle Sam."

In wine, Sam Ward's taste was exceedingly refined. He leaned somewhat towards the choicer Rhine wines — Rauenthaler, Scharzhofberger, and the peerless Metternich Schloss Johannisberger — and towards the more princely clarets — Lafite, Latour, Margaux, La Rose. However, Romanée Conti, Clos de Vougeot, and other top-notch Burgundies were given their full due on menus of his composing. As between the two classifications — the growths of Bordeaux and Burgundy — Sam perhaps found the Bordeaux more compatible: were they not, in their supreme qualities, virtual liquefactions of himself? The wine of Bordeaux — "at once rich and discreet, noble and smooth, simple and generous, not too grand in its seigneurial splendor to adapt itself to all tastes and savors, without losing anything of its lordly character" — was not this the personality of Sam Ward himself? The glorious vintages of Burgundy after all can be "as overwhelming as the company of the great"; but the subtle pressings of Bordeaux, like Sam, may be said to possess "the finest virtue of nobility, which is simplicity."

To behold Sam Ward enjoying wine was an arresting spectacle. Captain Keyes had early decided that "when Sam holds up a glass of old wine to the light and looks through it, the glow of his countenance makes all others look dismal by comparison." A writer for the *New York Tribune* recorded the step-by-step process — "the keen eye upon the claret to see that he wrought no harm to the precious fluid as he let it flow from one crystal to another; the delicate adjustment of finger and thumb to glass; the poise of the glass as he lifted it; the delicious contentment that spread over his features if both senses were satisfied; the appeal to his friends hard by to share in the delight; and the graceful invisible line in the air as he set it down."

The ritual varied with the time, place, and mood, for Sam was many hosts in one. He could sparkle with "a wit and grace that are to modern table-talk what a rare flagon of old Madeira, crusted with years, but brimming with the imperishable strength and perfume of eternal youth, might be to a gaudily ticketed bottle of machine-made champagne, effervescent, cheap, and nasty." This was the comment of one connoisseur. Should young people be present, Sam's glance would comprehend them benignly, for he turned naturally towards the freshness of youth. Or some older guest might evoke a memory out of the dead years, and Sam would silently take up his glass, hold it a moment to the light, carry it to his lips, and drink slowly, slowly, to the last drop; and the company would sense that it was a toast he drank, but to whom or what no one knew. Recovering, he would pick up the flow of conversation and dispense rapid obiter dicta upon cooks and epicures, all his remarks seasoned with erudition and drollery.

Conversation, and education in eating, Sam insisted, were elemental to a proper feast. A dinner, to him, should be a symposium, and a symposium was possible only among congenial spirits thoroughly grounded in the subject at hand. This required training. "It is only to the mental ear of the artist that a page of Mozart or Beethoven conveys its meaning," he illustrated. "No less difficult is it to convey to the average reader an adequate idea of the melting realities of a symposium. It is with the succession of courses as with the sparkling wit that enlivens the repast. The airy nothings, the *mots,* the repartees and spontaneous flashes of wit and humor that crackle like so many electric sparks, are as unrecoverable as the lost patterns of a kaleidoscope."

To conduce this perfect conviviality, as gratifying to the brain as to the tongue, the guests bring to the feast education, discernment, concentration, and good will; while the host, as gastronomer, must bring much more, — mastery of his subject, and the skill to present it without creating tedium. Just as the real length of a book consists not in the number of its pages, but in its ability or failure to sustain interest, so no repast can be too long that never abuts in satiety, the murderer of appetite. To stimulate and sustain appetite and attention, the gastronomer can employ supplements to the mere fare, namely, the company, surroundings, and conversation, and thus aerate and enliven a banquet with wit, charm, and trenchancy. To *enliven* — to infuse with life — is the definition of the role of divine alimentation.

The symposium, said Sam, is "the most civilized evidence of human refinement. Man the animal, struggling for existence, is more or less akin to the beast of prey. When he asks his brother or his companion to share his meal, he is at his first remove from the selfishness of instinct. The law of the strongest prevails among the brute creation. Ambition, love, avarice, all also are pure egotism. But the table, when shared with others, humanizes the purveyor, and develops and sustains innocent and unselfish motives."

This was his philosophy, profoundly felt.

To bring about the stimulating fusion of sense and spirit, conversation was indispensable, and Sam at times prepared his conversational effects the better to heighten his guests' enjoyment. This led some former trencher companions, turned sour and censorious, to insinuate that Sam Ward dealt in calculated portentousness, — witness his calling stewpans *alembics,* a carving knife a *bistoury,* a serving fork a *trident,* a spit a *wand.* But Sam Ward had more than one word at his command, and he liked to dramatize.

Some of the verbal garnishings he strewed upon his entrées were published in the *World* under the heading "Uncle Sam's Culinary Rhymes." ("To roast spring chickens is to spoil 'em, / Just split 'em up the back and broil 'em.") But when editor Hurlbert doctored Sam's limping meters, the author was nettled and thereafter kept his prandial effusions to himself, neatly assembled in a folder marked "Convivial Philosophy." Here are samples:

Seated at the festive table,
Eat no more than you are able.
But between the courses fair
Breathe to Evoë a prayer.

After you have swallowed soup,
Take of sherry one light stoup.

Father Bacchus, what we draw
From the bin we owe to Noah,
Noah, who first pressed the wine
Which thy worship makes divine.

The editorial pencil never hovered over these.

Like every conservator of wisdom, Sam dealt in aphorisms:

"No cook preserves his freshness of fancy and ingenuity of device more than two years. The fire uses them up and they become *routiniers, industriels,* et *non plus artistes.*"

"The great difficulty with cooks as with soldiers is their endurance under the *baptême du feu.*"

"A man may evolve a new religion from his inner consciousness, but not a new dinner."

"If any doubt exists in the mind of an intelligent man as to the salutary effect of a well cooked dinner, let him try a bad one."

His lore of gastronomy was immense. "The Greeks had sixty-two kinds of bread," he could point out, "and the Viennese baker at the Centennial Exposition [1876] gave us only three!"

"The Roman senators peeled their mushrooms with amber-handled knives in order to enjoy the emanation of their first aroma."

"In ancient French stories the peacock is styled a noble dish and its meat a proper food for kings and knights. It was not put on the table by the servants, but by the ladies themselves. I had one, at old Mr. Baum's in Mexico."

Sam was grateful that what he phrased as the "supposed hostility of Neptune to the Bacchus of Burgundy" had been disproved before his time. A Dijon merchant, he recounted, had sent around the world, in a ship that carried a French scientific mission to the

South Seas to observe the transit of Venus in the eighteenth century, several cases of his finest vintages. "When time enough had elapsed for their repose after their return, they were opened and compared with the stay-at-homes upon the shelves from which they had been taken. In every instance they were found to have improved remarkably in bouquet, savor, and tone."

Both his correspondence and conversation were larded with the vocabulary of gastronomics. Had he not pointed out to Seward the menacing cloud upon the horizon "no larger than a soup plate?" And once he assured his niece, Daisy Terry, "You and I together would make a lovely ham, — I the fat, and you the pink flesh."

The art of the cook Sam equated with that of any other ephemeral artist, such as the musician, the actor, the orator; but a cook's prerogative he rated much higher. A master chef, he said, "besides being the subtlest of natural chemists, should possess the method of a geometer, the symmetry of an architect, the harmony of a composer, the plastic sense of a sculptor, and the dexterous and tender fingers of a florist. He may aspire to be the highest of ephemeral artists, above the actor, the soloist, and the dancer, whose spell only endures, like the intensity of the Leyden jar, with their power to charm the public. Roscius may hold forth to a listless audience, Paganini may play to an unechoing throng, and Taglioni dance to a parterre grown critical, — while the leader of the culinary orchestra holds his congregation at his mercy. Imponderable thirst and impalpable hunger are his *claquers*, and his conscientious performances — always dress rehearsals if not first performances — are pre-assured of a *succès d'estime*, if not a crown of triumph. And this day after day — including Sundays — with varied but constantly recurring satisfactions denied to the concert room, the platform, the stage, the rostrum, and even the pulpit.

"You may quarrel with your tailor or your bootmaker, your upholsterer or your plumber," Sam stressed, "but never with the cook upon whose wits and pleasure depends that material *bien être* so indispensable to your moral and mental equilibrium. The contest is too unequal, and was so regarded by Eastern potentates, who, as well as cardinals in the days of the Borgias, had 'tasters' for every dish. In those days the results of culinary treachery were as rapid as nitroglycerine. Besides dyspepsia, a musty omelette, an overdone chop, or a negligently or maliciously confected hash at breakfast may clog the brain of the advocate, dim the perceptions of the physician, and reverse the tide of a man's fortune."

Cooks, being artists, Sam held, had moments of inspiration when they surpassed themselves, and the occasions when he had shared in such summital moments were treasured in his memory. "I remember unforgettably a *timbale de macaroni* at the Ashburton dinner which has never been equalled for my palate. Also, a saddle of venison with sauerkraut at a German society dinner, which, like Rubini's trill, has never been repeated. Then there was a *pâté de foie gras de canard de Toulouse*—the lid was never lifted while it was simmering."

If Sam Ward had a fault, his friends sometimes were tempted to say, it was the assumption of omniscience. Certainly his memory was prodigious, and upon occasion his information seemed encyclopedic. During a dinner at Washington, a disagreement arose over the number of Shakespeare's plays. Sam was appealed to; he volunteered to name them. One guest bet a bottle of champagne he could not, a second guest doubled the wager, and so on until a hamper of Veuve Cliquot was at stake. Calmly Sam called off the list, missed not a title, claimed the stakes, and had the wine drunk on the spot, while regaling the company with the history of champagne,—from the times when the name was given to a fruity red still wine down to the changeover to the white, sparkling vintage of modern times. Champagne, so designated, he related, made its public debut in the fourteenth century, "at a banquet offered at Rheims by Charles VI of France to Wenceslas, King of Bohemia and Rome, who came with a great retinue to negotiate a treaty. They sat down at table on the third of May, 1397, and kept up the festivity until the first of April ensuing,—with but few of those sober intervals upon which Father Matthews could have bestowed a *gratias*." Father Matthews was a crusading temperance advocate.

"The present exhaustive and economic cuisine of France only dates back one hundred years and is unlike the prodigal dietary of Rabelais," he went on. "It is the ingenious resultant of the thrifty forces of not more than four generations. Boulanger, the archetype of all restaurateurs, created the earliest of Parisian restaurants in the Rue Bailleul, and hung over its portal the semi-scriptural device —

"*Venite ad me omnes qui stomacho laboratis et ego restaurabo vos . . .*"

Gastronomical anecdotes "Uncle Sam" had for every occasion. He told of the country curate invited to a Lord Mayor's banquet at the Mansion House in London, who "did such justice to the hearty fare that an alderman, sitting nearby, was moved to beseech, 'My dear sir, let me entreat you not to waste that noble appetite on boiled mutton and turnips!' "

Gloomy reflections seldom were allowed to ruffle Sam's ease at table. Sir Samuel Romilly, the law reformer and epicure, being mentioned, Sam recalled that Romilly's son had once sent his father a brace of canvasbacks, which arrived in such prime condition that a year later Romilly exclaimed: "I shall never forget those canvasbacks; they did not seem ducks, but rather wingéd peaches!"

If old age were the topic, he cited Fontenelle, France's "popular science" writer in the seventeenth century, who lived to be one hundred and of whom his contemporaries said that he had a brain where his heart ought to be. "Which," Sam thought, "must have been a tolerably just criticism, — when Frenchmen found fault with egotism." Fontenelle shared his daily table with an aged contemporary, he recounted. "They differed enough on literary, scientific, and social topics to make their intercourse mutually agreeable. But when the Paris Halles [provision markets] entered the Zodiac of Asparagus, an annual controversy arose as to its preparation for the table.

"Fontenelle maintained that the attractive esculent ought to be served cold with an oil and vinegar dressing, while his *commensal* preferred it hot with melted butter. One day in May, at the height of the season, Fontenelle, going to the door of his apartment at sharp six to open it for his ever punctual friend, saw the latter at the foot of the stairway writhing in an attack of *apoplexie foudroyante.* His level head grasped the situation at once. He rushed to the kitchen and shouted to the cook, 'Toutes à l'huile aujourd'hui! [All with oil today],' and then went to the assistance of his poor messmate, upon whom the most prodigal attentions were lost.

"Ingenuity might readily find a defense for this apparent deadly egotism," Sam would suggest. "Fontenelle saw a dark sorrow, lowering not for a passing moment but destined to begloom the remnant of his days, and in self-defense made sure of the only consolation within his reach, — the way a lady takes salts, or my mother-in-law hot . . . well, never mind that. Fontenelle had a theory of life, that it might be prolonged far beyond the tables of mortality. He therefore considered his existence as an expanding Q.E.D. of this proposition, and felt bound to lose no pawn in this gambit with dissolution. The incident seems as natural as it is indubitably true. Fontenelle used to say, in the early spring — a season so trying to old trees and old men — 'Si j'attend la saison des fraises, je vivrai encore un an. [If I reach the strawberry season, I shall live another year].'" With his strawberry complexion, and creamy imperial, "Uncle Sam" looked as though he had many springs before him.

One subject upon which Sam could hold forth for hours, if he had an eager and sympathetic listener, was Delmonico's restaurant. Of that shrine of culinary and social supremacy he considered himself a founding father, for its span of existence coincided almost exactly with his own gastronomic birth, growth, and maturity. Once he roughed out a history of the place, but he never completed it. He himself remembered the little café at 24 William Street where the business had started; only coffee, chocolate, cakes, and bonbons had been sold there. But two years later the café became a restaurant, and one of Sam's friends earned a hundred dollars by translating the French menu into an English bill of fare, the two lists being printed on a single card in parallel columns as a guide for its mixed clientele. In 1835, while Sam Ward was exploring the eating places of Europe, the restaurant burned, and in 1837, just after Sam's homecoming to Bond Street, a new restaurant, called the Citadel, was opened by the Delmonicos at the corner of Beaver and South Williams Streets. There the cult of gourmandizing came into first flower in New York.

Fondly did Sam recall the palmy days when he had frequented the Citadel, first as a bachelor about town, later as an established, married banker. For the delectation of friends, he had contrived gastronomic surprises, the secrets of which he imparted only to Louis, the headwaiter of the Citadel, and to Lux, its chef. In his old age Sam regretted that he had forgotten the recipes for these "culinary jokes," except for one — *poulet à la Robert le Diable.* This was "a prime fowl, stuffed with *pâté de foie gras* and bread crumbs two days old, roasted before a Dutch oven, and basted with the exquisitely aromatic lard that protects the *pâté* and imbibes the combined perfumes of the liver and the truffles."

"I differed with my friend Lux upon certain points of high art, especially in his interpretation of the formula for *boudins à la Richelieu,*" Sam recalled. "But what availed discussion with that passionate advocate? Had I brought him over to my way of thinking, he would have been but a sullen convert, and of such is not the Kingdom of Friandise."

Delmonico's, like himself, had seen changes, not all of which either of them could approve. One was the great alteration in the drinking preferences of patrons. It was during the reign of the Citadel, Sam remembered, that "the *bar* began to usurp the functions of the *café.* The gloomy American system of tippling at the bar, like railway passengers tossing off a glass of ale during the 'ten minutes for refreshment,' left the marble tables, at which friends used to sit and chat, comparatively unoccupied," and the drinks "became Americanized into cocktails, slings, and smashes."

This degeneration Sam deplored. "We have disseminated our drinks through the Old World," he observed, "but to me it seems that while we have learned to diversify our repasts with every ingenious device of the Gallic cuisine, we have simplified our drinks, and old topers would stand aghast at the procession of well dressed men laconically confining their tipples to a 'pony brandy,' 'whisky straight,' or a 'whisky sour.' Sherry cobblers have gone out of fashion, cocktails are following in their wake, and the stately julep — which they 'build' instead of 'mixing' in the Old Dominion — is all but a memory of yesterday. While to call for the delectable whisky punch I drank at Delmonico's in 1832 would be as useless today as to order a case of Greek fire from the Imperial Pyrotechnist of Stamboul."

Sam made a cult of breakfasts. The preference dated back, he believed, to a shipwreck. It was quite a peaceful shipwreck: the steamboat on which he, a mere Round Hiller, was returning home with his Uncle Richard Ward, struck a rock in Long Island Sound and sank in shallow water. The passengers were taken off by farmers in boats, and in the kitchen of a nearby farmhouse, small Samuel, cold and hungry, was treated to a breakfast that made as warm an impression upon his memory as upon his midriff. "Shall I ever forget the savory incense of the first rashers of ham on the coals, which like the glory of the Lord filled the house?" Sam ruminated. "Candor admonishes me to say that saltier ham never assuaged the hunger of childhood. But the eggs were fresh, and I think I may date from that development the first germ of my consciousness of culinary equivalents. The ham seemed a cross and petulant wife, and the mellow eggs seemed to epitomize the manly virtues and the angelic patience of the suffering husband.

"In after life I remember meeting frequently at a *table d'hôte* two sententious old Frenchmen, one of whom invariably observed, when he had a *bouilli* with carrots, 'La carotte est l'ami de l'homme,' and the other as invariably replied, 'Je croyais que c'était le lézard.' I could never divine the parallelism between carrots and lizards, and in fact the pithy strophe of the one, and the anti-strophe of the other, had for me a mystic and Sybilline charm only comparable to that fascinating conic section, the hyperbola, with its asymptotes. I used occasionally to interject, 'L'ami de l'homme, c'est ni la carotte, ni le lézard, mais bien l'oeuf.' Ham without eggs must have been the torture of Tantalus. Certainly on the occasion of that shipwreck in Hempstead Bay, the eggs assumed in my thought the scriptural counterpart of the 'soft answer' which 'turneth away wrath,' and I realized then the proposition which I now enounce — '*point d'oeufs, point de déjeuner.*' "

As he took on age and inches, horizontally, Sam made this topic of breakfasts "one of those delightful projects in the air castles of the future" — he would write a book, he decided, on breakfasts he had eaten. But on further consideration he realized that "there is a Banquo at every feast" — too many companions with whom he had shared memorable breakfasts were ghosts now. So Sam's "Book of Breakfasts," like other projected labors of his life, was never accomplished.

* * *

Sam preferred to dine in company, although even when he sat alone at table, he could not be said to be dining without a friend, for between courses he would pull from his pocket the slim volume of Horace's poems, explaining, "When I have no other friend present, I invite my Horace."

And "Uncle Sam's" gourmandizing could always be set aside to accommodate a pretty woman: his badinage with women a third his age was as gallant as that of a young blade. His nephew, Marion Crawford, once was present when a lady (her name was Margaret) begged Sam to take her to a ball, since her intended escort had been prevented from appearing. Though he detested "the pomp and circumstance of pleasure," responded Sam, he could not resist so charming an invitation and would send word to put off another engagement. The lady protested that she would not permit him to slight his friends, but Sam shrugged that these were "only three or four old fogies at the club; they would talk my head off if I went." And while waiting for his carriage, he fenced with the lady in repartee.

"Are you fond of Dante?" asked she demurely.

"Very. Sometimes I buy a cheap copy and substitute the names of my pet enemies all through the 'Inferno' wherever they will suit the meter. In that way I get all the satisfaction the author got by putting his friends in hell, without the labor of writing, or the ability to compose, the poem."

"Do you do the same thing with the 'Paradiso'?"

"No, for my heaven admits none but the fair sex. They are all beautiful, and many of them are young."

"Will you admit me?" coaxed the coquette.

"St. Margaret has forestalled me. She has a paradise of her own, it seems, to which she has admitted me."

And off they drove to the ball, where "Uncle Sam," who had a faculty for catnapping, slept in a corner until Margaret was ready to return home.

It was the combination of this social adaptability and his peerless purveyance as an epicure that distinguished Sam as host. His own eating habits were classically simple. He tasted with relish, but sparingly, the many-course repasts which custom prescribed for public functions, but when dining alone he usually preferred a plain chop, or a single dish, such as a *rouleau* of truffles *en serviette,* washed down with a glass of sound wine. His breakfast ordinarily was a baked apple and tea, about the brewing of which he was extremely particular. He imported his own tea, China, usually. He would place a liberal quantity of leaves in a preheated earthen pot, pour on boiling water, let it stand a very few moments, then decant the tea into a second pot. About coffee he was just as exacting, storing it green and roasting it at the time of brewing. To this temperate eating he attributed his being able to slim down to one hundred seventy-four pounds towards 1880, — the first time he had tipped the scales at that figure in twenty years. His digestion remained incorruptible. "To think that I can go through such a banquet as Mr. Evarts gave last Monday," he told niece Daisy Terry, "twenty-two courses, and wake up like a singing lark, and that he, after a dinner at the club with me, should have suffered torments that still rack him!"

His reputation as a gourmet pleased him, and he was flattered that a drink he had concocted should be served widely and called a "Sam Ward." The recipe: fill with cracked ice a glass lined with a thin peel of lemon and pour in yellow Chartreuse. Chartreuse, preferably the yellow, was the only liqueur he cared for. He also was flattered by the appearance on the menus of many hotels and restaurants of dishes *à la Sam Ward.* Few people in history have had their names attached permanently to a dish, he would point out; and should his survive in this manner, that would be the sort of immortality he desired. In Boston, at least — where, oddly, he never was more than a transient visitor — his name has survived on bills of fare to this day. At the Somerset Club, where the cuisine is not trifled with, two dishes *à la Sam Ward* are highly popular. The recipes for these dishes, as he supplied them, follow:

Chicken Sauté Sam Ward

Using three 2-lb. broilers separate breasts and legs. Remove excess bones and sauté in butter until done. Remove chicken from pan and in the same pan sauté one pint of sliced mushrooms. Add one pint of cream sauce, salt and pepper, and let simmer for about five minutes.

To serve: Pour sauce onto a platter, arrange chicken on top of sauce with slices of crisp bacon on top of it. Serves 6.

Minced Chicken Sam Ward

Clean and boil one large fowl until done. Remove all meat from bones and chop into very small pieces with a heavy knife. Take one quart of fresh mushrooms and chop the same. Sauté mushrooms in butter until done, then add two cups of white wine. Reduce the wine to one-third. Add meat and one large cooked potato put through a grinder, which will bind the mixture. Add enough heavy cream for a nice blend. Bring to a boil and serve in a casserole with slices of crisp bacon on top. Serves 8 to 10.

At the well known Locke-Ober's in Boston, *Mushrooms Sam Ward* is a luncheon feature — grilled or sautéed mushrooms over a sliver of Virginia ham, all on toast, a cream sauce delicately flavored with sherry poured over, the whole placed under a bell glass and blended in the oven to "smoking hot" perfection.

Of course, in "Uncle Sam's" day the twin jewels in the diadem of American provender were canvasback duck and diamond-back terrapin. In preparing these masterpieces, Sam admittedly had no peer. His recipe for *Terrapin à la Maryland* (a dish he did not pretend to have invented, only never to have profaned) once was taken down by a newspaper reporter:

How to Cook the Toothsome Terrapin as it Ought to Be

Immerse the live terrapin in spring water, boiling hot, for five minutes, to loosen the skin. The skin is then removed with a knife, thoroughly polished to free it from any foreign substance, with a piece of chamois leather. Then replace the terrapin in the boiling water. When the claws become so soft as to pinch into a pulp by a moderate pressure between the thumb and forefinger, take it out and remove the bottom shell first, as the convexity of the upper shell catches the rich and savory juices that distinguish the terrapin from the mud turtle and the slider. Cut off the head and claws, and carefully remove the gall and sandbag. A little of the gall does not impair the flavor of the terrapin, but the sandbag requires the skillful touch of a surgeon, the heart of a lion, the eye of an eagle, and the hand of a lady.

Cut up the remainder into pieces about half an inch in length. Be careful to preserve all the juice. Put in a chafing dish, and add a dressing of fine flour, the yolks of eggs boiled so hard they are mushy, *quantum sufficit* of butter fresh from the dairy, salt to taste, red pepper, a large wine-glass of very old Madeira (to each terrapin) and a small quantity of rich cream. The dish, like everything else fit to eat except Roman punch and Stilton cheese, should be served smoking hot. Some persons have been known to season with spices, but this, like the rank perfume which exhales from the handkerchiefs of underbred people, is apt to arouse suspicion.

These recipes of Sam Ward's may be accepted as authentic. There are others, probably apocryphal, that have been ascribed to him, including one that may have been comprised in his "culinary jokes,"—the supposed recipe for boiling Smithfield ham in water to which *a wisp of new-mown hay* was added at the critical moment. And there was the oft repeated story of Sam's having taught the Potoyensee Indians to cook dog so deliciously they elected him their chief; a yarn that made a good conversation piece, but one for which Sam himself never claimed the merit of veracity.

Inevitably, of course, there were carpers; these maintained that Sam Ward's gastronomical fame was undeserved, or at best exaggerated. His onetime friend, Erasmus Keyes, during Sam's lobbying period joined this minority of croakers who sneered that Sam Ward had merely soaked up lore from cookbooks and was only superficially versed in gastronomy. With cookbooks Sam certainly was conversant; but his Lucullan erudition was not bookish, for to mere facts he added that "secret ingredient" which is the final resource of every master cook,—the condiment of his entire, variegated life.

One critic averred that "Uncle Sam" had been detected in the solecism of *repeating three white meats* in a menu, simply because he had been misled by their names, which *in print* appeared to signify quite different dishes. Another dissenter termed Sam Ward "old-fashioned" in his reliance on the sweetbread for dinner,—"a palpable error," this critic grimaced, "since there is no more tasteless viand, cook it as you may." This may be put down to a simple differentiation of taste, for palates other than Sam's have found the sweetbread neither insipid nor tritely "old-fashioned" when prepared as doubtless Sam Ward knew how. This same disputatious critic at least conceded, although grudgingly, that in London Sam Ward was accepted as a gastronomic authority; but standards there were dismissed with the assertion that at London "dining well means eating a good deal." The objector further said that he had questioned a celebrated Parisian gourmet about Sam Ward, and this judge of good eating had wiped his lips with the serviette carefully, then with gravy-dripping gravity eructed, "Never heard of him."

That was the dictum of a true gourmet, a man who lives for his palate alone. A gastonomer is altogether a different creature, and a gastronomer was "Uncle Sam." The evidence is ample of Sam's preeminence in the American hierarchy of the table, ranking second to none, and his scattered writings affirm his worthiness of association with the brightest luminaries of the French firmament. Although time and circumstances have given him less fame posthumously, it may be said safely that, as a host, Sam Ward was no bit inferior to Grimrod de la Reynière, and as a *raisonneur* and illuminator of gastronomy, he was on a par with his engaging contemporary, Charles Monselet. But none of the gastronomes of French renown were endowed with "Uncle Sam's" grace and wit (Talleyrand alone excepted), and not one possessed his unique power of personality, his charm.

NINE

"ON LYRICS AND LAFITE"

On March 14, 1881, Sam wrote to his sister Julia that he had been detained in Washington since the inauguration "by President Garfield's wish to see me. I called at the White House, had an affectionate reception. Everybody seemed glad to see me. Blaine especially kind."

Sam's hopes of a diplomatic appointment at last seemed likely to be realized. Then, on July 2, the President was shot by a disgruntled office-seeker, Charles J. Guiteau. At first it was hoped the wound would not prove fatal; for weeks the President hovered between life and death. Sam told Julia he was "backing divine Providence to win the race," and personally carried to the White House as a sovereign specific some hundred-year-old rum. He was anguished by the tragedy, and he gave way to grief when, on September 29, Garfield died. "His sufferings have endeared him to me in a way I should never have imagined," he confessed. "I am cut up root and branch. He has been a brother to me since I first knew him in 1865."

So, with Garfield's demise, Sam Ward's expectation of diplomatic recognition again was dashed.

The new President, Chester A. Arthur, Sam knew well as a New York attorney and political figure, and he rallied loyally to Arthur's support. In December he was "most warmly received" by the new occupant of the White House, and told Dudie: "Arthur is a gentleman of great practical experience and much ability, and I think his Administration will be a success. He has furnished the upper part of the White House most tastily, and for the first time since its erection it looks like a gentleman's habitation."

To maintain the dignity of the nation's chief representative had always been a desideratum with Sam, and in order that the entertainments at the White House should lack nothing, Sam forwarded a very special gift to the President that December of 1881, accompanied and explained by the following letter, written at 85 Clinton Place, in "Uncle Sam's" clearest chirography:

Dear President Arthur —

At the approach of Genl. Sherman on his march to the sea, the Charleston Jockey Club buried its old madeiras, which were saved by this inhumation, and about six years ago the wine was sold to a member of the house of Barings, who took it to London — where from British ignorance of the mode of handling such old wines, it never recovered from the voyage. At the time of Baring's purchase I and some friends of mine were in treaty for the whole lot, as we had been tempted by the high character of the samples sent hither. Three years ago Baring grew sick of his bargain & offered to redeliver the wine in N. York free of expenses, on being repaid its prime cost.

Mr. Keene & myself took it, and after a year's repose in demijohns the wine grew clear and was bottled.

Unluckily, the original catalogue has been lost — it may have fallen into Sherman's hands — and we have no descriptions of the years and vintages — none of it is less than 40 years old and some exceeds half a century.

The numbers sent to you yesterday are 3, 5, 6, 7 & 8 — one case of each of the 4 first and 2 cases of the last number.

The bottles should be taken from the cases and stood on end in a dry part of the cellar, when they will probably be ready for use in February, when it may be taken from the *cellis avitis*.

With great respect,
Affectionately
"UNCLE SAM"

This princely donation, made out of a full heart and a full bin, was not unique; for when Sam was in clover, everybody nibbled. Julia's summer place at Oak Glen took on the aspect of a Sam Ward museum: "Beautiful baskets of flowers . . . the latticework . . . the horse and equipage . . . We are quite 'sot up' by these generous gifts," wrote Dudie. "Your second basket of peaches arrived in time for Monday dinner, at which we entertained your grandson, Armstrong Chanler. He seems a very pleasant, well behaved fellow, inclining to the Astor type of countenance but in modified form. He asked about you with interest, calling you 'Grandpa Ward.'" And when Julia remarked on the banquets Sam was giving so profusely, he assured her that "you have brains and grace to offer, which are better than marble-cake."

His watchful benevolence brought rapturous acknowledgment from his niece, Laura Richards, now home from Florence and living frugally in Maine: "Was there ever such a good fairy as you? Here have Harry and I been puzzling our brains as to how we could manage a bookcase to meet the growing needs of our small family, and a pretty rug to replace an ancient carpet. And presto, comes your Christmas check . . . and we have our bookcase and rug with only the trouble of ordering them! . . . The whole affair savors of witchcraft. I picture you as a benevolent necromancer sitting in your chamber with your wand, conjuring up good things and pleasant surprises for all your friends, and then mounting your dragon car and whisking through the air to scatter gold and diamonds over your distant relatives."

It was not diamonds for Maud Howe but "a lovely great sapphire," and with it jeweled advice: "Never let people imagine that you make a convenience of them." John Elliott, a talented young Scots painter (who eventually would marry Maud), was "reduced to speechlessness" by a fantastically complete paintbox. For Julia Romana, "a beautiful teapot, a pearl, a pitcher, and a volume of Horace," while to Daisy Terry in Rome went a dark olive organdie, "feeling by intuition that a pretty costume is as desirable as one of Rivière's bindings to a book of poems"; together with a bottle of darker ink "so that I may more readily read your letters. Are your cheeks as pale as the ink, which almost defied a magnifying glass, in which your dear note of the 7th was penned?"

Another gift to Daisy, sent with special care, was some "primary Latin books" to get her started on the language — "the notation and solfeggi," he called them, "of the beautiful tongue which Horace and Virgil and Catullus informed with their genius that it might one day serve as the organ of Christian humanity. To you, who sneeze in Italian, it will be easy to lisp in Latin until you learn to warble." For lagniappe, he enclosed a classical anecdote. "In the last century, Frederick the Great went to Leipsic to see that great curiosity, unique then, a German poet. It was Gellert, author of 'The Fables,' whom the Gallicized king, reeking with the snuff of Voltaire and Maupertuis, looked upon with wonder. German was then called the language of horses! . . . So, when these older Latin poets, to whom I would add the later Lucretius, sailed into the sea of fancy and philosophy, they had the world to themselves, and having exhausted the resources of Roman thought and inspiration, they left no rivals."

Daisy answered her uncle's letters eagerly, and a brisk correspondence was maintained between them. Sam's letters were frequently reminiscent. Of Thackeray he told her, "I used to go out and in his house in Onslow Square like a tame cat." And further back in time was the recollection of a gay episode at Rokeby: "The time was when I could perform a play after once seeing it. I once played 'Marie Stuart' from memory before Mrs. Astor and Maddie at Rokeby and they really thought I was Ristori, and Maddie took me over to Mrs. Delano's and made me repeat the performance. This was in 1855. Since then the Astors and I have been strangers, and six of the family — William B., Mrs. A., Mrs. Carey and her husband, and Maddie and hers — [have died]. So goes the world! And your old uncle remains to pick out the thorns from under your feet!" The Careys were a daughter and son-in-law of the first John Jacob Astor.

Time had indeed mellowed Sam, and to Louisa Terry he avowed that he had at last learned to be patient: "Sufficient for the day is the good thereof. Harry Richards has been here," he went on. "I took him down to dine at Sutherland's. He is a nice fellow and his greatest merit is that his little wife adores him — a feat I have never been able to accomplish, and it is now too late."

Meanwhile, Lord Ronald Gower, at Cliveden, England, noted the receipt of a letter "from Uncle Sam offering me two thousand pounds for my Shakespeare monument." This was a Shakespeare bust, later expanded into the Memorial Monument at Stratford-on-Avon. Closer to home, Auntie Francis — Eliza Cutler Francis, Sam's mother's sister, whom he described to Julia as "the loveliest and honestest woman I ever knew" — was remembered with a whimsical greeting: "My dearest Auntie — To prevent miscarriage, which no one so well knew how to avert as our dear, good, blessed old Doctor — I warn you that I have sent a basket of pear (not grape) shot into the little fortress of your home, where I trust they will produce rosy cheeks and coral tongues, instead of the devastation of war, among the cherub regiment of Samuel the Patriarch" — said Patriarch being Samuel Ward Francis, father of an ever-increasing tribe.

But the truth, bit by bit, could no longer be disguised, namely, that Sam's wealth had brought him more cares than joys. He was in trouble again; in fact, as 1882 came in, he shuddered to see his fortune — his third fortune, the gift of Keene, the prop of his age — melting away, all through gullibility and misplaced business confidence. Sam had staked two promotion men in a scheme to build a fashionable seaside resort at Long Beach, Long Island, that would eclipse Long Branch, the New Jersey resort then at the zenith of its popularity. Sam was the venture's capitalist, and of course the project was laid out on a grand scale. Somehow, more and more cash seemed to be required, and Sam paid out and paid out, and still the demands did not lessen.

Julia was given glimpses of Sam's worry. "I have never been so wretched as since I got some money," he wrote her. "I continue pestered to death by everybody's business but my own, and shall some day die, like the donkey in the story, of *congojas ajenas,* as the Spanish call Other People's Troubles." And again: "I feel like the sick musician whose cat, crawling over the keys, struck the note sensitive, which he dragged himself out of bed to resolve into the corresponding chord, and expired. This morning I had the usual raft of shipwrecked madmen in my room . . . Since Garfield died I have had nothing but trouble." In desperation, he had returned to Wall Street. "I fag and fret downtown. People in shoals, to whom I have done kindnesses by the bushel, seem to expect a continuance of the same as a matter of course. Ah me! Time was when I was as good at dreaming as the best, but after having fought the battle of life for forty-five years I have nailed up that stop in the organ of fancy. I ought to go to some watering place to quiet my nerves and find out what repairs my old health requires to make it seaworthy, which it is by no means now."

Even Julia was not vouchsafed the whole truth, and to business friends, like S.L.M. Barlow, Sam presented a resolutely cheerful mien. When squiring celebrities out to Long Beach (in an attempt to give the place a cachet of fashion), he fancied himself a host at the glittering (and to him expensive) hotel there. "This flower of grace was never in my chaplet before," he confided to Barlow. "Quite a change from my little bar room in the Merced mines, about which poor Teresa Velez used to make such fun of me. I have come to the conclusion that the Boniface is the king of men."

From London Rosebery wrote to his "Uncle Sam" in affectionate reproach: "Where are all your promises to return? While waiting for papers to which to attach my respected name, I waste my sweetness on your desert air, desert in so far as you have deserted all your English nephews and nieces." Rosebery was in the government now, as undersecretary for Scottish affairs, but he was still Sam's "Sycophant," and he spiced his letters with high-spirited boyish jokes. But Sam could only reply with evasions, for certainly he could not afford to leave New York. But to Julia he bared more and more of his melancholy, writing to her on January 27, 1882: "I am never jolly on my birthday. I think such days should be spent in meditation and introspective contemplation . . . Our lives have been a continual making up for lost time, mine more than yours, because I wasted more precious years than you have weeks, and my pursuits have, I regret to say, been of far greater self-indulgence. Now that I am nearing the last goal I realize that the object of life is to be ready to graduate into the other world." But all his harassments could not alienate his sense of fun, and he chuckled to Dudie that Fletcher Harper, of the publishing firm, had complimented him upon the regularity of his attendance at Harper's church, and he had bowed in acknowledgment — but "some day he will address my double — some old chap with a head *nu comme un genou* [naked as a knee], as old Mr. Grymes used to say — and discover his mistake!"

Beset as he was by business vexations, and pestered by leeches who took his bounty as though it were "an annuity paid by a life insurance company," Sam kept up his interest in matters intellectual and social. Theosophy claimed his serious attention. He had so far advanced in the doctrine that he was receiving illuminations, he said, from "Koot Houmi," a mahatma of Tibet who was Madame Blavatsky's personal master of the occult. These mysterious communications, he averred, fluttered down inexplicably upon his writing table while he was in the bath; they were written on blue notepaper and had been transmitted over the "astral telegraph" which the Blavatsky devotees described so convincingly. Sam's nephew, Marion Crawford, had returned from India, and from Julia's house in Beacon Street cautioned his uncle tactfully: "I have no doubt of Koot Houmi, but be sure he is he and no other. The Tibetans have no postage stamps, but the Kashmirs have, and I am well acquainted with them, so let me see the missives before long."

Sam did not put his astral correspondence to this test, but from his belief in these supernatural manifestations he drew faith that Providence had been working in his behalf. "There is one circumstance which I think you will agree with me to be Providential," he wrote confidentially to Daisy Terry, "that, at so critical a period in the fortunes of the family, I should have been made by divine Providence the means of contributing to the welfare of all who are most dear to me. I shudder to think what might have been the straits to which your two aunts might have been put, had it not been providentially in my power to clear off the mortgage upon the ranch and pull the dear Beacon Streeters through their troubles."

Over young Crawford, Sam was deeply concerned. Frank, as the family sometimes called him, was twenty-six and at a loss what to do with his life. He must earn a living — but by what occupation? Louisa Terry had come from Rome to help get her son launched, if she could, and she called on Sam for help.

Nephew and uncle had not met since 1874, in London, and at first they did not hit it off. "Frank misapprehended my apparent nonchalance of manner," Sam told Louisa; while she admitted that Frank, no less, felt his uncle had "not found him *simpatico* . . . besides being awed perhaps by the reputation for wisdom that has gone abroad concerning you." But Sam soon thawed this reserve. He took Crawford to call on Longfellow, and the nephew began to understand his uncle's character when he saw him pull two bottles of Hochheimer from his overcoat pockets, and the friends — Longfellow with snowy pate and ancestral beard, Sam with massive bald dome and silvery goatee — embrace and settle down to a long, droll, gentle chat over the wine and cigars. After that, Loulie could write to "Bro. Sam" that "you have wholly won the big boy's heart and mind. After you had left us the other evening, Marion said, as though it were a new thing that no one of us had ever discovered, 'I consider my Uncle Sam to be altogether the most agreeable and the most remarkable and the most delightful man I have ever known.'" Smiles of amusement rippled between Sam's sisters at hearing this twenty-six-year-old's judgment, and Dudie twinkled: had she not proclaimed for half a lifetime that Sam was one of the most enchanting personalities who ever assumed human form?

Marion explained his silence during Sam's last visit, Louisa said, "by holding up the uselessness of trying to talk 'when such a man as Uncle Sam is present, who knows everything and says it in the best way.'" From then on uncle and nephew were mutually devoted, although Sam confessed to Louisa: "I am as puzzled about Frank's prospects as you are. He is full of talent, facility, and pluck, but does not know which way to turn to earn a dollar." To launch this brilliant but aimless nephew upon a suitable career henceforth became a major preoccupation.

Crawford came to New York and spent a good deal of time at 85 Clinton Place. Sam pushed him with editors, "deluged" him with magazines, got him book-reviewing jobs and orders for magazine articles, and kept him in pocket money. He also tried to get him a berth on the *New York World*, although warning Louisa that Hurlbert was "such a clever eel he can wriggle out of everything. A contract in black and white might bind him." Sam took his nephew to Hurlbert's fantastic apartment in the Gothic building of

New York University on Waverly Place, — vast rooms stuffed with a hodgepodge of *objets d'art,* good, bad, and indifferent, where few visitors were admitted; a first-rate Turner was the prize of the collection. Hurlbert was part-owner of the *World* now, but no contract was forthcoming, and Crawford did not feel that journalism was his forte.

It was no surprise when "Uncle Sam" took under his wing the most sensational, the most shocking, the most titivating visitor to America in 1882. This effete invader from the Old World was Oscar Wilde. The poet came to lecture Americans on aesthetics, — and on Wilde. His tour, conceived in ballyhoo and carried out with circus gaudiness, had originally been plotted as a device to resuscitate the dying box-office receipts of the Gilbert and Sullivan operetta, *Patience,* in which Wilde was supposed to be caricatured. Wilde turned the trip into a *tour de force* of self-exploitation, letting *Patience* take care of itself. Sam of course had met Wilde in England and knew about him, knew that he had studied under Ruskin at Oxford, that he had won coveted prizes while an undergraduate, and that he was a man of ability in spite of his calculated poses, — such as his highly publicized infatuation for Lily Langtry, the "Jersey Lily," whose pale beauty was sending artists into ecstasies and Wilde into newsprint columns.

Sam greeted the well-heralded arrival of Oscar in the U.S.A. with a poetical address published in the *World.* It was entitled "The Aesthetic: Samuel Ward to Oscar Wilde," and ran —

"Father, what is the aesthetic?"
  Asked a child.
Puzzled, he said, "Ask the hermetic
  Oscar Wilde."
"Oscar, what is the aesthetic?"
  Asked the girl.
" 'Tis," beamed Oscar, "this pathetic
  Suppliant curl;
Like a corkscrew sympathetic
  It will bore
Through the heart the most athletic
  To the core . . ."

Sam introduced Wilde right and left, dined him, and assured Barlow that he was "a remarkable man, with a woman's face and a great capacity to carry all the sail he spreads. A raconteur and a critic as acute as Ruskin, — and no prejudices." He matched Wilde at dinner against Evarts, who was famous for his table wit, and was delighted that Wilde was "able to return the shuttlecock, or if you like the lawn tennis ball, wherever it was projected." Evarts was not taken along when Sam trotted Wilde out to Long Branch to meet General Grant. During that dinner, Grant's son, Jesse, was far less taken up with notorious Oscar than with "Uncle Sam."

To Daisy Terry, Sam described Wilde as "an accomplished, original, and scholarly person of magnetic presence and fascinating manners, and I have adopted him among my nephews." While to Maud Howe, who, like numberless other young girls, was fluttered by the visitor, Sam reported that after "five hours on Tuesday at Hurlbert's dinner," he had had Oscar to dinner to "participate in the initial desecration of my rooms by the kindling of a range by a chef of the College of Cardinal Cooks . . . Wilde brought me a warm, enthusiastic letter from dear old Lord Houghton, and I can tell you that he is 'no slouch,' as old Valentine used to observe when he wanted to pay a high compliment to a man."

(Jim Valentine, Sam's race handicapper secretary of merry memory, was dead, juggernauted by a Broadway horse omnibus that broke both his legs. Gout supervened, and poor Valentine achieved the unhappy distinction of becoming the first man in medical history to succumb to an attack of the gout superinduced by collision with a horse. Sam and a host of friends mourned him.)

"Uncle Sam" had no doubt of Wilde's basic ability. "I predict that he will have a real success," he told Maud unequivocally, "as he has a substratum of solid intellectuality." He described the poet's getup — "extraordinary, long black hair hanging to the shoulders, brown eyes, a huge white face like the pale moon, a white waistcoat, black coat and knee breeches, black silk stockings and shoes with buckles. Until he speaks, you think him as uncanny as a vampire. But he talks like a man, and all he says has point, and, sometimes, *bite* in it. One thing is sure, he knows his business." Sam was positive about this, because Wilde had quoted some of Sam's own poetry and said he envied the author. "I therefore," declared Sam, "think that he knows his business. As Cooper's heroes say, 'I have spoken.' "

The aesthetic banquet "Uncle Sam" got up for Oscar made headlines. The table was bowered in calla lilies, and beside each plate lay a spray of lilies-of-the-valley, while the centerpiece was water lilies floating in a lake of Roman punch, — a touch that moved one of the convivialists to doggerelize —

> Tonight a Patriarch, with youthful feelings blest,
> Will be the host, fair Oscar Wilde our guest.
> The spotless lily, to the old man dear,
> Will decorate the feast, it doth appear.
> From out their bath of rum they'll shake their heads,
> Forgetting for the time their quiet beds;
> And ere the feast is o'er it may perchance, I think,
> To many guests seem that the lilies blink . . .

Rumors of high wassailing on this occasion spread afar, and in Washington Mrs. Henry Adams relayed the gossip she heard to her father. Quoting Henry James's fling at Oscar as "Hosscar Wilde, a fatuous fool, tenth-rate cad," she added, "We are told he was carried home drunk in New York from a dinner given him by 'wicked Sam Ward' at which a big bowl of punch bore floating lilies!"

Wilde's contrasting facets amused wise old "Uncle Sam." There was the epigrammatist, who delighted Marion Crawford by strolling into Sam's rooms and sighing: "Where will it all end? Half the world does not believe in God, and the other half does not believe in me." And there was Wilde in private, when he had no audience to play up to: Sam saw this side, too, and in writing to Daisy from the Park Avenue Hotel, Fourth Avenue at Thirty-second Street, he added a footnote: "I am writing at the hotel of Oscar Wilde, to whom I have just paid a visit and found him reading the Trois Mousquetaires."

Sam passed Wilde along to Julia in Boston, with the commendation: "I think him a sincere fellow with sweetness and dignity of manner and character, and forgive him his fantastic penchants, which he will outgrow." Sam blamed Wilde's exploiters for the poet's freakish behavior when on public show. Julia invited Wilde to luncheon and scandalized proper Boston. Brahmin Thomas Wentworth Higginson expressed indignation, in print, that a respectable home should have received this author of "a thin volume of very mediocre verse." Julia replied spunkily, in print, that if Wilde were really a bad man, as his detractors alleged, "to cut off an offending member of society from its best influences and most humanizing resources is scarcely Christian." As for her hospitality, "I am very glad to have had the opportunity of receiving Mr. Wilde in my house. I also take exception to the right which Colonel Higginson arrogates to himself of saying in a public way who should and should not be received in private houses."

Marian Adams took up this scandal, too, writing: "I am amused to see that Mrs. Howe and T. W. Higginson have fallen afoul of each other in the papers à propos of that vulgar cad Oscar Wilde. That Julia Howe should reform sinners by suppers and flattery is charming on the same principle that her moral brother Sam Ward gave him a feast in New York from which he is said to have been carried home drunk. What a cartoon for *Puck!* . . . I wish I could draw! I would support the family with a daily comic paper."

At Wilde's Boston lecture, sixty Harvard students tramped into the hall wearing wigs and knee breeches and carrying lilies and sunflowers, with Sam's grandson, Winthrop Chanler, in the van. The laugh, however, was on the students, for their prank had been well publicized in advance, and Wilde lectured that evening in trousers and conventional evening dress.

The lampooned, laughed-at writer then crossed the continent in a calliope-blare of press notices. In July he returned to New York, understandably victimized by migraine and insomnia. "Uncle Sam," the tireless prescriptionist, provided an infallible remedy, which really worked, and Oscar thanked Sam for a good night's sleep. "I am much better — felt well and happy — and very little pain of any kind: slept well also," came a bulletin from the revived invalid. "You are a magician, and a master of all things from finance to a dinner, and from lyrics to medicine." And shortly after that, an expression of fully restored vitality: "Will not you and Mr. Crawford dine with me to meet my young actor? 6:15 and come to the theater afterwards. I feel quite well, and in good spirits. Ever your affectionate and devoted . . ." Followed by an even livelier: "My dear Uncle Sam — Are you at home, and can I come up to see you? I have a book for you."

Then the "Jersey Lily" came to New York to appear in a play carefully timed to capitalize on the furor, and "Uncle Sam" constituted himself her escort. The Langtry cult in 1882 was a craze: not only was she startlingly beautiful, she was also controversial, because she had forsaken London society to seek a career on the stage. This breach of decorum had aroused the backbiters, — and since the back she offered to their mordancies was lovely beyond words to convey, spice was added to the pastime and the spectacle. Her acting talent was mediocre, but so compelling were her beauty and her presence, she never really failed in any play: audiences came to behold her and to worship.

The "Lily" won "Uncle Sam's" heart. To Daisy Terry he extolled her "calm and graciousness of manner. Like your Aunt Medora, her mouth is not well shaped, but she uses it with grace and simplicity. The head, neck, and shoulders are perfect, and her figure Junonian — not in its amplitude, but in symmetry and shape and dignity of carriage. Her voice is silvery and her laugh musical." And generously he wished her the success "she deserves for having stepped out of her brougham to seek independence on the stage."

Of course he got up a dinner for Mrs. Langtry at Delmonico's, which Oscar approved ("charming — but everything you do, from poetry to menus, is perfect. You are the great authority on lyrics and Lafite"). Bouquets, verses, and introductions showered upon the beauty, and "The Lily" loved it all. To greet her when she awoke came an effusion from "Uncle Sam:"

> O thou! who wilt the city take by storm,
> No matter whether weather's cold or warm,
> Or if thine acting to be real good or paltry —
> We only want to see thee, Lily Langtry!

Which called for a pretty reply, on perfumed notepaper —

O Uncle Sam! O Uncle Sam!
Oh! Please come to see me.
O Uncle Sam! O Uncle Sam!
How naughty you can be!
— Lily Langtry.

And Sam loved *that* — and dropped around to her hotel to offer compliments and counsel on the colors her frocks should be to set off her beauty.

These attentions on the part of "wicked Sam Ward" could not fail to reach the ears of Mrs. Adams, taking in the spectacle from Washington. Her pen raced through another gossipy letter, telling how Perry Belmont (August Belmont's son) was in town ("dined here twice — as he sat till a few minutes of seven of course he must dine as well as take tea") and "gives us the latest New York gossip . . . He had given Mrs. Langtry a supper, had driven her and dined with her at Hurlbert's with Mr. Evarts and old Sam Ward! But, alas, Mrs. Paran Stevens won't call on her and Mrs. Langtry says Mrs. Stevens is only a cook, and Lady Mandeville — one of the swiftest of all the swift American women in the Marlborough House [Prince of Wales] set — won't call on her either, and that settles her fate in New York socially, and really she's a bad lot and it's a wise decision."

Sam bowed out of Wilde's entourage towards the close of the latter's tour; he found it distasteful to be compared to Barnum exhibiting Jumbo. "It irks me much to go about as the courier of an elephant," he told Dudie. "I don't want to be eternally in the papers as his dry nurse." But he urged Wilde to persevere, in a parting exhortation:

Go it, Oscar! You are young,
Owning a conviction,
To which you have wisely clung —
Beauty is no fiction!

Longfellow was ailing, but from Craigie House he still followed Sam's metrical musings with interest and forbearance. Once Sam had written to him: "You are more or less a child of mine — at least, I have been the family physician to some of your bairns," and the poet might have returned the compliment. "A lovely letter from Longo this morning — a comment on my last two poems — to Oscar Wilde, and 'After the Ball,'" ran a note Sam wrote to Daisy Terry early in 1882.

Shortly after that the thread snapped: on March 24, 1882, Longfellow died.

Sam's last visit to Craigie House had been on Thanksgiving Day, the previous November. He had found Longo abed, where the poet said he had "constituted himself an invalid" after suffering a severe attack of vertigo. Sam had noticed that the "pearmain-apple hue of ruddy health, like a bunch of holly berries in a frame of snow," had faded from his friend's cheeks. During a half-hour chat Longfellow, in keeping with their practice of years, read Sam his latest poem, "Hermes Trismegistus," and "Hypolito" was as enthusiastic as he had been over "The Skeleton in Armor," urging that "the world be enriched" by its immediate publication. But he sensed that the lamp was burning low; hence word of Longo's death came as a grief, but no sudden shock.

Hurlbert, editor of the *World*, telephoned to Sutherland's, where "Uncle Sam" happened to be dining with Marion Crawford, when the news came, and asked Sam to write an appreciation for the morning paper. Hurrying to the *World* office, Sam dictated to Marion an article recounting the half-century of unbroken friendship, telling how they had met at Heidelberg, his marketing of Longfellow's poems, early and late, and how he had inspired some of the most famous pieces, — all memories filled with sweetness and loyalty. For *envoi* he quoted lines written by another poet-friend, Fitz-Greene Halleck, himself long since dead —

> Green be the turf above thee,
>   Friend of my better days!
> None knew thee but to love thee,
>   Nor named thee but to praise!

The next afternoon, upon returning from Wall Street to Clinton Place, Sam found awaiting him an appeal from Allen Thorndike

Rice, editor of the *North American Review,* for further Longfellow reminiscences, — but the manuscript would have to be in Rice's hands that evening in order to catch the May issue of the magazine, even then going to press. At the same time a telegram from Longfellow's daughter invited Sam to attend the funeral in Cambridge the next day. This would necessitate giving Rice the completed article by seven o'clock and catching the night train to Boston.

"We were up to the emergency," Sam told Daisy subsequently. He had dictated as Crawford wrote, and "though my bell was rung twenty-two times, and a cable about poor R——'s death, and I had to send a cable to Rosebery and another to President Arthur, on a merciful errand, Marion and I were through with our task by 6:30. . . . Rice was electrified by the celerity of our performance."

In this article Sam published the last letter Longfellow had written to him, about two months before the poet's death. It was in answer to a note from Sam, enclosing some of his "sportive fancies," including the gallant lines entitled "After the Ball." Almost upon his deathbed, America's great poet had read the following composed by his friend on the eve of "Samilasso's" sixty-eighth birthday:

AFTER THE BALL
An Impromptu to Mrs. Harry Hoffman

We met not "in a crowd,"
Although the music loud
Foretold the coming throng
Soon we should be among.
Something spoke in her glance —
"Come, let the others dance,
While you to me reveal
Thoughts with which mine can deal!"

Scarce had my lips begun
Ere she my heart had won!
Never such sweet replies

Sparkled in woman's eyes!
Drinking their luster in,
Unheard the dance's din —
She was upon a throne —
I with its Queen alone!

Then Hope, with unseen wings,
Fanned joy's Aeolian strings,
Till *I* the glare bewailed,
Longed that its light were veiled,
Veiled by a swift eclipse —
Dreamed I had touched her lips,
And thus became her thrall
In that gay festival!

And this had been Longo's response:

My dear Uncle Sam — "Whom the gods love die young" because they never grow old, although they may live to be fourscore years and upwards.

So say I, whenever I read your graceful and sportive fancies in the papers you send me, or in those I send you.

I am now waiting for your last, announced in your letter of yesterday, not yet arrived.

Pardon my not writing sooner and oftener. My day is very short, as I get up late and go to bed early — a kind of Arctic winter's day, when the sun is above the horizon for a few hours only.

Yes, the "Hermes" went to the "Century."

I come back to where I began — the perpetual youth of some people. You remember the anecdote of Ducis. When somebody said of him, "Il est tombé en enfance," a friend replied, "Non — il est rentré en jeunesse."

That is the polite way of putting things. But, old or young,

Always yours,
HENRY WADSWORTH LONGFELLOW

Il est rentré en jeunesse . . .
To all who knew Sam Ward, the accolade seemed just. "Fallen

into second childhood?" Not "Uncle Sam," ever! He had "gone back to youth" — or more accurately, as Longo's clairvoyant love had discerned, Sam Ward had never aged one day in spirit since that rollicking first meeting at Heidelberg.

Sam's private summing up of the long, fragrant friendship he did not publish, but he had it tucked away among his important papers. Four years previously, on Longfellow's birthday, February 27, 1878, he had sent the poet these spontaneous lines —

LONGO'S BIRTHDAY

When two and forty years ago,
We first met by old Neckar's flow,
Our hearts with youthful hopes aglow,
   How little did we dream
That like two shallops, side by side,
That drift adown a flowing tide,
We twain for two score years should glide
   Upon life's rapid stream.

And on this day that saw thy birth
I send this greeting, not in mirth,
But pensively, as smiles the earth
   Beneath this wintry sun;
For as to budding trees in spring
An ampler bole the seasons bring,
Each birthday hath an added ring
   Round my affection spun.

TEN

"IN THE STRAW" — AGAIN

LONGO'S passing came in the midst of increasing preoccupation on Sam's part with two insistent dilemmas — the struggle of his cherished young relatives to find their niches in life, and his own growing financial disaster. Maud Howe was trying her hand at fiction and journalism, while Marion Crawford ground out magazine articles on weighty subjects. For days at a time Sam abdicated his Clinton Place quarters to these two ambitious youngsters, a note to Julia reading: "I have not written you because I have given up my room all this week to Marion and Maud, and there has been no minute save the early morning when I was alone. These two children are so zealous with their pens that I have effaced myself to encourage them by giving them full swing . . . Frank has written two articles for the *North American Review*, which have both been accepted. This in addition to the one under my dictation [the Longfellow reminiscences], for which he will get the money." But for Marion such work was plainly a *pis aller;* it did not appear that he would make his mark as an economist or critic. Obviously he had talent, but it was assuming no definite direction.

Socially Sam introduced Crawford everywhere, and the younger man was a credit to his uncle. But Marion lacked the physical stamina that kept Sam going, and eventually Beacon Street was told: "Frank has been a good deal upset. I devoted my whole day yesterday to soothing him. He was too much out of sorts last P.M. to dine. I found him asleep on my sofa when I got home at 12 from the club." For a while Crawford went back to sober Boston and was placed on a diet, which he detested, while Sam cast about for a gainful occupation for his nephew.

Marion had brought a fund of stories from India. One of these

— about a diamond merchant, a Mr. Jacobs, whom he had met at Simla — fascinated Sam; it was filled with the sights, sounds, and odors of the Anglo-Indian world, against an exotic background of mysticism and suspense. Among Sam's numerous protégés was a young man named George Brett, who was in the New York store of Macmillan's, the publishers; Sam dropped in at the shop periodically to look over the new titles, and often he would buy books which Brett recommended.

When Marion had recuperated and returned to New York, Sam invited Brett to dine with them one evening at the Brevoort; and during the meal the conversation came around to Crawford's quandary as to what he should do in life. Sam led him to repeat the story about the Simla merchant, which Marion told charmingly. At the close, the enthralled Brett said earnestly: "There is no question what you should do, Mr. Crawford — write out that story!" To which Uncle Sam added: "Write it now!"

Crawford set to work immediately, working at his uncle's writing table at 85 Clinton Place, and finishing the task at his Aunt Julia's summer farm, Oak Glen. In a few weeks he turned out a novel which he called *Mr. Isaacs,* and in June Sam shipped the manuscript to Macmillan's in London. He was confident, writing: "Marion is not sanguine. I am. I believe in young aspirations, when they do not involve love or matrimony!" In August came the report: "Hurrah for Marion! Macmillan has accepted 'Mr. Isaacs!' "

The book had instantaneous success, both because of its novelty and because of the skill of the narrator. (It appeared only a few years before Rudyard Kipling would make use of the same exotic ingredients with startling effect.) For F. Marion Crawford, as he signed himself, it opened a career of wide popularity as a storyteller, that would bring him wealth, honors, and position.

One morning just after the book came out, the thrilled young author came down to breakfast at 241 Beacon Street and spread out before Julia and Maud a batch of newspaper reviews. "This," he said radiantly, with shy pride, "why, Auntie, this is fame!"

George Brett one day would head the American house of Macmillan.

No one was more delighted than Sam by the success of *Mr. Isaacs,* and Marion expressed warm-hearted gratitude by portraying his uncle to the life in a second novel, on which he set to work immediately. The portrait drawn in this book, *Dr. Claudius*, of "Uncle Horace Bellingham," was a photographically exact representation of "Uncle Sam" Ward as he appeared in 1882. "He was short, decidedly," ran the description, "but with a broad deep chest and long powerful arms. He was perfectly bald, with a wonderful cranium. A sweeping mustache and a long imperial of snowy white sat well on the ruddy tan of his complexion, and gave him an air at once martial and diplomatic. He was dressed in the most perfect London clothes, the whitest of linen, superb diamonds in his shirt, while a priceless sapphire sparkled in a plain gold setting on his broad, brown hand. He moved like a king and had the air of the old school in every gesture. His eyes were brighter than his diamonds, and for all his white beard and near seventy years, he was as young and fresh as the rose he wore in his coat,—a sight to do good to the souls of the hungry and thirsty, and of the poor, and those in misery."

A trait of Sam's—the secretiveness with which he went about performing his kindly actions—Crawford brought out in this delineation. When offered a tale of distress, Sam would listen attentively, stroking his beard, his head on one side, looking up in his peculiar way without lifting his chin, and nodding noncommittally. Meanwhile his brain would be weighing expedients and remedies; the benefaction would come later, as a surprise, thereby doubling his own pleasure. From his youth up, Sam had relished a touch of hocus-pocus in the management of affairs.

Some hocus-pocus more potent than his "ineptic" Wall Street incantations was becoming imperatively needed. As Marion's fortunes rose, Uncle Sam's sank, and to Julia he confessed miserably: "Long Beach is a sore thing, into which I was hurried half dazed by bad men whom I thought were good ones. I shall pull through, only I will confess I have never in my life endured such wretchedness . . . My *morals* never were so straight as now, and I ascribe it all to Emerson, who is the philosopher for men past sixty. Had we a calendar for philosopher-poets, Emerson could soon be canonized." Oddly, Sam had met Ralph Waldo Emerson for the first time at Longfellow's funeral; the Concord sage died a month later.

Daisy Terry, in far-off Rome, received complaints of endless worriment. "I am so horribly bored by the uncongenial muffs my business throws me into intimate relations with that I plunge into books and make them all shut up. It is a very queer thing to confess so late in life, but I am growing a conscience, — not one that makes cowards of us all, but a certain golden rule of life, adherence to which in all my actions I find a great serenity." In a backward glance at his ups and downs, he summed up his view of himself: "I have often been good by impulse and never very bad to others, but finding myself among people who do not know what real high principle is, I find it needful to lead a life of ascetic self-denial, in order to segregate myself from the crowd around me . . . I study Pascal with delight; the worldly wisdom of La Rochefoucauld arouses antagonism in me . . . To what wit I have always cultivated I add charity, and leave hope and faith to take care of me when they like . . . The truth is, I am preparing to emigrate, and am getting my team in order, so that I may hitch my horses and start at the crack of dawn . . ."

The emigration came sooner and differently from his expectation.

In a short while he was writing to Daisy, in an access of irritation: "I am making desperate efforts to extricate myself from all these business entanglements. If I did not potter and slave to care for my money, all of you might one day find yourselves like butterflies in a January world!"

To Julia, also, he poured out his exacerbation: "As usual, when I want to do most for one of my own people, the Devil turns up the wrong card! I am weary and overworked. Poor Byrne was found dead in his chair Friday morning. Mrs. Key arranged the funeral for which I sent the check . . . Unless I get out of this Niagara I shall probably go off the same way. Thank God, I am ready to cash in my checks at any moment."

In November he sent for Dudie: the crisis was beyond his ability to control. Julia spent a week in New York, reviewed Sam's predicament, and went home hoping that at least a modest income might be salvaged from the wreckage; she was indignant that Sam's two partners had "fooled away most of the $500,000 he lent them to start with."

In his extremity, Sam placed himself in the hands of his friends, Barlow, Hurlbert, and Butler Duncan, all of them competent businessmen. They found that Sam's fortune was gone irretrievably. What was more alarming, he had carelessly signed papers that might render him liable to much more. Their advice was unanimous: leave the country to avoid involvement in a nasty legal mess.

Consequently, on November 19, 1882, there went a hasty scribble to Dudie, whom Sam had promised to visit soon: "Sorry to disappoint you, but by Hurlbert's advice I am off for Europe tomorrow. This is to avoid servance of process. They intend to try to make me a full partner, and I don't want to get into the clutches of the law. I gave out I was going to Boston, just to get away noiselessly."

Yet even at this point, his care was for his family. Butler Duncan, he said, had bought the books and furniture at 85 Clinton Place, which provided a little cash. "John Sutherland will send Maud $500," he continued. "I enclose $50 to pay Marion's expenses to Canada when his book [*Mr. Isaacs*] appears. I add $50 for yourself. My address, which keep private, is care Charles Ellis, 36 Piccadilly, London. Not a word about my whereabouts." Then an afterthought: "I make your check $100. Affectionately, Bro. Sam."

Uncle Sam ruined — a fugitive from creditors! The world of Beacon Street turned wintry with consternation. From New York, Jerry the valet sorrowfully transported two bottles of Sam's century-old rum, the last remnants of his cellar. And for years to come, on great occasions — a new child, a new book — this hoarded ambrosia would be poured into tiny glasses and drunk in a toast — to the event — and to sunny Sam.

ELEVEN

A SOCIAL LION

So Uncle Sam had been cast into outer darkness. That was what Boston believed. But Boston was mistaken. The old man's arrival in England was greeted with shouts of joy.

Louis Jennings, former editor of the *New York Times,* whose hammering had helped to smash the Tweed ring, claimed first privilege in welcoming Sam, with a dinner at the Garrick Club. William Howard Russell, Sam's companion on that memorable swing through the Confederacy, embraced him, and Sam was delighted to remark that his friend had added scarcely a wrinkle to his mind or spirit. With the Earl of Dunraven Sam sat chinning until 1 A.M. And Lord Rosebery absolutely preempted his beloved "President" at breakfast every day, in Berkeley Square. To appalled Boston Sam wrote that nothing could exceed the kindness with which he was being all but smothered, while his British friends fully appreciated that, as in every one of his financial dilemmas, he had been cruelly sinned against, and hardly sinning at all. "I paint no false colors and tell them briefly how I have been robbed. It makes no difference to John Bull."

The amazing chance of being provided with a sumptuous flat in Piccadilly appeared to him a clear sign of Providential concern for his welfare. Charles Ellis, a friend who had gone to Tibet for some shooting, had written to Sam weeks before, extending the use of the flat; and Sam observed sagely that the letter, mailed at Omaha, Nebraska, "danced into my hands, doubtless by occult instrumentality, on the Monday when I was meditating what to do. So I accepted the offer and found a handsome apartment, with a man servant and a housekeeper, who are devoted to me."

But Rosebery perceived that the excitements of London life were not healthful for the old man in his tensely nervous state, and after a few days Sam was whisked off to Dalmeny Park in Scotland, where Lady Rosebery was awaiting the birth of her second child. From there Sam wrote gaily to Boston, "Lady Hannah summoned me to her bedside before I had been five minutes in the house, and her smile of gladness was a sunbeam of welcome." Within two days he found his mind "slowly recovering its tone," although he was quite "dazed by the continuous fondness of these kind friends for an old wreck like me."

His sixty-ninth birthday, on January 27, 1883, was fittingly celebrated, his room decorated with flowers, and at dinner there was brought in "a great round cake, as big as Fort Sumter, and on it four American flags and six candles." Sam made a speech, "as clumsily as any Englishman, I fear," and Rosebery gave him "a lovely set of studs and buttons for my shirt, gold with a pearl in each. So you will see I am coddled and spoiled, and can hardly realize that it is five weeks since I left New York . . . Like the fisherman whom Haroun al Raschid made caliph for a day, I rub my eyes every morning and my surprise hardly diminishes to find that this is not a dream. The constant dress parade is rather a strain upon the perpetual good behavior of an old Bohemian, but I am getting used to it."

(To Daisy Terry went a hurried confidential plea: "Can you send me a copy of the 'Battle Hymn'?" He had been called upon several times to recite it, he said, but somehow his sister's famous lines had faded from his memory, although Longfellow he could spout by the ream.)

The success of *Mr. Isaacs* in England made Sam purr. Gladstone's secretary told him not a copy was to be had in the circulating libraries, and said Gladstone had praised the book as "a literary marvel," although as a churchman he could not subscribe to its Oriental mysticism. Madame Blavatsky wrote a long letter, expressing surprise and pleasure, for while in India, Frank Crawford had been a sworn enemy of her cult. "She says the book must have been *inspired*," chirped Sam. "She little imagines what an atmosphere of occultism pervaded my rooms and still surrounds me . . . I am tempted to believe that Koot Houmi helped *project* it upon paper."

Friends were insisting that Sam write his memoirs, and he wondered whether Crawford might not serve as amanuensis, for "I don't feel up to the pen and ink work myself," he explained to Julia. "I am told the book would sell like hot cakes. So far as the *entrée* into any of the worlds here is concerned, I can put him *rectus* in any *curia.* Tell him this quickly. The thing is worth considering, for I cannot live forever."

But Marion was taken up with his own writing: his third novel, *An American Politician,* was in proof. He decided to return to Rome, stopping over in England for a few days. Sam met his nephew in London, and whirled him through a five-day drill that left the young man haggard — dinners with Indian nabobs, formal gatherings at Rosebery's place at nearby Epsom, The Durdans, and literary evenings at the Blue Posts tavern, an eating house in Cork Street noted for solid English fare and superb red wines. At one Blue Posts dinner, Oscar Wilde's friend, Rennell Rodd, sat between Crawford and Henry James; and afterwards Rodd and Marion wandered about in search of midnight adventures, winding up in a Covent Garden bar. Rodd, who was in the Foreign Office now, was moved to congratulate his friend on his drinking prowess, whereupon Crawford assured him that "the position of cupbearer to His Majesty our King and Uncle, which I have held more than once for six months at a time, would raise you to a wonderful perfection."

Then Crawford fled to Rome, convinced that Uncle Sam had been bent on introducing him to "the majority of the House of Lords." "You have no conception of what his life is like," he told cousin Maud. "I had five days of it, and never met anything less than a baron, never a commoner except Henry Irving and such people. His chambers reek with fat titles and the savor of many 'Right Honorables.' I couldn't stand it for a fortnight. He has promised to come on here, but I fear he will be kept in England by the train of princes and peers who so freely butter his dear old nose."

One change in his uncle Marion did report, and that was that he "rejoices in a complete set of teeth, which improves his utterance and his appetite." Sam had been overtaken by the minor infirmities of old age, eyesight and hearing both being somewhat dimmed; it was no longer possible for him to take pleasure in a performance of opera, although a concert played by an artist like Joachim could set his admiration aflame.

* * *

The pace Crawford found intolerable was only a warmup for Sam Ward, that London season. The Roseberys moved from Scotland to their English estate, Mentmore, where "Uncle Sam" could be even more sumptuously pampered. At all his residences, Rosebery set aside suites of rooms marked with "Uncle Sam's" name, for use at any time. Meanwhile, Lady Rosebery had successfully "cudgelled" Sam into beginning his memoirs, dictating his reminiscences to her. "She has constituted herself my amanuensis," Sam told Boston. "The first day she wrote nineteen pages, and since then I have gone on . . . hard work for me." Later, when he returned for a while to the flat in Piccadilly, a secretary continued the operation, and Sam reported cheerfully that "my scribe comes twice a day, takes down my dictation in pencil, and when he brings it to me in fair copy on the morrow I am surprised at its picturesque attractiveness . . . I reached the year 1836–37 this morning. It is odd how prettily some of my dictation reads."

One day in Piccadilly he received a shock. He had seen, he said, two Astor connections, "Mark Wilkes escorting a poor, infirm, dilapidated, and gray old woman, in whom it was difficult to recognize the dark-haired and pretty Eliza Langdon, whom I had not seen since 1840. I was shocked by the ravages of time upon a contemporary. She looked like old Mrs. Grymes . . . My time is getting short here below," he ruminated to Louisa Terry, "and I am enchanted to get back to my own thoughts and, perhaps, dreams of a better life. In truth, like Aramis, I have always preferred the convent or the monastery to the *corps de garde*. But what a responsibility to be alone with one's soul!"

As he dictated his Memoirs he looked back with detachment but no hint of amendment: "I only discovered at the age of forty what would have been my true vocation; at that of fifty what it might have been; and in the gray dawn of my sixtieth year, why my life had been a mistake and its pursuits an illusion."

The satisfactions of contemplation, however, were denied him, for "Uncle Sam" found himself the lion of the social season. "I have had to decline three distinguished dinners this week," he informed Boston lightly. "I dine today at Mrs. Phillips's, to meet Fanny Kemble's daughter. Tomorrow with the Royal Literary Fund at their annual banquet. Thursday at the Honorable Chandos Leigh's; on Friday at Rosebery's, and on Saturday with Henry Irving at his annual Lyceum dinner, and on the 12th with the Fishmongers Guild." He had been with the Duke of Sutherland to call on Lady Holland at Holland House, "the loveliest setting in all London. Thence to Argyll Lodge hard by, where I talked with *that* duke about America and with his duchess about asthma, for which I gave her an infallible cure." Down to Oxford to meet the Duke of Buckingham. Dining at The Durdans with the Duke of St. Albans and the Earl of Cardigan. Dining *en famille* with the Dunravens and their three little daughters — "they and their dog hung around me with confiding sweetness." At Stafford House to meet the Prince and Princess of Wales. And a week's visit to Trentham, "accepting the Duke of Sutherland's fifth pressing invitation" to luxuriate in that palatial pile — "sixty guest rooms, one needs the thread of Ariadne to find one's way among the bewildering complexity of passages, stairways, and corridors." He had caught the 5 A.M. train from London on a hot day, and arrived bristling with animation. Lord Ronald Gower showed him around the immense place, and at five-thirty the next morning Sam was up to catch the sunrise ("strange how few composers and poets see the sunrise, except when returning from a wassail"), ramble through the gardens and hothouses, admire the cattle, and revel in the fountains at play. Even the ex-Khedive of Egypt was less impressive than Sam Ward, who reported that "I was the guest of honor. Our dinner was charming, crowned with a profusion of cherries, hothouse grapes, and strawberries. The cherries melted in my mouth. They are larger than any grape. I wonder why they were not chosen as the forbidden fruit."

Back in London, a Western mining acquaintance was astonished by the unlimited attentions paid to Sam Ward, to all appearances an "unassuming old gentleman." When they drove out at the fashionable hour, it seemed that from every passing carriage and rider came nods for "Uncle Sam," as people vied for his recognition. At the Drury Lane Theater, Sam sat in a stage box, the Prince of Wales sat opposite, and shortly an equerry appeared with a request for Mr. Ward's company in the royal box. When Sam returned, his companions asked whether something important was in the wind; he smiled and said that the Prince was giving a garden party at Marlborough House the next day, to which several Americans had been invited, among them a charming miss to whom he had asked "Uncle Sam" to devote some attention.

At the Ascot races Sam had difficulty dodging the Prince and his betting book (Sam could no longer bet on a royal scale), but "he presented me to Lady Lonsdale, who immediately addressed me as 'Uncle Sam.' What with old acquaintances whom I did not recognize, and who rushed up to thank me for hospitalities I had forgotten, and with new ones male and female, I passed four very exhausting hours on my feet. Nor was the fatigue diminished by the very cordial shake of the Prince of Wales's hand: not having the king's evil, the royal touch did not revive me." At the close, Dunraven whirled him to the cars, "where we had to fight for our seats, and I felt, on getting home at 7 o'clock, like a raw recruit at the close of his first battle."

While in the toils of this fatigue, he vowed he would "retire from this gay and festive life. I have refused invitations extending towards the end of the month. My book is at too interesting a crisis to be sacrificed to social duties, in which I take no pleasure but only submit to from good nature, — which latter quality has been the bane of my life." But he was on hand the next day at "a frisk of dotards and dowagers," the *Conversazione* of the Royal Society at Burlington House. Then he breakfasted with Lord Houghton, and "Browning was there; he looks more like a bank president than a poet. He is fond of good cheer and strong wine. He seemed quite shocked when I told him that Ascot bored me with its throng of pretty women; that I went there to see another kind of race and was disappointed."

Before "Uncle" could retire, the irrepressible Hurlbert bounced into London, primed for gaieties. Jay Gould, the latest owner of the *New York World*, had sold the paper to Joseph Pulitzer; whereupon the "Member" had divested himself of his stocks, disposed of his art collection (at prices much in excess of its true value, the *New York Times* sourly intimated), and headed for Europe. He burst upon Sam like a *retarius* poised to ensnare social big game, and "Uncle Sam" opened the door of the arena.

In short order the "Member" contrived to "be received into three clubs — the Athenaeum, Travellers, and St. James's — to breakfast with me at Lord Dufferin's, with a score of notables — to dine at Lord Houghton's and Lord Wemyss' — and to accompany the Duke of Sutherland and myself to that castle of the Sleeping Beauty, Knole, Sevenoaks," Sam relayed to Barlow in New York.

"Yesterday I took Hurlbert to see my Laura of Grosvenor Square, and then to lunch at Lady Reay's — then launched him to dine at Twickenham with Mr. and Mrs. Labouchere, Henry Irving, and Ellen Terry, and they kept him all night. Today he lunched with Lady Galway and with Lady Hannah and the Sycophant — whilst he dines tonight with Lord Wemyss, so you may imagine he is busy . . . . Day before yesterday I saw the Member at six and we drove at eight to Stafford House to as charming a dinner as I ever enjoyed." There Cardinal Howard ("ex-Guardsman and possible future Pope") recalled that he had been Hurlbert's *cicerone* through the College of the Propaganda at the time of the Vatican Ecumenical Council of 1869.

Every place and everybody the entertaining Hurlbert brightened and bedazzled. With Sam he dined at the Garrick Club with "a rich Yorkshireman named Denison, long in India, who is called the 'Bengal Tiger,' and at 11:20 we went to the New Club, Covent Garden, where Sarah Bernhardt, after performing 'Fedora' at a matinée and in the evening, appeared in the club's private theater as 'Valerie the Blind Girl.' A strange juxtaposition," Sam mused. "I saw Mademoiselle Mars play the same part at the *Français* in 1835! And on the same stage where Sarah played I saw a troop of trained dogs perform in July of that year, when the audience consisted of two hundred revellers assembled at small tables munching broiled bones and drinking porter! And now the élite of London society, the majority of them ladies, mostly young, were assembled at half past twelve on a Sabbath morning to see this performance and partake afterwards of a *souper à la Régence!*"

One week of this "champagne and jollity," and "Hurlbert keeled over." He had been limping with a sore knee, and a doctor diagnosed gout, "at which the ex-editor leapt and swore like the Devil in a baptismal font. Finally, after various imprudences, I put him on the cars, with the Duke of Sutherland to look after him, who landed him at Dunrobin Castle [in Scotland], where he has been ever since, most of the time recumbent and writing charming letters about the shimmer of the sun upon the sea waves, the tender blue of the mountains, and the soft transparency of an atmosphere where figs and pomegranates ripen in the open air. I think that week of looking after my old friend, delirious with liberty and the affectionate interest of many new and old acquaintances, was more like being tied to the tail of a comet than anything in my previous experience."

Sam, to whom gout was inadmissible (he even doubted that Hurlbert had the gout), kept going. "Had I one spark of ambition," he reflected, "I could be a lion, though an old one. I really think these people like me."

In August he informed Barlow that the season had ended abruptly. "A week ago there were hours when it was dangerous to cross St. James's Street, Piccadilly, or Berkeley Square, and when Park Lane offered risks of broken ribs to unwary pedestrians. Today the London World has vanished like a flock of quail, and the solitude is almost phenomenal . . . I must confess to a feeling of loneliness since the departure of my chief darlings, the two Tennant girls, who have been to me the joys of the season."

The Tennant sisters were Laura ("my Laura of Grosvenor Square") and Margot, who became Margot Asquith. Rennell Rodd had introduced "Uncle Sam" to Laura Tennant ("that radiant little being — that wonderful woman-child," Rodd described her) and a sensitive friendship had sprung up at once between the old man and the nineteen-year-old girl. They corresponded regularly, although meeting often. "I never manage to ask you half the questions that lie like sealed letters in my heart waiting for your sympathetic fingers to open them," ran one of Laura's notes. "Goodnight, dearest Uncle Sam." Naturally Sam composed poems for both the sisters, in English and in French.

Periodic bulletins on the "Member's" circumstances peppered the letters with which Sam peppered S.L.M. Barlow. "Hurlbert is still an invalid and left Dunrobin for the hot springs not far distant . . ." "Hulbert kept on his back at Dunrobin by the village surgeon, but writes that he is attended by angels and dreams of a better life . . ." "Hurlbert, as I hear from his servant through mine, is able now to walk with his knee bandaged and is meditating a piratical voyage in some yacht or other . . ." "A telegram from the Member ordering a suit of knickerbockers — which looks like more walking . . ." "Hurlbert still at Dunrobin, has taken a moor and a shooting lodge and intends to keep open house after a little indulgence in hot soaking. I expect every day orders for more knickerbockers and when I reach Scotland shall not be surprised to find him in kilts . . ." "Hurlbert has taken to the rod — not the gun. The latter he was never familiar with, and the former he has been a stranger to since he left school . . ." "Hurlbert has been flying about like scud in a gale . . ."

To the ailing ex-editor Sam sent his "Mendacious Club" opinion of the disorder causing these capers and relapses: "I half suspect I was right *ab initio* as to your malady, of which I always doubted the gout. Habits of self-neglect are sure to engender morbid violations of the human equilibrium, which like real devils endeavor to escape where they can find a hole. Though if Mephistopheles was right, when he said in Faust's study 'the devils must go out by the door through which they entered,' I cannot understand why yours should have selected the knee, which has been bent to neither God nor woman for many a year past. Perhaps it is for that very reason in an abnormal state. Say you are sorry and I will forgive you."

Sam had been promising to come to Italy for a visit with the Terrys as soon as the London season ended; but then the Roseberys decided to take a trip around the world, and he felt he must stay and help them with their preparations, — letters of introduction, advice on ships, trains, clothing, provisions and a hundred other matters about which he, inveterate wanderer, was amply knowledgeable. Coincidentally, he kept in social circulation, and told Barlow of the pleasant evening he had passed with two New York friends and Aristarchi Bey, Turkish minister at Washington since 1873 and a great favorite there. After dinner they adjourned to the

Savoy Theater, "where I saw 'Iolanthe' for the first time with great pleasure . . . Aristarchi is more amusing than ever and wideawake and instructive, besides. His analysis of the cuisine of the London clubs and private houses established Delmonico's as far superior to anything here and equalled only by the Café Anglais in Paris. Prices about the same. All at the dinner were of the opinion that there are twenty cottages in Newport whose chefs are far superior to those of any twenty houses in London. This of course I ascribe to the extravagance of our people and the superiority of our markets. But in Paris the stranger has to pay for the Franco-German war, and the cooking is in inverse ratio to its cost — taste falling and avarice rising . . . I have told Rosebery that you and Mrs. Barlow insist on their resting for a few days at Glen Cove. I squeeze dear Lady Alice's hand and kiss her cheek. Uncle Sam."

There followed another rain of bulletins about the "Member." "Hurlbert has taken the loveliest of the Sutherland hunting and fishing lodges, Loch Hope, of which his notes and envelopes are hereafter to bear the superscription . . ." "Hurlbert still at Loch Hope, entertaining a large American party, with Lady Angelsey for its matron. The duke reports them as very gay, with Hurlbert for a host. He has sent to London for a wagon load of books, meaning to devote his seclusion to the fulfillment of a serious and mysterious literary project which I think stands a poor chance of being perfected."

On September 1 the Roseberys sailed for New York, to continue thence to California, Australia, and home by way of Suez and the Mediterranean. Sam saw them off at Liverpool and returned to London, where, on September 4, he sent Barlow the "last frantic letter" from the "Member," in which he "accepts the inevitable, — my departure for Italy. Nothing could exceed the persistent kindness of the duke and duchess's entreaties that I join them at Dunrobin, — but it's high time I went to my own people, who need me, and who will only believe, like St. Thomas, in the 'actual presence.' "

TWELVE

"TURN DOWN AN EMPTY GLASS"

THE change from cloudy London to gloriously sunny Italy revived Uncle Sam's spirit, if reviving had been necessary. He made the trip comfortably, "whirled through the St. Gothard summit to a sort of dreamy Elysium of cloudless skies and picturesque vales with fair fields teeming with culture and fertility." Reaching Sorrento on October 22, he found his family in the Hotel Cocumella, a former religious house perched on the cliff between Sant' Agnello and Sorrento, on the Gulf of Naples. With Louisa were four of her children — Marion Crawford, Daisy Terry and Arthur Terry ("17 years and 6 feet 3 inches, and graceful and handsome as he is tall"), and Mimoli Fraser with her two little boys. Hugh Fraser, Mimoli's husband, was kept by his diplomatic duties most of the time in Rome.

Sam was delighted by the reposeful setting. Trellised vines trailed between lemon and orange trees on the terrace, and for backdrop there was the breathtaking view across the bay, — emerald and indigo sea, sapphire sky, and Vesuvius, smoking lazily by day, at night tipped with a ruddy glow. Steps had been hewn in the rock leading down to a tiny beach two hundred feet below; at intervals these quaint interior staircases were lighted by windowlike openings, and on one landing Marion Crawford had established his workshop, — a table at which he wrote, with a jug of cool water on the floor beside him. Marion had been holding back his fourth completed novel, *A Roman Singer*, for Uncle Sam to read, — a duty Sam performed at once and gave the work his hearty approval.

Daisy told the Boston cousins that Uncle Sam had arrived "as jolly and brave as ever, in fact just his lovely old self, with an added halo and flavor of Oriental mysticism about him, which suits him very well." At noon, when the cliff threw a grateful shade, they all went swimming, Sam striking far out from shore with Marion; then he would swim back and perform diving stunts, blowing like a porpoise. While sunning himself on the rocks, he watched with amusement the antics of Mimoli's shavers taking their first lessons in the water. Afterwards, slowly climbing the grottolike stairways to the hotel, he would be ready to do justice to a bountiful luncheon; then, while the rest of the family dispersed to their siesta, he would sit in the blazing sun, soaking up its warmth, reading, smoking, or just gazing across the luminous blue bay.

Celebration of Daisy's twenty-first birthday had been held up until Uncle could be present, and his gift to her topped all — "the most superb sapphire and diamond you or any one ever saw since the beginning of the world," she raved to cousin Maud. The ambition and energy of this Terry daughter pleased Sam; beside her he felt lethargic, he said. "What a clear, limpid brain the girl has," he told Louisa.

In Crawford's lateen-rigged felucca, *Margherita,* he sailed to Capri and put in three deliciously lazy days, basking in the sun, smacking his lips over country meals, watching the bubbles drift up in the topaz-colored wine. Then back on the mainland he climbed Vesuvius with Marion — "did" Pompeii in a day, astonishing the guides with his knowledge of antiquity — and on the spur of the moment insisted on transporting everybody across the bay to try the seafood at a restaurant he liked. Mimoli drew special comfort from her uncle, for she was preparing to become a Roman Catholic, and her mother objected. Marion had entered the church while in India, and Daisy soon would follow; it was inevitable that Louisa's children, Roman-born and Roman-bred, should form Catholic sympathies. Sam, who respected all sincere faiths, although dogmatic about none, smoothed over the difficulty with Louisa, to Mimoli's relief.

Once Marion had finished his daily writing stint, he joined the others in merry doings, and any excuse was sufficient for a *festa.* A local troupe of tarantella singers and dancers, led by the mandolin-playing village barber and his wife, was called in to entertain Uncle Sam. The table had been set on the terrace, garlanded with carnations and verbena, and Chinese lanterns cast a soft glow. The hotel brought out the finest wine in the cellar, and Sam "went nearly crazy with delight" at the songs and vividly costumed dancers. In the midst of the performance, he demanded of Mimoli, "Why aren't the little boys here to enjoy this?" She explained that it was long past their bedtime, and one was still weak from a severe illness; but he sprang up, saying, "Well, I shall go and get Nino; he shan't miss it at any rate"; and in a few minutes he reappeared, carrying the boy wrapped in a blanket, smiling sleepily. "For the rest of the evening Uncle Sam held him on his knee, and the child laughed and sang with the singers and had his little sip of wine, — and repeated all the songs the next day," Mimoli recalled.

Fourteen days of this, then they broke camp: Louisa, Marion, and the Terrys returned to Rome, and Mimoli and Sam crossed over to Naples, where for several days they took in the sights. The riotous city put sparkle in his veins, Sam told Barlow, and when, after a week of sightseeing, he also went on to Rome, he experienced another transformation there. "The change is for the better and happier, if not for the gayer," he consoled himself, wishing he had Barlow along to share his tranquil enjoyment of the "divine Palestrina music" at St. Peter's.

But there was business pending in London, and since Marion wished to consult his publishers there, the two men set out together. The long train ride to Paris troubled Sam not at all — "no fatigue in sitting up two nights, as of old," he boasted to Barlow — and he reached London again after an absence of a month. He was delighted to hear that *Dr. Claudius* was selling well, and when Marion put into words all the gratitude he felt, but had neglected to express, the old man was touched; he told Julia he was preserving two of Marion's letters of appreciation especially, and he trusted that he had in fact demolished "the demon of cynicism" in Crawford "by having proved to him by example that loving kindness is existable without *arrière pensée*. If I have restored his faith in the possibilities of a gentler human nature, finding its chief happiness in promoting that of others, I shall have rendered him a far more precious service than in helping to make him a novelist. I cannot tell you the pride and happiness I feel in the two letters in question. I believe that were there a Heaven (which I don't dispute) and a gate to that Heaven and a St. Peter at that gate, I should only need to produce these two letters to have the portals flung wide open to so old and not impenitent a sinner as I am."

Rosebery was forwarding cheery accounts of his journey. He told of visiting the Barlows, and calling upon Andrew Carnegie at Pittsburgh, and George Pullman at Chicago, in both instances introduced by "Uncle Sam." Best of all was an overnight stay at the Mailliard ranch in California, "in company [Sam wrote proudly] with my grandson Wintie Chanler, whom Rosebery took quite a fancy to. It was very kind in him to pay this visit to my sister and pleasant to hear how much he enjoyed it."

To Sam any news of his grandchildren was manna. Earlier in the year he had been saddened by word of the death of Maddie's two youngest sons, Egerton White Chanler, and especially Marion Ward Chanler, who was only fourteen. Any relative bearing the name of his cherished brother, Sam held doubly dear.

The final week of October, 1883, he passed in Paris. The "untutored clumsiness" of a British dentist had garbled Sam's articulation to a point where it had become "painful to myself and chaotic to my listeners." But repairs by Parisian experts put things straight, and Sam was able to announce that he was "now like other men, and the change has revived my drooping spirits." The week spent in the French capital was crowded with activities, — devouring art and seeing friends. He listened to a young soprano and pronounced her "the new Malibran, the toast of the Parisians and worthy of all admiration." And as he was leaving for the railroad station, a note from the daughter of an old business associate cost him his dinner, when he sacrificed the time in order to call on her at the Meurice, breaking away at the last moment to catch the Channel train.

In London again, he rattled off for Barlow his jam-packed social schedule, although averring "everybody is out of town." He spent a day at the country place of Sir John Lubbock, the naturalist, where he learned "more of the true spirit of a naturalist than in all my previous life put together." Then Hurlbert erupted into town from

Scotland, "blazed with the steadiness of one of Edison's best 'electrics' until Sunday night, then betook himself back to Dunrobin, where he will find Billy Russell and a charming crew of convivialists to welcome him . . . Tonight I dine at your old stamping ground, the Blue Posts tavern," with Henry James, "who has been excessively kind to his brother novelist," Crawford. Marion now had finished reading the proofs of his fourth novel and was at work on the fifth, which Sam loyally predicted would be "the best of the lot."

Crawford's fame, he joked, had made him "a binary star," and Sam saw to it that their movement was never stilled. In one six-day period, they journeyed to Edinburgh and Dalmeny; the next day lunched with Charles Tennant, after which "his lovely daughter, the Princess Margot of my poem, drove us ten miles to Lady Reay's, where we were charmingly entertained." The day after that Lord Reay drove them to "contemplate the original Bears of Bradwardine as etched by Sir Walter Scott in 'Waverly.' After dinner that evening we drove ten miles to the cars, which brought us to London on Wednesday." That evening there was a dinner with George Du Maurier, Arthur Kinglake, and others to meet Crawford. Then it "so happened" that the Duke and Duchess of Sutherland were in town, and they entertained Sam and Marion at Stafford House with various Indian and naval dignitaries.

By this time Crawford, "unused to so much movement, was becoming rather the worse for wear," and Sam contributed further to Marion's indisposition by "taking him down on Saturday to spend the day with Tennyson at Haslemere." That visit Sam described with verve.

"It was my first interview with the Laureate, whom I had corresponded with more or less for twenty years. From the moment of our arrival until we were whirled to the station five miles distant, the spirit of our conference never flagged; and, as Commodore Vanderbilt said of Lord Palmerston, 'He shrank less than any man I ever met.' "

Tennyson read them a "long ghost story with thrilling effect, and talked a good deal with me about spiritual matters . . . His son (the unmarried one), Hallam Tennyson, is a splendid fellow, bright and genial, and the poet's wife most kind and gracious, but in appearance one resurrected from the grave, so pallid and ghost-like she seemed an apparition from another world."

The real excitement started when the visitors took their leave. Hurlbert was making another flying descent upon London, and "as I had invited Billy Russell and Hurlbert to dine with me at the Blue Posts that night, you can imagine my consternation at seeing the train leave the station as we drove up to it. There was no other until 6:40, so we chartered a carriage and drove ten miles to Godalming, where a way car took us to Woking, and the main train thence to London, after a steeplechase of four hours that brought us to the door just as Hurlbert was pulling the bell. He had arrived an hour before from Dunraven's castle. Billy Russell arrived shortly from Sandringham — and we stayed at the tavern until driven out by the small hours. The next day I breakfasted with the Duke [of Sutherland], who prevailed upon me to bring Crawford that night to keep them company. Billy Russell was there and our exchange of anecdotes and the adventures that befell us in the Confederacy before the war seemed very entertaining to all listeners. The next morning Crawford called in a doctor, who has been here twice a day since."

The medical attention was for Crawford. Sam felt no disability.

"Today I was summoned by Russell to pay a visit to Lady Angelsey, whom I once met at Newport at one of Ward McAllister's picnics, and who expressed a flattering wish to see me again," his report continued. "We found her at the Bath Hotel, Piccadilly. She was thinner but gayer than when she appeared to me as a young widow who had just put off her mourning. In fact, she seemed what the Methodist preacher called 'full of the Devil' — and with her were two pretty young women, not behind hand as a chorus."

There was a postcript to this — "Hurlbert rushed off yesterday to his third visit to Lord Portsmouth, having joined late the previous evening Russell and myself, who dined at the Garrick." The next word Barlow received said that Crawford had hobbled back to Rome, and Sam would follow "at more leisure."

The great event of that year and month of December, 1883, for Sam, was the publication of a new edition of *Lyrical Recreations*, under the imprint of Macmillan in London. The reappearance of his book, on the eve of his seventieth birthday, gave him much satisfaction. He had revised the text somewhat, in the light of the changes that had occurred during the twenty years since its first publication; some poems had been "judiciously omitted, and not a few new ones added, the judiciousness of which remains to be proved," he wrote to Barlow half apologetically. The edition was inscribed to *"The Earl of Rosebery, Decori Scotiae et Humanitatis,"* with a preface that skipped lightly enough —

The Muse I wooed at fifty-two
   Bore me these urchin lays,
Which raise their lowly heads anew
   Since quickened by thy praise.

Will they live on, to vindicate
   The memory of their sire,
Whom Fate compelled to leave to fate
   These foundlings of his lyre?

What care we? Ere the pyramids
   The priests of Isis sang,
While on the kingly coffin-lids
   The graver's chisel rang.

The priests are dust, the crumbling fane
   In piteous ruin lies;
In loving hearts the holy strain
   Of David never dies.

This "old friend in a new attire" was basically no gayer than its first version, although it was perhaps more tender. There was an acquired lightness of touch in the trifles addressed to what Daisy Terry called "Uncle Sam's chelas and fireflies," — the pretty women to whom he was continually sending "impromptus" and bouquets.

The theme of approaching death was retained and reinforced: "Antepenultimate," held over from 1865, ran —

Shall I sit and wait for Death
With a sigh at every breath
For the hours of gladness flown
From the present, drear and lone?
Yes, I'm weary of the fight . . .

And "Senescentia," a new poem, began —

All my being now is yearning
For the rapture of repose. . . .

How profoundly he had sensed the undertone of disillusion in his beloved *Rubáiyát* was made clear in "Lines Written in a Copy of Omar Khayyám" —

At night among the churchyard thistles
The boy with feigned bravado whistles;
And minor chords when Omar sings
Betray his path's environings,
And show, however brave their tread,
Our footsteps lead but to the dead.

As flow'ry meads delight the eye,
Though, 'neath the grasses, serpents lie,
His jubilees, with rapture fair,
Conceal a dreg-note of despair.
The cold stars glisten on his rhymes
To mock their muffled funeral chimes . . .

In tune with this elegy was a threnody for Siro Delmonico ("He lieth low whose constant art / For years the daily feasts purveyed . . ."). And to two fellow practitioners of the poetic art Sam paid his respects, but differently: for Edgar Allan Poe, a paean of praise ("Oh wayward, wierd, and mystic soul . . ."), and for Walt Whitman, the back of Sam's critical hand ("He who scorns the tuneful measure / Is a lout . . .").

Most satisfying, however, were the society verses and gallant trifles composed during recent months, in which Sam eschewed didacticism and saluted the objects of his admiration, for the most part young. Here Sam showed a talent that long practice had tooled to a fine edge. Such was "To Consuelo" —

Sweet mystery! This photograph,
In twilight caught, is thine;
Beneath I write its epigraph:
"The precious cup I may not quaff,
But I can bless the wine!"

"To Laura" was in French, as were several of the lighter bits —

Hélas! d'un si beau rêve
Que la durée est brève,
Trajet de météore!
M'apprenant qu'à mon age
L'amour devient mirage, —
Tithone sans Aurore.

This was the finial, ending the book with Sam's own Tithonus-like cricket-chirp. (In evoking the fable, did Sam in thought substitute for *Aurora* the lovely loved one who was ever young in his memory, while he aged, — *Medora?*) Sam was not wholly discontented with this testament to posterity, although no longer was he brash enough to dream of literary immortality. Presentation copies of the volume he sent out liberally, one special copy being forwarded to Washington in the diplomatic pouch of the American minister, James Russell Lowell, an old friend of "Uncle Sam." This gift was inscribed: "To Chester A. Arthur — President, Fisherman, and Fisher of Men — from his affectionate Uncle Sam," and the author described the contents appetizingly as "drops from my lyrical jelly-bag." (Eighty years later it would be an item in the rare book trade, especially prized because its pages were still uncut.)

This business being wound up, as Christmas approached, Sam advised "Carina Maudina Mia" in Boston: "I join our dear loved ones at Rome tomorrow, where I hope to recover sufficient tranquillity of mind to write you like a dear, sensible old uncle, which I used to be until circumstances not mentioned in Apuleius transformed me into the old livery horse, equally fit for a wedding or a funeral." As for any saying of his into which she might have read wisdom: "Perhaps the coming, or rather the advent, of age gives me mystical lore."

"Uncle Sam's" defection did not pass without protest from his friends in England. "Why have you deserted us when it is cold and leprous in Rome?" demanded Dunraven. "Here it is mild as milk, while in the North of Ireland, from which I have lately come, it is more like Florida."

Sam found Rome neither cold nor leprous. "My nineteenth day here, with only two cloudy ones," he assured Maud, adding that Marion was "fagging away at his novel," which of course would infallibly be the best yet.

Life at the Palazzo Altemps, where Louisa's family was crowded into rooms that contrasted sharply with their former spacious apartment in the Odescalchi, moved in a staid pattern. The family met at meals, but the rest of the day they scattered, pursuing their different vocations, and Sam found the days dull. "Most people are dull in this particular charnel house of the ages, where one's chief resource is the novelty of antiquity," he admitted privately to Barlow. Yet determined to be cheerful, he added: "But I never weary of walking in Rome, and am glad that I have kept this *bonne bouche* for the dessert of my life."

His rambles often took him into the studios of the artists who thronged the city; he enjoyed their zest, and while he could no longer afford to buy their works, he dealt generously with them in the commodity of sound advice. One group especially congenial was the cluster around the Spanish painter, José Villegas; John Elliott, the Howes' shy painter friend, belonged to this set. Good-naturedly Sam endeavored to draw that young man out. "I am making him see more of the world," he reported to Maud Howe; and to foster the intimacy he sat for his portrait to "Signorino Jacco," as the students nicknamed Elliott. At the same time, a Spanish sculptor, Mariano Benlliure y Gil, modeled a bust of the old man while Sam chatted in fluent Castilian, speaking it with the careless elegance and slight Parisian accent of a *boulevardier.*

The frugal fare provided at the Altemps aroused no enthusiasm in the veteran gastronome, although to Louisa Sam extolled it. The loss of her fortune had compelled Loulie to retrench painfully in her scale of living, and Sam, whose cellar had been famous, drank without demur the thin, sour Roman wine served regularly. He sensed that there was a difference now in his position within the domestic circle. Affectionate as they all were, his relatives had their own preoccupations, their own friends and interests, which he had never shared, or only transiently. Now, as a permanent dweller, he was no longer the focus of attention which he had been when he had appeared meteorically, attended by mystery and glamour; then everything had revolved around him, now he often was shunted into the background while concerns of which he knew little or nothing were under animated discussion. He was not resentful; he understood; but to play second fiddle was trying.

Whenever some distinguished guest was invited particularly to meet "Uncle Sam," his conversation would sparkle as brilliantly as ever and his reservoir of anecdote seem never to run dry. "When I was at Frankfort, in 1833," he might remark, apropos of the subject of fame and artists, "I asked the Countess Rossi — she was the diva Henrietta Sontag — whether she was not far happier in her new sphere as wife of the great Italian jurist, than as Sontag of the Opera. She exclaimed with great warmth: 'Moi, heureuse? Je donnerais toutes les couronnes du monde, et la tiare du Saint Père, pour une heure derrière la rampe et devant le parterre!' [I, happy? I would give all the crowns in the world, and the Holy Father's tiara, for one hour behind the footlights and in front of the pit!]."

At one dinner, that was graced by a prelate who had come to see the Uncle, the butler brought out one of the few remaining bottles of fine wine. He poured it without announcing the vintage. Sam lifted his glass, having no reason to expect anything but the ordinary table wine, and the others in the circle were edified by the look of sudden rapture that suffused his features as the bouquet penetrated his nostrils. "Château Lafite '67," he murmured, as if in prayer.

The incident marked a gap between the generations. When Sam had been mastering the mysteries of wine, in his eager youth at Paris, certain connoisseurs had been slangily called *côteaux* — experts whose palates were so exquisitely sensitive they could identify by bouquet and taste not only the vineyard from which a wine had come, but the very hillside (*côte*) on which the grapes had ripened. By the eighties the word, and almost the feat, had fallen into desuetude, and probably none of the witnesses of Sam's thrill of reverent recognition had before seen a *côteau* in action.

The truth was that Sam, the bohemian, was restless and a little bored with domesticity. His thoughts reverted continually to London, and he began laying plans to join the Roseberys when their ship touched at Malta, and sail back to England with them. Hurlbert was threatening to come to Rome, "to pass a season with Uncle Sam and prevent him from 'dilating with the wrong emotion' over alleged scenes of historic events," as the "Mendacious Club" "Member" wrote Barlow in January of '84. In February he arrived, and found "Uncle Sam sitting to a Spaniard for his bust and smoking cigarettes" with a *compadre* who resembled "the confessor of Lucretia Borgia, a charming woman abominably treated by the scribblers." Hurlbert and Sam's relatives were not compatible, and the "Member" said he might remain in Rome a fortnight, then "drop quietly down to join the Roseberys at Malta" with Sam.

On February 10 Crawford finished his current novel, and two days afterward left for Constantinople, under orders from Sam to take a thorough rest. Crawford's room at the Altemps was high in a tower, and since Mimoli Fraser was temporarily dispossessed of her apartment by workmen who were repairing the drains, Sam moved into Marion's eyrie and gave Mimoli his room.

Then Hurlbert changed his mind and decided to work back to England circuitously, by way of the Bosporus, the Danube, and the Seine, and on February 17 Sam set out for Malta alone. He was impatient to be on the move: only a few days before, while crossing the Piazza di Spagna with Elliott, he had paused to admire the artists' models and flower vendors, and rubbing his hands briskly together he had exclaimed, "Give me a clean shirt and a shilling, Jack, and I'm ready to start life all over again." He no longer coveted anything except affection.

* * *

But travel alone, at seventy, proved to be more taxing than the old man had foreseen. The train ride to Naples had been "cold and the journey lonely," he said in a note to Elliott, that was filled with wise counsels for the young painter. Yet Sam's spirit was buoyant. "I am glad to have gone away and recovered something of my old *drive*," he insisted. "It is a long time since I had to pack and unpack my own luggage, and what now seems a hardship will soon turn out a blessing."

To stop writing letters would have been for Uncle Sam to cease breathing, and Daisy Terry received regular reports of his progress. "It was time I struck my tent and recovered something of my old probity," he told her stoutly, although admitting that for the first time in his life he was finding a journey oppressive. At Messina, he had been struck by the cemetery, which he described half jocularly — "a square amphitheater, climbing the hill above the town and looking like an opera house. All the tombs have bas reliefs of the people inside, and some full-length statues. This early immortality will be a great help to historians." He had inquired the cost of sepulture, and had been informed that "for a grave which will have only one occupant the price was 20 francs, but for the right to a slab and an iron railing you must pay 150, and in the proscenium of this Temple of Death you must pay 1000 not to be disturbed, earthquakes alone excepted."

Unknown to Sam, the Roseberys had changed their route: they sailed from Suez directly to Marseilles, and from there continued overland to England. Hence Sam missed them at Malta, a place he found "cold, rainy, and rheumatic." But he visited the Templars church and bought English pipe tobacco for Villegas and Maltese laces for Louisa before heading slowly back towards Rome. The prospect of daily climbing the hundred and twenty-three steps to Marion's tower rather daunted him; and at Naples, when he ran into an old friend — Morton Frewen, brother-in-law of Lord Randolph Churchill — the two decided to take in the carnival sights. On Ash Wednesday, he wrote to Daisy that they had been peppered with confetti, had heard *La Gioconda* at the San Carlo Opera, and afterwards had gone to "a great omnium gatherum something like Barnum's [Museum], with a variety of shows within an enclosure which cost 3 francs to enter. There was a *café chantant* with 2000 people, where I heard a pretty woman, dressed like a page, sing a Neapolitan song that Haydn would have given his eyes for." A pretty woman and a pretty song — Sam Ward's tastes were steadfast. "But I feel like a lost sheep here," he concluded. So, after a farewell feast on succulent steamed mussels, he would strike out for Rome and Marion's tower.

The plan was frustrated when both Sam and Frewen became violently ill; cholera, the doctor termed it, although it was most certainly ptomaine from tainted seafood. Sam recovered partially first and summoned just strength enough to take his friend across the bay to Sorrento and arrange for adequate nursing there. Then he tottered back to Rome. Louisa took one look and had him carried up to the tower and put to bed.

For a while his life was despaired of. He would not accept the regimen prescribed by the doctor. Louisa wrote Julia that brother demanded his own remedies, "that he has picked up in various corners of the world, and it is difficult to persuade him that the amount of quinine desirable for breaking up a Guatemala fever can not be given to him." One night, Daisy Terry, sitting with him, saw his lips moving in an effort to speak. She bent low to catch what she feared might be his last words, and suddenly realized that he was asking her to read him Tennyson's "Come into the garden, Maud." So refractory was he, Louisa telegraphed Marion to hasten home; then she called in a nursing nun, Sister Marius, a tall, strong-minded, efficient French woman, to whom Sam submitted. Sister Marius, no less than the doctor, was nonplussed by the patient's extraordinary pulse: in normal health one hundred and twenty beats to the minute, under the stimulus of fever it became fantastic.

Even Sister Marius could not prevent Sam's carrying on a spirited correspondence, by dictation. He sent cheery messages to Boston and London, and assured Rosebery, who had reached home, that he would be seeing him at Dalmeny or Mentmore soon. He told Hurlbert, who was sojourning on the Riviera, that nothing could postpone his speedy recovery. And he worried about the portrait and bust completed by Elliott and Benlliure; he wanted the painting crated and shipped to London, and requested that photographs of the bust be forwarded to Rosebery, who he was sure would want to have it cast in bronze. Theosophist acquaintances he had picked up in Rome he desired to call, but they failed to come, — a failure noted with some complacency by the Terrys.

Crawford reached Rome on March 25; at first glance he was certain his uncle was dying. Marion was struck by the idealization of Uncle which Elliott had presented in his portrait, showing Sam in the features and guise of a sage, with venerable beard, eyes peering from under wrinkled eyelids into the distance with a faint twinkle, as though amused by some benignly secret joke. The capable hands were folded, and on the third finger of the right hand gleamed the fabled sapphire.

This painting, however, did not show the Sam who had been seen in Rome that winter: rather, it turned out to be an impersonal, although effective work of art for which Sam Ward sat as model. A likeness wholly realistic was the portrait bust made by Benlliure at the same time. In this bust "Uncle Sam" showed no deterioration, his vitality and alertness were unimpaired. Here was the commanding "King of the Lobby," erect and vigorous, — the sweeping mustaches and imperial, the imperious nose, the noble cranium, even the jaunty tie and suggestion of a twinkling, penetrating glance.

Despite his illness, Sam's vitality seemed unquenchable, and on May 8 Louisa wrote with relief to Julia that the crisis appeared to be past. The doctors felt that the patient might do better outside Rome during the approaching summer heat, and his thoughts reverted to a town he knew on the Italian Riviera, Pegli, some six miles ouside Genoa. There, he fancied, he might be invigorated by the sunlight and sea air; so preparations were begun to take him to Pegli. A night train was selected, and on the evening of May 10 Sam was carried down gently from the high tower. The villa had been made bright with lamps and flowers, and down flight after flight of steps Sam was borne on a litter, past curtsying servants, and out through the main gate to a carriage around which stood men holding flickering torches. It was a superb sendoff: and Sam enjoyed being the center of so much festivity and solicitude. He was cheerful as the carriage moved away. Accompanying him were Marion Crawford, Daisy Terry, and the devoted nun, Sister Marius.

After that brave departure, Louisa wrote again to sister Julia, mentioning that it was almost exactly three years since all four of them had been together in that wonderful reunion in Boston, when Sam virtually smuggled Annie across the plains for Dudie's birthday. "It was one of dear Brother's most successful coups," she recalled; "just one of those delicious surprises that one comes upon once in a lifetime." Looking back over Sam's amazing life, it seemed to Louisa that all that remained vivid in her memory was the innumerable acts of kindness he had performed for those he loved.

Travel was Sam Ward's best stimulant, and upon reaching Pegli he felt stronger. Crawford was relieved, also, that Uncle had ceased to allude to his Theosophist acquaintances; this Marion took as a sign of increasing tranquillity. Sam kept a worn copy of Horace at hand, with the *Rubáiyát,* and now and then read alternatively from these constant companions. Daisy would watch his eyes caressing the words in one book or the other; then they would turn and caress her. He seldom asked to have anyone read to him.

But it rapidly became evident that the bland Riviera climate was not helping him. On the morning of Monday, May 19 — eight days after they had arrived from Rome — Marion, writing to Rosebery, said that "there is too much sirocco, the air is too soft, and the whole atmosphere too enervating."

In the midst of this letter, Crawford noticed his uncle motioning to take down a message. "My uncle desires to know," Marion continued, transcribing Sam's words, " 'where you can put him up, should he be able to reach England by the end of next month, or sooner if practicable, to keep his *Death's-head and Crossbones* (his words) from scaring the children.' His only hope is in the English air, and his disappointment in this place seems very painful, and he seems somewhat discouraged. He adds, 'Please wire the exact spot in question, that he may make it the chief and central attraction of his fancy.' "

At this point Sam complained of a sharp pain; but this passed, and he said he would sleep a while. Crawford was anxious: a swelling in Sam's left hand and foot, which had bothered him for weeks, had subsided that morning, and Sister Marius considered the symptom ominous. Daisy came to sit with the sleeping patient, and Marion went to his own room.

In about an hour Daisy called, saying that Uncle was much worse. Marion hurried to the sickroom and found Sam awake, breathing heavily. Fixing his eyes upon his nephew, the old man said clearly, in a low voice, "I think I am going to give up the ghost."

Crawford darted away to summon the doctor; but when the physician arrived, Uncle Sam was beyond aid. Apparently suffering no pain, he gently receded, his heartbeat growing fainter and fainter, and two hours after dictating his last letter, with a long sigh he was gone.

In an adjoining room Daisy wept quietly, while the Sister of Mercy prayed. Beneath Sam's pillow lay the dog-eared Horace, and on the bedspread beside him, Khayyám, open at Omar's *envoi* —

> And when like her, oh Sáki, you shall pass
> Among the Guests Star-scatter'd on the Grass,
> And in your joyous errand reach the spot
> Where I made One . . .
> *turn down an empty Glass!*

ECHO CHAMBER

WHO can so well convey the mystery of a vanished personality as those who have felt its force?

Dazed by the abruptness of the end, Marion Crawford telegraphed the news to Rome, London, and Boston, and also to William Henry Hurlbert, at nearby Monte Carlo. The message struck Sam's "Mendacious Club" crony "like a thunderbolt." He boarded the first train only to discover that it did not stop at Pegli. Carried on to Genoa, he lay stranded there Monday night. Sleepless in the Hôtel de Londres, he scratched out his exasperation in a furious letter to Lord Rosebery. "The people who have encompassed our lost President all these weeks have persisted in their imbecility and perversity to the last. I have been trying in vain for the last week to get the exact address of our beloved Uncle at Pegli. I waited — and then comes this dreadful message from Crawford — still without any hint of where they were or what he proposes to do." At least, Hurlbert had ascertained that "no train has gone to Rome today bearing any such burden as I shudder to think of . . . Fagged as I am, I shall be up at six-thirty to catch the first train. All this one ounce of common sense on the part of C. could have spared me. But never mind that . . . I cannot make myself believe it."

Hurlbert reached Pegli the next morning, and the "ounce of common sense" was supplied. Crawford was numbed by grief and exhaustion, Daisy, too; neither was able to think coherently; Hurlbert took over the burden of making the dismal arrangements. There were complications, for Sam Ward was both a Protestant and a Freemason, and Italy was a Catholic country where the anti-clerical Freemasons formed a provocative and sometimes noisy opposition to both the church and the government. There were civil formalities to be complied with. Hurlbert told Rosebery: "The doctor, as soon as he saw the end had come, impressed upon Crawford the necessity of seeing the proper authorities without delay and preparing for the prompt, not to say almost indecently hasty, interment these people and the French insist upon in such cases. The question of a temporary or a permanent resting-place at Pegli Crawford referred to me, to be acted upon by us all jointly.

"In the little Protestant cemetery there was a vacant nook, shaded by noble ilex trees and oaks, alive with birds and bright with natural flowers. This was at once secured, and everything that must be done was done, not only without delay, but quietly and becomingly and tastefully . . . There came to us a modest, simple little German pastor, friendly and unpretending, who walked with us up the hill beneath the trees, and used the short, simple enough German service of the Lutherans over our dead, in the rich German tongue he loved . . . You know my feelings [for] these kinsfolk of our beloved President. But let me make haste to say that as far as Crawford is concerned, nothing could be more true, more tender, or more loyal than his bearing; no one could have shown more genuine feeling than his in these last cruel days. You may judge what I think of it and him when I tell you that after putting on my own finger the ring of the M.C. worn to the last by our dear Uncle, I gave Crawford mine, and told him I was sure you and I would be glad to have him wear it in lasting memory of his loving and gentle care of this dear friend."

On his side, Marion assured Julia that "Hurlbert came and showed more heart than I believed he possessed. He was very thoughtful and helped me a great deal. He seemed to think the Uncle would not have chosen another spot in which to rest from his long wandering. The beautiful little churchyard, between the Villa Doria and the Villa Pallavicini, is as lovely a spot as ever I saw. It was very solemn and impressive."

To Rosebery, in London, heart-stricken and reproaching himself for neglect of "Uncle Sam" during the last days, of failure to grasp the gravity of the illness, Crawford wrote: "There was a perfect dignity of peace about everything connected with the dear man's death and burial. Hurlbert came in the morning and he and I followed our dearest friend to his grave together. . . . The dear heart was gentleness itself during this later period, full of little forethoughts and tender words for all. Perhaps he knew he was nearer the end than we thought, for after we reached Pegli he almost always made me tear up his letters after reading them to him, a thing I never remember before. He has gone where there is no ingratitude any more, nor any pain for him — where he has that peace he so earnestly desired during the last months of his life . . .

"Do you remember in that letter he dictated to me for you he said, 'a quiet place, where my skull and crossbones will not frighten the children away?' Over the gate at the lovely burial ground at Pegli those emblems are carved, and as Hurlbert and I saw the last sods laid over him, the little children came and looked wonderingly over the wall."

In death, Sam remained the "Great Reconciler," the "Pacificator," which was the title in which he took most satisfaction. Marion confessed to Rosebery: "I have not always liked Hurlbert, but I shall never now forget his honest sympathy nor the genuine sorrow he felt and feels. Neither will I ever speak of him again except most kindly. I cannot write much. I am not well. . . . You will of course understand that it was better to make any such arrangements as were necessary at once. There are a great many things I will write to you about him when I am better able — how he loved you very dearly and how he spoke of you daily, almost hourly. I cannot thank you for the love you bore him, for words mean very little, only for his sake and dear memory I will ever honor you and give you such poor service as I am able."

Hurlbert cabled terse announcements to the press in London and New York, while Crawford notified the family. None was more overwhelmed than the "Old Bird." The dread telegram that arrived from Pegli on May 19 said, "Samuel Ward expired peacefully," and Julia entered in her journal: "Nothing could be more unexpected than this blow. Dear Bro. Sam had long since been pronounced out of danger . . . Latterly we have heard of him as feeble, and have felt renewed anxiety, but were entirely unprepared for his death." The next day: "Dark days of nothingness these, today and yesterday. Nothing to do but be patient and explore the past." And the day after that: "Had a sitting all alone with dear Uncle Sam's picture this afternoon. I thought it might be the time of his funeral. I read the beautiful 90th Psalm and a number of his bright, sweet lyrics. A sympathetic visit from Winthrop Chanler." The grandson who inherited most of Sam's charm and kindliness had come to talk with his aunt about the grandfather he scarcely knew.

A week later Julia's journal recorded: "Dear Brother Sam's death has brought me well in sight of the farther shore. May I be ready when it is my turn to cross." To Louisa, while her grief was yet green, she wrote despairingly: "The pathos of a life of such wonderful vicissitudes! I cannot half take it in. What must he not have suffered in those lonely days of wandering and privation, while I was comfortable in my household! . . . God knows, I had every reason to love him, for he was heroically faithful to his affection for me. Now I feel how little I appreciated his devotion, and how many chimeras, in my foolish, wool-gathering head, crowded upon this most precious affection, which was worthy of a much larger place in my thoughts . . . As I write, the tears come. The thought of his lonely funeral and solitary grave has wrung my heart at times, but sometimes I think of it as a place where one might be glad to be at rest. I believe he is in the heaven accorded to those who have loved their fellow-men, for who ever coined pure kindness into acts as he did?"

Julia would live another quarter of a century, into internationally honored old age, and every day Sam lived in her heart. A week before her death in 1910, she passed a pensive Sunday with her son and daughters, playing with still sensitive fingers while they sang, grouped around the piano, the student songs Sam had brought from Heidelberg seventy years before.

Of course the press marked the passing of a man who had been so much in the public's knowledge without ever holding public office or filling any readily assignable niche. *The Times* of London acknowledged Sam Ward to have been "almost as familiar a figure in some circles of London society as in his own country . . . the most charming of social companions and most genial of hosts." In a long, thoughtful appreciation, the *Saturday Review*, of London, spoke of him as "a social power, both in America and in Europe . . . Although he was a good American, he was of that class of Americans who, so to speak, bridge over the Atlantic — who help to make the New World intelligible to the Old, and the Old to the New. Few Americans have done as much as Mr. Sam Ward to foster good feeling in social life between the old and the new country."

The estimate a man's contemporaries place upon him at the moment of his passing often clarifies the impact he has made upon his times, for death can focus life's diffused rays into one clear beam. New York, the city of his nativity, the city of which he was always a proud citizen, almost unanimously recalled Sam Ward with affection. The *Tribune* detailed his eventful career and praised his charm, his scholarship, literary ability, linguistic brilliance, and of course his special attainments as the foremost American gastronomer of his generation. The secret of Sam's incomparable dinners, the *Tribune* rightly observed, apart from the food, was, first, the selection of the company, and secondly, "the exquisite tact and bonhomie with which he fused heterogeneous elements, and sent everyone away pleased alike with his host, his companions, and, chief of all, with himself . . . He fascinated all classes of men and women by the vast range of his information, and by a boundless capacity for diversified conversation."

The *Sun* reviewed the way successive fortunes had melted in Sam Ward's hands, and recounted some of the apochryphal yarns told about his prowess in diplomacy and cookery, commenting that Sam's "astonishing memory enabled him to retain every story that he heard, — and as to other stories that were never heard before, those were due to his inventive genius."

One dissenter, ironically, was the *New York World.* Under the aegis of Hurlbert, the *World* had been almost a personal mouthpiece for Sam, but now Joseph Pulitzer was making himself a millionaire by militant proletarianism, and Sam Ward, born rich and into the socially elect, provided a convenient target. "Now that he is dead," Pulitzer's paper caviled, "the world may be said to have lost the most elegant spendthrift who ever lived . . . Ward's first business stroke was characteristic of the history of the man. It was in marrying the daughter of William B. Astor . . . Practically, Sam Ward was a genteel adventurer all his life. His two marriages show it." And so on to the final, oblique sneer: "It is evident, however, that Sam Ward's powers decayed very fast, for in rapid succession he became the friend of Oscar Wilde, published a volume of poems, and died."

Against this were two full columns in the *New York Times,* racily and judiciously reviewing the "gastronomical pacificator's" history and achievements. "Uncle Sam's" striking appearance was recalled: "He moved with a dignified step which would attract attention to him in the midst of a crowd of strangers. He never remained a stranger long, however, for somebody was sure to recognize him, and 'There goes Sam Ward' would pass from lip to lip until the martial figure would become as well known as though he had been a hero whom everybody was anxious to honor." Sam's inviolable custom of spending everything he got on himself and his friends the *Times* noted: "He lived like a prince, entertained all the brightest and most celebrated men of the country, treating all alike, indifferent to their politics or religion . . . His gastronomical knowledge was his stock in trade, and upon it he lived like a potentate in Washington for nearly a score of years. The long, long roll of his friendships would have filled columns if confined to the famous alone, and there were hundreds of humble and unaspiring whose names were known only to himself."

The *Times* gave a sampling among the European friends alone; it ranged from Prince Bismarck to Hortense Schneider, the queen of Offenbach operetta; from Victor Hugo to the Czar of Russia; from Cardinal Newman to Ernest Renan; from Thomas Huxley to Pope Leo XII; from the Prince of Wales to Alphonse Daudet, Charles Reade, President Grévy of France, and the Emperor of Brazil.

As for Sam's lobbying and the money it brought him, the *Times* cheerfully testified: "Certain it is that Sam never had more than money enough to pay his daily expenses during the most successful part of his career as a lobbyist. During the Administration of Secretary McCulloch at the Treasury, he was a veritable power behind the throne, and seekers after legislation as well as legislators themselves understood it and bowed to his power." Still as hale and hearty as a young man when he had vanished from New York at sixty-eight, two years previously, it was said that even then, "when disengaged and left to his own whims, he was capable of clearing a big dish of truffles *en serviette,* with a quart of champagne to wash it down, and then going to bed and passing the night in dreamless repose."

"Uncle Sam's" conscience was clearer than many men's.

Yet, all in all, the man and his activities posed an enigma. The *Tribune* commented upon this, and tried in vain to resolve the contradictions in his character and career. Sam Ward's most remarkable accomplishment, the *Tribune* estimated, probably with justice, was "establishing himself in Washington at the head of a profession which, from the lowest depths of disrepute, he raised almost to the dignity of a gentlemanly business." Agreeing that he had been neither corrupt nor gross, and that he took open pride in the title "King of the Lobby," how then, the *Tribune* wondered, did he manage to escape falling into obloquy? "In short, what a puzzle was this universal favorite, whom the sternest moralist could not find it in his heart to dislike, and the boldest lobby agent could yet call his comrade; who lived by arts which nobody can respect, and adorned a questionable life with so much amiability, so much refinement, so much good breeding!"

In part the difficulty arose from Sam's refusal to fit into any one conventional pattern or category, although he touched upon many and adorned them all. His relatives tried to solve the riddle and found that their rules did not apply. To Julia Ward Howe, Marion Crawford gave his own best analysis: "I cannot tell what things he believed, though I think he was certainly no atheist. He did kind actions and thought kindly thoughts while continuing to speculate upon a system of ethics which in practice would probably be destructive of all morality. But he never came near the practice. He died as he had lived, full of thought and care for others, combined with a vagueness concerning all points of morality, which would have been terrible in a man less actively good than he was. My impression of him in his last days was that he was a better man than he ever made himself out to be. He died like a good man, and he was one."

Julia, who had always judged Sam by the inner light that shone through the tracery of his actions, measured him by that light in her final judgment, telling Louisa: "One of the lessons I have learned from Sam's life is that it is very hard for us to judge rightly the merits and demerits of others. Here was a man with many faults on the surface, and a heart of pure gold beneath."

A reputation based upon private actions, like the magnetism of personality, is as evanescent as the aroma of one of "Uncle Sam's" tantalizing dishes. Sam Ward left no major writings and no personal record beyond a voluminous correspondence, strewn over three continents. Ambitious most of his life for posthumous glory, he might have survived among scholars had he not been so punctiliously discreet. In his last years he had made a new will, leaving everything to Louisa, and instructing that his personal papers, including a diary covering his operations as a lobbyist in Washington, be destroyed. This was done. Had these secrets transpired, he might have been cultivated by historians and quoted often and at length; he preferred to make sure that others would not be embarrassed or hurt.

In his later years it became more or less the fashion to be condescending towards "Uncle Sam's" intellectual depth; his attainments in this field, it was sometimes said with the smile of toleration, were only blurred reflections from his studious youth. But there is evidence that to the end, Sam's mind was vigorous and his intellectual interests varied and by no means shallow. Just before his death, there arrived at Lord Rosebery's address in London Sam's last book bill, for purchases made during the London season of 1883 and thereafter, — a time when Sam was maintaining a social pace that knocked out the younger William Henry Hurlbert and F. Marion Crawford. This list attests to the scope of Sam's mental energies even in the last months of his life. The statement, dated "Christmas 1883," with subsequent additions, was rendered by James Bain, bookseller, No. 1 Haymarket, and listed the following purchases, all personal to Sam: Besant's *E. H. Palmer* — Swinburne's *Roundels* — *Geo. Sand* by Bertha Thomas — Goethe's *Conversations* — Lewes's *Life of Goethe* — Boyle & Manning's *Thibet* — Lord R. Gower's

Life of Lord Rochester—*Les Provinciales* (4 Languages)—*Quevedo* (in French) 2 vols—Beckford Sale *1318 Receuil de Porcès*—*Memoirs of Sir J. Campbell* (2 vols)—*L. da Vinci* (2 vols)—Hamilton's *French Dictionary*—Rich's *Babylon,* Ms. Beckford—*Quarterly Review,* July.

Just before leaving London for the last time, Sam added to his Horace collection by purchasing "Mattaire's *Horace,* 1715." Finally, from Italy, in 1884, he had ordered "*Emerson's Works,* Morley, Vol. 1," and on March 15, at the outset of his illness, appeared a final item on the invoice: "Binding *Lyrical Recreations,* morocco elegant." This was his last outlay for books, a presentation copy of his own verses. "Uncle Sam" gave only the best.

This was his valedictory. Within a few years Sam Ward had faded from the recollection of all except the few in whose hearts he was enshrined; with them his influence was perennial.

In 1890 a new United States envoy arrived in London—the first to carry ambassadorial rank—bringing a wealthy young Philadelphian as unsalaried private secretary. The young man's hope was to witness something of British official and social life, and his disappointment was keen when he learned that the Foreign Office refused absolutely to accredit any private secretary of any envoy; the privilege had been abused, and the ban was strict. Without hesitating, the new ambassador sat down and wrote a personal note to the Foreign Secretary, explaining the circumstances and requesting that an exception be made. Embassy officials were aghast at this shattering of diplomatic decorum, for until the ambassador had presented his credentials to the Queen, he did not exist officially. Nevertheless, at the ambassador's insistence, the note was carried to the Foreign Office; and the amazement of the embassy staff turned to stupefaction when a gracious reply, penned by the secretary himself, was returned, waiving the rule in favor of the eager young Philadelphian.

What had brought about this blithe overturning of the sacred rescripts of the British Foreign Office the embassy assistants never learned, but the secret was simple. The new ambassador was Thomas F. Bayard, Sam Ward's Senate friend, who subsequently had served as Secretary of State in Grover Cleveland's first administration. The Foreign Secretary was the Earl of Rosebery, Sam's faithful "Sycophant." The magic touch of "Uncle Sam" had accomplished the miracle, and the favor itself was the sort of kindly action in which Sam had shone.

From time to time, although at longer and longer intervals, other indications cropped up to show that Sam was not utterly forgotten. In 1917, for example, during the first World War, Maud Howe Elliott received from England an appeal for an autograph of her uncle. The appeal was on behalf of an unnamed collector, but Mrs. Elliott forwarded a letter in which Sam described a breakfast he had given for Sarah Bernhardt, and also had dwelt upon his last gift to Maud, — "a certain web of shimmering yellow satin." Sam had advised that Maud should not hesitate to wear it, as unsuitable to her coloring, for both Paolo Veronese and Rubens had painted fair-haired women in golden satins. An acknowledgment of this autograph came on stationery bearing a coronet: the collector was King George V, a son of the Prince of Wales of 1883 who had so appreciated "Uncle Sam."

Fifty-three summers after Sam had died, a niece and a granddaughter climbed the steep hill to the obscure God's Acre where he lay. There they found his grave, marked by a simple stone cross, and they read the epitaph:

ARCHIBALD, EARL OF ROSEBERY
WILLIAM HENRY HURLBERT
FRANCIS MARION CRAWFORD
IN LOVING REMEMBRANCE OF
SAMUEL WARD
BORN NEW YORK, U.S.A., JAN. 27, 1814
DIED AT PEGLI, MAY 19, 1884
And God gave him largeness of heart even as the
sands on the seashore

The armful of red roses they had brought was placed upon the tomb, and they left Sam to his slumbers.

So Hurlbert had wished it, when there had arisen discussion among Sam's friends and family about removing him to another resting place. For "Uncle Sam" had performed his most fabulous feat by the act of dying: miraculously he had endowed that worldly *abbate*, that dilettante opportunist, William Henry Hurlbert, with a heart.

Directly after Sam's funeral, Hurlbert, Crawford, and the others had returned to Rome, and from there, a few days later, the "Member" put on paper the pulse of his feelings, in answer to an anguished lament from Sam's "Sycophant":

"Don't tell me you could not write your letter — I cannot read it. It chills me like the first sight of that green place with the poppies and the ilex to which I walked with Crawford in the still early morning to see whether we should lay him there. You must not reproach yourself — you need not indeed reproach yourself for anything you wrote or left unwritten. He talked of you with Crawford on that last morning so tenderly, so lovingly — and now everything that is dim to us must be growing clear to him — and if you could know how he poured out his soul to me at times about you. But you know what his soul was and felt for you — I waste myself in idle words.

"My last note from him was so cheery and like himself that I was making ready to find him almost able to drive out with me upon the lovely hills around Pegli, when the tide so sharply and so suddenly turned and swept him beyond our reach forever! The nun who was with him to the last is kindness and good sense and practical, quiet skill all made flesh. She said to me: 'He had lived for two months on medical expedients and was gone within a week of his first taking to his bed, so far as the machinery of life was concerned.' Now that it is all over I am inclined to think she was right — and yet, perhaps, could we have taken charge of him from the first — but it is worse than idle to look back upon that. It is enough to know that at the end his sun set without a cloud of worry or of anguish — a golden soft sunset it was, over a sleeping blue Italian sea.

"Why should we move him? I am sure he would have loved this beautiful, quiet place. Hard by is the Villa Doria, where lives the old Principe. He had been most kind and attentive during the few days passed there — and before we came away we left instructions that the nook be sodded carefully and planted with flowers; and he will see that it is all duly and fitly done. Crawford and I propose that a simple cross of marble bearing his name and the proper dates be prepared and set up till we can all of us agree as to what action shall finally be taken to mark the spot . . .

"I went again yesterday with Crawford to look at Benlliure's bust. It is like, very like, — so like it is hard to bear. Crawford has broken down and gone into the mountains to recoup. I put my ring on his finger, and now I feel as if it were selfish in me to keep this I wear, which we took from the hand that was folded to rest from helping all who needed help, so many, many years. Will you take it and give me yours when I come to London? . . .

"This day week I had such a cheery letter from him — I sent it to you, did I not? And then came another as bright. And on Sunday last his sister here received a letter dictated by him so full of sense and spirits that all the house rejoiced to believe him going bravely on. None of us dreamed — none of us could have dreamed of this — and you must not for one moment reproach yourself for not divining what his very doctors failed to divine. He himself did not dream of it, I am sure. Believe me, it was to the hope of happy quiet days in England that he thought he was clinging. He wrote to me only the other day of such days. He talked of them to Crawford Monday week. Remember the sweetness of these thoughts and hope . . .

"If only you could have been with us that soft May day! But we will go there together some quiet future day. I told Crawford yesterday, and he agreed with me, that we had better leave the green place as it is with the poppies and the ilex till we make up our minds what shall be set there to witness how he was loved. If there be indeed any thought of these things of earth beyond that blue — he knows how precious is that place to us. And it will go hard with any that try to hinder us from keeping it as we would have it kept!

"I cannot write more. It seems all to be a nightmare in the sunlight — my head and my heart ache. I shall be more like myself, I hope, when I get up among the mountains of the Riviera again. Today I am going over to see his sister. Then I shall get away tonight — and I shall be glad to get away. It is walking in a vain show here and the streets are haunted."

DEBITS AND CREDITS

BIBLIOGRAPHY

INDEX

DEBITS AND CREDITS

WRITING the portion of a book headed "Acknowledgments" is usually a labor of obligation, performed dutifully but in a manner hardly expressive of the heavy sense of gratitude the author may feel. In the case of Sam Ward's biography, the task dissolves into a pleasure of recalling and noting a host of delightful experiences.

For this, the subject of the book principally is to be credited: mention Sam Ward, and smiling cooperation becomes the order of the day. To "Uncle Sam," his myth and his memory, let us therefore first of all say most heartily, "Thank you!"

The sources of any book that pretends to trace Samuel Ward's divagations through so many fields are bound to be as varied and as widely scattered as his own wanderings and activities, and merely to follow the more prominent of these traces involves journeys in time, space, and mental adjustment more or less corresponding to his own. This book does not attempt to run down every fact and rumor, — for time is limited, if space is not. But in the search for the truth about Sam the author has found that Sam's very name has been a talisman endowed with power to unlock private treasures and disclose data hitherto unknown or unnoticed. The result has been immensely to enrich the narrative and enhance the enjoyment of such readers as it may find, few or many.

Sam Ward has descendants and collateral relatives almost as the sands of the seashore (to employ one of his well-worn metaphors), and they are among his most fervent admirers, — which should not be surprising, inasmuch as his own traits of sympathy, charm, and eagerness to serve have been transmitted to the fourth and fifth generation of his line. Sufficient proof that Sam "survives" today.

Among those connected with Samuel Ward by family ties, the

author has encountered only the most generous and warmhearted cooperation. To nominate any one for outstanding mention would be invidious; yet none, surely, will cavil at giving place of precedence to Sam Ward's granddaughter, the late Margaret Chanler Aldrich. Besides being a woman of graciousness and ability in her own right, Mrs. Aldrich provided a living link with the subject of this biography: at the age of ninety-two, she remembered her grandfather vividly. With the utmost liberality she threw open "Rokeby" and the century-old accumulation of family records there for the fullest and most candid examination. It is regrettable that she did not live to see the completed book in which she took so affectionate an interest, although she was able to read the opening chapters. Without her perceptive collaboration, this work would be far leaner and less conformable to its model.

Upon a return visit to Rokeby, it was the additional good fortune of the author to examine a further mass of *Samiana* — his poems, scraps of tabletalk, menus, gastronomic notes, youthful exercises, photographs, letters to his daughter and to his wife Emily, and fragmentary diaries erratically begun and cast aside — which had been found after Mrs. Aldrich's decease. This wealth of unsuspected material, together with Rokeby and its contents, has descended to Mrs. Aldrich's own grandchildren; and it was with the eager assistance of Sam Ward's great-great-grandsons, Richard Aldrich and John Winthrop Aldrich, that the later documents were studied.

The lineal descendant of Samuel Ward who today heads one branch of the family is Rear Admiral Hubert W. Chanler, Sam's great-grandson. Admiral Chanler has placed the author and every reader under a substantial debt of gratitude by his action in making available the letters written by "Uncle Sam" to his niece, Margaret "Daisy" Terry (Mrs. Winthrop Chanler). The collection, bound in vellum, the author was enabled to study under most hospitable conditions at "Sweet Briar Farm," Admiral Chanler's home near Geneseo, New York, — the region to which Sam once thought he might retire and round out his life as a philosopher–gentleman farmer.

Also at Sweet Briar Farm is a remnant of Sam Ward's once ample library of classical authors, including a score or so of his prized editions of Horace. Some of these contain his penciled annotations as a bibliophile.

Of inestimable value was the sole copy known to exist of Sam Ward's unfinished Memoirs, — a bound proof, with minor corrections in Sam's own hand. This unique curiosity was most generously lent by Sam's great-granddaughter, Mrs. Lawrence Grant White, and proved of importance as well as informative interest, because of the flavor it imparts, as a dictated work, of "Uncle Sam's" conversational style in old age. Although typeset and a proof run off, the fragment was never published.

There is another branch of the Ward connection that has inherited the vitality characteristic of that remarkable clan, several members of which have contributed most materially to the progress and accuracy of this book from its inception. Among these, foremost has been Julia Ward Stickley, of Washington, D.C., the great-granddaughter and namesake of Julia Ward Howe. With indefatigable zeal, Mrs. Stickley led to sources and imparted family lore which have thrown light on hitherto dark stretches of Sam Ward's career. Her enthusiasm has been infectious and sustaining, her encouragement has never slackened.

Similarly generous of her time and material has been Mrs. Thomas Clark Howard, of Boston, another great-granddaughter of "Uncle Sam's" best loved sister. Mrs. Howard is the possessor of the Benlliure bust of Sam, as well as family letters and photographs, all of which were made available without question.

The inheritor of Sam's famous sapphire, and of his last portrait (the José Villegas painting), is Mr. Lawrence Terry, of Concord, Massachusetts, who has put himself out to render every assistance in his power. The trouble he took in obtaining an accurate jeweler's lapidary description of Sam's famous ring may set at rest misconceptions as to this detail.

In still another branch of this widespread family, Representative William S. Mailliard, of San Francisco and Washington, D.C., was spontaneously helpful in pointing out some of "Uncle Sam's" passages at arms with Congressional committees. In the Mailliard home in Washington hangs the Dresden portrait of Sam Ward as a dashing young man of society and science.

All the above persons had a proprietary interest in the subject because of kinship, and their assistance has been invaluable because, in compiling the life of any historical figure, family archives and oral tradition sometimes can supply not only facts nowhere else preserved, but also a verisimilitude which more formal sources are unable to convey.

The primary sources for a biography, of course, are the contemporary documents; and the search for these has led into scholarly fields. Here, again, the name *Sam Ward* has evoked instant and heartiest response. Sam Ward's circle of admirers in this century is far wider than the family circle only.

Sam's own documentation (mainly in the form of letters) is widely dispersed, and while much of it is known, undoubtedly more will come to light periodically.

The author acknowledges a peculiar debt of gratitude to Professor Allan Nevins for magnanimously opening, for use without restriction, the Sam Ward-S. L. M. Barlow correspondence contained in the Barlow Papers (including some letters of William Henry Hurlbert and Manton M. Marble) at the Henry E. Huntington Library in San Marino, California. This source was particularly useful in shedding light upon one of "Uncle Sam's" most hush-hush activities, — his lobbying in Washington in the years just after the Civil War. Owing to Sam's superlative discretion, this subject in all previous accounts had necessarily been left tantalizingly vague. The Barlow correspondence gives some definite clues to the sort of business undertaken by Sam, although even here the ineffable "Uncle" has left much to be divined. Still, every reader following Sam in his dartings around Capitol Hill will be under obligation to Professor Nevins for making possible this occasional clarification.

In this connection, appreciation should be expressed to Mr. S. L. M. Barlow, of New York City — the grandson and namesake of "Uncle Sam's" friend — for clearing up an ancestral misunderstanding. In most books of reference, Sam Ward's confidant, Barlow, is described as the grandson of a French émigré named Jean Brillot-Savarin (Brillat-Savarin?), which would be a fact of some pertinence, if true, because of Sam's and Barlow's eminence as epicures and gourmets. The present S. L. M. Barlow, after studying the family tree, reports that unfortunately there is genealogically no room for so distinguished a forebear as the great gastronome. How the error arose (it was current in the elder Barlow's lifetime) is today inexplicable.

A contribution calling for the warmest acknowledgment is that made by Mr. Max Pablo Ynsfran, of the Institute of Latin American Studies, at the University of Texas. This contribution illustrates the way traces of Sam Ward continue to pop up in unexpected places. Some years ago, while engaged in research in the National Archives of Brazil, at Rio de Janeiro, Mr. Ynsfran came upon the secret correspondence between Sam Ward and President López of Paraguay; and from that, and other sources available only in South America, he pieced together the episode which had remained unknown to Sam's contemporaries or to posterity. Mr. Ynsfran's permission to appropriate the fruits of his investigations at Rio and Asunción is a debt which can be noted although not repaid.

The William Henry Seward Papers at the University of Rochester were kindly placed at the author's disposal by Miss Margaret Butterfield, of the University's Library, together with her own preliminary study of the possible relationship existing between Sam Ward and Lincoln's Secretary of State. These papers have been of inestimable service in throwing light on this obscure period of Sam's life. Thanks to the zeal of Miss Butterfield, and the efficient help of her staff in abstracting the Sam Ward correspondence from the mass of Seward papers, one more gap (and a major one) in the narrative could be closed.

Unpublished letters written by Thomas Crawford to his wife, Louisa, relating to Samuel Ward, and unpublished correspondence of Marion Ward to Louisa Crawford, in reference to Medora Grymes and Sam's second marriage, were offered spontaneously by Mr. Thomas L. Gale, of the University of Pittsburgh; the originals were procured by Mr. Gale from Villa Crawford, the former estate of F. Marion Crawford, near Sorrento, Italy. These letters are of the highest value because of the glimpses they afford of Medora's character, and the Ward family's feeling about Sam's marriage; they help to bring into sharper focus the figure of Medora, which heretofore has remained shadowy and elusive.

Professor Carvel Collins displayed generosity in offering the results of his researches, incident to his editing of Sam Ward's narrative of the gold mines, published as *Sam Ward in the Gold Rush.* Professor Collins's version of Sam's 1861 text has been followed throughout.

Louise Hall Tharp is especially to be thanked, both for her personal encouragement and for background material contained in her admirable account of the Ward sisters and Sam, *Three Saints and a Sinner.* Maud Howe Elliott's *Uncle Sam Ward and His Circle* has been indispensable as a reference source. Of similar value have been the numerous memoirs, biographies, and miscellaneous works published by members of the highly ramified Ward-Howe-Chanler-Aldrich family connection.

Of the many other published works consulted, the Bibliography will give some indication.

Finally, a contribution that can only be designated as *hors concours,* is that made by Mr. Robert Lescher, this book's chief inspirer. But for his imagination, enthusiasm, expert guidance, and unremitting support, the work would never have been undertaken, continued, or brought to completion. For his long-suffering sympathy and innumerable acts of editorial and personal kindness, a most profound bow of gratitude! *Salaam!*

The staff of the Manuscripts Room of the New York Public Library is to be thanked for assistance in studying the Ward Papers there. The moving letters written to Lord Rosebery by F. Marion Crawford and William Henry Hurlbert, just after Sam's death, were located among the Rosebery Papers at Dalmeny Park and made available by the generosity of the Earl and Countess of Rosebery. Nor should the helpfulness and thoroughness evinced at the Library of Congress, the New-York Historical Society, the Somerset Club of Boston, the Museum of the City of New York, the Huntington and Bancroft Libraries in California, and the San Francisco Public Library be less than handsomely acknowledged.

To list the many more who have contributed to this book of many sources and many facets would superinduce tedium, — and no one more sedulously cultivated the art of never becoming a bore than "Uncle Sam." Permit the author, in this one respect at least, to emulate his subject.

BIBLIOGRAPHY

The question may be asked why in the course of the narrative no mention has been made of "The Diary of a Public Man," that teasing historical enigma, authorship of which the late Professor Frank Maloy Anderson believed he had traced to "Uncle Sam" Ward. Gaps in Professor Anderson's chain of deduction have been uncovered by the scholarly analysis of Roy N. Lokken. Also, it is the opinion of the present writer, based on the research required for this book, that neither the internal nor the circumstantial factors validate Professor Anderson's ingenious supposition. It is conceivable that Sam Ward may have had some hand in perpetrating a brilliant hoax (if it be a hoax, since even this has never been satisfactorily resolved); both his temperament and his admitted delight in a clever mystification would have fitted him for it. However, the authorship of the mysterious document is another matter, and its attribution to "Uncle Sam" seems unwarranted; therefore, speculation which could be nothing more than guesswork has been omitted from the biography. As a source reference for the world of Washington in Sam Ward's time, "The Diary of a Public Man" does have value, and it is an important item in the Bibliography.

MANUSCRIPT SOURCES

S. L. M. Barlow Papers, Huntington Library.

William H. Seward Papers, University of Rochester Library, Rochester, N.Y.

Samuel Ward Papers, New York Public Library.

Rokeby Papers, "Rokeby," Barrytown, N.Y.

Samuel Ward's Letters to Margaret Terry (Mrs. Winthrop Chanler), "Sweet Briar Farm," Geneseo, N.Y.

Samuel Ward's Memoirs (unpublished printer's proof with corrections in author's hand).

MAGAZINES

Harper's Weekly
Atlantic Monthly
Putnam's Magazine
Overland Monthly
Porter's Spirit of the Times
Saturday Review (London)
Vanity Fair (London)
The Nation
American Mercury
Saturday Evening Post
California Historical Society Quarterly
Massachusetts Historical Society Proceedings
New-York Historical Society Quarterly
Mississippi Valley Historical Review
Hispanic American Historical Review
Munsey's Magazine
North American Review

NEWSPAPER FILES

Principal dailies of:
New York
New Orleans
Washington, D.C.
San Francisco
The Times (London)

BOOKS

Adams, Henry, *Democracy, An American Novel.* New York: Holt, 1880.

——, *The Education of Henry Adams.* Boston: Massachusetts Historical Society, 1918.

——, *The Great Secession Winter of 1860–61, and Other Essays,* George Brookfield, ed. New York: Sagamore Press, 1958.

Adams, Mrs. Henry, *The Letters of Mrs. Henry Adams,* Ward Thoron, ed. Boston: Little, Brown, 1936.

Aldrich, Margaret Chanler, *Family Vista.* Privately printed, New York, 1958.

"All About Sam Ward." New York *Daily Graphic,* February 1, 1875.

Altrocchi, Julia Cooley, *The Spectacular San Franciscans.* New York: Dutton, 1949.

Anderson, Frank Maloy, *The Mystery of "A Public Man."* Minneapolis, Minn.: University of Minnesota, 1948.

Anon (pseudonym of Julian Osgood Field), *Things I Shouldn't Tell.* London: Everleigh Nash & Grayson, 1924.

——, *Uncensored Recollections.* London: Everleigh Nash & Grayson, 1924.

Armstrong, Hamilton Fish, ed., *The Poetry of New York.* New York: Putnam's, 1917.

Arvin, Newton, *Longfellow, His Life and Works.* Boston: Little, Brown, 1963.

Asbury, Herbert, *The Gangs of New York.* New York: Knopf, 1927.

——, *The Barbary Coast.* New York: Knopf, 1933.

——, *Sucker's Progress.* New York: Dodd Mead, 1938.

Asquith, Margot, *Margot Asquith, an Autobiography.* New York: Doran, 1920.

——, (Margot Oxford), *More or Less About Myself.* New York: Dutton, 1934.

Atherton, Gertrude, *My San Francisco.* Indianapolis: Bobbs-Merrill, 1946.

Aubry, Octave, *Eugénie, Empress of the French.* Philadelphia: Lippincott, 1931.

Bancroft, Frederic, *The Life of William H. Seward.* 2 vols. New York: Harper, 1900.

Bancroft, Hubert Howe, *History of California.* San Francisco: Bancroft, 1888.

Barrett, Walter, *The Old Merchants of New York.* 5 vols. New York: Knox, 1885.

Barrett, William E., *Woman on Horseback, the Biography of Francisco Lopez and Eliza Lynch.* New York: Stokes, 1938.

Barrows, Chester L., *William M. Evarts.* Chapel Hill, N.C.: University of North Carolina Press, 1941.

Barry, Davis S., *Forty Years in Washington.* Boston: Little, Brown, 1924.

Belden, Thomas Graham and Marva Robbins Graham, *So Fell the Angels.* Boston: Little, Brown, 1956.

Belmont, Perry, *An American Democrat.* New York: Columbia University Press, 1940.

Benson, George, "New York Journalists: W. H. Hurlbert." *Galaxy Magazine,* January 1869.

BIGELOW, JOHN, *Retrospections of an Active Life.* 5 vols. New York: Baker & Taylor, 1909–13.

BLAINE, MRS. JAMES G., *The Letters of Mrs. James G. Blaine,* Harriet S. Blaine Beale, ed. New York: Duffield, 1908.

BLAY, JOHN S., *After the Civil War.* New York: Crowell, 1960.

BOWEN, CROSWELL, *The Elegant Oakey.* New York: Oxford University Press, 1956.

BOWERS, CLAUDE G., *The Tragic Era: The Revolution After Lincoln.* Boston: Houghton Mifflin, 1929.

BOYKIN, EDWARD, *Congress and the Civil War.* New York: McBride, 1952.

BREVOORT, HENRY, *Letters of Henry Brevoort to Washington Irving.* New York: Putnam, 1916.

BROOKS, VAN WYCK, *The Flowering of New England: 1815–1865.* New York: Dutton, 1936.

——, *New England Indian Summer: 1865–1915.* New York: Dutton, 1940.

——, *The World of Washington Irving.* New York: Dutton, 1944.

BROWN, HENRY COLLINS, *Brownstone Fronts and Saratoga Trunks.—Recollections of Old New York.* New York: Dutton, 1935.

——, *From Alley Pond to Rockefeller Center.* New York: Dutton, 1936.

——, *Valentine's Manual of Old New York.* Valentine's Manual, Inc., Hastings-on-Hudson, 1916–1924.

BROWN, KARL, *A Guide to the Reference Collections of the New York Public Library.* New York, 1931.

BROWN, JUNIUS HENRY, *The Great Metropolis: A Mirror of New York.* New York, 1869.

BUTTERFIELD, MARGARET, "Samuel Ward, Alias Carlos Lopez." *University of Rochester Library Bulletin,* vol. XII No. 2, Winter 1957.

BYRON, LORD, *The Corsair.* London: Murray, 1814.

CARLISLE, HENRY C., *San Francisco Street Names.* San Francisco, 1954.

CARLSON, OLIVER, *The Man Who Made News — James Gordon Bennett.* New York: Duell, Sloan & Pearce, 1942.

CARPENTER, FRANK G., *Carp's Washington,* Frances Carpenter, ed. New York: McGraw Hill, 1960.

CARR, ALBERT Z., *The World and William Walker.* New York: Harper & Row, 1963.

CARSON, JAMES PETIGRU, *Life, Letters and Speeches of James Louis Petigru.* Washington, D.C.: Lowdermilk & Co., 1920.

"*Catalogue de la Bibliothèque de Samuel Ward, Jr.*" (Ms). New York Public Library.

Catalogue of the Art Collection Formed by the Late Samuel Latham Mitchell Barlow. New York, 1890.

Catalogue of the Artistic and Valuable Collection of Mr. William Henry Hurlbert. New York, 1883.

CECIL, ALGERNON, *British Foreign Secretaries, 1807–1916.* London: Bell, 1927.

CHAFETZ, HENRY, *Play the Devil.* New York: Potter, 1960.

CLAY, MRS. CLEMENT C., JR., *A Belle of the Fifties. Narrated by Ada Sterling.* New York: Doubleday, Page, 1905.

CHANLER, JOHN WINTHROP, *Emigration and Expatriation are the Citizen's Practical Declaration of Independence.* Speech delivered in the House of Representatives, February 6, 1868. Washington, D.C.: Government Printing Office, 1868.

——, Speech on *The Paris Exposition of 1867.* Delivered in the House of Representatives, March 14, 1866. Washington, D.C.: Government Printing Office, 1866.

CHANLER, JULIE, *From Gaslight to Dawn.* Privately printed, New York, 1956.

CHANLER (Chaloner), JOHN ARMSTRONG, *Four Years Behind the Bars of "Bloomingdale," or the Bankruptcy of the Law in New York.* Privately printed, Roanoke Rapids, N.C., 1906.

CHANLER, MRS. WINTHROP, *Autumn in the Valley.* Boston: Little, Brown, 1936.

——, *Roman Spring.* Boston: Little, Brown, 1934.

——, *Winthrop Chanler's Letters.* Privately printed, New York, 1951.

CHESNUT, MARY BOYKIN, *A Diary From Dixie.* Boston: Houghton Mifflin, 1949.

CLEMMER, MARY, *Ten Years in Washington.* Hartford, Conn.: Hartford Publishing Co., 1883.

CLEWS, HENRY, *Fifty Years in Wall Street.* New York, 1908.

Coblentz, Stanton A., *Villains and Vigilantes.* New York: Wilson-Erickson, 1936.

Coleman, Evan J., "Gwin and Seward — A Secret Chapter of Ante-Bellum History." *Overland Monthly,* November 1891.

——, "Senator Gwin's Plan for the Colonization of Sonora." *Overland Monthly,* May 1891.

——, "Senator Gwin's Plan for the Colonization of Sonora: Postscript." *Overland Monthly,* August 1891.

Collins, Carvel, *Sam Ward in the Gold Rush.* Stanford, Calif.: Stanford University Press, 1949.

Collins, Frederick L., *Money Town.* New York: Putnam, 1946.

Corti, Egon Caesar, Count, *Maximilian and Charlotte of Mexico,* translated by Catherine Alison Phillips. 2 vols. New York: Knopf, 1928.

Crawford, F. Marion, *The American Politician.* New York: Macmillan, 1884.

——, *Dr. Claudius.* New York: Macmillan, 1883.

——, *Katherine Lauderdale.* New York: Macmillan, 1893.

——, *Mr. Isaacs.* New York: Macmillan, 1882.

——, *The Ralstons.* New York: Macmillan, 1893.

Crewe, Marquess of, *Lord Rosebery.* New York: Harper, 1931.

Crow, Duncan, *Henry Wikoff, the American Chevalier.* London: MacGibbon & Kee, 1963.

Curtis, George Ticknor, *The Life of James Buchanan.* 2 vols. New York: Harper, 1883.

Daley, Maria Lydig, *Diary of a Union Lady, 1861–1865,* Harold Earl Hammond, ed. New York: Funk & Wagnalls, 1962.

Da Ponte, Lorenzo, *Memoirs of Lorenzo da Ponte.* Translated by Elisabeth Abbott, edited and annotated by Arthur Livingston. Philadelphia: Lippincott, 1929.

Davis, Elmer, *History of the New York Times, 1851–1921.* New York: New York Times, 1921.

Dennett, Tyler, *John Hay: From Poetry to Politics.* New York: Dodd Mead, 1934.

Derby, J. C., *Fifty Years Among Authors, Artists, and Publishers.* New York: Carlton, 1884.

Devol, George, *Forty Years a Gambler on the Mississippi.* New York: Holt, 1906.

DeVoto, Bernard, *Easy Chair* article on "The Diary of a Public Man." *Harper's Magazine,* May 1945.

——, *The Year of Decision: 1846.* Boston: Little, Brown, 1942.

"The Diary of a Public Man — Unpublished Passages of the Secret History of the American Civil War." *North American Review,* August-November 1879.

Dies, E. J., *The Plunger.* New York: Covici & Friede, 1929.

Donald, David, *Charles Sumner and the Coming of the Civil War.* New York: Farrar, Straus & Cudahy, 1961.

Dunraven, Earl of, *Past Times and Pastimes.* 2 vols. London: Stodder & Houghton, 1922.

Eldredge, Zoeth Skinner, *The Beginnings of San Francisco.* San Francisco, 1912.

Elliott, Maud Howe, *John Elliott: The Story of an Artist.* Boston: Houghton Mifflin, 1930.

——, *My Cousin, F. Marion Crawford.* New York: Macmillan, 1934.

——, *This Was My Newport.* New York: Macmillan, 1938.

——, *Three Generations.* Boston: Little Brown, 1923.

——, *Uncle Sam Ward and His Circle.* New York: Macmillan, 1938.

Elliott, Maud Howe and Laura E. Richards, *Julia Ward Howe — 1819–1910.* 2 vols. Boston: Houghton Mifflin, 1916.

Elson, Henry W., *Sidelights on American History.* New York: Macmillan, 1899.

Eskew, Garnett Laidlaw, *Willard's of Washington.* New York: Coward-McCann, 1954.

Fairchild, Mahlon D., "Reminiscences of a Forty-Niner." *California Historical Society Quarterly,* March 1934.

Fiske, Stephen, *Off-Hand Portraits of Prominent New Yorkers.* New York: Lockwood, 1884.

Forney, J. W., *Anecdotes of Public Men.* New York: Harper, 1873.

Fortier, Alcée, *A History of Louisiana.* 4 vols. New York: Goupil, 1904.

Fossier, Albert A., *New Orleans: The Glamour Period, 1800–1840.* New Orleans: Pelican Publishing Co., 1957.

Francis, John W., *Old New York, or Reminiscences of the Past Sixty Years.* New York: Middleton, 1866.

FRASER, MRS. HUGH, *Reminiscences of a Diplomatist's Wife*. New York: Dodd Mead, 1912.

FULLER, ROBERT H., *Jubilee Jim, the Life of Colonel James Fisk, Jr.* New York: Macmillan, 1928.

FURNAS, J. C., *The Road to Harper's Ferry*. New York: William Sloan, 1959.

FURNEAUX, RUPERT, *The First War Correspondent: William Howard Russell of The Times*. London: Cassell, 1944.

GALE, ROBERT L., *Thomas Crawford, American Sculptor*. Pittsburgh: University of Pittsburgh Press, 1964.

GOUVERNEUR, MARIAN (Mrs. M. C.), *As I Remember — Recollections of American Society During the Nineteenth Century*. New York: Appleton, 1911.

GOBRIGHT, L. A., *Recollections of Men and Things at Washington During a Third of a Century*. Philadelphia: Claxton, Remsen & Haffelfinger, 1869.

GOWER, LORD RONALD, *My Reminiscences*. 2 vols. London: Kegan Paul, Trench, 1883.

——, *Old Diaries: 1881–1901*. New York: Scribner's, 1902.

GRAHAM, R. B. CUNNINGHAME, *Portrait of a Dictator: Francisco Solano López (Paraguay 1865–1870)*. London, 1955.

GRANT, JESSE R. (with Henry Francis Gardner), *In the Days of My Father, General Grant*. New York: Harper, 1925.

GRISCOM, LLOYD C., *Diplomatically Speaking*. New York: Literary Guild, 1940.

GUEDALLA, PHILIP, *The Second Empire*. New York: Putnam, 1923.

GWIN, WILLIAM M., "Memoirs of Hon. William M. Gwin," William Henry Ellison, ed. *California Historical Society Quarterly*, March-December 1940.

HALL, FLORENCE HOWE, *Memories Grave and Gay*. New York: Harper, 1918.

HALL, HENRY MARION (ed.), "Longfellow's Letters to Samuel Ward." *Putnam's Magazine*, 1907.

HAMILTON, GAIL (Mary Abby Dodge), *Gail Hamilton's Life in Letters*, H. Augusta Dodge, ed. 2 vols. Boston: Lee & Shepard, 1901.

HARRISON, MRS. BURTON (Constance Cary), *Recollections Grave and Gay*. New York: Scribner's, 1911.

HART-DAVIS, RUPERT (ed.), *The Letters of Oscar Wilde.* New York: Harcourt Brace, 1963.

HATFIELD, JAMES TAFT, *New Light on Longfellow.* Boston: Houghton Mifflin, 1933.

HEGERMAN-LINDENCRONE, L. de, *In the Courts of Memory.* New York: Harper, 1911.

HENDRICK, BURTON J., *Statesmen of the Lost Cause.* New York: Literary Guild, 1939.

HIBBEN, PAXTON, *Henry Ward Beecher, An American Portrait.* New York: Doran, 1927.

HIGGINSON, MARY THACHER, *Thomas Wentworth Higginson.* Boston: Houghton Mifflin, 1914.

HIGGINSON, THOMAS WENTWORTH, *Cheerful Yesterdays.* Boston: Houghton Mifflin, 1898.

——, *Letters and Journals of Thomas Wentworth Higginson,* Mary Thacher Higginson, ed. Boston: Houghton Mifflin, 1921.

——, *Contemporaries.* Boston: Houghton Mifflin, 1921.

——, *Malbone: An Oldport Romance.* Boston: Fields, Osgood, 1869.

HOBSON, ELIZABETH CHRISTOPHERS, *Recollections of a Happy Life.* New York: Putnam, 1917.

HOLDEN, W. H. (ed.), *Second Empire Medley.* London: British Technical & General Press, 1952.

HOLT, HENRY, *Garrulities of an Octogenarian.* Boston: Houghton Mifflin, 1923.

HONE, PHILIP, *Diary,* Bayard Tuckerman, ed. New York: Dodd Mead, 1910.

——, *Diary,* Allan Nevins, ed. New York: Dodd Mead, 1936.

HOWE, JULIA WARD, *Passion Flowers.* Boston: Ticknor & Fields, 1853.

——, *Reminiscences, 1819–1899.* Boston: Houghton Mifflin, 1899.

HURLBERT, WILLIAM HENRY, *France and the Republic.* London, 1890.

——, *Ireland Under Coercion.* Boston: Houghton Mifflin, 1888.

JAMES, ROBERT RHODES, *Rosebery.* London: Weidenfeld & Nicolson, 1963.

JEYES, SAMUEL HENRY, *The Earl of Rosebery.* London: Dent, 1906.

JOHN, EVAN, *Atlantic Impact, 1861*. London: Heinemann, 1952.

KEMBLE, JOHN HASKELL, "The Genesis of the Pacific Mail Steamship Company." *California Historical Society Quarterly*, September-December 1934.

KENNEDY, ELIJAH R., *The Contest for California in 1861*. Boston: Houghton Mifflin, 1912.

KEYES, ERASMUS DARWIN, *Fifty Years' Observation of Men and Events*. New York: Scribner's, 1884.

KING, GRACE, *Creole Families of New Orleans*. New York: Macmillan, 1921.

——, New Orleans: *The Place and the People*. New York: Macmillan, 1895.

KING, J. L., *History of the San Francisco Stock and Exchange Board*. San Francisco, 1910.

KINGSLEY, CHARLES, *Two Years Ago*. 2 vols. London, 1857.

KOENIG, LOUIS W., *The Invisible Presidency*. New York: Holt, Rinehart & Winston, 1960.

KORNGOLD, RALPH, *Thaddeus Stevens: A Being Darkly Wise and Rudely Great*. New York: Harcourt Brace, 1955.

LAMB, MRS. MARTHA J., *History of the City of New York*. 3 vols. New York: Barnes, 1877.

LAMON, WARD H., *Recollections of Abraham Lincoln*. Washington, D.C., 1911.

LANGTRY, LILY (Lady de Bathe), *The Days I Knew*. New York: Doran, 1925.

LATHAM, MILTON S., "The Day Journal of Milton Slocum Latham." *California Historical Society Quarterly*, March 1932.

LEE, JAMES MELVIN, *History of American Journalism*. Boston: Houghton Mifflin, 1923.

LEECH, MARGARET, *Reveille in Washington, 1860–1865*. New York: Harper, 1941.

LEWIS, LLOYD, *Sherman, Fighting Prophet*. New York: Harcourt Brace, 1932.

LEWIS, LLOYD and HENRY JUSTIN SMITH, "The King of the Lobby." *American Mercury*, February 1935.

——, *Oscar Wilde Discovers America (1882)*. New York: Harcourt Brace, 1936.

LEWIS, OSCAR, *Sea Routes to the Gold Fields.* New York: Knopf, 1949.

LOKKEN, ROY N., "Has the Mystery of 'A Public Man' Been Solved?" *Mississippi Valley Historical Review,* December 1953.

LOLIÉE, FRÉDÉRIC AUGUSTE, *The Gilded Beauties of the Second Empire.* Adapted by Bryan O'Donnell. London: John Long, 1909.

——, *The Romance of a Favourite.* Translated by William Morton Fullerton. New York: Appleton, 1912.

LOMASK, MILTON, *Andrew Johnson: President on Trial.* New York: Farrar, Straus & Cudahy, 1960.

LONGFELLOW, ERNEST WADSWORTH, *Random Memories.* Boston: Houghton Mifflin, 1922.

LONGFELLOW, HENRY WADSWORTH, *Hyperion, a Romance.* New York, 1839.

——, *Kavanagh: a Tale.* Boston, 1849.

——, *Poetical Works.* Boston: Houghton Mifflin, 1893.

LONGFELLOW, SAMUEL, *Life of Henry Wadsworth Longfellow.* 2 vols. Boston: Ticknor, 1886.

LOW, FREDERICK F., *Reflections of an Early California Governor.* Sacramento, Calif.: Sacramento Book Collectors Club, 1959.

LYNCH, DENNIS TILDEN, *"Boss" Tweed: The Story of a Grim Generation.* New York: Boni & Liveright, 1927.

MCALLISTER, WARD, *Society As I Have Found It.* New York: Cassell, 1890.

MCCABE, JAMES D. JR., *Great Fortunes, and How They Were Made.* Cincinnati and Chicago: Hannaford, 1871.

MCCULLOCH, HUGH, *Men and Measures of Half a Century.* New York: Scribner's, 1888.

MARTIN, EDWARD SANDFORD, *The Life of Joseph Hodges Choate.* New York: Scribner's, 1920.

MARTIN, EDWARD WINSLOW (pseudonym of James Dabney McCabe), *Behind the Scenes in Washington.* Philadelphia: Continental Publishing Co., 1873.

MINNIGERODE, MEAD, *The Fabulous Forties: 1840–1850.* New York: Putnam, 1924.

MOORE, JOHN BASSETT, *History and Digest of the International Ar-*

bitrations to Which the United States Has Been a Party. 6 vols. Washington, D.C., 1898.

MOORE, JOHN WEST, *The American Congress, a History of National Legislation and Political Events, 1774–1895.* New York: Harper, 1895.

——, *Picturesque Washington.* Providence, R.I.: Reid, 1886.

MORRIS, LLOYD R., *Incredible New York.* New York: Random House, 1951.

NASATIR, ABRAHAM A., *French Activities in California — An Archival Calendar-Guide.* Stanford, Calif.: Stanford University, 1945.

NEVINS, ALLAN, *Frémont: The Pathmarker of the West.* New York: Longmans, Green, 1955.

——, *Hamilton Fish: The Inner History of the Grant Administration.* New York: Dodd Mead, 1937.

——, *History of the Bank of New York and Trust Company.* Privately printed, New York, 1923.

——, *The War for the Union,* Vol. 1: *The Improvised War.* New York: Scribner's, 1959.

——, *The War for the Union,* Vol. 2: *War Becomes Revolution.* New York: Scribner's, 1960.

NICHOLS, ROY FRANKLIN, *The Disruption of American Democracy.* New York: Macmillan, 1948.

NICOLAY, HELEN, *Our Capital on the Potomac.* New York: Century, 1924.

NOYES, ALEXANDER D., *Forty Years of American Finance.* New York: Putnam, 1909.

O'CONNOR, HARVEY, *The Astors.* New York: Knopf, 1941.

O'CONNOR, RICHARD, *Gould's Millions.* New York: Doubleday, 1962.

O'MEARA, JAMES, *Broderick and Gwin.* San Francisco, 1881.

PAGE, THOMAS JEFFERSON, *La Plata, the Argentine Confederation, and Paraguay.* New York: Harper, 1859.

PETERSON, HAROLD F., "Edward A. Hopkins: A Pioneer in Paraguay." *Hispanic American Historical Review,* May 1942.

PHELPS, ALONZO, *Contemporary Biography of California's Representative Men.* San Francisco, 1881.

PIERCE, EDWARD L., *Memoir and Letters of Charles Sumner.* Boston: Roberts Brothers, 1893–94.

A *"Pile" — A Glance at the Wealth of the Monied Men of San Francisco and Sacramento Cities.* San Francisco, 1851.

PLUME, J. V. (attributed), *Re-Union of the Pioneer Panama Passengers, June 4, 1874: the 25th Anniversary of the Arrival of the Steamship Panama at San Francisco.* San Francisco, 1874.

POORE, BEN: PERLEY, *Perley's Reminiscences of Sixty Years in the National Metropolis.* 2 vols. Philadelphia: Hubbard, 1886.

——, (ed.), *The Trial of Andrew Johnson, President of the United States, Before the Senate of the United States.* Washington, D.C.: Government Printing Office, 1868.

POPE-HENNESSEY, JAMES, *Monckton Milnes.* 2 vols. New York: Farrar, Straus & Cudahy, 1955.

PORTER, K. W., *John J. Astor.* Cambridge, Mass.: Harvard University Press, 1931.

PRYOR, MRS. ROGER A., *My Day: Reminiscences of a Long Life.* New York: Macmillan, 1909.

——, *Reminiscences of Peace and War.* New York: Macmillan, 1924.

RACOWITZA, PRINCESS HELENE VON, *An Autobiography.* New York: Macmillan, 1911.

RAINE, PHILIP, *Paraguay.* New Brunswick, N.J.: Scarecrow Press, 1956.

RANDALL, RUTH PAINTER, *Mary Lincoln.* Boston: Little, Brown, 1953.

RAY, GORDON N., (ed.), *The Letters of William Makepeace Thackeray.* 4 vols. Cambridge, Mass.: Harvard University Press, 1949.

——, *Thackeray: The Age of Wisdom.* New York: McGraw Hill, 1958.

RAYMOND, E. T., *The Man of Promise, Lord Rosebery.* New York: Doran, 1923.

RECTOR, GEORGE, *The Girl From Rector's.* New York: Doubleday, Page, 1927.

REID, T. WEMYSS, *The Life, Letters, and Friendships of Richard Monckton Milnes, First Lord Houghton.* London: Cassell, 1890.

Reports of Committees of House of Representatives, 40th Congress, 2nd Session, Report #44 (May 25, 1868), "On Raising of Money to be Used in Impeachment." Washington, D.C., 1868.

Reports of Committees of House of Representatives, 43rd Congress,

2nd Session, "On Pacific Mail Subsidy Bill" (January 1875).

RICHARDS, LAURA E., *Samuel Gridley Howe.* New York: Appleton-Century, 1935.

——, *Stepping Westward.* New York: Appleton, 1931.

RIPLEY, ELIZA, *Social Life in Old New Orleans.* New York: Appleton, 1912.

ROBINSON, LURA, *It's an Old New Orleans Custom.* New York: Vanguard, 1948.

RODD, SIR JAMES RENNELL, *Social and Diplomatic Memories 1884–1893.* London, 1922.

ROSEBERY, Lord, *Lord Chatham, His Early Life and Connections.* New York: Harper, 1910.

ROTHSCHILD, SALOMON DE, *A Casual View of America — The Home Letters of Salomon de Rothschild.* Translated and edited by Sigmund Diamond. Stanford, Calif.: Stanford University Press, 1961.

RUSSELL, WILLIAM HOWARD, *The Civil War in America.* Boston, 1861.

——, *My Diary, North and South.* New York: Harper, 1863.

——, *Pictures of Southern Life, Social, Political, and Military.* New York, 1861.

——, "Recollections of the American Civil War." *North American Review,* 1898.

SCARLETT, P. CAMPBELL, *South America and the Pacific.* London: Colburn, 1838.

SCHRIFTGIESSER, KARL, *The Lobbyists.* Boston: Atlantic Monthly–Little, Brown, 1951.

SEITZ, DON C., *The Dreadful Decade.* Indianapolis: Bobbs-Merrill, 1926.

——, *The James Gordon Bennetts.* Indianapolis: Bobbs-Merrill, 1928.

SEVIER, O'NEIL, "Sysonby, The Race-Horse of 1905." *Munsey's Magazine,* November 1905.

SEWARD, FREDERICK W., *Reminiscences of a War-time Statesman and Diplomat.* New York: Putnam, 1916.

——, *Seward at Washington.* 3 vols. New York, 1891.

SHERMAN, W. T., *Memoirs.* New York: Webster, 1891.

SICHEL, PIERRE, *The Jersey Lily: The Story of the Fabulous Mrs. Langtry.* New York: Prentice-Hall, 1958.

SMITH, ARTHUR D. HOWDEN, *John Jacob Astor.* Philadelphia: Lippincott, 1929.

SMITH, BEVERLY W., JR., "All-Time Champ of the Lobbyists." *Saturday Evening Post,* December 23, 1950.

SMITH, MATTHEW HALE (Burleigh), *Sunshine and Shadow in New York.* Hartford, Conn.: Burr, 1868.

SOULIÉ, MAURICE, *The Wolf Cub: The Great Adventure of Count Gaston Raousset-Boulbon in California and Sonora, 1850–54.* Translated by Farrel Symons. Indianapolis: Bobbs-Merrill, 1927.

STEEDMAN, REAR ADMIRAL CHARLES, *Memoirs and Correspondence,* Amos Lawrence Mason, ed. Cambridge, Mass., 1912.

STEVENS, JOHN AUSTIN, *Albert Gallatin.* Boston: Houghton Mifflin, 1883.

STEVENSON, LIONEL, *The Showman of Vanity Fair.* New York: Scribner's, 1947.

STEWART, GEORGE R., *Revolution in San Francisco.* Boston: Houghton Mifflin, 1964.

STOKER, BRAM, *Personal Reminiscences of Henry Irving.* 2 vols. New York: Macmillan, 1906.

STRONG, GEORGE TEMPLETON, *The Diary of George Templeton Strong,* Allan Nevins and Milton Halsey Thomas, eds. New York: Macmillan, 1952.

SWANBERG, W. A., *First Blood — The Story of Fort Sumter.* New York: Scribner's, 1957.

——, *Jim Fisk: The Career of an Improbable Rascal.* New York: Scribner's, 1959.

——, *Sickles the Incredible.* New York: Scribner's, 1956.

TALLANT, ROBERT, *The Romantic New Orleanians.* New York: Dutton, 1960.

THARP, LOUISE HALL, *Three Saints and a Sinner.* Boston: Little, Brown, 1956.

THOMAS, BENJAMIN, and HAROLD M. HYMAN, *Stanton: The Life and Times of Lincoln's Secretary of War.* New York: Knopf, 1962.

THOMPSON, LAWRENCE, *Young Longfellow.* New York: Macmillan, 1938.

TREFOUSSE, HANS L., *Ben Butler.* New York: Twayne, 1957.

TROWBRIDGE, J. T., *My Own Story.* Boston: Houghton Mifflin, 1903.

Van Dusen, G. G., *Thurlow Weed: Wizard of the Lobby.* Boston: Little, Brown, 1947.

Van Wyck, Frederick, *Recollections of an Old New Yorker.* New York: Liveright, 1932.

Vesey, John Henry, *Mr. Vesey of England,* Brian Waters, ed. New York: Putnam, 1956.

Villard, Henry, *Memoirs of Henry Villard.* 2 vols. Boston: Houghton Mifflin, 1904.

Wagenknecht, Edward Charles, *Longfellow: A Full-Length Portrait.* New York: Longmans, Green, 1955.

Wagner, Harry Raup, "The Life of Ferdinand C. Ewer, May 22, 1826–October 10, 1883." *California Historical Society Quarterly,* December 1934.

Wallace, Edward S., *Destiny and Glory.* New York: Coward-McCann, 1957.

Ward, John, *A Memoir of Lieutenant-Colonel Samuel Ward.* Privately printed, New York, 1875.

Ward, Samuel, "Days with Longfellow." *North American Review,* May 1882.

——, "Incidents on the River of Grace, by Midas, Jr." *Porter's Spirit of the Times,* New York, 1860–61.

——, *Lyrical Recreations.* New York: Appleton, 1865.

——, *Lyrical Recreations.* London: Macmillan, 1883.

——, (attributed), *Exploits of the Attorney-General in California, by an Early Californian.* Privately printed, New York, 1860.

Wasburn, Charles Ames, *History of Paraguay.* 2 vols. Boston: Lee & Shepard, 1871.

Warshow, Robert Riving, *The Story of Wall Street.* New York: Greenberg, 1929.

Watson, Douglas S., "The San Francisco McAllisters." *California Historical Society Quarterly,* June 1932.

Watterson, Henry, *"Marse Henry": An Autobiography.* 2 vols. New York: Doran, 1919.

Weber, Carl J., "The 'Discovery' of Fitzgerald's *Rubáiyát.*" *University of Texas Library Chronicle,* Austin, Texas (Summer 1963).

Wecter, Dixon, *The Saga of American Society: A Record of Social Aspiration, 1607-1937.* New York: Scribner's, 1937.

WEED, THURLOW, *The Life of Thurlow Weed: Autobiography and Memoir by Thurlow Weed Barnes.* Boston: Houghton Mifflin, 1883.

——, *Letters from Europe and the West Indies, 1843–1852.* Albany, N.Y. 1866.

WEEKS, LYMAN H., ed., *Prominent Families of New York.* New York: The Historical Co., 1897.

WELLS, ANNA MARY, *The Life and Times of Thomas Wentworth Higginson.* Boston: Houghton Mifflin, 1963.

WELLS, EVELYN, and HARRY C. PETERSON, *The 49ers.* New York: Doubleday, 1949.

WERNER, M. R., *Tammany Hall.* New York: Doubleday Doran, 1928.

WIKOFF, HENRY, *Reminiscences of an Idler.* New York: Fords, Howard & Hulbert, 1880.

WILKINS, THURMAN, *Clarence King.* New York: Macmillan, 1958.

WHITNEY, J. PARKER, "Memoirs of a Sportsman." *Forest and Stream,* 1906.

WILLIAMS, ROGER L., *Gaslight and Shadow: The World of Napoleon III 1851–1870.* New York: Macmillan, 1957.

WILLIAMS, T. HARRY, *P. G. T. Beauregard: Napoleon in Gray.* Baton Rouge, La.: Louisiana State University Press, 1954.

WILSON, JAMES GRANT, *Thackeray in the United States.* 2 vols. New York: Dodd Mead, 1906.

WILSON, RUFUS ROCKWELL, and OTILIE ERICKSON WILSON, *New York in Literature.* Privately printed, Elmira, N.Y., 1947.

YNSFRAN, MAX PABLO, "Sam Ward's Bargain with President López of Paraguay." *Hispanic American Historical Review,* August 1954.

——, *La expedición norteamericana contra el Paraguay.* Mexico City: Editorial Guarania, 1958.

YOUNG, JOHN P., *San Francisco, a History of the Pacific Coast Metropolis.* Chicago: Clark, 1912.

INDEX